David Miles was Chief Archaeologist at English Heritage from
1999 to 2004. Previously the Director of Oxford Archaeological
Unit and an Associate Professor of Stanford University, he is a
Research Fellow of the Institute of Archaeology, Oxford and a
Fellow of Kellogg College, Oxford. As consultant to the Historic
Royal Palaces Agency, he has organised excavations in the Tower
of London and Hampton Court. His principal projects at English
Heritage include Stonehenge, coastal and maritime surveys, and
the National Mapping Programme, using aerial photography to
explore the English landscape. David Miles is the author and co-
author of many books and articles on history and archaeology
including *An Introduction to Archaeology*, *An Atlas of Archaeology*
and *The Countryside of Roman Britain*. He was a columnist for the
Oxford Mail and *Oxford Times* for ten years and frequently broadcasts
on radio and television. He is a Fellow of the Society of Antiquaries
of London and Scotland.

Every layer they strip
Seems camped on before

'Bogland' SEAMUS HEANEY
Opened Ground: Poems 1966-1996 (1998), Faber, London

I have crossed an ocean
I have lost my tongue
from the roots of the old one
a new one has sprung

'Epilogue' GRACE NICHOLS
Staying Alive (2003), Neil Astley (ed.), BloodAxe Books

'Britons sent out testicles – sorry, tentacles.'

Malapropism said by West Indian lady,
17 April 2002

THE TRIBES OF BRITAIN

DAVID MILES

PHOENIX

To Jess and Joey:
our contribution to the Tribes

A PHOENIX PAPERBACK

First published in Great Britain in 2005
by Weidenfeld & Nicolson
This paperback edition published in 2006
by Phoenix,
an imprint of Orion Books Ltd,
Orion House, 5 Upper St Martin's Lane,
London WC2H 9EA

An Hachette UK Company

Revised edition

12

Copyright © David Miles 2005, 2006
Maps copyright © Ken Wilson 2006

Picture research by Brónagh Woods

A CIP catalogue record for this book
is available from the British Library.

ISBN 978-0-7538-1799-5

Printed and bound in the UK by
CPI Mackays, Chatham ME5 8TD

The Orion Publishing Group's policy is to use papers
that are natural, renewable and recyclable products and
made from wood grown in sustainable forests. The logging
and manufacturing processes are expected to conform to
the environmental regulations of the country of origin.

www.orionbooks.co.uk

CONTENTS

Introduction to the Paperback Edition

For an author to stray outside his or her area of specialisation is always a dangerous journey. It is inevitable, though, in a book such as this, when you seek to survey half a million years of history. In *The Tribes of Britain* I wanted to tell one of the possible stories of the people of the British Isles and Ireland; emphasising our interaction with the rest of the world and combining the evidence of archaeology, demography, history, climatology and biological sciences. These are rapidly developing areas of research, and so there are subjects where I have lingered somewhat behind the times, been cautious in my interpretations or brief to the point of simplicity. Nevertheless I have tried to present the big picture in a personal and readable way. I am grateful to those who took the trouble to point out mistakes in the first edition. Any survivors remain my responsibility.

I am grateful to Kate Shearman and Jenny Page at the Orion Publishing Group for their patience and efficiency in pulling together the paperback edition.

As climate change, immigration, birth rates, ageing and threats of bird flu continue to dominate our newspapers, I hope that *The Tribes of Britain* will help to put these issues into perspective. Our ancestors have been there before us.

DM, April 2006

Introduction

> The knowledge of past events has further virtues, especially
> in that it distinguishes rational creatures from brutes, for
> brutes, whether men or beasts, do not know — about their
> origins, their race, and the events and happenings in their
> native land.
>
> HENRY OF HUNTINGDON, *The History of the English People, c.*1130–55

IN *Monty Python and the Holy Grail* the Pythons posed a serious question: 'Who are the Britons?' They might well ask. As an archaeologist, I have spent the best part of thirty years tracing the lives of ordinary Britons — by which I mean the people who have lived in the British Isles since the end of the Ice Age twelve thousand years ago, and even earlier, back half a million years to the first hominids to colonise this land.

Over two thousand years ago explorers and traders from the Mediterranean world first recorded for posterity the names of the inhabitants of these remote north-western islands: they called them 'Pritani'* — or 'Britanni', as Latin-speakers mispronounced it — though the locals may not have thought of themselves by that name. They probably identified with their tribes, such as the Cantii, whom Julius Caesar encountered in what is now still known as Kent, or the Parisii, in Yorkshire, or the Atrebates, in Hampshire, who, if their tribal names are anything to go by, had connections with what is now northern France. The earliest written reference to Ireland, though, called its inhabitants 'Hierni' or 'Iverii', which can be translated as the 'People of the Fertile Earth'. This is the kind of name which, around the world, people give themselves — like the Lakota of the American Great Plains, whose name means 'The People'

---

* In modern Welsh the name for Britain is 'Prydain'. Pytheas sailed around the Atlantic coast from Missilia (Marseilles) and first recorded the 'Pritannic Isles', north of the land of the Celts, about 320 BC in his book *On the Ocean* (Peri tou Okeanou).[1]

but who are better known, at least until recently, by their nickname, the Ojibwa word 'Sioux', meaning 'Enemy'.

Outsiders have a habit of assuming the worst about strangers, or even neighbouring tribes. When I was a child in Halifax we thought that people in Leeds spoke oddly, so we tagged them 'Loiners', for the way they pronounced 'lane'; and I firmly believed that the people of Hull never went anywhere without their ammunition of empty beer bottles. Strabo (c.64 BC–c.AD 21) was a collector of observations and travellers' tales, who probably himself never ventured beyond the Mediterranean. Nevertheless, in his early-first-century *Geographica* he put back the Irish tourist industry by a few centuries when he informed his readers that the Irish were man-eaters – the men, that is – who also had sex with their mothers and sisters.

Strabo admitted that he had no trustworthy witnesses for this slander; but like all good tabloid journalists he adopted the principle: when fact meets legend, print the legend. So *Geographica* created the model for travellers' tales which would be repeated for centuries, sending a frisson of danger and self-satisfaction through generations of readers in the safety of their armchairs.*

Until about the sixteenth century, when the ideas of the Renaissance made a degree of academic rigour fashionable, most historians or annalists preferred a good story to the truth. In the Roman tradition it was not so much what you said or wrote that counted but the rhetorical power with which you delivered the message. Roman writers could only guess about the origins of the Britons, though the fact that they were the first literate commentators on non-literate (prehistoric) communities gave their words authority for centuries. Tacitus, whose father-in-law Agricola was governor of the Roman province of Britannia, speculated:

> However, who the peoples who inhabited Britain originally were, native or immigrants, as usual among barbarians, has been too little investigated. Inferences can be drawn from the physical shape. The reddish hair of the people who inhabit Caledonia [Scotland] and the size of the limbs indicate a Germanic origin. The swarthy faces of the Silures [a Welsh

---

* Such clichés also justified the maltreatment of conquered traditional communities and occasionally came home to roost. The whalers of the *Essex*, sunk by a bull whale in the Pacific in 1820 (and the origin of the Moby Dick story), decided not to make for the nearest landfall, the Marquesas or the Society Islands, because they were convinced that hordes of hungry cannibals awaited them there. In fact since 1797 Tahiti had been the possessor of an enormous mission chapel. Ironically the *Essex* survivors resorted to cannibalism themselves, consuming their shipmates to avoid starvation.[2]

tribe], their generally curly hair and their location facing Spain* suggest that ancient Iberians came across and settled these areas. Those closest to the Gauls are similar to them, either due to continuing effects of heredity or, where lands jut out opposite one another, the climatic conditions gave shape to the inhabitants' bodies. However, it seems probable that the Gauls colonised the neighbouring island.

As the most famous and widely read author of the ancient world, Homer was often plundered for origin myths; Trojans – Aeneas or his offspring – supposedly headed west after the fall of Troy, providing credibility and a pedigree for innumerable dynasties and cities. As Christianity took hold, the Bible developed a similar role, though, not surprisingly, it has little to say specifically about the spread of Noah's offspring to the wild west of Europe.

One writer who took a relatively hard-headed approach, ignoring the Homeric and biblical myths, was Bede, the first historian of the English, writing from his monastery in Jarrow in the early eighth century. He starts his *Ecclesiastical History of the English People* with a no-frills account of British origins, proposing that they came from Brittany; that the Picts in the north originated in Scythia – he means Scandinavia, not the people whom Herodotus describes as living near the Black Sea. He goes on to describe the movement of peoples since the departure of the Romans from the province of Britannia: the Scots have colonised western Scotland from northern Ireland and the Angles, Saxons and Jutes have crossed into southern and eastern England from the Continent. With all these newcomers Britain is a veritable Tower of Babel, where five languages are spoken: British, Pictish, Scottish, Anglian and the *lingua franca* of the educated religious elite, Latin. As a good Christian Englishman, Bede had to explain why his pagan Germanic ancestors were able to overcome the resident Christian Britons: this was a punishment from God, for the errant ways of the British, he explained. Norman commentators, such as Henry of Huntingdon, used the same explanation for William the Conqueror's victory over Bede's English descendants.

Later medieval accounts of the peopling of the British Isles tend to draw on classical and biblical explanations. The earliest written Irish records – in the *Book of Invasions of Ireland* (*Lebor Gabala Erenn*), documented in the eleventh-century *Book of Leinster*, tells of a series of colonisations starting with a granddaughter of Noah just before the Flood.

---

* The Roman map of western Europe had Britain orientated to face the Iberian Peninsula.

Following the deluge, descendants of Japhet and Magog arrived, but these people were wiped out by plague. The semi-mythical tribes the Fir Domnann, Fir Galeoin and Fir Bolg, who had escaped servitude in Greece, came next; then the Tuatha De Dannan, also descended from Magog, who brought their knowledge of magic and the arts from the north. And finally the Sons of Mil, the Gaels, successfully invaded. One of their ancestors went off to Egypt and married the Pharoah's daughter, Scota. This couple gave birth to Gaedel Glas, ancestor of the Gaels, who concocted the Gaelic tongue from the seventy-two languages of Babel. His descendants colonised Spain and from there spotted Ireland. Mil and his seven sons set out for this land on the horizon and there established the major dynasties.

This hotchpotch of classical and biblical allusions may not contain a word of truth, nor even mythical echoes of real events. This has not, however, prevented generations of historians from arguing about it; and for many years a similar myth dominated beliefs about British origins. This was set out in its most widely read version by Geoffrey of Monmouth, in his medieval best-seller *Historia Regnum Brittaniae* ('The History of the Kings of Britain') composed in Oxford about 1133. He seems to have drawn some of his inspiration from the Welsh tradition compiled supposedly by Nennius in the ninth century as the *Historia Brittonum*. From this source Geoffrey tells the story of Britto (Brutus), who was told by the goddess Diana, in a dream, of an island in the sea, beyond the setting of the sun, once inhabited by giants. 'Now it is empty and ready for your people … A race of kings will be born there from your stock and the round circle of the whole earth will be subject to them.'

Britto landed at Totnes, in what was then called Albion, but he modestly changed the name to Britain in honour of himself. A few giants still hung around the place but they were packed off to caves in the mountains. In Cornwall, where they were especially numerous, the giants were killed or, in the case of Gogmagog, engaged in a fatal wrestling contest. Needing a capital, Britto located a suitable spot on the Thames and established Troia Nova ('New Troy') which came to be known as Trinovantum, then Caer Lud – the 'City of Lud'. According to Geoffrey, when Julius Caesar arrived off the shores of Britain, he exclaimed: 'By Hercules, those Britons come from the same race as we do, for we Romans too are descended from Trojan stock.'

Geoffrey's fantastic saga contains the stories of many of England's national heroes – King Coel, Leir, Merlin, the builder of Stonehenge, and Arthur. If most of this now seems like the stuff of myth and legend, in the medieval world such stories had a serious as well as an entertaining purpose. Britto/Brutus, for example, was portrayed as the King of all Britain, who divided the land between his three sons: the eldest, Locrinus, took Loegria (England); Kamber inherited Kambria (Wales) and Albanactus, Albany (Scotland). If Geoffrey of Monmouth had been regarded as a prototype J. R. R. Tolkien – merely a masterly story-teller drawing on High Church symbolism and legends – then the three kings would have had no more significance than hobbits. But to medieval England Geoffrey had delivered the national story: England was top dog; Wales and Scotland should acknowledge their inferior positions in the national pack. When England's King Edward I attempted to take advantage of the deaths of Alexander III in AD 1286 and the Scots heir Margaret four years later, Geoffrey of Monmouth's tale was submitted as relevant evidence to the Pope. It was wheeled out again by the three Henrys – IV, V and VI – and even in 1547, when the English attempted the so-called 'rough wooing', to persuade Mary Queen of Scots into the sickly marriage bed of Edward VI.

Britto/Brutus was an important pillar in the origin myth of Tudor ancestry. This did not stop the Italian scholar Polydore Vergil pointing out the spuriousness of Geoffrey's so-called history; but a good story trumps a spoilsport historian no matter how right he or she may be. Spenser's *Faerie Queen*, Shakespeare's *Cymbeline* and *King Lear*, Dryden's *King Arthur*, Malory's *Morte d'Arthur*, Tennyson's *Idylls of the King* and a string of Arthurian novels and films in recent decades have subsequently helped to keep the Geoffrey legend of British origins intact in the popular imagination, albeit re-shaped and revised for new audiences.

These myths and accounts, the earliest written records, are most interesting for what they tell us about the way people have manipulated the past to justify dynastic power, political ambitions or even the primacy of a particular place of pilgrimage. As an archaeologist, I have attempted to explore the British past often through quite mundane material – everyday objects such as broken pots, food refuse, fragments of stone or metal tools, or the organic remains of plants and wood preserved in anaerobic bogs; and, of course, the bones of human beings. I have been fortunate that my work has taken me to many different parts of the world, from Canada to the West Indies, the Orkney Islands to sub-Saharan Africa. Some of these fragments of the human jigsaw puzzle have been several hundred thousand years old, others created in the lifetime of my own parents. Plans, maps, documents and diaries, words committed to paper, papyrus, parchment, slabs of stone and leaves of wood bring us close to past lives; but physical evidence, whether thoughtfully placed in graves or haphazardly discarded as rubbish, is the mainstay of archaeology.

Such stuff can project us further back into the distant prehistoric past or illuminate the contemporary world. What we look like, what we wear and what we eat tell us a lot about ourselves and other people: our sense of identity and belonging; who we think we are.

Working in different parts of the world I have constantly been impressed by the way people absorb ideas, culture and each others' genes like a sponge, creating something new from the parts they have gathered — Comanche Indians took the horse, the weapons and the women of European neighbours to create a spectacular Plains culture; Black Africa absorbed Islamic and Chinese trade goods to make the Swahili civilisation of Kenya. Prehistoric Britons adopted farming from the Continent and created a culture of circular temples from Wessex to the Northern Isles, which probably generated Geoffrey of Monmouth's giant legends. Britain as much as anywhere is a laboratory of change — a place joined to the Continent, then separated by rising seas; a place peripheral to world civilisation then central to it; a place of thinly scattered population and now one of the most densely populated parts of the globe. A place where some of its tribal languages have stuttered to extinction and another has spread across the globe. A place created by immigrants which excels at xenophobia; which has one of the richest histories in the world but still suffers from amnesia. Britain may be a group of islands, but it lies just off the world's largest land mass. Unlike, for example, Tasmania, isolated for 13,000 years, Britain is accessible.

I have also been struck by the closeness of humanity — how similar we are to each other; how, in vastly different times and places, we respond and adapt in similar ways to the pressures of climate, the need for food and water, the desire for status and, unfortunately, hostility to others — to those defined as being outside the tribal circle and at odds with the approved moral order. I witnessed the evidence of such clashes in Canada, around Georgian Bay, north of Toronto, when searching out and excavating Indian settlements occupied in the seventeenth and eighteenth centuries. There the French and the British, the Huron and the Iroquois exchanged furs, tobacco and weapons, swapped genes and lethal microbes, adopted the religions and languages of the most powerful, and slaughtered each other in competition for all of the above. I saw a mass grave of Huron Indians who had died from smallpox. Several years later, excavating in St Nicholas's Church in Sevenoaks, Kent, with a team of Oxford archaeologists, we uncovered the body of Lord Amhurst, 'the Conqueror of Canada', victor over the French in North America and the man who is sometimes credited, if that is not a grossly inappropriate word, with the invention of germ warfare — he had infected blankets distributed to the Indians, so spreading the smallpox whose devastating impact was so clear in the mass grave in Ontario.*

In death, Amhurst, the English hero whose portrait hangs in that peculiarly British institution the National Portrait Gallery, lay alongside his French neighbours in Sevenoaks. These were Huguenots, rejects from the dominant Catholic French tribe, who had sought refuge in England, created a new British identity and in their way contributed just as much to the creation of the British Empire as Lord Amhurst himself. Such burials and memorials tell us a lot about who people want to be, how they wished to be perceived by posterity. This message to the future may come from the dead themselves, or from those who organised the ceremony, a medium for the living to assert their own identity.

Westminster Abbey is an iconic English building which echoes with such messages. The building itself was founded and then remodelled by two kings — Edward the Confessor and Henry III, both of whom wanted the English to be more like the French. Inside, on the wall of the south cloister, there is a stone memorial, scarcely noticed by most visitors, to a Frenchman who was proud to be, first, a Protestant and, second, a subject of England. This memorial is a testimony to the endlessly shifting and fascinating subject of tribal, national and religious identity. It begs the question posed in *Monty Python and the Holy Grail*: 'Who are the Britons?'

The memorial reads:

> Sacred to FRANCIS LIGONIER etc.
> Colonel of dragoons, a Native of France, descended
> From a very ancient and very Honble
> Family there; but a zealous Protestant
> And subject of England, sacrificing himself
> In its defence against a POPISH PRETENDER
> At the battle of FALKIRK in the year 1745

The memorial to Francis was placed by his brother, Sir John Ligonier. Eager to assert the family's successful new identity, he describes himself as a Knight of the Bath and General of Horse in the British Army. There is no doubt where the Ligoniers belong: they are well and truly part of the British Establishment of the mid-eighteenth century.† Of course,

---

* Amhurst cannot really be said to have invented germ warfare: 700 years earlier Guillaume le Bâtard, better known in his forcibly adopted country as William the Conqueror, knew the trick of hurling rotting corpses into besieged castles.

† It was Field Marshal Lord Ligonier who put forward General Jeffrey Amhurst and Major General James Wolfe for their posts in the Canada campaign.

even the term 'British' is a source of endless confusion and debate. The Ligoniers had washed up in England because of the internecine religious wars in France and the competitive struggle between Catholic France and its Protestant neighbours. Out of this emerged a marriage of convenience between two historically antipathetic parties: England and Scotland.

As recently as 1700 Sir Edward Seymour, Tory leader in the English House of Commons, had shunned the northern neighbour: Scotland, he said, was a beggar and '... whoever married a beggar could only expect a louse for her portion'.[3] That pretty well summed up the traditional English attitude. But within a few years, faced with the increasing problems of national security and a powerful Continental aggressor, England became a suitor. In spite of popular opposition in Scotland, the powerbrokers there appreciated that a union was potentially good for their wallets. So the Anglo-Scottish Union took place on May Day 1707. The Treaty declared: 'That the Two Kingdoms of England and Scotland shall ... Forever after be United into One Kingdom by the name of Great Britain'.

England and Scotland were not destined to settle down and live happily ever after. While a Scot such as James Thomson (1700–1748) wrote 'Rule, Britannia' and embraced the imperial partnership, others resented the whole enterprise. Francis Ligonier died in the fateful year of '45, when the Jacobites, supporters of the deposed Catholic royal house of Stewart,* led by the Young Pretender, rose against the Union, the English and their German monarch George II of Hanover.†

Ironically, Ligonier fell at Falkirk, the site of an earlier and more famous battle, in 1298, where William Wallace was defeated by the Plantagenet King Edward I, conqueror of Wales, campaigner in France and the monarch who expelled the Jews from England. William Wallace's brutal execution was lovingly and sadistically recreated by Mel Gibson in his entertaining travesty of British history, the film *Braveheart*. Gibson, a

---

* The Jacobites took their name from 'Jacobus', the Latin for James, the given name of many Stewart kings. The Stewart family took their name from their role as 'stewards' to the Norman Scottish Bruce dynasty.

† George was obviously a man with a keen eye for genetic improvement. His son Frederick, born in Hanover, wished to marry Princess Wilhelmina of Prussia. George II forbade the marriage, saying: 'I did not think that ingrafting my half-witted coxcomb upon a mad woman would improve the breed.' He was scarcely fonder of his kingdom than he was of his son. 'I am sick to death of this foolish stuff and wish with all my heart that the devil may take all your bishops, and the devil take your Minister, and the devil take your Parliament and the devil take the whole island, provided I can get out of it and go to Hanover.' Nevertheless he was the last British sovereign to fight alongside his troops – though they were Austrians, Hanoverians, Hessians and Dutch as well as British, at the Battle of Dettingen, in 1743.

Catholic Australian, portrayed Wallace as an archetypal ancient Briton: long-haired, woad-daubed and over a millennium out of time. *Braveheart* may have appealed to nationalistic Scots and glorified their national martyr, but it did little to help anyone's understanding of relationships and identity in medieval England and Scotland.*

Wallace and Francis Ligonier were individuals with complex identities caught up in the web of history. They led dramatic and violent lives in history's spotlight. Most people who have lived in the British Isles remain historically anonymous, but they are no less influenced by the pull of history, by environmental and economic pressures and political events. Individuals shape history and are shaped by it. Our cultures and identities, where we live and even the size of the population are moulded by millions of individual decisions. In many atlases Britain appears centre stage and overly large. In fact, this small group of islands, separated from each other and the Continent as sea levels rose at the end of the Ice Age about nine thousand years ago, lies at the extreme north-western tip of the European land mass. Another finger of land projects from Eurasia on the eastern side, mirroring Britain in size and location: the Kamchatka Peninsula. At various times in the past both places were underpopulated and remote from the focal points of history. To the classical world of Greece and Rome, Britain was *Ultima Thule*,† a mysterious, exotic place at the margin of the known world. Britons typified barbarism. Britain was the boondocks. Probably no educated Roman, such as Pliny the Younger, who witnessed the Vesuvian eruption, or even Julius Caesar, who twice sailed by the White Cliffs of Dover and landed on the south coast, could have imagined that Britain, one of the last parts of the world to be settled by *Homo sapiens*, slow to adopt farming and a latecomer to the use of metal, would become an imperial power on a scale to surpass Rome, the heart of a world economic and industrial revolution and possessor of a capital city whose population would exceed Ancient Rome's by ten times. So how did Britain's population grow and change? Where did its people come from? How did they interact to create the shifting, multiple identities of Britain? And how can we find out? This is the subject of this book.

---

* One relationship which is certainly out of kilter in the film is Wallace's affair with, and implied impregnation of, Edward's French wife Isabella. At the time in which the film is set she was unmarried and living in France. Robert the Bruce, the Scots leader, was, just like King Edward, descended from Norman invaders. He took his name from Breaux, in the Cotentin Peninsula north-west of Bayeux. In the film the English are demonised, as they are in Gibson's contribution to American history *The Patriot*, where he refashions history for the benefit of his primary audience, conveniently portraying the American revolutionaries as sympathetic towards black people.
† Iceland is also a contender.

In recent history my own family is probably fairly typical. I think of myself as a Yorkshireman, British, English (but not the same as southerners even if I do live in London), European (I split my time between France and England), ex-Catholic, and certainly Americanised – I was brought up on a diet of westerns, in the cinema and on television. As a child I fantasised that the millstone grit outcrops of Yorkshire's Calder Valley looked like Monument Valley in John Ford movies such as *Stagecoach* and *The Searchers*. I knew the tribes of America, from Apache to Zuni, long before I heard about the tribes of Ancient Britain – the Atrebates or the Votadini; that is about as far as we can go in the alphabet soup of British tribes. I also think of myself as an archaeologist, which means I belong to an international tribe (the men wear beards!).

Although I identify closely with Yorkshire, few of my family originated there. In the nineteenth century the Mileses – my great-grandfather – came from Ipswich to work in the textile trade. My grandfather, William Miles, married a Naylor, a local family who had intermarried with Irish immigrants, the Mulligans. My mother's family, the Grahams, were Scots and Irish. My great-grandmother, however, spoke with a Welsh accent. She was Mary Bannon, who lived in St Asaph's and married James Garrick Graham, a ship's cook from Edinburgh. He died young, so Mary attempted to walk with her three children to the West Riding, where she had relatives who had moved there from western Ireland in pursuit of work. When Mary reached Manchester, she was picked up as a vagrant; the two oldest boys were taken away from her and placed in a Catholic Boys' Home, St Joseph's, run by Jesuits. My grandfather, Joseph Leo, stayed there from the age of seven until he rejoined his mother eight years later. His two elder brothers joined the army; one of them was eventually posted to India, where he married a local woman. Joseph Leo, my grandfather, married Emma Jane McEvoy* from another family of Irish immigrants. In 1914 he volunteered to join the Leeds Bantams – recruits from industrial Yorkshire who were under 1.62 metres (5 feet 3 inches) tall – and lost his leg, aged twenty-one, fighting at Vimy Ridge, near Arras. Joseph Leo died when he was 48; and I never met him, but he was a vivid presence in my childhood because my mother talked about him a lot.

My two children have more complicated genes. Their maternal great-grandmother, Rufka Fischman, left Bialystock† – now in Poland, then

---

* Emma Jane, James, Sarah and Ellen were the four surviving children of their mother Sarah McEvoy, *née* Gallagher, who gave birth to nine children in the last decade or so of the nineteenth century.

† The name will be familiar to anyone who has seen the musical *The Producers*. The hero, Max Bialystock, is a typical go-getting Jewish wise-guy.

part of the Russian Empire – in 1901 along with her mother and five sisters. As Ashkenazi Jews they probably had not had the surname long. In Poland surnames were allocated to Jews from 1844. Families who could pay enough to the officials were rewarded with pleasant or impressive names – names that included flowers, such as Rosenthal, or precious metals, such as Goldberg.

Rufka's father and two brothers had already gone ahead to find work in London before sending for the family. While researching this book my wife and I visited the Immigration Museum on Ellis Island, in New York. Displayed there were photographs taken in Bialystock shortly after the family left – they showed bodies in the street, victims of the Tsar's pogrom against the Jews. The Fischmans were certainly economic migrants; but were conditions so awful and threatening that they would now be considered 'genuine refugees' by our tabloid newspapers? Fortunately they came at a time when the barriers to entry were not prohibitively low; but they were gradually descending, as the British increasingly saw immigrants as a problem. The Fischmans anglicised their name to Fisher. Yet, like many people, the older ones felt the need to protect their own genetic and cultural identity. When Rufka married an English gentile, George Axford, they did not attend the wedding; instead they held a funeral for her.

My children's maternal grandfather, Morien Morgan, was also an economic migrant of a sort. He left Bridgend, in South Wales, to be educated as one of the first generation of aeronautical engineers at Cambridge University. As with my own generation, education took him away from his home town. Nevertheless he always thought of himself as a Welshman and sounded like one. He may have lived in England for nearly fifty years, but he would have failed the rugby union test.* It was obvious where Morien's sporting loyalties lay.

When I first met Morien, I asked about his unusual name. He told me that he had been born on the same day that his uncle Morien had left for Australia, who had the name from a well-known bard in the Eisteddfod. I was pleased to be able to tell him that the original Morien was a British hero who had died fighting Yorkshiremen at the Battle of Catterick in the sixth century. Morien's deeds were recorded in the epic poem 'Y Gododdin' – a great fighter 'though he was no Arthur'.

---

* Norman Tebbit, when a Conservative minister, implied that immigrants were not fully British if they still supported the cricket teams of their native lands. Even in 1995 (not 1895!) an article in *Wisden Cricketers' Almanack* assured its readers: 'Asians and negroes do not feel the same pride and identification with England as the white man.' The urge to play for England was a 'matter of biology'.[4]

I don't think my father-in-law was much of an Arthur either. More a Merlin. He helped put the Spitfires into the Battle of Britain and later launched Concorde.

So over the past five generations my family has moved about the British Isles or arrived from overseas looking for work, avoiding trouble, marrying locally, gravitating away from the countryside and often, like so many people, towards London and the industrial towns. We include Catholics, Jews, Methodists, Anglicans and Hindus; and we speak English with a variety of accents that give away our place of origin and our class. In tribal Britain we still identify ourselves most when we open our mouths. In a recent survey British people agreed that immigrants could become British – but most importantly they must learn to speak English. The then Home Secretary, David Blunkett, agreed. There are some people descended from Britain's earliest inhabitants – Welsh, Highland Scots, Cornish, Irish or Manx – who might like to see immigrants learning to speak one of Britain's older Gaelic languages; but the tide is flowing strongly for English, not just around the British Isles but across the world – another surprise for Julius Caesar, for when he landed in Kent, in 55 BC, no one spoke English.

The idea for this book came when I lived in Oxford, just over the ancient bridge that separates the tower of Magdalen College and the gates of Britain's oldest Botanic Garden from the hunched terraces of Cowley Road and Iffley Road. People who only know Oxford from television have a very clichéd image of the place – of Inspector Morse in his timeless Jaguar, cruising empty, litter-free streets between honey-coloured college walls and always finding a parking space. In fact it is a busy, commercial city, which has constantly burst its boundaries from the Anglo-Saxon defences to the twentieth-century ring road. It has horrendous traffic, the usual drink and drug problems, but disappointingly few murders.

When I moved into one of the Iffley Road terraces, built in 1852, the year Oxford's railway station opened and twenty years after the area had been hit by a cholera epidemic, my mother was genuinely puzzled. She had a Yorkshirewoman's disdain of terraced houses, which she had escaped in the early sixties for the respectability of semi-detatched suburbia. She couldn't understand why I would want to move back into the inner city – even Oxford's. Most of my mother's generation would have agreed with her; there were certainly few of them left in our triangle of Oxford known as St Clement's. When the local residents' association met in our kitchen, there was one old lady who had lived in the area all her life, and the family next door who were the third generation in their house. Everyone else was a relative newcomer — from various parts of England, Ireland, Jamaica, Bangladesh, Pakistan, India, the USA and France — the New Britons. We used to joke that English restaurants and local accents were endangered species in the centre of Oxford.

Most people assume this rich cultural mix is a recent phenomenon, mainly due to post-war immigration from the old Empire — or new Commonwealth. If you looked over Magdalen (still pronounced 'Maudelen' in the fourteenth-century fashion) Bridge, there, apparently, was the evidence, in mellow Cotswold stone, for the antiquity and stability of 'Olde England'. But Magdalen Tower grows out of a deep, dark and complex mulch: newcomers, conflict and change are fundamental to Oxford's — and Britain's — history. At the Oxford Archaeological Unit where I worked we had the opportunity to excavate close to the base of the tower. We uncovered the foundations of an earlier impressive building, the Hospital of St John the Baptist, set up in the thirteenth century with the support of Henry III, patron of architecture and promoter of Westminster Abbey.* In Oxford to facilitate the new hospital, Henry needed to provide a site. Even though the city was crowded, there was one conveniently 'available' on the banks of the River Cherwell. All Henry had to do was confiscate it from its owners, Oxford's Jewish community, who could expect no favours from their monarch and supposed protector.

In Henry's reign the Jews were being pressured to convert to Christianity. The newly arrived Dominican order of friars[†] — Christendom's blackshirts — provocatively set up their headquarters in Oxford's Jewish quarter. On 17 May 1268, Ascension Day, the Jews were accused of desecrating Oxford's processional cross. So their leaders were imprisoned and forced to pay for a new gold cross, which was then prominently displayed opposite the synagogue. In such times it was not difficult for Henry III to confiscate part of the Jews 'garden' for the Hospital of St John the Baptist, though he did leave them an area for their cemetery, which now lies beneath the Botanic Garden. They were not to have the use of it for long. Twenty-two years later, in 1290, Henry's son, Edward I, expelled the long-suffering Jews from his kingdom and their Oxford

* His grand project was the new Westminster Abbey, designed to house the relics of Edward the Confessor and as a coronation church. He was inspired by Rheims Cathedral, where the French crowned their kings, and the jewel-like Sainte Chapelle in Paris, in which Louis IX intended to house his new collection of relics, which included the Crown of Thorns and the True Cross.
† The Dominicans were founded in 1216 by the Spaniard Domingo de Guzman (St Dominic). They arrived in Kent in 1221 and within a fortnight reached Oxford, attracted to the centre of learning where they specialised in preaching and theology. Their most illustrious member in Oxford was Roger Bacon.

property eventually passed to a newish institution named Balliol College.*

While I was living next to Magdalen College School, a piece of ground was stripped to build a new extension. This provided a keyhole into another layer of Oxford's far from somnolent buried history, revealing the remnants of Civil War earthworks, from the 1640s, when General Fairfax successfully besieged the Royalist city. One result of the Parliamentary victory was that Cromwell re-admitted the Jews into England. Like many other immigrants, the Jews introduced the British to new tastes in food. Jacob the Jew opened the first coffee house in England, in 1651, at the Angel Inn, just up the High Street from Magdalen College. The Angel became one of Oxford's great coaching inns; unfortunately it succumbed to the British fondness for redevelopment at any price – the mock-Elizabethan-style Examination School, which opened on the site in 1882, went three times over budget. It was, however, the site of one of England's first urban archaeological excavations, which revealed a lunar landscape of crater-like pits. We now know that these were medieval rubbish dumps, where Oxford's inhabitants, lacking rudimentary public services, simply poured their ordure into holes conveniently and unhygienically dug into their back lots.

As an archaeologist I cannot help but think in four dimensions – and the fourth dimension is time. As you walk through Oxford there is a city beneath your feet, streets on which Anglo-Saxons walked a thousand years ago, now buried three or four metres deep; and beneath them the cold gravel terraces sown with the teeth of extinct mammoths. It is no wonder that Philip Pullman set his marvellous *His Dark Materials* trilogy here. But to understand the past and our ancestors we also need to remember how people have thought about history, about the British and other people, in relatively recent times. We can constantly find ourselves being snagged on discredited but persistent theories. Like brambles, some historical ideas refuse to go away.

At the Examination School excavation, for example, the pioneering Victorian archaeologists revealed what, to us, are bog-standard medieval rubbish pits; but they saw them through the distorting lenses of their own theories: the pits were 'an ancient British village'! They visualised their ancestors as simple folk – semi-naked, ancient Britons daubed with woad, like Mel Gibson, and easy meat for those well-organised, empire-building proto-Victorians, the Romans. The idea had got about that ancient Britons lived in pit dwellings, where they crouched, hobbit-like,

* John Wycliff's college; the intellectual home of the heretic Lollards and, arguably, the Peasant's Revolt (see p. 282).

in holes in the ground, beneath conical thatched roofs. So pits meant ancient British 'pit dwellings'. It took Gerhard Bersu, a distinguished German archaeologist kicked out of his country by Adolf Hitler, to explain to the British that in the Iron Age the Britons used pits as underground grain stores and they lived in highly desirable, comfortable, if rather communal, roundhouses. Thanks to a German émigré, we now know that our ancestors were not the simpletons of prehistoric Europe.

But the Victorian view of British pedigree was not just a matter of pits and post-holes. In 1900 William Z. Ripley of the Massachusetts Institute of Technology produced *The Races of Europe*, in which he indulged in the Victorian fondness for classification and the assumption that virtue was visual and physically apparent. 'The aristocracy,' he pronounced, 'everywhere tends to the blond and tall type, as we should expect.' In contrast, the old British types display 'irregularity and ruggedness', large mouths, brow-ridges and big noses 'not delicately formed'. Ripley believed that on a trip through Britain at the start of the twentieth century, 'one could spot these distinctive types: both ancestry and character were written into the physiognomy of the population'. Human beings could be mounted like moths, butterflies and beetles on the basis of their appearance and the measurements of their skulls.

When I reopened a prehistoric long barrow on White Horse Hill, Oxfordshire, originally excavated in 1855, I found that the skulls had been removed from the bodies. The purpose of this exercise in Victorian headhunting was to collect and meticulously record contributions for one of the great works of nineteenth-century pseudo-science, *Crania Britannica*, a lavishly produced compendium of British skulls published in 1856, three years before Darwin's *On the Origin of Species*, by Joseph Barnard Davis and John Thurnam.*

In Denmark, Christian Thomsen, attempting to organise the prehistoric antiquities in the National Museum, developed the Three Age System – of Stone, Bronze and Iron – so that he could order his material

---

* The leading proponent of craniometry – the science of skulls – was Samuel George Morton of Philadelphia. He built up a skull 'library' of more than a thousand specimens, from the measurements of which he developed his theory of racial origins and published *Crania Americana* in 1839. He argued that the races developed separately, prior to the Great Flood and the dispersal of Noah's sons. The Caucasian type – led by the Teutons and Anglo-Saxons – was supreme. The Hottentots were like 'lower animals' and the Chinese 'a monkey race'. When Stephen Jay Gould recalculated Morton's measurements of Caucasian and Indian cranial capacity or brain size, he found the former were inflated and the latter underestimated. Morton's *New York Tribune* obituary emphasised his international status: 'No scientific man in America enjoyed a higher reputation among scholars throughout the world.' Nevertheless, he persistently, even if transparently and unconsciously, mis-measured to suit his own racial theories of white (Anglo-Saxon) superiority.

in a relative, if not precise, chronology. Scandinavian craniologists working with this system claimed to be able to distinguish Stone Age skulls from later Bronze Age ones. William Wilde, Oscar's father, applied this distinction to the Irish in his book *The Beauties of the Boyne and its Tributary the Blackwater* (1849) and claimed to be able to distinguish the waves of invasion set out in the *Book of Invasions*: the pre-Celtic Fir Bolg from the Celtic Tuatha De Dannan, whose arrival Wilde assigned to the Bronze Age. In Britain Davis and Thurnam pronounced that the inhabitants of Stone Age long barrows were long-headed ('dolichocephalic') and those interred in the Bronze Age round barrows, conveniently, were round-headed ('brachycephalic'). Many archaeologists assumed this represented the arrival of a new ethnic group into Britain: the Celts.

From skull shape and size Victorian 'anthropometrists' declared that they could not only identify racial types but measure intelligence, predict behaviour, identify criminals and lunatics as well as ancient British types still surviving in the modern population. The new technology of photography enabled scientists to assemble galleries of such stereotypical characters for the benefit of the police. And the surviving ancient British types were destined to be ruled by their superiors – those of Roman, Anglo-Saxon or Norman blood. This kind of racial determinism dominated later nineteenth-century historical and anthropological thinking. Human skulls provided a measurable means to define races scientifically. Different races occupied different levels on the cultural ladder. So scientific racism defined a global cultural hierarchy. For neo-Darwinians, poor performers, such as American Indians, Tasmanians, even British Celts, were destined for subjugation and ultimately extinction.

Joseph Barnard Davis and John Thurnam, the compilers of *Crania Britannica*, considered their measurements and pronounced: in western Ireland 'the peculiar character of the natives proclaims their descent from a primeval race'. *Punch* cartoons would soon display the simian Paddy for the amusement of its tall, blond, delicately featured English readers. The Irish, according to the calculations of Davis and Thurnam, 'are wild, superstitious, vengeful, addicted to extravagant legend, and timidly susceptible to every impression which can arouse their fatalism, or their fears'. Then, conveniently, they delivered the conclusions: 'They are the children of the British populations, incapable of ruling themselves in any high sense, and requiring a fostering hand to carry on their improvement of which they stand in perpetual need.' In Britain we are still living with the problem this attitude created.

So if the population of the far west of the British Isles was some kind of inferior specimen, like Neanderthals, or mountain gorillas clinging to their remote fastnesses, what of the rest? In the north of England and parts of Scotland the locals were the finely bred offspring of Vikings: 'An acute, shrewd people, active, industrious, vigorous, enterprising, trustworthy ... clean and respectable ... most unlike the Celtic races.' That is the verdict on the fine folk of Cumberland. So what is normal for Norfolk? Courage, determination and large hat sizes — clearly a sign of intelligence for Davis and Thurnam. And so the isobars of racial superiority could be drawn around the British Isles.

The Victorian obsession with collecting, measuring and classifying was typified by Dr John Beddoe, president of the Royal Anthropological Society of London. He was the repository of statistics collected by doctors and clergymen from around Britain. From them emerged his great work in 1870, *On the Stature and Bulk of Man in the British Isles*. Beddoe was largely responsible for propagating the classical myth of the small, dark Welshman, which is still repeated today, but he created an impressively 'scientific' term — the 'index of nigrescence': essentially, tall, fair people in the north-east degenerate into short, dark ones in the south-west. And in between there are also odd pockets of 'physical degeneration' — such as Nottingham, where the ancient aborigines supposedly survived in a sea of racially superior Teutonic newcomers.

'Degeneration' was initially a term used by naturalists in its literal Latin sense, indicating departure from an original genus or type. J. F. Blumenbach (1752–1840) was the German naturalist who, following in the systematic footsteps of his teacher, the Swedish botanist Carl von Linné, and the creator of modern systematic biology, classified *Homo sapiens* into four varieties, or races. His publication *De generis humani varietate* appeared in 1776, the same year as the American Declaration of Independence. Twenty years later Blumenbach modified his original system to one based on five types.[5]

He concluded that the people of greatest beauty were light-skinned and originated near Mount Caucasus, in Russia. He explained: '*Caucasian variety* I have taken the name of this variety from Mount Caucasus, both because its neighbourhood, and especially its southern slopes, produces the most beautiful race of men, and because ... in that region, if anywhere, we ought with the greatest probability to place the autochthones [original forms] of mankind.'

Hence the light-skinned people of Europe and western Asia were classed as Caucasian — the original God-given form of *Homo sapiens*. From their homeland humans spread across the globe, encountering different climates, diseases and other pressures, both cultural and natural, which promoted 'degeneration', or change.*

White people who moved from their temperate homeland into the tropics would become dark-skinned; conversely, black slaves transported, say, to North America would eventually become white. So to Blumenbach race was a fairly superficial matter and, liberally for his time, he argued that people were essentially, mentally and morally, the same. He especially noted the abilities of black writers such as Phillis Wheatley, brought as a slave from west Africa to Boston, who earned a reputation as a poet on both sides of the Atlantic.[6]

> *A* PHILLIS *rises, and the world no more*
> *Desires the sacred right to mental pow'r;*
> *While, Heav'n-inspir'd, she proves her Country's claim*
> *To Freedom, and her own to deathless Fame.*[7]

Nevertheless, even for Blumenbach the Caucasian provided the racial gold standard from which others departed, or degenerated. The most liberal of nineteenth-century thinkers, such as Darwin and Alexander von Humboldt, could not quite discard the attitude that Caucasians were top of the evolutionary tree and lesser tribes were destined to wither on the branch. If Hitler stretched such views to their ultimately horrifying conclusion in the twentieth century, it is also a salutary reminder to see how widespread they were, and how they could be expressed by a forward-thinking British intellectual. H. G. Wells pronounced in 1902:

> And how will the New Republic treat the inferior races? How
> will it deal with the black? ... the yellow man ... the Jew? ...
> those swarms of black, and brown, and dirty white, and yel-
> low people, who do not come into the new needs of
> efficiency? Well, the world is a world, and not a charitable in-
> stitution, and I take it they will have to go ... And the ethical
> system of these Men of the New Republic, the ethical system
> which will dominate the world state, will be shaped primarily
> to favour the procreation of what is fine and efficient and
> beautiful in humanity — beautiful and strong bodies, clear
> and powerful minds ... And the method that nature has fol-
> lowed in the shaping of the world, whereby weakness was
> prevented from propagating weakness ... is death ... The
> Men of the New Republic ... will have an ideal that will make
> the killing worth the while.[8]

---

* Blumenbach believed that cultural habits, such as binding the heads of children, would eventually change skull shapes in descendants by 'inheritance of acquired characters'.

In the mid-nineteenth century the supposed science of racial determinism provided a convenient buttress for racists (notably advocates of slavery in America), for European imperialism and for the active mistreatment or neglect of primitive peoples classed as backward natives. Such theories also provided support for the developing interest in eugenics expressed by H. G. Wells — the idea that the human population could be improved by limiting the breeding opportunities of its less capable, 'inferior', members. Or worse.

By 1910 the anthropologist Franz Boas had substantially undermined the credibility of scientific racism. He showed that skull shape was essentially influenced by environmental factors and could, therefore, change from one generation to another. The skull was not a marker of fixed racial affinity. Nor did slight variations in cranial capacity make much difference to intelligence or dictate what language you would speak. No matter how advanced particular societies were around the world — politically, socially, technologically — people on average were pretty much as smart as each other. At various times, for all kinds of complex historical reasons, various groups, whether Romans, Chinese, Iraqis, Spaniards, British or Incas have ruled their particular roost; but not because they were inherently more intelligent or worthy. Britons have been at both ends of the cultural spectrum.

In *Richard II* (II, i, 40–50) Shakespeare put the ultimate patriotic speech into the mouth of John of Gaunt, creating a timeless image of enormous emotional appeal if one of limited historical and geographical accuracy:

> This royal throne of kings, this sceptr'd isle,
> This earth of majesty, this seat of Mars,
> This other Eden, demi-paradise,
> This fortress built by Nature for herself
> Against infection and the hand of war,
> This happy breed of men, this little world,
> This precious stone set in the silver sea,
> Which serves it in the office of a wall,
> Or as a moat defensive to a house,
> Against the envy of less happier lands;
> This blessed plot, this earth, this realm, this England …

Shakespeare was pandering to his Tudor audience drawing a contrast between their time and that of the recent and nasty Wars of the Roses — when the rulers of the English Eden persistently soiled their own patch. Nevertheless, Shakespeare's rousing and comforting phrases have been burnished and hallowed by some of England's most widely read historians, such as Churchill or Arthur Bryant, and broadcast to the nation, for example by the impressive BBC Radio 4 series *This Sceptered Isle* (in 1995–6).*

Norman Davies[9] has, notably, emphasised how Anglocentric is this interpretation of British history, ignoring not only the important roles of Ireland, Scotland, Wales and the smaller islands, but the extent to which Britain is an interesting place precisely because of its cultural mix and its openness. There are times when the Channel has played the part of a moat, defended by the wooden walls of the fleet against Napoleon's giant armies, or by squadrons of Hurricanes and Spitfires. Far more often, though, the sea has acted as a highway linking Liverpool to Dublin and North America, Whitby to London and Australia, Kirkwall to Reykjavik or Oslo, Cork and Cornwall to Brittany.[10]

The outside world does not bounce off the White Cliffs of Dover; rather it washes around them and into the inlets of the Thames, Ouse, Humber and Trent, the Tyne, Forth, Clyde, Dee, Mersey, Severn and Shannon. Nowhere in Britain and Ireland is far from the sea or from one of its arteries. Islands such as mainland Orkney or Man are also literally 'precious stones set in a silver sea'; historically, the inhabitants of these maritime crossroads could reach out into the world and the world could come to them.

Daniel Defoe (in *The True-Born Englishman*, 1701) created another often-quoted image of Britishness: he was closer to the historical mark with his description of 'that heterogeneous thing, an Englishman':

> *In eager rapes, and furious lust begot,*
> *Betwixt a painted Briton and a Scot:*
> *Whom gend'ring offspring quickly learnt to bow,*
> *And yoke their heifers to the Roman plough:*
> *From whence a mongrel half-bred race there came,*
> *With neither name nor nation, speech nor form*
> *In whose hot veins now mixtures quickly ran,*
> *Infus'd betwixt a Saxon and a Dane.*
> *While their rank daughters, to their parents just,*
> *Receiv'd all nations with promiscuous lust.*
> *This nauseous brood directly did contain*
> *The well-extracted blood of Englishman ...*

* Churchill's ripe, cigar-and-brandy prose echoed through the fifty-five episodes of this series – at least the words concocted mainly by the team of underpaid and under-credited writers who put together Churchill's *History of the English-Speaking Peoples*. Churchill was a brand as much as an author.

For Englishmen to boast of generations
Cancels their Knowledge and lampoons the Nation.
A true born Englishman's a Contradiction,
In Speech an Irony, in Fact a Fiction.

Like Shakespeare Defoe knew his audience. In August 1714 Prince George Lewis of Hanover, hardly a true-born Englishman, ascended the throne of his adopted country as King George I.

The catastrophe of Nazi Germany discredited but unfortunately did not entirely eradicate the racial theories that had played such an important part in western historical thinking. Post-war archaeologists were still, though, wedded to the idea that Britain had been subject to waves of invasion bringing technological change: from Neolithic farmers with their sheep and cereals, the first metallurgists glugging mead or beer from their distinctive pottery beakers – hence 'Beaker Folk' – to the waves of horse-riding sword-wielding Celts of the Iron Age. In early historic periods Angles, Saxons, Jutes, Scots, Vikings, Danes and Normans justified the historical fondness for invasion hypotheses, or the *1066 and All That* approach to history.

During the 1960s the simplistic idea that British history was dominated by invasion-induced change came under concerted attack. In particular, the growing impact of radiocarbon dating, and the calibration process that provided more confidence in the dates, undermined some of the traditional assumptions. At Christmas 1962, when I was fifteen, I received a massive book on World Archaeology written by the leading experts of the day. In it there was a reconstruction drawing showing the building of Stonehenge. The local natives – all adult men (no women and children) – provided the brawn; an architect from Mycenaean Greece provided the brains. Shortly afterwards this image was discredited. Radiocarbon dates put the megalithic sites of Britain centuries and even millennia earlier than the architectural achievements of Mycenae. Tombs such as Maes Howe in Orkney could not be crude northern copies of the so-called Tombs of Agamemnon or Klytemnestra in Mycenae.

Academic fashion shifted in favour of indigenous development: essentially, the continuity of local populations developing their own social organisation and adapting to new technologies. Archaeologists also began to question the meaning and mechanisms of change in early historic periods. Bede confidently described the arrival of Angles, Saxons and Jutes. But did this mean simply change at the top? – the rise to power of a new, incoming elite, as happened when William and his warrior band of Normans and Flemings took control of England? Or was there an Anglo-Saxon mass movement of people — a smaller-scale version of the European colonisation of North America? From the 1970s most archaeologists favoured the former explanation, though some continued to question why, in that case, there was such a massive culture change in southern and eastern England in the fifth century. And why do we speak English; not Gaelic?*

Victorian racial theories had proved to be ludicrous, all that skull-measuring a waste of time. Now the dating of prehistoric Britain was on a sounder footing, the old invasion explanations no longer made sense. Nevertheless, the questions of origin and change remained. We needed new ways of tackling them.

I was in my first year of primary school, constructing castles out of wooden bricks, when two Cambridge researchers came up with the twentieth century's most significant shape: the double helix. James Watson and Francis Crick had cracked 'the structure of the molecule at the heart of all life'.[12]

In the 1970s gene cloning and manipulation took off and it became possible to determine the order of bases along DNA molecules. This meant that the messages of genes, previously only picked up by cells, could now be read by humans. When I was at school, would-be archaeologists were advised to study history and Latin. My eccentric interest in biology was frustrated by the school timetable: biology clashed with Virgil. So it wasn't until 1968, at university, when I had a girlfriend (and, reader, I married her) who was studying genetics that I read her copy of Watson's *The Double Helix*, his candid account of the discovery of the structure of DNA. I wish I could say that I immediately spotted this new tool for exploring the past. Unfortunately I didn't have a clue. It was not until the 1980s that I began to appreciate the possibilities of the new subject of archaeogenetics.

Since then, molecular archaeology and genetic science have burgeoned, creating new pathways into history. Big questions are being asked: about the origins and expansion of *Homo sapiens*, our relationship to Neanderthals, the human colonisation of the Americas and the Pacific, the spread of farming and farmers across Europe, changes to diet and the impact of diseases. Oxygen and zinc isotopes are helping to identify prehistoric immigrants such as the Amesbury Archer, buried near Stonehenge, and his neighbours at Boscombe Down, who appear to have started their lives in the west, perhaps in Wales. Molecular archaeology

---

* The vast majority of the words in the *Oxford English Dictionary* derive from languages other than Old English. However, words deriving from Old English make up 62 per cent of those most commonly used.[11]

and DNA studies are a little like a runaway steam train: sparks are flying in all directions and it is difficult to stay on the rails. There are also a lot of loud hooting and excitable claims — often announced by press release, exclamatory and simplistic. The fact is that glamorous new techniques — like the Victorian measurements described earlier — can sound impressive and still generate garbage. So we still need to be careful of over-enthusiastic scientists proclaiming spectacular results.

A question that particularly interests me — because I have spent a not insignificant proportion of my life on my knees excavating Anglo-Saxon burials — is to what extent the local population of Roman Britain was replaced by Bede's incoming Anglo-Saxons. Genetic work on long-established south-eastern English families suggests that they match fairly closely with people in the Low Countries and are significantly different from the populations of Wales and Ireland. This is taken to support the image — which a lot of archaeologists considered old-fashioned and discredited — of fierce, pillaging Germans driving out the native Brits, indulging in ethnic cleansing either by slaughtering the men or driving the native 'waelas' — or foreigners, in Anglo-Saxon — into the fastnesses of the west. Recent genetic sampling has been taken to support this idea. But does it? Or is this a case of an historic event, real or imaginary, being rolled out to explain a set of data? In the nineteenth century burnt layers in towns such as London or Colchester were routinely ascribed to Boudicca's rebellion as if no one else ever lit a fire.

In the case of English genes matching those of the Low Countries there could be other explanations and contexts besides fifth-century Anglo-Saxon immigration and invasion. We have little or no genetic information about the Mesolithic population of Britain, but archaeological evidence suggests links between Britain and north-western Europe, when both were part of a continuous land mass. Such links could have been reinforced with the spread of farming, by contacts in the Iron Age and in the middle Saxon period. In other words, the people facing each other across the Channel and the North Sea could have a long history of economic and genetic exchange. When populations are isolated for a long time, they become more genetically distinctive. In the North Sea province this is not the case, but to pin the similarities on one episode may not be good history.

Genetics present enormous opportunities for understanding our past. However, it is worth remembering some of the basic precautionary principles when attempting to rewrite history from genes[13] — for example, the fact that small populations are more likely to become genetically distinct; and while rare genetic varieties are more likely to survive in large populations, they can become dominant in small gene pools.

People mainly exchange genes with their near neighbours, unless there is a strong cultural barrier, such as religion; but this is more often breached, as in my family, than religious orthodoxy admits. Jews, like most people, tend to have close genetic links with the communities they live closest to.* There are more likely to be genetic differences between populations isolated by distance or substantive physical barriers such as deserts or mountain chains.

Regional populations can, however, have strong genetic badges of identity, for example hair colour. My brother's two children look distinctly different from mine because they have inherited the fiery red hair of their mother — literally a Ryan's daughter. Tacitus's observation that the Caledonians had reddish hair — from which he assumed their Germanic origin — is supported by modern surveys: the Scottish population has the highest incidence of red hair anywhere in the world. This is probably a characteristic that goes back a long way, to when the population of north Britain was relatively small and isolated — perhaps when Mesolithic hunter-gatherers spread into areas newly released from the ice. Populations in Britain then increased, but most of the expansion probably came from the growth of internal communities. Recent isotopic analysis indicates that immigration continued, though on what scale is uncertain. However, as the mitochondrial DNA that Bryan Sykes extracted from the tooth of a young Upper Palaeolithic hunter buried in Gough's Cave, Somerset, showed: 'There was more of the hunter in us than any one had thought.' This DNA, from 13,000 years ago, matched the commonest sequence found in modern European populations.[15]

So, rather than tidal waves of invasion scouring the genetic beach of Britain, results like Gough's Cave suggest a basic continuity of population from the Upper Palaeolithic. The historical models of the nineteenth century were influenced by the dramatic changes imposed on the local population of America, Africa and Australia by technologically and numerically superior European powers. Such drastic changes should not be taken out of context, however. They happen when small native populations are overrun by much larger immigrant groups, especially when the newcomers bring fatal diseases to which the locals are not immune, and when the newcomers have impressive technology — from the steel swords

---

* This makes a nonsense, of course, of Nazi racial theories. Most Jewish gene pools show that non-Jewish men and their Y chromosomes, rather than women, did most of the mixing from outside. This also demonstrates the sense of the Jewish tradition of transmitting Judaism through the female line; to be a Jew by birth you must have a Jewish mother.[14]

and horses of conquistadors in South America to the Maxim machine-gun in South Africa.

In pre-modern Britain these factors did not apply. None of the known invaders of Britain – whether Romans, Anglo-Saxons, Vikings or Normans – arrived in prodigiously large numbers or with dramatically different technologies from the Britons. The Romans imposed the most obvious changes, thanks to organisational superiority. With them came foreign soldiers, traders and slaves from across the empire – from Africa, Syria, Spain and Greece. But Britannia's population remained substantially British. Another scenario which cannot be ruled out is what historians sometimes call 'systems collapse': where society fundamentally breaks down and the population plummets. This is a possibility in the fifth century as the Roman Empire disintegrated. Did the Angles, Saxons, Jutes and Scots simply move into a land where a demoralised population was failing to reproduce itself?

In researching this book I have often been struck by how many books on prehistory and history never mention population. For early periods it is not a straightforward subject – as someone once said, 'One guess is as bad as another.' Nevertheless, population – its size, make-up, rate of change – is fundamental to the understanding of any society. Prehistorians cannot work with the precision of those who have access to censuses or recorded birth, death and marriage statistics. They can, however, make estimates based on settlement densities, lifestyles, the productivity of the land, the human impact on the landscape and cemetery data. Cemeteries supply archaeologists with basic demographic evidence, providing that bones are reasonably well preserved, for example in alkaline soils. Inhumation – burial of the body, as opposed to cremation – also enables more information to be garnered from the skeleton, such as age at death, sex, height and robustness, and family relationships. Only occasionally, where disease or trauma has impacted on the skeleton itself, can the cause of death be determined. On well-preserved adult females the number of births can sometimes be estimated from pubic scars. From a totally excavated cemetery, where the dates of use can be estimated, it becomes possible to calculate the size of the contributing community. But opportunities for complete cemetery excavations, especially large ones, are limited; and in many cultures and periods people are not helpful to archaeologists: they dispose of bodies in ways that leave little or no trace – leaving them exposed, placing them in rivers, burning them, or clearing out burial chambers.

For those of us accustomed to the crowded British Isles estimates of early prehistoric population are remarkably low, for example as few as

1,200 in 9000 BC, rising to 5,500 in 5000 BC.[16]

With the onset of farming the population of Britain had the capacity to expand as new foodstuffs became available and the span between births shortened. Perhaps by 2000 BC – as the great stone ring at Stonehenge was constructed – there may have been about a quarter of a million Britons and fifty thousand Irish people. By the end of the Bronze Age, a millennium later, farming had clearly intensified, with the kind of demarcated landscapes of boundaries and enclosure that I describe at White Horse Hill (see Chapter 2). At this stage the population may have doubled to half a million.

If we move forward another millennium or so to about the late third century, when a substantial part of the British Isles was under Roman rule, recent estimates put the population of mainland Britain at about 3.5 million. These are all speculative figures based largely on settlement size, density and land use.[17] If they are not accurate as numbers, at least they indicate the general trend.

Most demographers – those who scientifically study human populations, their size, structure and development – would regard this as pretty crude stuff. In later periods marriage, birth and death records and, from 1801 in Britain, censuses allow much more sophisticated analyses of population: of birth and death rates, the impact of disease, age of marriage and fecundity. However, even with the most recent census there can be problems. Where I live, in Westminster, ironically the home of the National Office of Statistics, the local authority believes that several thousand people have disappeared from the 2001 Census. Densely populated urban areas with a lot of young, mobile people still prove difficult to count.

There is no doubt that the human population grew very slowly for a very long time. About ten thousand years ago there were probably about 4 million people in the world. Some of them were just beginning to come to terms with domesticating plants and animals and manipulating the carrying capacity of their environment. By the time of Christ, when agriculture had spread across much of the globe, there were probably over 200 million people. Five hundred years later, with the collapse of the Roman Empire, plagues and major unrest across Eurasia, the world population had probably fallen by a few million. In the Middle Ages it grew modestly; then, hit by serial plague again, it fell back in the fourteenth and fifteenth centuries. At this time the most distinctive thing about Britain's population was how small it was compared with those of European neighbours such as France and Italy. In AD 1600 the world population was about 560 million. The decline in plague mortality levels and improvements in agriculture boosted the numbers of Europeans, including the British, who started to colonise new lands, particularly America. The effects were catastrophic for indigenous populations (and slightly reduced growth at home), but rapidly expanding European communities in the thinly populated Americas and later Australia more than made up the losses in terms of numbers. As a result of migration and the Agricultural and Industrial Revolutions of the later eighteenth century, world population had soared to 945 million by 1800. A century later, in 1900, it had reached over 1,650 million. Twentieth-century warfare, starvation and disease knocked back the growth slightly, but medical advances, urbanisation and industrialisation meant that by 2000 the world population had topped 6,000 million.[18]

In 1927 the world supported 2 billion humans. It had taken 123 years to double from one billion, but only another thirty-three years to reach 3 billion, followed by fourteen years to hit 4 billion in 1974. And 5 billion in 1987, when the United Nations celebrated by declaring Matej Gaspar, a boy born in Zagreb, the world's five-billionth human being. We don't seem to have identified the six-billionth.

Through the Middle Ages and early modern period various statistics collected by rulers or by the Church provide a basis for population estimates, and have allowed historical demographers to reconstruct important demographic factors such as the varying ages of marriage, numbers of children, death rates and the causes of death and migration patterns. It was not until 1801 that England undertook its first census. By this time population growth was a hot topic. From about 1650 to 1800 the population of Britain and Ireland had increased dramatically, stimulated by land reclamation, agricultural productivity and the onset of the Industrial Revolution. Commentators such as David Hume (1752) and Robert Wallace (1761) had taken up the issue of whether a rapidly growing population was a sign of society's health. Was the growth of industry, urbanisation and the restructuring of social classes a good thing or not? Was modernisation a blessing or a curse?

The most influential commentator on these issues was Thomas Robert Malthus, a Cambridge graduate and a country curate. He was not looking for personal fame, because when he published his essay on the *Principle of Population as it Affects the Future Improvement of Society*, in 1798, he remained anonymous. Malthus sounded a warning note:

I think I may fairly make two postulata. First, that food is necessary to the existence of man. Secondly, that the passion between the sexes is necessary, and will remain nearly in its present state ... I say, that the power of population is indefinitely greater than the power in the earth to produce subsistence for man. Population, when unchecked, increases in geometric ratio. Subsistence increases only in an arithmetical ratio.

Malthus believed that humans have a powerful natural urge to increase their population but ultimately are checked by the lack of food. He also believed that poverty and low wages were a consequence of population growth. Increase the food supply, you get more people and more poverty. Sensible people will foresee the consequence and plan their families. Malthus meant them to do this by abstinence; he firmly objected to contraception, and waited until he was thirty-nine and had a secure university post before himself marrying. Poverty, he argued, was the fault of the poor for not trying harder, and welfare (the Poor Laws) only perpetuated the misery. Sharper suffering would encourage people to practise self-discipline.

Two centuries later the Malthusian argument still continues. Malthus, though, failed to see that technological progress could lead to improved food supply and a higher standard of living.* Like some other theoreticians he does not seem to have been a very sensitive observer of his fellow human beings. However, by promoting a national debate, by making population controversial, Malthus had the effect of spreading the knowledge of birth control, of which he so disapproved, amongst nineteenth-century Britons. The ultimate result was to sever the link between sexual intercourse and fertility, which Malthus took for granted.

The acceleration in population growth since the mid-eighteenth century has been principally due to the decline in death rate – fewer people die each year than are born. Medical advances have played a part, mainly in the twentieth century, but the principal cause has been improved standards of living: better food and drinking water, warmer and cleaner clothes, improved housing and hygiene.[19]

As the death rate dropped in economically developing countries like Britain, within a generation or two the fertility rate declined as well. In other words, in modernised societies people have fewer children. This is not a new phenomenon. Over two thousand years ago prosperous Romans adopted the same small family structure. As Pliny wrote to one

---

* Providing, as Marx and Engels argued, that the capitalist factory owners did not cream off too much of the profits or replace the workers with machinery. They believed that growing population would lead to increased dissatisfaction and, ultimately, the revolution. Marx did his bit by producing eight children.

of his friends: 'In our time most people hold that an only son is already a heavy burden and that it is advantageous not to be overburdened with posterity.'

I have gone through life on the crest of a mini population wave — the post-war baby boom, which peaked in the late 1950s and then rapidly declined through the 1960s to a trough in the 70s and 80s. This has caused a new outbreak of anxiety about the population: falling birth rates and rising life expectancy leading to a greying of the population. As baby-boomers surge into their sixties, attitudes to ageing will change, especially if the elderly stay fit and relatively prosperous, and exert their numerical strength politically: Youth tribes will be replaced by Grey tribes. On present trends, by 2050, 20 per cent of the population — 12 million people — will be over seventy and another 8 million aged between sixty and seventy. Already there are more over-sixties than under-sixteens in Britain. This has given rise to a pensions crisis. None of my grandparents lived more than five years beyond retirement — in the 1950s that was typical. Now the elderly frequently enjoy two or three decades of life beyond retire-ment age; and supporting each of them are 2.5 workers, half the number per pensioner as at the start of the twentieth century. The cost of caring for old people in 1995 was £11 billion; the Royal Commission on long-term care estimates this will quadruple by 2050.

It is unlikely that British families will suddenly begin to have signifi-cantly more offspring — the cost of child care and housing, the concern to maintain standards of living, the desire and need for parents to work are likely to inhibit that. So tough issues will have to be faced with unpopular consequences: increasing taxes, and raising the retirement age. Britain is also an attractive destination for the youthful populations of the world's poorer countries. In Africa, the Indian subcontinent and south-east Asia, the demographics are very different from those of the West. While the median age of Europeans is thirty-seven, that of Africans is eighteen. America has maintained a more youthful population and boosted its in-dustries with a relatively open-door policy, including turning a blind eye to illegal immigration.* Britain, in contrast, has often seen newcomers as a problem. It has no Statue of Liberty nor an Ellis Island-style immigra-tion museum to celebrate the arrival of its huddled masses. But the White Cliffs of Dover are not a wall behind which the natives shelter. Our genes and our history tell a different story.

---

* In the 1990s over 13.5 million new immigrants arrived in the US, mostly in California and the southern states.

One In the Beginning

'NO SUBJECT HAS lately excited more curiosity and general interest among geologists and the public than the question of the Antiquity of the Human Race.' These words were written by Sir Charles Lyell in *The Antiquity of Man*,[1] published in 1863. So great was the public curiosity and interest that the book ran to three editions in its first year. This was not surprising: Darwin's *Origins of Species by Means of Natural Selection; or the Preservation of Favoured Races in the Struggle for Life* had appeared only four years earlier, in 1859, and Lyell, as much as anyone, demonstrated the evidence in support of Darwin's theory of evolution.

Nevertheless, while able to describe discoveries of early humans on the Continent, in the Somme and Rhine valleys, Lyell had to admit: 'Yet the oldest memorials of our species at present discovered in Great Britain are post-glacial ...' But with typical Victorian optimism, and rotundity of expression, he urges his readers not to despair 'on the grounds of any uncongeniality in the climate or incongruity in the state of the animate creation with the well-being of our species'. We have no evidence, says Lyell, because 'we have made no investigation'.

Unfortunately his readers took this to heart; soon they were scrabbling in every cave they could lay their hands on. The result is that many of Britain's important cave sites are now badly disturbed, burrowed into by Victorians whose enthusiasm ran ahead of their forensic abilities.

In spite of his denials that much work had taken place, Lyell was only able to produce the evidence for his book because others had already started. He singled out for approval Dr Falconer and Lieutenant Colonel E. R. Wood, who had 'diligently explored of late years' the ossiferous caves of the Gower Peninsula in South Wales. The Gower was a famous hunting ground — more significant than Lyell realised. In 1822 Daniel and John Davies found the bones of exotic animals, including a mammoth's tusk in Goat's Hole Cave, Paviland. The illustrious William Buckland, Professor of Geology at Oxford and Dean of Westminster

Abbey, was informed and in January 1823 he came to look for himself. In the course of his week's digging he found what has since become one of the most famous human burials in Britain: the 'Red Lady' of Paviland.

Buckland, in his *Reliquae Diluvianae* (1823),* wrote that the skeleton was covered 'by a coating of ruddle' — red ochre — which stained the bones and the earth around. Also on the body, 'where the pocket is usually worn', were a group of periwinkle shells (*Nerita littoralis*), and over the ribs many fragments of ivory rods and rings also stained with red ochre.

Buckland first suggested that the partial skeleton (it had no skull) was that of a male — probably a customs officer, murdered and hidden by smugglers. By the time of publication he had changed his mind, and came up with one of the best-known names in British archaeology. The ochre-stained skeleton was now the 'Red Lady of Paviland', supposedly a woman of ill-repute who plied her ancient trade among the frustrated Roman troops based in the camp above the cave. Buckland, as Dean of Westminster, preferred to admit the existence of fallen women rather than the possibility of antediluvian men. We now know that Buckland's story does not hold up: the 'Red Lady' is a male and anatomically a modern human, like us;† the shells and ivory are typically Palaeolithic (Old Stone Age) forms of decoration, and the supposed Roman camp is a prehistoric promontory fort. But it is only too easy to indulge in the convenient wisdom of hindsight. In 1823 the 'Red Lady' was the first human fossil to have been discovered anywhere in the world.

In 1995 Steven Aldhouse-Green, Professor of Human Origins at the University of Wales, began a campaign to re-examine the Paviland Cave, the skeleton and the many finds.[2] The Oxford Radiocarbon Laboratory re-dated the skeleton to about 26,000 years ago. This is a period (known as the Gravettian to archaeologists) of harsh climate, when humans were only intermittently present in Britain. The 'Red Lady' may have come at a time of 'biomass expansion', when herds of animals were so prolific that human hunters followed them into the cold, extreme-north-west peninsula of Eurasia — the ends of the earth. They were well equipped with hafted weapons, their flint blades fixed with resins. Their stone tool

---

* Buckland was a catastrophist, who believed in the biblical flood, hence his title, which translates as 'Evidence of the Flood'. For Buckland, animals such as mammoths were extinct because Noah had not managed to get them into the Ark. Lyell was a pupil of Buckland's at Oxford, but represented the new geologists who broke away from catastrophism and promoted uniformitarianism, the idea that the processes which impact on the earth today, such as erosion, were the same in the past.

† By a 'modern human' I mean *Homo sapiens sapiens*, the species to which all human beings belong.

kit has been compared to a Swiss Army knife: gear for cutting, boring, scraping, piercing and chiselling.[3]

We know little about their clothing, but, like the modern Inuit or the prehistoric Iceman shot by an arrow and left to die in the Alps five and a half thousand years ago, such people must have been kitted out to cope with the tough conditions. These highly effective hunters also, about this time or a little later, invented the spear-thrower, or *atlatl*, to launch projectiles with greater force and accuracy, as well as the boomerang.

The 'Red Lady' was an adult male who died in his later twenties. He was about 1.77 metres (5 feet 8 inches) tall and relatively robust – though a lightweight compared with the stocky Neanderthals who lived in northern Europe before the arrival of modern man. The earliest anatomically modern humans in Europe were gracile; they had the lightweight build that originally evolved in a warm African environment. The Paviland man's ancestors, and ours, probably arrived in Europe 10,000 years before him and his build shows that the modern *Homo sapiens* was adapting to the colder conditions in which he found himself. In contrast with the common image of Stone Age hunters, the Paviland man did not eat only meat; we can tell from his bones that he ate plenty of seafood too.

Today the Paviland Cave is not easy to reach: it involves scrambling down a limestone sea cliff to an entrance that is only accessible at low tide. But when the dead man was buried the cave was well inland, perhaps 100 kilometres from the sea, which was at a much lower level than today. During cold periods water remained trapped in the ice and sea levels fell; as the climate warmed, as it has in the past 13,000 years, the sea level rose – and it continues to do so today, with potentially dangerous consequences for the future. Twenty-six thousand years ago the Paviland Cave would have provided shelter and a strategic lookout over a game-rich plain. So why was he eating fish? Interestingly bear bones from the cave show that these animals also gorged on fish. Both the 'Red Lady' and the bears were probably catching migrating salmon in the ancient River Severn, which ran nearby; and salmon runs are a prolific source of protein. In pursuing salmon as well as the game on the mammoth-plains of South Wales the Paviland man buried in the cave displayed the key survival qualities of modern humans: versatility and adaptability.

These people did not live by fish nor meat alone (the bread delivery would not arrive for another 22,000 years, see page 65): they had a creative cultural life and evidently contemplated the afterlife as well. The members of his small community buried the Paviland man with ceremony, laid out in a grave, his garments covered with red ochre, which is commonly used to symbolise the power and life-giving properties of blood. He is not the only Gravettian burial to be found without a head. Already the skull may have played a particularly important role in symbolising the power of ancestors. It is the start of a long tradition of treating human remains in symbolic ways, of using bones to convey cultural and spiritual messages. From the beginning, people have been fascinated by the questions: Where do I come from? Who were my ancestors?

For Bryan Sykes, Professor of Genetics at the Institute of Molecular Medicine in Oxford and a leading researcher into human origins, the lack of a skull could have presented a problem. For hunters of mitochondrial DNA like him, the protected interior of the tooth is the best place to search. Nevertheless he managed to recover sufficient material from other bones to show that the 'Red Lady' had a DNA sequence that matches the commonest present-day European lineage.[S4]

As we will see later in this chapter, this contributes to an ongoing heated debate: Are today's Europeans, including Britons,* more closely related to these Upper Palaeolithic hunters, or to later migrants, the first farmers, coming ultimately from the Near East and south-western Europe with the Neolithic package of domesticated plants and animals in the millennia after 10,000 BC?

To understand early humans in Britain we need to understand climate change and its impact. This is not to say that even the earliest hominids – our fossil ancestors – were simply flotsam on the tide of nature. They were social and creative creatures who exploited and adapted their environment. Nevertheless the collection of islands which we know as the British Isles and Ireland were the extreme peninsula of a continental land mass and subject to enormous, and sometimes rapid, climatic fluctuation. As a result, hominids repeatedly inhabited and abandoned Britain, often, but not always, influenced by the extremes of climate that caused ice sheets to grind over Scotland and as far south as the Chilterns. In the past half a million years people have come in and out of Britain like the tide, along with animals as varied as mammoths, cave bear, hyenas and water voles. In some periods Britain was an island; at other times it was attached to the mainland of Europe. During one of its insular phases, from about 128,000 years ago, Britain was exceptionally warm. Hippos wallowed beneath Trafalgar Square. And yet there were no people, so far as we can tell on present evidence. This suggests that it was not the presence of ice sheets alone that influenced the fluctuations of hominid population. Climate change frequently appears in today's newspapers as

---

* Of course, many contemporary Britons, as I discuss later, have their recent ancestry in Africa and south-east Asia, but the argument about genetic origin here concerns the indigenous European population who have lived in the area for thousands of years.

if it is something new. In fact we live in a period that has been remarkably stable over the past 13,000 years. The long-term picture, though, is one of major variation on a world-wide scale.

There have been about nine major advances of the ice in the past 800,000 years, which, in the coldest phases – the glacials – have covered much of Britain and northern Europe. The glacials were separated by warm stages (interglacials). Within these major climate stages there were also more rapid fluctuations, episodes of warming (interstadials) and cooling (stadials). The British Isles have gone from glaciers and arctic tundra to warm intervals comparable to the weather in, say, northern Spain today. At present we are living in one of the longer interglacials, which started about 13,000 years ago, when the last Ice Age came to an end. This morning, as I am writing this in the south of France, my local newspaper, *Midi Libre*, carries an article mocking the British (*'Les Brittaniques sont des gens étranges!'*) for not only talking about the weather all the time but even betting on it. Yet as the British know,* weather is fundamental; and we now know a lot more about its history, thanks to deep-sea cores, ice cores, such as those from Greenland, and long-term sequences of pollen, which indicate the changing pattern of vegetation.§

Ice cores, like tree rings, can give a very precise picture of temperature fluctuations because they provide an annual record – in the case of the Greenland cores for 110,000 years continuously. The big surprise from these cores has been the amazing speed at which climate can change.

The mystery of the Trafalgar hippo and the absent hominids may now be explained by our more detailed knowledge of climate during the second-to-last interglacial period. Instead of a 10,000-year-long warm spell this was, in fact, a period of remarkably unstable climate. At one point, for just seventy years, temperatures plunged to glacial levels;⁵ and there were 10°C shifts in average temperature within just a few years. The average hominid probably preferred somewhere a little more predictable and avoided the extreme ends of the continental land mass such as Britain.

Megafauna, such as hippos, give an indicator of climate; but big animals are relatively rare and hard to find. If we want to use animal remains to spot climate change and the appearance of interglacial warm stages, then we need something small and common. The answer is the vole. The so-called 'vole-clock' is based on the fact that voles are prolific, short-lived, very sensitive to environmental change and that they evolve rapidly in response to it. About 600,000 years ago grassland spread over much of the continent of Europe. Successful voles adapted by developing rootless

* And the French were about to find out: shortly afterwards the hottest summer on record (2003) began and thousands of elderly French people died of overheating.

back teeth which grew continuously. The old voles (*Mimomys savinii*) eventually disappeared and the new ones, of the genus *Aruicola*, dominate the record. Boxgrove (Sussex), the earliest hominid site in Britain, has been dated to a warm stage half a million years ago, thanks to the vole *Aruicola terrestris cantiana* (which takes its names from Kent and its Iron Age tribe the Cantii).

Boxgrove is not far from another famous, or rather infamous, site associated with what was once believed to be the first Briton, Piltdown Man. In 1912 Britain's imperial rivals France and Germany had already discovered their early ancestors at Cro-Magnon and in the Neander Valley, near Heidelberg.*

Britain was lagging behind in the race to possess the earliest European. Then Charles Dawson, a local solicitor, found some skull fragments, along with elephant and hippo, in a gravel bed at Piltdown Common, Sussex. England had its own fossil man. In the following months Dawson uncovered more material including a jawbone. Remarkably the skull was big-brained and human-like, while the jaw resembled an ape's. This put the earliest Englishman, named scientifically as *Eoanthropus dawsonii* ('Dawson's Dawn Man'), earlier on the ancestral tree than the French and German candidates. At the end of 1912 this caused an enormous stir. In the following decades, as more hominid fossils appeared, the Piltdown Man began to look suspiciously odd. In 1953 scientific tests proved the suspicions correct: the remains had been cobbled together from a human skull and an orang-utan jaw with the teeth filed flat and artist's pigments used to make them look suitably ancient. Piltdown Man was a forgery, and not even a very good one. The finger has been pointed at almost everyone involved, from Dawson himself to Sir Arthur Conan Doyle and most recently Martin Hinton, a zoology curator at the Natural History Museum. But the Piltdown forger remains as elusive as Jack the Ripper.

A couple of weeks before writing this I sat down in London with Professor Chris Stringer of the Natural History Museum and a group of scientists from the Ancient Human Occupation of Britain Project (AHOB[6]). I was feeling pleased because I was able to tell them that English Heritage had just bought Boxgrove Quarry, the famous site of Britain's earliest hominid remains dating to about 500,000 years ago.[†]

---

* In German 'Neanderthal' simply means 'Neander valley'. When German spelling was modernised, 'thal' became 'tal'. I retain the original spelling by which the hominid remains were classified.
† Because of the definition of a monument – as a built structure – in British legislation, Boxgrove, one of the most important archaeological sites in Europe, cannot be protected by scheduling. English Heritage has had to buy the site to protect it.

Chris wanted to discuss the possibility that hominid sites as early as 700,000 BP (Before Present) might exist on the East Anglian coast and a theory that human artefacts found there with distinctive voles might belong to a warm period even earlier than Boxgrove. Could hominids have expanded from Africa and arrived in Britain 200,000 years before the conventional date? The answer may lie in an organic deposit containing hand axes, animal bones and botanical material on the Norfolk coast, which is currently being washed away by the North Sea. This is potentially a key site for hominid origins in Britain.

However, at present, the oldest known human remains in Britain still come from Boxgrove in Sussex, dating to about half a million years ago. Although Palaeolithic sites in Britain are rare, some, like Boxgrove, are extremely well preserved. Archaeologists usually deal with long-term processes, but at Boxgrove the actions of individuals, events which may have lasted for only minutes or a few hours, are captured under the sediments that eroded from the chalk cliff above and rapidly formed a protective blanket. There was an open grassy plain below the cliffs where large herbivores, such as horses, grazed and kept the landscape open. Predators included lions (much bigger than today's), hyenas, wolves, bear – and a large hominid known to us as Boxgrove Man. He is represented by his gnawed tibia. There were also two teeth from another individual. A leg bone may not look much, but it showed that its owner was male, powerfully built and, judging from the analysis of the bone cells, or osteones, probably in his forties. He stood nearly six feet (1.8 metres) tall and had the legs of a sprinter. He belonged to the species *Homo heidelbergensis*,* the northern descendant of *Homo ergaster* who had come out of Africa about one and a half million years ago.§

Boxgrove Man had the heavier build of a hominid who had evolved to deal with the colder northern conditions, but not to the same extent as his descendant of 300,000 years later *Homo neanderthalensis*.

On one particularly well-preserved area of ground surface five members of the Boxgrove clan sat around the carcass of a horse. They were knapping flint, found nearby, with antler and quartz hammers; in about fifteen minutes they each produced a hand axe – a perfect butchery tool to skin and dismember the horse. Any one of us examining such a flint axe would assume the maker was both skilled and intelligent.‡ The Boxgrove evidence suggests that the hominids had killed the horse with wooden spears rather than scavenging the carcass, and that the group cooperated in defending it from the other rival predators, while a small task

* Named for a lower jawbone found at Mauer, near Heidelberg, in 1907.

force set about rapidly butchering the dead animal. When the job was done, after maybe three hours, the specially made tools were simply discarded on the spot. It must have been easier to make a hand axe when one was needed than to carry such a heavy object about. The clan probably wanted to move away from the kill site as quickly as possible with their valuable prize to eat it communally. We are not sure if they had fire and there are no traces of shelters. Yet these first British hominids were powerful characters, well organised, capable of short-term planning, making the tools for the job and looking after themselves in a hostile environment. Except, of course, that somewhere along the line Boxgrove Man's leg ended up being gnawed by a wolf.

The period of Boxgrove occupation was followed by the very severe Anglian glaciation, which wiped out much of the British fauna. The Anglian glaciation also had a major impact on the landscape as we know it: the large Bytham River which flowed across central England and through present-day East Anglia was swept aside by the ice. The Bytham River valley was probably the main corridor through which early hominids entered Britain from the Continent. In its place a new river developed further south, in front of the Anglian Ice Sheet: the ancestral Thames.

The Anglian Ice Sheet also had another even more fundamental impact upon Britain. A chalk land-bridge linked Dover and Calais. To the north of it the waters of the Thames and the Rhine poured into the North Sea basin, creating a huge lake which ponded up against the Anglian ice wall. Eventually the rising waters of this dammed lake broke through the Dover/Calais ridge, severing Britain from the Continent. This island status did not last: lowered sea levels in the subsequent climatic cold stages reinstated the land-bridge; but the channel – the Straits of Dover, or La Manche – created by the Anglian outpouring became a permanent feature, like a moat waiting to be flooded.

After the 50,000-year-long Anglian glacial stage the climate warmed and hominids re-colonised Britain. At Hoxne, in East Anglia, plant pollen is well preserved in the lake sediments and there are hints that hominids were setting fires in the forest to open up the landscape and

† During the construction of the Channel Tunnel Rail Link another site appeared at Ebbsfleet, in Kent. Four hundred thousand years ago a group of *Homines heidelbergenses* chased a type of elephant (*Palaeoloxodron antiquus*) into a bog. They then cut it into slices with flint blades which the archaeologist Francis Wenbow-Smith said were like Stanley knives. No hand axes were found. This type of butchery tool has also appeared at Clacton, Essex – again without hand axes. This could be the first evidence of multiculturalism in Britain: one hominid species, but different groups, with distinct sets of stone tools representing cultural variation. In the long run, the hand-axe users won out, but how and why we do not yet know.

encourage the browsing animals upon which they preyed. Anatomical remains are scarce, but a fragment of skull from Swanscombe (Kent) has a distinctive depression on the back that is a characteristic of Neanderthals. The Swanscombe hominid is usually characterised as a pre-Neanderthal, an ancestor of the best known of all early hominids.

As we can see with the Swanscombe skull fragment, Neanderthal features evolved gradually in the *Homo ergaster* ancestors who left Africa and colonised Asia and Europe over a million years ago. Neanderthal anatomical characteristics were fully developed by about 130,000 years ago. They flourished for about 100,000 years and by 30,000 BP they were extinct.

The first observers of the bones found in the Feldhof Cave, above the Neander Valley, in 1856 were puzzled by their robustness, bandy legs and protruding brow ridge. Speculation varied: the skeleton was that of a congenital idiot, or even a Cossack horseman. Darwin's colleague Thomas Huxley proposed, correctly, that human evolution was the explanation.

With more remains to study we now have a better idea of what Neanderthals looked like. Most obviously they were strongly built, barrel-chested and fairly short: males averaged about 1.69 metres (5 feet 6 inches) and females about 1.60 metres (5 feet 2 inches). Neanderthals had particularly short forearms and lower legs, which suggests that they evolved to conserve body heat in a cold climate. Their pronounced bow legs, often commented on, are an indication of strong musculature, which anyone who has watched Olympic weightlifters in action will have observed. In spite of their powerful bodies Neanderthals suffered a lot of physical injuries and did not live long; not one is known to have outlived forty years of age (assuming our age-evaluation techniques are reliable). Life was tough and relatively short, but not necessarily brutish. It seems likely that Neanderthal bands cared for their orphaned young and their injured. In spite of their large brains, however, their system of communication was probably simpler and language less well developed than those of modern humans, judging from their throat and mouth anatomy.

Neanderthals occupied a wide area, stretching from the mountains of Uzbekistan westwards through Israel, from the northern Mediterranean countries to northern Europe. Skeletal fragments of about five hundred Neanderthals have been found in total. Evidence is limited in Britain, but the most north-westerly Neanderthal occupation site known is at the Pontnewydd Cave in North Wales. The remains of an adult and two children aged about twelve and nine are those of early Neanderthals of about 240,000 years ago.* They shared the steppe environment with wolf, bear,

---

* This is very early and, strictly speaking, these people are ancestral to fully developed Neanderthals.

leopard, rhinoceros, horse and bison. Hand axes, spear tips and scrapers from the cave illustrate the tool kit necessary to kill and butcher their prey and prepare skins. The Neanderthals also lit fires for protection, warmth and cooking. This may sound like classic cave-man behaviour, but in fact the Neanderthals' main living area was probably outside under the shelter of the cliff. Much of the occupation debris was later pushed into the cave by the advancing glacier and so preserved, while ice gripped the land.

In spite of the scarcity of Neanderthal bones in Britain the distribution of elements of their distinctive flaked-stone tool kit shows that they were active across much of the southern half of the country. Neanderthals made some sixty-three different types of stone tools, including knives, scrapers for preparing hides and points for drilling holes. Most of these stone tools are scattered finds, moved about by the action of ice and water. Recently, though, there has been a remarkable discovery in a gravel quarry at Lynford, Norfolk.[7] There, within the glacial terrace deposits, was a hollow filled with dark organic material. Fortunately, as the large extraction machines ate into the gravel, John Lord, a local amateur archaeologist, spotted the hollow in the quarry face. When he looked more closely he realised that it was littered with animal bones and flint tools.

When I visited Lynford, archaeologists from the Norfolk Archaeological Unit had exposed the skeletons of three mammoths and a woolly rhinoceros. Eventually the bones of horse, deer, reindeer and brown bear also appeared, some badly worn, gnawed and scavenged, some split for their nourishing marrow and scarred by flint tools. About forty-four mint-fresh, flint hand axes lay among the bones, still sharp enough to slice through hide and flesh after 60,000 years.[8] Like the Boxgrove people the Lynford Neanderthals had sharpened their hand axes to butcher these animals and then, like the Boxgrove people, simply discarded them. Some were of a distinctive triangular shape, known in archaeological jargon as the *bout coupé* type. This is a form found only in northern France and Britain – indicating that the Neanderthal groups in the extreme north-west had developed a distinctive culture of their own – the first identifiably British (and northern-French) manufactured object.

Finding these was an enormous piece of luck – a mere speck of Neanderthal landscape surviving in a cold dry grassland valley scoured by glacial meltwater. Needles in haystacks had nothing on Lynford. It still remains to be seen whether the Neanderthals had hunted and killed the mammoth, or whether they were scavenging carcasses that were opportunistic finds. At La Cotte, on the Channel Islands, Neanderthals drove mammoth and rhino over a granite headland to their deaths. Like Boxgrove, the Lynford quarry is a rare opportunity to glimpse one of these fragile, preserved moments – a miraculous snapshot from our deep past. It may yet provide forensic evidence to tell us if Neanderthal hunters were able to tackle such substantial animals as mammoths. Considering the effectiveness of the Boxgrove ancestors with the spear and the size of the Neanderthal brain, my money is on the Neanderthals as big-game hunters.

Clearly, Neanderthals were, for over 100,000 years, a successful species – not the shambling brutes so often portrayed in films, paintings and stories such as H.G.Wells' 'The Grisly Folk',[8] or even the innocent, if sympathetic, incompetents of William Golding's *The Inheritors* (1961). They survived in the fluctuating climate of Eurasia for approximately four times longer than we modern humans have so far existed.

But how many Neanderthals were there? Clive Gamble has modelled their territories, 'landscapes of habit', which he assumes to cover about 5,000 square kilometres. If the absence of evidence from this period in Scotland and Ireland is blamed on glacial erosion rather than the real absence of people, then the total hominid population for the British Isles would fall between about 6,000 and 27,000 individuals.[§] The population density would have varied through time and with the resources available in different regions. Nevertheless, Clive Gamble's estimate provides us with a general idea of the number of people in Middle Palaeolithic Britain at any one time.

But who were these early people? and how do they relate to us? The young man buried in the Paviland Cave 26,000 years ago, for example, was clearly not a Neanderthal. Even lacking a skull, his skeleton has all the characteristics of a different hominid. He is *Homo sapiens sapiens*: one of us. So what happened to the Neanderthals in Europe and Britain? Is the 'Red Lady' an evolved form, a descendant of Neanderthals? or has a new hominid arrived on the block?

These questions encapsulate one of the hottest debates about human origins. Essentially there are two sides to this argument. The 'multiregional evolutionists' believe that *Homo ergaster* spread out of Africa a million or more years ago, colonised much of Eurasia and the Far East, and evolved gradually into modern humans in each region. According to this argument we and the 'Red Lady' are related to Neanderthals.

The other camp, sometimes known as the 'Garden of Eden' faction, propose that *Homo sapiens sapiens* is a new species that evolved from *Homo ergaster* separately, and entirely within Africa. About 100,000 years ago these slim-bodied, big-brained hominids expanded out of Africa into

Asia, reaching Australia about 60,000 years ago — 20,000 years before they discovered Britain — and eventually colonising the entire globe except for Antarctica.

The biological evidence tends to support the 'Garden of Eden' or 'Out of Africa' theory. The earliest modern human skeletons appear in Africa first and in areas close by, such as Israel, about 100,000 years ago,* many millennia before the disappearance of Neanderthals in Europe and archaic hominids in eastern Africa.

Recent research on DNA also provides support for this theory — that modern humans evolved in Africa and as humans have been there longest. Africans display the greatest genetic variety. Geneticists calculate that modern humans are descended from an African population of about 10,000 people. With such a population bottleneck, and a dose of bad luck, Homo sapiens sapiens could easily have become extinct like other hominids. Instead Svante Pääbo of Leipzig's Institute for Evolutionary Anthropology writes: 'Thus from a genomic perspective, we are all Africans, either living in Africa or in quite recent exile outside Africa.'[10]

Modern humans (Homo sapiens sapiens) lived alongside other hominids for many generations, but gradually the others disappeared, possibly as a result of human aggression but more likely because the new highly mobile, versatile, fast-talking quick-thinking hominids out-competed the old ones.† In the case of Neanderthals they may even have been out-bred: there is some evidence that their gestation period was several months longer than ours.

I am, of course, falling into the trap of an egocentric species: assuming modern humans were a major factor in the disappearance of Neanderthals. There could be other factors such as climate change or disease that specialists have so far failed to observe. It is sometimes assumed that human aggression could have led to genocide, but so far no forensic evidence, no Palaeolithic smoking gun, has appeared to condemn Homo sapiens sapiens for Neanderthal murder.

So what happened to the Neanderthals? If they did not evolve into modern humans, could they have interbred with them and simply been absorbed? The DNA evidence suggests this is unlikely: no evidence has been found that Neanderthals contributed to the gene pool of current humans.§

As a cautious scientist Pääbo does not rule out the possibility that

---

* Sites such as Klasies River Mouth in South Africa, Ono in Ethiopia and on Mount Carmel in Israel.[9]

† For example, while the Neanderthals were skilled stone-tool makers, flaking tools from a core, the newcomers were even better, making a wider range of blade tools.

somewhere in Europe or Asia Neanderthals or *Homo ergaster*-type hominids interbred with modern humans; but if they did, no trace has yet been found, and the interaction cannot have amounted to much in terms of its overall contribution to the modern gene pool.

The most likely scenario on present evidence is that modern humans replaced archaic humans with no interbreeding; and for the past 30,000 years, only one hominid (*Homo sapiens sapiens*) has lived on the planet.*

In the key period for the emergence of modern humans in Europe (around 45,000 to 30,000 BP) much of the north was under ice and the central areas were tundra or steppe landscapes. Vast herds of bison, horse, reindeer, mammoth and woolly rhino presented an attractive target for human hunters. At this time of low sea level much of the North Sea basin was dry land, linking Britain and the Continent. Flint tools and animal bones fairly frequently turn up in the nets of trawlers from this now drowned world, which the Exeter University archaeologist Bryony Coles has named 'Doggerland'.[11]

This period saw modern humans develop a much more sophisticated culture than any of their predecessors: new forms of stone tools, standardisation and improved knapping technology, which themselves reflected greater use of animal bone, wood and hides; a huge increase in the use of jewellery and bodily decoration as seen in the Paviland burial – *Homo sapiens* was a *fashionista* from the beginning.†

Across Europe evidence appears of musical instruments (bird-bone flutes; and surely drums must have been used?), formal burials, portable art, such as Venus figurines (females modelled with pendulous breasts and rounded figures), animal carvings and, above all, the cave art best known from the spectacular animal paintings in northern Spain, southern and central France, in caves such as Altamira, Chauvet and Lascaux. In comparison Britain is not in the big league of Palaeolithic art galleries, though the first example of cave art, including the engraved image of an ibex, has recently been located at Cresswell Crags, Derbyshire, in a narrow gorge which, like Cheddar, must have provided a sheltered habitat for humans about 12,000 years ago.[13] This is now the most northerly cave art known, though it is misleading to regard it as specifically British – Britain was part of the Continental land mass at the time; and there is no evidence that the ibex lived this far north. The image would not be out of

---

* I did say this is a fast-changing subject. In 2004 the remains of a small hominid were discovered on the Indonesian island of Floris. This may be a remarkable survival of an isolated species but its precise status remains to be clarified.

† The recent discovery of pierced, ochre-stained mollusc shells, about 75,000 years old, in Blombos Cave, South Africa, suggests that the development of human symbolic thinking and language may have developed earlier in Africa.[12]

place in France or Spain. Most likely the hunter-artist was highly mobile and familiar with both the art and the animals of the south. Like me, he or she may have had a habit of heading towards the Mediterranean to escape the gloomy British winter.

These new humans seem to have thought differently from the old: in symbols, stories and metaphors, placing great emphasis on art, bodily decoration and the ritual treatment of the dead. For the first time people could speak prose and poetry,* convey emotion through music and imagine powers greater than themselves.

David Lewis-Williams, based on his studies of rock art and shamanism in South Africa, warns against seeing these early humans as scientists in skins. Cave art, he argues, is a projection into the rock of hallucinations, the products of altered states of consciousness. The human mind had developed the ability to experience trance states — whether chemically induced, through physical stress, through hyperventilation or with prolonged music and dancing. These mental states are generated by the neurology of the human nervous system. They are wired into the brain; but the content is cultural: bulls and horses at Lascaux, lions at Chauvet. Out of this need to explain shifting states of consciousness emerges a world-wide phenomenon among hunter-gatherers: the shaman, a person with special powers of communication with the spirit world, which existed above and below the everyday one. Shamans, by channelling the power of the elements, could influence the weather, heal the sick and influence the behaviour of animals. In a hard and erratic world they provided some sense of security and control, and formed the origin of the world's religions.

The most spectacular products of Upper Palaeolithic (Aurignacian) people appear in the areas of milder climate, south of Britain. However, from the sheer quantity of material and sites it is evident that human populations expanded rapidly from eastern and southern Europe and into France and Britain. For a time, as I explained earlier, Neanderthals and humans lived side by side until eventually Neanderthals disappeared. Humans increased in numbers as their efficiency as hunters improved — with better tools and weapons† and increased ability to communicate and

---

* Steven Mithen, of Reading University, has argued that the new generalised form of human intelligence was fuelled by fully developed language and resulted in the attribution of meaning to images.[14]

† It is sometimes suggested that the bow and arrow were invented about this time, but there is no clear evidence for it. However, the site of a mass slaughter of reindeer at Stellmoor, near Horbury, Germany, dating to about 12,000 BP produced over a hundred pine arrow shafts. These were cleverly designed to break halfway along the shaft when they struck, leaving the arrowhead in the victim so that the loose main shaft could be recovered and reused. The Stellmoor hunters made powerful bows from a single piece of fir; such bows, requiring considerable strength to pull, may have promoted the hunting of larger mammals as a male activity.

co-operate. The climate also improved for several thousand years from 43,000 BP at the time when modern humans first colonised western Europe. As they had migrated out of Africa into the eastern Mediterranean about 100,000 BP, it is an intriguing question why it took them so long (about 50,000 years) to move northwards.

An upper jaw and two teeth are all that remains of the earliest modern human from Britain. But that was enough for Oxford University's Radiocarbon Laboratory to date these fragments to about 31,000 BP, or possibly a little earlier. The jaw came from Kent's Cavern in South Devon, where it was found, in 1870, in another of those exercises where Victorian excavators treated caves like Augean stables. Fortunately at Paviland the burial of the 'Red Lady' shows us that fully fledged modern humans, after evolving in Africa and developing their culture in western Asia and north of the Mediterranean, did reach Europe's north-westernmost peninsula, Britain – 20,000 years after they first arrived in Australia.

The last Ice Age in Europe was at its most extreme 18,000 years ago. Britain, gripped by cold, was an uninhabited polar desert and humans lived south of the Loire (where the scattered populations are estimated at one person per 20 square kilometres). About 13,000 years ago the climate warmed; but the Ice Age was not quite finished with Britain: from about 10,800 BC the temperature plunged again into a final thousand-year cold spell. Exactly when and how humans returned to Britain is not certain; but return they certainly did. There is well-preserved evidence of a group of Late Glacial humans in Gough's Cave, Cheddar (Somerset), dated to the centuries either side of 12,000 BP.

The Cheddar bones have revealed some fascinating insights into how Late Glacial hunters treated their dead. These people, who were so expert at skinning and butchering reindeer and other animals, did the same thing to their own: the bodies had been expertly scalped, dismembered and defleshed, leaving fine cut-marks and scrapes on the bone. This kind of behaviour may seem strange to us, but it is not uncommon around the world for corpses to be exposed and defleshed, sometimes as a way of releasing the soul. The flesh and the brain may be ritually consumed, though there is no clear evidence for that at Cheddar. Cheddar people ate venison, but we cannot say for certain that they were cannibals. Once the body had been reduced to bones, these were buried in the floor of the Cheddar cave.

The landscape was very different in post-glacial Britain. Eighteen thousand years ago half of the land was covered by ice. Ben Nevis was invisible beneath a glacier 1,800 metres thick. The rest was uninhabitable. By 10,000 years ago the ice had retreated and new plants and animals, including people, colonised what was still the extreme-north-western peninsula of the Eurasian land mass. Conditions in Britain were increasingly attractive, benefiting from the presence of the North Atlantic Drift. The warm waters of this oceanic current, known as the Gulf Stream further south, flow up the east coast of the United States until, off Newfoundland, they collide with the cold wall of the Labrador Current and are pushed eastwards across the Atlantic. This boundary, between warmer southern and colder Arctic waters, is the Polar Front. It is fundamental to the climate of Britain and to all those determined creators of semi-tropical gardens from Tresco Abbey (Isles of Scilly) – 'like the big greenhouse at Kew with the roof off' – to Inverewe in Wester Ross.

Today the Polar Front lies to the north of Iceland – hence the mild, wet, frost-free areas along the west coast of Great Britain and southern Ireland. Ten thousand years ago it ran across the Atlantic from the north-western tip of Spain. In less than a thousand years (by 7000 BC) it shifted to the north of Shetland. The moderating climate successively attracted dwarf birch, pine forest and, finally, a temperate climax woodland of predominantly oak, hazel and lime over the southern and central parts of the islands. Nevertheless, many species of plants and animals – such as the fabled snakes missing from Ireland – did not make it into Britain before the land-bridge was severed by the rising sea level.

Below the North Sea today lie the low hills and estuaries of Doggerland, the drowned world between Britain and Denmark where once herds and hunters moved in annual rituals. One day in September 1931 evidence of this northern Atlantis appeared in the net of the trawler *Colinda*. Fishing over the Ower Bank, off the Norfolk coast, she brought up a block of peat. This in itself was evidence that the seabed was once dryish land. But when the *Colinda*'s captain – evocatively named, as if by Melville or Bunyan, Pilgrim Lockwood – broke open the peat, inside he revealed clear evidence for the presence of human hunters: a serrated barbed point carved from red-deer antler. This has since been dated by radiocarbon calibration to about 10,000 BC.

At that time Doggerland would have covered an area about the size of England, a tundra landscape across which vast herds of reindeer and horses plodded, where salmon spawned in its prolific rivers. As the climate warmed, oak woodland colonised the valleys and hills. Red deer, roe deer and wild pig replaced the barren-ground reindeer. It remained an ideal hunting ground. But every year the sea rose imperceptibly, about 30 millimetres, gradually reducing Doggerland in size until, about 8,000 years ago, the North Sea waters poured again through the channel moat separating the British peninsula from the

Continent.* Britain and Ireland were once again islands, as they have remained ever since.

Around the shores there is still plenty of evidence of these coastal changes: waterlogged stumps of prehistoric trees in the Thames estuary, or Cardigan Bay, where the sea has drowned magnificent ancient forests. As the crushing weight of ice was lifted from the north, Scotland breathed, and still breathes, a sigh of relief that lifted its land beyond the reach of the sea and raised the terraces of ancient beaches high and dry. In contrast, south-eastern England, like the opposite end of a slow-motion see-saw, continues to sink. Without the Thames Barrier the chambers of the Houses of Parliament would soon suffer the fate of Doggerland; and as global warming promotes more extreme sea surges, the present barrier may not be enough to protect London from the funnelling effect of the Thames estuary.

Archaeologists call this post-glacial period the Mesolithic or Middle Stone Age. Once it was considered a something-or-nothing period, an interlude between the age of the heroic Palaeolithic hunter cave painters and the inevitable rise of Neolithic (or New Stone Age) farmers. The Mesolithic in Britain was literally put on the map by Grahame Clark, who published *The Mesolithic Age in Britain* in 1932. This was principally a study of the stone-tool technology of the period, of which microliths, or small triangular flint blades, are the most diagnostic feature. The Mesolithic hunters and foragers made arrowheads or compound tools such as spears, harpoons and sickles by inserting these blades into wooden or bone handles. The microliths functioned like the teeth of a saw or a shark, providing effective weapons and cutting and piercing tools.

Archaeological fieldworkers, trawling the surface of ploughed fields, find such stone tools by the thousand, as if the land has been sown with dragons' teeth. Mesolithic bands clearly exploited the whole of the British Isles, scattering their small but almost indestructible flint blades behind them, as they shot at birds and deer, opened shellfish, sliced through rushes and sharpened stakes, cut firewood and cleaned animal hides. Occasionally we can literally walk in their footsteps where the tracks of Mesolithic hunters and their prey survive impressed in the mud of Morecombe Bay and the Severn estuary. On the other hand their dwellings and settlements remain illusive and often difficult to interpret when found.

The hunter-gatherer camp site at Star Carr, on the edge of the Vale of Pickering about 5 miles south-west of Scarborough, is a type-site of the Mesolithic, one of the best-known prehistoric excavations in Europe

---

* As a result of this global warming the North Sea rose 130 metres in total.

amongst professional archaeologists. Yet few of the holidaymakers heading to the nearby seaside have heard of Star Carr, which lies anonymously in the countryside. Between 1949 and 1951, however, Grahame Clark revealed the wealth of evidence left by these elusive people. The survival was remarkable because their camp site stretched alongside a now disappeared lake. As peat formed on the damp margins it provided a protective, airless blanket, preserving pollen, charcoal, insects, organic materials and animal bones. For Clark this was forensic heaven. And it was the first archaeological site in the world to be radiocarbon dated.

Star Carr added new dimensions of archaeological visibility to the cultural life of Mesolithic communities in Britain, revealing them as skilled dwellers in the woodland environment, not just manufacturers of stone tools who scattered them in confusing patterns. Star Carr is also an object lesson in the problems of archaeological interpretation: why it is not always straightforward or even possible to calculate how many people were doing what and where in the deep prehistoric past. At Star Carr the stone tools do provide patterns — most of them are end-scrapers for cleaning the fat from the inside of animal skins, and burins, or piercing tools, for punching holes through leather. On the hills above, on the North Yorkshire Moors, the flint scatters are often made up of lost arrowheads and other hunting tools. The successful hunters returned to camp sites such as Star Carr, where the carcasses could be processed and divided among the community. Clark wanted to know what time of year this had taken place and he thought the animal bones discarded around the camp would tell him. In particular, he found red-deer skulls with their antlers attached. As red deer shed their antlers in April, he concluded that they had probably been killed in the winter and carried to the winter base camp by the lake.

Since 1951, however, the Star Carr evidence has been reinterpreted many times. The latest, but probably not the last, word on the bones contradicts the winter theory: the pattern of tooth eruption in the deer showed that they had been killed in early summer.[15]

Detailed analysis of the peat beds has also provided a fuller picture of the Mesolithic environment at Star Carr and how this early Yorkshire clan exploited it. Birch woodland surrounded the lake, which was fringed with reeds. Soon after 9000 BC people began, annually for eighty years, to set fire to these reeds. After a gap of a few decades they returned and began the process again. However, the lake was shrinking. Colonised by willow, aspen and eventually hazel, it was turning into the marshy 'carr' that gives the place its name today (though today intensive farming and drainage are increasingly desiccating and destroying these rare and valuable wetlands). About the middle of the ninth millennium, after almost

500 years of use, the foraging community finally deserted Star Carr.

This was a landscape in which people lived well, hunting red deer, roe deer, wild boar, elk and auroch (large wild cattle). The lakes provided fish and wildfowl; the forests were rich in hazelnuts, berries, roots and tubers, and at the coast there was a plentiful supply of shellfish, seabirds and their eggs, edible seaweed and larger prey. The people who lived in the new British forests were not the pathetic foragers portrayed by Darwin. They were adapting to a constantly changing environment and creating a new and distinct culture. Some of the best evidence for this distinctiveness has come from the earliest settlements known in Ireland. These proliferate in the north-east, where the best supplies of flint are found, sealed in chalk trapped under the sheets of volcanic lava which form the Giant's Causeway. Most of Ireland was probably colonised quickly by people initially crossing from southern Scotland, but because of the quality of the flint around Lough Neagh and Strangford Lough Mesolithic sites are easier to find there.

Excavations in the 1970s at Mount Sandel near Coleraine (Co. Derry) uncovered the earliest man-made structures known in Ireland, radiocarbon dated to between 7000 and 6500 BC. These ten structures were like the benders of modern travellers or Apache wickiups: a circle of wooden poles bent over and covered with hides or vegetation. The best preserved were about 6 metres across with a central hearth, around which the family could gather for warmth and cook. As at Star Carr, the Irish group at Mount Sandel returned each year, probably as part of a structured cycle of movement designed to exploit different resources through the seasons. On their returns the Mount Sandel people rebuilt one of the huts four times on the same site.

Fortunately, these Irish hunters were a tidy lot and disposed of their rubbish around the camp site, often in old storage pits initially used for caches of hazelnuts. Wild pig seems to have been the favourite source of meat, supplemented by mallard, grouse, wood pigeon, snipe and thrush. They also trapped eagle and goshawk, perhaps for their feathers rather than their flesh. The camp overlooked the River Bann, not far from the sea, which was a rich source of trout, salmon, eel and sea bass. The range of resources – salmon in spring and summer, eels in autumn, hazelnuts and wild pig in autumn and winter – suggests that this prolific landscape could have supported a year-round base camp at Mount Sandel.

Times were not always so good for Mesolithic hunters, especially in what might seem the unlikely setting of Uxbridge, West London.[16] Just over 9,000 years ago a group of a dozen people set up camp there and lit a fire. They needed the warmth as it was the depth of winter. The hunters sat in two arcs, on either side of the fire, side-on to the wind. Food was scarce in the forest, but they had with them a cache of red-deer bones from the legs of at least fifteen animals, probably collected over several weeks of hunting. The meat had previously been stripped from the carcasses, but the bones were kept so that the nutritious, protein-rich marrow was available at the toughest time of the year, when hunter-gatherers frequently lost weight. As they sat on either side of the fire the little group split the bones to extract the marrow and threw the ends of the shafts behind them. It seems from the distribution of material that the members of the clan had their specialist jobs – wood, bone or leather working, with the flint-knappers at the ends of the arc to keep the sharp waste fragments away from the central area. The winter was not a time of plenty, but the Uxbridge people had clearly developed a strategy for dealing with it.

Because Scotland was so severely affected by glaciation, the evidence of early human occupation is scarce. In fact the earliest settlement known was one of those chance discoveries that make archaeology such an interesting and, at times, frustrating activity. You look for one thing and find another. At Cramond on the Firth of Forth a team of amateur archaeologists from Edinburgh were excavating around a Roman bathhouse. Unexpectedly, they came across a well-preserved deposit of chert-stone tools and hazelnut shells. This proved to be Scotland's oldest site of human occupation. Radiocarbon dating of the hazelnut shells showed that Mesolithic hunter-gatherers were living there about 8500 BC. Their camp lay on a bluff above the confluence of the Rivers Forth and Almond, ideally placed to exploit the resources of the rivers, the seashore and the forest.

The first Scots were technologically advanced; they were using so-called 'geometric'-style microliths, which do not appear in England until about 7800 BC. So did this new technology come from the north? Unfortunately, the soils at Cramond are acidic, so animal bone is not preserved. At Sand in Wester Ross there is better evidence for the activities of hunter-gatherers: a midden or dump of mainly limpet shells accumulated outside a coastal rock shelter along with red-deer and bird bones. We have no images of these hunters, but like all humans they cared about their appearance, making jewellery from boars' tusks and cowrie shells and gathering dog whelks, which are a source of purple dye. They were also at home on the sea, capable of fetching material from the Isles of Rhum and Skye.

Recently remarkable new evidence of the longevity of Mesolithic settlements has been rescued from the eroding cliff tops at Howick, on the Northumbrian coast near Bamburgh. The settlers dug a hole 6 metres across and 0.7 metres deep into the underlying sand and built up a perimeter wall with the material. Strong timber posts were then set into the floor to support a pitched roof about 6 metres high at the apex, covered in thatch or turf.*

Inside, the occupants sat around a central hearth into which they tossed the remains of food, the bones of grey seal, wild pig, birds and even fox. Many of the remains were paw bones, which would have been collected when the animals were skinned. There were also masses of hazelnuts around the fire. When Clive Waddington, the excavator, from Newcastle University, contacted me with news of this discovery, I did not hesitate to arrange a programme of radiocarbon dating. After all, this was one of Britain's earliest domestic houses, and hazelnuts, because they are quickly gathered and consumed, provide particularly good dating material. The forty dates that we obtained showed that the house was built around 7800 BC and used for about 150 years.

These were not transitory people: they really belonged to this land. Remarkably, a very similar building, Scotland's earliest house, was also found at the same time as Howick was being excavated, 40 miles to the north at East Barns, in East Lothian, near Dunbar. These places show that Mesolithic hunters were not simply mobile nomads living in temporary shelters or tents. Clearly where conditions were favourable they either lived in permanent sites or created places which could be visited regularly at appropriate times of the year.

The Howick building was discovered because the settlement was eroding from a cliff top into the sea. At the time it was occupied the sea level was about 4.5 metres lower than today and the coastline would have been about 300 metres further out.† This means that many Mesolithic sites could now be underwater. This was confirmed recently by divers from the Hampshire and Wight Trust for Maritime Archaeology. Exploring along the foot of an underwater cliff in the Solent, they came across freshly dug lobster burrows. In the lobsters' spoil heaps were scattered Mesolithic flint tools, which marked the first submerged prehistoric camp site, where Mesolithic flint-knappers had sat working and tossed their waste material behind them. Two thousand years later, about 6500 BC, the rising sea swept into the Solent valley, drowning the abandoned camp site and the forest that surrounded it: dozens of fallen oaks still lie on the seabed, victims of earlier global warming.

It is difficult, from the fragmentary archaeological information, to

---

* The house has been reconstructed at the Maelmin Heritage Trail site on the A677 near Milford.[17]
† The distance varies around the coast depending on local topography.

calculate the numbers of hunter-gatherers in post-glacial Britain. However, Christopher Smith analysed the density of their activities across Britain (excluding Ireland).[18]

Smith was brave enough to attach numbers to his population survey, but in some ways observable trends rather than specific numbers are more reliable at this period. He estimated a population of 5,500 maximum for Britain in 5000 BC, which is low compared with the estimates of 10,000 to 27,000 for the Middle Palaeolithic hominid populations of Britain and Ireland (between 300,000 and 35,000 years ago).[19]

We know that Mesolithic numbers are distorted by the invisibility of many of their settlements, flooded by rising sea levels or hidden beneath the flood silts of rivers such as the Thames. Nevertheless Smith produced some convincing trends: the British population increasing in the centuries prior to the final cold snap, the Loch Lomond episode; a reduced population in the cold period, followed by increasingly rapid growth in the four millennia up to the start of the Neolithic and farming.*

Surprisingly perhaps, for tens of thousands of years our ancestors were a relatively rare species, constantly knocked back by climate change, and making relatively little impact on the planet. The number of people in the world 10,000 years ago was probably in the region of 4 million. Growth rates were extremely slow through most of the Stone Age, perhaps as little as 0.001 per cent, rising to 0.1 per cent in the Mesolithic, on the eve of the expansion of agriculture. Hunter-gatherers live at very low densities, as they are dependent on the natural productivity, or carrying capacity, of the land they inhabit. Carrying capacity can be calculated broadly for different environments – deciduous woodland, for example, has a maximum primary productivity of 2,500 grams per square metre per year, and tundra as little as 100 grams per square metre per year. Given that humans in temperate latitudes use about 2,200 calories per day (and half as much again in cold conditions) and most of the biomass in deciduous forest comes in the form of wood and leaves, then animals, supplemented by nuts, berries and tubers, must have been an important part of the Mesolithic diet. For much of the year large animals such as red deer tend to be very lean – good for protein, but lacking the carbohydrate-rich fat that humans also need.

The small island of Colonsay, off the west coast of Scotland, is not at first sight a particularly appealing destination for Mesolithic seafarers. Why bother with an island that was not apparently even colonised by deer? The clue lies in the name 'Hazel Island' ('coll' is Gaelic for 'hazel').

---

* About 1,100–1,200 people at 9000 BC; 1,200–2,400 by 8000 BC; 2,500 to 5,000 by 7000 BC, and 2,750 to 5,500 about 5000 BC.

When Steve Mithen of Reading University dug test pits on the island, looking, with great persistence, for Mesolithic settlement, he came across a large circular pit (or possibly the sunken floor of a hut like those found at Cramond and Howick) 4 metres across, with a neighbouring cluster of smaller pits. The big hole was packed with over 100,000 hazelnut shells, roasted in the smaller pits and eventually, after an orgy of nut-eating, discarded along with apple cores. So Colonsay, with its prolific supplies of nuts, provided the ideal supplement to the protein-rich Scottish diet of about 6700 BC.

To the south of Colonsay lies the small, inhospitable island of Oronsay. Along the edge of what was the southern coast about 6,000 years ago (9 metres higher than today) there are a series of mounds made up principally of shells discarded by Mesolithic foragers. Most of these are from limpets, one of the least appetising of British shellfish, usually only eaten in emergencies. Most likely the limpets were used as bait to catch saithe – a type of cod, whose bones are common among the more visible shells. The presence of otoliths – small bones found in the fish's ear – provides a seasonal calendar. Their size indicates the age of the fish and the season when the fish died. The saithe were being caught in autumn – the same period that the hazelnuts were gathered on Colonsay; but the hunters seem to have been present all year round on windswept Oronsay, either as permanent settlers or regular visitors, catching bull grey seals in spring, sea otters for pelts and large numbers of seabirds. The Oronsay shell-middens have attracted archaeologists for over a century – they contain not only shells, but also rare examples of Mesolithic human remains. Studies of these bones indicate that the Oronsay people existed on an entirely marine diet of fish, seabirds, seals and shellfish.

So from one end of the British Isles to the other hunter-gatherers lived successfully on the natural resources of the forest, rivers and sea; but they did so in relatively small numbers. From studies of hunter-gatherers who retained their way of life into recent times we know that the family unit grouped with others to form a band. Such bands varied in size from fewer than fifty people, but averaged about 300, with an average density of 0.15 persons per square kilometre. Most members of bands, especially of small ones, sought marriage partners outside their immediate group, in the mating network which we call a tribe. A tribe commonly consisted of about four bands with an average population of about 900 – though these figures varied enormously in the North American groups that formed the basis for the study. Such bands and tribes were relatively egalitarian – leaders were occasionally chosen on the basis of experience or charisma to head up war bands or delegations – but most work parties were self-selecting, shared their spoils in common and people held little in the way of private property. Mesolithic people were the original, and genuine, communists.

These tribes had language, ancestors and culture in common; they occupied relatively stable territories and probably signalled their identity through dress, hairstyle and bodily decoration. At Star Carr, for example, a tribe of a thousand might have occupied an area of about 70 by 100 kilometres − the area of the North Riding of Yorkshire. They must have had a name for themselves and probably a clan totem and certainly a common language, though we do not know what this was or even if it bore any relationship to a modern tongue. The bands would have moved on a shifting seasonal and annual cycle, in pursuit of whatever foodstuffs or other commodities were available. Only in the most favourable environments might some groups have remained relatively static.

In many respects the people of Mesolithic Britain seemed to be living the Good Life. Yet all was about to change as the new lifestyle of farming spread across Europe. While the hunters, fishers and plant-gatherers of Britain pursued their traditional ways, life had changed in central Europe and the Mediterranean. Domesticated animals − sheep, goats, cattle and pigs − and cultivated plants such as wheat and barley now formed the basis for a new economy, new beliefs and new relationships between humans and the land.

About three years ago I went to take a look at the construction site of the new Channel Tunnel Rail Link, which will eventually join Britain, at high speed, to the Continental rail network. At the base of the North Downs in Kent there were the beginnings of a gigantic cutting into the chalk. Scores of archaeologists shepherded mechanical diggers, which, like long-necked brontosauruses, grazed on the hillside eating into what had once been the bed of a warm Cretaceous sea.

In one area the archaeologists had resorted to the tool of their trade, the trowel. They were on their knees in obeisance before the remains of a long, rectangular pattern of circular dark post-holes and curved slots. This was a rare discovery in Britain: a longhouse of about 3900 BC − when farming first arrived in Britain. This impressive structure was well preserved beneath 5 metres of hillwash or colluvium − soil which had gradually slipped down the slope of the chalk scarp as a result of prehistoric agriculture: prehistoric farmers had cleared the forest, ploughed the shallow soils and generated erosion. The Neolithic, or New Stone Age, is the period when farming − the domestication and control of key plants and animals − first appears in Britain: the so-called 'Neolithic Revolution'.

Unlike the Industrial Revolution* this one did not begin in Britain but in western Asia, and took some 6,000 years to reach these islands.

Textbooks often assume that with agriculture people settle down, create villages, take up specialisations, from potting to priesthood, and thus develop a class system. Unfortunately, in northern Europe, including Britain, it does not seem to work quite like that. Evidence of permanent settlement and substantial buildings is scarce. So the big timber structure at White Horse Stone in Kent was a particularly interesting discovery. It was also a discovery that would not have been made without the Rail Link construction. The deep blanket of hillwash made it invisible to archaeological techniques such as field-walking, geophysics and aerial survey – which is why it is essential for archaeologists to be included in big construction programmes. These are a potential window into the past, but someone has to be there to look through it.

For about 100,000 years modern humans subsisted by hunting wild animals and by collecting wild plants. While northern Europe was still in the grip of the last Ice Age, hunter-gatherer communities in the Euphrates valley – in present-day Syria – began to interfere more radically with the wild grasses, whose grains provided them with some of their basic foodstuffs.† By collecting seeds and transposing them into specially prepared beds, the ancient Syrians developed the first domesticated crops and they became the world's first farmers, or gardeners. The cultivators selected the natural mutations with the qualities they most desired, such as large seeds. Rapidly these plants began to differ from ones in the wild and domesticates, the ancestors of wheat, barley and rye, can be recognised both from their physical characteristics and their genetic make-up.

At Abu-Hureyra hunter-gatherers had lived for about 400 years, dependent on wild plants and animals. This confidence in the environment must have been shaken when there was a sharp reversal in the pattern of climatic improvement and the wild plants became more scarce. However, the ability of modern humans to adapt came to the fore and the community began the process of domestication by planting and tending wild cereals in more favourable plots. The Abu-Hureyrans are the earliest agriculturalists to be dated so far but they were not alone: around 12,000 years ago the trick of domestication appeared also in China and the Far East with other plants, and from the Euphrates it spread through western Asia and into Greece

* The term 'Industrial Revolution' was first coined by Arnold Toynbee, father of the well-known historian, in the 1880s and was picked up by V. Gordon Childe for the Neolithic in the 1920s.
† The earliest evidence for plant domestication, in the form of cereal grains, comes from the site of Abu-Hureyra in Syria, dated to about 11,000 BC.

(between 9000 and 8000 BC). In the Euphrates valley domestication also involved local animals – first sheep and goats, then pigs and cattle.

In 1965 the well-known Cambridge prehistorian Grahame Clark, whom we met at Star Carr, published the first map, using the limited number of radiocarbon dates then available, to plot the spread of the Neolithic across western Asia and Europe. With its epicentre at Jericho the waves of agriculture rippled across Europe, into Greece, along the Danube, into the northern European plain at a rate of about 1 kilometre a year, finally breaking upon the shores of Britain after several thousand years. Recently this exercise has been undertaken again, using the much larger radiocarbon database now available of just over 2,600 samples from 715 sites and a more sophisticated statistical analysis.[20]

The new analysis confirms the general trend that agriculture spread across Europe from western Asia, starting about 12,000 years ago and belatedly arriving in Britain 6,000 years later. However, the current was far from a regular flow. It may have averaged 1.3 kilometres per year, but in reality the spread of agriculture pulsed and eddied at different rates: sometimes moving quickly, at other times stalling as local groups resisted or ignored the supposed advantages of the 'Neolithic package'; but this term is mere jargon, a construct of archaeologists not the people who lived in northern Europe 6,000 years ago.

In fact the term 'Neolithic', or New Stone Age, was invented by an energetic Victorian, Sir John Lubbock, later Lord Avebury. Lubbock was not a professional scholar; rather he was a politician and a banker. In Victorian Britain he was best known for his Bank Holidays Act of 1871, and for a while bank holidays were known as St Lubbock's days. Lubbock was also a seriously competent natural historian, archaeologist and workaholic. Charles Darwin wrote to him: 'How on earth you find time to do all you do is a mystery to me.' One of the things Lubbock managed to fit in was his first book, published in 1865, *Prehistoric Times as Illustrated by Ancient Remains and the Manners and Customs of Modern Savages*.

He wrote:

> From the careful study of the remains that have come down
> to us, it would appear that Prehistoric Archaeology may be
> divided into four great epochs:
> That of the Drift; when man shared the possession of
> Europe with the Mammoth, the Cave Bear, the Woolly-haired
> Rhinoceros and other extinct animals. This I have proposed
> to call the 'Palaeolithic' period.

The later or polished Stone Age: a period characterized by beautiful weapons and instruments made of flint and other kinds of stone; in which, however, we find no trace of the knowledge of any metal, excepting gold ... For this period I have suggested the term 'Neolithic'.

The Bronze Age, in which bronze was used for arms and cutting instruments of all kinds.

The Iron Age, in which that metal had superseded bronze ...

Lubbock goes on to say that his classification only applies in Europe and 'some nations, indeed such as the Fuegians, Andamaners, etc., are even now, or were very lately, in an Age of Stone'.

Lubbock coined the term 'Neolithic' to account for the technological changes in stone-tool manufacture, the way later prehistoric, post-glacial communities of Europe ground or polished their axe heads. In the 1920s the great Australian archaeologist Gordon Childe broadened the approach and introduced the term 'Neolithic Revolution' to describe the transition from hunting and foraging to the domestication of plants and animals. After Childe the Neolithic was synonymous with farming. His term deliberately echoed the 'Industrial Revolution' to imply that there had been a rapid and dramatic transition to a new way of life. If you bought into the Neolithic package, it came with domesticated plants and animals, permanent settlements, proper architecture and pottery as well as polished stone axes. And with it mankind took the ultimate giant leap to a civilised life: of towns, craft specialists, class structures, priesthoods, kings, surplus food and an increasing population. As Lubbock's book title indicates, the alternative was savagery. For the evolutionary-minded the advantages of the Neolithic Revolution were self-evident.

But the picture is now not so simple. The Victorians had a low opinion of hunter-gatherer, or foraging, societies. Lubbock specifically refers to Fuegians – the inhabitants of Tierra del Fuego, whom his friend Darwin observed on the *Beagle* voyage as 'stunted in their growth, their hideous faces bedaubed with white paint, their skins filthy and greasy, their hair entangled, their voices discordant, and their gestures violent. Viewing such men, one can hardly make one's self believe that they are fellow creatures.'

And in *Prehistoric Times* Lubbock reflects, though does not entirely support, the arrogant and racist views of his sources. And, to be fair to Darwin, while the great man inevitably saw the Fuegians through contemporary Victorian lenses, he did accept them as fellow humans.

Natural scientists in the nineteenth century, such as Darwin, Huxley and Alexander von Humbold, could travel the world as ships' doctors or naturalists; but while they were able to collect plant and animal specimens, they neither had the training, inclination nor time to study and communicate with the indigenous peoples whom they only superficially observed. To mid-Victorian gentlemen these hunter-gatherers were human failures, destined for extinction.

In this they were not so far wrong. Today fewer than 0.001 per cent of humans still live by hunter-gathering and most of them survive in remote or marginal areas – in Australia, New Guinea or South African deserts, the circumpolar zone or tropical rainforest. These are the last remnants of a way of life that was universal amongst humans for tens of thousands of years. As such, modern foragers are not typical of those who followed a hunter-gatherer lifestyle in the forests of post-glacial Europe. Nevertheless anthropologists living and communicating with groups such as the !Kung!San bushmen of Botswana find people whose lives are full of humour, interest, imagination and human foibles. Their lives were not, as Thomas Hobbes would have it, simply nasty, brutish and short. Nor was it all work. Even in the Kalahari – an environment increasingly desiccated by global warming over the past 10,000 years – hunters and gatherers could sustain themselves on approximately thirty hours of effort per week.

Some archaeologists have presented the Neolithic transformation as a wave of advance sweeping across Europe, pushed by farming communities, the new frontiersmen whose ancestors came from the Near East, through Turkey into Greece, the Danube region, the south of France and northern Europe. Others disagree and prefer to see the Neolithic not as a revolution or a simple package of domesticated plants, animals, pots and settled villages, but as a variety of resources and cultural elements that indigenous Mesolithic people could adopt or reject as they saw fit. Certainly the large timber house which we discovered at the White Horse Stone site in Kent represented as revolutionary a structure in the English countryside as the Channel Tunnel Rail Link does today. But was this built by local people picking up ideas from the Continent? or was the massive timber building the work of immigrant farmers, like the Amish in the film *Witness*, raising a new barn in a new world? Archaeologists have argued about immigration versus local development for decades. Recently a dimension has been added to this debate in the form of the new science of genetics.

Since the disappearance of the Neanderthals we all belong to a single species that spread out of Africa from about 125,000 years ago and dispersed around the world. Genetically we are all similar, but with observable differences. These differences take the form of random genetic mutations, which are usually of little significance in themselves but provide a kind of fingerprint which allows us to trace our ancestry. These mutations occur at a predictable rate, so the greater the differences between two human populations, the greater the amount of time since those populations split off from each other. As a result, each one of us contains the history of our ancestors within our own genetic material. By mapping the genetic variability of humans around the world geneticists can begin to track their dispersal, migrations and interrelationships. At least that is the theory. In practice there are lots of complicating factors in what is a new science, still in its infancy but nevertheless one of the most exciting breakthroughs in the study of life since Darwin.

One of the pioneers of this new science of historical genetics is Luigi Luca Cavalli-Sforza, who in the 1950s began to analyse blood-group frequencies as a way of assessing relationships between modern humans. In the sixties he was able to show that European populations were closer to each other than they were to Africans and subsequently he showed that this divergence occurred about 33,000 years ago. At that stage the original homeland of humans was still uncertain.

In the 1970s Cavalli-Sforza teamed up with the archaeologist Albert Ammeman to chart the rippling effect of the spread of agriculture across western Asia and Europe. At the end of the last Ice Age there was a period of rapid climatic change that produced Mediterranean seasons: long, dry summers and short, wet winters. I am experiencing one of the former as I write this book in the south of France. It was 42°C yesterday. And the book I am reading in the evenings is appropriately titled *Grasses*. This kind of climate suits grasses, which produce seeds early in the year and then lie dormant during the hot summer. I am interested in their aesthetics — grasses can look beautiful if I can keep the goats out of our garden — but Mesolithic foragers were attracted to the energy packaged in the seeds, which could be harvested and then stored for the rest of the year. The prolific production of seed by wild grasses such as *einkorn*, the wild prototype of wheat, encouraged the foragers to stick close to their basic food supply. As global temperatures increased and the eastern-Mediterranean climate continued to dry, and the grass strands began to thin out, these foragers began to experiment with planting seeds in prepared beds — and perhaps watering them as I did this morning, using my bath water to conserve an increasingly scarce resource.

The relatively simple act of planting marked a turning point for us humans: with it we start to take control of nature and of our habitat. We opened the Pandora's Box to our future. By controlling energy supply in this way we also greatly increased our potential population density. No longer were we dependent on the natural and limited carrying capacity of the land.

Fifty thousand years ago the human population was perhaps a mere 10,000 individuals. By the time those first seeds were planted in the Near East it had struggled up to perhaps 10 million in 40,000 years. Thanks to farming, the world population rose to over 500 million in the mid-eighteenth century, the eve of the next global leap forward for humans: the Industrial Revolution, which was launched in Britain. Why should this be so? Human populations expanded, albeit slowly, as we crossed out of Africa to exploit the new world of Australia, Europe, Asia and America; but the available natural resources limited population expansion, and humans could easily overexploit these resources, especially when the species they hunted or gathered were teetering on an ecological knife-edge as a result of climate change.

Hunter-gatherers had low birth rates, partly because with the relatively rough, fibrous foodstuffs available to them they did not have the pappy baby foods that make early weaning a possibility. Unless there are palatable alternatives, children rely on their mothers' milk up to the age of about four. Frequent breastfeeding stimulated the production of prolactin, a hormone which reduces fertility and the chances of early pregnancy. So spacing between births in hunter-gatherer clans tends to be about four years. For such mobile people, where women were often the gatherers of the largest source of calories, more than one dependent infant at a time would have been a real and sometimes unacceptable handicap. For the independence of both mother and child, weaning from the back was as important as weaning from the breast. Because natural resources can fluctuate annually – there might be a disastrous nut harvest or a prey population could collapse suddenly – it is in the interest of hunters to restrict their own population to considerably less than the normal carrying capacity would allow. This reduces the risk of starvation in the inevitable lean years.

Farming changed all that. On the new frontier there was an infinite amount of land to be cultivated. More people meant more labour to cut down forest, clear the land, harvest larger areas and look after more animals. With animal milk and the cereals from domesticated grasses human infants could be weaned in half the time and the birth intervals reduced. Humans have been very selective in what they chose to domesticate – usually plants with high-density food parts, which can be bred by selection to increase in size the part we want to eat – as with emmer wheat, rice or corn. In the same way relatively few species of animals have come to live in the farmyard — sheep, goats, cattle, pigs, chickens — animals that were relatively sociable, docile and meaty, or capable of generating secondary products, such as milk and wool, or work, in the cases of some of the domesticates we rarely eat, such as dogs, donkeys, llamas and horses. None of the major Eurasian domesticates, except perhaps the pig, were native to Britain. All had to be shipped in.

Agriculture was not an unmixed blessing for humanity, however — let alone for the species that were swept aside by its advance. Farming requires hard work, and in a bad year of harvest failure or animal disease results can be disastrous. Horticulturalists and arable farmers also find it easier to overindulge in carbohydrates — it is harder to resist food when there is a store full of the stuff. Hunters traditionally are lean and fit, though their cuisine would earn no Michelin stars. In comparison farming communities eat more, grow larger, put more effort into the rituals of cooking — and grow larger still. Obesity was a Neolithic disease; and it was not the only one. The proximity of humans and domestic animals meant that new diseases could leap the species barrier — influenza from fowl, measles, smallpox, tuberculosis.

Forest clearance for agriculture generated drastic ecological changes (and continues to do so), which promoted the spread of malaria and schistosomiasis. Settled populations of humans and animals pollute the ground and water supplies so that typhoid, cholera and hookworm flourish. Large and dense human populations also allow bacterial and viral diseases to recycle themselves around a plentiful supply of victims. In the longer term Old World farming communities became relatively immune to many of the Neolithic diseases. These often became diseases of childhood, until passed on with disastrous consequences to New World populations such as those of America or the Pacific regions.

Nevertheless, the immediate impact of the Neolithic was population expansion: farming provided an ecological advantage that stimulated population growth. The ripples of Neolithic expansion also reflected the spread of the agriculturalists themselves and their genes. In other words, year by year pioneer farmers simply swamped the hunter-gatherers like the rising sea levels. The descendants of Cain outbred those of Nimrod and spread across Europe.* In the 1970s archaeologists were still reacting to discredited invasion hypotheses and did not readily adopt what looked like old wine in a new genetic bottle. A lot of archaeological evidence suggested that hunter-gatherers in Britain, Scandinavia and north-west

* By 1994 Cavalli-Sforza and his collaborators had developed their data and their arguments on what they called 'demic diffusion' in an outstanding publication: *The History and Geography of Human Genes*.

France adopted agricultural practices gradually rather than being replaced by immigrants.

The theory that Near Eastern farmers and their descendants had technologically, culturally and genetically moved across Europe from the south-east, in Greece, was also supported by Colin Renfrew, in a book that resurrected one of the great questions of linguistics: 'Where and when did the Indo-European family of languages originate?'[21]

Renfrew's proposal was that the original proto-Indo-European language came out of western Asia with the first farmers and spread with the flocks of sheep and fields of corn. The new dominant culture brought with it a new language and probably new religious ideas, ideals and a new dominant world view. In a few out-of-the-way pockets the old hunter-gatherer way of life clung on, according to Renfrew − reflected today in the survival of pre-Indo-European languages such as Finnish and Basque.

This linguistic theory came in for a fierce drubbing − if Indo-European existed in the eighth millennium BC, why did its subsequent offshoot languages contain common words for social hierarchies (kings, for example) and technologies such as metalworking, which did not exist at the time the original language was supposed to have spread?[22] Also, languages can diffuse without the benefit of mass migration − for example English throughout India and much of Africa − neither the European Neolithic nor the subsequent languages required the migration of people of western Asian origin. This still leaves a big question unanswered: When did the first recognisable British languages − the ancestors of Welsh, Irish, and Scots Gaelic − arrive in these islands?

The migration of farmers across Europe was also questioned by a group of historical geneticists based in Oxford, led by Bryan Sykes.[§] His team looked at DNA from over eight hundred individuals across Europe. They identified seven major genetic clusters into which fit 95 per cent of modern native Europeans. These seven clusters varied in age between 45,000 and 10,000 years. The results suggest that European origins are more complex than indicated by the migrating-farmers model. Only one cluster among Sykes's groups seemed to originate among the pioneer farmers of western Asia. The other six groups, each of which was between 23,000 and 50,000 years old and constituted 85 per cent of modern native Europeans, originated during the Ice Age. According to Sykes, there had been some immigrant farmers who had followed the urge to go west − into the Mediterranean and the Danube − but most Neolithic farmers in Europe were the descendants of Mesolithic hunter-gatherers. Farming and domestication had been passed on as an idea, rather than being brought by waves of new people.

This clash of opinions about the genetic map of Europe led to one of those fierce debates which occasionally brighten up the lives of academics. While there are ongoing arguments, more recent research suggests the two views are not incompatible. Cavalli-Sforza now estimates that pioneering farmers, surfing the wave of advance into Europe, contributed some 28 per cent to the gene pool; Sykes puts the figure at 20 per cent. So on present genetic evidence it seems that significant numbers of west-Asian farmers moved into south-east Europe; but the majority of the population, especially in Britain and northern Europe, can trace its ancestry back to Ice Age hunters – like Adrian Targett, the Head of History and two of his pupils at Cheddar School, in Somerset, whose DNA was found to match that recovered from the tooth of the 9,000-year-old man buried in the caves at Cheddar. At present the most likely scenario is that colonisation or immigration of early farmers was a major factor in south-eastern Europe but that local adoption of agriculture with immigration on a reduced scale became increasingly the pattern towards the north and north-west of Europe.[23]

From about 5500 BC an innovative and distinct farming culture spread rapidly from the Hungarian plain through Poland and Germany into France and the Netherlands. This new habit spread at about a kilometre a year. It has been suggested that these early farmers had a thrusting frontier mentality and ideology, rather like that of nineteenth-century pioneers in America, expressed by Horace Greeley in his famous phrase: 'Go west, young man!' And these people spread a remarkably uniform package – the same style of timber longhouse, for example, was built from Hungary to France for several centuries – not unlike the spread of Romanesque churches 6,000 years later.

Archaeologists, with little regard for euphony, call the farming culture the Linearbandkeramik (or LBK) after its distinctive pottery decorated with incised lines. These farmers sought out the best soils, cleared areas of woodland and constructed their rectangular timber halls, between 10 and 40 metres long. Cattle were the favoured animal. Perhaps like many African herders today the LBK cowboys regarded their cattle as wealth and status on the hoof, not simply a source of milk, blood or meat. While cattle browsed in the surrounding woodland the domestic pigs rooted through its floor. Where I am writing I can look out over oak woodland that is home to a family of wild boar. Just now the floor of the wood looks as if it has been ploughed – this is the sign of the boars at work before the hunting season starts. The introduction of larger populations of domestic but still tough and athletic pigs must have helped considerably to open up the European wildwood. Surprisingly pollen analysis does not suggest that the woods themselves were rapidly and extensively cleared. This would make sense if LBK communities were not so much stable villages as mobile herders, seasonally moving through the forest and returning to the longhouses which may have functioned as communal centres and cult houses rather than simply as family homes. Significantly, when some of these LBK buildings went out of use they were mounded into houses for the dead and transformed into tombs.

Interestingly, our Channel Tunnel Rail Link house, which closely resembles the LBK buildings, is at a site known as White Horse Stone, named after one of the group of megalithic tombs in the Medway valley of which Kits Coty is the best known. These monumental Neolithic tombs are the earliest human structures still visible in our landscape. Their long rectangular shape, with chambers to take the bones of the earliest British farmers, mirror the LBK architecture of the Continent, but were created to house the dead. The timber longhouse found on the rail route was massive, 18 metres long and 8 metres wide with curving walls. Inside are two rooms, on either side of a central entrance. About 3900 BC* the building stood prominently on the slope of the North Downs overlooking the plain below. Today the landscape is open, but 5,000 years ago the builders created a clearing in the forest so that they could erect the longhouse, which was then in use for about a century.

Was this then a family house, a communal or cult building for a clan group practising semi-mobile herding and small-scale arable farming? Certainly they left very little rubbish or domestic debris. So was this a ceremonial building placed near the tombs of their ancestors? An even more impressive Neolithic building was first discovered by aerial photography in the dry summer of 1976 at Balbridie, on Deeside in Scotland.[24]

This was a massively built structure with curving end walls and large internal posts: the widest Neolithic building in Europe and the longest in Britain at 24 by 12 metres. It probably stood a little later than its White Horse Stone predecessor, coming to an end somewhere about 3500 BC.† Remarkably, the excavators recovered nearly three-quarters of a million charred cereal grains from this building, including bread wheat – an unusual crop at such an early date in Britain. Archaeologists tend to assume that cereal production was of minor importance in the early Neolithic, but Balbridie suggests otherwise. The building resembles structures in the Aisne valley in France and, as with the White Horse Stone longhouse, we cannot rule out the possibility that immigrant farmers sailed across

* Radiocarbon dates from the post-holes indicate a date range from 3940 to 3530 BC.
† Other substantial early Neolithic buildings are known at Lismore Fields, Derbyshire, at Callander in Perthshire and at Tankardstown, Co. Limerick.

the Channel with their cattle, pigs, sheep and sacks of seedcorn. The domestic animals, which were not native to Britain, clearly had to be shipped across the Channel — just as we know from DNA studies that pre-historic cattle were brought far greater distances, over 1,000 kilometres, across the Indian Ocean from southern India to contribute to the gene pool of African cattle.[25]

Archaeologists continue to argue about whether farming was brought to Britain by Continental immigrants carrying the Neolithic package of domesticated plants and animals or whether the knowledge and ideas of domestication slowly spread through the native hunter-gatherer popula-tion with little influx of new people.

Both suggestions may be correct. At White Horse Stone and Balbridie the buildings show Continental influence and parts of eastern Scotland arguably have overseas links. Some areas show a close overlap of early farming and Mesolithic activity; others do not. There seems to be no continuity, for example, in the Tyne valley and in Invernesshire — as if hunter-gatherers and farmers were separated in space and time. A differ-ent pattern emerges on islands off the west coast of Britain — such as Islay, where every archaeologist would like to do fieldwork, lubricated with the universe's finest whiskies. There, as on the Isle of Man, Mesolithic and Neolithic materials often occur on the same site, suggest-ing that local people had transformed their way of life.[26]

The islands of the west and north also have remarkably early settle-ments and extensive field systems, such as the Scord of Brouster in Shetland, where early Neolithic farmers grew barley, raised sheep and manured their fields with their refuse and seaweed gathered from the shore. Shetland seems to have been divided into massive field systems before most of southern England. In recent years the Celtic tiger econ-omy of Ireland has generated an enormous number of archaeological excavations ahead of development. As a result, several substantial rect-angular Neolithic houses have been found in clustered communities as well as extensive field systems. At Corbally, Co. Kildare, three houses were well constructed of posts and planks set in deep foundation trenches. Two of these were 11 metres long with hearths in the bigger of the two rooms.

So why does the radical change to farming seem to be happening more quickly and extensively on what to English people may seem to be out-of-the-way places? The answer may be location, location, location: places accessible in the western seaways and open to influences from Spain, west-ern France and Brittany. Domesticated sheep, cattle and cereals had to come over from the Continent by boat and from a maritime perspective the western islands are not remote. Recently I stood on a high point of the Isle of Man. The weather was clear and it felt like the centre of the universe; the coasts of Ireland, Scotland and England were all clearly visible. The Mesolithic people of this region had to be skilled seafarers to exploit the resources of the islands. They probably had more long-distance contacts than land-locked hunter-gatherers and were quicker to learn about and adapt to the new life-ways of farming. A historian discussing trade in eighteenth-century Orkney and Shetland noted how the locals sold their knitwear and woollen goods to Dutch and Danish herring fishermen and had links with Edinburgh, Newcastle, London, Norway, Hamburg, Spain and Portugal. His conclusion – 'the world was wide for these little islands' – is probably a universal truth.[27]

New discoveries like the White Horse Stone longhouse in Kent are causing a rethink of the Neolithic in the south. In Orkney, permanent Neolithic settlements with planned, domestic interiors have been known for years – sites like Skara Brae on the mainland and Knap of Howar on Papa Westray dating to the mid-fourth millennium BC. But Britain is often viewed from a southern perspective and, ironically, the importance of maritime communications forgotten.

The evidence of Neolithic communities in Scotland is particularly rich and varied. Substantial and comfortable houses were built of local sandstone slabs in a landscape in which timber is and was in short supply. The most famous of the Orkney sites, Skara Brae, was spectacularly well preserved beneath encroaching sand. This well-planned settlement was occupied for over 600 years from about 3100 BC. The community of six houses linked by passageways and with communal drains was sunk into an earlier rubbish mound, with massively thick walls to protect the inhabitants from Orkney's notorious winds. The similar houses at the Knap of Howar were occupied even earlier than Skara Brae from about 3600 BC: the earliest of Orkney's Neolithic settlements. Skara Brae's oval houses had a living space about 6 metres across (roughly 36 square metres). The numbers who lived in each probably varied depending on family circumstances. The arrangements of hearths and box-like beds are remarkably similar to those in traditional Orkney homes even as recently as the nineteenth century. When making assumptions about living space it is worth remembering one observation made in an Orkney house in 1847. A visitor, observing a single box bed, asked where the parents and six children slept. The answer was: together, in one bed. One of the Skara Brae houses was certainly less crowded, as it had five beds. The huddled, cell-like structures with central hearths, storage bins, impressive stone dressers and beds provide clear evidence of family homes and clustered communities not available in England. In the Scottish Neolithic there is no reason to doubt that there were prominent farmsteads and hamlets practising mixed farming and taking wild resources where they were worthwhile, particularly seabirds and deer.

Ireland also provides evidence for communal effort in order to clear and organise land on a large scale. The Ceide Fields in County Mayo are bounded by stone walls up to 2 kilometres long and 200 metres apart, forming blocks up to 7 hectares in size. These fields seem to have been intensively cultivated and grazed for about 500 years from 3700 BC. Then, a few centuries later, as the climate deteriorated, blanket bog crept over them, wiping out the chances of future cultivation and preserving the best example of organised Neolithic land use in the British Isles.

At present we can say little about the scale of colonisation of Britain by Continental farmers. It seems likely that the indigenous Mesolithic population adopted various aspects of plant and animal domestication quite rapidly about 4000 BC, possibly stimulated by contacts with the Continent or by the presence of immigrant farmers. The changes were not simply economic: farming brought with it a new cosmology, new ways of looking at the world, at nature, the land and the gods. In the first two millennia of farming in Britain it appears from the archaeological record that as much effort went into cultivating the gods as went into cultivating the land.

If archaeologists may have underestimated the speed and extent of the farming transition in southern England, the evidence is less ambiguous in the north and west. In Ireland the impact is clear, in an environment where there were probably no large mammals immediately prior to the Neolithic – the Irish elk had died out in the last cold spell and wild cattle and red deer may not have made it into Ireland before the post-glacial sea-level rise. Pollen diagrams consistently show a decline from about 3900 BC in the pollen of forest trees such as elm, oak, pine and hazel with a corresponding increase in grasses and weeds of disturbed ground such as ribwort plantain.*

The elm decline may have been due to the introduction of Dutch elm disease, but it corresponds to a sharp fall in other woodland species and the appearance of cereal pollen in small quantities. Because cereals do not disperse much pollen it is easy to underestimate their importance to early farmers, but at least seven querns – stones for grinding corn – were found in association with a house at Ballygalley, north of Larne. The farmers there also had stone tools made of material from the island of Arran, off the coast of Scotland, and axes from Cumbria and Cornish

---

* This last plant, a classic indicator of woodland clearance, also crossed the Atlantic with European farmers to America, where it was known to north-east-coast Indians as 'white-man's footstep'.

greenstone. As I mentioned earlier, people, animals, plants and tools were on the move, especially across the sea lanes between the north-western islands and peninsulas of Europe.

Nothing shows this more clearly than the distribution of polished stone axes made from porcellanite, a distinctive blue-grey stone found on Rathlin Island and at Tievebulliah, high up a mountainside in County Antrim. Many of these axes found their way into the western islands of Scotland, to the Isle of Man and into English river valleys, notably the Thames. Similarly the greenstone, so precariously won from narrow geological bands high on the crags of Langdale in the English Lake District, was widely distributed across Britain. These axes are the physical manifestation of a long-gone network of social relations, of marriages, gifts and exchange across the entire British Isles.

If calculating the population of a single Neolithic bed presents problems, then estimating how many people lived in Britain and Ireland as a whole in the fourth and third millennia is even more difficult; and modern demographers, with their battery of census statistics, might think it foolhardy even to try. However, the Neolithic is the first period in the history of Britain when we find any significant number of human burials surviving in the archaeological record. This is because the earliest British farming communities constructed impressive communal tombs. They were our first monument builders, marking their territories with great mounds which housed the bones of their ancestors.

The adoption of farming, with new foodstuffs such as dairy products, a more controlled carbohydrate supply, improved storage with ceramics, woollen and linen clothing, and a need for an expanding labour force all resulted in a substantial boost to human birth rates and growth in population. Whereas hunter-foragers in temperate north-west Europe may average one person per 10 square kilometres, it is not unreasonable to expect simple agriculturalist populations to achieve in the region of 3 to 10 people per square kilometre. Obviously Britain was a new frontier around 4000 BC, but over the next two millennia farmers spread across the entire landscape.

We do not know the details of their cosmology, the names of their gods and festivals; but clearly these farmers were driven by an enormously powerful belief system that brought order and meaning to a dangerous and potentially chaotic universe. The houses of the living are still relatively rare but those of the dead are not. Neolithic people right across Great Britain, Ireland and the islands put enormous effort into providing monuments of great variety and complexity to house their ancestors, or later as foci for ceremonies, processions and communal gatherings; and these show strong regional distinctiveness, partly because of natural resources, such as the sandstone of Orkney or the sarsen stones of Wessex, but also in that these people used the subtleties of architecture to express tribal and religious identity.

The most spectacular monuments, which are still visible today, are the megalithic tombs, like West Kennet, near Avebury, Wayland's Smithy on the Ridgeway (Oxfordshire) and the magnificent tombs of the Boyne valley in Ireland. These burial mounds were not simply functional places for the disposal of the dead: they were probably focal points for religious ceremonial and communal gatherings – places where people sought to influence the annual cycles of growth and rebirth reflected in the movement of the Sun and Moon. For our purposes they present the best evidence for the size of the Neolithic population and its demography.

One problem for archaeologists today is that many megalithic tombs have been disturbed in the past, often by early tomb-raiders in the nineteenth century rummaging through the burial chambers in search of spectacular grave goods which did not exist. In the south of England the best evidence comes from the tomb of Hazleton North (Gloucestershire), first opened and meticulously excavated between 1979 and 1982 by Alan Saville and his team. It is not often you get a chance to see an undisturbed Neolithic tomb opened for the first time, so I visited Hazleton, on the top of the Cotswolds, several times during the excavation. My most memorable trip was by aeroplane, to photograph the barrow when it had been fully exposed. Unfortunately, the only plane I could lay my hands on at short notice had low wings (for a clear view the plane's wings should be above the cockpit). As we banked in tight circles above the barrow I peered frustratedly through the camera lens and shouted at the pilot, 'The bloody wings are still in the way.' He solved the problem instantly – by flipping the plane upside down. As my stomach went through 180 degrees the image of the Hazleton barrow was permanently imprinted on my brain. More importantly for British archaeology, Alan Saville recovered 9,000 human bones, mainly in fragments, from within the Hazleton tomb's two stone-lined burial chambers. In the northern entrance passage there were two articulated bodies. One became known as the 'flint-knapper' because he had been buried with a worked core of flint under his right elbow and a hammer-stone for striking the flint by his left knee. This man had died at the age of thirty-five to forty, and had signs of arthritis and two healed fractures. Within the stone burial chambers the human remains were far more difficult to interpret: thousands of bone fragments were piled like the scattered pieces of a nightmare jigsaw puzzle. Forty-one individuals were buried in the two Hazleton chambers, twenty-two men and women and nineteen children. Most of the Hazelton people died young: only two were over forty-five.

The Hazelton tomb was built about 3800 BC and used for only a few generations, perhaps up to 150 years. With only forty-one burials this means that not everyone in the Hazleton clan was buried in the communal tomb. There were traces of cremations, so perhaps others were disposed of in ways that left little or no archaeological record. Maybe only people of a particularly significant clan ancestry were laid in the tomb, or those that died close to an important festival. Archaeologists have often argued that Neolithic bodies were first exposed until the flesh disappeared from the bones. The appropriate bones were then selected for burial in tombs and in other important communal centres. This does not appear to have been the case at Hazleton or other similar tombs such as West Kennet.* Instead the bodies were placed in the chambers and then later the bones were moved to make room for new occupants. Sometimes the tomb-organisers collected and stacked particular bones in groups. At West Kennet vertebrae were found in one corner and skulls piled against a rear wall. The scale of burial at Hazleton is matched at other tombs in southern England, notably another well-excavated Cotswold tomb at Ascott-under-Wychwood (Oxfordshire).†

None of the Cotswold–Severn megalithic tombs has produced evidence of more than fifty interments.

Orkney once again provides a very different picture.[28] There the thriving Neolithic population is well-represented in the tombs: 16,000 human bone fragments at Isbister and 13,500 at Quanterness, representing at least 342 individuals in the former and a minimum 157 in the latter. This looks like a much better sample of the local population than is available in England. Forensic examination of the bones shows that burial in Orkney tombs was not reserved for any particular sex or age group.

Compared with most modern, western populations, the Isbister people died young, many in childhood and the majority by the age of thirty. Few reached the advanced age of fifty. In fact infant mortality was probably more pronounced than the bone evidence suggests, because infants below about eight months were not interred in the tombs. For those that survived birth the average life expectancy was about twenty years — compared with over sixty-seven years for males and seventy-two years for females in the 1952 life tables for England and Wales. Life in Neolithic

---

* This Wiltshire tomb is one of the so-called Cotswold–Severn group.
† West Kennet contained the bones of about twenty adults and thirteen children (some had been lost to barrow-diggers), and Ascott-under-Wychwood contained thirty-six or thirty-seven adults and ten children.

Orkney may seem, to modern readers, extremely hazardous, but it is comparable with many pre-modern groups.

Life expectancy for various cultural groups (after K.Weiss[29])

Group	General range of life expectancy
Australopithicus	about 15
Neanderthals	about 18
Proto-agriculturalists	20–7
Contemporary hunter-gatherers	22–9
Classical and medieval society	22–9
Sweden 1780	38
UK 1861	43
Sweden 1903	54
Sweden 1960	73

When I work in non-western countries such as Tunisia and Egypt I am always struck by the sheer numbers of children. Neolithic Orkney, and the rest of Britain, must also have been an incredibly youthful society. Unlike in modern societies, women here died earlier than men, mostly between the ages of fifteen and twenty-four, because of the hazards of childbirth and the strain of child-rearing. In Orkney by the age of forty men substantially outnumbered women. In spite of the hardships the Neolithic population grew relatively rapidly, and where land was restricted population control was probably already practised. Infanticide and abortion were unfortunate realities.

Because we have a signficant sample of prehistoric Orcadians it is possible to generalise about their lifespan and also their size. The Orkney men averaged 1.74 metres (5 feet 7 inches) tall and the women about 1.64 metres (5 feet 3 inches). This is slightly smaller than the modern population, though diet could have been responsible for this. No one seems to have had an easy time: their musculature was particularly well developed, suggesting that everyone, including children, was physically active. At Isbister, cliff-climbing for birds' eggs would explain some of the physical evidence seen on the bones. There were some advantages to the Neolithic lifestyle: only nine Orkney teeth out of 1,537 showed signs of decay; but the five people who had abcesses in their molar sockets would have suffered agonies.

Neolithic children were put to work at an early age. One small Isbister woman, less than 5 feet tall, had carried such heavy loads that her legs had become bandy like a weightlifter's and the bones misshapen. Her burdens also generated osteoarthritis in her ribs and degenerative diseases in the upper back. Death at the age of about thirty-five must have come as a blessed relief as she had a massive and painful cyst in the roof of her mouth. Her body was already that of an elderly woman. One group of women from Isbister had particularly pronounced neck muscles at the back of the skull and often a depression in the cranium, both of which could have been caused by the habit of carrying heavy loads supported on a head band. Others carried loads on straps on one shoulder and under the opposite armpit. This partly accounted for a remarkably high rate of osteoarthritis among Orkney people, even some as young as six and thirteen. Farming led to increases in the human population, but it did not make life easy for most people; and the obsession with creating megalithic houses for the ancestors may not have helped.

So how large was the Neolithic population of Britain? On the basis of their impact on the landscape, the number of monuments they constructed and the observable birth rates it is probable that between 4000 and 2000 BC the population grew steadily. Pollen diagrams, which show some forest regeneration, suggest that there could also have been setbacks. Growth was not necessarily constant.

Smith's Mesolithic estimates for Britain (excluding Ireland) put the numbers of hunter-gatherers in 5000 BC at a mere 2,750 to 5,000. In the next millennium it is particularly difficult to make any reasonable calculation of population, though figures in the order of 140,000 have been suggested for the early Neolithic populations of Britain and Ireland.[30] So far no one has produced a detailed and reasoned calculation, though as evidence continues to increase rapidly, this may soon be possible.

One approach to the relative scale of prehistoric communities is to calculate the amount of effort it takes to build their monuments. The Hazlelton tomb, carefully constructed from quarried limestone, is quite a small feat of construction compared with later spectacular monuments such as Stonehenge. The modern excavators estimated that the Hazleton community spent 8,000 to 14,500 work-hours to extract the stone and build their 50-metre-long cairn. West Kennet, the most impressive tomb in southern England, required about 15,700 hours.[31]

Building teams of five to ten workers could have constructed the smaller tombs, which is not an unreasonable input for even a small-scale clan. In some tombs there are several burial chambers, which might indicate that more than one clan group — tribal relatives, perhaps — came together to create the earliest and longest-surviving monuments in Britain; but monument building was becoming competitive. The works of man began to increase in scale as the population grew. British society was changing and becoming more complex and more stratified. Some people wanted to lead the tribe and to display their status for all to see.

Two The Ancestral Land

THE SMALL MARKET town of Amesbury, not far from Stonehenge, is expanding. New houses are sprouting across the fields. In the summer of 2002 a team from Wessex Archaeology[1] stripped off the thin topsoil from an area destined for a new school. They revealed a Romano-British cemetery and two odd, irregular-shaped pits, which the excavators thought might be holes where trees had once stood. They turned out to be a lot more interesting than that. As the archaeologists trowelled downwards, they exposed the well-preserved flexed skeleton of a man aged between thirty-five and forty-five with a spectacular collection of grave goods clustered around him. The man clearly belonged in the early Bronze Age, the time when Stonehenge was at its peak. Some of the objects were particularly characteristic of this period: four finely decorated pots of a type known as 'beakers'; a black stone wristguard typically worn by prehistoric archers to protect themselves from the strike of the bowstring (and another red one lay by his knees) and a set of fine flint arrowheads, probably originally attached to shafts in a quiver. Not surprisingly the man was immediately christened the Amesbury Archer. He had been sent into the afterlife with three copper knives, some of the earliest known in Britain, and a smooth black 'cushion' stone, which would have been used for working metal. The Amesbury Archer had lived at the start of the new age of metalworking.

This was already a remarkable burial, the richest known from the period; and it was to get better. A few metres away there was a second burial of a young man in his early twenties. Unusually, just inside his jaw lay a pair of gold basket-shaped 'earrings'. There are only seven pairs of these known in Britain, though they have also turned up across the Continent. In spite of being called earrings, these truckle-shaped objects were probably normally worn as hair ornaments, wrapped around the plaits of vain Bronze Age men. This young man, though, seems to have worn his on a string around the neck: he must have been proud of such rare, glitzy objects. After all, no one had ever seen gold before. The young man had an unusual skeletal anomaly in common with his older neighbour: both had foot bones joined together that are usually separate. Could this mean that the two were related? Radiocarbon dates placed the older burial at about 2300 BC; the younger one was fractionally later. So we could have a father and son or two brothers. At present the relationship has not been confirmed by DNA analysis.

The decorated pots buried with the Archer highlight one of the big issues in the study of European prehistory. These beakers, which were used as drinking vessels and contained a potent alcoholic brew such as mead, appear across Europe in the late third and early second millennium BC. The argument arises because some prehistorians have taken the pots to indicate people: 'Beaker Folk' spreading out from the Rhineland and Low Countries across the Continent as far as Scandinavia, and to Italy and into Britain – another of these putative invasions that archaeologists used to identify so readily. But such pots need not have arrived with new people, any more than Coca-Cola bottles in a rubbish dump need indicate an American invasion. Instead beakers could reflect cultural influences, the spread of high-status objects, and the appearance of new habits such as elite drinking parties. Two thousand years later the prestige of Rome clearly generated the spread of another type of fine beaker with glass vessels, both associated with wine drinking. British chieftains who wanted to be in fashion looked to the Continent and to Rome.

In the early Bronze Age British society was changing. The beakers are probably elements in a package of fashionable objects adopted by people anxious to display their prestige and emphasise increasing social inequalities. Across Europe about 2000 BC the *nouveaux riches* demanded their equivalent of the Rolex watch and the Armani suit; but in Britain these beaker elements are not found alone: they combine with local traditions, and were absorbed into existing British regional cultures. It looks as if beakers were adopted by the Brits. Another argument against a major incursion of newcomers is that some distinctive changes, such as the construction of round barrows for single burials and the use of metal, appeared even before the beakers. The changes in skull shape (which nineteenth-century anthropologsts thought so important) from long to round heads can now be accounted for by gradual genetic change in the native population. So, recently prehistorians have turned against the idea of an invading horde of Beaker Folk, bringing their boozy habits and flashy ways across the Channel after 2500 BC. Instead they interpret the beakers – along with knives, gold earrings, shale and jet buttons, triangular arrowheads,* wristguards, bronze daggers and whetstones — as part of elite display. Early Bronze Age men, both in Britain and on the Continent, dressed the part.

At least the important ones. At Barnack (Cambridgeshire) one male, at the centre of a group of burials, was equipped with most of the relevant status symbols; but of the fifteen people who surrounded him only three had any grave goods. And women were never buried with the new metal daggers. At Barnack, the community dug a circular ditch round the group of burials and piled up the spoil to form a barrow. Hundreds of barrows still dot the countryside, often in clusters or lined along prominent ridges. Thousands more disappeared, ploughed flat by generations of farmers, until archaeologists began to fly over the countryside and spotted the distinctive dark circles in crops of barley and wheat.†

The Amesbury Archer is the richest beaker burial known in Britain in terms of the number and variety of objects in his grave. He is also early for a Beaker burial: radiocarbon dating placed him between 2400 and 2200 BC. This is exactly the period when the builders of Stonehenge were hauling massive sarsens‡ into place to construct the most distinctive phase of Britain's most famous monument. Not surprisingly, news of the Amesbury Archer flashed around the world. The *Daily Mail*, not usually noted for its coverage of archaeology, asked: 'Is this the King of Stonehenge?'

We can only speculate about the social structure of early Bronze Age Britain. Certainly to talk of kings at this period is an anachronism, though some prehistorians have argued for the existence of chieftains or 'Big Men' capable of controlling and directing their communities — the Amesbury Archer may have been such a person; but as forensic work continued on

---

* Leaf-shaped flint arrowheads were in service for centuries, but now a new, barbed and tanged form appeared.

† Thanks to crop marks we now know that early Bronze Age barrows existed across Britain and are as common in the valleys of the Thames, the Trent and the Nene as they are on the chalk downland of Wessex. Crop marks have been mapped on a large scale since the 1940s but were observed even in the nineteenth century by antiquarians on horseback. They form because crops can sink their roots into the buried ditch fill, extract moisture and nutrients and so grow taller and take longer to ripen. Cereals such as barley, which grow tightly packed, produce a more detailed image than plants such as brassicas. Each plant acts like a pixel in a newspaper photo, reflecting changes in the subsoil.

‡ The meaning fo the word 'sarsen' is much debated. One theory suggests that it comes from 'saracen'. Medieval people gave the name of the most famous pagans of their day to the massive pagan stones in the countryside. Geologically sarsen is a hard sandstone, which erodes out from beneath the chalk and litters the dry valleys of the downland, where prehistoric people collected it for their monument building. There are no sarsens known to occur close to Stonehenge. They were probably brought from the Downs above Avebury. The so-called 'bluestones', a variety of igneous rocks, were used in the preceding phase.

his bones he had other tales to tell. Oxygen isotope analysis[§] of his teeth showed that he was not a local. In his childhood he lived in a colder climate, probably in central Europe close to the Alps. He was an immigrant; but why he came to Britain we do not know. Was there intermarriage between European elite families? The younger person in the nearby grave was raised on the Wessex chalkland, so could he have been a British-born son? Perhaps the Archer was a pilgrim to the great religious centre of Stonehenge; or an economic migrant who possessed the arcane knowledge of metallurgy, giving him the status of a miracle worker, a prospector who arrived in Britain in search of tin and copper ores. Moreover, he possessed another interesting feature. Sometime in his life he suffered an injury to his left leg, which became withered and must have caused him to limp — a coincidence maybe, but in European mythology the smith god, known as Hephaestus in Greece and Wayland in the north, is always portrayed with a limp.

The discovery of the Amesbury Archer has, however, reopened the debate about the movement of people in early Bronze Age Europe. One man does not make an invasion of Beaker Folk; yet his presence emphasises that prehistoric Britain was not isolated from the Continent either. What we need, of course, is more information from other early Beaker burials. Oxygen isotope analysis of a fair sample of human remains could yet tell us if the Archer came alone or as part of a rush of prospectors.[*]

It is remarkable how often, when an unusual discovery such as the Amesbury Archer appears, something similar turns up almost immediately. Archaeology seems to suffer from the London bus syndrome. Shortly after finding the Amesbury burials Andrew Fitzpatrick of Wessex Archaeology was called out to the nearby Boscombe Down airfield, where human bones and fragments of beaker lay scattered on the spoil heap of a freshly dug water pipeline. The grave uncovered at Boscombe Down really was unusual; it held seven people: three adult men, a male teenager and three children. The oldest of the men, aged thirty to forty-five, lay on his side in a crouched position. One of the three children, who was about three years old, had been cremated. The bones of the teenager and the other two men (aged twenty-five to thirty) had been laid both above and below the older man, and some of their bones, such as those from the arms and skulls, were clustered together. The bones of the younger men showed signs of wear, as if they had previously been exposed and brought from elsewhere to this grave. The skulls all had distinctive small Wormian bones — a feature which not all of us possess, but which tends to run in families.

* Such work has been undertaken in Bavaria, where 17 out of 69 Beaker individuals sampled (8 out of 38 males and 8 out of 24 females) were found to have originated elsewhere.

Could we have here a group of men who were related? A 'Band of Brothers', the newpapers called them, echoing the title of a recent American television series about World War II. In the grave with the three men, the teenager and three children were seven beakers of an early type, decorated with impressed cord decoration. There were also five barbed and tanged arrowheads and a boar's tusk — the Amesbury Archer had four. The Boscombe band must be virtually contemporary with the Amesbury Archer (about 2300 BC but radiocarbon dates are still awaited). So where did they come from?

Analysis of the Boscombe teeth (only three of them so far) looked at both oxygen and strontium isotopes. The high strontium levels indicate that the three men grew up in an area with a high radiogenic background: somewhere with ancient rocks such as granite. In Britain this points to Cornwall, Wales, the Lake District or Scotland. The oxygen isotopes indicate a climate somewhere between the extreme south and north of Britain. There is evidence that all three men spent the early part of their childhood in one place and then moved — but certainly not straight to Wessex.* This could mean that their families migrated from the west, or that children were sent to live with other members of an extended family or with political allies.

Because the Boscombe family originated in the west and were interred so close to Stonehenge, inevitably links were made with the Preseli Hills of Pembrokeshire. This is the source of the man-size bluestones which were set up at Stonehenge from about 2400 BC. But if these people originated in the Preseli Hills, why should they — and their three-tonne local rocks — end up at Stonehenge? One scenario links Beakers and the earliest metalworking in Britain. We now know that copper miners operated in south-west Ireland, on Ross Island in County Kerry, from about 2400 BC, and Beaker pottery turns up there. For prehistoric sailors crossing the southern part of the Irish Sea the Preseli Hills stood out as a prominent landmark. With their outcrops of exotic stones they may have had mythical significance to these people. The network formed between Continental prospectors and British and Irish tribes who controlled access to supplies of copper and tin explains the links between Europe, Wessex, south-west Wales and Ireland. The Salisbury Plain people, with their great temple, were not themselves naturally rich in metal ores, but they may have played the role of middlemen in this developing west-European axis. And along the sea lanes of the metal-seekers they trans-

---

* The chemical signatures are different in the earliest teeth, the premolars (which form after the milk teeth have gone by about the age of six) and the third molars (which erupt about the age of nine to thirteen). But neither has a Wessex signature.

ported the magical stones of the west from the land of the setting sun.*

This is a period when the tribes of Britain – and individuals – become more competitive, struggling for power and prestige. In the Neolithic period communities constructed tombs to demarcate their small-scale territories. Groups came together to create causewayed enclosures, tribal gathering places surrounded by ditches dug in sections, like a string of sausages. These were often sited in quite out-of-the-way places: in marshes, between streams or on hilltops. In causewayed enclosures like Windmill Hill, near Avebury (Wiltshire), Etton (Cambridgeshire) and Abingdon (Oxfordshire) young men and women could have posed in bouts of mutual admiration. Perhaps there was some form of competitive dancing, wrestling or stick-fighting to allow the girls to spot the man of the moment and the mate of the future? Animals, too, could be exchanged,[2] and the ancestors, whose selected bones were also present in the causewayed camp ditches, remembered through songs and epic tales. Neolithic society was not, however, without its stresses. Some causewayed camps, such as Hambledon Hill (Dorset), clearly came under attack and were showered with arrows.

The competitiveness of the early Bronze Age is even more transparent. There are individual tragedies: the man whose burial we excavated at Barrow Hill, Radley (Oxfordshire) lay flexed in a shallow grave, surrounded by his Beaker finery, including a set of delicately crafted flint arrowheads. Unfortunately for him, the arrow that struck his spine was considerably more robust and deadly than those in the burial set. Such signs of aggression are fairly common in this period. Archaeological evidence also points away from the community-based ideologies of the Neolithic towards more powerful individuals: men with weapons, jewellery and even spectacular garments such as the gold cape from Mold (Flintshire).

The glistering of gold is the ideal symbol of power, status and permanence; and much of the stuff came from Bronze Age Ireland and Wales, along with supplies of copper. Little is known about early gold and tin mining; but the largest copper mine in Bronze Age Europe can be reached by a tramway from Llandudno, the coastal resort in North Wales. Halfway along the tram's journey passengers alight for the Great Orme copper mines, where Tony Hammond and a local team have been re-excavating since 1987.[3] The archaeologists-cum-speleologists have, so far, surveyed nearly 7 kilometres of Bronze Age underground tunnels, and an estimated 8–10 kilometres still remain unexplored. The shafts,

* Geoffrey of Monmouth had Merlin dismantle an Irish stone circle and magically transport the stones to Stonehenge. A coincidence or a garbled three-thousand-year-old folk memory?

tunnels and galleries penetrate 70 metres beneath the earth. On the surface there are a quarter of a million tonnes of waste, hauled out by prehistoric miners three and half thousand years ago. Radiocarbon dates from
the collagen in bone tools and from wood charcoal in the mines indicate
activity around 1600–1200 BC.

As the archaeologists grubbed their way into the mineshafts, they
found the miners had abandoned their tools where they had used them –
mainly cattle-rib bone gouges stained green with the copper, and stone
hammers. The 33,000 bone tools and 2,400 hammers are a vivid testimony to the determination of these early Welsh miners and the value of
the thin seams of copper. Some shafts were only half a metre across. As
an ex-caver, and the smallest male in the team at 124 pounds (it was a
long time ago!), I could get through passages off-limits to everyone else
except a young girl who was even slighter than I was. Those Bronze Age
miners at Great Orme must have included bantamweight men, or women
and children.

The only known Bronze Age smelting site in Britain (dated to 1580
BC) was found nearby eroding out of a cliff and perched precariously
above the sea. Analysis of the copper slag showed that malachite and
chalcopyrite ores were used – evidence that the smiths were capable of
managing the complex smelting processes involved.

Great Orme is unusual in continuing to operate into the late Bronze
Age and the Iron Age. Most dated copper mines in Britain are at their
peak several centuries earlier, like Mount Gabriel in County Cork, which
flourished from about 1800–1500 BC. North and mid Wales and south-
west Ireland have, in recent years, produced considerable evidence for
prehistoric copper mining, much of it seasonal and small-scale, especially in the mid-Welsh uplands. Such mines are a rare occurrence in
England – only two are known: at Alderley Edge and Ecton in North
Staffordshire. The big mystery is south-west England. Where are the
copper mines of Cornwall and Devon? Perhaps swathed under the debris
or destroyed by the prolific output of the nineteenth- and twentieth-
century mining. Another possibility is that the Cornish exploited tin, gold
and their rich agricultural lands – leaving the even more gut-wrenching,
claustrophic job of copper mining to their less well-endowed Welsh
neighbours across the water.[4]

The Welsh also extracted lead. The earliest-known mine at Copa Hill,
Cwmystwyth, in mid Wales was a sophisticated operation with five-
metre-long sections of alder and oak 'launder', or drainage gutters, linked
together as an aqueduct to divert streams away from the workings.[5] Lead
mining began at Copa Hill about 2000 BC and continued, on and off, for

six hundred years until climatic deterioration and blanket bogs over-whelmed the place. The hammerstones found at Copa Hill came from 20 miles away (near Aberystwyth), which suggests that the miners travelled from there too. They could have been pastoralists who moved inland during the summer, like the copper miners, to undertake lead mining seasonally.

Ireland produced distinctive copper axe heads toughened with arsenic alloy. Bronze only appeared when metalworkers discovered the knack of adding about 10 per cent of tin to molten copper. They hammered this alloy of copper into shape when hot in order to manufacture harder, more durable objects, particularly spears and axes; but these hard, shining ob-jects, unlike anything ever seen before, were not always utilitarian. Some were elaborately decorated with geometric patterns, which also appear on the gold jewellery. Irish gold lunulae, or crescent-shaped collars, made of beaten sheets of the metal, are particularly magnificent. Over eighty have been found in Ireland and across the west and south-west of England. There are also circular discs of beaten gold, decorated with sun symbols, which usually have two buttonholes in the centre, so presumably they were sewn on to garments. In middle Bronze Age Britain and Ireland there was clearly an elite, perhaps priestly chieftains, bedecked in this gorgeous new material which did not tarnish and glowed like the sun. Later in the Bronze Age Irish gold production increased − if the preva-lence of jewellery made from solid gold bars rather than thin sheet is any-thing to go by. The streams running off the hills of County Wicklow were the most likely setting for this Irish gold rush.

Gold, copper and tin became essential elements in the panoply of European prestige goods. Fortunately, as objects rarely retain their status when they become common, these materials were rare. This necessitated long-distance exchange and the creation of alliances across Europe. The Irish lunulae, for example, are found in Cornish soil. We do not know how often Bronze Age ships cut across the Irish Sea to get them there, but cross they did, perhaps to return with cargoes of Cornish tin, which was needed by Irish bronze smiths. There is no direct evidence that tin was mined in Cornwall as early as the mid-second millennium BC, but early mines have a habit of disappearing into the maw of later and larger ones. So we cannot be sure when Cornish tin mining began. Central Europe was certainly one source and bronze scrap, for re-use, entered Britain from the Continent. Divers have found cargoes of metalwork (but no wrecks) in Langdon Bay, off Dover (Kent), and Moor Sand, Salcombe (Devon). These worn and fragmented objects were types rarely found on land in Britain, presumably because such material was melted down and transformed into weapons or tools, which appealed to their British users.

There were no traces found of the prehistoric ships which carried the metalwork cargoes off Salcombe and Dover. However, in 1992, when a new road was cut across the waterfront at Dover, a middle Bronze Age sewn-plank boat appeared, magnificently preserved in the waterlogged, airless deposits of a silted, prehistoric creek.[6] A boat like this, now beautifully displayed in Dover Museum, comes as a startling reminder that the seas around Britain were not a barrier, but could be a highway, a means of cheap, long-distance communication. Nowhere in Britain is more than 70 miles from the sea, and most inland areas are accessible by rivers. Prehistoric craft are rare; the survival of one such as the Dover boat is a minor miracle, against the overwhelming odds of time and the third law of thermodynamics (everything rots!). However, the Dover boat is not a unique survival. Three or four craft from North Ferriby, on the north shore of the Humber, are an equally remarkable find. There are fragments of another at Caldicot Castle, Gwent, which provides evidence that oak-plank boats, fastened with yew lashings, were plying the tidal estuaries and perhaps the coasts of England around the mid-second millennium BC. Other craft such as the flat-bottomed plank boat from Brigg, on the River Acholme (a tributary of the Humber), dated to around 800 BC, carried cargoes along inland waterways. The clearest evidence for this comes from a Bronze Age barge found at Shadlow (Derbyshire) on the River Trent in 1998. The craft was at least 14 metres long, about the same size as the Dover boat, and the same age, dating to about 1300 BC. The barge carried a cargo of sandstone slabs, which originated from a source about 3 kilometres upstream, material for a nearby stone and timber causeway.

There are indirect indications of sea travel, of craft that hugged the coast with bulky cargoes and ballast: the stones in Puncknowle Barrow (Dorset) had travelled 30 kilometres (19 miles) along the coast; pots made in Brittany and the Lizard, Cornwall, appear in graves in Wessex; jet from the East Yorkshire coast, amber from the Baltic and shale from Dorset turn up in burials hundreds of miles from their places of origin. If the objects moved, then people had to move with them.*[§]

A common theme in many societies is the respect and reverence shown to ancestors. Across central Asia into northern Scandinavia, in southern Africa and South America, among hunter-gatherers, herders and simple farmers the shaman helps the living by communicating with the dead. In

---

* This is certainly true where objects cross the sea. In some cases it is possible to argue for 'down-the-line' trade: a kind of long-distance pass-the-parcel, where people trade or give gifts to their next-door neighbours.

a trance state he draws on the power of the ancestors: to cure sickness, to promote fertility or for protection during hazardous journeys. The ancestors convey confidence to the living; they link the past, present and future. We cannot be certain what prehistoric people in Britain believed and thought: they left no written record. Stones and pots do not speak directly. But certainly there are many signs that ancestor worship was prevalent. Valuable objects were placed in burial mounds: at Bush Barrow near Stonehenge, the gold cup from Rillaton (Cornwall) and another recently found at Ringlemere in Kent. These were not always buried as grave goods with individuals, but may have been put into an existing barrow as offerings to the ancestors. Some barrows are covered with animal-bone debris, as if a community of pastoralists had gathered there to celebrate a great feast of the dead. So Bronze Age barrows and their contents may not simply reflect the status of an individual buried within, so much as the continuing relationship between the living and the dead.*

So was the population increasing? As usual in prehistory, any estimate is an exercise in imprecision. What we can say is that people were making an increasingly visible impact on the landscape. In an area like the upper Thames valley, for example, we can locate Neolithic ceremonial monuments regularly sited along the valley: henges and cursuses (long processional avenues)† at Lechlade (Gloucestershire), Stanton Harcourt (Oxfordshire), possibly under the city of Oxford, north and south of Abingdon and Dorchester. By the early Bronze Age each one of these sacred landscapes became clustered with barrows, and there are also concentrations at new sites. Groups of semi-mobile pastoralists created these ancestral burial gounds to mark out their territories which were about 5–10 kilometres apart. Similar patterns appear in other river valleys where aerial photography provides a detailed picture.‡

In prehistoric Britain, as in the world of Christendom, some religious places were more important than others: areas such as the peninsulas between the Lochs of Stenness and Harray on mainland Orkney, the Boyne valley in Ireland, Thornborough and the Swale valley in Yorkshire and, of course, Stonehenge and Avebury. These are prehistoric Britain's major cult centres.

There have been various estimates as to how many working days it would take to build these monuments. Silbury Hill (part of the Avebury

* The Stonehenge landscape has also been interpreted in this way.[7]
† Cursuses are remarkable linear monuments, the first large-scale monuments to be built across Britain. Some are laid over Mesolithic remains and incorporate earlier ancestral sites. They seem to encapsulate time and movement in the landscape as ritual processions.[8]
‡ In Wessex territories have been estimated at 30 kilometres across and in the Ouse valley (Bucks/Beds) there are about eighteen territories similar in size to the Thames examples.

complex) stands 40 metres high and covers 2.2 hectares (5.4 acres). It is the largest man-made prehistoric mound in Europe. Five hundred people working every day for ten years (or 5,000 for one year) could have built this monster. Obviously a substantial community, or even a group of communities in co-operation, must have come together to perform such a feat. Near Stonehenge, by the River Avon, is another less well-known henge, at Durrington Walls. This had massive wooden structures inside it requiring the timber from 3.5 hectares (8.5 acres) of mature forest. Durrington Walls needed almost a million man-hours to complete it – about three years of hard labour for a hundred people. These are major achievements of civil engineering and community effort.*

Shortly after I first started work as Chief Archaeologist at English Heritage I was walking along Hadrian's Wall when my mobile phone rang. It was bad news: the Druids (modern, living ones) had taken over the timber circle of Seahenge and were refusing to allow the excavation to continue. Seahenge was one of the most interesting sites I have ever been involved with – if one of the most troublesome. Over the next few weeks I spent many hours with the Druids and neo-pagans explaining our views, and I even ended up giving evidence in the High Court, where one of them put a curse on me (but I am not superstitious – touch wood!). The early Bronze Age timber circle had recently appeared on the coast of north Norfolk, near Holme-next-the-Sea – exposed as the sea eroded the shoreline. The press immediately named the site Seahenge and hordes of people came to see it. The neo-pagans, and others, felt that we should leave the circle alone.† I thought we had a duty to record this unique monument before the sea destroyed it. The reason I mention Seahenge here is because of a remarkable discovery by Maisie Taylor, the wood expert who minutely studied the timber. She found the distinctive imprints of fifty-one different bronze axe blades on the wood. Now Seahenge is a small structure, only 6 metres across, but with it we had the first direct evidence for the number of workers involved in the construction of a prehistoric monument. Maisie's timber fingerprints showed fifty-one woodworkers each with their own axe. Other members of the community must also have helped with the haulage. Perhaps about a hun-

* Henge monuments, stone and timber circles and barrows are spread across the British Isles. Not all are on the Stonehenge scale. Devil's Quoits, a henge with a stone circle inside it at Stanton Harcourt (Oxfordshire) was 110 metres across and required an estimated 26,000 man-hours of work. The grandest sarsen phase of Stonehenge needed 30 million man-hours or 2,000 workers for five years. I use the term 'man-hours', but in these youthful societies children and women would doubtless have been members of the work gangs.
† The circle is actually more of an oval, egg-shape.

dred people in total came together to build their local shrine near the sea.

Seahenge is a classic example of a liminal place: somewhere on the boundary – in this case, on the margins between the land, the sea and the sky. The fifty-five split-oak timbers in the outer circle stood shoulder to shoulder, with only a small entrance. The bark remained on the outside. Inside, the oak was raw and cut. So for anyone climbing inside it would feel and smell as if they had entered into the heart of an oak tree. Within stood a massive inverted tree stump, placed in a pit with its roots in the air. In several shamanistic societies, from India to Lapland, inverted trees provide a communication channel into the underground spirit world. This may be the function of these wooden walls and upside-down oak tree. Prehistoric monuments cannot speak, but Seahenge comes close; and it even provides us with its precise date: the oak was cut in the spring of 2049 BC and the outer timbers in the spring of 2048 BC, a year later.[9] Perhaps these Norfolk people put the oak in the ground first and then built the timber palisade, three or four metres high, the following year.

So the distribution and size of monuments can give us some idea of the scale of the groups who built them. In the upper and middle Ouse and the Thames valleys there could be population densities of about ten people per square kilometre. If major territories held about 3,500 people, then only a few received barrow burial, perhaps one in forty-four in the Ouse valley. In Dorset and Wiltshire there are at least 4,000 barrows, probably built over about thirty to forty generations and containing an average of three burials, say 400 burials per generation (20–30 years) across the Wessex region. One estimate puts the population of Wessex, with five territories based on the big monuments, at 34,000. Across the country, however, there must have been enormous variation. River valleys attracted prehistoric communities; other areas, such as the uplands of the north-west, contained far fewer people. Early Bronze Age Britain may have had a total population of about a quarter of a million, with perhaps another fifty thousand in Ireland.[10]

THE TALE OF THE WHITE HORSE

> *Before the gods that made the gods*
> *Had seen their sunrise pass*
> *The White Horse of the White Horse Vale*
> *Was cut out of the grass.*

For the poet and writer G. K. Chesterton, who composed these words, the hill-figure of the White Horse at Uffington symbolised the state of

England. He associated it with the White Horse banner of Wessex and the Christian King Alfred's victory over the army of the heathen Danes at nearby Ashdown in AD 871. So long as the horse remained pristine in its whiteness, Albion would flourish.

Another, less mystical but more muscular Christian, Thomas Hughes, also saw the White Horse as symbolic of the state of the nation. A native of Uffington, Hughes wrote in the opening chapter of his best-known book, *Tom Brown's Schooldays*, 'And then what a hill is the White Horse Hill! There it stands right up above all the rest, nine hundred feet above the sea, and the boldest, bravest shape for a chalk hill that you ever saw. Let us go to the top of him and see what is to be found there.'

For several years in the early 1990s I took Hughes's advice; I wanted to see what could be found there. White Horse Hill is one of the most dramatic landforms in southern England. The steep scarp of the Berkshire Downs faces across the Vale of the White Horse to the Thames and the Cotswolds beyond. The sheer slope is the result of an ancient collision: the tectonic plates of Africa and Europe collided; the shock waves shunted up the Alps; the impact rippled as far as southern England, so that the Downs, the Chilterns and the Cotswolds reared up to face to the northwest.

Towards the end of the last Ice Age, about 13,000 years ago, the freeze-thaw effects generated enormous sheets of slurry, which further sculpted and scoured the White Horse slope. As a result the landscape is a natural theatre in which people can create and re-create their own dramas.

The dramatic potential of the landscape was first exploited about 5,000 years ago when prehistoric farmers built a long barrow high on the steepest part of the slope. But they did not place it, as you might expect, on the very top. Instead the low, whale-backed, burial mound was precisely sited on a false crest — not particularly apparent as you stand on the site, but from the valley below it is clearly silhouetted against the sky.

This was a trick well known to generations of mound builders. A millennium later early Bronze Age barrow builders also made sure their tumuli were prominent against the skyline. The biggest effort of all went into sculpting the ramparts of Uffington Castle, the hill fort that crests the highest point of White Horse Hill and can be seen for miles. The hill fort builders were making a statement: they were the Kings of the Castle; this land was their land.

The most spectacular element in the landscape at White Horse Hill is the Manger, a narrow, steep-sided dry valley which forms a natural amphitheatre. The back wall of the amphitheatre acts as a screen for one of the most remarkable images of the English landscape: the Uffington

White Horse. The horse is sinuous, made up of abstract elements as if with a few giant brush strokes. It is totally unlike the other prosaic and static horse figures which can be found, reluctant even to plod, across Wiltshire, Dorset and Yorkshire. The Uffington beast is sleek, an image of almost feline grace and speed.

In taking up Thomas Hughes's challenge to see what was on the hill I had no desire to destroy the mystique or dilute the power of the landscape, but I did want to learn more about it — to understand the interplay of geology, climate, biology and human action that had created this powerful place. Speculation about it has been rife for over three hundred years.

Unlike its Wiltshire progeny at nearby Cherhill, Westbury and Marlborough, the Uffington Horse is certainly old.* There are references to it in a string of medieval charters, and more particularly it features in a fourteenth-century manuscript in Corpus Christi College, Cambridge, the *Tractatus de Mirabilibus Britanniae*, as second only to Stonehenge as one of the Wonders of Britain.

So if the White Horse was a wonder, and presumably a mystery, to medieval manuscript writers, how old is it? When I began to walk around the horse in the late 1980s, trying to figure out how to tackle this question, there were three commonly repeated theories: The idea first mooted in the eighteenth century was that the horse commemorated Alfred's victory over the Danes; a second proposed that it was made by pagan Anglo-Saxons in about the sixth century; and the favourite, because it had been carefully and logically set out by one of the great figures of recent British archaeology, Professor Stuart Piggott,[11] was that the White Horse belonged to the late Iron Age, the century or two before the Roman conquest. Virtually no one ever mentioned a fourth theory, almost a throwaway remark by Morris Marples, that the horse might have been created even earlier, by the peoples of the late Bronze Age or early Iron Age.[12]

Stuart Piggott, like Hughes, was a native of the Uffington area and a one-time neighbour of the poet John Betjeman.† Shortly before his death, when I used to visit him to talk about the possibilities of new scientific

---

* Most White Horses were carved in the eighteenth or nineteenth centuries. The Red Horse of Tysoe (Warwickshire) might have been older but has now disappeared.

† The poet of nostalgia addressed one of his verses to Piggott:

> *When evening air with mignonette was scented*
> *And picture windows had not been invented,*
> *When shooting foxes was still thought unsporting*
> *And White Horse Hill was still a place for courting ...*

Piggott himself was not at all nostalgic. He wrote brilliantly about the past, but had no illusions about paradises lost.

dating techniques, he was completely hard-headed and open-minded about his own theory. Actually he did not regard it as his: he credited Anna Fairchild, daughter of William Stukely, the surveyor of Stonehenge and the promoter of Druids. Anna visited White Horse Hill in 1758 and wrote to her father, 'The figure of the horse on the side of the hill is poorly drawn, though of immense bulk but very much in the scheme of the British horses on the reverse of their coins.'

Anna was right: the segmented horse with its beaked head, galloping to the viewer's right, does bear a close resemblance to the horses that appear on Iron Age coins. These are the earliest coins in Britain. The prototype of most of them is the so-called Macedonian philippic – a coin minted for Alexander the Great's father – one of whose functions was to pay Celtic mercenaries recruited into the mighty Macedonian army. As a result the philipic, the silver dollar or krugerrand of its day, infiltrated into third-century BC barbarian Europe and stimulated the production of new tribal coinage. It is these coins that provide us with the earliest evidence of British tribes, their names and the names of their rulers, when Britain emerges from the anonymity of prehistory.

The gold staters and silver drachmas of Philip II had the head of Apollo on one side and a chariot drawn by horses on the other. Gaulish and eventually British tribes adapted the coin designs so that the chariot often all but disappeared – represented merely by a small wheel, probably a sun symbol. The horse, in many cases, became an abstract form which, as Anna Fairchild recognised, bore a similarity to the Uffington Hill figure.

In 1981 I approached the guardians of the White Horse – the National Trust and the Government's Inspectorate of Ancient Monuments (now English Heritage) – with a suggestion that we might investigate this most enigmatic of archaeological problems. I did not get a very positive response. The general idea was that the builders had carved the horse into raw chalk – scratched like a sgraffito image. So how could it be dated? Archaeologists need strata, layers, to provide a context for objects like coins or pottery which provide the building blocks of chronology; or organic material such as bone or charcoal to provide samples for radiocarbon dating. The horse did not look very promising.

However, I did get permission to carry out a detailed survey. A group of us took a weekend off from excavating in a Thames-side gravel pit to experience the airy pleasures of the downs. We decided to camp overnight on the plateau just below the White Horse in order to be able to start our survey as early as possible in the morning. When I emerged from the tent just after dawn, I was met by a remarkable sight. A thick, slowly billowing mist filled the vale. A white sea lay below us, its shoreline within a few paces of our tents. Above floated the White Horse, bathed in the light of the rising sun. It was a magical morning — and an interesting weekend, but unfortunately not one that provided a conclusive argument to convince the sceptics that further investigation was worthwhile.

The decisive discovery came months later, not on the hill, but in a far from magical office block in London's Elephant and Castle, a place where ancient Ministry of Works files went to die. During World War II the White Horse had been covered over so that it would not provide a landmark for Luftwaffe pilots (the military mind moves in mysterious ways!). I wanted to check the files to see if we could discover exactly what had been done to the horse. To my surprise we struck gold. There was a precise and beautifully executed drawing of a small trench excavated into the head of the horse. The accompanying section showed that it was not merely scratched into the underlying geology but formed from a deep trench packed with successive layers of chalk and interleaved with slivers of silt. The implications were obvious: this archaeological layer cake could provide opportunities for stratigraphic excavation and dating.

Over the next three years we tried out every technique we could think of at White Horse Hill. Big excavations are rather like an autopsy: a dramatic intervention. Our idea was to use non-intrusive geophysical and aerial surveys followed by carefully targeted keyhole surgery to answer key questions with the minimum of interference. The White Horse Hill is, after all, protected as a Scheduled Monument and a Site of Special Scientific Interest. We did not want to damage or remove any more evidence from the site than was absolutely essential.

As it turned out, White Horse Hill became a window into late prehistory. Thanks to a new technique — Optical Stimulated Luminescence (OSL dating) — we were able to date the silts deeply buried in the belly of the horse. The dates centred on 800 BC — the end of the Bronze Age and the beginning of the Iron Age. The adjacent hill fort of Uffington Castle proved to have been built about the same time. It was a time when there was a lot happening.

Aerial photographs showed that on the downs, to the south of White Horse Hill, long ditches divided the land into large parallel blocks. These were the same configuration as the present-day parish boundaries, which, since the tenth century, have divided the White Horse country into strips. These traditional English parishes gave people access to all the important local resources: river, meadow, arable, woodland and pasture. But the blocks visible on our aerial photographs were not medieval. They belonged to the late Bronze Age. Almost three thousand years ago local communities carved the downs into estates, each dominated by a hill fort. At Uffington, not content with erecting ramparts around the highest point in the local landscape, the local tribe also marked the wall of the Manger, and the source of their river, with the White Horse banner.

From the fourth to the early second millennium BC the inhabitants of this land had marked their territory with burial mounds. Now, around the turn of the second and first millennium BC, times were changing. The population was growing fast; the landscape had been extensively cleared of trees; grassland was being exploited more intensively and increasingly large areas were put under the plough. At the same time the climate was deteriorating: Britain was becoming colder and wetter. There was increasing pressure on land as moorland expanded in the north and west, heathland spread over old agricultural land in the south and water tables rose in the valleys. With these pressures came increasing territoriality and competition for land among people led by mounted warriors, armed with swords and spears. British tribes were jostling for space and emphasising their presence. Their impressive hilltop ramparts still mark the British and Irish landscape.

White Horse Hill shows in microcosm the changes which were happening across the British Isles in the later Bronze Age and into the Iron Age, from about 1500 to 500 BC. The builders of henges, barrows and megalithic monuments were mainly pastoralists, moving with their herds and flocks through a landscape with few artificial boundaries. We cannot document the population with any precision, but the signs are that it was increasing. The best indication comes from the evidence of intensified agriculture taking in more and more land. The second millennium BC is a period of major change in Britain, when the landscape begins to fill with settlements, fields, boundaries and trackways. There is good evidence also for the development of settlement hierarchies, and for seasonal and specialist sites.

Recently there have been dramatic advances in our understanding of human settlement in late prehistoric Britain, its scale and regional variety. For the first time in British history we can get some idea of the detailed settlement geography of specific areas. When I started my career as a field archaeologist, one of my professional heroes was Chris Taylor — a prolific landscape historian with the Royal Commission for Historical Monuments (England). Chris was not an excavator; he used the evidence of his eyes and worked on a big scale, surveying large areas of Dorset and Cambridge, looking at the patterns of fields, villages and trackways. There was one thing, though, about which, I am glad to say, he was wrong.

In 1972 he made a gloomy prediction that in areas such as the Thames valley the evidence for landscape change would be irrevocably lost by the end of the century because of the scale of development. What we did not appreciate in 1972 was that the best evidence lay blanketed beneath the alluvial flood silts of our rivers, and that, by taking the opportunities presented by building sites of the late twentieth century, archaeologists would be able to explore beneath the alluvium, and into many areas covered by urban and suburban sprawl.* Some of these projects, such as the Eton Rowing Lake, the Reading Business Park and the extension of Heathrow Airport have generated excavations on a scale that was almost inconceivable in 1972.

Archaeologists now suffer from almost a surfeit of data, especially that from the many small-scale, developer-funded projects. But this data has huge potential. Dave Yates, a researcher at Reading University, has shown how we can reinterpret prehistory. He combed the archives of local-authority Sites and Monuments Records and of archaeological field units to produce a brilliantly detailed picture of Bronze Age settlement in the Thames valley and much of eastern England.[13]

From the many keyhole projects across south-eastern England he opened up doorways into a previously closed world to reveal the prehistoric landscapes of Staines and Uxbridge, Carshalton and Southend. A clear pattern has now emerged in the middle and lower Thames and on either side of the Thames estuary. In the middle to late Bronze Age power and influence shifted from Wessex into this area and into the east of England. The landscape of the Thames valley became covered with ditched and hedged fields, integrated with droveways, water holes and settlements. Intensified animal husbandry seems to be the basis of the economy and to cope with their hoofs, trackways are metalled for the first time at Yarnton (Oxfordshire), Cranford Lane (Hillingdon) and Hays (Dagenham). The patchwork of fields created diverse micro-environments allowing Bronze Age farmers to develop strategies for specialised crops such as flax and beans for rotation, and to ensure that they were not vulnerable to the failures that can visit those who are over-dependent on monoculture.

The largest block of intensively settled later Bronze Age landscape lies around the Thames–Colne confluence on the gravel terraces west of

---

* This came about because in 1990 in England (and later in Scotland, Wales and Ireland) government Planning Policy Document no.16, entitled 'Archaeology and Planning', put the responsibility for archaeological investigation and protection on to developers. Since then thousands of evaluations and excavations have been funded in advance of housing, road, railway and airport construction and gravel extraction.

London. In this area Bronze Age communities were intensively exploiting the largest area of lower-terrace gravel anywhere in the Thames valley. This land was essentially free-draining, but there was easy access to water in the rivers or by digging water holes no more than a metre deep. Pressure on such desirable land was intensive, and even islands in the flood plain were exploited, if necessary by building bridges. And these islands may have had symbolic, religious significance: places for offerings and ceremonies; little Avalons.

This was not an egalitarian society of peasant farmers. A defended enclosure dominated each block of intensively exploited land, or a riverside settlement controlled access along the waterway, such as the site at Runnymede, where there were metalworkers and exotic materials such as amber and shale, imported by ships plying the Channel and North Sea. At Queen Mary's Hospital, Carshalton, a late Bronze Age ringwork physically dominates what David Yates called the 'regimented landscape' below: every late Bronze Age field, and the animals and people in them, could be observed from the ringwork.

These broad patterns have been reconstructed from many small-scale excavations, but at the Reading Business Park, by the M4 motorway, a large settlement complex reveals the scale and character of occupation. This is another intensively exploited block of land, at the junction of the Thames and Kennet, again dominated by a ringwork at Marshall's Hill, on the high ground above Reading near to the present-day University campus. This is the site of one of the earliest field systems in southern Britain, laid out before 1000 BC, though most motorists crawling past it on the M4, by the intersection for Reading South, would not be aware of it.

There are clusters of Bronze Age roundhouses of remarkable regularity on each of the dry islands. The British seem to have had a particular fondness for circular houses. They are ubiquitous in later prehistory yet rarely seen on the Continent. There may be practical reasons, but circularity is a constant theme and to our prehistoric ancestors may have symbolised their universe. When the *Sunday Times* covered this story they described them as 'Bronze Age Barrett Homes'. You could have any kind of house you liked providing it was round, 8 metres across and had a south-east facing entrance. In one of these clusters there were sixteen roundhouses laid out in fairly regular lines; next to them were water holes and groups of four-post structures, thought to indicate above-ground granaries. A mound of burnt stones 85 metres long and 25 wide bounded the northern edge of the settlement along the edge of a watercourse. These 'burnt mounds' are widespread in later prehistoric Britain. In Ireland they are thought to be the remains of special feasting sites, where large haunches of meat were cooked in tanks of water brought to the boil by hot stones. In England the evidence is less clear; saunas, textile production and domestic rubbish disposal are some of the explanations for them.

Nevertheless, the sheer scale of late Bronze Age settlement and agriculture in the lower Thames valley is impressive; and other regions have similarly sophisticated farming landscapes. One of the best known is at Flag Fen, on the fen edge near Peterborough. Here Francis Pryor has shown that hedged banks and ditches, trackways, funnels, gateways and paddocks were carefully designed to control large flocks of sheep.[14, 15] The sheer scale of pastoralism in parts of Bronze Age Britain has revolutionised our view of prehistoric communities in the south-east of England.

This process is most developed (and most investigated by archaeologists) in eastern and south-eastern England, but other parts of Britain were caught up in these trends. Much of the Wessex downs are covered with extensive regular field systems. Some survive as earthworks on army ranges and steep slopes; others can only now be seen as ploughed-out soil marks on aerial photographs. Even the higher chalklands are covered by these fields and the impression is that there was little open grazing land outside this formal control. The scale and regular orientation of these blocks also speak of some central authority and basic surveying skills. In spite of the scale of the fields there are few contemporary settlements; possibly they lay in the neighbouring river valleys. The historical cliché, commonly reported in twentieth-century textbooks, that valleys were impenetrable forest and swamps in prehistoric Britain, is clearly old hat — the Vale of Pewsey, for example, is full of sites.

David Field, who has surveyed much of this area for English Heritage has pointed out that with this 'investment in land, place became static'. Daily experience became restricted by boundaries and plots; fields took on the character of place rather than space: more domesticated, civilised, with specific owners and probably, though we will never know them, possessing names.[16, 17]

If the communities of the Thames valley were seriously raising cattle, then sheep may have been the major business of the downs. One of the most interesting discoveries of recent archaeology will never take pride of place in a museum gallery. It is an enormous pile of sheep manure. The late Bronze Age/Iron Age (800–600 BC) midden at East Chisenbury (Wiltshire) is 200 metres across, 3 metres deep and covers 2.5 hectares (6.2 acres). In among the sheep manure are vast quantities of neonatal lamb bones. From an admittedly small sample, it is calculated that there are enough meat bones in the tip to feed 10,000 people for over a century. The East Chisenbury midden suggests that downland sheepfarming

3,000 years ago was on a par with that of the early historic period. The mound itself must have been a prominent monument to fertility: perhaps another focal point for communal feasting. It is interesting that the broken pots in the mound were flat-based – the sort usually used by people with furniture – rather than the round-based pots which mobile herdsmen pushed into the ground. These people were not simple nomads. Animal rearing was a big business where spring lambs were reared for consumption, their mothers' milk taken for milk and cheese and, judging by the many spindle whorls in the midden, wool was spun on a large scale for textiles.

Bronze Age farmers even colonised upland areas which today seem more suitable for ramblers and grouse shooting. On Dartmoor stone-clearance cairns indicate earlier forest clearance. But by about 1400 BC systematic enclosure spread over all but the highest moorland, incorporating watercourses, and grazing land was organised into estate-like blocks. These territories were demarcated by linear boundaries, known locally as reaves, some of which can be traced continuously for 5 to 10 kilometres.[18]

In Scotland the Royal Commission on the Ancient and Historical Monuments of Scotland (RCAHMS) has surveyed extensive later Bronze Age landscape in lowland and upland Perthshire, Sutherland and Skye, where roundhouses integrated into field systems are visible as earthworks. Although none of these complexes has been excavated on the scale of those in the Thames valley, the survey of almost 100 hectares (247 acres) of enclosures, roundhouse groups and hundreds of clearance cairns at Balnabroich (Strathardle), Perthshire, shows that land-use intensification was developing in Scotland, though not, so far as we can see, on the Dartmoor scale. But if burnt mounds, however they are interpreted, are a type of fossil of this period, they are prolific in Scotland, where over five hundred are known.[19]

The main difference between Scotland and the south is that, while unenclosed farmsteads are common in Scotland, including many on islands such as Islay, the Orkneys and Shetlands, there is no evidence as early as the later second millennium BC for the high status, dominant ringworks found in Essex and the lower Thames valley. Defended sites such as hill forts do not appear until about the eighth century BC. It seems that the process of economic intensification and social differentiation was not so developed in Scotland.

Late Bronze Age communities across the British Isles had pushed their settlements and agricultural land to a high-water mark of activity in the late second millennium BC. They were soon to find themselves in retreat. In the lower Thames valley that remarkably intensive pattern of land use proved unsustainable and was almost entirely abandoned in the early years of the first millennium BC. The reasons were probably complex and varied, but an undoubted factor was the climate.

In comparison with changes at the end of the last Ice Age, more recent shifts in climate have been relatively minor. Nevertheless, the onset of the Sub-Atlantic phase, as it is known, about 3,000 years ago, is significant. There were certainly lower summer temperatures, a decrease in evaporation (specialists argue whether there was an increase in rainfall, but at any rate the ground became significantly wetter), a rise in sea levels and the onset of peat growth on upland moors and lowland rivers. These changes were most important because they came at a time when people in Britain had extensively cleared the forest cover, intensified their farming practices and extended them onto the upland moors, valley floors and coastal margins. Overgrazing may have further exacerbated the problems.

Some of the best evidence for what is happening to the climate comes from peat bogs such as Tregaron Bay (Cardiganshire), in Wales. Here, as in many others, we see renewed and rapid peat growth, from about 1250 BC and continuing for some 800 years. Conditions improved around 400 BC and stayed that way until about the fifth century AD.

Farmers abandoned their fields in areas like Dartmoor, western Ireland, upland Scotland and the Pennines as blanket bog spread across the land. Soil became less fertile as it was leached of nutrients like iron, promoting acid podsols and iron pan, which impedes drainage. Tree cover was further depleted as it failed to regenerate and moorland bog expanded.

Blanket bog spread over many areas of Scotland and the islands that had been settled and cultivated: in Perthshire, on Islay, Jura and Shetland. Local small-scale human activity – damaging the soil structure, overgrazing, impeding drainage – may have had greater impact in specific places than climate change alone.[20] In contrast, ultra-pessimists have argued for a major depopulation of Scotland as a result of an act of God: the eruption of the Hekla volcano on Iceland in 1159 BC, generating a nuclear-winter-type event. This, though, is highly contentious, and few vulcanologists or archaeologists support the idea of a depopulated Scotland.

In the valleys rising water tables made settlements such as the huge Reading Business Park complex uninhabitable. In addition, increasing erosion off the cleared and cultivated slopes led to run-off into the valleys and increased alluviation (flood silts); the dry valleys filled with colluvium (hill-wash). Land was also lost around the coast. On the Gwent

Levels of south-east Wales Bronze Age people had pushed out onto the drying land. From about 1200 BC marine transgression and worsening storms destroyed their settlements. In the Somerset Levels prehistoric farmers had colonised the lowlands and built timber trackways across them. Two periods of sea-level rise (1220–900 and 800–470 BC) drowned most of the levels until medieval monasteries reclaimed them. In southern Britain the heathlands of Surrey and Dorset were the result of these processes. Ironically some of Britain's most loved landscapes, which many people assume to be natural, were created by human mismanagement and the over-optimistic colonisation of precarious landscapes by our Bronze Age ancestors.

The writer L. P. Hartley, in his novel *The Go-Between*, wrote the famous words: 'The past is a foreign country: they do things differently there.' This is certainly true in later prehistory. The Britons had some odd habits. Most characteristically they discarded vast quantities of valuable objects – weapons, tools, shields, even new boats – into rivers and marshes. The British Museum, Reading Museum and the fine new prehistoric gallery in the Museum of London contain vast quantities of prehistoric metalwork found in the River Thames. There have been various explanations: casual losses when people attempted to cross rivers, battles, or material eroded out of the river banks. In the past most of this stuff was found during dredging, so its context was uncertain. Recently several spectacular discoveries in wetlands have thrown light on the behaviour of prehistoric people. They were deliberately placing these valuable objects in shallow water as offerings to the gods. Evidence has been accumulating that from about 1700 BC there was a major shift in the belief systems in western Europe and Britain.

As we saw earlier in this chapter, British communities in the fourth and third millennia BC put enormous effort into the construction of ritual and ceremonial centres related to their ancestors and to the movement of the Sun and Moon. From the middle Bronze Age such monuments were no longer maintained. Instead increasing emphasis was placed on the ritual importance of rivers and watery places. Valuable objects are not only found in the Thames, but also in rivers such as the Witham, the Shannon and in the margins of the Fens. As early as 1882 John Evans suggested that the Wilburton (Cambridgeshire) hoard 'may have been thrown into the water as precious offerings to the gods'.[21]*

Flag Fen has provided the most vivid evidence of such offerings. There, rows of piles ran for over a kilometre from the fen edge to a dry

---

* For a contrasting view see Colin Pendleton (2001), 'Firstly, let's get rid of ritual', in Joanna Bruck (ed.), *Bronze Age Landscapes: tradition and transformation*, Oxbow Books, pp. 170–78.

island at Whittlesey. The Flag Fen people felled about 2 million trees, which they then split and transported to make this amazing structure. Its function was unclear, until excavators and metal detectorists realised that there were over three thousand bronze swords, spears and tools in the water by the platform. Some of these artefacts were bent and broken, deliberately snapped to emphasise the owner's sacrifice. Other objects – such as one bronze sword – were unused or even unfinished. A set of bronze shears nestled inside a specially made wooden box. Several generations of the Flag Fen community built and remodelled the causeway between 1365 and 967 BC; from it they reverently placed metalwork into the water, not as large hoards or casual losses, but in hundreds of deliberate and individual offerings.

The Irish were also generous to their gods and anxious to display their status. Large cauldrons, flesh hooks and burnt mounds indicate that competitive, high-status feasting was a feature of the developing Irish chiefdoms, and their metal offerings in rivers and watery places are even more spectacular than in Britain. The remarkable Downs (Co. Offaly) collection of supposedly 177 objects (the precise number is uncertain as the objects – 'a horse-load of gold-coloured bronze antiquities' – were recovered from bogland in the 1820s). This looks like a Flag Fen type of site where offerings were made over a long period. Among the swords, spears, axes and knives there was a bucket possibly imported from central Europe. Twenty-six bronze horns were more characteristically Irish. These great curving instruments, probably imitating cattle horns, are not found in the rest of Britain. Prehistory rarely makes a noise: in this case it is a cross between those of a bull and a didgeridoo.

Their wealth in livestock and animal products may explain how these highly organised societies could afford to sacrifice so much of their valuables and weaponry into the water. But it does not explain why. The evidence of climatic deterioration in the later second millennium BC – and even of a volcanic or comet-inspired catastrophic event[22] – may have encouraged a later prehistoric water cult. The water may also be the ultimate resting place of the dead. Enormous quantities of prehistoric metalwork – from Bronze Age rapiers to the spectacular Battersea Shield, now in the British Museum, occur in the lower Thames in the same stretches where human remains, including many skulls, have been found.[23]

Was the Thames a sacred river, a British Ganges, into which the dead were placed? This could also explain the scarcity of burials on land. Except for a few areas like East Yorkshire, human remains become almost invisible in the archaeological record in the last few centuries before Christ.

Flag Fen is not the only place where timber platforms and ritual deposits are known. I can almost see one from where I am sitting now, looking out over Vauxhall Bridge, in London. Close to the bridge a line of massive timber stumps are all that remain of a Bronze Age causeway linking the south bank of the river with a dry island, which once stood in the Thames. The sacred Thames was even better preserved several miles upstream at Dorney (Buckinghamshire). There, Eton College constructed an Olympic-sized rowing lake, which cut across an abandoned, silted bend of the river. Since the nineteenth century the Thames has been routinely dredged. Most of it, historically speaking, is now a sterile canal, its contents scoured away. So an ancient channel such as the one found at Dorney is an archaeological treasure trove, a Holy Grail for wetland archaeologists.

Three thousand years ago the braided river at Dorney divided the valley floor into three islands. As at the Reading Business Park, the area was intensely settled and divided into fields. Some of the earliest timber bridges ever found in Britain, constructed between 1400 and 1300 BC linked the islands and river banks. (Unfortunately the huge oak timbers had grown so quickly that the tree rings were uncharacteristic, and useless to us for dendrochronology.) This bridge may have stood for several centuries. Then five more were built in a short stretch of the river from 800 to 400 BC and the last by 200 BC. It seems that each bridge lasted about a century before it was replaced by another alongside. In that period the river fluctuated. Around 500 BC it became a boggy hollow crossed by a trackway of wattle hurdles and brushwood placed alongside an older bridge. Then the water levels rose and a new bridge was needed. Humans were not the only builders: just downstream there was a beaver dam. Fish eagles were probably on their way to extinction in the area as humans increasingly hunted and disturbed them.

One of the most fascinating aspects of the Eton Rowing Lake project is the light it throws on the ritual use of the Thames. The bridges were not merely functional; as well as linking settlements and fields, they also acted as platforms on which ceremonies must have taken place, and from where local people could place offerings into the water. On one sandbank there were three upright poles, two with complete late Bronze Age pots at the base, human bones and animal skulls. Five human leg bones with smashed ends, cut-marks and traces of gnawing may indicate ritual cannibalism. Did Old Etonians eat their relatives? (As I write, the jury is still out.)

The Thames is not the only English river where prolific quanities of offerings were made. The famous Witham Shield, with its strange animal decoration, is one of many precious objects to come from the river near Lincoln. When I visited the excavation of a timber causeway at Fiskerton, a log boat 7.2 metres long lay in the mud. Not unusual on a river bank, you might think. But this one, judging by the fresh adze marks, was unused, and it had been deliberately pinned down under the causeway and the water. From around it had come a large collection of Iron Age tools, weapons and strange objects the like of which I had never seen before. The timbers at Fiskerton proved to be suitable for dendro-chronology and they revealed some staggering dates.[24] The various rebuilds to the causeway, when new timbers were inserted, closely co-incided with total lunar eclipses. The earliest was in the winter of 457/6 BC — an eclipse would have been visible on 12 January 457, then ten years later, and so on. Some of these renewal phases coincided with eclipses which would not have been visible from the site, so the rebuild did not follow the eclipses; they predicted them. These are preliminary results, but if they prove to be accurate, they will transform our understanding of the astronomical capabilities of prehistoric Britons. Fiskerton also throws interesting light on the persistence of British beliefs. Offerings continued to be made into the water from the fifth century BC, through the centuries when Britain was occupied by the Romans and into the Middle Ages, when the Witham valley was ringed with monasteries. Several of these sat near the ends of prehistoric timber causeways. In Roman Britain the most famous water-cult centres at Aquae Sulis — Roman Bath — whose name means 'The Waters of the God Sul'. The monastery at Glastonbury may also have been placed over an ancient water shrine. Even Heathrow airport, I always notice as I rush for a plane, has a pool where travellers cast their coins. Clearly water has made a deep impression on the British pysche.

So deep that even human sacrifices were made into it. One of the most evocative discoveries ever made in Britain is the well-preserved naked body of a man, found in the bog of Lindow Moss in Cheshire.*[25] Lindow Man died violently in his early twenties. His killers struck him from behind, twice on the top of his head with a narrow-bladed axe. The wound became swollen, so the blows did not kill him outright. However, they were not finished with him yet. The killers tied a cord tightly around his neck, cutting the cord closely on either side of the knot. They were evidently not flustered or in a hurry. Then they inserted a stick under the cord and garrotted their victim until his neck broke. Finally they slit his

* Radiocarbon dates suggest that he was killed and placed there at the end of the Roman period, in the fifth century AD, but it is more likely that he belongs in the Iron Age. Radiocarbon dating is notoriously unreliable for the Iron Age.

throat with a short, deep cut through the jugular vein. This looks more like a blood sacrifice than a murder committed in anger.

Lindow Man was placed face down in the bog, naked except for a fox-fur band around his left arm – was this a clan symbol perhaps? He was a well-built young man about 1.68 metres (5 feet 6 inches) tall with a full head of medium-length hair, a short beard and sideburns. He was no heavy-handed son of toil, as his fingernails were neat, round and unworn. Before his death he had eaten a griddle cake made of emmer and spelt flour (these are typically Iron Age cereals). Lindow Man had been healthy, though infected with worms, and he had mistletoe pollen in his gut. The Roman writer Pliny said that the Druids, the priests/judges of Britain and Gaul, held 'nothing more sacred than the mistletoe'.* Lindow Man suffered a horrific death. Had he transgressed the rules of his tribe or was he a sacrifice, to bring his people or his captors good luck? Whatever the reason for his death he remains the best preserved Briton from prehistory.

Among the weapons deposited in rivers in the early Iron Age are long slashing swords of a type which could have been used by mounted warriors. Around 1000 BC horse harnesses begin to appear in quantity and it is in this period that Britons began to ride for the first time (and wear trousers). The domestication of the horse transformed human capabilities. Once mounted, 'people could move further and faster and ... take more with them than ever before'.[26] The rider has a sense of power and superiority; an armoured sword- or bow-wielding horseman is a fearsome opponent, as the Aztecs and Incas discovered when confronted by the Spanish conquistadors, who credited their horses, as much as God, with their spectacular victories.

Irish slashing swords of the earliest type, the so-called Ballintober swords, are commonly found in the lower River Thames and suggest that there were contacts between the two areas. These swords, armour and horse gear point to mounted warriors either riding on horseback or carried in chariots. The importance of the horse in the late Bronze Age would account for its appearance as a tribal symbol on White Horse Hill. Next to the White Horse is a hill fort, a great earthwork enclosure originally topped with timber and later stone ramparts. In the first millennium BC such hill forts dominate the downlands of southern Britain, the Welsh borders, and continue up the Pennines into central Scotland. This is also the period when iron appears for the first time. Not surprisingly,

---

* Pliny, *Natural History XVI*, 95. Tacitus (*Germania*, 12, 1) also wrote about the Germans that they pressed down cowards, shirkers and sodomites under a wicker hurdle into the slimy mud of a bog.

prehistorians used to identify these changes with the apearance of new-comers, the horse-riding, sword-wielding Celts, blazing a trail from Continental Europe. The Iron Age was once synonymous with the Celts. Now many archaeologists not only doubt the existence of the invasions; they also question the existence of Celts in prehistoric Britain.[27]

Who are the Celts? This is a hot subject among prehistorians, linguists and art historians. A couple of pro-Celtic authors called it 'a sterile debate', yet railed against those who were 'at pains to deny the existence of any such thing as pre-Roman culture, let alone Celts, a point of view which reflects England's insular, "outsider" approach to the concept of a united Europe and a positively racist approach to the definition of British'.[28]

The earliest reference we have to the Celts, from the mid-fifth century BC, is by Herodotus, who is justifiably known as the 'father of history'. Unfortunately this curious, conscientious and well-travelled Greek did not, by his own admission, know much about northern and western Europe. His detailed accounts of the Scythians, north of the Black Sea, are vivid and accurate; but the 'Keltoi' are only mentioned briefly, in rela-tion to an inaccurately placed source of the Danube, supposedly near the Pyrenees.* Putting together the scraps of evidence from various Greek authors it seems likely that 'Keltoi' was a name applied generally to the barbarian tribes of northern and western Europe.

The Greeks had a high opinion of themselves and their language: non-Greek speakers who gabbled unintelligibly — 'bar-bar-bar' — were hence 'barbarians'. To the south, in Africa, were the Libyans, to the east the Persians, to the north-east the Scythians and to the north-west the Celts. Like Africa, northern Europe was to a considerable extent *terra incognita* for Herodotus. In lumping together the myriad European tribes he attempted to categorise the unknown in much the same way as later Euro-peans classified the indigenous people of mainland America as 'Indians'. This is not a name these people originally used to describe themselves — though they may have come to do so under the influence of the cultur-ally, economically and politically dominant group.

In a similar fashion 'Celt' is a category identified by Ancient Greeks, and under their influence adopted by the Romans. Both also used the term 'Galatai', or 'Galli' (in Latin), a word that probably derives from 'Keltoi'. At any rate, to classical writers both words meant much the same

---

* In the *Histories*, Book Two, 33: 'The Celts live beyond the Pillars of Hercules and are the neighbours of the Cynesians who are the westernmost European people.' In Book Four, 49, he reverses the order: '[The Ister] rises in the land of the Celts, who live beyond the Cynesians, fur-ther west in Europe than any other race.'

thing: the barbarian peoples who lived in northern and western Europe. In the classical world view, beyond the civilised Mediterranean, there were generalised barbarian peoples symmetrically arranged to the north, south, east and west. Many modern historians, however, have taken the terms 'Celt'/'Gaul' at face value and assume that late prehistoric western Europe was some kind of Celtic European Union.

Classical writers had little interest in the ethnic subtleties of barbarian peoples. Over centuries they repeated standard clichés about the Celts: they were drunkards, wore trousers and their hair long; they were tattooed, childish, aggressive, foolhardy and not steadfast. They had gory religious rituals, practised human sacrifice, headhunting, and had reprehensible sexual habits — and, in Britain at least, still tore around the countryside in chariots.

In more recent times Celts have been romanticised into mystical and musical denizens of a never-never land. As J. R. R. Tolkien wrote: 'Anything is possible in the fabulous Celtic twilight, which is not so much a twilight of the Gods as of the reason.'[29] Other historians write of the Celts as if they were a consciously culturally, politically and linguistically unified people whose power and authority spread across Europe and beyond. 'At that time a territory stretching from Ireland to Galatia* was in Celtic hands. This rapid expansion over an enormous area implies great fecundity and a great spirit of adventure.'[30]

This is a misleading perception of western Europe in the later prehistoric centuries and fails to take into account the great variety of people who lived there, their social and political differences and the complex changes which these societies underwent at different times and at different rates. Nevertheless, in terms of language, religious beliefs, technology, art styles and their inherent symbolism, the late prehistoric peoples of western Europe — conveniently labelled as Celts — also had much in common.

Defining ethnic identity is always a problem, especially in prehistory. We are on more secure ground when using 'Celtic' to describe a family of languages. In 1786 William Jones pointed out, in a talk to the Royal Asiatic Society of Bengal, that Sanskrit had clear affinities with Greek and Latin. He proposed a common origin for them and other related languages, such as Persian. Hence the idea of a family of languages derived from a common Indo-European ancestral language was born. A branch of Indo-European had been identified several decades before in the late seventeenth century by Edward Lhuyd, curator of the Ashmolean

* Galatia is an area in central Turkey settled by a Gallic group to whom St Paul subsequently wrote his letters to the Galatians.

Museum in Oxford. He appreciated that Irish, Scottish, Gaelic, Breton and Welsh were closely related and in 1707 grouped them together as 'Celtic'. After more than a thousand years the Celt was reborn.

From the presence of place names such as 'dunos' (*dunum* in Latin),* river names such as 'Avon',† and personal names which appear in classical sources (for example, 'Cartimandua' and 'Cassivellaunus'), it is clear that Celtic languages were spoken across much of western Europe. The earliest mention of the British Isles occurs in later references to the *Massalliot Periplus* (the description of a voyage from Marseilles, which was written about 600 BC‡).

Great Britain is named as 'Albion' and Ireland as 'Ierne', both Celtic words. The Old Irish 'Eriu' and modern 'Eire' are derived from the earlier name which the Greeks transcribed as 'Ierne'. 'Albu' was the word used for Britain by the Irish as recently as the tenth century AD.**

Another navigator from Massalia, Pytheas, wrote of the northern isles about 320 BC in his book *On the Ocean*. The original text does not survive, but he is quoted by later writers: Polybius, Strabo and Avienos. Admittedly they tend to regard Pytheas as a teller of traveller's tales, though his reputation has been validated by recent historians.[31] Pytheas refers to the Pretanic islands, a name which recurs as 'Pretannia' in the more coherent account of Britain given by the Greek author Diodorus Siculus (the Sicilian) in the first century BC. In his *Geographica*, Strabo uses the same 'P'-word, except in Book 1, where he adopts the now more familiar 'B' spelling. At least it is more familiar if your first language is English. The early Celtic pronunciation has, in fact, survived among modern Welsh speakers, whose word for the island is 'Prydain'.

Early classical navigators came to an island called Albion where the people were known as the Pretani. This Celtic word probably means the 'Painted People', or the 'Tattooed Ones'. So the first name we have for the people of Britain refers to their fondness for bodily decoration.

The Irish were even more remote than the Britons, and subject to wilder stories. Strabo has this to say: 'Concerning Ierne I have nothing certain to tell, except that the inhabitants are more savage than the Britons,

* There are at least sixteen 'dun' names in Britain and many more on the Continent. An example is 'Camulodunum' – the fortification of the war god Camulos – at modern Colchester, Essex.
† The British word 'abona' means river, hence Welsh 'afon' and Cornish 'avon'. There are seven 'Avons' in England and Scotland and several in Ireland.
‡ The words of the *Periplus* survive in the *Ora Maritima* of Avienus, written in the fourth century AD.
** The *Periplus* uses these words in the context of describing the trading activities of navigators from Tartessos (in southern Spain, probably near the mouth of the Guadalquivir River). The Tartessians traded with the people of Oestryminides (probably Brittany), who in turn traded with two large islands beyond, Albion and Ierne.

since they are man-eaters, and since they count it an honourable thing when their fathers die to devour them, and openly to have intercourse not only with other women, but with their mothers and sisters as well; but I say this only with the understanding that I have no trustworthy witness for it.'[32]

When Edward Lhuyd grouped his British languages together, he recognised that they were related to Gaulish. As classical writers such as Caesar equated the Galli and the Celts, Lhuyd adopted the latter term as the family name for the language group; but no ancient source ever suggested that Celts lived in Britain and probably no ancient Britons would have thought of themselves as Celtic. Lhuyd realised that in Britain there were essentially two branches of the 'Celtic' language group: Irish/Scottish, or what he called Q-Celtic (it is easy to recognise from the use of the 'Q' sound in *Mac* – 'son of'), and Welsh/Cornish/Breton, or P-Celtic (who use *Map* to mean 'son of'). Lhuyd developed a theory to explain the two linguistic branches. The Irish/Scots had colonised Britain first and then later arrivals speaking P-Celtic had pushed them westwards.

This invasion hypothesis was to dominate thinking about late prehistoric Britain for more than two and a half centuries. It also generated a persistent but irrelevant, or at least misplaced, question: When did the Celts arrive in Britain? Barry Cunliffe states sensibly: 'The only way to rephrase it and still to retain the spirit of the enquiry is, "At what stage and by what process did the language group commonly referred to as 'Celtic' reach, or emerge in, western Europe?"' Until the 1960s archaeologists were confident that they knew the answer: those horse-riding hill-fort builders brought it. And they were followed by successive waves of Continental invaders. Such an explanation for change in the first millennium BC assumed a heartland for Celtic civilisation, from which conquerors emerged to irradiate their subjects with the benefits of their superior culture. It all seemed to smack of nineteenth-century imperialism. By the 1970s the idea was discredited.

Now the 'invasion' explanation is seen as grossly simplistic: at the same time objects like swords and shields do not move by themselves. This was brought home to me when I first visited the little local museum at Chatillon-sur-Seine, in Burgundy. As I walked into one of the galleries I was stunned by the huge bronze vessel dominating the room. I had often seen photographs, but I was still unprepared for the sheer scale of this marvellous object. It was the famous Vix crater, made in Greece or a Greek colony about 500 BC and transported in labelled sections across the Mediterranean, up the Rhône into central France. On its arrival, craftsmen put the pieces back together again to form a colossal vessel over a metre and a half high and weighing 280 kilograms. Around the neck of the vessel is a parade of armoured Greek warriors and chariots. Gorgon heads glare balefully from the massive tendril-like handles. The crater was designed to contain a virtual wine lake, a cornucopia of hospitality. No one suggests that the Vix crater indicates a Greek invasion of Gaul. It is far more likely that this unique vessel was brought by a Greek trader or diplomatic mission from Massalia, as a gift for a Gallic chieftain.* Vix lies on a strategic hinge, a land-bridge between the southward-flowing River Rhône/Saône, and the northward- and westward-flowing Seine. The rulers of such an important area for trans-Gallic trade must have been worth cultivating by traders who were increasingly penetrating northwards with the enticing products of the Mediterranean world.

As we have seen, later Bronze Age Britain was well populated and intensively farmed. For generations Britons had created monuments, exploited their land and worshipped their gods. The evidence points to the continuity of people, places and traditions. Yet we should not discount the influence of the Continent, and the possibility that some people from the European mainland came to settle. In the late Iron Age tribal names (first recorded by Roman authors), such as the Parisii in Yorkshire and the Belgae in the south, indicate the presence of groups whose origins may be in Gaul. Archaeological evidence also points to one possible group of immigrants in East Yorkshire. On the Yorkshire Wolds, near Driffield, there are distinctive groups of square barrows. Some of these contain the bodies of men with swords, and even with wheeled vehicles – chariots, waggons or carriages, depending upon which terminology is in fashion.†￼This distinctive Iron Age group, dating from the fourth to the first century BC, is known as the 'Arras culture', after the small Yorkshire village of Arras,‡ where a cemetery was found. Similar burials are known in the Marne valley in the Champagne region of France. So the Yorkshire charioteers are sometimes assumed to be invaders from that area.

Ian Stead of the British Museum excavated many of these burials and came down against this theory. While the barrows are similar to those in the Marne, all other aspects of the local culture, including the burial rites, are clearly native to the area; and the local settlements show a long history of continuity. But there is, here in East Yorkshire, the tantalising possibility of some cultural, economic or political contact with Iron Age Gaul.

* It was found in the tomb of a small woman in her mid-thirties with a deformed leg and a twisted face.
† Men were not the only proud possessors of vehicles. At Wetwang Slack a woman with a badly deformed face (like the Vix woman) was buried about 300 BC with a two-wheeled carriage decorated with coral from the Mediterranean.
‡ Not the town of Arras in northern France.

British carriage burials are characteristic of Yorkshire. However, recently one has turned up in Scotland, at Newbridge, amongst the industrial sprawl west of Edinburgh. We do not know the sex of the occupant, as only fragments of tooth enamel have survived the acidic Scottish soil. Yorkshire carts were usually dismantled to fit the grave, but the Newbridge vehicle was buried intact. No barrow covered the burial, but it lay close to the large Bronze Age barrow on Holy Hill – the continued use of an ancestral landscape?

When Julius Caesar came to Britain in 55 and 54 BC he was surprised to find the native warriors still dashing around the batttlefield with great panache in their chariots. To him this was an archaic form of warfare. The Arras vehicles, though, are fine examples of British workmanship and show that in the Iron Age there were skilled craftsmen specialising in wood. The earliest known British wheel comes from Flag Fen, dating to 1300 BC (though wheels could have arrived 2,000 years earlier), but the finest example of the wheelwright's art was preserved in the mud of the Trent valley at Holme Pierrepoint, near Nottingham. Different woods were chosen for their distinctive properties: ash for the felloe, or outer ring, which was constructed of six sections joined by oak dowels and secured with an iron tyre. The spokes were of oak and radiated from a central hub made of birch. By the first millennium BC much of the British wildwood had been cleared. What remained was managed woodland, exploited with considerable skill and knowledge, in a landscape of farms and fields.

After about 500 BC, in spite of the loss of land to environmental deterioration, there are vast numbers of Iron Age settlements across Britain and clearly the population was expanding. The sheer number of enclosed sites is impressive.

In Wales, for example, there are almost six hundred hill forts and other fortified enclosures, the largest over 6 hectares (15 acres), forming a continuous band along the Marches from Moel Hiraddug in the north, overlooking the Wirral, past Old Oswestry, the Breiddin, the Wrekin and Croft Ambrey to the Severn Estuary. The pattern is repeated on the opposite side of the Severn, where massively defended hill forts dominate the Mendips. Much smaller enclosed sites, of around 2 hectares (5 acres) or less, are also thickly spread across the fertile coastal lowlands of Wales, particularly in Pembrokeshire, and in Cornwall. There is also enormous regional diversity of settlement types across the British Isles and the people were probably equally diverse, with different dialects, dress and habits. On the chalklands of the south some hill forts are abandoned as others become dominant. Tribal territories were probably merging.

While some hill forts contain few houses and were perhaps cult centres or places for seasonal gatherings in the tradition of causewayed enclosures, others, such as Danebury (Hampshire),[33] were packed with roundhouses and may have had a population of a few hundred. Even such inhospitable sites as Mam Tor or Pen-y-Gent – both high on the Pennines and commanding wide views – had clusters of roundhouses. In North Welsh hill forts populations of thirty to fifty people per hectare have been suggested. Having spent many years poring over the British countryside, it is my impression that Britain in the Iron Age was as densely occupied as it was at the time of the Domesday Book.

This high population seems to have had relatively few problems in feeding itself. Hill forts such as Danebury and hundreds of farmsteads across lowland Britain contain underground grain siloes or storage pits, dug into the ground, capped with clay and capable of holding one to two tonnes of grain apiece. The storage is efficient because the grain gives out carbon dioxide, which acts as an insecticide. Above-ground Roman granaries suffered far greater losses to grain weevils and other pests. With my Oxford colleagues I excavated many of these pits in Thames valley farmsteads. They provided fascinating detail about late prehistoric farming, mainly because when the farmers cleaned these pits by setting fire to them, they inadvertently preserved large numbers of grain and weed seeds by carbonising them. By sieving the soil we could not only see what food plants were grown, such as spelt wheat, bread wheat and barley, but we could also chart the development of arable agriculture. Arable weed seeds act as environmental indicators. So, for example, we observed that common spike rush (*Eleocharis palustris*) increased later in the Iron Age, indicating that the farmers were bringing the flood plain of the Thames into cultivation. And they were also growing more winter wheat to increase productivity, but sometimes having problems with nitrogen deficiency in the soil. Overall, though, the picture is of an expanding population solving its nutrition problems through increasingly productive farming.

While the population was thriving across much of Britain, there were a few regions where it remained persistently low, at least to judge by the lack of known settlements in some areas, such as the north-west of England. Julius Caesar stated that the inhabitants of the inland areas of Britain were not arable farmers, 'but live on milk and flesh and clothe themselves in skin'. This was probably a garbled second-hand account, as he never observed much of Britain north of the Thames for himself. Archaeologists have also sometimes assumed that in the northern and western highland zone animal husbandry was completely dominant. It is clear, though, that arable cultivation was common in the highland zone, which includes a mosaic of fertile lowlands from the coast of Wales to the Scottish islands and the lowlands of Scotland and north-eastern England. Pollen evidence indicates extensive clearances, some for arable fields. The farmers at Thorpe Thewles, north of the River Tees, lived within a small gated enclosure, which contained several roundhouses. They kept cattle but seem to have had a thriving arable component to their farm. Charred grain – mainly six-row barley and spelt – was present in large quantities and indicated processing of cereals rather than consumption. The Thorpe Thewles farmers must have ground their grain into flour, because they left fragments of querns scattered about the farmyard. These were made from stone from the Pennines and North York Moors and were traded around the region.

The Thorpe Thewles farmers must have been seen as soft lowlanders by some of their less privileged neighbours. The hardiest Iron Age farmers, or the most desperate, sought a living on the higher slopes of the Cheviots, driven by the pressures of the increasing population and shortage of good land. Small farmsteads, surrounded by irregular enclosures, carved out fragments of the most difficult terrain. The corrugated surfaces of lazy beds show that these small-scale peasants had no plough or plough team, but relied on hoes and spades to cultivate their intransigent land. These people must have been vulnerable to bad weather, crop failure and disease.

Not all the inhabitants of the north and west of Britain had such a tough life as the Cheviot smallholders. In the more fertile coastal strip of Scotland and the Scottish islands local clan leaders developed the most spectacular architecture in Britain – the elegant stone tower house, or broch, such as Mousa in Shetland, Gurness in Orkney and Dun Carloway on Lewis.* Brochs are such distinctive buildings that it used to be assumed that they were exotic introductions created by newcomers. However, now it seems that they come towards the end of a long tradition of stone house building, including wheelhouses, in northern Scotland, which culminates in the great towers of the late centuries BC. Brochs are not easy to date and recent evidence from one at Scatness, in Shetland, suggests that their origins may be earlier than previously thought. Charred barley in the construction levels has been radiocarbon dated to between 400 and 200 BC.

Brochs combined hollow-walled construction, containing staircases, with the circular form of roundhouses to reach heights of more than 10 metres. At a few sites, particularly on Orkney, clusters of stone roundhouses, little hamlets, clung to the skirts of the towering broch – perhaps

---

* I call the broch builders 'clan leaders', but their status is much debated. Some argue that these are high-status sites, others that they are simply the vernacular houses of farming families.[34]

the homes of the dependents sticking close to the elite residence. But there are so many brochs the residents could not have been very elite.

So why build these impressive towers? One of the most remote areas that I ever worked in was the Mani – the southern finger of the Greek Peloponnese, which points towards Cyprus and Africa: the opposite end of Europe to the Scottish islands, but with some similarities. This is a tough, stony, sea-girt promontory. From about AD 1600 local competition for land and power became so great and vendettas so intense that feuding clan leaders built taller and taller tower houses. At first these were for defence from small-scale attacks; but gradually the prestige of the family came to be symbolised by the height of its tower. If similar pressures led to the construction of brochs, then the sheer difficulties of moving about during a period of active blood feuds would explain the storage capacity of brochs: Scalloway in Shetland, for example, had huge quantities of grain.

The broch dwellers ate more than barley and oats.* Bone refuse shows that young pigs, calves and red deer were favoured foods. The large number of calves butchered early is evidence that milk production was important; pork is frequently the preferred meat of elite groups and hunting red deer is often restricted to aristocrats. But even aristocrats cannot keep the mice away: the earliest known house mouse on Shetland appeared in a late Iron Age wheelhouse. Shortly afterwards the cat arrived in the northern isles.

The heat seems to have gone out of the north by about AD 200. Possibly hostility to the Romans or the opportunities for raiding and trading southwards caused rival clans to merge together and join the Pictish confederation. At any rate, people stopped living in towers.

Ireland shows many similarities to Atlantic Britain, with many ringworks, promontory and hill forts and crannogs – dwellings built on artificial platforms in loughs and lakes. Unfortunately, precise dating in Ireland is notoriously difficult, and the Iron Age (lacking a Roman occupation) extends into the Christian period. The most distinctive aspect of late prehistoric Iron Age society is the existence of famous, long-lived 'royal' or ritual sites. The 'Félire Oéngusso' ('The Martyrology of Oengus') – a calendar of saints written about AD 830 – boasts of the triumph of Christianity and the abandonment of these great pagan centres – Tara (Temair), Navan (Emain Macha), Rathcroghan (Cruchain) and Knockaulin (Dun

---

* Cultivated oats (*Avena sativa*) was a new crop in the late Iron Age islands; as it grows successfully in poorer soils it allowed Iron Age farmers to extend their arable and increase their carbohydrate yield. It also provided extra winter fodder for animals and was particularly useful as a food for pigs and horses – the favoured beasts of the elite.

Ailinna). Irish literary sources refer to them as royal palaces, forts, assembly places and cemeteries.

Archaeology reveals large oval enclosures, often with internal ditches, like British henges, with a long sequence of ritual activity. The Hill of Tara, for example, is a prominent two-kilometre-long ridge with over sixty discrete monuments, where the Irish people carried out their ceremonies from the fourth millennium BC to the fifth century AD. The Navan complex was the focus for the legendary capital of Ulster, Emain Macha. A great hill fort dominates the area: known as Haughey's Fort, its construction started about the thirteenth century BC. Close by is an artificial pool of the same date known as the King's Stables, into which ritual offerings were made: clay moulds from the manufacture of bronze swords, human, cattle, pig and dog bones. As in Britain, Irish religion demanded sacrifices into the water.

Less than a kilometre to the east there is an almost circular enclosure of 6 hectares (15 acres), sited prominently on a drumlin ridge. Traditionally this is the site of Emain Macha, the capital of the Ulster kings. Excavations of two circular earthworks within the larger enclosure produced spectacular yet strange results. Inside one circle there was a roundhouse which stood between the mid-fourth century BC and the late second century BC and was rebuilt nine times. A massive forty-metre-diameter structure of concentric timber posts replaced the roundhouse. The final act in the construction of this monument was to lever an enormous central post, about 13 metres long, into place. Dendrochronology on the surviving oak rings dated this monster to late 95 or early 94 BC. In succeeding years worshippers seem to have gradually built up a stone, clay and turf cairn around the internal posts, probably as a series of ritual deposits, which eventually reached nearly 3 metres in height and 37 metres across. The outer timbers were then deliberately set on fire and the whole sacred site was capped by a mound of turf, to create a tumulus-type structure.

Like Haughey's Fort, the Navan enclosure also had a ritual pool to the north-east. In the nineteenth century ditch diggers turned up human remains and four large bronze horns. Only one of the horns survives, but it is a magnificent example nearly 2 metres long and decorated with curvilinear tendrils.

Tara and Navan provide a fascinating and tantalising glimpse into long-lived Irish ritual practices. Like many settlements, fortifications and religious sites in Britain they give an impression of native communities attached to their land but undergoing social and economic changes. If these communities were stable, in the sense that generations continued to occupy the land of their ancestors, they nevertheless had a network of long-distance connections through trade, alliances and probably marriage. The old adage 'Fog in the Channel; Continent cut off' certainly did not apply in prehistory. Among the shale armlets, bronze sickles, axes, pins and sword fragments at Navan, which indicate long-distance trade, there was one particularly startling discovery: the skull of a Barbary ape (*Macaca sylvanus*), an animal which began its life in North Africa. Traditionally, exotic animals are suitable prestige gifts from one ruler to another: from Haroun al Raschid, the great caliph of Baghdad, who sent an elephant to Charlemagne, to the president of Turkmanistan who gave John Major one of his more memorable fiftieth-birthday gifts in 1993: a Turkman stallion.

As the Roman Empire expanded into the western Mediterranean and north of the Alps it became a powerful centre of gravity which tugged even the distant British Isles into its orbit. The literate classical world begins to make references to these remote barbarians; and in the chilly north the charms of Mediterranean civilisation exerted their attractions − wine, oil, fruit, glossy tableware, glass, silver jugs and bowls. In the first half of the first century BC Roman merchants had increasing contact with the previously underdeveloped markets of Gaul. As the market frontier advanced, barbarian communities adapted to exploit the new opportunities. The first amphorae of wine were shipped into Britain. Several key points of contact between Britons and Gallic traders are known on the south coast, at Hengistbury Head (to the south of Chichester Harbour), Mount Batten, near Plymouth, and most recently Cleavel Point/Green Island in Poole Harbour.[35] It is usually assumed that Gallic traders simply sailed their boats onto the beach to unload at low tide. In Poole Harbour, however, there is evidence for a more sophisticated timber mole allowing ships to draw alongside in sheltered water. Radiocarbon dating has not yet provided very precise dates for the origin of the mole, though the excavators suggest a surprisingly early date around 250–200 BC, for what is Britain's earliest known, specially constructed cross-Channel port.

More is known about the trading activities through Hengistbury Head (Dorset) thanks to Barry Cunliffe's excavations.[36] The site was a kind of ancient British Hong Kong, isolated on a headland but with good sea and river communications into the territories of the two neighbouring tribes. Hengistbury was also conveniently sited to collect local iron and Kimmeridge shale and salt, while drawing in silver, lead, tin and copper from the south-west. Its hinterland was rich in corn and cattle. The Greek geographer Strabo listed Britain's most useful export commodities in the early first century AD: metals, hides, corn, hunting dogs and slaves. If that is what the Britons exported, what did they get in return? Sherds of resilient amphorae show the arrival of Italian wine along with yellow and purple raw glass – and another taste of the sunny south: figs.

Breton pottery at Hengistbury suggests that the Continental trading links in the first century BC were via the north Armorican coast (Brittany). Strabo says that the curious Romans sent a war galley to follow a Phoenician vessel to discover the British trade route – a route which must also have provided a channel of communication for tribal elites on either side of the Channel. At least it did according to Julius Caesar. In his account of the Roman campaigns in Gaul in 54 BC he writes of questioning two Belgic emissaries, Iccius and Andecumborius. According to them, an earlier king of their neighbours, the Suessiones (a tribe from the Paris area), one Diviciacus, had been the most powerful man in the whole of Gaul and had also exercised power in Britain. The Belgae, they said, were originally German in origin (Belgium is named after them) and another powerful tribe in northern Gaul was the Atrebates,[37] whom we find in late Iron Age Hampshire and Berkshire.

In his account of Britain Julius Caesar described an episode of immigration:

> *Britannia pars interior ab eis incolitur, quos natos in insula ipsi memoria prodicum dictunt, maritima pars ab eis, qui praedae ac belli inferendi causa ex Belgo transierunt (qui omnes fere eis nominibus civitatum appellantur, quibus orti ex civitatibus eo pervenerunt) et bello illato ibi permanserunt atque agros colere coeperunt.*[38]

['Inland Britain is inhabited by tribes said by their own tradition to be indigenous to the island, the coastal part by tribes that migrated at an earlier time from Belgium to seek plunder. (Most of these latter are called after the names of the states from which they came.) And after the raids they stayed there and began to cultivate the fields.']

Much has been made of this brief statement: the Belgic invasion, supposedly in the early first century BC, has often been elevated to the status of an historical event and the coin- and wheel-thrown-pottery-using inhabitants of south-eastern Britain identified as Belgae. There are many archaeological reasons to doubt this major incursion of northern Gauls. However, there may have been limited settlement in the area around the Solent – a cremation cemetery, at Westhampnett, began in the early years of the first century BC, and the name of the town known to the Romans as Venta Belgarum ('Market of the Belgae' – modern Winchester) are obvious clues.

For the first time, with the Roman commentaries, we have a written account and the names of British tribes and people. '*Hominum est infinita multitudo*' ('The population is innumerable'), writes Caesar. Buildings are set close together and there are many cattle. The Britons have a taboo against eating hares, fowl and geese, which they keep as pets (the first record of the British fondness for animals). Caesar also tells his readers that the Britons use bronze and gold coins, as well as standard iron ingots, as currency.

Coinage appears in Britain from about 125 BC and opens a new dimension, throwing light on international contacts, tribal groups and influence, and providing the first insular evidence for the names of people and their rulers. The earliest coins in Britain, such as the so-called 'large flan' type of the Gaulish Ambiani tribe, appear in the south-east. Hengistbury Head shows there were contacts between Brittany and south-west Britain. Then, in the first century BC, the short Channel route into south-eastern Britain became increasingly important. Gallic coins were ultimately derived from the gold staters of Philip II of Macedon and were probably first acquired by Gallic mercenaries operating in the armies of Macedonia. The naturalistic Greek designs showing the head of Apollo, and the horses and chariot on the reverse, were eventually abstracted by the craftsmen of north-west Europe into miniature master-pieces of Celtic art. Caesar's report on the British influence of the Suessiones is reflected in the distribution of their coins, marked with a characteristic triple-tailed horse, from about 60 BC.

Early coins tend to be of high-value gold and may represent diplo-matic gifts or the reward for periods of mercenary service. In the early first century BC the development of a market economy in Kent generated the need for British-made, low-value, small change. The prototype of these bronze coins, probably belonging to the tribe later known as the Cantii (hence the modern county name: Kent), derived from prototypes produced in Marseilles, which featured a charging bull and the mint mark 'MA'. For the first time the British were exposed to writing, in the form of Latin script.

In the 70s and 60s BC several other tribes in southern Britain followed the example of the Cantii and adopted coinage – the Atrebates in Hampshire/Berkshire, the Durotriges in Dorset and the Catuvellauni/Trinovantes north of the Thames, the Iceni in Norfolk and the Corieltauvi in Lincolnshire and the east Midlands. Until recently some ten thousand Celtic coins were known from Britain. Recently I was invited to visit the British Museum. There, spread across a large table, was a fabulous collection of gold coins, some a rich reddish colour, but all looking mint-fresh. These came from a cluster of hoards, amounting to another four thousand coins, recently found in east Leicestershire. Most of these belonged to the Corieltauvi tribe,* who had buried them in a previously unknown ritual sanctuary. The Corieltauvians had constructed a pallisade across a prominent ridge, which they entered through a two-way gate. Inside they held great feasts, gorging mainly on pigs. By the gate they buried their valuable caches of coins and, just inside the palisade, another cache included an elaborate silvered Roman cavalry helmet. Was this an official gift to a Corieltauvian leader or had he led a group of retainers onto the Continent and allied them with the Roman conquerors of Gaul in the 30s or early 40s AD?

Eighty or ninety years earlier Caesar had been concerned that the British were providing help to their Gallic cousins. In 51 BC Caesar smashed the Gallic tribal alliance at Alesia, in Burgundy. As a result of Caesar's campaigns, some Gauls fled to Britain. Commius, an ally of Caesar's turned bitter enemy, came here, establishing himself at Calleva ('The Settlement in the Woods' − Silchester). His name appears on the first British coins to indicate a tribal dynasty. He famously said that he never wanted to see another Roman in his life.

However, Caesar's expeditions and the ultimate conquest of Gaul had its impact in Britain. The defeat of the Venetii tribe in Armorica reduced the south-western trade route. Instead the cross-Channel connections, now to Roman Gaul, became stronger. Judging from the decline of their coinage, the Cantii did not benefit; perhaps they were punished for opposing Rome. Instead allies such as the Trinovantes/Catuvellauni, north of the Thames estuary, became politically and economically powerful and the main benefactors of trade with Rome.

British coinage circulated mainly within discrete tribal areas, allowing us to plot the political geography of southern Britain. The Catuvellauni, to the north of the Thames, and the Atrebates, to the south, became the dominant groups, as the first Emperor Augustus brought stability to Gaul. Beyond, to the west and north, the Durotriges, Dobunni, Corieltauvi and Iceni also minted their own coinage. As tribal society in late Iron Age Britain changed and political units became larger, new types of sites appeared. Enclosed *oppida* − large defended areas of land − developed in more accessible nodal points. At Dyke Hills, at Dorchester-on-Thames, a massive bank and ditch cut off an area of over 40 hectares (99 acres) in a bend of the Thames, by the confluence with the River Thame. Inside was packed with roundhouses.

---

* The Corieltauvi were previously known as the Coritani.[39]

Even larger 'territorial *oppida*' enclosed vast estates, usually by rivers. At Verulamium (St Albans) and Camulodunum (Colchester) there were elite dwellings, farmsteads, ritual centres* and industrial areas. These are the first settlements in Britain with documented place names (on coins), and although Roman towns ultimately developed on or close to these sites, they do not generally display the conventional characteristics of urban places. Only at Calleva (Silchester, Hampshire) is there good evidence for a nucleated settlement with a street plan, whose inhabitants might justifiably have considered themselves Britain's first town-dwellers.

In the late Iron Age, as Continental links with the south-east become more pronounced, clusters of cremations, with imported pots and toilet instruments, appear around St Albans and the Chichester area. There are also some spectacularly rich burials accompanied by Roman wine amphorae, drinking vessels and silverware for ablutions, gaming sets and feasting equipment. Weapons were notable for their absence. Instead these British rulers signalled their fondness for the Roman luxuries of life. It was a signal that did not go unnoticed across the Channel.

---

* The first architecturally distinct cult buildings appear, such as the temples excavated at Heathrow, Hayling Island and Thetford.

Three Romans in Britain

A WIFE'S TALE

> *Claudia Severa Lepidinae suae salutem iii idus Septembres soros*
> *ad diem sollemnem natalem rogo libenter facias ut venias ad nos*
> *iucundiorum mihi diem interventu tuo factura ...*
>
> ['Claudia Severa to her Lepidina, greetings. On 11 September, sister,
> for the day of celebration of my birthday, I give you a warm invitation to
> make sure that you come to us, to make the day more enjoyable for me
> by your arrival ...']

NINETEEN HUNDRED YEARS ago Claudia Severa, the wife of a Roman
officer, Aelius Brochus, wrote to her friend Sulpicia Lepidina. Sulpicia
was the wife of another officer, Flavius Cerialis, commander of the garrison
of Vindolanda and prefect of the Ninth Cohort of Batavians. In cordial
terms Claudia invited her fellow memsahib, stationed with her husband
on the remote north-western frontier of the empire, to join her for her
birthday. This simple message is one of the most remarkable survivals
from Britain during the period of its Roman occupation – the first time
that we can hear the words of ordinary people. Britain has emerged from
prehistory.

Archaeologists found Claudia's message in a soggy patch of ground at
the fort of Vindolanda into which the military secretaries had dumped
the garrison's redundant archives in the period before the building of
Hadrian's Wall. Most of the letters, lists and accounts at Vindolanda were
written in ink on thin wooden tablets, the size and shape of modern post-
cards.* Normally such vulnerable and fragile objects would disintegrate
within weeks; but at Vindolanda the words invested in an airless north-
British bog have miraculously survived.

These everyday letters send very different messages about life in the

---

* The ink was a mixture of carbon, water and gum arabic. Limewood is most commonly used
for the tablets, which could be folded together to protect the inner surface.

Roman army from the usual propaganda displayed on arches and monuments such as Trajan's Column.* Trajan's Column is heroic and dramatic, a display of power: muscular soldiers throw pontoon bridges across the Danube, massacre barbarians, pile up plunder and make sacrifice to the gods. This is imperial muscle at its mightiest. Life in the Vindolanda documents is much more routine and mundane, yet no less interesting for that: requests for leave, concerns about impassable muddy roads, lists of foodstuffs. One letter says: 'I have sent you some socks, two pairs of sandals and two pairs of underpants. I hope you are getting on well with your messmates.' This sounds like a soldier's anxious mum who has made a trip to the Roman equivalent of Marks and Spencer. In another an officer writes to ask for a strong hunting net, reminding us that these expert cavalrymen probably spent more time relieving the boredom of garrison life by chasing boar and deer than hostile tribesmen. An altar found in nearby Weardale gives thanks to the hunting god Silvanus and records the deeds of Gaius Tetius Veturius Micianus, prefect of a cavalry regiment stationed at Lancaster, who bagged a remarkable wild boar which had eluded all others.

Among the Vindolanda documents there are no accounts of battles, or even skirmishes with local tribesmen. One memorandum refers disparagingly to the 'Brittunculi', which we can translate as 'the little Brits' or 'wretched Britons'.[1] This might be a contemptuous reference to hostile local tribesmen or, alternatively, to a recruiting officer's low opinion of native conscripts. By AD 100 British soldiers were serving overseas in the Roman army.[†] Nevertheless, the stalwarts of Imperial Rome dismiss their new subjects with the casual slang of colonial troops of any age. The period of Roman control over England and Wales is the first in which we have written accounts of events, people, motives and mistakes. It is a truism that history goes to the victor. The voices that we hear are virtually all those of the Roman rulers. The majority of the population, ordinary Britons — farmers, peasants, shopkeepers, slaves, children — are virtually silent.

The Vindolanda documents reveal the administrative arrangements, the practical needs and the social life of the Vindolanda garrison and its relationship with the Roman network in northern Britain and beyond.

* Trajan's Column, which illustrates his campaigns in Dacia, can be seen in Rome, or even more clearly in the Cast Courts at London's Victoria and Albert Museum where a nineteenth-century plaster cast captured the images before they were subject to twentieth-century pollution – and there is a viewing platform, as the Romans originally intended.
† The 'ala Britannica' and 'ala I Brittonum' units, recruited in the first century, served in Pannonia on the Danube. The 'cohors I Brittonum' served in Trajan's Dacian Wars and the 'cohors I Cornoviorum' were recruited from the Cornovii tribe, who take their name from the 'horn' of the Wirral Peninsula.

There is remarkably little interaction with their British neighbours. Yet those who made up the garrison were not themselves Roman, or even Italian, by birth. In fact they had only been members of the Roman imperial club for a century or so. Most of the troops were Batavians or Tungrians from the Low Countries (modern Netherlands and Belgium) around the mouth of the Rhine, part of what Julius Caesar called Gallia Belgica.*

Batavian troops were celebrated horsemen and after Caesar's conquest of Gaul they made valuable recruits into the Roman army. Ancestrally these Belgae were culturally and genetically far closer to the 'wretched Brits' whom they now regarded with neo-imperial disdain. Yet only thirty years earlier the Batavians had risen in revolt against Rome. The general Petillius Cerialis had crushed the uprising and been rewarded by a posting to Britain as governor, where he began the suppression of the north of Brigantia (the Pennine area of Britain). His Batavians at Vindolanda were now agents of Rome, identifying with the colonial masters but led by their own tribal aristocrats.[2, 3]

One of these was Flavius Cerialis, the prefect of the Ninth Cohort of Batavians, whose wife received the birthday invitation. By his name shall we know him. This loyal servant of Rome had discarded his barbarian family name. Instead he or his father had adopted that of Rome's ruling Flavian dynasty, probably around AD 70. At the time of the Batavian revolt it is likely that this aristocratic family had sided with Rome and been rewarded with citizenship. Flavius Cerialis may have taken his second name, or cognomen, from Petillius Cerialis himself. By adopting such Roman names the Batavian family publicly declared its allegiance. Tribal elites across northern Europe had to take a gamble when faced with the aggressive power of Rome: co-operate or resist. Clearly Flavius Cerialis and his family had sided with the victors.

The Vindolanda evidence shows how acculturated they were, in language, habits and taste. Not surprisingly the commander's wife came from a similar background to her husband. The clues also lie in her name. Sulpicia Lepidina was probably a member of a family granted citizenship during the year-long reign of the Emperor Servius Sulpicius Galba (AD 68–9). This is typical of Rome's strategy of imperial control: to acquire new territories with the aid of troops recruited from those areas

* Tacitus reports that the Batavians (their name means the 'Better Ones') were a German tribe, part of the Chatti from the area east of modern Cologne, who split off and migrated to the Rhine mouth to become crack Roman troops. Their principal settlement, Batavodurum – 'The Fort of the Batavians' – was rebuilt after the revolt of AD 70 as Noviomagus – 'New Market' – now the site of Nijmegen. The Tungrians occupied the land to the south of the Rhine delta and their name survives in the name of modern Tongres, between Liège and Maastricht.

most recently absorbed into the empire. In a mere forty years the Batavians and Tungrians were fully paid-up members of the Roman Empire, which provided them with opportunities for advancement; and because of their newly acquired literacy and bureaucratic habits we can glimpse tantalising fragments of their world in the fort at Vindolanda and its imperial network.

Perhaps most illuminating, in comparison with the testosterone-fuelled activities of Trajan's Column, is the evidence for the domestic and family life of the military. Tacitus, the historian who is one of our major literary sources for Roman Britain, voices the traditional view in the form of a speech by the hard-bitten Caecina Severus to the Roman senate: 'An entourage of women involves delays through luxury in peacetime and through panic in war. It turns the Roman army into a likeness of a procession of barbarians. Not only is the female sex weak and unable to bear hardship but, when it has the freedom, it is spiteful, ambitious and greedy for power.'[4] Clearly some ramrod-stiff Romans did not approve of taking the women along during the serious business of empire-building.

Nevertheless, Roman officers' wives dutifully accompanied their husbands on the frontier – and brought their children too. Claudia Severa, who so looks forward to a birthday visit, also sends the best wishes of her young son (*filiolus*). Further evidence is supplied by the small sandals, a child's sock and school exercise books left buried within Vindolanda. A misspelt quotation from Virgil's *Aeneid* (IX, 473), written in childish capitals, even has a schoolmaster's terse comment written across it: '*Segn[iter]*' – 'slack'. Virgil was the ideal author for the trainee imperialist. He instructed, in the *Aeneid*: 'Your task, Roman, never to be forgotten, will be to govern the world under your dominion. Your skills will be to establish civilisation where there is peace, to grant mercy where there is submission and to crush by war when there is defiance'. This was Rome's approach to her provinces in a nutshell.

So how did these families from Continental Europe find themselves in the remote highlands of northern Britain? And what impact did their presence have on the British who lived, voicelessly, around them? Roman soldiers and the imperial officials were not numerous in comparison with the native population, but over three and a half centuries they helped transform the culture of southern Britain and were in turn transformed themselves. More than at any time in prehistory the British Isles were open to the influences of the outside world and to the arrival of newcomers from Continental Europe, Asia and Africa. The Roman Empire was a mighty engine of change. But the influences did not pulsate in one direction. Through technology, religion, language and the arts, the empire itself became a mosaic formed by the complex of cultures within and even beyond the imperial frontiers.

The Roman invasion of Britain was launched on 22 March AD 43, when an armada of a thousand galleys and transports set off across the Channel from the port of Gesoriacum (Boulogne) on the coast of Gaul. The fleet carried 40,000 troops, a massive army by ancient standards – the might of Rome to be impressed upon the barbarian tribes at the edge of the known world: a tough imperial hammer to crack a small British nut. Rome's fourth emperor, Claudius, did not intend to fail in his mission.

So why was he going to all this trouble, amassing huge resources, absenting himself from Rome – a city seething with his enemies – undoubtedly taking considerable military, economic and political risks to conquer such remote offshore islands? Most obviously Claudius was attempting to mirror the achievements of his illustrious ancestor Julius Caesar. Almost a century earlier Caesar had made two surprisingly rash expeditions to Britain in 55 BC and 54 BC to warn off the Brits, who, he says, had been fighting alongside the Gauls. No doubt he also hoped to impress his readers and political rivals in Rome with his bold adventures at the edge of the known world. He was clearly unaware of any harbours like Poole, as part of his fleet drawn up on the beach was smashed by storms. Nevertheless, the expeditions resulted in our first detailed written account of Britain, in Caesar's *De Bello Gallico*. At the second attempt Caesar crossed the Channel with eight hundred galleys, five legions, two thousand cavalry and a collection of Roman merchants with an eye to the main chance. Like hungry gulls behind the plough they hoped that turmoil would churn up good opportunities. They already knew that British chieftains in the south had developed a taste for their wares.

In the initial encounter the Romans were somewhat confounded by the light mobile chariots from which British warriors cast missiles, then dismounted to fight. As the Romans marched to cross the Thames, a few groups surrendered because of their hostility to Cassivellaunus, the British leader, but the whole expedition petered out with no clear resolution. Caesar imposed a tax on the British, as if they were Roman provincials. There is no evidence they ever paid it.

During this time southern Britain was changing. The presence of a great empire just a few hours' sailing time away was bound to have an effect on British life. Caesar's expeditions were a warning to the British not to meddle in the affairs of their Gallic allies and kinsmen. Following Caesar's assassination a prolonged civil war distracted Rome from any ambitions in the north; but in 27 BC Octavian emerged from the troubles as the first emperor of Rome. His rival, Mark Antony, was dead and so was Rome's traditional republican system of government. In Tacitus's words: 'He found the whole state exhausted by internal dissension and established over it a personal regime known as the Principate.'[5]

The new emperor, renamed Augustus, established administrative systems in Gaul and a network of roads and river transport, which stimulated trade between the Channel coast and the Mediterranean. Roman-manufactured goods, ceramics, glass, wine and oil now flowed through the Roman arteries of Gaul, aided by a common currency, language and bureaucracy, unhindered by the old patchwork of Celtic tribal rivalries. The Thames estuary was the new gateway into Britain and the tribes who controlled the entrance dominated access to Continental luxuries. For many years historians and archaeologists assumed that these tribes were Caesar's enigmatic Belgae.

Augustus probably maintained diplomatic links with Britain to ensure that the south coast stayed in the hands of friendly tribes. North of the Thames the Catuvellauni were ambitious and aggressive (their name means 'Men Good in Battle'). To keep them in their place Rome cultivated their southern neighbours and rivals the Atrebates. Commius's 'sons' (as they describe themselves on their coins) seem to have befriended Rome while excelling at sibling rivalry: Tincomarus, the 'Big Fish', was ousted by Epillus in AD 7 and Epillus in turn by Verica in AD 15. Augustus was pragmatically indifferent to their domestic squabbles, provided the Atrebates stayed loyal to Rome, and the balance of power in southern Britain was not disturbed. To the Romans the rest of Britain and Ireland beyond the trading gateway was remote and irrelevant. The Atrebatic rulers were permitted to style themselves with the Roman title 'Rex'. Epillus, for example, issued coins with the inscription 'rex calle[vae] — King of Calleva; and Verica emblazoned a vine leaf on his, surely reflecting some sort of identification with the pleasures of Mediterranean culture.

Coin evidence is no substitute for detailed political accounts; nevertheless it provides us with the earliest names of the players in the first-century British power struggle. As a form of propaganda the coins do not always tell the literal truth: is a 'son' of Commius a genetic descendant or a political aspirant to a famous name? But they provide a crude indicator of tribal territories, alliances and the political geography of southern Britain in the decades before the Roman invasion of AD 43.

Tincomarus seems to have lost out in the local power struggle and, playing with fire, looked to the superpower across the Channel for help. Augustus includes him in a long list of supplicants recorded in his biography *Res Gestae Divi Augusti* — 'The Achievements of the Deified

Augustus'. Augustus did not reel in the 'Big Fish', because he had far more pressing military problems on his strategically important German frontier. The ambitious Catuvellaunian leaders, from their tribal heartland north of the Thames, took advantage of Rome's distractions.

There is evidence from the coinage that the Catuvellauni expanded their sphere of interest to the west, united with or absorbed the Trinovantes to the east and took over their royal centre Camulodunum (Colchester – 'The Fortress of Camulos', a British war god). The ruler of the expansionist Catuvellauni was Cunobelinus – Shakespeare's radiant Cymbeline, styled by the Roman historian Suetonius 'King of the Britons'. He calls himself the son of Tasciovanus, who had minted coins at Verulamium, the present-day St Albans.

Cunobelinus shifted his royal seat eastwards to Camulodunum – then a relatively new foundation, located to exploit Continental trading networks. It covered a peninsula of about 30 square kilometres, flanked by rivers and massive earthen ramparts. This was huge compared with earlier defended hilltop sites or the contemporary hill forts of the west and north. Within this great territorial *oppidum* there was a royal complex at Gosbecks and nearby an aristocratic burial ground. The grave goods in the great mound known as the Lexden tumulus illustrate the impact of Rome on Camulodunum's tribal leaders of the early first century. The contents include chain-mail armour, Roman bronzes, furniture, fifteen Italian wine amphorae and a medallion encasing a silver coin of the Emperor Augustus, minted about 17 BC. Here lay a chieftain who had developed a serious habit for the luxuries of Rome and probably a diplomatic link with its ruler. The chieftains of the Catuvellauni sustained their power and their lifestyle on the backs of their hard-working peasantry, supported by a retinue of warriors whose loyalty had to be constantly rewarded. Aggressive and expansionist states, led by rulers eager to exert their status and reward retainers with Roman objects of desire, might also have raided inland Britain for slaves, in the same way that African rulers on the west-African coast supplied European traders in the eighteenth century. Strabo notes that some British leaders 'procured the friendship of Caesar Augustus by sending embassies and paying court to him'. The silver medallion of Augustus buried with the Lexden ruler may have been the physical symbol of this dangerous friendship.*

In the early first century AD the ambitious Catuvellaunian kings expanded their sphere of influence into Kent, which became the fiefdom of Cunobelinus's son Amminius. Like Verulamium and Camulodunum,

---

* Addedomarus is one candidate for this royal burial, but the date of the tomb cannot be precisely established.

Canterbury functioned as an *oppidum*, a centre for the elite, a gateway for Roman luxury goods and a base for traders from the empire. As a result of some undiagnosable internal family quarrel Amminius fled to the embracing tentacles of Rome. Augustus's successor, Tiberius, had died in AD 37 and the new emperor was the famously psychotic Gaius Julius Caesar, better known to posterity as Caligula ('Little Boots' — a nickname given to him as a child by doting troops in his father Germanicus's camp). Amminius's arrival provided Gaius with an opportunity to reopen the British question. But Rome was not in a position to provide an effective challenge to Catuvellaunian ambitions in southern Britain.

This changed three years later on 22 March AD 43 with the assassination of Caligula. On first impressions the new emperor, Claudius, was hardly the face to launch a thousand warships. Until the age of fifty he had led a secluded life, an embarrassment to the imperial family because of his physical impediments. Nevertheless, as the only surviving male adult of the imperial Julio-Claudian family, the Praetorian Guard declared him emperor. His appearance may have been unprepossessing but Claudius was well read and intelligent. He appreciated how to construct and manipulate a suitably imperial image, and anyway, few subjects of ancient empires and kingdoms ever saw their rulers in the flesh. They were known by their deeds and their carefully manipulated icons on coins and statuary. Rome was a warrior state, its wealth, history and power built on 200 years of conquest. Claudius needed to reinvent himself as a conqueror; Britain provided the ideal opportunity. Still exotic and remote, beyond the ocean, the end of the inhabited world, Britain was a reminder of the bravura of the all-conquering Julius. A successful expedition there would establish Claudius as a worthy Julio-Claudian successor.

The army, the most powerful institution in Rome, could make or break emperors. A British expedition would keep the army occupied; victory would allow Claudius to stuff its mouth with gold. Conveniently he had the invader's perfect excuse: an invitation. According to the historian Dio Cassius, it came from another exiled British ruler, Verica (or Berikos) of the Atrebates: 'A certain Berikos, who had been driven out of the island as a result of an uprising, had persuaded Claudius to send a force there.'[6]

Following the death of Cunobelinus, who ruled the Catuvellauni for at least thirty years, his sons Togodumnus and Caratacus pursued an expansionist policy even more vigorously than their father, probably with less respect for what seemed an indecisive and ineffectual Roman authority across the Channel. Their father and uncle, Epaticcus, had already made incursions into northern Atrebatic territory, around Calleva (Silchester). Now the aggressive new leaders expelled Verica from his kingdom (perhaps in AD 42) and, with the westerly tribe, the Durotriges, took control of the south coast.*

Rome's century-old pragmatic policy of maintaining a friendly trading zone across the Channel from Gaul was in tatters. Claudius, a fragile and unlikely emperor, needed to silence the schemers, doubters, rivals and republicans in Rome. The time was right for a full-scale invasion of Britain. Claudius put together a crack team under the command of Aulus Plautius, a distinguished professional soldier, fresh from service in the Balkans. Four legions were drawn from the empire's toughest frontier, along the Rhine–Danube.† The total force consisted of about 40,000 men.[8]

A fifth legion stood in reserve to accompany the emperor himself once the invasion force had securely established itself in Britain. From inscriptions, tombstones and archaeological evidence we know it included Thracian cavalry and archers (natives of Bulgaria and Albania) and eight cohorts of Batavians from the Low Countries (some of whom eventually garrisoned Vindolanda), troops whose skills included an ability to swim rivers such as the Thames and the Medway in full gear.‡

Aulus Plautius divided his fleet into three to facilitate landing and provide flexibility in case of resistance. The south coast of Britain is not an easy landfall for a large fleet, lying parallel to the main direction of wind from the west.[9] Today the creeks at Richbrook (Rutupiae – the name means 'muddy creek') Kent which sheltered the Roman invasion fleet are completely silted up and the dried-out mud-flats are dominated by a Viagra factory.

The landings were, it seems, unopposed and the main British opposition, led by Caratacus and Togodumnus, retreated to a river, generally assumed to be the Medway, where they mustered their forces. A further onslaught from the Roman army drove the British back towards the Thames, where Togodumnus was killed. Some tribes were quick to see the advantages of siding with the new foreign power and eleven British kings surrendered.** With the main opposition in retreat and his new tribal allies onside, Aulus Plautius sent for the emperor. Claudius arrived in style to preside over his victory, buttressed by his gleaming legionary

---

* There is archaeological evidence that the Isle of Wight (Vectis) had close links with the Durotriges, the tribe centred on present-day Dorset.[7]

† II Augusta and XIV Gemina from the upper Rhine army based in Strasbourg and Mainz, XX Valeria from Neuss on the lower Rhine and IX Hispania from Pannonia.

‡ Auxiliary regiments were made up of native troops from Rome's subject territories. For auxiliary troops the army provided regular employment and a route to Roman citizenship and status.

**According to Dio Cassius, who lists the king of the 'Bodunni', probably a textual error referring to the northern Dobunni based in present-day Gloucestershire and west Oxfordshire.

guard, and trailing a large retinue of Roman aristocrats, many of them potential rivals and plotters whom he wisely kept at hand during his absence from Rome. To complete his durbar and impress the local Britons Claudius brought a troupe of north-African elephants, with which he paraded into Camulodunum.

The surprisingly determined sixty-three-year-old emperor had achieved his aim. News of his victory was sent post-haste to Rome, where the senate awarded Claudius and his son the title 'Britannicus' and permission to hold a triumph – a celebratory procession through Rome, which was the ultimate accolade of a victorious general. Coins stamped with a triumphal arch inscribed 'de britann[is]' carried the message of the conquest around the empire. A full-scale commemorative arch marked the site of Claudius's departure from Boulogne (Gesoriacum); another was erected in Rome to remind the citizens of their leader's glorious exploits. Even in Asia Minor, two cities, Aphrodisus and Cyzicus, kowtowed to the emperor by setting up memorials. Around the empire Rome's subjects associated the name of Claudius with the remote, exotic islands of Britannia.*

Claudius had only spent sixteen days in Britain. But for Rome's troops, administrators and new subjects it was a sentence of three and a half centuries. At the end of his brief visit he authorised Plautius 'to subjugate the remaining areas'.[10] Quite what areas were intended we do not know. And Claudius may have had only the vaguest idea himself. There was no grand strategy behind his imperial adventure in Britain, only pragmatism and short-term politics. As the ever-cynical Cicero replied to his brother, who had taken part in Caesar's second expedition: '*De Britannicis rebus cognovi ex tuis litteris esse nec quod metuamus nec quod gaudeamus.*'[11] ['About matters British I understand from your letters that there is nothing there about which we should either tremble or rejoice.']

Cicero's complacency was misplaced. At the time of the Roman invasion many distinctive tribes, speaking different dialects of Celtic and with varying ways of life, occupied Britain from Cantium in the south to the northern isles of Orkney. The Roman imperial machine was not inevitably all-conquering; and the Romanised way of life was not self-evidently beneficial to those upon whom the empire sought to impose itself. Rome, in fact, failed to conquer Britain as a whole. Claudius's imperial agenda only succeeded in the easily penetrated, agriculturally productive, rich underbelly of the south and east.

---

* Claudius's 'invasion of Britain was the greatest event of the reign, and one of his prime claims to rule, as his systematic exploitation of it shows'. Barbara Levick (1990), *Claudius*, Batsford, London.

During the period of Roman rule Britain can conventionally be divided into three zones: the civilian district, the military zone and the barbarian territory beyond. This conforms to some extent to the highland/lowland zone model promoted in the 1930s by Sir Cyril Fox in his influential book *The Personality of Britain*.[12] South and east of the imaginary line between the Rivers Tees and Exe lie the lowlands of young rocks, low hills and flat fertile valleys suitable for agriculture. Large populations of productive peasants could easily be subdued, controlled and taxed, whether by tribal chieftains or by Roman governors. To the north of the Tees–Exe line life was different, among the landscapes of old rocks, higher hills, moors and mountains, steep remote valleys and higher rainfall. Here the small-scale, scattered communities depended principally upon their herds of cattle and sheep. Like hill tribes from the Pyrenees to Afghanistan, those of Wales, the Pennines and Scotland were independent-minded, tough and resistant to tax collectors. They could be defeated by superior forces, but not controlled in the long term. As the legionaries moved north and west in Britain, the imperial project reached the limits of its viability.

If Wales was tough, Caledonia was impossible. The upland tribes continued a more traditional way of life, living in small, scattered groups with fewer large regional centres and without their own coinage or wheel-thrown pots. These were the people most resistant to Rome's influence. In Wales, Cornwall and Devon and the north-west, native settlement continued relatively unchanged. In the north the frontier fluctuated between the Solway–Tyne, marked by Hadrian's Wall from the second century, and the Antonine Wall, about 120 kilometres to the north. Ultimately Rome had to draw the line at Hadrian's Wall. Barbarian Caledonia was a step too far, its land too poor, its people too hard to succumb either to Rome's over-stretched armies or its blandishments.

During the three and a half centuries that the Romans occupied the province of Britannia, half of the British Isles remained outside their control. In Caledonia (Scotland), there were military interludes, of which Agricola's campaigns of AD 79/80 to 83/4 are the best documented, thanks to the writings of Tacitus. These culminated in the battle of Mons Graupius in north-eastern Scotland and the crushing defeat of the Caledonian tribes under Calgacus.* But within three years Rome's forces had withdrawn into the southern uplands and shortly after that to the Tyne–Solway isthmus.[13]

---

* An occasion for another stirring speech composed by Tacitus and placed in the mouth of a freedom-loving native leader.

The construction of Hadrian's Wall in the early AD 120s* separated the Romans and the barbarians, according to Hadrian's biographer. In practice the wall was a demarcation line through which tribesmen could only pass by surrendering their arms. Beyond the wall, to the north, the Roman army maintained military bases and close diplomatic ties with the tribes of southern Caledonia, such as the Votadini. Under Antonius Pius between AD 139 and 142 the Romans re-occupied southern Scotland and built a turf barrier, the Antonine Wall, and a massive ditch across the Forth–Clyde isthmus. It functioned for only a couple of decades. Finally, between AD 208 and 210, the Emperor Septimus Severus and his son Caracalla undertook another major campaign in Scotland, only to retreat to Hadrian's Wall. Rome's direct control of what is now Scottish territory was relatively short-lived and exclusively military in character. In spite of Mons Graupius, the highlands and islands were never held. In fact the Romans only had eyes for the most productive agricultural land south of the highlands,[14] which had the capacity to support their garrisons.†

Forest clearance and increasing numbers of native settlements and fields indicate an expanding population. However, only the tribal elites seem to have had any substantive contact with the luxuries of the Roman world. Like the pre-conquest tribal rulers of the south they clearly had an appetite for bullion, coinage and booze, judging from coin hoards and silver vessels found in tribal centres like the great hilltop enclosure of Traprain Law, south of Edinburgh. By the fourth century there are signs that the small-scale Caledonian tribes were merging into larger confederations, which would come to present a threat to their southern neighbours.

Scotland's limited appeal to imperial Rome is not reflected in Tacitus's optimistic account of Agricola's campaigns there. In fact, he writes, with only one legion his father in law could have conquered Ireland. It never happened. Strabo in his *Geographica*, written in the early first century, places Ireland, or 'Hibernia', at the limits of the inhabited world. He then proceeds to disparage the Irish as total savages leading a wretched existence in a foul climate. Tacitus, on the other hand, reported that Ireland was much like Britain and that its harbours were well known from the merchants who traded there. Because of the trade links Ptolemy, shortly after AD 100, was able to detail Irish tribes, settlements and rivers. He mentions the Rivers Vidva, Bouvinda and Senos — probably the Rivers Foyle, Boyne and Shannon. He attempts to transcribe Irish tribal names

* It ran for 80 Roman miles (117 kilometres) from Wallsend on the River Tyne to Bowness on the Solway Firth.
† Probably about 25,000 troops in the first century and slightly fewer at the time of the Antonine Wall.

such as Robogdii in the north-east (probably the Dal Riáta of Antrim and later Argyll) and the Voluntii (the Ulaid). While Ptolemy mentions the cult centre of Emain Macha, none of his place names can be identified with the great earthworks of Tara (County Meath), Ireland's principal ritual centre. Ptolemy places a tribe that he calls the Iverni in the south-west. These people are the most likely source of the early Greek name for Ireland – Ierne – and the Irish word for the island – Eriu (Eire).[15]

Ptolemy's geographical knowledge of Ireland suggests that traders plied routinely across the Irish Sea. One site which could potentially throw light on the character of this contact is the promontory fort at Drumanagh (County Dublin). Roman coins from the site indicate that this might have been a trading centre and a focal point for Romano-British traders – or alternatively a launch pad for Irish raiders of the kind who seized St Patrick from his father's farm. Well-dated archaeological evidence for the first four centuries AD in Ireland is unfortunately scarce. The scatter of Roman coinage, occasional burials with Romano-British and Gaulish objects and ritual deposits of imported goods hint at the contacts. But it is only with the arrival of Christian bishops and the mission of Patrick that substantial changes to Irish society can be observed.

The tribal structure of Britain influenced the Roman strategy for occupying the island. Within a matter of three to four years the invaders pacified the south-eastern zone from the Exe to the Humber. A new Roman road, the Fosse Way, marked the frontier, a line cut with the precision of a Stanley knife, which symbolised Roman control and power, an imperial scar across the tribal face of Britain. And the positioning was remarkably subtle: it linked key military bases from Isca (Exeter) in the south-west, past Corinium (Cirencester), Ratae (Leicester) and Lindum (Lincoln), where it joined Ermine Street, the road from London, and continued as far as the Humber at Winteringham. Both ends of the Fosse frontier could be supplied by sea. The road itself provided a rapid-transit system in an almost straight line for 350 kilometres.

This frontier enclosed the richest agricultural land in Britain, inhabited by the most populous and politically advanced tribes, who were easy to control and easy to tax. Or so it seemed. At Camulodunum (the name Latinised from 'Camulodunon') the Twentieth Legion built a fortress. A small garrison of Thracian cavalry, recruited principally from Bulgaria, kept an eye on the royal compound at Gosbecks.

The tombstones of two individuals, some of the earliest marked graves in British history, confirm the presence of these forces. Marcus Favonius Facilis was a centurion of the Twentieth, and Longinus a cavalryman of the First Squadron of Thracians. Longinus's tombstone is particularly fine, carved with the standard cavalry image: a calm, upright rider mounted on a well-controlled horse, which neatly steps over a fallen barbarian. The iconography represents not only Longinus's specific identity as a cavalryman, but the mythic representation of the rider conquering death, triumphant over evil. Here we have the first example in Britain of the image that will develop, in a Christian context, into the familiar picture of St George and the Dragon.

Longinus is also one of the first ordinary individuals – a sergeant not a king, queen or a general – to leave us some personal information. Not very much – nothing about his character, motivation or cause of death – but we do know from the formal inscription on his tombstone, a telegram from the grave, that he was the son of one Sdapezematygus, clearly the native name of a tribesman recently drawn into the empire. Longinus came from the district of Sardica (Sofia) and he died aged forty after serving in the army for fifteen years. He made a will in which he left money to mark his grave. For his family there was a foreign field in Britain which was for ever Bulgaria. Ironically, Longinus's name has survived for posterity because his tombstone was one of those desecrated in Boudicca's revolt, to be discovered centuries later.

Thanks to the desire of these Roman soldiers to memorialise themselves we have evidence of other cavalrymen like Longinus: Sextus Valerius Genealis, a Frisian from the Low Countries, Dannica from Upper Germany – both buried at Colchester – and Lucius Vitellius Tancinus, a Spaniard and, judging by his tripartite name, a Roman citizen.

While I was writing this book I went to visit the excavations at the Roman fort and town of Alchester in Oxfordshire, directed by my friend Eberhard Sauer. Eberhard is an expert on the Roman army and at Alchester he had, remarkably, found the timbers of a Roman fort dated by tree rings to AD 44. When I arrived, he hurried me to the site office. There was the top half of an impressive first-century Roman tombstone which the excavators had just found, re-used as a fragment of masonry in the later Roman town wall. Unfortunately the tombstone had been snapped through the middle of the inscription. 'Never mind,' I said to Eberhard, 'with your luck you'll find the other half.' A couple of days later he did. The inscription now reads:

Dis Manibus
L[ucius] V[alerius] L[uci filius] Pol[lia tribo] Geminus For[o]
Germ[anorum]
Vet[eranus] Leg[ionis] II Aug[ustae]
an[norum] [L?] h[ic] s[itus] e[st]

he[res] c[uravit]
e[x] t[estamento]

['To the souls of the departed
Lucius Valerius Geminus, the son of Lucius, of the Pollian voting tribe
from Forum Germanorum
veteran of the Second Augustan Legion
who died at the age of 50 lies buried here
his heir had this set up
according to his will.']

This Lucius was a veteran of the Second Legion which, under its commanding officer Vespasian, went on to become the scourge of south-west Britain. Lucius came from Forum Germanorum, a small town in northern Italy, a principal recruiting ground for the Roman army in the mid-first century. While we cannot be precise about his time of death, it is likely that he joined the legion while it was based in Strasbourg and then took part in the invasion of Britain.*

The physical remains of Roman soldiers have rarely been excavated in Britain, but one exception is the fascinating military cemetery at Brougham near Penrith (Cumbria). Here the Roman army built a fort in a strategic location on the road to Carlisle in an area thick with British ritual monuments. Between AD 200 and 310 the garrison buried its dead – men, women and children – in a cemetery east of the fort. What is most extraordinary about these burials is that they clearly belonged to an ethnic group practising their own distinctive rituals. The bodies were burned on elaborately decorated biers and surrounded by grave goods – glass drinking cups with men, small samian cups (red ceramic vessels from Gaul) with children and 'antique' samian bowls with adults. The dead went into the afterlife with joints of meat and even whole carcasses of cattle, sheep, dogs, geese and fowl. But most singular of all: military equipment and horses were placed in the adult graves, including those of women. Hilary Cool has investigated the scene in great detail and came to the conclusion that these people were Pannonians – horse-riders from the Danube area between modern Austria and Hungary. The women, with their distinctive jewellery and hairstyles, must have been an exotic sight in northern Britain – especially if, like east-European Amazons, they rode the horses and carried the weapons found in their graves. Or were these things simply ethnic or tribal badges, the signs of a people who had joined the Roman army but still wished to proclaim their identity in an alien land? [16]

* Tombstones dedicated to deceased veterans have also been discovered in Chester, Caerleon, Lincoln, York and Gloucester.

In the south-east lowlands centrally organised tribes who resisted were easily conquered. Many simply sided with Rome. All were then controlled through the tribal aristocrats who had decided that their interests lay with the new masters.

As the army moved west and north the smaller-scale pastoral communities put up a stiffer defence. There is stark evidence for the fate of the British, of the Durotriges tribe, who resisted at the hill fort at Hod Hill in Dorset. This was one of twenty hill forts that tried to hold out against the invader. The Second Legion under its general (and future emperor) Vespasian stormed the ramparts and cut down the defending Durotriges. The legion rained its ballista bolts — mechanically hurled spears — on the natives' roundhouses; and British bodies bear the scars of the Roman war machine.

Rome's policy, however, was to absorb the conquered, provided they accepted their fate, into the empire; and in particular to win over and utilise the tribal rulers. At Gosbecks (Colchester, Essex) there is evidence that the royal family — or at least a pro-Roman faction — was allowed to retain its position. Richly furnished British burials at the Stanway site date to before and after the conquest. One, of about AD 50, included a rare set of medical instruments — a surgical kit of scalpels, forceps, needles and a surgical saw. Was this a Briton trained as a doctor, accompanied by the tools of his trade? He also had the trappings of Roman luxury: an amphora, wine strainer, a pottery dinner service, and a gaming board set out with the glass counters for a game of *ludus latrunculorum* — 'the game of little bandits'.

Nearby, the contemporary, so-called 'warrior's grave' also contained an impressive collection of grave goods: over twenty pottery vessels, glassware, a spear and fragments of a shield. Like the 'doctor', the occupant also had the means to pass the time pleasantly in the afterlife, with a folding wooden board and a bag of twenty glass counters. Close by these was a third, even more significant grave. It held a small ceramic inkpot. Is this the burial of the earliest known literate Briton? These graves show the British elite in the south-east adopting Roman taste, fashions, foodstuffs and education.

An earlier generation of archaeologists, influenced by their own experience of the British Empire, portrayed first-century Britain as a blank canvas onto which Roman strategists could place the slide rule of imperial control. Now, thanks to several decades of fieldwork, we can see that the whole of Britain was a well-populated landscape of settlements, farms, fields, tribal and cult centres and routeways. The site of Lincoln, for example, was of great importance to the Roman army, at the point where the River Witham cut through the Jurassic scarp. It controlled access to the Wash and northwards to the Humber. But this was not neutral or un-occupied territory. The Lincoln area was already an ancient cultural landscape, a sacred place marked by burial mounds, where for genera-tions the Corieltauvi and their ancestors had placed offerings to the gods in the River Witham and where there was already an important river crossing.[17]

Even the name is British. 'Lindon' (transformed to 'Lindum' in Latin) means the 'Place by the Pools', a reference to the sacred waters where the Witham cut through the limestone ridge. We can now appreciate that Corieltauvi society was complex, one that minted coins at its tribal centre at Old Sleaford, 25 kilometres south-east of Lincoln on the edge of the Fens, and managed a productive economy based on animal rearing, agri-culture, iron manufacture and salt production. Into this ancient and intricate society and densely populated landscape bulldozed the Roman army. We have no written records to tell us about the impact on the British people who lived here, but it must have been traumatic. Though there are no signs of resistance and slaughter, the Romans nevertheless arrived as an army of occupation, taking an iron grip on the land, im-posing a web of military bases and rigidly straight roads with the legion-ary fortress of Lindum at the centre. The sacred pools of Lindon became a military zone – a situation paralleled at Isca (Exeter), Glevum (Gloucester) and Camulodunum (Colchester), and later at Caerleon, Wroxeter, Deva (Chester) and Eboracum (York).

Following the death of Claudius in AD 54 and the accession of Nero, the Roman army pressed beyond the Fosse Way into the hill country of Wales. In AD 58 a new governor arrived in Britain. Suetonius Paullinus was an Italian professional soldier who had led his troops in the Atlas Mountains of Algeria. Through his Africa campaigns he had learnt the hard way how to tackle tough, independent-minded hill tribesmen like the Silures and Deceangli of North Wales. In two seasons of campaigning the Romans took a grip on the mainland of Wales. British refugees fled to their sacred island of Mona, or High Island (Anglesey) – a centre for Druids, the British and Gallic priesthood so hated and feared by the Romans. The historian Tactitus, in his *Annals of Imperial Rome*, conjures up a vivid description of the attack on Mona: as the Roman troops strug-gled to reach the beach, 'the enemy lined the shore in a dense armed mass. Among them were black-robed women with dishevelled hair like Furies, brandishing torches. Close by stood Druids, raising their hands to heaven and screaming dreadful curses.' Tacitus conjures up a dramatic and terrifying scene for his readers in Rome, made all the more spine-tingling by the reminder that it was the Druids' habit 'to drench their altars in the blood of prisoners and consult their gods by the means of human entrails'.

Of course the voices of those on the beach are silent – probably a crowd of frantic, disorganised tribesmen, desperate women and elderly priests confronting the faceless and remorseless ranks of the best-armed and -trained troops in the world. British resistance did not last long: 'Onward pressed their standards and they bore down their opponents,' Tacitus told his readers.

No sooner had Paullinus dealt with the British tribes in Wales than he received shocking news: the Iceni under their Queen Boudicca had revolted and the south was in flames. Boudicca was the widow of the Icenian King Prasutagus, who ruled by a treaty arrangement with Rome.*

On his death, with no male heir, he bequeathed half his kingdom to the Emperor Nero, probably in an attempt to retain as much as possible for his wife and daughters. To no avail. With the governor campaigning in Wales, authority principally rested in the hands of the procurator, Decianus Catus, a ruthless and acquisitive tax gatherer. The greedy imperial bureaucrats, backed by the procurator's troops, moved in to carve up the old kingdom and the estates of the Icenian chieftains. As discipline broke down, thuggish Roman soldiers raped the daughters of the dead king and Boudicca herself was flogged. The Iceni rose in revolt, joined by their southern neighbours, the Trinovantes, who had had to put up with the land-grabbing of arrogant and overbearing legionary veterans at Camulodunum.

Their tribal centre had become a physical manifestation of Roman power – a *colonia*, or planned town, for Roman veterans. While retired soldiers took tribal land for themselves the Britons were forced to fund grandiose public buildings, notably the temple of the imperial cult devoted to the Divine Claudius.

The British attacked Camulodunum and burnt down the new town. The survivors holed up in the solidly classical imperial temple, an unfortunate place for a last stand as the building was a symbol of all that the Iceni and Trinovantes hated about Rome. They had paid for it themselves with the aid of loans. According to one Roman source it was the demands for repayment by loan sharks, such as the millionaire Seneca, that added fuel to the fires of discontent.

After sacking Camulodunum Boudicca's army moved on to Verulamium and London. Boudicca did modern archaeologists a favour: she

---

* Rome had treaty arrangements with three tribal groups: Prasutagus and the Iceni in the east, the Atrelates/Regni in the south and Queen Cartimandua and the Brigantes in the north.

burnt everything in sight. The charred horizon of AD 60 provides a snapshot of the early Roman attempts to introduce urbanisation to Britain. The blanket of ash caused by the great destruction acts as a time line within archaeological excavation and fossilises the evidence of the mid-first century beneath. While Camulodunum and Verulamium were formal, legally constituted Roman towns, established on the sites of important tribal centres, London 'did not rank as a Roman settlement but was an important centre for businessmen and merchandise', according to Tacitus. Excavations at No. 1 Poultry, in the City, revealed densely packed timber buildings for merchants and workshops. Dendrochronology confirms that London's grid of streets was first established about eight years before Boudicca's war, by about AD 52. London was a frontier boom town. Nevertheless the tough-minded Paullinus, who had marched directly back there from Wales with his troops, decided not to defend it.

Instead, with a force of 10,000 legionaries and auxiliaries, he chose his own ground somewhere north-west of London, to encounter Boudicca's huge but raggle-taggle British force. The tribesmen rolled up, laden with plunder, accompanied by their families grandstanding in carts around the edge of the battlefield. Tacitus puts stirring Latin rhetoric into the mouth of the British-speaking Boudicca, full of noble, freedom-loving sentiments designed to appeal to his republican-minded readers in Rome:

> We British are accustomed to women commanders in war.
> I am descended from mighty men. But I am not fighting for
> my kingdom and wealth now. I am fighting as an ordinary
> person for my lost freedom, my bruised body and my outraged daughters … you will win this battle or perish. This is
> what I, a woman, plan to do! Let the men live in slavery if
> they will.*

In the slaughter that followed Tacitus quotes one report that 'almost eighty thousand Britons fell'. According to another Roman historian, Dio Cassius, Boudicca fled, died of illness and was given a rich burial – a tantalising prospect for archaeologists. No grave has been found, but we do have a likely site for Boudicca's royal compound.[18] Sited on a promi-

---

* Tacitus is intelligent and well informed: a brilliant writer. Yet, as a member of the senatorial class that has lost power and influence under the principate, he is deeply cynical about the new imperial ruling class – a collection of mad and bad emperors, bribing soldiers and employing ex-slaves as their henchmen – the old sterling virtues of freedom-loving Romans are represented now only by a few stalwarts of his own class, such as his father-in-law Agricola. Barbarians, unpolluted by Roman corruption, also serve a purpose in his writings as noble savages. As a master of rhetoric and a Latin wordsmith Tacitus composes ringing phrases that would be applauded by his educated audience more for their effect than for their accuracy.

nent hill near Thetford (Norfolk), a site of ritual activity for millennia, an enclosure was impressively enlarged around AD 60 and set within eight concentric lines of hedging. There were three roundhouses inside, one of which had a towering two storeys. It was probably from here that Boudicca launched her defence of Britain.

In the aftermath of the Boudiccan affair a new official, Caius Julius Alpinus Classicianus, took up the post of imperial procurator (finance officer) and proved to be more understanding of the British predicament.* As a result of his statesmanlike and courageous intervention a new generation of more principled and less rapacious administrators and governors took control in southern Britain. Nevertheless the British rising in the south caused the Romans to retrench. Garrisons withdrew from Wales to Glevum (Gloucester) and the network of forts between London and Lindum ensured that the eastern tribes could not rise again. Much of the fenland of East Anglia was probably confiscated and managed as imperial estates.

In spite of the almost disastrous events of AD 60 Rome continued with its tried and tested policy of co-opting local elites, promoting self-government through urban centres and taxing a preferably docile population, the vast majority of whom were peasants and country dwellers. Urban centres were fundamental to this approach to imperial rule. In Britain official towns were established with imperial authority: *coloniae*, for retired veterans, and *civitates*, capitals to act as formal centres for tribal territories. At Colchester, Gloucester and Lincoln, after the legions moved northwards and their fortresses were decommissioned, the Roman authorities established new towns with colony status.† The fortresses at Lincoln and Gloucester already possessed land confiscated from the local tribes in the early years of the conquest, so this could be granted to veterans with the minimum of aggravation to the British community.

This policy was popular with soldiers approaching retirement in their old stamping grounds, the province which they had got to know and where they had established relationships with local women and with

---

* Classicianus was probably a Gaul, from near Augusta Treverorum (Trier), a member of a provincial aristocracy which had experienced the transition from conquered subjects to active members of the imperial ruling class, from barbarian 'them' to 'one of us'. He persuaded Nero to undertake a commission of enquiry. As a result Paullinus, hero and hard man of Rome, was diplomatically shipped out. Classicianus died while serving in Britain and was buried in London. His elaborate tombstone, described by Professor Shepherd Frere as 'a precious national possession', is in the British Museum.

† The dates of these decisions are uncertain but probably between AD 84 and AD 98. If Agricola had established Lincoln's *colonia* before AD 84, then his son-in-law Tacitus would have almost certainly mentioned it in his biography.[19]

colleagues. At the earliest fortress at Camulodunum about 50 per cent of the legionaries were Italians; by the time Glevum was decommissioned the proportion of Italians was about 20 per cent, with the rest from more recently incorporated provinces.[20] Ultimately troops came to Britain from as far away as Bulgaria and North Africa.

After AD 70 increasing numbers of provincials joined the army, not just as auxiliaries but also as members of crack legionary units. These troops may have had more in common culturally and even linguistically with their British neighbours than first-generation legionaries. Nevertheless, on discharge they acquired land or a cash grant and played their part in developing the emerging Romano-British culture. The earliest recorded citizen of Lindum (and the earliest evidence of the town's name) did not remain there. Marcus Minicius Marcellinus of Lindum, leading centurion of the Twenty-Second Legion, dedicated a structure in Mainz to the goddess Fortuna, between AD 81 and 95. A third-century occupant of Lincoln, Aurelius Senecio, set up a tombstone there to his wife, Volusia Faustina, who died aged twenty-six years one month and twenty-six days. He must have played an important role in Lincoln life, for he describes himself as a decurion, one of the hundred members of the local government (*ordo*) of the city, the provincial equivalent of the Senate in Rome.

The four *coloniae* of Britain

Colchester	Colonia Victricensis	founded c.AD 49
Gloucester	Colonia Nervia Glevensium	founded AD 97
Lincoln	Lindum Colonia	founded by AD 90
York	Eboracum	founded by AD 237

While the *colonia* at Lincoln initially depended upon veterans to make up its senior citizens, 50 miles to the south Leicester (Ratae) became the Corieltauvi's *civitas*, or tribal capital, with the native aristocracy providing members of the *ordo*, or town council. This was mirrored across the civilian province, even in the doggedly British wild west at Carmarthen (Moridunum), the town of the Demetae tribe in west Wales, at Exeter, Isca Dumnorum – a legionary fortress until about AD 75 then the *civitas* of the Dumnonii, and at Wroxeter, the *civitas* of the Cornovii.

In such traditional tribal areas the Roman authorities may have had to provide financial stimulus for urbanisation, much as recorded by Tacitus in what is probably the most famous passage in his biography of Agricola, his father-in-law and governor of Britain:

The winter which followed was spent in the prosecution of sound measures. In order that a population scattered and uncivilised, and consequently ready for war, might become accustomed by comfort to peace and quiet, he would exhort individuals, assist communities to erect temples, market places (*fora*), houses; he praised the energetic, rebuked the indolent, and the rivalry for his approval took the place of coercion. He also began to train the sons of chieftains in a liberal education, and to give preference to the natural talents of the Briton as against the trained abilities of the Gaul. As a result the nation which used to reject the Latin language began to aspire to rhetoric. The wearing of our dress became a distinction — the toga came into fashion. Gradually the Britons went astray into alluring vices: to the promenade, the bath, the well-appointed dinner table. Their simple natures gave the name '*humanitas*' to what was their slavery.

Some historians have seen this passage as a mere filler in Tacitus's account of Agricola, a winter's tale told between the serious business of campaigning. But the passage throws up interesting questions about the Roman attitude to empire, to the conquered Britons and the British response. The Romans did not have a textbook for imperialism (though they did have them for other things, such as agriculture and architecture). Their approach was opportunistic, flexible and pragmatic. The Agricola passage, however, reflects the priorities: scattered country dwellers are potentially dangerous and difficult to tax; civilisation and government require towns; a market place promotes economic activity. In temples the proper rites for the deified emperor, the principal Roman gods, the Capitoline Triad (Juno, Jupiter and Minerva) and even local gods, can be practised. Rome was tolerant of native religions providing they did not become a focal point for rebellion. Religion melded society together and Roman soldiers were as likely to make offerings to local native deities as to the classical gods. The system depended upon the co-operation of the tribal elites and Tacitus tells us that in southern Britain they adopted the style of the Roman rulers in language, dress and food. In the rhetoric of republicanism this amounted to slavery.

Education played an important role in cultivating imperial exclusiveness. The Romans believed in training their future leaders from a young age and Agricola's approach to the Britons was not new. When the rebel Sacrovir captured Autun in AD 23 he took as hostages 'the most well-born of the three Gauls who were there receiving a proper education'.[21]

According to Suetonius, there was a similar school for young Germans. Agricola himself had been a schoolboy in Marseilles, by which time the southern coast of Gaul, according to several Roman commentators, had become almost like Italy.

Education began with the study of Latin. Agricola says that the British had a facility for languages; they picked up Latin quickly when it suited them. Their native tongue in southern Britain was Gallic, or P-Celtic. This remained the language of the countryside and the majority of people during the four centuries of Roman rule. But for would-be rulers and administrators Latin was essential – the language of literacy in the western empire, of administration, Roman law and the army. Many Britons must have been bilingual. In the Roman world a primary education was available for the sons and daughters of the elite. Secondary education, particularly in rhetoric and literature, was aimed at the boys. School and a thorough grounding in classical education would set them up for life. The many happy hours spent reading Virgil provided them with the right world view, the appropriate quotation and the ability to mix comfortably in civilised Roman society.

Agricola does not mention the girls. In spite of the British role models, Boudicca of the Iceni and Cartimandua of the Brigantes, women were expected in Rome's deeply patriarchal society to play a domestic role. One, at least, bucked the system. Martial, the famous writer of epigrams, writes approvingly (for a change) of Claudia Rufina, a British woman in the later first century, who was so sophisticated that the hawk-eyed matrons of Rome took her for an Italian.

Teachers were often Greek slaves or freedmen (or if not Greeks, a Greek name conveyed the right impression). We only have the name of one teacher in Britain: Demetrius of Tarsus (St Paul's home town). He sailed to the western isles in AD 82 and lived in Eboracum (York). He was obviously not alone. Inscriptions, gravestones, graffiti, names inscribed on objects, adverts, notices and letters became commonplace in towns. However, Britain, along with northern and central Spain, has the lowest density of inscriptions in the Roman Empire and most of those were found around Hadrian's Wall, inscribed for the army or individual soldiers. For whatever reason – expense, refusal to identify with the Roman world, widespread illiteracy – most Britons did not commemorate their lives and work, or their gods, to the same extent as Roman subjects who lived closer to Italy.

Agricola's 'sound measures' also included the promotion of new towns. The Roman plantations at Colchester, London and Verulamium imposed the Mediterranean model with a grid of streets, a forum, basilica and bathhouses. These elements characterised the officially recognised towns, the *coloniae, civitates* and *municipia*. After their destruction by Boudicca's forces, these alien urban transplants recovered relatively slowly. With a display of imperial confidence the Roman authorities had established the veteran colony at Camulodunum (Colchester) within six years of the invasion. There was a considerable delay before they launched the next two, at Lindum (Lincoln) and Glevum (Gloucester). In fact, what urban development can be recognised in the first century, at places such as Chichester, Bath, Silchester and Canterbury, seems to depend upon local initiative rather than official planning. In the later first century, as the Roman army ground westwards and northwards, it left behind a network of roads like a spider spinning its web, which influenced the siting and layout of new towns. The roads and urban street grids were articulated for the convenience of traffic through those places which today end in 'chester/cester' (an early English adaptation of *castrum* — 'fort' — because they had defensive walls): Winchester, Cirencester, Dorchester, Leicester, Chichester and Silchester (which had started early but was re-modelled). At Verulamium a new *forum basilica* rose from the ashes in AD 79, reflecting the renewed sense of Roman optimism at this time, which was also evident in the willingness of veterans to commit to life in the two new colonies of Lindum and Glevum.

These remarkably similar model towns were dotted across the province, but relatively few Britons lived in them. Even at their peak the larger towns Verulamium and Corinium probably only had populations of up to 10,000, with perhaps double that at London.* Most were considerably smaller. In the early decades many urban inhabitants were probably merchants, craftspeople and manufacturers following in the wake of the army — particularly in the settlements, or *vici*, which sprang up outside military bases to provide troops who were oversexed, overpaid and over here with drink, girls and fast food. Most unofficial towns, such as Chesterton (Durobrivae), grew organically, with no formal planning or imperial promotion; and towns were not initially popular with the country-dwelling rural aristocracy.

London recovered quickly from the disaster of AD 60–61 through a combination of official support and sheer economic energy. On elevated ground at a crossing point of the tidal Thames, the city rapidly overtook Camulodunum and Rutupiae (Richborough) as the gateway to southern Britain. The site of London straddled the boundary between several British tribes and there seems to have been no major pre-Roman

* The excavations at No. 1 Poultry revealed a densely populated town, reaching an estimated 10,000 population by the end of the first century and doubling thereafter.

settlement there. However, a wooden drain under an east–west street with a tree-ring date of AD 47 indicates that Londinium came into existence by or before AD 50. Shipping, buoyed in on the tidal Thames, could dock here; the wharves and warehouses attracted traders, shopkeepers and small-scale manufacturers both to the north bank and to the new thriving settlement on the dry island of Southwark.

The presence of Classicianus's tomb – the diplomatic procurator who calmed things down after the Boudiccan rising – shows that London was probably already the provincial capital. The next four decades were a period of rapid development. Impressive new buildings appeared for the first time in the city: the *basilica*, or court, the governor's palace, public baths at Cheapside and Huggin Hill, a fort for the governor's military garrison in the north-west corner of the town and a wooden amphitheatre nearby at the modern Guildhall site. The amphitheatre was remodelled on a grander scale in the early second century – perhaps about the time of the Emperor Hadrian's visit in AD 122. The retaining wall of the arena was rebuilt in Kentish ragstone and tile to a height of about 2.5 metres, enough to keep the spectators safe from the entertainment – wild animals and gladiators – in the arena. The capacity of London's second-century amphitheatre was about 6,000, so a large proportion of Londoners could attend their earliest and bloodiest sporting arena.

Thanks to a recent discovery, we know for certain that the occupants of Roman London were from the beginning a mixed bunch and known in Latin as 'Londinienses' – Londoners. The word was inscribed on a small, broken plaque found in Southwark. The text reads:

NUM[INIBUS] AUGG
DEO MARTI CAMULO
TIBERINIUS CELERIANUS
C[IVIS] BELL[OVACUS]
MORITIX
LONDINIENSIUM
… [PRI]MUS …

['To the Powers of the Emperors
And to the God Mars Camulus
Tiberinius Celerianus
A citizen of the Bellovaci
Moritix (a rare Gallic title which might mean a 'sea captain')
Of the Londoners.']

This Tiberinius presumably lived in London but was a citizen of the Bellovaci tribe from the region north of Paris. As a Romanised Gaul he dedicates his inscription both to the deified emperors and to Mars Camulus – the classical and Celtic war gods combined.* The fact that the inscription refers to 'Londoners' – the people rather than the place – suggests that London was not a chartered town with its own *ordo* or council. It may, however, have been an imperial domain under the control of the emperor.[22]

The names of several hundred Roman Londoners are known from inscriptions, tombstones, graffiti and letters. Some were certainly slaves, like Amencletus, who dedicated an elaborate and expensive tombstone to his wife Claudia Martina, who died at the age of nineteen. He refers to himself as a 'slave of the province', a job most probably connected with the governor's office, with responsibility for helping to organise the cult of emperor worship. His name is Greek and means 'Irreproachable', but slave bureaucrats, like teachers, frequently had Greek names regardless of their origins. Judging from his job (and the fine tombstone), Amencletus was a rather superior slave; and his wife was a free woman and a Roman citizen.

Our modern image of slavery is defined by the harsh treatment and lifelong status of plantation slaves in the southern states of America and the West Indies. In the Roman world slavery was a universal but complex institution. Certainly in the mines, the fields and the arena slaves often led brutally short lives. Some slaves, though, both male and female, exploited their education, training, natural abilities and attractiveness to undertake important jobs, to buy their freedom by a relatively young age, or to marry their owners. Slaves were nevertheless regarded as property and London must have had a slave market. A business letter from a certain Rufus implies as much. He addresses the letter to Epillicus (a British name) and instructs him to make sure 'to turn that girl into cash'.†

The ambiguity of servile status in the Roman world is emphasised by a remarkable discovery made in 1994 at the No. 1 Poultry site: the first deed of sale of a slave to be found in Britain. Written coldly in legalistic Latin on a wooden tablet of silver fir (*Abies alba*) the document states:

> Vegetus, assistant slave of Montanus the slave of the August Emperor and sometime assistant slave of Secundus, has bought and received by *mancipium* the girl Fortunata, or by whatever name she is known, by nationality a Diablintian, from Albicianus [...] for six hundred denarii. And that the

---

* Camulus's name appears in Camulodunum (Colchester) – 'The Fortress of Camulus'.
† These lines were written in Latin on a wooden tablet found in the Walbrook – *diligenter cura[m] agas ut illam puellam ad nummum redigas* – translated by Professor Ian Richmond.

girl in question is transferred in good health, that she is
warranted not to be liable to wander or run away, but that if
anyone lays claim to the girl in question or to any share in
her, [...] in the wax tablet which he has written and sworn
by the genius of the Emperor Caesar [...].

So we have here what Dr Tomlin, the translator, terms the 'logbook' of a human being. A slave girl named Fortunata was sold to Vegetus, himself both a slave and an imperial official. She was a Gaul, from the tribe of the Diablintes, who lived north of the River Loire, around modern Mayenne.* She was sold for 600 denarii, a substantial price and the equivalent of one and a half years' salary for a legionary.† Fortunata's age is not specified, but at that price she was probably a young woman being sold into domestic service or destined to become Vegetus's concubine.

It may come as a surprise to modern readers to realise that the purchaser, Vegetus, was himself a slave, and assistant to another slave, Montanus. Both of them belonged to the emperor (not named, but probably Domitian or Trajan) and were officials in the imperial household. In other words, they were the equivalent of civil servants in the Roman Treasury or managers of the imperial estate. Vegetus and Montanus are also the first imperial slaves to be specfically named in Britain. Although Vegetus was himself a chattel of the emperor and not a Roman citizen, he was clearly richer and more influential than most other people in Roman Britain. But while he could purchase Fortunata for his own use, technically she belonged to the emperor.

Either or both of these slaves, who briefly enter the illuminated stage of history, might ultimately have purchased their freedom – or been granted it in an emperor's will. The diverse relationships in the multicultural society of later first- and second-century Britain are most clearly illustrated in the remarkable tombstones of a married couple, Regina and Barates. Barates was from Palmyra, the magnificent Syrian caravanserai whose traders imported luxury goods into the empire from the Persian Gulf and India. Barates himself was in the business of dealing in flags and ensigns for the army, a business that presumably thrived where troops were concentrated along the northern frontier. He set up a very fine and expensive tomb at South Shields to 'Regina, the freedwoman of Barates, alas!' The inscription on her tombstone tells us that she was his freedwoman, wife, and a Catuvellaunian by nation, who died at the age of

---

* Their tribal captial was Noviodunum, modern Jublains.
† There is only limited evidence of Roman slave prices, e.g. a six-year-old girl in Dacia in AD 139 cost 205 denarii; 600 denarii is at the top end of the known range.[23]

thirty. So this well-off Syrian merchant had married a woman whose origins were in the St Albans area, a member of the tribe who had led the resistance to the Roman invasion and one who for some reason had been enslaved and then freed.

Barates wanted us to know that his wife lived in some style. On the tombstone she appears well dressed, wearing fine jewellery, a British torc, or ring, around her neck; she has a substantial jewellery box and an overflowing basket of food. Regina is the first British trophy wife. How much older Barates was we do not know, but according to his tombsone he died at the age of sixty-eight.

From evidence across the empire we know that most freed slaves were women, many like Regina marrying their masters. Slavery existed in Britain before the arrival of the Romans,* but in the Roman Empire it was institutionalised and taken for granted. Philosophers rationalised that no one was free, so slavery was just a matter of degree. Certainly it was fundamental to the imperial economic system, fed by generations of con-quest.† In Italy this was reflected in the growth of huge rural estates, or latifundia, on which slaves provided the majority of the labour force. The extent to which the rural economy of Britain was slave-driven is much less certain. Presumably the large villa estates, which expanded substan-tially in the later third and fourth centuries, utilised slaves classed as 'a speaking tool' (*'instrumentum vocale'*) in the words of Varro, the Roman writer on agriculture; but we have no evidence of numbers, and the only slave in the entire Roman Empire whose own words have survived was the well-off son of a Romano-British estate owner, captured by raiders at his home and shipped to Ireland to work as an enslaved shepherd. The experience of Patricius, or St Patrick, as we now know him, is a reminder that even in the less Romanised parts of the British Isles slaves were a valuable commodity.

Recently we discovered one of the most exotic characters ever found in Roman Britain. A body, buried in the cemetery of the rough frontier supply town of Catterick, appeared to be a woman. The skeleton was

---

* Julius Caesar implies that the majority of Britons were of almost servile status, but this is probably an exaggeration. Strabo lists slaves among British exports and there were slave chains amongst the cult offerings found in the bog at Llyn Cerrig Bach (Anglesey).

† For two centuries Rome mobilised more of its adult male citizens, a greater sustained effort of militarisation, than any other ancient state. The result was disastrous for small Italian farmers. Many were recruited and died in the service of the state; others were pushed off their land by wealthy magnates with slave muscle to exploit. Slave raiding in Britain may have been stimu-lated by the increasing demand for Roman luxury goods among native elites. Diodorus Siculus reported that 'Italian merchants regarded the Gauls' taste for wine as a godsend. They take the wine to them by ship up the navigable rivers ... and it fetches fantastic prices' – a slave for a sin-gle amphora of wine.[24]

decked in elaborate jet jewellery. Closer inspection, however, revealed 'her' to be a young man. The most likely explanation is that he was a priest of the oriental cult of Cybele – a fertility goddess who required her male servants to suffer castration and then dress as women.

Roman Britain was a multi-cultural place with an exotic mixture of peoples and religions. On Hadrian's Wall and in London the Persian cult of Mithras the bull slayer thrived among soldiers and traders. This mystery religion, which emphasised the contrasts of light and dark, good and evil, appealed to men with its secretive, Masonic ways. Another oriental cult attracted a wider constituency. Christianity cultivated women and the urban poor. By the fourth century, and once the Emperor Constantine had given his official approval, Christianity took hold in towns such as Silchester, London and Cirencester – and among better-off villa owners like St Patrick's family. At the Lullingstone villa (in Kent) the family established a chapel in an upstairs room complete with wall paintings showing themselves at prayer. In the Hinton St Mary villa (in Dorset) the owner even included an image of Christ (looking rather like a square-jawed Hollywood idol) in their mosaic floor. The majority of country dwellers (*pagani*) were conservative about religion. They stuck to the old ways.

Although urban centres took root with varying degrees of vigour across much of Britain in the period of Roman occupation, the vast majority of the population – probably 90 per cent or more – were peasant farmers. In many parts of Britain, particularly in the north and west, the traditional ways of life changed relatively little. But the tribal elites, who controlled the most productive farmland, increasingly reflected their status and their cultural and political allegiance to the empire in new forms of architecture. From the later first century they began to move into that most desirable of residences, the Romanised villa. The first, and one of the most impressive, of these buildings was the magnificent, palatial establishment at Fishbourne, built in the AD 60s and remodelled on a more magnificent scale a decade later. Here foreign masons, craftsmen and gardeners constructed a residence like no other seen in Britain; it would not have been out of place among the seaside palaces of Rome's magnates around the Bay of Naples. Fishbourne lay 3 kilometres west of the new town at Chichester – Noviomagus ('New Market'). Close to the sea a guild of metalworkers – '*collegium fabrorum*' – dedicated a temple to Neptune and Minerva, guardians of sea and land, at their own expense. Their gift was authorised by Tiberius Claudius Togidumnus, 'King and Legate of Augustus in Britain', or '*Rex magnus Britanniae*' – 'the great King of Britain' – according to the inscription set up to record the event.

Togidumnus was probably the successsor of Verica as ruler of the

Atrebatic kingdom around modern West Sussex, Hampshire and even as far as Bath. As a favoured client king (his Atrebatic people were now renamed the 'Regni' — 'People of the King') his territory was rapidly favoured with the trappings of Roman civilisation. The benefits of co-operation with the new imperial power were visible to all in bricks and mortar, in marble and mosaics. A string of smaller luxury villas appeared on the south coast at this time, at Angmering, Southwick, Pulborough and Bosham,* probably belonging to other co-operative tribal notables, such as Tiberius Claudius Catuarus, who lost an inscribed gold ring at Fishbourne.

These buildings were alien transplants. However, in the later first and second centuries Romanised farmhouses built of stone, tile and mortar sprang up in the Chilterns around Verulamium, Essex, Kent and in the Cotswolds — desirable residences for the British tribal elites and probably a minority for Roman officials. The distribution of these solid farm-houses, at their peak between AD 270 and 350, indicates the high-water mark of Romanised influence in Britain. Some of the richest, in Somer-set and Gloucestershire, with underfloor heating systems, bathhouses and mosaic pavements, provided a level of comfort not seen again in the domestic architecture of Britain until the nineteenth century. Large entrance halls, spectacular dining rooms and private quarters linked by corridors reflect both the public role of their owners as rural gentry and estate owners and the increasing importance of privacy and social differentiation. But Romano-British villas, of which about a thousand are known, range from the palatial, such as Woodchester and Chedworth (Gloucestershire), to more modest, workaday farmhouses. By the fourth century they were all, however, the centres of working estates. Unfortun-ately we have no documentary evidence to tell us about their ownership, value, productivity, or the size of their landholdings.

Recent archaeological excavations have produced detailed biological evidence which throws light on production and consumption in these villas. Clearly new crops and foodstuffs appeared in Britain and new technologies. Hay meadows appeared for the first time, giving greater control over animal feed, and with them large iron scythes such as those found at the Barnsley Park villa (Gloucestershire), Great Chesterford (Essex) and Farmoor (Oxfordshire). New breeds of sheep required shearing rather than plucking and shears become a common tool of the Romano-British farmers. There was an enormous increase in the supply

---

* This villa was made of stone brought from near Paris and lay close to the church from where, a millennium later, Harold Godwinson departed for Normandy on a trip which led to another invasion of Britain.

of iron generally — nails, brackets, hinges, locks, keys, knives and saws appear in hugely greater quantities on these farmsteads than on earlier Iron Age farms.

The staple crops of the Iron Age: spelt wheat (*Triticum spelta*) and emmer — hardy and adapted to the damp climate — continued to be cultivated along with breadwheat (*Triticum aestivum*) and clubwheat (*Triticum compactum*). Oats and two-rowed barley remained the principal fodder crops. With the Roman army and traders came more diverse Mediterranean plants, which must have brought increased variety to the British diet — particularly herbs such as coriander, cumin, fennel, dill, rosemary and opium poppy. Most farmsteads and gardens in Roman Britain grew these. More exotic spices were imported. At Vindolanda a soldier called Gambex paid two denarii for an order of pepper, which could have made the journey across the Indian Ocean from Calicut to the Red Sea port of Berenice. The taste for olive oil became more widespread and was principally supplied from the Guadalquivir valley until in the third century the Spanish trade, interrupted by barbarian incursions, was replaced by North African supplies. Spain and North Africa were also major suppliers of *liquamen* and *garum*, sauces produced from fermented fish mixed with salt to produced an intense flavour, rather like Worcestershire sauce, which is made from anchovies. A recently discovered pottery container from Carlisle was labelled as best-quality sauce from North Africa. A Spanish amphora found in Gloucester had 'G.IIIIC' painted on the neck, meaning four *congii* (13.13 litres) of *garum*. Another at the No. 1 Poultry excavations in London contained '80 measures of fish sauce made from best quality tuna matured for two years'. This came from Cadiz. A Southwark amphora had the 'finest fish sauce from Antipolis' (Antibes, in the south of France, where you can still find the best, and most expensive, bouillabaisse in the world).

As the British developed a taste for Mediterranean food, they also used new pottery vessels in the kitchen, such as *mortaria*, or bowls with abrasive grits in the base, which are ideal for grinding spices and making sauces. Early *mortaria* manufacturers, such as Sollus at Brockley Hill, on the road from London to Verulamium, stamped their wares with their names.* Many of these literate potters were probably immigrants from Gaul taking advantage of the expanding Roman market. Other distinctive

---

* The names of about 250 potters working in Roman Britain are known, mostly manufacturers of first- and second-century *mortaria*. A few, like Caius Attius Marinus, had the *tria nomina* (three names) of a Roman citizen. He worked in Camulodunum and then moved to Radlett, in Hertfordshire. Some, like Malliacus and Vediacus, had Celtic names; and Tamesubugus, working near Oxford, took his name from the nearby Thames.

pots – such as the lidded casseroles found in northern Britain, for example in Carlisle, which were used by North African troops – are clues to new immigrants. They retained a taste for the slow-cooked stews of their homelands; but their cuisine did not spread among the natives.

Some Mediterranean products, such as olives, could not thrive in the British climate and had to be imported. There is, though, evidence for the cultivation of vines, albeit on a small scale. Vine trenches, supports and pollen turned up on a farm at Wollaston (Nottinghamshire) and potters made amphora at Brockley Hill (Middlesex) for retsina produced in the Verulamium area. Local production was probably minor compared with the cargoes carried by Roman ships into the bustling port of London.*

Most Brits probably preferred beer, judging from the vast numbers of quart vessels which litter their settlements and the many malting kilns found on farmsteads. And it was good stuff: when the Emperor Diocletian attempted to establish price controls across the empire, in AD 301, his edict priced British beer at four denarii a pint – twice as much as Egyptian beer.

While no population or census statistics survive from Roman Britain, the archaeological evidence indicates an expanding population and increasing exploitation of available land. Even in southern Britain there were areas where Romanised villas were few and far betweeen and peasant farmsteads predominated. In the fenlands, along the Severn estuary, on the low-lying ground of the upper Thames valley, and the Solway Plain – the trend to drain wet fertile soils, which began in the Iron Age as the climate improved, continued. Factors such as population increase, tax demands by the empire and the growth of the consumer market encouraged farmers to dig hundreds of kilometres of drainage ditches to increase productivity. Peasants could acquire new land by clearing upland forest: pollen diagrams reflect the decrease of woodland through the Roman period and deposits of alluvium (flood silts) in the major river valleys show that soils now exposed and ploughed were eroding from the river catchment areas. Some areas were more highly populated than today: on Salisbury Plain there is a remarkable survival (thanks to the presence of the army and the absence of arable farming) of Romano-British village earthworks linked by networks of lanes.†

From aerial photography and geophysical surveys it is literally possible

* The *Madrague de Giens* wreck, a routine cargo vessel, which sank off the south of France, carried 6,000 amphorae holding 144,000 litres of wine.
† The Salisbury Plain military training area is one of the best-preserved stretches of countryside to be found anywhere in the Roman Empire. It is literally possible to walk along hollow lanes, from the prominent earthworks of one village, such as Chisenbury Warren, to another. See D. McOmish et al. (2002).

to draw plans of the Romano-British countryside, in the Fens of Cambridgeshire and Lincolnshire and in the Vale of Pickering, in York-shire, as detailed as a modern Ordnance Survey map. The sheer scale of land use and settlement reveals a countryside with a higher density of people than exists today. These peasant villages, such as Chisenbury Warren (Wiltshire), sprang up from the second century. Similar earth-works have now almost entirely disappeared in the Fens as a result of modern arable farming. When fenland peasants raised their eyes to the skyline, they would have seen a towering Roman building dominating the flatlands, as Ely Cathedral does today. This structure, at Stonea Grange, may have been the headquarters of the imperial estate for which these peasants laboured.

We know most about occupation in river valleys such as the Thames and the Nene, where large-scale excavations have preceded gravel extrac-tion. At Claydon Pike (Gloucestershire), east of Corinium, military engin-eers laid out a network of minor roads along the valley floor which linked new nucleated, rural settlements. British ranchers had exploited this area for at least three centuries, but now their scattered farmsteads were aban-doned. At Claydon Pike, at a crossroads, the authorities built two large aisled barn-like buildings unlike anything ever seen before in the British countryside. These were set up inside a gated compound, alongside a shrine, in the later first century. Around these the existing native fields and drainage ditches were re-aligned and quickset hedges planted. Before, the native herders had allowed their cattle to wander and to over-graze the pasture. Now, animals were excluded from the fields, which instead produced hay. Soldiers did more than fight. Here the presence of military equipment, high-value coinage, glassware and an unusually large number of Spanish amphorae suggests that they policed this productive estate. Perhaps the land was a military pasture (*prata*) where they raised fodder, bred animals and produced hides for military use. Alternatively, the soldiers could have been protecting a tax-collection depot – a collect-ing point for agricultural products requisitioned from the local commu-nity. At any rate, by the fourth century the land had been sold back to the locals. They lived in a small villa surrounded by box hedges and the pas-ture had become a mixed farm growing cereals and flax. The family were probably local Dobunni and they were buried in a nearby cemetery, where some of them were decapitated after death in the native manner.

In another area which has been investigated in detail, the Nene valley around Wellingborough and Peterborough, land is densely occupied with villas, villages and pottery production centres.* Villas such as those at Redlands Farm and Raunds have typical Romanised buildings but they also retain stone-based roundhouses, the native vernacular form of build-ing which persists even in this highly Romanised area.

In the north and west traditional small-scale pastoral communities were relatively immune to the blandishments of Roman civilisation. There was enormous regional variation of settlement in Cornwall, Wales, the uplands of northern England and Scotland. Here people remained firmly native in character and Roman-style objects – coins or ceramics – are a rarity. In the Yorkshire Dales stone-walled field systems show that large areas were systematically exploited in the Roman period, but between the Roman forts the natives lived in small-scale farmsteads of round-houses and walled compounds. For those of us accustomed to excava-tions of vast quantities of Roman artefacts in the south, their material poverty comes as a surprise. Once, when I visited the excavation of one such farmstead at Reeth, in Swaledale (Yorkshire), a digger excitedly brought a worn sherd of pottery to Professor Andrew Fleming, the site director. Andrew showed it to me and asked: 'Do you think it's Roman?' 'What do your Roman pottery fabrics look like?' I enquired. 'I don't know,' he said: 'that's our first piece of pottery.'

Similarly, in areas such as Cornwall surveys of enclosed native farm-steads, so-called 'rounds', show a remarkable density of sites occupied between the second century BC and the fifth century AD. These indicate an increasing level of population, particularly in the second to fourth cen-turies, even in those areas that remained British in character. Recent surveys have revealed as many as two 'rounds' per square kilometre on the most fertile lowland and there are an estimated 1,000 rounds in Cornwall.†[26]

It used to be assumed that the population of Roman Britain was rela-tively small at about one million. It is now clear from the sheer density of settlement found by aerial survey and during modern development, that this is too conservative an estimate.‡ The population was, arguably, at least similar to that of the early Norman period or even comparable to the peak prior to the Black Death.

* Villas could have industrial as well as agricultural functions: iron working, salt and pottery manufacture, as well as fish farming and horticulture.[25]

† The location of these rounds can sometimes be determined by place names which incorpo-rate the words 'ker' or 'dyn' meaning 'fort' in old Cornish. At Trethurg Round, near St Austell, the best-excavated and -published of these sites, the enclosure contained roundhouses and a large elongated oval building – another example of local British vernacular architecture. There may have been as many as sixty people living in this round at its peak in the second to fourth centuries, but population densities are based on very speculative figures for the occupancy of floor areas.

‡ About one settlement per square kilometre observed in the Lincolnshire Fens and four times that in the Nene valley, similar to the upper Thames, Solway Plain and East Lothian.

One calculation breaks down the population as follows:[27]

Site types	Total population estimate
Major towns (25)	120,000
Small towns (80)	200,000
Army (at its peak)	60,000
People in *vici* attached to forts	40,000
Countryside	2 million
Total	2.5 million

Other estimates are higher – for example, a total of 3.6 million, assuming 3.3 million in the countryside.[28] Because of the lack of dating evidence, estimates for Scotland and Ireland are even more difficult, but figures of 250,000 and 500,000 respectively are not unreasonable. The vast majority of these people were natives whose ancestors had lived in Britain for millennia. Perhaps between 100,000 and 200,000 people in Britain were soldiers, administrators, merchants, slaves and craftsmen from the rest of the empire.

These figures can be taken as rough estimates. We do, however, have more specific forensic evidence for Roman Britons – in the form of their burials – than for any earlier period. This is because burial grounds were systematically and predictably placed outside towns alongside the main roads and close to villas and villages. A recent survey[29] analysed 5,716 individuals from fifty-two Romano-British sites, an almost tenfold increase in comparison with scarce Iron Age human remains.* The average height of Roman Britons in this sample was 1.69 metres (5 feet 5 inches) for men, and 1.59 metres (5 feet 2 inches) for females. Skeletal evidence suggests that most of the population was reasonably well fed. In fact richer diets may have increased problems for a minority, as gout appears in Cirencester, along with dental disease and DISH (a bone disease exacerbated by a richer diet).

New infections in Britain include leprosy, tuberculosis, gout and rheumatoid arthritis. Roman towns had relatively good water supplies and sanitary facilities compared with those of medieval and early modern Britons. Nevertheless, evidence from York and London shows densely crowded and often filthy conditions in urban backstreets in which rats, parasites and infectious diseases could flourish. Most infectious diseases that kill people leave no evidence on the skeleton. Similarly we have little accurate information about the average age at death, though it is clear that infants were highly vulnerable, not least to the infanticide which was

---

* Most human remains come from alkaline soils in the south and east. The old rocks of the north and west generate acidic soils in which human bone degenerates.

practised in the Roman world. There is a great deal of evidence that children were loved and cherished, but at the same time babies were also frequently disposed of at birth and buried in some corner of the farmyard or in the cellar.[30]

Some of the best-analysed groups of burials came from the small town of Baldock (Hertfordshire) where, unusually, life-table modelling is possible from the Iron Age through the Roman period.[31] A remarkable drop in the death rate suggests a significant increase in living standards in the Roman period. There is also a leap in population growth. However, a huge increase in the death rate in the second century may reflect the great plague recorded in AD 166. Rises in the mid-third century also coincide with known plagues in AD 251 and 271. But not everyone was equal: the Wallington Road group had a high mortality rate for infants and also young adults of seventeen to thirty; and the expectation of life at birth was surprisingly low at twenty-six years — considerably less than the lowest modern figure at thirty-eight years in Sierra Leone and Guinea (in 1984). In contrast, at the nearby Royston Road cemetery, 478 aged burials showed a life expectancy at birth of forty-one years. These people led relatively long and comfortable lives, while their neighbours, the Wallington Road group, suffered from malnutrition, trauma and stress to their bones. These were people who undertook hard manual work. So we may be looking at agricultural slaves or the lowest level of peasants: people who were overworked, undernourished and vulnerable to public-health crises. Nevertheless, overall the Baldock population rose through the Roman period, as did the population of Britain as a whole.

The Roman occupation of southern Britain lasted from AD 43 to about 410. For those who lived in impressive villas the empire brought relative peace and prosperity; for the majority, though, life consisted of hard work and taxes. Society had never been more stratified, with extremities of wealth and poverty. However, for much of the period improved long-distance and local transport, an international currency, intervals of peace, increased agricultural productivity, improved water supply and a modicum of public health led to increasing population until the later fourth century. By then, however, Roman Britain was in trouble. Across Europe the empire was in a state of military and economic collapse. Coinage dried up, wages went unpaid, industries collapsed, towns decayed, villas fell into a state of disuse, ditches were no longer cleared. Roman Britain was in a state of crisis; the barbarians were at the door.

Four New Tribes, New Kingdoms

ONE FRIDAY AFTERNOON in August 1974 I was excavating a Romano-British farmstead near Abingdon, in Oxfordshire. One of my colleagues, Charlie Chambers, returned from an expedition to a nearby gravel pit at Berinsfield, just north of Dorchester-on-Thames. He had been to investigate some Roman fields, the remains of which were rapidly disappearing into a gravel quarry. We particularly wanted to know if there were any waterlogged biological deposits there that might tell us about the landscape contemporary with our farmstead.

'I've found a Roman well,' Charlie said, 'and there are some human bones on the spoil heap.' Immediately we jumped into our Land Rover and returned to the quarry. When we arrived it was like walking on a pebbly beach. A massive dragline had just stripped the topsoil away, revealing the yellow gravel surface below. Narrow, dark, rectangular marks were clearly visible, scattered across the gravel — the outlines, familiar to any archaeologist, of human graves.

I knelt down on the nearest one and cleaned over the surface with my trowel. Immediately the blade caught on something hard and metallic. It only took a few moments to reveal the pyramidal shape of an iron boss, the centrepiece of a circular wooden shield — a type classified by archaeologists as early Anglo-Saxon, dating to about AD 500. Under it would, almost certainly, be the skeleton of an adult male.

Over the next three weeks a team of forty people — professional archaeologists, local volunteers and students from Oxford — worked almost every hour of daylight to uncover the burials of 118 individuals, mostly inhumations, or bodies laid in graves, but also four cremations placed in hand-made pots.

These people were distinctive in death. Many of the men and boys over about twelve were buried with long iron-tipped spears, knives and circular shields of lime wood, with heavy iron bosses of the kind that I had found in the first moments on the site. Some of the women wore swags of amber and glass beads, suspended between gilded saucer brooches that pinned their woollen dresses at the shoulder.[1]

The richest burial was of a young woman (in Grave 102). In life she had suffered from a painful abscess on the left side of her mouth and so chewed on the right. Any archaeologist knows that if modern life has one blessing, it is dentistry. When her relatives had placed the young woman in her grave, they had covered the body with rushes, probably cut from the banks of the nearby River Thame. She had worn a woollen dress and been wrapped in a heavier woollen cloak. A linen shroud had covered her face. All this could be detected from forensic evidence: slight fragments of textiles mineralised where they came into contact with metal.

Her jewellery marked her as a young native woman of the Gewisse, the West Saxon tribal group that occupied the upper Thames valley from the late fifth century.* The two large saucer brooches were typical badges of identity, worn by Gewissan women in the later sixth century; cast in bronze, decorated with an abstract central sun symbol, then gilded. Around her waist a belt, long since rotted away, had been held by a heavy copper-alloy buckle, typically Frankish in style and more often worn by women in Kent around 550–600. The great square-headed brooch on her left shoulder was very distinctive, decorated with stylised male heads with pointed beards, stylised human masks and biting animal heads. The prototypes of such brooches are found in Scandinavia and the closest parallel in Britain is from an grave in Alfriston, Sussex.

The swags of amber beads covering the girl's chest probably came from Scandinavia directly. Amber was found on the shores of the Baltic and traded into Britain. The beads were not merely decorative: their warm orange colour and magnetic properties when rubbed probably marked amber out as a curative material with magical properties suitable for amulets. In a harsh world of primitive medicine the girl in Grave 102 needed all the help she could get. And that was not much: she had died at the age of about eighteen.

Conventionally we refer to the people buried in cemeteries like Berinsfield as Anglo-Saxon. Their grave goods, style of dress, weapons, pottery and the settlements they lived in mark them as culturally different from the people who inhabited southern and eastern England under Roman rule. If their fifth-to-seventh-century cemeteries are plotted on a map of Britain, they clearly congregate in the lowland zone of Britannia.

Our young Berinsfield woman wears an amalgamation of Germanic

---

* Bede refers to the 'Gewisse' in about AD 620 and later calls them 'West Saxons'. Their name probably derives from the adjective '*gewis*', meaning 'sure' or 'reliable'. John Blair suggests this is a nickname translated as 'The Trusties'.[2]

styles, fused together to create a new English identity. If she could speak, would her words be in Old English – a Germanic language – rather than the Gaelic and Latin used by the townspeople of Roman Dorchester, a century and a half before her death? Were her grandparents German immigrants, or local Britons who had adopted an Anglo-Saxon lifestyle? Certainly she represents a fundamental change that took place in Britain after AD 400 – a change that affected the population, its culture, religion and language. So how had this come about?

Two hundred years before the Berinsfield women died, the Roman province of Britannia prospered, especially during the reign of the Emperor Constantine, whose elevation to power came while he was based in York.* The countryside was productive, villas flourished and the population expanded. But in Continental Europe all was not well.

The western Roman Empire had systematic and deep-seated problems which worsened in the later fourth century. Since Gibbon wrote his magnificent and polemical *Decline and Fall of the Roman Empire* historians have speculated about the reasons for Rome's collapse. Gibbon blamed Christianity; others have put the problem down to vice and corruption, expensive bureaucracy, an army increasingly staffed by foreigners, political instability, desertion of the countryside, peasant revolts, environmental deterioration and increasingly powerful barbarians swarming across the frontiers. Some or all of these could be parts of the cause. Like the collapse of the USSR, in our own lifetime, empires crumble for complex reasons, which do not develop overnight and can be difficult to observe. Collapse can be sudden and unpredictable. In the mid-fourth century Britannia temporarily benefited from her relative stability and distance from the Continent's problems. We know, for example, that British products were exported to mainland Europe, as in AD 359 the Emperor Julian sent 600 ships to requisition British supplies for his pressured garrison in the Rhineland. There is also some evidence that wealthy Gauls migrated to Britain to escape the troubles.† But Britain could not avoid the fundamental problems for long. The Roman Empire, with its wealthy houses, hoards of silverware and bullion, rich temples and agricultural estates, provided a magnet for the expanding populations of barbarians beyond its frontiers. If tribal leaders needed to supply their warrior retinues with treasure and feasting, and feed their burgeoning communities the target was obvious.

According to the historian Ammianus Marcellinus, by AD 364 raiding

* It is unlikely, though, that his mother, Helena, was British, as is sometimes claimed.
† There are villas with Gallic architectural elements in the Cotswolds and dedications to Gallic deities such as Mars Thincsus.

on Britain was becoming endemic, as Saxons in the east, the Irish in the west and the Picts from the north battered the island. This culminated, in June 367, with the event known to the Romans as the *barbarica conspiratorio* — 'the barbarian conspiracy' — when Picti, Scotti and Attacotti from Ireland combined together to deliver a concerted blow against Britannia while the Saxons hit the Continental mainland.* We do not know by what diplomatic means or language (Latin?) these tribes communicated. However, they did seem to have a remarkable awareness of Rome's frailty. They launched their big push when the Emperor Valentinus lay on his sickbed in Trier, and the administration of the western empire was in a shambles. The barbarians overran the countryside, looting villas and villages. They killed Nectaridus, the commander of Britain's Saxon shore defences and left Fullofaudes, the commander in the north, stranded in their wake. Only the defended towns of Roman Britain, with their powerful walls, were able to hold the looters at bay.

The authorities repaired the extensive damage and in reaction built watchtowers on the north-east coast to flash warnings of attack. Clearly trouble came from the sea. New forts also guarded the west coast at Cardiff and Lancaster, supplementing similar ones that already existed in the east. These were known as the 'forts of the Saxon shore', part of a defence system which ran from the east coast around to Porchester, in Hampshire, a clear indication of where the authorities believed the problem to lie. As well as fortifications on land the Roman authorities also had their fleet, the *classis Britannica*, routinely patrolling this coast. As there is no evidence of Saxons living on Britain's east coast, it is most likely that the name 'Saxon shore' indicates Germanic pirates, proto-Vikings, who constantly probed for weakness with seasonal raids along the coast. Ammianus tells us the Britons were now 'dancing for joy'. Too soon: the Saxons had not gone away for good.

Piracy, raiding and trading had a long tradition among the tribes of maritime northern Europe. The Vikings in the eighth century are the historical headline-grabbers, but for centuries Germanic and Scandinavian

---

* Ammianus refers to two tribes of Picti, the Dicalydonas and Verturiones. The Attacotti appear to be linked with the Scotti in Ireland. St Jerome portrays them as barbaric pagans incarnate, indulging in multiple marriages and cannibalism. St Jerome writes: 'I, myself, as a young man in Gaul saw that the Attacotti, a British tribe, eat human flesh, and, even though throughout the woods they might find herds of swine and oxen and cattle, it is their custom to cut off the buttocks of the herdsmen and their wives, their breasts too, and to judge these alone as culinary delicacies.' Jerome was in Gaul about AD 370, at the time of Attacotti raids, but there is some doubt about the reliability of his account. Ammianus may also have exaggerated the seriousness of the barbarian conspiracy, as it was the contemporary emperor's father, Count Theodosius, who was responsible for mopping up the problems. By the late fourth century units of Attacotti are recorded serving in the Roman army.[3]

people had been taking to the seas to the consternation of their neighbours. One of the earliest records of Germanic maritime ability relates to the Usipi, a Rhenish tribe recruited into Agricola's army in western Britain. In AD 83 this cohort rebelled, seized three galleys and sailed them around the north of Scotland, down the east coast and across the North Sea in an attempt to reach home. Unfortunately for the Usipi, they fell into the hands of the Frisians, who sold them into slavery. However, they have gone down in history as the first recorded circumnavigators of Great Britain, and the first Germanic recruits in Britain to betray their paymasters.

The investment in new coastal defences shows that around AD 370 Rome did not intend to abandon Britannia. As a productive land rich in crops, animals, metals and men the province was still valued. Not all Britons supported the empire in its ambition to retain the province. Besides the hostile Irish, Caledonians and Picts, some well-to-do British citizens also sought their independence, according to the Greek historian Zosimus. Rome was no longer the overwhelming power it had been and some Britons did not take kindly to decision-making from the Continent. Britannia had traditionally retained a large Roman army, but now the forces began to fragment as troops were withdrawn for expeditions into Europe to counter barbarian attacks or support rivals for the imperial throne. In Britain some of the forts, such as Birdoswald on Hadrian's Wall, began to look less like disciplined military garrisons and more like villages. These outposts became isolated. The troops set themselves up as private armies to protect their own patch at a price. In such unstable times local warlords appeared, such as Vortigern, whose name in Gaelic means 'Mighty King' — tough leaders who took the initiative for their own defence, and no doubt enforced payment and drafted recruits, willing and unwilling, from their own communities.

So who were the enemy? In Rome they were already in the streets. Alaric and his Gothic army of turncoats sacked the city in AD 410. Only six years earlier these Goths had been the strong right arm of the Roman Emperor Theodosius. In Bethlehem St Jerome put into words the feeling of a generation: 'When the brightest light on the whole earth was extinguished, when the Roman Empire was deprived of its head, when ... the whole world perished in one city, then I was dumb with silence.'

Other Germanic tribes — the Alans, Vandals and Sueves — had piled against the Rhine frontier pressured by nomadic Huns moving westwards out of the Asiatic steppes.* As the Rhine froze in December AD

---

* The age of migrations did not only impact in the west. Other tribes of Huns moved against the Chinese Empire. Changing climate may also have been a factor in central Asia.

406, this cold mass of displaced people drifted across the ice bridge into the relative haven of the empire. In the following year the Vandals moved through Spain and into North Africa. Because of these movements of people historians often refer to this era as the 'Migration Period'.

In spite of the shock Rome, under its final emperors, tottered on for another sixty-six years, but it was in no position to influence events in Britain. The year AD 410 is traditionally seen as the end of Roman Britain. An imperial edict of Honorius in that year instructs a number of places to defend themselves. 'Brettia' is usually assumed to be Britain. However, the other places mentioned in the edict are all Italian towns and 'Brettia' may well be Bruttium, in southern Italy. This makes sense. Following their away victory in Rome the Goths headed south, drawn by the wealth of Italy and the rich pickings in Africa across the stepping stone of Sicily.

The centre of imperial power shifted eastwards to Constantinople and Britain was left out in the cold. Contemporary written sources for Britain are scanty − a few Roman and Greek authors and chroniclers provide bald accounts and passing references to this remote area of the old empire. Because written accounts, and other evidence, were thought to be thin, historians have also labelled this time as the 'Dark Ages'. Increasingly, though, archaeology is shedding light on the period, a fascinating time of enormous change and diversity and not simply an unfortunate gap between the classical and medieval worlds. And there are some written sources. Around AD 540 to 550 (or possibly a few decades earlier) a British cleric, Gildas, wrote a tract entitled *The Ruin of Britain* (*De Excidio Britanniae*).[4]

He is the nearest we have to a contemporary voice. And what a voice. Gildas is no reasoned, objective historian. He shrieks in anger and rage from his monkish cell in Wales or the West Country (Dorset is the best guess). His work is a sermon, a lament, a polemic and a fierce denunciation of the moral weakness of British rulers in the face of the barbarian threat. As a history of the fifth century it has its shortcomings − it names only one British person, one place and one date (which is wrong). Although imperial rule was long gone Gildas was well educated in the classical tradition. He wrote in Latin, which he calls '*lingua nostra*' − 'our language'; but it is the sort of language that would not have been approved of in Agricola's first-century schools, or by the schoolmaster who corrected childish texts in Vindolanda: 'As the Romans went back home, there eagerly emerged from the coracles that had carried them across the sea valleys the foul hordes of Scots and Picts, like dark throngs of worms who wriggle out of narrow fissures in the rock ... they were readier to cover their villainous faces with hair than their private parts ... with clothes,' Gildas rants in his typically intemperate style, like a thundering biblical prophet. 'The proud tyrant [probably Vortigern] and his council decided that the ferocious Saxons (name not to be spoken!) hated by man and God should be let into the island like wolves into the fold, to beat back the peoples of the north ... a pack of cubs burst forth like the lair of the barbarian lioness, coming in three keels, as they call warships in their language.' Gildas has an aversion to personal and place names, but he has a bestiary at his command.

Gildas describes a period of slaughter and pillage, but does not imply that the British were erased from the land. Out of the troubles one British leader emerges who is not lashed by the vitriol of Gildas's tongue: Ambrosius Aurelianus, a descendant of good Romano-British stock. Under Ambrosius's leadership the British fought back, culminating in a victory at Mount Badon (possibly in the south-west, near Bath), which temporarily halted the Saxon advance. Gildas tells us that the battle took place in the year of his birth, forty-three years previously. The linear earthwork, the Wansdyke, which can still be seen cutting across Wiltshire, may have been the physical British barrier against the Saxons. In later sources, such as the Welsh chronicler Nennius, the Battle of Badon is associated with Arthur, that betwixt-and-between figure of the Celtic twilight. It is possible that Artos/Arthur – 'The Bear' in Celtic, was the *signum*, or nickname, of Aurelianus himself. A bearskin cloak would have been a distinguishing element of his uniform as a Roman general.

Gildas's sermon was a warning to the petty kings and rulers of western Britain that if they did not mend their ways God would unleash the Saxon hordes once more. His literary and religious models were biblical; and they were later seized upon by Bede, the most important historian of the early English, to justify the actions of his own forefathers – to portray the German migration into a promised land as a replay of Exodus.[5] Bede's English were the new chosen people. Their inevitable destiny was to rule Britain.

Bede (673–735), condemned as 'venerable' to generations of British schoolchildren, was born and brought up in the north-east, in the territory which was given to the monasteries of Jarrow and Monkwearmouth in AD 682. His parents, about whom we know nothing, handed their son, as a seven-year-old, to the care of Abbot Benedict and hence into the new monastery at Jarrow.

Bede spent the rest of his life there. Physically it was a narrow, cloistered existence. He rarely travelled; he was probably a conservative, cautious character, not a leader or an administrator. He loved to teach and read and write: the perfect academic, sitting in his monastic college yet at the centre of an international information network. But he was the first and greatest Anglo-Saxon historian. The title of his most famous work, *The Ecclesiastical History of the English People, (Historia ecclesiastica gentis Anglorum)* may not sound like bedtime reading, but it is, in fact, a vivid portrayal of Anglo-Saxon England, full of memorable stories.[6] Its theme is the conversion of the English by Roman Christians and their ultimate victory over their Celtic brethren and rivals. Like Tacitus, the greatest historian of the first century, Bede works in a Roman tradition; he is always anxious to explain his sources, even and especially if he is sceptical about them; and like Tacitus he has a point of view — in his case that of a Roman Catholic priest and monk living within the kingdom of Northumberland. To Bede it was God's will that his pagan ancestors should be unleashed on the British. Like the Israelites, the Anglo-Saxons wandered through the wilderness to the promised land. Destiny led them to punish the wicked British, who were too slothful to convert their pagan oppressors. Bede was their historian and their spokesman. The English then accepted the word of God, brought by Augustine and his mission from Rome in AD 597 in fulfilment of the prophesy of Isiah 49: 'Listen, O isles, unto me; and hearken, ye people so far.'

The phrase 'economical with the truth' could have been invented to describe Bede's work. British Christians, who had kept the faith alive and converted Ireland and much of the north and west, receive little credit. Bede is Rome's man. He is also a great historian who draws his readers into the world of Saxon kings and their warrior retainers, of monks and peasants, timber feasting halls, blood feuds and fatalism.

Bede is our primary source of information about the origins of his people and why they came to Britain. There is an obsessive interest in the myth of migration, of the pagan forefathers who braved the sea. Almost 470 years after the landing of Julius Caesar, he tells us, Roman rule came to an end in Britain. The garrisons had been led away 'by rash tyrants' and the country lay exposed to attack by 'two savage alien races, the Scots from the west (Ireland) and the Picts from the north'. Bede describes a scene of horror and slaughter followed by starvation, refugees fleeing their homes, chaos and the breakdown of civilisation. The Britons appealed to Rome for help with the famous phrase: 'To Aetius, thrice Consul, come the groans of the Britons ... The barbarians drive us into the sea, and the sea drives us back to the barbarians. Between these, two deadly alternatives confront us, drowning or slaughter.' But, according to Bede, Rome had its own problems with the Huns and plague in the east.

In Britain a respite from Irish and Pictish raids followed by a good harvest only generated dissolute behaviour on the part of the British, who indulged in lying, drunkenness and violence. British Christians even 'threw off the gentle yoke of Christ'. Bede describes a terrible plague which struck 'this corrupt people' and destroyed so many that the living could scarcely bury the dead. Then this 'wicked nation', in attempting to stave off the Scots and Pictish raiders, 'agreed, with the advice of their King Vortigern, to call the assistance of the Saxon peoples across the sea' – a decision ordained by God as a punishment for the British.

In the period after AD 449 three longships of Angles or Saxons, led by Hengist and Horsa, arrived in the east, supposedly to protect the country. Instead they sent word back home that the British were a soft touch and there was lots of fertile land. 'A larger fleet came over with many warriors.' Bede tells us that 'these newcomers were from the three most formidable races of Germany, the Saxons, Angles and Jutes'. From the Jutes are descended the people of Kent, the Isle of Wight and the mainland opposite, who 'are called Jutes to this day'. The East, South and West Saxons (hence Essex, Sussex and Wessex) came from Old Saxony and the Angles from Old Saxony, 'which remains unpopulated to this day'. The East and Middle Angles, Mercians and all the Northumbrian peoples are descended from the Angles. Ordained by God, the Saxon protectors proceeded to pillage and destroy, butchering all before them, enslaving their prisoners, while survivors in desperation fled overseas: 'God's just punishment on the sins of the nation'. Bede took it for granted that his ancestors were Anglo-Saxon and came from the three great tribes or peoples, the Angles, Saxons and Jutes. In a later passage (Book V, chapter 9), he refers to Frisians, Rugians, Danes, Huns, the Boructuari and Old Saxons (but not the Angles or Jutes). Some historians have taken this to mean that these more varied groups also contributed to the Anglo-Saxon melting pot in Britain. However, it is far more likely that Bede was listing pagan inhabitants of Germany in his own time, who were appropriate subjects for missionary activity, not early immigrants into England.

The Bede story of the Saxon arrival, or *adventus*, is clear and certainly vivid. For him this is a version of Noah's flood – sweeping away the unclean so that the kingdom of God could be reborn. As far as he is concerned, the Germanic newcomers are his own ancestors and he speaks their language: English. Bede is an admirable historian, but he is also creating and propagating a national-origin myth. We cannot take the myth at face value. The Anglo-Saxons, themselves then largely illiterate, did not keep objective historical records of their fifth-century activities. The *Anglo-Saxon Chronicle*, first written down in the ninth century on the instructions of King Alfred and on into the years after the Norman Conquest, was principally designed to be a powerful propaganda tool for the royal house of Wessex, to legitimise the ancestry of King Alfred and his successors. The 'arrival' story has all the elements of a myth: three tribes arriving in three boats, led by two men called 'Mare' and 'Horse': Hengist and Horsa. This is the stuff of legend and 'the three ships seem about as historical as the Three Bears'.[7]

So can we penetrate these fragmentary accounts, ideological battle-fields and ancestral myths to understand how the population of Britain changed in this most fundamental of periods from the fifth to the eighth centuries? There are two essential issues: the role and fate of the native British population and the scale and nature of immigration, from Ireland into northern Britain and Wales, from the Continent into Britain and from south-west Britain into Armorica, or north-west France.

In spite of his skill as a historian it is important to remember that Bede was a man of his time, limited by the available evidence, his preconceptions, and influenced by the culture in which he lived. To Bede worthwhile history was written in the context of a hierarchical society of kings, who traced their ancestry back to the god Woden. Monks belonged within their tribe as much as warriors. Like bards in the king's household, they created a history of royal genealogy not an account of the population as a whole. Bede says that in his time there were in Britain 'five languages and four nations – English, British, Scots and Picts. Each of these have their own language, but they are all united in the study of God's truth by the fifth – Latin – which has become a common medium through the study of the scriptures.'

In spite of the impression given in many history books, Pope Gregory and Augustine, in AD 597, were not the first to bring Christianity to Britain. They just had the best story. Bede tells the tale – and it may be no more than a tale concocted in Whitby Abbey to appeal to an Anglo-Saxon audience – that Gregory saw some fair-haired boys for sale in the Roman slave market. He was told that they came from Britain, where people were still ignorant heathens: 'They are called Angles.' 'That is appropriate,' Gregory replied, 'for they have angelic faces.' And their province is Deira (Northumberland – Bede's own). 'Good,' said Gregory. 'They shall indeed be "*de ira*" [saved from wrath] and called to the meaning of Christ.' This is a typical piece of Anglo-Saxon wordplay: to see messages in names. It may be partly because of the 'Angles' pun and his own origins that Bede entitles his nation 'English'; to earlier commentators, the Germanic incomers were usually called 'Saxons'. The Gregory story also serves to play down the significance of British Christians, who during the previous two centuries had developed their own distinctive style of Christianity.

Christianity thrived in the towns and villas of fourth-century Roman Britain, as witnessed by magnificent treasures such as those from Mildenhall and Water Newton. In the fifth century it spread into the British west and north and took hold in the countryside there. In the south-east there is evidence of a Christian community in Verulamium in the early fifth century. The Germanus who came to Verulamium in AD 429 was Bishop of Auxerre and an ex-soldier. He was sent by Pope Celestine to tackle the British ruling group about the touchy subject of heresy, particularly the teachings of Pelagius. Pelagius was probably the most famous Briton of his day, notorious in Rome for his unorthodox views. Pelagius's version of Christianity emphasised the role of the individual. Grace did not simply come from God. Church fathers such as Augustine loathed this 'porridge-eating Briton'. According to Jerome he was like Cerebus guarding the gates of Hell, which naturally were in Britain. Procopius, in Constantinople, keeps up the bad press. Fishermen in Gaul, he reports, row the souls of the dead over to Britain, which is cut in two by a wall. Beyond, the weather is awful and the country full of wild animals. People who go beyond the wall die immediately because the weather is so severe. Germanus's expedition to Verulamium was probably part of a short-lived and unsuccessful strategy to bring Britain back into the western empire and to exert Roman control over the wayward Church.

Carrying the word of God to the Irish barbarians, amazingly, fell to one of these British slaves. Patrick, as his name (Patricius) implies, was an upper-class Briton, abducted at the age of fifteen from his family's villa estate near Bannaventa and dragged off to northern Ireland. Patrick's father (Calporinus) and grandfather (Potitus) were Christian clerics, a deacon and a priest respectively. The whereabouts of Bannaventa is uncertain. Archaeologists often claim that it lay in the south-west; but more likely Patrick's home was somewhere near Carlisle, at the western end of Hadrian's Wall. Remarkably, Patrick wrote two biographical works, the only slave from the ancient world to do such a thing. Even more remarkably, both of Patrick's writings survive. The first, the *Epistola*, or 'Letter', was addressed to the troops of a British chieftain, Corotocus, denouncing them for the massacre of some of Patrick's converts. The second, the *Confessio*, is an account of his life, apparently justifying himself against some unspecified criticism. He tells how, in his youth, he had little time for Christianity. His faith strengthened during his five years in Ireland as a slave, working as a shepherd. Following his escape, Patrick made his way to Gaul, trained as a priest and determined to convert his former captors. This was a remarkably revolutionary idea: to take Christianity to the barbarians. Needless to say, Bede never mentions Patrick.

Patrick's missionary career in north-eastern Ireland probably occupied the last three decades of the fifth century. There are hints of others – early saints such as Auxilius, Ciaran and Declan – working further south, about whom we know next to nothing. We should not, however, believe the story I was told as a child in St Patrick's School, West Vale (Yorkshire): that the conversion of Ireland was a one-man job. Even a dedicated missionary like Patrick would probably have made little impact in an unreceptive society of tough war bands, warrior leaders and petty kings. Significantly, though, the Irish themselves had opened up the channels of communication to Britain. As well as pirate raiders, such as those who captured Patrick, there were others who came to settle: the Deisi of southern Ireland into south-west Wales, north Wales and possibly Cornwall. Ogham inscriptions with Irish personal names testify to their presence. Christianity may well have flowed into Ireland, principally along the routes established by kin and family on both sides of the Irish Sea. This created a fertile breeding ground in which Patrick and his colleagues could flourish.[8]

Patrick writes, apologetically, in Latin. He is self-effacing about his literary abilities and classical education. As this is a commonplace of classically educated gentlemen, we should probably assume the opposite of what he implies. Patrick, Gildas and other members of the western-British elite went to considerable lengths to preserve the Latin language, which, as Bede, stated, became the conduit for Christianity. In a changing world of fragile alliances, weak kings and tyrannical, yet vulnerable, warlords, Christianity provided continuing order in this world and the promise of better things to come in the next; but at the same time as it spread in the north and west, Christianity disappeared in the pagan Anglo-Saxon south-east.

In the west the tribal rulers who emerged in the fifth century created new strongholds, such as Dinas Powys and Castle Dore, Fowey, refortified ancient hill forts at South Cadbury and Congresbury, in Somerset, and established trading posts such as Tintagel, still with maritime links to the Mediterranean world. Distinctive pottery from the east Mediterranean, North Africa and Gaul arrived on these sites, containing wine and oil to lubricate the wheels of loyalty and power. Christianity fostered these links to the exotic Mediterranean world, and assisted tribal rulers to acquire prestige goods and redistribute them as gifts to retainers. Red slip tableware and so-called 'B amphorae' turn up at Tintagel and around the south-west peninsula in relatively large quantities around AD 500; traces also appear in Ireland at the royal site of Clogher, in County Tyrone, and the ring fort of Garranes in County Cork, in Scotland at Dumbarton Rock, the royal stronghold of the Dal Riáta, and the early monastery of Whithorn.[9] The Christian communities of the south-west of England, Wales and the Scillies may have provided the gateway for luxury goods delivered by merchants arriving from the Mediterranean and from Gaul. These potsherds are the physical evidence of the continued movement of people and ideas in the so-called Dark Ages. A sole historical record tells that John the Almoner, pontiff of Alexandria, had a sizeable fleet of ships. One of his vessels, loaded with 20,000 bushels of grain, was driven by storms onto the British coast. There the grain was exchanged for tin (which suggests the crew were in the south-west) and the metal shipped back to Egypt. This is the only historical account of the trading voyages, otherwise identified by potsherds in the half-century after AD 500. There is no account of British links eastwards with the Saxon enemy. Yet eighth-century Saxon coins – *sceattas* – contain up to 8.5 per cent of tin. The most likely source is British Dumnonia.

Around AD 500 Gildas chastises the western British as wicked backsliders, but he takes it for granted they are *Christian* wicked backsliders. Christianity was brought to the southern Picts by the Briton Nynia, better known as Ninian. Sometime in the fifth century he was posted to the see of Whithorn, or Candida Casa (the 'White House'), in Galloway, just across the Solway firth from the Romano-British community which produced Patrick. Ninian was probably another example, like Palladius, of a bishop appointed to a Christian community beyond the old empire, this time exploiting the Irish–Caledonian connection. An inscribed stone of about AD 450 indicates that a man called Latinus founded a church at Whithorn. Bede records Nennius's presence, though only in a couple of sentences, qualified by the phrase 'as they say'. He was not about to blow the trumpet on behalf of British Christians.

Nennius, like Palladius, ministered to a resident Christian community. It is doubtful that he converted the Picts. The revolutionary idea of carrying God's message to pagans was Patrick's – 'a slave in Christ to a foreign people', as he describes himself.

We know little about the Irish Church in the years following Patrick's ministry either from historical or archaeological evidence. There are hints in place names. Names like Donnybrook (Dublin) derive from the Latin *dominicum* – *domnach* in Irish – meaning a church building. The

Latin word in this sense was only current until about AD 600 so presumably indicates an early church site. *Sen chell*, derived from the Latin for 'old church' survives in the name Shankill. The name refers to a church that was old in 670, when lots of new churches were appearing. Along with new churches, Irish Christianity needed schools to teach Latin from scratch to a population unaccustomed to the language. In the heart of the empire schools had existed for centuries; in Ireland they had to be created. The pursuit of learning became an Irish obsession. St Columbanus, who was born about AD 545, devoted himself to his books and became the first Irishman to leave behind a substantial body of writing. His command of Latin was impressive.

Christianity's success in Ireland was not a foregone conclusion. In the Roman world the Church moulded itself into the imperial system. It had a hierarchy of bishops based on *civitates* and the principal provincial towns (Lincoln, Cirencester, York and London in Britain). The Church identified itself with the destiny of Rome. Ireland was tribal, familial and rural – a land of shifting allegiances, no fixed boundaries and no written laws. Thanks to Christianity, Ireland's literary tradition, in Latin and the vernacular, is the finest and most prolific in early medieval Europe, and it is sufficiently detailed to allow us to reconstruct the political geography of Ireland in the seventh and eighth centuries. Though we know little about Irish events while the Romans were in Britain, it is evident that substantial changes had taken place since Ptolemy's time (about AD 100). In the south (Munster) the Iverni, or Erainn, tribe, who gave their name to the island, had given way to a dynasty known as the 'Eóganachta' – 'the people of Eógan'. A later origin myth, which may contain a grain of truth, says that these people were Irish settlers in Britain, who had returned and established their tribal capital at Cashel.*

In the south-east the kingdom of Laigin was pushed back from the River Boyne after about AD 500 by their northern neighbours the Uí Neill, who claimed descent from the heroic Niall of the Nine Hostages (Noigiallach). By the eighth century the Uí Neill had also expanded towards the north-west, pushing back the Ulaid and Dál Raita, some of whom migrated to Scotland (though the habit of movement across the narrows between north-east Ireland and Scotland was probably long established). The powerful Uí Neill controlled the ancient ritual site of Tara, so their over-king held the title 'King of Tara'. They probably also held Emain Macha, the other important sacred centre. Not surprisingly, the early Christian centre of Armagh, associated with Patrick, was

---

* The name derives from the Latin word *castellum*, the root of the English 'castle'. This is not a word normally used in Ireland, so may have been brought from Britain by Eogan's people.

established close by, while St Secunius sited another Christian centre near Tara. It did no harm for Christians to identify with the tribal traditions.

Ireland was littered with petty kings, tied by kinship and clientship to more powerful rulers above, their retainers and family below. Kings were owed tribute (in the form of labour and food). In return they provided success in battle, plunder, gifts, charisma and a channel of communication to the gods. Their role was secular, religious and fragile. Failure in warfare or in the fertility of herds and crops could bring about their downfall. These kings ruled and ministered over tribal groupings known as *tuath*, of which there were as many as two hundred in fifth-century Ireland. In such a fragmented country power and allegiances constantly shifted.

Tradition and order were controlled by tribal wise men, the *brithemu*, who delivered the law, and bards, or *finlial*, responsible for tribal memory in the form of poetry and epics such as the *Taín Bó Cuailgne* (the story of Cuchullain and the cattle raid of Cooley), Ireland's equivalent of the *Iliad* or the Anglo-Saxon *Beowulf*.[10] In a land without coinage cattle were the principal source of wealth. Stealing them was an Irish national sport. For the Christian Church Ireland was a totally new experience, providing none of the usual classical foundations on which to build. But build it did, exploiting the Celtic fascination for monasticism. Ireland's principal churches were controlled by monks rather than bishops and were grouped together into *paruchia*.

The early history of monasticism is almost completely obscure. It grew in the historical gloom of the sixth century, probably transported from southern Wales, where Roman estates and schools, such as Llantwit Major, continued regardless of the political and military collapse of the empire.

Ireland and Wales seem to have had close contacts. A group of the Deisi, for example, an amalgamation of people whose name means 'The Vassals', migrated from the Waterford/Tipperary area to Dyfed. This is recorded in a late eighth-century document known as *The Expulsion of the Deisi*. Inscribed stones recording Irish names in the Irish Ogham alphabet are found in southern Ireland and south-west Wales (Dyfed), dating roughly to 400–480. The sea lanes between these two areas are precisely the ones which operated in the early Bronze Age, so contact in the fifth century should come as no surprise. The Welsh saints David and Cadoc influenced the Irish Christian fathers such as Finnian of Clannard. Finnian taught a generation of men who went on to found monasteries themselves: Brendan of Clonfert, Ciaran of Clonmacnoise and Colum Cille of Durrow, a high-ranking member of the Uí Neíll clan.

Colum Cille, or Columba, founded the great monastic centre at Iona in the Hebrides in AD 563, a bridgehead for the conversion of Pictland and the Anglian kingdom of Northumberland, where King Oswald requested an Ionian bishop to come and minister to the English. Bede, rather scathingly, reports Wilfrid of Ripon's words: 'The Iona monastery was isolated at the uttermost ends of the earth.'

Influential Christians were not all men. The most distinguished house of nuns was St Brigid's at Kildare. In spite of Bede's disdain, many of these Celtic monasteries became rich establishments, closely associated with the royal families and centres of productive agricultural estates worked by tenants. The monks themselves produced marvellous works of art in honour of God — superb metalwork like the Ardagh Chalice and manuscripts like the *Book of Kells*, now in Dublin. The more ascetic monks, though, retreated to cells in the wilderness, notably on the barren, wave-lashed rock of Sceilg Mhicil, off the south-western peninsula of Kerry, to follow the tradition of Egyptian anchorites.

Ireland became a powerhouse of Christianity. Like Colum Cille in Iona, many other Irish monks became *peregrini pro Christo* — 'pilrims for Christ': St Fursa went to pagan East Anglia and established a monastery in the old Roman fort of Cnobesburh, or Burgh Castle, Suffolk. Later he went on to France, dying in Peronne (Picardy), where the Irish became so familiar that it was known as *Peronna Scottarum* — 'Peronne of the Irish'. Columbanus left Ireland with a retinue of twelve monks for France in AD 591 establishing monasteries there and in Lombardy where he died at Bobbio (northern Italy) in 615, by then one of the great founders of western monasticism. In the ninth century Irish scholars held distinguished positions in Europe's great scholastic centres, in the imperial schools of Charlemagne, where Dicuil wrote works on geography and astronomy; at Liege, Sedirlius Scottus produced works on philosophy, theology and grammar, and in the palace of Charles le Chauve ('the Bald') in Laon Irish scholars clustered around their academic superstar Johannes Scottus Eriugena.

Like Patrick, who received his adult Christian education in Gaul, the Welshman Samson also had close links with the Continental Church. British communities from Wales and the south-west transplanted themselves in numbers that cannot be quantified into Armorica, which was renamed Brittany. Samson attended a Church council in Paris in about AD 561. According to his biographer, he had been persuaded into the monastic life by St Illtud at his monastery in Glamorgan. However, the balmy coastal plain of South Wales was not arduous enough for Samson. He took himself to the remote island of Caldey, off the Pembrokeshire coast.

His example persuaded the rest of his large, aristocratic family to enlist in droves for the monastic life; and with them came their rich estates, whose wealth was devoted to the work of God. Samson's biographer illuminates a society at the edge of the known world, but far from isolated. By ship they sailed to Cornwall, Brittany and to Ireland to found yet more churches. Like the farmers, megalith builders and metal prospectors of prehistory, these pilgrims for Christ used the western seas as their highways and channel of communication. In Ireland and Wales monasticism fitted well with the system of kinship and clientage. Land belonged to the kin group (the *fine*) and so monasteries became tribal, family concerns. In an uncertain and hostile world monasticism offered shelter, protection and certainty. For the academic and artistic it offered fulfilment. For the ascetic it provided discipline and self-denial. In the sixth century the monastic life was new, flexible and exciting. It was not yet institutionalised and certainly nothing like that of the great monasteries which dominated Europe in the high Middle Ages. From the ruins that survive we can see Irish monasteries which resemble fortified farms and others like remote birds' nests clinging to Atlantic crags.

In spite of their staggering achievements, the influence of British and Irish Christianity was to be short-lived. Marching from the south were the properly tonsured clerical forces of the Roman Pope. They were to win the day.

The British and Irish Church was dynamic, but it was also idiosyncratic. The Roman Church represented international, ecumenical Christianity, allied to the memory and the surviving culture of the Roman Empire. Columba's form of tribal Christianity brilliantly suited sixth- and seventh-century Ireland and northern Britain; and it was a shot in the arm for European Christianity. Yet in a world of increasing political sophistication, of larger and more powerful kingdoms, growing population and urbanisation, the pan-European Roman Church suited the times. The clash between the British and the Anglo-Roman Church focused particularly on the issue of the date of Easter, a subject close to Bede's heart. Like most theological and liturgical arguments, including haircuts, this one was, in reality, a power struggle between the rival Churches. The argument was settled in AD 664, at the Synod of Whitby. The winner was inevitably Rome. In Iona the monks sulked. They refused to kowtow to Rome for almost forty years, but their influence on the mainland was a thing of the past.

I began this chapter with a description of the burials at Berinsfield (Oxfordshire). Archaeologically these are classic pagan Anglo-Saxons:

women with saucer brooches and amber beads; the men with shields and spears buried in family groups from about AD 450 until about 650.[11] An obvious interpretation on the basis of cultural objects is that these were Germanic immigrants, invaders who gradually swamped the native British and took over their land in the south and east. But this traditional view is now highly contentious. Many scholars argue that there was no significant change in population. The natives, influenced by an Anglo-Saxon military elite, simply adopted the clothing, jewellery, language and religion of their rulers. Even the days of the week changed, commemorating the Germanic gods Tiw, Woden and Thor, while the name of the goddess Eostre was retained for the principal Christian festival of Easter.

Can modern scientific methods throw light on this problem of population change? Are the British the ancestors of the English? or should we look to the Low Countries and Germany for both cultural and genetic roots? The obvious starting point would be with the well-preserved skeletons. Unfortunately these do not help very much with ethnic identity: north-west Europeans are physically much alike. There are variations of height and colouring within populations, but the distinctions between them are not sufficient to enable us to say with certainty from skeletal evidence either: 'These people are Germans' or 'British'.

Nevertheless, this does not stop researchers from trying. Heinrich Harke, a German archaeologist based at Reading University, tried to tackle the problem by looking closely at the mature male burials from our Berinsfield cemetery.[12] He came to the conclusion that those equipped with weapons were taller than those without.* So Heinrich suggested that the tall characters were immigrant Saxons and the smaller, unarmed men were native British. Now this thesis has caused some controversy. Critics have argued that the sample is not statistically meaningful; that high-status weapon carriers could be taller not because of ethnic origin but because they had a better diet. It was amusing to hear Heinrich describing the varying reactions to his idea in Germany and Britain. In Germany, he said, archaeologists refused to believe in the survival of any British; in Britain (younger) archaeologists refused to believe in the arrival of any Germans.[13]

The Berinsfield cemetery is the first Anglo-Saxon population to be the subject of biomolecular dietary analysis. Using stable carbon and nitrogen isotope analysis of bone collagen, it is possible to estimate the sources of dietary protein. Both women and men had a healthy diet and lots of animal protein, though the young weapon-bearing men under

---

* Young boys and old men also had weapons, which were probably a mark of status rather than an indication of their being active warriors.

thirty ate the best food. It is possible that the supposed 'British' had the worst diet – though the scientists say – and in this case it is true: 'More research is needed!'

Another approach to the physical remains was to examine the metrical variation between teeth from a wide variety of Roman and Anglo-Saxon cemeteries.[14] This research suggested that there were greater differences between regions than there were between the periods; that in each region the Roman-Britons and Anglo-Saxons came from the same parent population.*

I was interested in these results because we excavated not only the Anglo-Saxon cemetery at Berinsfield but also the sub-urban Romano-British cemetery of Dorchester, a mere 600 metres to the south. While one cemetery (Berinsfield) was littered with Anglo-Saxon jewellery, weapons and pots, its burials scattered in family groups, the other (Queensford) was a typically well-ordered Roman cemetery with lines of burials inside a rectangular enclosure and with very few grave goods. Culturally they could not have been more different. And the use of both cemeteries may even have overlapped in the fifth century.

If these were the same people, why are the burial rites so different? At present there is a conflict between the archaeological evidence for cultural change and the scientific evidence for continuity of population. Earlier we encountered the stable isotope analysis of teeth with the Amesbury Archer, who had migrated from central Europe. The large-scale application of this technique to Anglo-Saxon burials might help clarify these issues, but it has not yet been done.†

Another obvious approach would be through large-scale DNA analysis. It needs to be emphasised that DNA is not a magic wand.[16] DNA studies have answered some big questions, such as: 'Did modern humans interbreed with Neanderthals?' and smaller-scale ones, such as: 'Are these the remains of the last Russian Tsar and his family?' There have, however, been many problems of contamination and preservation when attempting to sample ancient remains. In the case of the Anglo-Saxon problem, the research would need to be both detailed and extensive, finding samples from well-excavated, well-preserved burials in several countries.

An alternative approach would be to work backwards from DNA samples of modern populations, the method adopted to study the expan-

---

* Another researcher who has examined many burials in Wessex recently came to the conclusion that population had not changed.[15]

† The *Meet the Ancestors* programme carried out stable isotope analysis from an 'Anglo-Saxon' burial at Bamburgh, on the north-east coast, and claimed that he had originated in western Scotland.

sion of Neolithic farming populations discussed earlier. As we saw, the results from this are still contentious. The difficulty with the Anglo-Saxon question is that it is neither large-scale (like the Neanderthals) nor small-scale (like the Tsar), but somewhere in between. And there is another issue: the peoples of north-west Europe seem to be descended from common ancestors who lived between 40,000 and 17,000 years ago, when Britain was part of the north-west European land mass.[17]

Since then there have been many episodes when Continental Europeans could have entered the British Isles and intermixed with the local populations. In other words, Britons and Anglo-Saxons are not genetically very different. There could be greater differences between people in North and South Wales than between, say, Norfolk and Denmark — especially when the gene pool is also muddied by the later arrival of Vikings.[18]

There is the danger with DNA results that observed differences may be associated with a particular known historical event when, in fact, there could be many alternative explanations. Results from small samples can also be contradictory. One project, based on Y-chromosome data so looking at the male line, in Wales and Ireland concluded that there has been continuity from the Upper Palaeolithic to the present with, possibly, some female immigration.[19] Another group of researchers (also based in University College, London, like the previous group) examined DNA samples from modern men living in towns in a band stretching from Wales across England. They observed a clear difference between the Welsh and the English, and noted that the English bore a close similarity to people in Frisia.[20] There could be many explanations for these results, though superficially they suggest that while the Welsh are natives the English are 'newcomers' to the British Isles.

So archaeologists, historians and geneticists continue to argue fiercely about the process of change in the post-Roman period — in particular about whether waves of new immigrants swept into the country or a resident population simply changed its ways and its language. Were the British driven westwards, leaving their lands to be colonised by hostile English barbarians, or did they remain, largely as native peasantry, adapting to the culture of their masters?

So where does this leave our young woman from Berinsfield? To an earlier generation of historians there is no problem. She is the descendant of Germanic immigrants or invaders, who took control of the Thames valley in the later fifth and sixth centuries. To some, more recent, archaeologists she is a Briton, now acculturated as a result of Continental influences to adopt Germanic dress and funerary styles — rather like the children in the nearby Berinsfield estate today: dressed in blue jeans and baseball caps, but certainly British, not American. No one has yet quite won the argument, but on present evidence it seems that Germanic warriors did attack Britain and then migrate and begin to settle, some with families while others intermarried with the British. The number of Continental immigrants probably varied in different regions with most in the south and east and far fewer in the north and west. Gradually, however, over about two centuries the Germanic Anglo-Saxon culture became dominant.

Some advocates of the 'dominant elite' model suggest that the invaders could have been as few as 10,000 to 25,000. In contrast, the 'mass migration' model, with the movement of whole communities, implies that at least ten times this number arrived. Transport would have been necessary; and it was available in flat-keeled, clinker-built vessels – the form of efficient seagoing Saxon ships. Powered by both oars and sail, they could land their human cargoes on the beaches or deep within the estuaries of Britain. The problem for archaeologists is that after about AD 400 the Roman Britons become almost invisible. Coins are no longer minted or imported, industrial pottery is, apparently, not manufactured and vast numbers of settlements are abandoned. It seems that the market economy collapsed and towns and rural villas become dilapidated. Any rebuilding, such as in the city of Wroxeter, was in timber. For the most part people abandoned the urban and Roman way of life. If there were some three million people in Roman Britain at its peak, what happened to them?

The most likely scenario is that the native lowland population had fallen dramatically by the mid-fifth century. The demographic impacts would have been less pronounced among the highlanders of the north and west, who were less dependent on the Roman infrastructure. The Romano-British aristocracy, as Gildas confirms, recruited German muscle to support their faltering society. Over some fifty years the opportunities for these bodyguards and the raiding war bands became more transparent: whole families and communities shipped out from their Continental homelands, which were increasingly beleaguered by rising sea levels, and seeing opportunities in a new land. This is not to say that the British in the east and south disappeared, swept away by ethnic cleansing. It is far more likely that they were absorbed into the newly developing English communities.

The words you are reading are the most telling argument against the minimalist elite model. They are in English;[21] and so are the names of most villages, fields and towns in the east and south of England today. Military conquests by the Romans and the Normans did not have this fundamental impact on the language and place names of a numerically dominant resident population.

Modern English is a Germanic language, which developed from the Old English spoken by the Anglo-Saxons. One argument suggests that if only a small Germanic elite had arrived in Britain, then the population would have continued to speak their Celtic languages, Latin, or some form of amalgamation of the two, as do the French and Spanish. The counter-argument is that people can change their language without moving from their ancestral land or being swamped by numerically superior incomers. This can be seen today as native languages disappear and people, influenced by a dominant culture, adopt English, Spanish and Chinese, for example. This certainly happened in Cornwall, where the spoken Celtic language disappeared by the eighteenth century without a mass incursion of English.

The earliest Anglo-Saxon settlements, in the upper Thames valley around Abindgon and Dorchester-on-Thames, East Anglia, Kent and Sussex, occupied good agricultural land which had been cultivated for millennia. The native population must, for the most part, have adopted the traditional role of the peasantry, an underclass culturally, physically and politically dominated by the newcomers. The Anglo-Saxons called them '*wealhish*' – 'foreigners'; and the word then came to be used specifically for the Britons (hence 'Welsh'). It appears in place names in eastern England such as Walton: 'The Village of the Welsh', and Wallingford: 'The Ford of the Welsh People'. Eventually, as the Anglo-Saxons campaigned in the west and took prisoners, the word took on the meaning of 'slave'. A few *weahlish*, by force of personality or through the fortunes of marriage alliances, may have done better. Some Anglo-Saxon leaders, the founding fathers of the English kingdoms, have British names, such as Cerdic (Caradoc), Ceawlin and Cenwealh (whose name incorporates *weahlish*).

In the course of the seventh century Anglo-Saxon culture became completely dominant in the lowlands, though genetically perhaps two-thirds of the population were of British descent. After the peaceful post-Mount Badon interlude recorded by Gildas, Anglo-Saxon military expansion continued in the north and west. Elmet, in South Yorkshire, fell to Edwin of Northumbria in the AD 630s. In 658 the *Anglo-Saxon Chronicle* records: 'Cenwealh fought against the Britons at Peonnan [probably in Somerset] and put them to flight as far as the river Parret.' In this phase of the development of Engla-land (the 'Land of the English) we are witnessing a process of assimilation by military conquest rather than wholesale population change.

In the south in the sixth and seventh centuries most people must have looked distinctly English: their dress, their language and their settlements would identify them. Female dress accessories functioned as clear badges of ethnic identity. A traveller in sixth-century England would probably have known whose territory he or she was travelling through by the dress of the local women – though, as we know from documented examples, appearances can be deceptive and ethnic identities can shift and change: a Catuvellaunian slave can become a Roman matron. Ethnicity is not shaped in the womb but in the head. Increasingly from the fifth through the sixth and seventh centuries native Britons were absorbed into the Anglo-Saxon world.

Not far to the west of Berinsfield is the site of the first Anglo-Saxon settlement to be excavated in Britain, at Sutton Courtenay. This was found in a gravel pit in the 1920s by E. T. Leeds of Oxford University. Leeds recognised dark marks in the yellow gravel, but these were playing-card-shaped and about 3 by 2 metres across. They proved to be one of the classic indicators of Anglo-Saxon settlement, the *Grubenhaus*, or sunken-featured building: a simple wooden, thatched or shingled building sitting over a shallow pit.

In some cases these pits were planked over to create a floor with a cavity beneath. In others the floor may have been on the base of the pit. As the buildings fell out of use, these pits were backfilled with rubbish – a treasure trove for desperate archaeologists, who are otherwise starved of material on Anglo-Saxon settlements. It is within these pits that we find most of the pottery, animal bones, tools and carbonised plant remains that make up the physcial evidence of Anglo-Saxon activities outside cemeteries. The sunken-featured buildings frequently contain evidence of textile production: clay and even lead loom weights, spindle whorls and bone thread pickers. For Anglo-Saxon women, textile manufacture was an important activity – from carding and spinning wool and flax to weaving on vertical warp-weighted looms (hence the doughnut-shaped weights, which were suspended from the bottom of the warp – the vertical threads).

Textile manufacture was economically important and also a mark of identity – hence the words 'spinster' and '*wif*-man' ('weaving person'), from which comes the modern English 'wife'. Some high-status Anglo-Saxon women went to their graves with weaving battens – sword-shaped implements used for beating up the weft on vertical warp-weighted looms. In contrast a male (in Old English 'man' means a person regardless of gender) was a '*weap*-man' ('weapon-person') and the spear and shield were marks of the male role. Judging from grave finds, boys over the age of about twelve had come of age and were regarded as '*weap*-men'.

At Sutton Courtenay E. T. Leeds recognised the *Grubenhauser* as typically Germanic – they are a regular feature of Continental settlements, where they are used as work sheds and animal byres. However, he failed to recognise larger timber halls or longhouses. For many years it was assumed that the Anglo-Saxons lived in glorified dog kennels. In fact there are much more substantial houses at Sutton Courtenay, but they were hard to recognise in the difficult, messy conditions of a gravel pit in the 1920s and 1930s. More recently aerial photography has revealed the foundations of these impressive buildings and metal detecting suggests that the site developed by the seventh century into a market.

Nevertheless, the timber halls of Anglo-Saxon England, reconstructions of which can be seen today at West Stow in Suffolk, differ from the longhouses on Continental settlements such as Feddersen Wierde. These were aisled buildings, usually with stalls for cattle, and up to 25 metres long. Such a building could house twenty cattle at one end and a family at the other, linked by a central corridor. In the milder English climate such integrated accommodation for animals was not necessary: Anglo-Saxon halls were modified principally for human use and perhaps influenced by local Romano-British methods of building.

Perhaps the most evocative passage in Bede's *History* conjures up the image of an Anglo-Saxon hall. Paulinus is attempting to convert King Edwin of Northumbria. One of the King's retainers speaks:

> Your Majesty, when we compare the present life of man with that time of which we have no knowledge, it seems to me like the swift flight of a lone sparrow through the banqueting hall where you sit in the winter months to dine with your thanes and counsellors. Inside there is a comforting fire to warm the room; outside the wintry storms of snow and rain are raging. This sparrow flies swiftly in through one door of the hall, and out through another. While he is inside, he is safe from the winter storms, but after a few moments of comfort, he vanishes from sight into the darkness whence he came. Similarly, man appears on earth for a little while, but we know nothing of what went before this life, and what follows.

Continental villages of the fourth and fifth centuries mostly have a clearly planned layout, arc densely settled and show signs of a social hierarchy. In contrast, early English settlements sprawl over the countryside with little constraint on space or coherent planning and every sign of rude equality.

North of Sutton Courtenay, for 5 kilometres along the Thames as far as Radley, are some of the earliest and most thoroughly investigated Anglo-Saxon settlements. There are scattered sunken-featured buildings and water holes. Some are inside the earthworks of the Iron Age *oppidum* and small Romano-British town of Abingdon; others are placed around the demolished villa at Barton Court Farm, along with small timber halls. The largest Anglo-Saxon settlement, at Barrow Hills, Radley, spreads between the mounds of a major prehistoric barrow cemetery and across a late Romano-British cemetery. These settlements were used by loosely based family or kin groups. In this landscape there is no clear evidence of the Britons who once farmed every square metre. If they were still present, the Anglo-Saxons showed no fear of them — the Germanic settlements could not have been more vulnerable to attack; they seemed to be able to put down a building wherever they pleased. Early settlements in other areas are similarly profligate with space. At Mucking, on the windswept terrace above the Thames estuary to the north, there are similar settlements. The first generations at Mucking may have earned a living policing the natural gateway into south-eastern Britain on behalf of the surviving British authorities — or they may have been freebooters. A rare example of more coherent planning, with specialised activity zones, is the early Anglian settlement at West Heslerton. A massive geophysical survey between the medieval/modern villages of West and East Heslerton has revealed other large-scale Anglian settlements, but still sprawled across the fields of their abandoned Romano-British predecessors. This is not to suggest that the Britons had vanished like will-o'-the-wisps. While some were absorbed into Anglo-Saxon communities or survived in lowland enclaves, most developed a distinctive post-Roman culture in the north and west.

At the opposite end of Britain great changes were taking place in a region of almost Balkan complexity. Confusingly Scotland is named after an Irish tribe — the Scotti, also known as the Dal Riáta. The short seaway between northern Ireland and Scotland was a highway rather than a barrier. Gaelic- (Celtic-) speakers from the Antrim tribe of the Dal Riáta crossed over from about AD 500 to Kintyre, but this was probably just one event in a long process of movement. According to the foundation-tradition legend, the new Gaelic kingdom in Argyll was established by Fergus Mor mac Eira. We know little else about him.

South of the Forth–Clyde there were several British tribes, recorded by the Romans: the Selgovae, Novantae, Damnonii and Votadini. By the sixth century these had developed into the British kingdom of Strathclyde and Rheged, in south-west Scotland, and Gododdin in the Lothian.

The Gododdin followed that tradition started by Calgacus at Mons Graupius: they lost gloriously. The epic poem *Y Gododdin* is an account of their defeat by their southern neighbours the Angles at Catraeth (Catterick, Yorkshire). The tale was written down in Wales and it may have been a Welsh scribe who added to the description of the hero Morien that, though brave, 'he was no Arthur'.

North of these British kingdoms, the descendants of the Caledonian tribes were called the Picti ('Painted Ones'), a name first recorded in AD 297. They were probably a confederation of the Maeatae, Caledones and other tribes of the highlands coming together, like the Saxons, in reaction to the threats and opportunities of the Roman Empire.[22]

To Gildas the Picts were 'a foul horde'. To modern historians they are 'a problem', a mysterious people, speaking a non-Indo-European language and carving weird symbols on standing stones. Most of this is untrue. They were, in fact, a northern barbarian people, similar to their neighbours. They occupied a harsh land but were skilful sailors, farmers and hunters with widespread connections; and they spoke a form of P-Celtic, like the British and Welsh, though their Dal Riáta neighbours spoke Q-Celtic, so St Columba, from Ireland, needed an interpreter to speak to the Picts.[23]

Nevertheless, the missionaries of Dal Riáta seem to have successfully converted the Picts, whose bishopric at Abernethy was dedicated to St Brigid of Kildare. The bit about the weird carvings is true. The Picts conveyed messages through the medium of stones incised with vigorous images of birds, fish, snakes, mirrors, horsemen, strange zigzags and crescent-moon shapes. The symbols are also found on cave walls and on magnificent jewellery all the way up the east coast of Scotland above the Firth of Forth, into the glens and across to Orkney and Shetland. The enigma of the Picts has also been reinforced by the idea that they disappeared. They became a lost people. In fact they were subsumed into the Scottish kingdom of Alba (originally the name for Britain as a whole) after AD 900.* Their genes survive. From 900 it is reasonable to call the people of the north 'Scots'.[24]

The geography of Pictland is demarcated not only by the symbol stones but also by place names. Except in the far north, where a later generation of Viking names predominates, Pictish settlements are marked by 'Pit' names, as at Pitlochry or Pitmadden. Other Pictish place names can be recognised by the words '*pert*' (wood), '*caer*' (fort), '*pren*' (tree), '*aber*' (river mouth or confluence) and a few others. On the west coast the Irish

---

* In AD 906 Scone is specifically mentioned as a ceremonial centre where the royal and ecclesiastical powers are united.

Gaelic speakers introduced their own names, such as '*achadh*' (field or settlement) '*sliabh*' (mountain) '*baile*' (settlement) and, most distinctive of all, '*cill*' (church), usually combined with a saint's name.

Pictish settlements are not easy to date, but a variety have recently been recognised from aerial photography, fieldwork and excavation. At Carn Dubh, above Pitlochry, prehistoric roundhouses were replaced by sub-rectangular buildings in the mid-first millennium. Similarly shaped ones of the same date were also found at Pitcarrick, in Perthshire. These were longhouses, with a central soakaway at one end, possibly where the beasts were kept. The duns and brochs that dominated the landscapes of the highlands and islands in the Iron Age and Roman period went out of use by the fourth century. In many cases settlement continued but in the form of less dominant cellular roundhouses or linear houses. At Gurness, in Orkney, a shamrock-shaped house, with discrete cells and a central hearth, is reminiscent of the Neolithic houses of Skara Brae.

The brochs and wheelhouses dominated the landscape. The new farmsteads of Pictland were more modest and self-effacing, suggesting that social and political changes were taking place. Earlier buildings reflected the pride and status of local kin groups. After the fifth century authority became more centralised. The new confederacies generated client relationships, authority figures, power centres and prestige goods. As in the Roman world, the role of the farmer and the peasant was to be taxed. In Dal Riáta the document known as the '*Miniugud Senchasa Fher nAlban*' ('The Explanation of the Genealogy of the [Gaelic] Men of Britain') was written in the mid-seventh century (the earliest surviving copy dates to the tenth century). It contains a mixture of origin legends, military assessment and survey to clarify how much tribute could be extracted. Individual households and their land were the basis for raising tax and military dues. Households were grouped together, often in fives into estates, under a minor noble whose responsibility was to ensure that his lord received his due. Increasingly the Church became an important player in the political system of Scotland.[25]

The histories of saints contradict the image of the supposed Dark Age as a closed barbarian world. When the raggle-taggle armies of Roman Britain departed, they did not turn out the lights of civilisation and close the doors behind them. Life went on. It is clear that there were movements of people – raiders, pirates, monks and families seeking new lives. Irish people moved across the sea to the west coast of Britain and the British crossed to the newly named Brittany; and people from the tribes of coastal Germany and the Low Countries moved into Britain. The scale of these movements is almost impossible to estimate.

Where archaeologists have been most active — in northern Germany, the Netherlands, southern and eastern England — it appears that populations not only moved, they decreased. There is clear evidence for the decline of towns, the abandonment of long-established settlements and the neglect of intensive farming systems. Technology took a step backwards. Although the land continued to be farmed, there was an expansion of grazing and low-energy agricultural systems.

This all suggests that in fifth-century Britain, particularly in the lowlands, there were fewer people about. Anglo-Saxon settlements such as West Stow, Sutton Courtenay and Mucking were profligate with land because it was going spare. The inhabitants did not defend or demarcate them with boundary ditches. Fifth-century cemeteries, like the settlements, indicate small, scattered populations with relatively limited hierarchical differences. The population of Roman Britain, about three million at its peak, may have declined to less than half.

Britain did not stay like this for long. Many factors combined to boost the human population: plenty of good agricultural land, developing technology, the rebirth of towns and trade, and social and political factors. The Church increasingly expected celibacy from its priests, but not its congregations. Nevertheless, as we can see in Mediterranean Catholic countries today, religious ideology does not boost birth rates without the co-operation of women. The success of the Roman Church was one element in the interlinking threads of seventh-century European society. The other was the decline of tribal, kin-based societies, the emergence of new states, more powerful centralised kingdoms, with pronounced social hierarchies. In these societies individuals had greater flexibility and choice. They were less constrained by tradition; entrepreneurship was possible. Trade was stimulated by the hierarchy's need for prestige goods to display social difference. The rulers created more efficient and demanding bureaucracies, helped by a literate Church, to generate income. The Church promoted skills not only in learning and the arts, but also in building, carving, woodwork, glass-making and metallurgy. Many early monastic sites, such as Whitby, looked almost like small towns, with specialist craft and industrial areas. The sound of hammers must have been as noticeable as the sound of bells, the smell of ovens and smithies as characteristic as that of incense.

Population growth is ultimately dependent on the food produced by farmers. From the sixth century the conditions were right for agricultural expansion and intensification. The incentive existed once again to produce more food, and more people to produce more food. Breadwheat, with its higher productivity and ease of threshing, and rye in more difficult areas, were common staples. Barley was needed particularly for brewing. Fibre crops such as hemp and flax were important, as well as wool in textile production. The excavated hamlet of Wicken Bonhunt provides a vivid picture of rural production in about AD 700. Oats, wheat, barley, peas and beans were the main crops. The bones of 295 fowl were recovered, mainly geese, but also ducks, doves and, most surprisingly, a peacock. The excavator suggests that egg production was a speciality. The remains of six hundred pigs, mainly heads, were found as well as a hundred sheep and twice as many cattle. The usual collection of Anglo-Saxon paraphernalia – heddles, loom weights, spindle whorls – indicated textile production.

Wicken Bonhunt seems to have been a thriving, productive settlement. It was re-ordered in about AD 700 in a way which is characteristic of settlements in Anglo-Saxon England. Hall-type houses became bigger and more impressive. At Cowdrey Down, Hampshire, the substantial timber halls had a new style of construction: posts set in continuous trenches. At Yarnton, near Oxford, and Higham Ferrers (Northampton-shire) the new-style halls had a separate private sleeping chamber at one end. Such houses suggest that villages were becoming more hierarchical. In these settlements space was demarcated more rigidly, with fences, ditches, banks and hedges. Even at settlements occupied since the fifth century, such as Yarnton and West Stow, this concern to mark out property is evident. Others are abandoned as part of what is sometimes called 'the Anglo-Saxon settlement shift', a move to more nucleated settlements.

The emergence of English class consciousness also appears in the documentary evidence. Anglo-Saxon law codes and wills provide a guide to social ranking. Most of the evidence relates to men, though women could hold land in their own right, like the Yorkshirewoman Asa, who appears in the Domesday Book, or Aelfgifu, who owned fifteen estates in and around Buckinghamshire in about AD 970. And unmarried aristocratic women often played important roles in the Church, such as Hild, Abbess of Whitby Abbey.

The value of a man's life was reflected in the monetary value placed on it by the law, his *wergeld*, or 'man's price'. These complex payments appear in the earliest law code of Ethelbert of Kent in the early seventh century and in Alfred's law code of the late ninth century. The highest rank was the king ('*cyning*' in Old English has the word for 'kin' at its root: 'the leader of the *cyn*'). His *wergeld* was many times (about twelve) that of a noble, a disincentive to assassination. Then came the *ealdorman* (or *gerefan* in Northumberland) and *eorl* – a man of superior rank. The followers of the king were granted *heriot*, or gifts of weaponry — which included swords, spears, chain mail, helmets and horses — and were known by that name. During the reign of Alfred the term 'thegn' becomes used frequently for high-status men, with a *wergeld* of 1,200 shillings. Some thegns held huge estates, while others were much more modest in their possessions.

The ordinary freeman was a *ceorl* — place names such as Chalton (Hampshire) and Chorlton (Lancashire) commemorate them — and his *wergeld* was 200 shillings. He was obliged to contribute food, rent or *feorn* (from which we get 'farm') to the king's retinue. On most estates there was a farm steward or *geneat*, who oversaw the *cottars*, landholders who paid no rent but had to work on the lord's land and provide military service. The great mass of peasants, the *gebur*, had even more onerous duties. The number of slaves, or *thralls*, is uncertain, but they were owned by the higher ranks down to *ceorls*. Not surprisingly, few places are named after *thralls*, but there is an exception which proves the rule at Threlkeld (Cumbria) — 'The Spring of the Slaves'.

Across Britain there is evidence of more complex, status-conscious societies. In the north and west traditional building styles such as the brochs and wheelhouses of Hibernia, Orkney and Shetland were abandoned and new-style settlements appeared. Crags and hilltops such as Dundurn, Dunadd and Clatchard Craig were defended. The new rulers were fond of re-using Roman building materials, sometimes carted several miles. The British established a new acropolis — Al Cluith — at Dumbarton Rock. At these fortified sites complex monumental approaches and layers of defence emphasised the status of the ruler. These are probably the archaeological manifestations of the growth of kingship. In spite of the origin myths in the *Anglo-Saxon Chronicle*, littered with the alliterative descendants of Woden, Hengist and Horsa in Kent, Cerdic and Cyrnic in Wessex, Stulf and Wihtgar on the Isle of Wight, there is no good evidence of actual fifth-century Anglo-Saxon kings. These probably first emerged as part of the struggle for land between kin groups that wracked England between the fifth and eighth centuries. The first kingdoms were relatively small. The Warwickshire territory of the Stoppingas ('People of Stoppa') around Wootton Wawen can be reconstructed from an eighth-century Mercian charter of King Aethelbald. In Essex the eight parishes named Roding ('People of Hrotha') were a similar-sized micro-kingdom, about 12 to 15 by 6 kilometres.[26]

These units were gradually absorbed by the winners in the royalty stakes. The Rodings and the Stoppingas became examples of what Bede calls *'regiones'*, or districts of the larger kingdoms of East Anglia and

Mercia. The presence of bishops, for example in Suffolk, Norfolk and the Isle of Ely, also reflects the existence of earlier units in what became the larger kingdom of East Anglia. By the seventh century the patchwork of petty kingdoms had been stitched together to form seven big players in England: East Anglia, Sussex, Essex, Wessex, Kent, Mercia and Northumbria (an amalgamation of the former kingdom of Bernicia and Deira). Out of these, Mercia and Wessex soon became dominant, muscling for power across their common Thames frontier.

Similar processes were under way in the north. The Scots Dal Riáta, the British of Strathclyde and the Anglians all struggled for power with each other and with the Picts. In the mid-seventh century three Pictish kings seem to have been British. Shortly afterwards the Anglians hold sway in Pictland and in AD 672 the army of their King Ecgfrith massacred many of the Pictish aristocracy. A Briton – Bridei mac Bile, probably from the Strathclyde group – is then found leading the Picts against the Anglians and defeating them at the Battle of Nechtansmere (near Dionnichen) in AD 685. The politics of the period are both complicated and obscure. The Picts emerge as dominant in the region under Oengus mac Fergusa (729–61), who took the stronghold of Dunadd and seized control of Dal Riáta. By the end of the century their fortunes were reversed: Dal Riáta was back in the driving seat.

The Dal Riáta rulers were, in the words of one historian (Lynch, 1992), 'middle-ranking kings of an increasingly fissiparous set of peoples, located within a small but difficult territory'. Nevertheless, in the ninth century, under Cinead mac Ailpin (Kenneth MacAlpine) they took control of much of Caledonia and gave the kingdom their name: Scotland.

After the collapse of the Roman province of Britannia fifth-century England reverted to small-scale tribal communities. It was once thought that place names could point towards these early English communities, notably those which included the suffix '-ingas' – names like Hastings, meaning 'People, or Kin, of Hasta', Reading: 'Kin of Raida', and Godalming: 'Kin of Godhelm'. Now we realise these '-ingas' names do not belong to the very beginning of English settlement; they appear later and could instead indicate the earliest English petty kingdoms, when tribal societies evolved into larger political groups.

As the tribes struggled with each other for dominance, competitive chiefdoms developed into kingdoms. We know little about the details of this process, the emergence of the first English kings; but there are hints in a document known as the *Tribal Hideage*. Bede tells us that the hide was originally a unit of land of one family. In other words, the land allocated by a kin group to its adult male members. By the time the hide appears in written sources it has evolved into a unit of taxation: it is part of the political, bureaucratic world of kingdoms and is used to assess tribute. The *Tribal Hideage* incorporates a seventh-century tribute list for the south-east Midlands and includes a number of folk groups, like the *Cilternsaete* — 'the dwellers in the Chilterns'. These people are never mentioned again, presumably because they were swallowed into the maw of the new English kingdoms which started to emerge from the late sixth century.

There is further archaeological evidence for increasing status and the emergence of a royal elite in the form of massive timber halls, rich barrow burials, high-status exotic objects and eventually massive engineering projects such as Offa's Dyke, with which, imitating Hadrian's Wall, King Offa of Mercia separated his English kingdom of Mercia from the Britons of Wales.

Few royal settlements have been investigated in England. The best known and best excavated is Yeavering, in Northumberland. This early seventh-century royal residence is probably the palace complex of King Edwin, called by Bede 'Ad Gefrin'. Yeavering began as a modest settlement but was rebuilt to reflect the increasing power and status of the Northumbrian King Aethelfrith (592–616) and was enlarged in the reign of Edwin (616–32). The King's great hall stood prominently on a plateau above the River Glen. Around this great hall were other halls. Nearby was a large double fenced enclosure 150 metres across — a kraal to hold the royal herds.* Uniquely, Yeavering had a timber grandstand, like a section of a Roman theatre, where the retainers could sit in elevated seats to hear royal pronouncements. Bede records one of them when he describes how the recently converted Edwin travelled to Ad Gefrin with the missionary Paulinus in the late AD 620s. During his thirty-six-day stay Paulinus preached to the Anglian people, who flocked in from the surrounding countryside. The converted were baptised in the waters of the River Glen, Northumbria's chilly equivalent to the River Jordan.

Kings did not stay long in royal residences like Ad Gefrin. They progressed around their territory: to be seen; to live off the larders and stores of their subjects. The residences themselves did not necessarily last long either. Ad Gefrin was soon abandoned, according to Bede, and another residence built nearby at Maelmin. Aerial photography has revealed a complex of impressive timber halls at modern Millfield, which is probably this later royal palace of Maelmin. As they progressed, kings carried their symbols of status and power with them in the form of lavishly

* Another has recently been found at Higham Ferrers (Northamptonshire).

bedecked and mounted retinues, standards, furniture and textiles. No discovery better illustrates the wealth, pretensions and glittering pomp of those who ruled in seventh-century Britain than the ancestral burial ground of the East Anglians at Sutton Hoo (Sussex). Here twenty burial mounds dominate the high ground above the River Deben.

In 1939, on the eve of World War II, archaeologists opened Mound 1. They found in the sand the impression of a magnificent and elegant ship 27 metres long. A burial chamber in the ship had been packed with the accoutrements of a very important person. Archaeologists still argue about who this was. The most likely candidate is Raedwald, the King of the East Anglians and the High King of England, who was buried in about AD 625.[27]

There was no body. This is because bone dissolves in the acidic soils of Sutton Hoo and only recently have archaeologists realised that 'sand bodies' can be identified and modelled from the stains they leave in the ground. Around the probable burial position in Mound 1 the archaeologists, in 1939, found the kit of a lavishly bedecked warrior: a coat of mail, a superb pattern-welded sword, a battleaxe, a helmet of a Scandinavian type and a Roman-style tunic with gold-and-garnet shoulder clasps. The dead person was provided with entertainment in the next world: musical instruments, drinking horns, a cauldron and chain for feasting, Byzantine bowls and plenty of cash — imported from the Continent, as the East Anglians still did not produce coinage of their own. The most evident symbols of status were a massive gold buckle and great whetstone mounted by a bronze stag. Bede says that on his progresses King Edwin was preceded by an object called a '*tufa*'. Perhaps this whetstone, a symbol of the king's role as 'swordgiver' to his retainers, was a royal standard.

Many objects in the grave reveal that this was a society with wide international connections. Hanging bowls of British workmanship, Scandinavian influences in armour and jewellery, Merovingian coinage and objects from the Byzantine world show that East Anglia was not remote and isolated. In ships such as that in Mound 1 the East Anglians could have travelled up the coast to Northumbria, down to the Thames estuary or crossed the North Sea to their ancestral homeland.

The objects from the classical world, such as a stack of silver bowls, may have been diplomatic gifts. The two silver spoons inscribed 'Saulos' and 'Paulos' could be presents to mark the conversion of King Raedwald. Unfortunately for the donor, Raedwald's attachment to Christianity was fragile. Under pressure from his relatives he decided to hedge his bets and return to the pagan religion of his ancestors.

Sutton Hoo is not just a royal burial ground. Recent excavations have shown that it had a long history and includes Anglians of varying status, including a warrior with a horse and, most miserably, the victims executed on the official gallows. At Sutton Hoo the King of East Anglia had the power over life and death, at least for other people. And at this time other mounds are set up to mark the burial place of powerful rulers: at Taplow (Buckinghamshire) by the Thames, on the Cotswolds and in the territory of the Pecsaete — the 'People of the Peak', around Bakewell (Derbyshire). Here, high on a ridge, was set the Benty Grange barrow, in which a man was buried with chain mail, silver fittings and, most spectacularly, a helmet with a boar crest.[28] With these prominent barrow burials we see the emergence of English kingship.

One of the most fascinating recent discoveries in British archaeology appeared at Prittlewell, near Southend (Essex), just north of the Thames estuary. Here, in October 2003, archaeologists from the Museum of London uncovered a wooden burial chamber 4 metres square and 1.4 metres deep. Inside this underground wooden room the mourners had laid the body of a man, probably on a bed. Nothing remained of the body (as at Sutton Hoo, the soils were acidic), but his shoe buckles indicated where he lay. And later, in the laboratory, the investigators found traces of tooth enamel from soil samples taken at the head end. A sword and shield suggest the body belonged to a man; but he had other spectacular objects: a solid-gold belt buckle, a gold-fringed tunic, two gold coins from Merovingian France. One of them was made by a moneyer called Vitalis, in Paris. The dead man also had a folding stool of a type later associated with kings and emperors, two drinking horns, rare glass jars, a board game and a lyre. Most remarkably, there were bronze vessels hanging on the chamber walls from iron hooks. One was a flagon from Byzantium (Constantinople); there was also a Coptic bowl from the eastern Mediterranean, an 'antique' cauldron and a hanging bowl with enamel decoration from Ireland or northern Britain.

The obvious question is: Who was he? Two gold-foil crosses from the burial suggest that he was a Christian. The other objects indicate that he was buried between AD 600 and 650. It is early days to identify the 'Prittlewell Prince' with any certainty, but Bede provides a tantalising clue. He describes how Ethelbert of Kent was converted to Christianity in AD 597. In 604 Augustine appointed Bishop Mellitus to preach in the province of the East Saxons, whose capital was London, 'a trading centre for many nations'. Ethelbert's nephew Sabert 'ruled the province with this uncle's authority'. When Sabert accepted the new faith, Ethelbert built a church dedicated to St Paul in the city of London. Ethelbert died in AD 616 and was buried in Canterbury. Sabert died the same year, but Bede does not say he was buried in St Paul's. He does, however, record that Sabert left three sons — all pagans. These three banished Bishop Mellitus from London and encouraged the people of Essex to reject Christianity and return to the old gods. The excavators of Prittlewell suggest, believably, that our man in the tomb is Sabert, given a pagan-style send-off by his sons.[29] His burial was rich but not so splendid as that in the Sutton Hoo ship burial. But then Sabert was an under-king, merely a ruler of Essex; Raedwald was the High King of all England.

Sutton Hoo and Prittlewell highlight the growth of kingship in a hierarchical society, the complex international connections of the Anglo-Saxon world and the emerging role of Christianity. At Lechlade (Gloucestershire), by the confluence of the River Thames and its tributary the Leach, an ancestral burial ground shows that these trends were penetrating into more local, modest levels of society. These peoples were from the same Gewisse tribal group that we met at Berinsfield, but were now becoming part of a West Saxon kingdom. By about AD 500 they had spread into the upper reaches of the Thames valley. In the late 630s the Italian bishop Birinus, according to Bede, came to Britain to proselytise among the English. He intended to travel further inland, but finding the Gewisse to be 'completely pagan', Birinus decided to put his efforts into converting them. Cynegils, the local king, was baptised. 'Oswald, the most holy and victorious king of the Northumbrians happened to be present,' says Bede (Oswald is the Northumbrian monk's hero), and gave his daughter as a wife to Cynegils.

In the generation following these events at Dorchester-on-Thames the burial rituals at Lechlade underwent considerable changes. The ancestral cemetery continued in use, but now the bodies lay facing east, reflecting the Christian belief that on Judgement Day the dead should rise to meet their maker. There are family groups with few grave goods, but there are some with outstanding quantities. In other words, the Lechlade community has become more class-conscious. Some of the men go to their graves, like Raedwald, armed to the teeth with spears, shields, knives and *seaxes*, or machete-like swords. The wealthier women change most of all. Instead of the amber beads and saucer brooches of their great-grandmothers, they have fine-gold pins with garnet mounts, amethyst beads, large cowrie shells — and even more textile equipment. Many of these objects have travelled along the same route as Birinus: from the Mediterranean, via Gaul (Merovingia) and Kent, and up the River Thames. These Gewisse, or West Saxons, have shifted their cultural focus from their ancestral German homeland to the south-east, to Kent, and the Roman world beyond. The northern pagan symbols such as amber and gilded suns have disappeared. In their place come garnets, the colour of the blood of Christ, and amethysts, the colour of Heaven, still used today for bishops' rings. The gold pins and chains found beneath the chin suggest that these English women were modestly dressed, with wimples around their heads. By about AD 700 they abandoned this ancestral burial ground and established a new Christian cemetery, probably near the site of the present Lechlade parish church of St Lawrence.[30]

The presence of King Oswald of Northumbria at the baptism of the Gewissan King Cynegils was no coincidence. The Gewissans had a powerful enemy to the north and west, the expanding Anglian kingdoms of the Midlands and the Cotswolds. As the kingdom of Mercia, these people under Penda (626–56) would eventually overrun the Thames valley. In the late 630s an alliance between the Gewisse West Saxons and Northumberland made sense. Together they became part of 'the Europe-wide club of civilised Christian people'.[31]

Out of the collapse of Britannia the people of Britain and Ireland – Gaels, Picts and English – created a vibrant mix of cultures, far more exciting and original than anything seen in the soviet province of the Romans. This so-called Dark Age shone with the jewellery of Sutton Hoo. Out of this multicultural and multilingual mix emerged one of Britain's greatest works of art, the *Lindisfarne Gospels*, made about 715–20 on Lindisfarne (Holy Island).[32] Its stunning, ornamented 'carpet' pages, influenced by the Coptic art of Egypt, resemble the prayer rugs of Islam – which is not surprising, as Bede reveals that Northumbrian monks also used the prayer mat (*oratorio*).

The release from the Roman Empire seems to free the imagination of the British, and the presence of the Church and their own competitive royal families provide a focus for their creativity. At the end of his *History of the English Church and People* Bede describes a time of peace. Admittedly, he says: 'The Britons for the most part have a national hatred for the English, and uphold their own bad customs' (he means the date of Easter). Nevertheless, 'Peace and prosperity prevail – let the countless isles be glad.' But the age of piracy and migration was not yet finished with Britain. If the artist-monks of Lindisfarne could have lifted their eyes from their glowing pages to penetrate beyond the horizon of the North Sea, they would have known that the undeserved anger of God was about to descend on them.

Five The Viking Legacy

AS AN ARCHAEOLOGY student I spent the early summers, for three years, excavating in Orkney. In Kirkwall, the islands' capital, I was struck by the appearance of the children. They were nearly all blond. The narrow streets beneath the grimly magnificent red-sandstone Cathedral of St Magnus had Norse-sounding names. The Orkney families I got to know best were the Foubisters and the Isbisters, also good Norse names. Orkney seemed different from mainland Scotland: the appearance, accent and names of the people echoed Scandinavia.

The answer to this ethnic distinctiveness is inscribed on the stone slabs inside the great prehistoric tomb of Maes Howe, west of Kirkwall. Names here clearly belong to men and women of Norse origin, many of whom settled in Orkney even if they remained inveterate travellers. These form the largest collection of Norse inscriptions in Britain: thirty inscriptions were carved at different times, probably over several centuries, in the spiky runic letters used by the Norsemen. Runic letters are a modified form of the Roman alphabet – modified not for pen, brush or quill-wielding monks and clerks but for dagger- and axe-carrying Vikings.[1]

Armed with their metal blades the Vikings could cut these angular letters into stone, bone or wood. The runic alphabet first appeared about the second century AD. In Scandinavia and their overseas territories the Norse carved runes on commemorative tombstones and crosses, on jewellery, charms and amulets, or on wooden tally sticks to record business transactions. A comb case made of deer antler in about AD 1000 and found in Lincoln is marked in runes: *kamb : kopan : kiari forfastr* ['Thorfastr made a good comb']. Terse but rhythmic: easy to carve with a knife point.*

---

* There are about 2,500 runic inscriptions known in Sweden, far fewer in Denmark and Norway; they occur in Britain, Ireland and western Russia, but surprisingly not in Iceland, which is the source of many sagas – the finest Norse literature.

In the often bleak and windswept Orkney landscape the Maes Howe tomb provided a convenient shelter for those caught in bad weather. To while away the time until the storm blew itself out Norsemen carved graffiti on its walls. One such event is actually recorded in the *Orkneyinga Saga* — the history, or tales, of the Orkney people. Earl Harald and his men were travelling from Stromness: 'During a snowstorm they took shelter in Orkahaugr [the Norse name for Maes Howe] and there two of them went insane.' Howling winds and a spooky tomb proved too much for these sensitive souls.

Some visitors to Maes Howe had their minds on more obvious Viking attractions: women and treasure. 'Ingigerth is the most beautiful of women,' wrote one admirer. Another left the tantalising message: 'It is true what I say, that treasure was carried off in the course of three nights.' Another chose to boast about his literary skills: 'These runes were carved by the man most skilled in runes in the western ocean with the axe which belonged to Gaukr Trandilsson in the south of Iceland.'

It is believed that the skilled, if immodest, runesmith who left his marks on the south wall of the tomb was a certain Thorhallr Asgrimsson. According to *Njal's Saga*, his great-great-great-grandfather was the killer of Gaukr Trandilsson. About two hundred years later Gaukr's axe was still in his murderer's family and still being put to good use. Its owner, Thorhallr, appears himself in the *Orkneyinga Saga*, as the captain of the ship that brought the Earl of Orkney, Earl Rognvald, back home from the Crusades in 1153.

The Norse left obvious traces of their settlement at the site which I helped to excavate. Skaill lies almost 30 kilometres east of Maes Howe, on the easternmost edge of Mainland, the largest island of the Orkneys. The setting was spectacular, overlooking a broad, sandy bay where seals monitored us from offshore and terns and guillemots behaved like extras in Alfred Hitchcock's *The Birds*. If we approached too close to their nests they would dive-bomb us — or worse, vomit up their stomach contents. The place name Skaill — from Old Norse *skali* — can mean a hall. In Orkney it usually refers specifically to a high-status place in a good location. Our Skaill certainly was well placed: bordering on an accessible beach, with a sheltered bay in front and good agricultural land behind. We found the hall, but only by dint of shovelling away tons of sand under which it was buried.

The buildings were unlike anything I had seen in the south: the thick walls were fronted with stone, the interior cavities filled with turf stacks to provide effective insulation from the piercing Orkney winds. The main building, a long rectangular hall, had a huge central hearth. On each side there was a raised bench or platform for sitting, working, drinking, tale-telling and sleeping. In long, dark Orkney winters the Skaill family probably stirred from its comforting fug as little as possible. Such buildings are typical of Norse settlements. which lie in a great arc across the northern Atlantic from Norway to Greenland to L'Anse aux Meadows in Newfoundland.

People had lived in Skaill long before the Norse arrived. In the sand dunes there were traces of a Pictish settlement; even earlier, the first prehistoric farmers who had built Orkney's spectacular stone circles and Maes Howe itself had left their rubbish dumps. Norse settlers probably first arrived at Skaill in the early ninth century. Two centuries later Skaill had come up in the world: it was the home of Thorkel Amundason, foster-father to Orkney's most powerful nobleman, Earl Thorfinn the Mighty.

One of our problems excavating and understanding Skaill was that much of the archaeological evidence had been eroded away by the sea. Around the coast of Britain, particularly along the east coast where the rocks are soft, important evidence is continuously lost. Occasionally someone is in the right place at the right time to spot the archaeology at the key moment: as it is exposed but before it falls into oblivion. This happened to Julie Gibson, the archaeologist for Orkney, when she went to Scar, on the little island of Sanday, to check out reports of human bones on the beach. On arrival she found what appeared to be the outline of a boat in the sand, studded with lumps of iron that resembled the rivets used in Viking ships. Julie realised that it would only take another storm to erase the remains of the boat for ever. Unfortunately it was late in the year. I excavated in Orkney in June, when it scarcely even became dark. At Scar the excavators had to work through November, when daylight scarcely existed. This is the time of year for curling up by the hearth. Nevertheless, by Christmas Eve the archaeologists had recorded what proved to be a fascinating boat burial laid inside a stone-lined pit. Two days later a storm wiped away most of the remains.

As at Sutton Hoo, the impression of the boat was also marked in the sand by its iron rivets. The Scar boat was no spectacular longship, but a workaday rowing boat 6.3 metres in length. In style it resembled boats from Scandinavia; and closer investigation proved that is where it came from. Soil lodged between the planks contained igneous rock particles which, geologically, could not have originated in Orkney. This material was included in the caulking, which sealed the boat when it was constructed. Norwegian Vikings must have brought the Scar rowing boat to Orkney nested inside their longship, on a voyage from Norway.

The three people buried within the boat may have made the same journey. They were an unusual trio: a man in his thirties, an elderly woman and a child of about ten. The grave goods suggested that both man and woman were of some status; certainly neither was a slave, consigned to everlasting duty in the afterlife. Perhaps all three had died in an accident or been struck by some virulent illness, though their skeletons provided no clues to the cause of death.

The man was curled into the prow of the boat, accompanied by his sword in a sheepskin-lined wooden scabbard. There was a set of arrows; any wooden bow would be long gone. To keep up appearances he had a bone comb, and to pass the time in the afterlife – only marginally longer than an Orkney winter – there was a set of twenty-two antler and bone gaming pieces. The old woman carried objects that reflected her relatively high status, but she was nevertheless prepared to be useful. As well as a gilded brooch, she had an iron sickle, a pair of iron shears, a soapstone spindle whorl and a cooking spit. Most remarkable of all was a complete whalebone plaque 28 centimetres long and 20 centimetres wide.

The plaque is decorated around the edge with key-pattern bands which merge into two elegant dragons' heads. These confront each other on one side of the plaque, like well-mannered sea monsters emerging from the deep. The Scar plaque is unique in Scotland – the only complete one of its kind – but it rivals the finest examples from Norway. A clue to its use comes from a fragmentary plaque discovered on the Isle of Arran. This was accompanied by two smooth, heavy, glass balls, like small curling stones, designed to fit in the hand. Eleven of these glass objects have been found in Scotland and over forty in Norway. We know their purpose, partly from forensic examination, but also because such tools remained in use into the nineteenth century. The glass balls are linen smoothers, whose function was to impart a high gloss to the white linen caps worn by Norse and Scottish women. The plaque, carved out of a solid piece of whale rib, was probably the equivalent of a small portable ironing board, on which the caps could be placed for glazing, as it is called.

In the last decade of the eighth century the prophesy of Jeremiah (1:14) seemed to be coming true in Britain: 'Out of the north an evil shall break forth upon all the inhabitants of the land.' In the south King Offa organised the defence of Kent against heathen seafarers in AD 792. The following year the Norsemen struck the monastery of Lindisfarne. The Viking era had begun.[2]

At first the raids were sporadic, on the north-east coast of England, the west coast of Scotland and the Hebrides and the north-west coast of England.

The *Irish Annal* for AD 794 makes no bones about the impact: 'devastation of all the islands of Britain by the heathens'. Islands were particularly vulnerable and also provided useful staging posts. Viking settlement took hold of the Orkneys and Shetland, perhaps in the early AD 800s; the Isle of Man and Anglesey provided bases in the Irish Sea.[3] Iona was so frequently attacked that the monks fled back to Ireland with the remains of Columba – not surprisingly: in 806 sixty-eight of the Iona community were massacred. In 825 the Vikings captured the Prior of Iona, Blathmacc mac Fliand, who had stayed behind after most of his brethren had left for Ireland.

A poem in praise of Blathmacc described him as a man of royal descent, 'the hope of his homeland', who had abandoned the life of a secular ruler to devote himself to God.* Blathmacc refused to reveal the whereabouts of the precious relics of Columba, supposedly buried on the island, so the Vikings killed him. Many of the treasures must have already gone with the fleeing monks, to Kells, County Meath, the new refuge and main house of the Columban group. The magnificent illuminated gospels, created in Iona and preserved in Ireland, became known as the *Book of Kells*.

The *Annals of Ulster* record only seven years of Viking raids between AD 800 and 820, two of which are against Iona. The intensity increased after 820 – in 821 a large number of women captives were carried off; the monastery of Bangor was attacked in 823 and 824. By the 830s the raids were extending southwards and inland along the Irish river systems. The famous monastery of Clonmacnoise, almost in the centre of Ireland, was hit by the Vikings on 6 March 835. Not that such attacks were exclusively triggered by Norsemen. Only two years earlier the neighbouring Irish King of Munster, Feidlimid mac Crimthainn, had attacked Clonmacnoise and its companion monastery Durrow, massacring the monks and burning the monasteries' fields.

By AD 837 the Viking threat had become seriously well organised: two fleets of sixty longships, each crewed by thirty men, sliced into the heartland of Ireland along the Boyne and the Liffey. Three thousand Vikings was a force to be reckoned with for the small, fragmented kingdoms of Ireland. Nevertheless, the southern Ui Neill mustered an army to take them on, probably near Drogheda. The Irish suffered heavy losses and the *Annals* tell, for the first but not the last time, of warfare 'from

---

* The poem was composed by the German scholar and Abbot of Reichenau on Lake Constance.[4]

Shannon to the sea'.* As the raids intensified, the Viking ambitions grew. In Ireland the first signs of colonisation came with the establishment of *longphorts*, or naval bases, from AD 841, at Linns, County Louth, and Dublin (the Irish name means 'Black Pool').† It would be a mistake to assume that the *longphorts* represent the start of some Norse grand strategy. The Vikings were themselves mixed and fissile groups, ready to split and pursue whatever opportunities arose. Nevertheless, they were clearly becoming more confident and able to operate on a bigger scale, as their political and military systems became more sophisticated. Yet by establishing bases they enabled the Irish forces to strike back at them.

The impact of Vikings as raiders and settlers varied in different parts of the British Isles at different times, depending on local circumstances. In the northern isles settlement probably began early in the years after AD 800. The place names of Orkney and Shetland are almost entirely Scandinavian – not just of the towns and villages, but of all the headlands, cliffs and bays that seafarers would need to recognise from offshore as they navigated around the islands. These names closely resemble those of Norway, not out of sentimentality for the old country, like those given to New York, Boston or Exeter by English colonists in North America, but rather because the words were practical and descriptive, such as Sandvik ('Sandy Bay') or Lerwick ('Muddy Bay'). For these Vikings the northern isles provided convenient places to colonise. From them they could continue to launch their devastating raids on the lands to the south.[5]

It is clear that Orkney was one of the stepping stones by which the Norse people of Scandinavia spanned the northern seas, as far as Iceland, Greenland and Newfoundland. The archaeological evidence, the place names and written language clearly indicate the presence of the Norse: of mariners, warriors, farmers and the women who ran the households, manufactured textiles and raised children. But these Norse people are also familiar to us as Vikings – better known for smashing skulls than pressing linen. Are the men who broke down in Maes Howe the same fearsome pirates who terrified Christendom? The answer is, of course, 'Yes and no.' In Orkney the Norse speak for themselves. We gain a more balanced view of their lives through their writings and from their archaeology, especially in the northern isles. In the south, in England, Wales and Ireland, we hear about them through very different voices.

---

* The *Annals* also give the name of a Viking leader for the first time: '*Saxoilbh, toisech na nGall* – 'Saxolfr, chief of the foreigners'.
† They also established bases and proto-towns at Wicklow (Vikinggalo), Wexford (Veigsfjorthr) and Waterford (Vethrafjorthr), Limerick (Hlymrekr) and Cork.

The first of these is the *Anglo-Saxon Chronicle*, which is one of our major sources for this period; but as we saw with its semi-mythical accounts of English origins, its interpretation is not without problems. The *Chronicle* was compounded from a variety of annals, now mostly lost and unidentifiable, pulled together in Wessex during King Alfred's reign, probably in the AD 890s. Seven different versions now survive. The compiler of the first *Chronicle* used unknown sources, already a century old, for his information. Annual entries come across like a telegram from the past – bald and terse. The first reference to Scandinavians in England occurs in the year AD 789. In this year King Brihtric married Offa's daughter Eadburh. 'And in his days there came for the first time three ships of Northmen. The reeve rode out to meet them and tried to force them to go to the king's residence, for he did not know what they were; and they slew him. These were the first ships of Danish men which came to the land of the English.'

Other versions of the *Chronicle* tell us that these first 'Northmen' actually came from 'Haeredalande' (Horthaland, in western Norway). Another source provides more detail, identifying the place of this first landing as Portland in Dorset. Ethelweard, the Wessex chronicler, gives us the name of the unfortunate reeve: Beaduheard. He rode to the coast from Dorchester, with a small retinue, and made the fatal mistake of assuming that the newcomers had arrived to trade and would, therefore, need to be escorted to see the local king to obtain suitable permissions. The origin of these first raiders remains a matter of dispute. By the time the *Anglo-Saxon Chronicle* itself was compiled, the Danes, with their large occupying armies, had become the big problem for Alfredian England – did the later chronicler refer to the new arrivals as 'Danish men' because the Danes dominated the thinking of his own time? The south coast of England is off the beaten track for Norwegian sailors. A Danish home-land would make more sense for these new arrivals at Portland.

However, there is no doubt about the next recorded raiders in England. They were definitely Norwegians; and their arrival on the north-east coast generated an outburst of purple prose from the usually laconic chronicler:

> 793. In this year dire portents appeared over Northumbria and sorely frightened the people. They consisted of immense whirlwinds and flashes of lightning and fiery dragons were seen flying in the air. A great famine immediately followed these signs, and a little later in the same year, on 8 June, the ravages of the heathen men, miserably destroyed God's church on Lindisfarne with plunder and slaughter.

The Lindisfarne raid sent shock waves through Christendom. Violence was an everyday occurrence, but this was different. Heathens had despoiled one of British Christianity's most sacred places. Three hundred years later, in the early twelfth century, Simeon of Durham described these raiders as 'stinging hornets' and 'ravenous wolves' who smashed holy relics, hacked down nuns and priests and looted monastic treasures. His language is reminiscent of the earlier diatribes of Gildas – and it created the image of rapacious Vikings which has since launched a thousand historical novels, romantic paintings and lurid films.

News of the Lindisfarne sacrilege rapidly spread abroad, to the most important court in northern Europe, that of Charlemagne ('Charles the Great'). The Frankish king's adviser was one of the great intellectuals of his day, the Englishman Alcuin of York. Alcuin was so appalled that he sent off not one but seven letters – to the Archbishop of Canterbury, three to the King of Northumbria, Ethelhard, and others to the Bishop of Lindisfarne, the monks at Jarrow and a priest at Lindisfarne. 'It has been nearly three hundred and fifty years that we and our fathers have lived in this most beautiful land,' wrote Alcuin, overlooking the fact that he was himself an early example of the brain drain and resided on the Continent. 'Never before has such a terror appeared in Britain and never was such a landing from the sea thought possible.'

Like Gildas when describing Anglo-Saxon aggression, Alcuin blamed the victims. God was punishing the Christian monks for not keeping up to scratch. Nevertheless, the psychological impact of the raid is evident from his letters, as it is from the portents described in the *Anglo-Saxon Chronicle*. Alcuin was genuinely shocked by the news, in his own words: 'to behold the church of St Cuthbert splattered with the blood of the priests of God'.

This was only the beginning. The following year the Norsemen returned, this time to strike again the monastery where Bede himself had spent his life. Jarrow, on a bluff above the River Tyne, was as vulnerable to attack from the North Sea as the island of Lindisfarne. But this time there was fierce resistance. The *Anglo-Saxon Chronicle* provides the bare bones of the events: '794. And the heathens ravaged in Northumbria and plundered Ecgfrith's monastery of Donemuthan. One of their leaders was killed there, and some of their ships were broken to bits by storms, and many of the men were drowned there. Some reached the shore alive and were immediately killed at the mouth of the river.'

On this occasion the late St Cuthbert, it was said, had strengthened the arm of the English. The Vikings were not invulnerable; and they would not receive Christian charity – rather the strong right arm of God's agent.

So who were these raiders from across the North Sea? Nowadays we call them Vikings — a word that suggests long-haired thugs in horned helmets, but one that was rarely used by contemporaries.* To the Anglo-Saxons they were more often Nordmanni ('Northmen'), Dani ('Danes') or heathens. Nationality in modern terms was meaningless, as it was only in this period, in the eighth to tenth centuries, that nation-states began to emerge in the Scandinavian homelands of these raiders. The meaning and origin of the word 'Viking' is uncertain: in Old Icelandic, *vic* referred to a bay or an inlet; it is also the name of the region near present-day Oslo. So were Vikings originally people from southern Norway, or did the name describe pirates who lay in wait, their ships hidden within creeks, ready to pounce on hapless trading vessels? In Icelandic a *vikingr* was a pirate and to go on *a viking* meant to go on an expedition. So not all Scandinavians were Vikings, any more than all later Englishmen had careers as buccaneers with Henry Morgan and Captain Kidd.

The first use of the term in Old English, in fact, referred to piratical activity in the Mediterranean (and by whom it was perpetrated we do not know). The *Anglo-Saxon Chronicle* uses the term *wicings* on only five occasions, in describing relatively small raids. For several succeeding centuries, through the Middle Ages, the word was not used at all. Vikings disappeared from the English collective memory, only to be resurrected in the eighteenth century and elevated by literary romantics and popular histories in the nineteenth century. As the historical novels of Sir Walter Scott captured popular imagination, the Vikings were reinvented. One of the best-known Viking sites in Shetland — Jarlshof — has a name that is a pure Scott concoction: invented by Sir Walter when he visited the ruins of the seventeenth-century laird's house in 1814 and set the opening of his novel *The Pirate* on this dramatic site. Others contributed to the fantasy and Viking stories became commonplace in school textbooks and in popular fiction, not only in Britain but also on the Continent. A picture in *The History of France for Primary Schools* (*L'Histoire de France des Écoles Primaires*, 1895) is typical: sword- and axe-wielding Norsemen hack down venerable bearded monks and women and children who lie in pools of blood, while they haul their loot and slaves back to the dragon-prowed longships.

The operas of Wagner not only created the sound of the Valkyries and the Teutonic gods; their stage-sets generated the popular image of Germanic pagans. As a result, winged and horned helmets are indelibly, if fictitiously, engraved in most people's image of the Vikings. Pre-Raphaelite artists were also attracted to the romance of the Vikings. William Morris

---

* In fact, the Vikings shaved their hair, leaving a tuft at the front, and wore conical helmets. There is no evidence for horns or wings.

visited Iceland in 1871 and 1873 and translated several Icelandic sagas.* He said of the *Volsunga Saga*: 'This is the Great Story of the North, which should be to our race what the Tale of Troy is to the Greeks.' Morris's business partner and fellow painter Ford Maddox Brown also tackled Viking themes such as *The Expulsion of the Danes from Manchester* (*c*.1880, in Manchester Town Hall). As a result the Vikings are established in the British national myth and we still question the extent to which they were plunderers, traders, or even genetically our own ancestors.

The vivid, if lurid, nineteenth-century images are direct descendants of the accounts by English, Irish and French monks. The Vikings, at the time of the early raids, provided no written records of their own to tell us about their motivation, or to describe events from their point of view. In recent years there has been a reaction on the part of archaeologists and historians, an attempt to revise the image of Europe's most ferocious rapists and pillagers. Instead, York's Jorvik Viking Centre emphasises more positive roles for the Vikings – or, more accurately, the Norse – as promoters of international trade; as craftspeople and town builders; as masters of maritime communication from Newfoundland to Russia to North Africa and the Black Sea. This shift of emphasis helps to bring the Viking world into sharper focus, but though Viking piracy may have become an historical cliché, for the people who lived around the shores of Britain, Ireland and France in the eighth and ninth centuries, the threat was real – and especially shocking because to these Christian communities it appeared that God was inflicting his wrath upon them. Ireland, with its rich monastic culture, was especially vulnerable to Norwegian raids. One Irish monk left his thoughts, in his own language, in the margin of a Latin grammar:

> *Is acher in gaith innocht*
> *Fo-fuasna fairggae findfolt*
> *Ni agor, remm mora minn*
> *Dond laechraid lainn va Lothlind*†

> ['The bitter wind is high tonight
> It lifts the white locks of the sea;
> In such wild winter storm no fright
> Of savage Viking troubles me.']‡

* The Icelandic sagas, like Homer's *Iliad* and *Odyssey* are stories – literature set in a distant past – which cannot be treated like objective history.

† The Irish word for 'Viking', 'Lothlind', refers to their raiders' place of origin: Lothland, or Rogaland. Most of the Norse loan-words in Irish also come from the dialect of this part of south-west Norway.[6]

‡ Translation by R. Flower (1947), *The Irish Tradition*, Oxford, p. 38.

According to the *Anglo-Saxon Chronicle*, there were sporadic hit-and-run raids by 'Northmen' from about AD 789 to 864. Irish monasteries of the north and east coast such as Rathlin (Rechru) were attacked from 795. The *Annals of Ulster* record 'the burning of Rechru by the heathens', and that Skye was overwhelmed and laid waste. In the same year probably the same Vikings plundered Iona of its treasures and livestock, their compatriots returning again in AD 802, 806, 807 and 825. Iona had the misfortune to be sited, like a convenient service station, on the Viking seaway down the west coast of Scotland. These raids were carried out by relatively small numbers of Viking ships – anything from three to fifty, with crews of up to fifty men apiece, working in shifts, two men to an oar. In spite of the *Chronicle*'s emphasis that the raiders where 'heathenmen', the Vikings were not on some pagan equivalent of a crusade. They were after loot; and monasteries were the best place to find it. Lindisfarne, Jarrow and Iona were not simple places of prayer and poverty. These monasteries were great landowners. Like the royal families, with whom they were closely associated, the monks needed to reflect the status and power of their Lord, their founders and themselves through the visible display of objects of great value. Beautiful objects such as illuminated gospels and church silver made suitable diplomatic gifts for kings and bishops – and irresistible targets for Viking thieves.

Bede criticised the nuns of Coldingham (their abbess, Abbe, about AD 680, was the sister of the Northumbrian king) for spending their time 'weaving delicate clothes with which to adorn themselves like brides and make friends with visiting men'. A century later the habits, in both senses of the word, were not much different. In 786 an English Church Council, not for the first time, condemned male and female ecclesiastics for their 'elaborate dress dyed with the colours of India'.

Faced with repeated Viking threats, the monks of Lindisfarne left the island in AD 875, taking the body of St Cuthbert and his relics to the mainland for safe-keeping.* Since 995 they have rested securely, providing a focus of devotion, at the great cathedral of Durham.†

---

* Cuthbert came to Lindisfarne in AD 664 from Melrose, which was strategically sited on the Tweed valley route to Iona. After the Synod of Whitby which decided the Easter question in favour of the Roman dating system, it was Cuthbert's role to reconcile the British (Celtic) and Roman differences. Because of Bede's comments, these have been exaggerated. Celtic Christians were the opposite of introverted isolationists and did not harbour pre-existing antipathy to Rome.[7] The Whitby Synod did not lead to the entire rejection of the Celtic Christian tradition. Cuthbert himself retreated, in the latter part of his life, to his hermitage on the Farne Islands, his 'gateway to resurrection' through ascetic contemplation, where he died alone in AD 687

† Excepting the attentions of Henry VIII's commissioners in 1539/40, who were relatively restrained in the face of such saintly authority, but probably removed the *Lindisfarne Gospels*, which can now be seen in the British Library.

St Cuthbert's superb pectoral cross is made of gold and garnets, with the central boss of shell which originated in the warm waters of the Red Sea or Indian Ocean. The garnets probably followed a similar route, from India via Byzantium,* along with the ivory used to make the saint's liturgical comb. Cuthbert's body was wrapped in Byzantine cloth of silk from the Orient and accompanied by a gospel book bound in beautifully moulded leather. Other gospels, such as St Wilfrid's, were encased in gold- and jewel-encrusted covers which reflected the sumptuous pages of decoration in the *Lindisfarne Gospels*, the earliest surviving translation of the gospels into English, the *Book of Kells* or the *Book of Durrow*. It was the jewels rather than the pious reading matter that attracted the pagan Vikings. They were, though, well aware of Christian practice: they co-ordinated their raids with Christian feast days, when the sacred vessels and the congregation could be captured.

Monasteries were not only home to important, lordly monks who loved display; they were centres for industry and craftsmanship, which accumulated precious stones, gold, silver and sumptuous textiles as the raw materials for their manufactures. Even Bede, who extolled the simple life, on his deathbed left presents of pepper, incense and precious spices from the remote Orient. The monasteries were channels for exotic materials from as far afield as India, Italy, Spain and France. Their stone buildings were often the most substantial in the region and also acted like banks or vaults for other people's valuables.

It is not surprising that the Vikings were attracted by the scent of such luxurious piety. But why in the last years of the eighth century? The arrival of these fierce raiders from the pagan north came as a shock to the Christians of Britain and mainland Europe. Previously the Norsemen had stayed close to home in the fjords of Norway and the islands and inlets of Denmark. But things were changing in Scandinavia. Historians have sometimes emphasised population pressure as the main motivation for Viking expeditions and, certainly, agricultural land was restricted along the narrow coastal strip of Norway with its steep fjords. However, it is probably an oversimplification to assume that population growth was the prime factor. In parts of Scandinavia there were still large areas into which farming, grazing and forestry could expand. There were other reasons for raiding.

The small-scale tribal societies were becoming increasingly complex. Like late Iron Age southern Britain or seventh-century Anglo-Saxon England, Scandinavia was going through the initial stages of state

---

* Bohemia is another possible source.

formation. Ironically, it was increasing contact with the south that helped to generate these changes. The southern, Christian kingdoms had themselves begun to cast an eye on Scandinavia with motives which were not entirely pure. The pagan north was the source of desirable furs, walrus ivory, timber, amber and potential converts to Christianity. Luxury goods such as Rhenish glass and coinage, together with new political and social ideas infiltrated the north. Increasing contact with southern neighbours generated change and the process of eighth-century modernisation. Petty kings and their retinues became engaged in a vicious struggle for power. This internal competition generated a need for wealth and prestige. By boosting their reputations, distributing gold and silver, foreign luxuries and weapons to their followers, these would-be dynasty builders could recruit even more retainers to their side, or eject their rivals. The easiest way to fuel these ambitions or relieve the frustration of defeat was by raiding richer soft targets in Britain and France.

Vikings could descend on their prey suddenly and without warning because of the effectiveness of their craft. The longship, the *dreki*, or dragon-ship, is the emblem of the Vikings themselves: swift, manoeuvrable, capable of penetrating the rivers of Europe or drawing up on the beaches through shallow water. Thanks to their ships, the Vikings could literally turn up out of the blue.

The pagan Vikings have left no records of their shipbuilding, but fortunately some of the vessels themselves survive. To the Vikings their ships were more than mere transportation – they were symbols of status and of myth. As such, ships, some of which have been discovered and excavated, were often used to bury their dead, especially the more important members of society.

One such acted as the burial chamber of a royal woman who died in the ninth century. The well-preserved Oseberg ship epitomises the elegance of Viking craft. Decorated with intricate carvings and with a tendril-like curvilinear prow, this ship looks as if it has been grown and cultivated rather than built. However, the Vikings would not have braved the North Sea in this delicate little creation. The Oseberg ship, 21.6 metres long and 5 metres wide, was probably a royal barge for use on sheltered waterways, the Viking equivalent of the encrusted coach in which the Queen today progresses down the Mall.

The even-better-preserved Gokstad ship, also found near Oslo and excavated in 1880, was a less ornate and refined vessel, but still beautifully proportioned: clinker-built with a shallow draft and a central keel. A massive central timber known as a 'mast fish' gripped the mast in place. The overlapping planks, or strakes, were held with iron nails whose ends were flattened over a washer, or rove. When the timbers rot away it is these corroded nails that mark out the shape of the ship in the ground, as at Sutton Hoo. The Gokstad ship also contained a small four-oared boat, a *faering* 6.5 metres long, similar to that found at Scar in Orkney.

Viking shipbuilding was part of a long north-European tradition of creating seagoing vessels, which includes the fourth-century Nydam and the seventh-century Sutton Hoo ships. Such vessels enabled the people of northern Europe to raid, trade, migrate to new lands with their families or intermarry with foreigners. The phase of raiding from the late eighth century was followed by trading and colonising expeditions. The *Laxdaela Saga*, written down in Iceland in the thirteenth century, tells the story of how one family came to leave Norway and settle in Scotland. A powerful chieftain, Ketil, fell foul of King Harald Finehair. He decided to abandon his home with his family rather than risk assassination. The sons wanted to go to Iceland, where, they said, the rivers flowed with salmon and the seas were full of whales. But Ketil had other plans: he preferred to go west across the sea to Scotland because he thought it was a good living there. He knew the country well, for he had raided there extensively. Actually he had probably used Scotland as a seasonal base from which to raid Ireland.[8]

As the Vikings developed trading links and overseas colonies in the Faroes, Iceland, Orkney, Ireland and England, they required seaworthy vessels capable of carrying cargo, animals and greater numbers of people. Such a vessel was Skuldelev 1 (deliberately scuppered in the narrows of the Roskilde Fjord to prevent a sea-borne attack on the Danish royal town of Roskilde), which could be operated by a twelve-man crew. These were still open boats and sailors and passengers were exposed to the elements. When close to land the vessels were probably beached at night so that the crew could cook and sleep on terra firma. On longer voyages across the North Atlantic the Vikings had to make do as best they could, living on dried and salted rations, sleeping wrapped in animal skins or in cosy two-man sleeping bags.

How the Vikings navigated out of sight of land we do not know — possibly with a mixture of dead reckoning and celestial observation and skilled observation of nature, clouds, seabirds and inshore fish. Some suggest that they used the magnetic properties of feldspar crystals. There is no doubt, though, that Vikings, like Polynesians, had mastered ocean navigation. The North Atlantic is dotted with a convenient series of stepping-stones: from Norway it is 230 miles to the Shetlands, another 190 miles to the Faroes; 240 miles beyond lies Iceland and another 190 miles take the voyager to Greenland. Fortunately this was a period when the climate was relatively mild.* Whatever the motivation – land-hunger, a desire for plunder and status, escape from rivals, or sheer curiosity and the urge to explore – within a few decades, from the late eighth century to AD 900, the Vikings had established themselves across the North Atlantic from Norway to America.

We know this from archaeological evidence and from the later sagas; but the Vikings were not always the first to find these northern islands. Irish monks had reached the Faroes at least a century earlier. Their motivation was clear and certainly different from that of the Vikings: the *peregrinato pro Christo*, or 'pilgrimage for Christ', drove them selflessly into the unknown – pilgrimage as a form of penance, and a spiritual quest into the northern equivalent of the desert.

When the Vikings landed on the Faroes, they found the Irish monks waiting for them, enjoying the peace and solitude. But not for long. Another of Charlemagne's Irish intellectuals has left us a clear account. Dicuil, in AD 825, wrote a treatise, *Liber de mensura orbis terrae* ('On the Measurement of the Earth'),[10] in which he says that there are islands to the north of Britain. He continues:

> A devout priest told me that in two summer days and the in-tervening night he sailed in a two-benched board and landed on one of them. Some of these islands are very small, nearly all are separated from one another by narrow stretches of water. On these islands hermits sailing from our country Scotia [Ireland] have lived for nearly a hundred years. But just as they were always deserted from the beginning of the world, so now because of the Northmen pirates they are emptied of anchorites and filled with countless sheep and a great variety of sea-fowls.

The names Papey and Papos in south-west Iceland point to the early arrival of Irish monks, who must have criss-crossed these same seas like the Vikings, with less panache, but as much fortitude, in their leather-covered currachs.

The place name 'Papa' – as in Papa Westray (Orkney) and Papa Stour (Shetland) – records the presence of these Christian fathers on even the tiniest of Atlantic islands; they even landed on the backs of whales, according to a joke in the semi-mythical account of St Brendan's voyages. They may also have reached Iceland, whose position was recorded

* From about the ninth to the twelfth centuries there was a climatic optimum. As the climate thereafter deteriorated, the Norse found the conditions in places like Greenland much more difficult and even impossible.[9]

by classical writers Polybius, Pliny, Strabo and Tacitus as six days' voyage from Britain. Bede repeated this information in his writings on time: a land where there is no night at the summer solstice, nor day at the winter solstice, and which lies one day's journey south of the eternal ice.*

The Vikings arrived in the Faroes via Orkney and Shetland sometime in the first two decades of the ninth century. They probably found the poor Irish hermits scarcely worth robbing. The real wealth of the islands, as Dicuil writes, was to be found in sheep, as the Norse name Faereyjar, or 'Sheep Islands', implies. Fish, fowl and pilot whales also allowed the Norse settlers to eke out a living. Viking reports about the attractions of Iceland varied. According to the *Landnamabok* – the Icelandic 'Book of Settlements' – which records the Viking landholding, two early arrivals, Naddod the Viking (sailing from Norway and leaving in the autumn for the Faroes) and Gardar Svararsson (packed off from home by his mother), found the land to their liking. The third arrival, Floki Vilgerdarson, sailed from Shetland. He spent so much time fishing that he failed to make hay and his livestock died during the winter. After a tough few months he sailed for Norway. 'When asked about the place he gave it a bad name' – hence it was known as Iceland.†

In spite of its off-putting name, Norse settlers could not keep away. For a period of sixty years from AD 870 there was a surge of immigrants from Norway and the British Isles. These were not raiders or summer visitors: the new Icelanders meant to stay – and so they did, becoming the only independent, self-supporting Norse community overseas and one which, thanks to its rich saga tradition, culturally at least outshone the homeland.

The *Landnamabok* was probably written down in the twelfth century, and the earliest surviving edition dates to a century later. However, it records the names of 400 original settlers, their places of origin, family information and some of the idiosyncracies of individuals such as Rolf the Thick and Thorkell the Tall. The leader of the settlers, according to the book, was Ingolf Arnarson. His brother Hjorleif separated from him

* Dicuil was even better informed: 'It is now thirty years [from AD 825] since clerics, who had lived on the island from the first of February to the first of August told me that not only at the summer solstice but in the days round about it the sun setting in the evening hides itself as though behind a small hill in such a way that there was no darkness in that very small space of time and a man could do whatever he wished as though the sun were still there, even remove lice from his shirt.'

† A note of caution: archaeology has not been able to confirm the presence of Irish clerics from excavations in Iceland, where the word '*papa*' is used as a nickname for puffins. It is also possible that the 'Papa' names were brought to Iceland by the Vikings themselves, who had adopted them from Orkney.

to settle further west. As Hjorleif had only one ox, he ordered his slaves to pull the plough needed to break the land for the first sowing. This was too much even for slaves, who attacked Hjorleif and his men, killed them and carried off the Viking belongings and their women to an offshore island. When Ingolf discovered what had happened to his brother, he went after the slaves and killed the lot of them.

The *Landnamabok* suggests that these leaders arrived in Iceland with their families and their retinues of servants and slaves. They staked out an estate – as much land as they could walk around in one day – which was then subdivided amongst the followers, under the lordship of their leader.

Interestingly, of the 400 settlers mentioned by name as many as 7 per cent came from islands off Britain, mainly Ireland and the Outer Hebrides. Some of these, such as Cetil One-Hand, are specifically named as Irish ('*Iskr*'). The Norsemen also had Irish wives and concubines, as well as Irish slaves, or *thralls*. Even one of the great saga figures, Njall (or Neil), the wise but doomed lawgiver, was probably of Irish descent.

The historical evidence for Norse and Irish/Scottish intermarriage is confirmed by various DNA studies of the Icelandic population. Genetic profiling of over 16,000 Icelanders, using mitochondrial DNA, indicated that over 60 per cent of the women among the original settlers came not from Scandinavia but from Scotland or Ireland. Other genetic tests suggest that about 20 per cent of the men were also Scots/Irish.* The mitochondrial DNA results suggest that some of the Norse who settled in Iceland had previously lived in Scotland or Ireland and married local girls, or that they captured them during raids. Modern Icelanders have made much of this Irish element in their genetic make-up, even suggesting that it has contributed to their literary genius.

The *Landnamabok* has to be treated with caution as a source. It is not an objective and accurate census. The 400 settlers represent the leading men or families only, not the total population of Iceland. Estimates of this vary for Iceland in the settlement period, but figures around 20,000 to 30,000 seem reasonable, rising to perhaps 60,000 in the later Viking period. It is clear that the Norse settlers rapidly exploited every square metre of useful land, from Reykjavik ('Smoky Bay'), where Ingolf himself set up home, to Iceland's Pompeii, the valley of Thjorsardalur. This once-fertile valley, home to twenty Viking farms, was blanketed by ash from an eruption of Mount Hekla. Farmhouses, such as that excavated and reconstructed at Stong, show how these Viking farmer-sailors lived.

---

* While Norse women made up 35 per cent of the female ancestors of the inhabitants of Orkney and 12 per cent of the people of Skye and the Hebrides.[11]

Thick turf walls and roofs of live grass enclosed a twelve-metre-long hall, a living room, dairy and lavatory. The design is similar to the Viking buildings I helped excavate and which are found throughout the northern isles, in Orkney, with central hearths and side benches. This style of turf hut continued into the nineteenth century. In 1863 Sabine Baring-Gould described the roofs and walls of Reykjavik as 'of mouldy green as if some long-since inhabited country had been fished up out of the sea'. These single-storey Icelandic turf farmhouses, roofed with flowering grasses and appearing to grow out of the hillsides, were still commonplace in the landscape during William Morris's grand tour. It was seeing a traditional Icelandic loom, still a feature of the living room, that persuaded him to install one into his own house.

In Iceland Norse farmers, with their Irish and Scottish wives and slaves, colonised a virgin land as settlers rather than as raiders. Further south, in the populous islands of Britain, they were faced with a more complex situation; and for archaeologists the evidence for population movement and cultural and genetic interaction is more difficult to interpret.

Jarlshof, in spite of its fake name, is the best-known Viking settlement in Shetland, thanks to extensive excavations in the 1930s. The Vikings took over a site which had been occupied for millennia. It lay on the southernmost tip of Shetland, on the promontory known as Sumburgh. This Old Norse name — *Svinaborg* — may mean 'The Fort of the Pigs' and refer to the earlier broch — the stone fortified tower — still visible to the first Viking settlers. They selected Jarlshof as a place to establish a farmstead for the same reason as their Pictish predecessors: it had easy access to the sea, a good fresh-water supply, fertile land and plenty of building stone and turf — the ideal base for a family of farmers, fishermen and pirates.

Their lives may have followed the pattern described in the *Orkneyinga Saga*, which portrays the seasonal round of Svein Asleifarson.[12] In the spring he had more than enough to occupy him, with a great deal of land to sow, which he saw to himself. When that job was done, he would go off plundering, in the Hebrides and in Ireland, on what he called his 'spring trip'; then back home just after midsummer, where he stayed till the cornfields had been reaped and the grain was safely stowed away. After that he would go off raiding again and not come back till the first month of winter was ended. This he used to call his 'autumn trip'. While the men were away having a good time the women would look after the farm.

The Jarlshof farmstead had a typical Viking longhouse, with a barn, a smithy and possibly a sauna. Over the generations some of these buildings were abandoned or re-used, while new ones were built. The excavations produced a great deal of evidence of daily life: fishing weights, oil lamps, bone dress pins carved with animal heads, haircombs, spindle whorls and loom weights. These last were often made from steatite, or soapstone, a form of talc which can be easily carved and was one of Shetland's most important natural resources. It must have reminded the Vikings of home, as Norway also had plentiful supplies. The Norse had a name for steatite: *kleberg*, which also means a loom-weight stone. One of the main soapstone quarries is at Cunningsburgh ('The King's Stronghold'), an old Norse name which reflects the importance of the traditional landowner and the Viking tendency to take over important Pictish places. The open-cast quarries at Cunningsburgh still retain the shapes of the bowls which were cut from the soapstone and then hollowed out.

The Jarlshof farm thrived for centuries: breeding and rearing sheep, cattle and pigs, typically using everything but the squeal, if the archaeological evidence is anything to go by. The Shetland Norse also had dogs and ponies — a little larger than today's Shetland ponies — which they must frequently have loaded onto their ships to transport to more remote islands. When William Morris visited Iceland, they were still the main form of transport. Fishing was also important at Jarlshof and Viking ship technology improved access to the deep sea. The Vikings hauled in large cod, saithe and ling. On Orkney two deep middens show the growing importance of deep-sea fishing to the Viking settlers. Dried and salted 'stockfish' was subsequently traded across the North Sea and into England.

We do not know the names of the early Norse inhabitants of Jarlshof. However, we do have, unusually, some human images scratched as graffiti onto fragments of stone. Along with sketches of boats there is a profile of a bearded man with curly hair and a large staring eye. The style, such as it is, resembles that of the Pictish symbol stone at the Brough of Birsay, with its three Pictish warriors carrying spears and ornate square shields. If the Jarlshof drawing is of a Pict, it raises the question of what happened to the native inhabitants of Orkney and Shetland. The landscape was completely relabelled in the Norse language; a Norse dialect survived in Orkney until the eighteenth century. A cross-slab from the churchyard at Culbinsgarth, on the Shetland island of Bressay, provides a clue to the cultural and genetic mixing that must have taken place. The inscription is in Ogham, the form of writing invented in Ireland and used in Pictland: it includes the Gaelic words for 'cross' and 'son' and the Norse word for 'daughter'.

The population must have become a true mix of native British and Norse. There are clues in the archaeological evidence that the two ethnic groups lived side by side, and intermarried. For example, the Vikings used steatite and wooden vessels but did not make pots.* However, at Old Scatness in Shetland, a typical Viking settlement, steatite vessels are found alongside Pictish barrel-shaped pots. Could this indicate Pictish wives feeding their Viking husbands in their local fashion?

The Norse also came to settle on the northernmost mainland of Scotland, across the Pentland firth.† They gave this area the name Katanes (now Caithness), meaning 'Headland of the Cats'. Beyond this was Sudreland (Sutherland) – 'The South Land'. Its native inhabitants spoke Gaelic and to them Caithness, where the Norse settled, was Gallaibh – 'Among the Strangers' – and the Hebrides Innse Gall – 'The Islands of the Strangers'. The Norse farmers in Orkney and Caithness probably used native Picts to work their land either as slaves (like the colonisers of Iceland) or as a peasantry, much depressed on the social scale.

The Icelandic *Landnamabok* provides a specific and reliable example of what happened to one high-ranking Celtic family whose fate was to be caught up in the Viking maelstrom. Erp was the son of Earl Lelduin of Argyll and Muirgeal, the daughter of an Irish king. His father was killed by Earl Sigurd the Mighty of Orkney and his mother Muirgeal was enslaved. In captivity she became the faithful handmaid of Earl Sigurd's wife and was then sold 'for a high price' to Aud the Deep-Minded, one of the leading women in saga literature and an Icelandic matriarch. Muirgeal and her son, Erp, were among the slaves transported to Iceland with Aud. Most of them were subsequently freed and some became founders of important Icelandic families. Aud said of Erp: 'It has never been my wish that a man of such high birth should be called a slave.'

The slave trade was an essential feature of Viking raiding and *thralls*, or the unfree, were an important element in Norse society until the twelfth century. Viking slavers hunted far afield for their prey. If the English turned the Welsh into slaves, the Vikings did the same for the Slavs (hence our modern English word 'slave'). From the Baltic and the Atlantic to the Mediterranean and the Black Sea, the Vikings made a serious business out of slavery, routinely exchanging captured slaves with Islamic merchants and dragging off Picts, English and Britons to their base in Dublin.‡

* This is not strictly true. In some places, unusually, Vikings picked up the craft from their neighbours. However, most Viking settlements are 'accramic'.
† The Pentland Firth, the stretch of water separating the Orkneys from mainland Scotland, was known to the Vikings as Pettlandsfjodr – 'The Fjord of the Picts'.
‡ In AD 871 Ivarr the Boneless and Olaf the White brought 'a great multitude' of slaves, according to the *Annals of Ulster*.

The Irish *Fragmentary Annals* records that while the Viking Ragnald and one of his sons remained in Orkney, his two other sons sailed southwards. They returned with black slaves from North Africa:

As fdda dna ro badar na fir ghorma sin i nEirinn

['And these black men remained in Ireland for a long time.'] [13]

This is not as far-fetched as it might seem. In AD 844 a Moorish embassy paid a diplomatic visit to a Norse Court in Ireland following a Viking attack on Seville. It is also worth remembering that several centuries earlier someone brought a Barbary ape to Tara.

The Vikings did not, of course, have a monopoly on slave trading. Slavery was institutionalised in the Roman Empire and Irish slavers from the north-east of the island captured the sixteen-year-old Roman Britain Patrick. Slaves appear in some of the earliest English law codes: those of Ethelbert of Kent, set out between AD 597 and 616. Gregory the Great, who is famously said by Bede to have seen Anglian slaves in Rome, also records in a letter of 599 that Jewish slavers were doing business in northern Gaul, where, presumably, they would have acquired English and British slaves. In spite of supposed Christian disapproval, slaves are still recorded in the Domesday Book in 1086. The internecine wars between Anglo-Saxon tribes and the conquest of British kingdoms, particularly in the south-west, furnished a regular supply of captives. Bede tells the story of the Mercian nobleman Inma, who was taken on the battlefield by Northumbrians in AD 679. Instead of killing Inma, his captors sold him to a Frisian slave trader in London. Fortunately Inma was wealthy enough to buy his freedom. For the poor, slavery was a constant threat: a father could sell a son under the age of seven into slavery; beyond that age he had to have the son's agreement. According to Kentish law, criminals could also be punished by enslavement: for theft, fornication and kidnapping monks.

Most of the Anglo-Saxon records of slavery involve the capture of fellow countrymen. Christian Anglo-Saxons were not supposed to sell their co-religionists across the sea, in case the enslaved fell into heathen hands and were prevented from practising their religion. Clearly such sales did take place and people were shipped abroad against their wishes. Marseilles was a major slave-trading port and the life of St Eligius records him freeing Saxons (probably English) there in AD 641. The most famous Anglo-Saxon slave, Balthild, may also have been purchased in Marseilles. We know her story because she was exceptionally lucky, becoming the wife of the Merovingian King Clovis II (639–657). Balthild was said to have been bought for a pittance, as a house slave for a retainer in the royal palace named Herchinoald. Like many attractive female slaves, she caught the eye of the master. With her transformation in status she was able to sponsor monasteries near Paris and in Picardy, which she stocked with English men and women whose freedom she had purchased herself. Documentary sources suggest that while Balthild's good fortune may have been exceptional, she was one of many English slaves on the Continent in this period.

The London slaver who puchased the Mercian captive Inma was a Frisian. Frisians were well known as traders and middlemen in many commodities, including people. A Frisian colony appears in York in the mid-eighth century as the town prospered. The Anglo-Saxon word for Briton — *wealh* (hence, 'Welsh') — is clearly used to refer to slaves in tenth-century West Saxon texts. This may have resulted from the Anglo-Saxon expansion from Wessex into south-west Britain and the large-scale enslavement that followed.

A satirical verse by Warner of Rouen, composed about 1020, tells of the bawdy adventures of a Celtic poet Moriuht, an eleventh-century Tom Jones, who was captured by a band of Danes. They sold him at Corbridge (on the line of Hadrian's Wall, it was strategically placed between the English, the Scots and the Norse kingdom of York.). There he was bought by a monastery of women, with predictable results. Forced to flee when his industrious activities came to light, Moriuht was taken by Danes again and sold to a widow woman on some Continental Saxon slave market. After seducing her, he departed for Rouen — another major trading centre — near where he redeemed his own wife from slavery. Although this is a satire and fantasy, Warner of Rouen based it on the real context of a flourishing slave trade in which Corbridge and Rouen featured as markets. Another was Bristol, where slaves brought from across the country were sold to Ireland. The Norse place names in South Wales and along the Severn estuary testify to the importance of the Bristol Channel for the Vikings.*

The Church's attitude to slavery was ambiguous at best: some churchmen were major owners. However, Wulfstan, Bishop of London and Worcester and Archbishop of York, was one Anglo-Saxon who determinedly opposed the Bristol trade in the early years of the second millennium: 'You might well groan to see the long rows of young men and maidens whose beauty and youth might move the pity of a savage, bound together and brought to be sold.'[15] After the Norman Conquest Wulfstan's campaign was eventually successful when William agreed to outlaw the

---

* Names like 'Milford (Haven)' – 'The Sandbank Fjord'; Gateholm – 'The She-goat Island'; Fishguard – 'The Enclosure for Catching fish', and Lundy – 'Puffin Island'.[14]

Anglo-Irish trade – somewhat unwillingly, as he received four pence on every slave sale. The slave trade, but not slavery itself, was prohibited in England at the Westminster Council of AD 1102. That did not stop the Irish, Welsh and Scots raiding England in search of fresh victims.

After seventy years or more of raiding, the Scandinavian threat to Britain and Ireland took an even more sinister turn for the local rulers and their subjects. Full-scale armies began to arrive with an eye to acquiring land and power on a long-term basis. These Danish armies were no longer attached to the umbilical cord of rivers and their mother ships; from AD 865 they criss-crossed the country at high speed, unfailingly detecting weaknesses in the Anglo-Saxon kingdoms that they encountered. Northumberland, indulging in a civil war at just the wrong time, was the first to succumb. There is a particularly significant entry in the *Anglo-Saxon Chronicle*: '876. And that year Healfdene shared out the lands of the Northumbrians, and they proceeded to plough and to support themselves.' The Norse were settling down and taking over Northumbrian estates.

The following years saw the Danes acquiring land across much of England. In AD 877: 'Then in the harvest season the army went away into Mercia and shared out some of it, and gave some to Ceolwulf'; and three years later, in 880: 'In this year the army went from Cirencester into East Anglia, and settled there and shared out the land.'*

Armies do not often leave much trace in the archaeological record but there is an exception at Repton (Derbyshire). In AD 873–4 the Great Army of the Danes overwintered there, next to a monastery and the mausoleum of the Mercian royal family built in the eighth century. In the later ninth century, part of the mausoleum was re-used as a charnel house. A mound edged with stones and about 13 metres across was placed on top in such a position that it could be seen from the River Trent. Repton was excavated by the Oxford archaeologists Martin Biddle and Birthe Kyølby-Biddle, who discovered the skeletons of four adolescents in the top of the mound.[17] These looked remarkably like human sacrifices. The charnel house beneath contained a confusing mass of human remains, which included 249 left femurs and 221 skulls, many of which belonged to young men. The excavators believed that they had found the remains of soldiers of the Danish army who had

---

* Four hundred human skulls and other bones found in pits in the churchyard at Buttington (Montgomeryshire), on the bank of the Severn near Welshpool, may be the victims of the Battle of Buttington recorded in the *Anglo-Saxon Chronicle*. Here the Welsh and English combined to besiege the Danes until, when some had died of starvation, the desperate defenders broke out and a bloody fight took place.[16]

fallen in various encounters with the English and been brought to Repton. Sceptics counter that the bones may simply be those of both recently and long-dead inhabitants of the monastic cemetery, disturbed when the Danish army dug a massive ditch around the Repton site to defend their winter camp.

Nevertheless Repton does have other burials whose Scandinavian origin can hardly be doubted. To the east of the church, beyond the monastic cemetery, was a small group of individuals whose ethnic and religious identity was clear from their grave goods. One of these, the first to be buried, was a man of about forty. He had been killed when an axe or sword had sheared into the top of his left leg. He went to his grave wearing two glass beads around his neck and a silver amulet in the form of Thor's hammer — a typical Viking object. He also had a sword in a wooden scabbard, strapped with leather and lined with fleece — a clever device to ensure that the blade was kept oiled as it was drawn out of the scabbard. Between his thighs and close to his fatal wound there was a wild boar's tusk, a symbol of virility and power, and a jackdaw's humerus (a magical replacement for his own leg?). If the jackdaw was a substitute for a raven, then this man went to his grave with attributes of Thor, Frey and Odin — the Viking triad of gods. Yet he was placed close to a Christian shrine, as if seeking to maximise his protection in an uncertain afterlife.

He was not the only one to hedge his bets. There are several possible Viking burials in English churchyards. At Wensley (Yorkshire), for example, one man buried near to the church was accompanied by a sword, spear, knife and a sickle. Another, close by, had five silver pennies and a gold ring. The coins date the burial to the AD 870s, suggesting that these men were fallen warriors from the Great Army.

The Scandinavian soldiers of the Great Army practised a different burial rite at Heath Wood, Ingleby (Derbyshire). Here they erected fifty-nine barrows, within a short space of time, on a ridge overlooking the River Trent. Inside the barrows various excavators have found cremation hearths, male and female bone fragments, and offerings of animals — dogs, sheep, cattle, horses and pigs. The burnt grave goods include swords and wire embroidery of a kind known from Sweden.[18] It is to Sweden and northern Jutland that we have to look for similar cremation cemeteries in barrows. Heath Wood is unique in England. Interestingly the nearby village has a Scandinavian name: Ingleby means 'Village of the English'. With their burial ground the soldiers seem determined to emphasise their own identity and ethnic origin.

The woman known as the 'Pagan Lady' excavated on St Patrick's Isle, at Peel on the west coast of the Isle of Man, illustrates the problem of recognising ethnic identity. She was buried within the protective void of a 'lintel' grave, capped and lined with stones, close to St German's Cathedral. She died in middle age; about 1.65 metres (5 feet 5 inches) tall, she suffered from osteomalacia, caused by vitamin D deficiency, which resulted in her having pronounced bow legs. The archaeologists called her the Pagan Lady because of her rich grave goods. She had a necklace of seventy-one glass, amber and jet beads and a pendant, another group of two amber beads and a perforated ammonite, an iron knife, a bone comb, shears and a cooking spit of iron, a pillow filled with feathers and a pouch with needles inside. Traces of goose feathers found on the iron spit may have come from a brush of the type used to sweep out ovens and hearths within living memory on the Isle of Man and in Scotland. As the Nobel Prize-winning Irish poet Seamus Heaney wrote in his poem 'Mossbawn', describing a woman baking: 'Now she dusts the board with a goose's wing.'[19] Goose wings were also used to baste joints of meat, which might explain the association with the iron spit. This is the only spit from Viking Age Britain, though they are frequently found in Danish and Swedish graves in the Scandinavian homeland.

So was the Pagan Lady a conscientious Viking housekeeper, Norse by birth, or a Briton acculturated by marriage? Lacking genetic or other scientific data, it is not possible to be certain. The Isle of Man, a prominent landmark in the Irish Sea with good sheltered harbours and a fertile coastal plain, was strategically well placed to attract Viking seafarers and settlers.* It commands an inland sea. The written records tell us virtually nothing about early raids or colonisation on Man, but there is plenty of archaeological evidence: ship burials, carved stones and hoards of silver. Most of this evidence points to the presence of Viking men, perhaps only settling in the late ninth century on Man (and in north-west England) after a hundred years of activity in the Irish Sea region. The distribution of their sites suggests that they took over the best land from the native Gaelic speakers.

While the Norse who settled in England more or less abandoned the use of runes, the Christian Norse on Man developed a rich tradition of carving stone crosses inscribed with them.† Another fascinating fusion of

---

* In the 1980s, when I was involved in the excavation of Eynsham Abbey, in Oxfordshire, I met two remarkable clergymen. One was the son of J. R. R. Tolkien, who claimed, believably I must say, to be his father's inspiration for Bilbo, the hobbit. The other was the retired Bishop of Sodor and Man, who was writing a history of Eynsham Abbey. 'Sodor' is derived from the Viking word '*sudreyjar*' – 'the southern isles' – and refers to the Hebrides. In the Viking world view, the Isle of Man was the southernmost of these convenient maritime staging posts between Great Britain and Ireland.

† Forty-eight crosses are known on the Isle of Man dating to between AD 930 and 1020.

pagan Viking and Christian images appears on the Gosforth Cross (Cumbria), which shows a crucifixion scene with Mary Magdalene in the traditional guise of a Valkyrie — wearing a trailing robe, and with a long pigtail. On the other side of the cross is a portrayal of Ragnarok, the Viking last trump, when evil breaks its bonds and the earth is cleansed by fire. The wolf Fenrir is shown attacking Odin, while the evil god Loki is chained beneath an enormous serpent.

It is generally assumed that Viking men intermarried with local Manx women and quickly adopted Christianity. One exception may be the man buried at Balladoole. This Viking lay in his eleven-metre-long boat, its mast projecting out of the ground, within a Christian graveyard, inside an earlier Iron Age enclosure. The grave is visible today marked out with boulders in the shape of a longship, sited spectacularly to overlook the sea. The Viking was not alone in his last resting place: near him was a young woman, possibly a slave, who appeared to have been sacrificed. A similar grim rite was witnessed at the opposite end of the Viking world by Ibn Fadlan, ambassador from Baghdad (Islam's greatest city) to the Bulgars, in whose country he arrived on 12 May AD 922. Ibn Fadlan knew these Vikings as the 'Rus' — merchants who sailed down the Volga to the Caspian Sea, and from whom Russia takes its name. An international trading centre grew up at Bulgar, on the Volga. The Rus merchants built wooden huts to house up to twenty people. They set up idols and left food offerings to their gods to encourage successful trading. The men were tall and blond, tattooed up to their necks, and carried axes, swords and knives. Their women showed off their status by wearing beads, large brooches and neck rings. The fastidious and highly civilised Ibn Fadlan did not think much of the northerners' hygiene: they defecated immodestly, like wild asses, rarely washed (and then disgustingly in basins rather than running water). They were fond of combing their hair, of having sex with their slave girls in front of other people and sacrificing them on funeral pyres — which Ibn Fadlan describes in graphic detail. The Rus brought furs, ermine, marten, sable, fox, squirrel and hare from their northern homelands and from near the Arctic Circle. On the Volga they met Arab traders and exchanged their goods for Kufic coins, thousands of which found their way to Scandinavia and into Britain. Even a small statue of Buddha made in the sixth or seventh century in India turned up in Helgo, a trading centre in central Sweden.

The Rus illustrate the difficult issue of shifting ethnic identity. In the mid-ninth century the Rus were certainly Scandinavian, mainly Swedish. A century and a half later they were Slav, absorbed into the surrounding community by marriage. Though Slav-speaking, they often retained

Scandinavian names and political links to the old country. Jarpslav of Kiev married a Swedish princess and gave his daughter in marriage to Harald Hardrada. If Harald had emerged victorious from his confrontation with the English King Harold at Stamford Bridge in 1066, England would have had a Rus-Slav queen.*

This cultural and genetic intermixture is clear in the archaeological record of the Isle of Man. The Pagan Lady of Peel is the only candidate there for an actual Viking woman. Most Viking men married Manx women and, like the Rus, forged a new, mixed identity. In England there are surprisingly few obviously Norse burials (about twenty-five are known, mostly in northern England, compared with thousands of Anglo-Saxon burials).[20]

This is probably because the Norse rapidly converted to Christianity, intermarried and otherwise adopted a local identity. Their status was probably far more important to them than their ethnicity. The few Viking women who appear in England must have stood out. They wore distinctive apron dresses held at the shoulder by enormous gilded brooches shaped rather like tortoise shells.[21]

The incredibly wide international connections of the Vikings, stimulated by raiding and trading, are reflected in the coin hoard discovered in Croydon (Surrey) in 1862. It included West Saxon, East Anglian and Mercian pennies as well as Carolingian *deniers* and Arabic coins. This was probably the personal loot of a warrior in one of the great armies reported in the *Anglo-Saxon Chronicle*. After about AD 850 the scale of Norse attacks increased and the *Chronicle* describes the army of 865 as 'great', though estimates of its size vary considerably from ten to forty thousand. It was led by two brothers, Ingwaer and Healfdene, who appear in the Irish *Annals* as 'Imbar' and 'Alband'. Imbar/Ingwaer is probably the saga hero Ivarr the Boneless, 'King of the Norsemen in all Britain and Ireland' and the founder of the Irish Sea kingdom, which included the great trading centres of Dublin and York.

Healfdene was killed in Ireland in AD 877, trying to keep a grip on this northern proto-empire, but not before he had shared out Northumbrian land among his followers. The following year the Danish army forced their main opponent in southern England, Alfred, to seek refuge in the fens of Somerset. Alfred deserves his title 'Great' (the only English king to receive the Roman title) because of his legal, intellectual and military efforts. It was his fightback that pushed the Danes back into eastern

* England did, however, gain a Polish queen mother: the mother of King Cnut (Canute) was Polish.

England – and his biographer Asser who made sure that his achievements were appreciated by posterity. Alfred defeated the Danish leader Guthrum at Eddington (Wiltshire) and, in AD 886, imposed the Treaty of Wedmore, a very 'English' thing to do – Danish society had not attained this sopisticated level of literacy and diplomacy.[22] The treaty established the boundary between Wessex and Guthrum's territory: 'Up the Thames; then up the Lea and along the Lea to its source; then in a straight line to Bedford; then up the Ouse to Watling Street.'

Later in the tenth century the area to the east became known as the Danelaw, to distinguish the territory where Danish legal custom applied and where there was an integrated and well-established Anglo-Danish community. With the Treaty of Wedmore, Guthrum accepted both Christianity and the Christian ideal of kingship. His coins bore his new baptismal name of 'Athelstan'. In the meantime Alfred used the period of peace to build up his defences: his peasant army worked shifts – half on duty, half off – so that it was always at the ready; he constructed a fleet of innovative ships (said to be neither Frisian nor Danish in design) and established a network of defended towns, or *burhs*, along his frontier – probably inspired by those built by King Offa in Mercia almost a century earlier.* As a result, nowhere in Wessex was more than 32 kilometres from a *burh*. Urban centres had disappeared with the collapse of Roman Britain. A few centres of international trade like London, Ipswich, York and Hamwic (Southampton) developed in the seventh and eighth centuries; but ironically the Viking threat stimulated town life across southern and midland England.

The *Burghal Hidage*, a document of about 914–18, written during the reign of Alfred's son Edward the Elder, lists thirty Wessex *burhs* and another three outside the kingdom. Some of these disappeared once their defensive role was redundant. Others developed into successful commercial and administrative centres. Some of these revived Roman towns (chosen because of their defences) – in Chichester, Winchester, Exeter, Bath, Porchester and Southampton. Several had natural defences or overlooked the sea, such as Langport and Watchet, in Somerset. Others were placed inside Iron Age hill forts, notably Cadbury (Somerset); and some controlled the Thames frontier, laid out like rectangular Roman sites, at Cricklade (Wiltshire), Oxford and Wallingford. Wareham (Dorset) also has the same distinctively regular plan and defences. Within these towns some of the earliest English streets were systematically laid out and

---

* Offa, imitating Carolingian defences, created *burhs* in his kingdom of Mercia in the AD 780s at Gloucester, Chester, Hereford and Tamworth to block access upriver to Viking longships.

metalled. Winchester had 8.6 kilometres of streets requiring 8,000 tonnes of flint cobbles.

As a result of his careful planning and foresight, Alfred was able to see off the next Viking attacks on Wessex in the AD 890s. The *Chronicle* records: 'By the grace of God, the army had not on the whole afflicted the English people greatly.' The tenth century brought a period of relative peace to England; it was only towards the end, when Russia was no longer available for raiding, that the Scandinavians turned their attention back to England. The *Anglo-Saxon Chronicle* provides us with a southern, Wessex view of the world; it has relatively little to say about the north. Irish and Welsh sources tell of the settlement of the Wirral by Norwegians, led by Ingwiwndr, who had been expelled from Dublin in AD 902. In the Irish and north-British world, competition was not only between Irish, native Britons and Vikings, but also between rival Norsemen, Danes and Norwegians, hungry for power, wealth and territory.

In the south Alfred, the King of Wessex but never of England, nevertheless did as much as anyone to create a sense of English identity. He halted the Norse tide and reversed it and, by encouraging the translation of Latin religious works into English, promoted what until then had been the minor tongue of a relatively remote people. He has rightly been called the father of English prose. Alfred also had the good sense to have competent children, particularly his daughter Aethelflaed and his son Edward the Elder. It was Edward who expanded his authority from Wessex across England, taking control of the Danelaw and its Danish occupants by AD 918. Edward's son Athelstan was brought up in Mercia and was able to consolidate his traditional seat of power in Wessex with the old enemy in the Midlands. With this solid power base he could look northwards. Chester had a period of prosperity, as a multi-ethnic community including Hiberno-Norse traders, who made their homes near the River Dee. Under the control of King Athelstan (924–90) Chester became the most productive mint in England with twenty-four moneyers working there between 924 and 939. Chester's prosperity was based on the trading network around the Irish Sea, which was disrupted by renewed Viking attacks from 980 when the city was sacked. In 926 Athelstan married his sister to Sihtric, the Norse King of York. Inconveniently, Sihtric then died leaving a son from an earlier marriage, Olaf, as his heir. The boy's uncle, Guthfrith, the Norse King of Dublin, crossed the Irish Sea to support him. Athelstan decided to move against Northumbria: he defeated his Norse rivals and razed the fortifications of York; the kings of Strathclyde and Scotland and the lord of the fortress of

Bamburgh accepted his authority. Shortly afterwards the Welsh princes were paying annual tribute to Athelstan, 'Basileus of the English'.*

The arrangement with the Scots did not last long. In AD 937 the Strathclyde Scots, and the Dublin Norse joined together to attempt to quash the upstart English power. They invaded England and fought a battle at Brunanburh, which, to the great delight of the Irish, they lost. Along with Hastings and Bannockburn, Brunanburh ought to be recognised as one of the great battles of British history – unfortunately we do not know where it took place (Bromborough, on the Wirral, is a strong possibility). Nevertheless, for the first time the old Anglo-Saxon rivals, Wessex and Mercia, fought together as an English army to defend their new kingdom from the northern threat. In spite of the victory neither Athelstan nor any of his successors before the Norman Conquest had firm control over Northumbria and its earls.†

So much for a brief outline of the politics and the battles; but who actually lived in the areas supposedly settled by the Norse, where according to the *Chronicle* 'they proceeded to plough'? The distinguished historian of Anglo-Saxon England, Sir Frank Stenton, writing in the 1920s, 'argued for a massive settlement of Scandinavians', who fundamentally altered the social, economic and genetic make-up of eastern and northern England.[24] This, according to Stenton, was evident from the place names, Scandinavian legal and administrative terms, the presence of large estates called 'sokes' and the large number of free peasants recorded in the Domesday Book in 1086. Underlying this was the deep-seated assumption among many historians that English liberties had Germanic roots, transplanted by Anglo-Saxons and further propagated by the Norse. From them originated the pioneering freedom-lovers who had gone on to colonise America.

Since the 1960s there has been a reaction: that invasions *per se* are an inadequate explanation of change, and that the image of Anglo-Saxon individualism and liberty is a gross simplification. The scale of the Norse settlement has also been called into question. Place-name maps can give an overly simplistic impression. Draw a line from Chester to London across the map of England and it might appear that to the north and east everyone was Norse and English, or British to the south and west. Recent detailed studies show that place-name distribution is far from straightforward. There are four principal categories of Scandinavian place

* William of Malmesbury later wrote that the North Welsh annually paid 20 pounds of gold, 300 pounds of silver and 25,000 oxen, hounds and hawks.[23]
† The lords of Northumbria held the Anglo-Scandinavian title 'earl', the equivalent of the English *ealdorman*, until Cnut established the title in the south.

names. The commonest are *by*-names – Ferriby, Whitby,* Selby, for example – whose suffix is the Danish word '-*by*', meaning a farmstead or village (the English equivalent is '-ton'). There are about 850 of these *by*-names with particular concentrations in North Yorkshire, Lincolnshire, Derbyshire, Leicestershire, Northamptonshire and on both sides of the Solway firth. There is a more discrete group east of Norwich. Many of these are attached to a personal name, the vast majority of which are Scandinavian.

The second group of Scandinavian names includes the element '-*thorp*', an Old Danish word for a secondary settlement, and therefore later in date than *by*-names. Yorkshire has 155 of these. The third group of place names are known as 'Grimston hybrids' because they contain a Scandinavian element such as the personal name 'Grim' and the English '-ton'. These names are thought to indicate English settlements taken over by Scandinavian settlers. A fourth indicator of the Scandinavian presence is those English names for which a Norse pronunciation has been adopted, such as Shipton/Skipton, Cheswick/Keswick, or church/kirk.

We cannot assume a direct correlation between Viking occupiers and Scandinavian place names. There was a Scandinavian element in the original English settlement of the fifth to seventh centuries; some of the names could originate from then, although they might not be recorded until the Domesday Book in 1086. Some place names might have been given by Scandivanian speakers and not the occupants, such as Ingleby, 'The Village of the English', near to the Viking burial mounds described earlier. England was a densely occupied place when the Scandinavians arrived, and many places were simply renamed. Only a few weeks before writing this I visited the excavations at Whitby Abbey and saw evidence of dense industrial settlement of the Anglian seventh century, now unfortunately falling into the sea. The original name (Fari-sinus) must have been changed in the ninth or tenth century.

The existence of such a large number of personal names, plus '-by', '-ton' or '-thorp' can be explained by the changing pattern of landholding. The large estates common up to this period were broken up and distributed to individuals. The new names reflect newly reorganised properties under new ownership. They do not reflect mass migration of Scandinavians colonising new territories.[25] When the leaders of Viking

* The name 'Whitby' can be confusing. The Synod of Whitby took place in the seventh century when the place was known, according to Bede, as Streon ae shalch, or Fari-sinus ('The Haven of the Watchtower'). The Roman lighthouse, or pharos, had long since fallen into the sea. The Danes changed the name to Whitby, and this name was applied to the earlier synod.

armies allocated territory to their followers, it helped the resident farmers and those expecting to collect taxes to know who the owner was. That is not to say that the Scandinavians were all absentee landlords: there are many loan words in English taken from Danish which refer to farming and suggest that new techniques and practices were introduced. The Vikings were practical people who did not mind getting their hands dirty. As had happened in Russia, however, the English Vikings quickly adopted the local language, suggesting that they were in a minority.

However, regional patterns seem to vary. One group of people who have left some evidence of their ethnic allegiance are moneyers, who recorded their names on coins. At the time of Alfred (871–99) there were no Scandinavian names among the moneyers; half a century later, under Eadred (946–55), they amounted to 15 per cent. During the reign of Ethelred II (978–1016) 5 per cent of moneyers had Scandinavian names nationally, but in York they amounted to 75 per cent, in Lincoln 50 per cent, in Chester 25 per cent and in London 7 per cent. This evidence cannot be treated as a census. Moneyers with Scandinavian names may have been English-born but following the local fashion in having 'appropriate' names for landowners, merchants or craftspeople. We can take these names, however, as an index of Scandinavian influence.

The Vikings came to Britain as pirates, but in the course of the next two centuries they exerted much more significant and positive influence. In some areas, such as Orkney, they came to dominate the population. Their attempts to conquer England, Ireland and northern Britain stimulated fundamental political and cultural changes. They caused the break-up of great estates, stimulated a new property market and encouraged country-dwellers to move into new urban centres. Offa and Alfred established *burhs* as new towns and the Vikings in their turn also created defensive market centres. The *Anglo-Saxon Chronicle* for AD 942 lists the five Boroughs of the Danelaw: Derby (changing its English name: Northworthy), Leicester, Lincoln, Nottingham and Stamford.

The small number of earlier trading *wics*, such as Hamwic, provided a means for kings to control and tax the economic activity of international traders. The Mercian and Wessex *burhs* were initiated as defensive sites, but their strong boundaries also provided a means to control the entry and exit of traders and develop regional market centres. The first Law Code of Edward the Elder, Alfred's son, states: 'No one shall buy or sell except in a market town'; and traders and customers had to use coins whose production was also controlled by the king. It was appropriate that when we dug a trench across New Inn Hall Street in Oxford to expose one of the earliest street surfaces in the city, there lay a silver coin of

Edward the Elder himself, stuck to the cobbled surface of quartzite pebbles.[26]

The vast majority of British people were country-dwellers. These new towns had small populations ranging from a few hundred to very few thousands. But now there were opportunities for craftsmen and traders; and it was in the areas where the Danes took over and reorganised rural estates that most people, albeit in relatively small numbers, took the opportunity to adopt urban life. This is not to say that the Vikings were inveterate town planners. There were no towns in some of the places where they were numerically dominant, such as the Isle of Man and Orkney. Their most successful foundation, however, was Dublin, in the ninth century, which became one of the richest trading centres in northern Europe over the next hundred years. For Viking seamen Dublin was ideally placed to link the northern isles, Chester, Wales, the Severn estuary, France and Spain. Dublin's name did not mean 'Black Pool' for nothing: its soggy, anaerobic ground has proved a gold mine for archaeologists. As in York, marvellous evidence survives of timber buildings, craft activities and even the filthy conditions in which town-dwellers existed. Parasites such as tapeworms and whipworms seem to have been an inevitable fact of life. Towns generated wealth not longevity.

Nevertheless, if at the beginning of the Viking Age there were fewer than a dozen towns, by 1066 there were over a hundred. Probably no more than 10 per cent of English people lived in these towns, about the same proportion as in Roman Britain at its peak.[27]

Urban life had begun to revive with the emergence of trading centres in Middle Saxon England known as *wics*. The best known archaeologically are Hamwic (Southampton), Gippeswic (Ipswich), Eoforwic (York) and Lundenwic (London). In London the early international trading centre, 'the mart of many nations' mentioned by Bede, developed as a beach market.[28] Boats were pulled up on the Thames waterfront of the Strand, near to present-day Charing Cross Station, thus avoiding the dangerous, tumbledown Roman walls of the city. It then spread to present-day Covent Garden and Whitehall. Other such markets probably developed along the Thames at Chiswick, Greenwich, Woolwich and Twickenham, judging by their '*wic*' place names.

These *wics* had none of the elegant public buildings and spaces of Roman towns: they were basic and functional markets. Hamwic, for example, was founded about AD 700, a site of about 45 hectares (112 acres) enclosed by an earthwork to demarcate the commercial area. The authority of the king, rather than this earthwork, protected the town. Inside there was a regular street system bounded by timber houses and workshops. Judging from the imported pottery, the traders of Hamwic had connections with France, the Rhineland and the Low Countries. Many of the population of 2,000 to 3,000 people were craftworkers processing raw materials. By AD 900 Hamwic was in decline as Winchester and then Southampton prospered.

The arrival of the Vikings put these embryo towns at risk. The traders needed defences. In the ninth century Lundenwic was abandoned, its boundary ditch infilled by AD 867. The traders moved inside the nearby refurbished Roman defences. At Hamwic they retreated to higher ground 500 metres away, developing the town now known as Southampton, while royal and ecclesiastical official functions were centred on Winchester.

The new name of London — Lundenburh — emphasised its defensive function, as one of Alfred's fortified *burhs*, established in AD 886, as part of his strategy to provide bulwarks against the Danish armies. At Lundenburh Alfred granted land next to the new prime trading site at Queenhithe to the Bishop of Worcester and Archbishop of Canterbury.[29] In this way he developed a commercial partnership with powerful ecclesiastical lords from opposite ends of his sphere of influence. It took until AD 1000 before London began to prosper as a port with the construction of timber docks against which ships could be securely moored. By 1050 London was a major international port, with outlying settlements at Southwark and Westminster (as opposed to the east minster of St Paul's). New churches reflect the Scandinavian connections, such as St Olave in the Jewry or St Nicholas Acon, a small church between Lombard Street and St Nicholas Passage, named for its founder, a certain Haakon.* A grave slab carved with a fantastically vibrant dragon (originally painted blue, brown and white) came from St Paul's Cathedral churchyard. Along the edge it is incribed in runes (a rare English example): 'Ginna and Toki had this stone set up.' These two were probably the widow and son of a Dane who lived and died in London in the eleventh century. The slab, which captures the spirit of the Norse, now lives in the Museum of London.

York has a similar trajectory. The *wic* site was abandoned in favour of the defensible area between the Rivers Ouse and Foss, where the Roman fortress walls survived at least in part. With the fall of Northumbria to the Great Army in AD 866, York became the base for Danish campaigns against the English kingdoms. But the Scandinavians were also deeply

---

* Both of these churches were founded after about 1040. St Nicholas Acon was built within an existing tenement over rubbish pits dated to about 1040. St Olave's is dedicated to one of King Cnut's victims, so is unlikely to have been built until after Cnut's death.

involved in long-distance trade – much more so than the English, let alone the Irish and British. Viking Age York expanded across the River Ouse over the site of the Roman *colonia*. About AD 900 a bridge and the new Micklegate – 'Great Street' – linked the two areas of the town. Ironically, the name 'Micklegate' also links York, the place where Constantine the Great was crowned emperor, with his new capital of the eastern empire, Constantinople. To the Rus Vikings Constantinople, or Byzantium, was Mickligardr – 'The Great City'.

Micklegate crossed to Ousegate and Coppergate ('Street of the Coopers' or 'Woodworkers'), the site of major archaeological investigations into this period. The long narrow tenements of Coppergate, established in the early tenth century, have remained in use as property boundaries in York for almost a thousand years. Timber post and wattle buildings stood end on to the street. Initially metalworkers dominated the area, using iron, gold, silver, copper and lead. The back yards were full of rubbish and cesspits – a boon for archaeologists. When these buildings were rebuilt more densely, with planks and sunken floors, the craft activities shifted to woodworking and jewellery, suggesting that the hazardous industrial metalworkers had had to move to a less vulnerable area. As in Dublin, the urban environment at York was extremely squalid – the combination of rotting rubbish, dung and decomposing timber buildings built up an organic layer at the rate of 25 millimetres a year. Ibn Fadlan, our Arab commentator who had such a low opinion of Viking hygiene, would not have been surprised.

Alfred and his sons ensured the success of the kingdom of the Anglo-Saxons. Wessex had absorbed the south-eastern counties of Kent, Surrey, Essex and Sussex in the mid-ninth century.* Under Alfred it expanded northwards to absorb its chief rival Mercia. Now the Angles and Saxons were united and Gloucester and Winchester were the principal administrative centres while London generated wealth as the international trading centre. Alfred's son Edward the Elder and grandson Athelstan extended the kingdom of the Anglo-Saxons into the Danelaw, to York and Northumberland. For the first time something resembling Bede's vision of a united Christian England was a reality. Athelstan was 'King of the English' on his coins. Hywel Dda, ruler of the West Welsh and Owain, King of Gwent, accepted his overlordship, even if the

---

* The counties, or shires, developed as administrative units in the eighth and ninth centuries. A shire was first mentioned in the Laws of King Ine of Wessex dating to about 688–94, but the unit became explicit in the next century. The area around the trading centre of Hamwic, 'Hamtunsir' (Hampshire), is documented in AD 750. Wiltshire is the territory around Wilton, and Somerset was centred on Somerton (now in Devon).

majority of Welshmen continued to regard the English as their oppressors. And in Orkney the Norse retained their ethnic and political identity.

In spite of his victory over King Constantine of the Scots and the Norse of Dublin at Brunanburh in AD 937, Athelstan could no more hold the Celtic north than could the Romans. However, by the reign of King Edgar (959–75) Northumberland was firmly attached to a unified kingdom of England. England, it seemed, had at last successfully absorbed the Vikings. The Norse had settled down, and adopted English religion, language,* writing and even families. Their new towns added prosperity to the kingdom and their presence helped to create a new Anglo-Scandinavian identity in England. In the mid-tenth century the kingdom appeared peaceable and relatively prosperous.

Events in Europe were to change that, however. The powerful Scandinavian states turned away from Russia and looked once again to the prosperous West. England was vulnerable as, first, King Edgar died (in AD 975), then his son was murdered and Ethelred (the Unready) succeeded to the throne. The Scandinavian armies demanded protection money – Danegeld. On St Brice's Day, 13 November 1002, Ethelred 'ordered to be slain all the Danish men who were in England ... Sprouting like cockles amongst the wheat they were to be destroyed by a most just extermination.'[30] In Oxford the Danes sought sanctuary in St Frideswide's Church. The English burnt it down around them.

Thanks to the mortality rate amongst the English royal house, and the rivalries and factionalism of the royal advisers, the kingdom fell into the hands of the Dane Cnut (Canute) in 1016. In spite of its failure to eject the new invaders, England was essentially well organised and administered: the shire system of Wessex had been extended across the county; it had flourishing towns, a sound currency, a regulated legal system and an expanding population. England was a modern European state. Fortunately Cnut was an anglophile and in spite of ruling a vast 'North Sea Empire' spent most of his time in England. He married Ethelred's wife Emma and cultivated English advisers. Nevertheless, on his death in 1035, the big problem still remained: Who would succeed to the throne of this desirable kingdom?

* Danes did, however, add a number of Danish loan words to English, e.g. 'egg'.

Six New Norsemen

WHEN I TAKE students around Oxford to look at the topography of the city, we always start on a high spot: the top of the motte of Oxford Castle. From there we look out over the city, with its spires, towers and car parks, across the Thames valley into the old county of Berkshire and territory of Wessex. Oxford Castle is not well known, even to local residents – principally because until recently most of it was inside one of Her Majesty's prisons. Like many castles, Oxford's came to house the county gaol.

So most people in Oxford pass this conical grass-covered mound without realising that it is the city's principal monument to the Norman suppression of England, erected in the years following the Battle of Hastings and the unexpected triumph of William of Normandy.

In the years before the Norman invasion Oxford was a prosperous trading town, with about 5,000 inhabitants, Anglo-Saxons mixed with Danes who had survived the St Brice's Day massacre. Important Anglo-Saxon aristocrats had houses there as well as wealthy burgesses like Saegrim and Swaetmann, the moneyer. The growing town had thrust through its eastern defences, constructed to provide a bulwark against the Danish armies, and expanded down the High Street. Towards the river in Holywell twenty-three 'men with little gardens' clustered around the church of St Peter-in-the-East, presumably cultivating vegetables for the townspeople. And the city had at least five watermills. In the suburbs archaeologists find unusually large quantities of a distinctive shelly pottery known as 'St Neot's ware' and manufactured in the Danelaw region. It is possible that Oxford's Danish community lived in these peripheral areas. With Cnut's conquest of 1016 the status of the Danes in Oxford would have improved and Danish house-carls supervised the shire court in the 1050s. A man buried in a stone coffin in St Aldate's Church wearing a fine Viking-style ring of plaited gold may have been one of Oxford's high-status Danes during Cnut's reign.[1]

Cnut's Danish garrison may have lived in the eastern suburban settlement of St Clement's. The cult of St Clement was particularly associated with Denmark (as in St Clement Dane's in London, probably a garrison church) and with seafarers and traders in the late tenth century. Human and horse bones and Danish horse gear found by Magdalen Bridge in 1884 may indicate their cemetery.*

The Norman invaders found the gates of this cosmopolitan town open, but inside the English were hostile and disgruntled. Those who lived in the south-east quarter of the town would have had a particular reason to resent the arrival of these mail-clad horsemen with their brutally cropped hairstyles. The Normans under Robert D'Oilly proceeded to raze that part of the city, flattening the people's houses and closing streets, in order to create an open building site for their new castle. The locals were then dragooned into digging and throwing up the massive earthen mound, or motte, as a platform for a timber tower to dominate the town. The Normans had little interest in the English except to exploit them. Oxford was soon taxed to the hilt and lay half in ruins.

When my Oxford colleagues and I excavated the castle at Mayenne, in northern France (which also fell victim to William), the local town council commissioned a *bande dessinée* about the château – a lively French tradition of illustrated story-telling best known outside of France for the *Tintin* and *Astérix* comic books. The earliest surviving *bande dessinée* hangs in Bayeux, in the form of the famous tapestry (though a good copy can be seen in Reading Museum), which tells the story of the Norman invasion of Britain. The tapestry contains vivid scenes of castle-building, sieges and escapes. It also depicts the typical Norman castle with its earthen motte, and elevated lookout tower on top. Below the motte was a defended courtyard, or bailey, packed with storehouses, workshops and accommodation for men and horses.

Standing on the Oxford motte one can sense the resentment that this towering demonstration of Norman power must have caused to the local English living in its shadow. But the motte was not exactly a monument to Norman confidence. The castle's location, in the south-west corner of the Anglo-Saxon *burh*, then overlooking the Thames, reflects the unease of the occupants. They could easily escape out of the back if the wrath of the city-dwellers turned into outright and overwhelming aggression.

Like all successful conquerors, the Normans had God on their side; and to show their appreciation of divine assistance, almost as soon as the castle was erected, in 1071, they founded the chapel of the collegiate foundation of St George within its walls. Today the great rubble tower of

---

* The horse gear includes stirrups, which appeared in western Europe in about the eighth century. This small technical improvement made the armoured knight possible.

St George still survives, part of the castle's defensive curtain wall, though it may originally have been constructed as an entrance tower of the English *burh*.

Here, in the College of St George, Geoffrey of Monmouth wrote one of the most influential works of the Middle Ages: the *History of the Kings of Britain*. His fantastical, mythical, part-historical and highly readable account put British history on the literary map of Europe. Geoffrey, probably born near Monmouth and of Norman/Breton stock, concocted a glorious British past, a land 'inhabited by five races of people, the Norman-French, the Britons, the Saxons, the Picts and the Scots'. According to Geoffrey, the first Briton was a Trojan – Brutus, grandson of Aeneas, who was told in a dream:

> Brutus, beyond the setting of the sun, past the realms of
> Gaul, there lies an island in the sea, once occupied by giants.
> Now it is empty and ready for your folk. Down the years this
> will prove an abode suited to you and to your people; and for
> your descendants it will be a second Troy. A race of kings will
> be born there from your stock and the round circle of the
> whole earth will be subject to them.

One of these kings was an obscure and fleeting British character from the dark days of the Anglo-Saxon invasions. Geoffrey elevated him – Arthur, no less – into the greatest and most chivalrous figure of Christendom and in so doing attempted to unite the native British under the leadership of their divinely anointed Norman kings. Arthur is presented as a power-ful king who could exert his authority in Europe – a model for a modern monarch. The medieval world overlooked the irony of reinventing a defender of Britain as a propaganda tool for its Norman conquerors.

The new arrivals were not the only players in the complicated dynastic and racial struggles of Britain in the eleventh century. Early in 1066 it was far from clear who would come out on top in the contest for England. The Normans were part of a network of power, marriages, alliances, landholding and money-grabbing that stretched from Ireland and Britain to Scandinavia, France and into eastern Europe. Many of the major players in this web were descended from Vikings. The Normans, as their name implies, were Norsemen, Scandinavian raiders who had settled in Francia, married local women, descendants of the Gauls and Germanic Franks, and adopted Christianity. In AD 911 Charles the Simple, King of West Francia, granted land in the Rouen region to a war band led by Hrolf, or Rollo. Over the next fifty years, thanks to fresh im-migration from Scandinavia, aggression and diplomatic marriages, the

Norse expanded their territory in northern France until the duchy of the Normans stretched from the borders of Brittany to the Loire. Throughout this period they became increasingly Gallicised — Duke William Longsword (927–43) had to send his son to Bayeux to learn Danish because it was no longer routinely spoken around Rouen. The great grandsons of men who had ravaged the monasteries of Europe now allied themselves closely with the Church and the Pope. The Norse pioneering spirit and energy were harnessed to the modern eleventh-century French feudal system of unified state-building, driven by military power dependent on heavy cavalry and motivated by a fervent belief in Christianity. For the Normans the Pope became their strongest ally, whether they were fighting in Sussex, Sicily or against the Seljuk empire in the east.

While the Normans were establishing their duchy in France, the Danes resumed attacks on England after fifty years of relative peace. In the face of such a powerful invader the English resorted to paying protection money, a tried and tested response to Norse aggression. Danegeld became an increasingly expensive way of buying off the problem. There were other ways. Ethelred, for example, tried to ally himself with the Normans, under Duke Richard, who, in the time-honoured way, married off one of his sisters, Emma, to Ethelred in 1002, to put the seal on their partnership.

Emma's career is fundamental to an understanding of the Norman world, of the role of elite women, and of the duchy's eventual conquest of England half a century later. Power flowed through aristocratic bloodlines. A daughter of one duke of Normandy and the sister of another, Emma was Ethelred's queen in England until his death in 1016. A son by that marriage was Edward the Confessor, the future King of England.

A year after Ethelred's death Emma married Cnut (Canute), who had exploited the divisions among the English aristocracy and, backed by the men of Wessex, defeated the English candidate for the throne at Ashingdon on 13 October 1016. Following a great conference at Oxford, where Cnut agreed to uphold English law, he married the widow Emma to further cement the bonds with the legitimate English royal family — and, as it happened, with the rulers of Normandy as well. Emma already had two sons by Ethelred: Edward (the future 'Confessor'), born in 1005, and Alfred, born about seven years later. Emma presumably decided that her young sons would remain healthier if they were well away from their powerful new Danish stepfather, so she sent them into the care of their Norman uncles, Duke Richard II and Robert the Magnificent (1027–1035). Robert, the father of William the Conquerer, was a strong supporter of his nephew Edward's claim to the English throne. It was this long succour of Emma's sons that stimulated the Norman interest in the issue of the English royal succession, which was to come to a head with Duke William.

For twenty years England had been ruled by a Norse king, while Viking earls controlled northern Scotland and the Isles. In Ireland, though, Norse influence, based on Dublin, waned as Brian Boruma (941–1014) (his nickname comes from *borum*, meaning 'of the cattle tribute') struggled to unify the famously fragmented country. Grateful monks at Armagh referred to him as *Imperator Scotorum* (Emperor of the Irish) – a unique and short-lived title. In less than a decade he had met his death in battle at Clontarf, on Good Friday, 23 April 1014. The forces ranged against him were Irish Leinstermen, with Norse allies from Dublin, the Isle of Man, the Western Isles, Orkney and Shetland. Brian's Munster army won the day, but he lay dead on the battlefield. Clontarf was a battle between Irish rivals rather than with Norse invaders, as it is sometimes presented. Nevertheless, Brian Boruma has entered Irish mythology as a national patriot and defender of his country, a romantic hero to the Irish and especially to his descendants the O'Brians. Ireland remained locked in its constant kingly struggles.

Emma and her son Edward the Confessor provided William with the genetic and political bridgehead to England. After two decades of rule by Cnut the English establishment was firmly linked with Norse interests. The English lords looked to Cnut's sons for the succession. Unfortunately, by 1042 both of them were dead. This left the way clear for Edward to return as king to England. Aged thirty-seven and after twenty-six years in Normandy he needed English friends – and he found one in the most powerful earl in the country, Godwine of Wessex. Edward married Godwine's daughter Edith and cemented the relationship by granting earldoms to her brothers Swein and Harold (the future Harold II). Although Harold is often called the last English king, his ancestry is a typical aristocratic cocktail: Scandinavian blood flowed in his veins through his mother Gytha and grandfather Jorl Thorgills. Edward could trace his ancestry to the pagan Saxon founders of the Wessex dynasty, but his friends were Norman and he brought them over to keep him company at court. He also promoted Norman clerics, in particular Robert of Jumièges to the archbishopric of Canterbury.

Over the next decade Edward and the Godwines, the mightiest earls in England, jockeyed for power. At one low point, in 1051, Godwine and his family sought refuge in Flanders and Dublin. This coincided with the consolidation of Duke William's authority in Normandy and it may have been at this time that Edward raised the question of the English succession with his cousin William. After all, Edward had no children and there was no love lost between him and the ambitious English earls. However, Godwine and his sons could not be kept down. Harold and his brother Tostig between them controlled lands from the old family heartlands in Sussex and the Isle of Wight to Northumberland and the Scottish and Welsh borders, where they acted as a buffer against the troublesome British.

Thanks to the Godwinesons' authority, Gruffudd ap Llewelyn, the only Welsh king to hold the whole of Wales, and King Malcolm in Scotland recognised King Edward as their overlord. However, Gruffudd did not last long when Harold decided to punish him for his raids into England. The unified kingdom of Wales came to an end in 1063, thanks to Harold's brutal campaign and with Gruffudd's murder in Snowdonia. To remove her from any further dynastic manipulation Harald married the widowed Queen of Wales, Ealdgyth, himself.* He had no ambitions to rule the turbulent mountainous land of Wales: the Welsh could rule themselves, provided they remained fragmented and too weak to cause trouble in England.

The succession was never going to be straightforward, with a childless king and potential Saxon, Scandinavian and Norman contenders. Harold did not help matters by falling into the hands of William in Normandy and, contentiously – depending on whose version of the story you choose to believe – swearing an oath of allegiance to the Norman duke over a casket of holy relics.

When William announced his intention to seize the English throne by force, following Harold's supposed betrayal, the propaganda surrounding the oath issue provided the excuse for the Pope to give his support to William. The enterprise then had something of the moral force of a crusade, and persuaded many waverers and sceptics to take up arms in the name of William, and God – as well as Mammon. William was also able to claim that anyone in England resisting his rightful claim to the throne was a traitor and their lands could be rightfully seized.

King Edward's grand project, the magnificent Romanesque Minster of St Peter's, Westminster ('west' in contrast to the 'east' Minster of St Paul's), was consecrated on 28 December 1065. This was a Norman church built before the Norman Conquest, much influenced by Jumièges.[2] Within a week the old king – for so he seemed though only aged about sixty – was dead. On his deathbed he nominated Harold as his successor .

---

* Ealdgyth was the granddaughter of Lady Godiva of Coventry.

The Witan – the assembly of English nobles – took the pragmatic decision to uphold the dead king's recommendation and offer the throne to Harold, the richest, stongest, most experienced candidate. Harold's coronation followed Edward's funeral on the same day, the Feast of the Epiphany, 1066. Harold was taking no chances that other candidates might press their case. Needless to say, they did. First in line was the Scandinavian contender, Harald Hardrada. His claim was through Cnut's line, and he was an aggressive six-foot-four-inch arch-opportunist who had already fought his way from Norway to Byzantium and back. He seems to have gathered his forces in Orkney and met up with Harold's exiled brother Tostig – an embittered wretch who had so oppressed and alienated his unfortunate subjects when Earl of Northumberland that even Harold agreed he had to go – which he did, stuffed with gold and bile, demanding revenge and an appropriate station in life.

King Harold had gathered his army and fleet on the south coast to await William. As the year dragged on, tides and weather did not favour the Norman armada, which remained stuck on the French side of the Channel. Harold had about 16,000 troops, made up of 3,000 crack professionals – the axe-wielding, mail-clad *huscarls** – and the bulk of the army – the *fyrd*: part-timers who owed forty days' service a year to their king. As Harold's forces became increasingly frustrated at the lack of a visible enemy (and concerned for their farms, which needed tending), he decided to disband them on 8 September. Then, on 19 September, came the news from Harold's friends in the north: Harald Hardrada had arrived.

King Harold's drive northwards, gathering his scattered army as he went, was a feat worthy of Julius Caesar at his most forceful. On 29 September he was at Stamford Bridge, a few miles east of York, ready and waiting when Harald Hardrada turned up. In the ensuing battle Harald, Tostig and most of their army were cut to pieces. Only twenty-four ships, of the hundred that had gathered in Orkney, were needed to transport the survivors home.

Hardrada, with his vast experience and fearsome reputation, must have seemed like England's deadliest enemy in 1066. In comparison William was relatively untried. But on 27 September, the day after the Stamford Bridge carnage, William was on his way to England. With him was the largest invasion force since Aulus Plautius and his Roman legions had landed in AD 43. The fleet consisted of 400 troop carriers, supported by cargo ships laden with equipment. The Bayeux tapestry

---

* *Huscarls* had originally come to England as the personal retinue of Cnut.

shows shipwrights felling trees and constructing longships (supposedly in eight months). Billowing sails then drive the fleet across the Channel, the boats filled with horses, docile as rocking horses, a contrast to the twisted, mangled animals on the battlefield.

Critics, with the benefit of hindsight, have accused King Harold of precipitately returning to the south to tackle William. Why did he not take his time, gather an army, potentially of 40,000 men, and overwhelm the Norman invaders in his own time? But Harold, confident after his victory over the mighty Hardrada, must have wished to snuff out the overweening Norman invader, who was not just ravaging England but Harold's personal family estates in Sussex. William, after all, was something of an upstart: the presumptive leader of a relative newcomer in European power politics. Normandy was not in the same league as the wealthy, well-organised kingdom of England.

William had landed close to the old Roman fort at Pevensey. In one of his ships he carried a prefabricated wooden castle. Once on English soil he built a motte and erected it. This was the first of many such Norman nails in the English coffin. By rushing to engage with William, Harold hoped to put a stop to the Norman depradations. The Bayeux tapestry does not shirk the brutality of war: among the depictions of dismembered troops there is a particularly affecting image of the civilian victims – a mother and child departing their home, which is being put to the torch. Harold was probably no sentimentalist, but such treatment of his own people must have been hard to stomach for a proud lord. Besides, it was becoming late in the year for campaigning; if William was not tackled now, he would be in England through the winter.

So on 14 October 1066 Harold determined to complete the task of repelling all invaders. Fatefully, in England's most famous battle, 10 kilometres north of Hastings on the ridge known as Senlach, he failed.

Losing a battle in the eleventh century did not necessarily mean losing a war or a country. Hastings was decisive not only because the English were defeated but because Harold and his two brothers, Leofwine and Gyrth, were killed along with many of the English nobility. With the death of the King and the two Godwineson earls the regime simply deflated for lack of credible leadership. Harold's mistake was to take command of the battle himself, instead of staying in reserve to fight another day. England's relative sophistication and its well-coordinated administration, designed by Alfred and his successors to raise taxes and resources in the face of the Danish threat, now proved a disadvantage. Firstly, the rich state attracted the attention of confident power-hungry warlords like Hardrada and William. Secondly, such a centralised power could fall with the removal of its head. In contrast, a fragmented, hydra-headed society such as Ireland was much more difficult to take over.*

The survivors of the Norman army perhaps numbered about 5,000 men – relatively few compared with the English population of about 2 million. William needed to import more supporters from the Continent if he was to keep them down. Nevertheless, the total number of Norman immigrants and their cohorts may not have amounted to more than 5 per cent of the total population.

Nor were the invaders all Norman: others who had joined William's crusade to the land of opportunity included Flemings, Bretons and French.[3] Later Italian and Jewish bankers and merchants were to follow.

The Normans also brought with them a new, upper-class fashion for surnames. These were still relatively rare and restricted to baronial families but over the next three centuries became commonplace. In the decades immediately after the Conquest surnames seem to have mainly served to clarify the right of ownership to land and as such can indicate the family place of origin in France or land acquired in England.[4]

William de Warenne, an important figure at Hastings, had extensive family lands in Normandy and took his name from Varennes, near Dieppe. His reward from the Conqueror included enormous estates in Sussex, Norfolk and Yorkshire and the title of 'Earl of Surrey'; but most Warrens today are of more humble origin, taking their name from someone who lived near a rabbit warren. Rabbits were another alien invader that came into Britain with the Normans. Other Norman surnames included the Mortimers – from 'Mortemer' (Seine-Maritime) – the family who were to become great marcher lords on the border with Wales. Another marcher family were descendants of Roger de Montgomerie, who came from St-Germain-de-Montgomery in Calvados. His son, also Roger, followed him to England in 1067 and was granted estates in Sussex including Arundel Castle and the earldom of Shrewsbury. When he built a powerful castle in the Welsh Marches he named it and the associated town Montgomery after the family's estate in Normandy.

People of French origin continued to migrate into England throughout the Middle Ages, as surnames become more widespread. Not everyone today with a name such as Mortimer can claim to have arrived with the Conqueror. In fact, scarcely anyone can. As David Hey emphasises: 'The fact of the matter is that it is impossible to prove descent in a male line from an ancestor who fought at Hastings unless your name is Malet

---

* For similar reasons the Romans in the first century found the advanced south of Britannia easier to conquer than Wales or Caledonia.

or Mallet(t).'[5] William Malet and his son Robert were retainers of William long before the Conquest. Such men did well out of the conquest of England. As Henry of Huntingdon wrote in the later twelfth century: 'In the twenty-first year of William's reign there was hardly a nobleman of English descent left in England but all were reduced to servitude and mourning, so that it was a disgrace to be called an Englishman.'

For William's troops the invasion of England and the Battle of Hastings were a risky gamble. It paid off, and now they expected to collect their winnings, in the form of landed estates. Over the next two decades there was an enormous shift in the ownership of land in England as William redistributed the estates of 4–5,000 native aristocrats to his nobles. Harold's estates in Sussex, the south-west and Herefordshire went to William fitzOsbern, and in Kent to William's brother Odo, Bishop of Bayeux and commissioner of the famous tapestry. Out of the 180 or so tenants-in-chief who held large estates worth over £100 a year a mere two were English. At the next level, about 100 out of 1,400 medium-sized landholders were English. Some 6,000 sub-tenants are recorded in the Domesday Book and far more of these are English, but many of them now leased land that they had owned freely before 1066. The decline of the power and influence of the English in their own country is also reflected in the Church. By 1080 only one out of sixteen bishops was English; and many of their seats were moved from traditional centres such as Dorchester-on-Thames (Oxfordshire) and Selsey (Hampshire) to the bigger towns, which became centres of administration. The Normans not only removed the English from power; they destroyed the English symbols of power and culture. In particular a massive building programme replaced great Anglo-Saxon churches such as the Old Minster at Winchester. It left the impression that the Anglo-Saxons never built much more than timber halls, until archaeology revealed the impressive footprints of the Winchester Old Minster and St Augustine's, Canterbury.*The Norman aristocracy shunned the English, who became second-class citizens in their own land, rarely married local women and spoke a different language.

The decline of the English is reflected in the increasing adoption of Norman first names. Anglo-Saxon parents gave their children names before baptism, and the sacrament simply endorsed them. About the time of the Norman Conquest, however, early infant baptism became the

* The surviving church tower at Earl's Barton (Northamptonshire) gives some impression of the Anglo-Saxon achievement. It held a chapel on the ground floor and the residence of a thegn above. Like St George's tower in Oxford, it probably acted as a gateway tower to a defended *burh*.

norm and the emphasis seems to shift to saints' names and the names of godparents. Anglo-Saxon names were enormously varied and, for example, in Devon about 562 different ones are recorded. Some royal houses repeated particular patterns, like the fondness for 'S' — Saebert, Seaxred, Saeward — in Essex, while other royal families had favourites such as Edward, Edgar and Edwin (repeating the first element in the father's name). Pet names were common: Trumwine becomes 'Tuma' and King Saebert's family called him 'Saba'. Simpler Anglo-Saxon names were made up of one element such as '*beorn*' ('man' or 'warrior') and '*wulf*' ('wolf'). Other names had two elements: for example, Edward, meaning 'Happy Guardian', Ethelflaed — 'Noble Beauty' — and Ethelthryth — 'Noble Strength'. The upper echelons tended to use the longer, more impressive, two-element names.

Until late in the eleventh century English children were usually given Germanic names: Anglo-Saxon and Danish names were similar in type and meaning. The typical Norman names were also Germanic but modified by French influences — names such as Henry, Geoffrey, Robert, Roger, Odo and William (the first person in British history to be labelled a 'bastard'), or Matilda, Millicent and Rosamund. But fashions were changing under the influence of European Christianity: biblical, saintly and Latin names spread throughout western Europe and into Britain. By the later eleventh century there were lots of children called Andrew, Matthew, Maurice, Laurence, Stephen and even Pagan (meaning 'Country-dweller'). Biblical names such as Moses and Isaac were used by Jews, who followed the Normans into London, Lincoln and Southampton, but they also became popular with Gentiles. Inevitably the English began to imitate their masters and adopt popular Norman names, especially royal ones such as Henry and Robert. The old names could even become a handicap. The almost saintly Bartholomew, the hermit of the Farne Islands, was born in Whitby in the early twelfth century. His parents gave him a good Viking name: Tosti. As he grew up, other children made fun of this name and he became known as William; then he adopted Bartholomew as his religious name. By the 1220s in Lincolnshire, deep in the old Danelaw, only 6 per cent of some 624 tenants listed around Louth had Anglo-Saxon or Norse names. But there were 86 Williams, 59 Roberts and 40 Johns. By the thirteenth century the group of favoured names had become much smaller, with John, Peter, Thomas and William at the head of the field for men and Elizabeth, Mary and Anne for women.*

It is not surprising that by this period surnames, or bynames, had become commonplace among all classes of Englishmen — with a restricted number of first names they were needed for more specific identification. The fashion spread from the Norman aristocracy first to upper-class Londoners, from the mid-twelfth century and slowly through the countryside in the fourteenth and early fifteenth century. In the late fourteenth century there were still country-dwellers − for example in Lancashire at the time of the 1379 poll tax − known as son of someone or, in the case of women, by names such as 'Agnes Spenserdoghter' and 'Eva Jacksonwyf'.

After 1066 and for several centuries, settlers continued to arrive in Britain and their place of origin can be detected by locative surnames such as 'French', 'Fleming', 'Flanders', 'Burgoyne' ('from Burgundy'), 'Brabham' and 'Bremner' ('from the duchy of Brabant'), or, more specifically, 'Villiers' ('from Villiers-le-Sec', Calvados) and 'Saville' ('from Sainville', Eure-et-Loir). Not all these French immigrants came during the Conquest. The Courtenays of Devon (but not those of Oxfordshire) came with Eleanor of Aquitaine, the new wife of Henry II, in 1152, and acquired huge estates in the south-west by marriage. French surnames do not always relate to places of origin. Some started as nicknames − flattering ones, such as Durant ('Steadfast') and Fortescue ('Valiant Warrior') and others less so, such as Corbet ('Little Crow') or Gifford ('Chubby Cheeks').

On Christmas Day 1066, in the new French-style Westminster Abbey built by Edward, William swore on the Bible to 'hold this nation as well as the best of any kings before him did, if they would be loyal to him'. Initially it seemed that the English would pragmatically accept the change at the top. Their country was a sophisticated state and William needed the co-operation of the middle-ranking English reeves, sheriffs and other officials if the all-important bureaucratic system of tax raising and law enforcement was to be maintained. Yet the positions at the top − the earldoms, baronies and bishoprics − were reserved for Normans. New laws also favoured Normans; for example, heavy communal fines were imposed on the English if a Norman was assaulted. In comparison with the Danes, the Norman regime was more oppressive and its changes at the top more radical.

---

* The royal family provides the most continuous guide to the fashion in names. Mary first appears with King Stephen's daughter in the 1130s, as the cult of the Virgin becomes more popular. Henry II promoted Joan and John in the 1160s for John the Baptist. A poll tax return for the Sheffield (Hallamshire) area in 1379 lists the forenames of 715 men. These in order of popularity and frequency of use are John 236 (33 per cent), William 137 (19 per cent), Thomas 85, Richard 67, Robert 64, Adam 35, Henry 28 and Roger 17. Only 20 forenames were used among the 715 Yorkshiremen and of these over half were called John or William. Edward was the only English name to retain its popularity.[6]

As part of the great Norman land-grab William adapted the system that he found in place. William himself took lands worth twice as much as those held by Edward the Confessor. The royal estate was valued at £11,000, or one-sixth of the landed revenues of his entire kingdom. In the eleventh century land was not private property: it was held as an 'honour' in return for duties to the king or to the aristocratic tenants-in-chief, who themselves owed duties to the king. By holding such extensive estates William was ensuring his personal network of interest stretched across the whole country.

However, he ensured that the pyramid of hierarchy was broadened below himself. The English super-earldoms, notably that of the Godwinesons, which towered above the middle-ranking thegns, were dismantled. In the new Norman world there were about two hundred tenants-in-chief. These were earls and barons who had their 'honours' directly from the king. Next in rank were about a thousand landowners with estates valued at £5 or more and then up to seven thousand lesser lords. There were now more lords with the rank of earl than had existed before the Conquest, but William had the sense to restrict their influence. Normally they were specifically related to a shire, like the English *ealdormen*; hence the new name 'county', from 'count', the Continental term for an earl. This system did not depend simply on the good will and the docility of the English labouring peasants or townspeople. The lid was held firmly in place by military might. A rash of castles spread across the country. As the *Anglo-Saxon Chronicle* glumly reported for 1067, while William returned to Normandy as the conquering hero to check on the home front:

> Bishop Odo and Earl William* stayed behind and built castles
> far and wide throughout the country and distressed the
> wretched folk and always after that it grew much worse. May
> the end be good when God wills.

The greatest symbol of Norman power was the White Tower, the Tower of London, erected in the south-eastern corner of the country's largest city, to dominate the local population. This was the most impressive secular building constructed in Britain since the departure of the Romans, and to make the point it was literally built of alien Norman stone, shipped over from Caen. Many more castles were needed, not only to suppress the still turbulent English but also to control the Celtic west and the ambitions of King Malcolm III of Scotland. The distribution of castles

---

* That is, William fitzOsbern, who became Earl of Hereford.

A fanciful portrayal of a tattooed Pictish man painted in the late sixteenth century by John White. White was one of the first artists to draw native Americans, who provided him with analogies for his depictions of Ancient Britons.

The statue of Boadicea (or Boudica) and her daughters, sculpted by Thomas Thornycroft and erected by London County Council in 1902. Britain's first warrior queen, freedom fighter and anti-European stands appropriately on the Victoria Embankment (Boudica means Victoria) charging towards the Houses of Parliament.

A Roman gold aureas, which provided the model for subsequent English coinage, portrays the head of the Emperor Claudius, who ordered the invasion of Britain in AD 43. The reverse shows the victory arch built in Rome to celebrate his triumph *De Britannis* – over Britain. Claudius on horseback is flanked by trophies of weapons.

A silver penny of Aelfred, King of Wessex. The coin shows Aelfred in the style of a Roman emperor, with the Latin title *Rex* (King). The reverse has a monogram of the name LONDONIA. The coin was probably issued about 879–80 to mark Aelfred's control of London, following a treaty with the Danes.

Seeing the Bayeux tapestry, said Hilaire Belloc in 1914, is one of those moments when time itself is 'telescoped up'. This vivid cartoon strip illustrating the Norman Conquest may have been made by English craftswomen commissioned by Bishop Odo of Bayeux or Edith, sister of the defeated King Harold.

William Blake (1757–1827), author of the archetypal English verse *Jerusalem*, here depicts *St Gregory and the British Captives*. Bede's apocryphal story of English slaves in Rome – 'not Angels but Angles' according to Pope Gregory – supposedly launched Augustine's mission to convert the Anglo-Saxons. Bede may have invented Gregory's pun and at the same time established the name 'Angli' or English.

In this scene an English woman and child flee their home, put to fire by the Normans.

A thirteenth-century manuscript illustrates an attack on the Jews.

The horrors of the plague, Europe's and Britain's greatest demographic disaster, the Black Death (1346–1353) depicted in an engraving of 1348. People and their animals flee the corrupted air of the town (though villages were even more vulnerable) and pass an elderly man inflicted with buboes or sores.

Hogarth's *Noon* (1738), Huguenots leave their church 'des Grecs' in Hog Lane, Soho. The sobriety of the French Protestants contrasts with the loose ways of the local Londoners on the left, and the English fashionistas who ape courtly French manners (*right foreground*). The kite hanging from the church roof (*top right*) symbolises the flight of the Huguenot refugees.

Jewish men in London's Whitechapel (1954) cross the road in front of a Number 25 Routemaster, the London icon finally taken out of service in 2006.

James Gillray's *United Irishmen in Training* (1798), another bunch of brutal French revolutionaries in the making, according to England's fiercest satirist.

Sawney in the Bog House (June 1779) by James Gillray (1756–1815), who was himself half-Scottish. The finest caricaturist of the eighteenth century savagely lampoons the unsophisticated kilted Scot. Such caricatures of the Scots had been popular in England from about 1745.

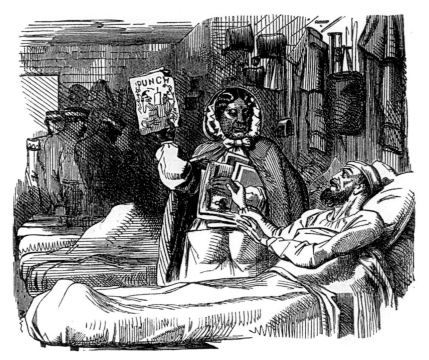

Mary Seacole, the Jamaican nurse who ministered to the British troops in the Crimean War, as depicted in *Punch* (20 May 1857).

The Cenotaph, St George's Plateau, Liverpool, sculpted by Herbert Tyson Smith and unveiled in 1930. This is one of the most powerful of the First World War memorials emphasising grief and loss. This side, facing Lime Street, shows civilian mourners in everyday dress, with military gravestones receding into infinity.

Modern Britons 1: An Anglo-Sikh gentleman in his West Midlands allotment. He carries a bunch of coriander, a herb popularised in the twentieth century by Indian restaurants.

Modern Britons 2: A supporter of St Helens rugby league club with his greyhound. Rugby league, a sport predominantly played in northern England, is also remarkably Americanised.

reflects the particular concerns of the Norman ruling minority and also the location of the Norman-French population. Along the south coast castles such as Lewes and Hastings controlled the important access routes to and from the Continent. Others sprang up where the English had been dispossessed of their land. From their secure bases Norman horsemen could patrol and dominate their new territories; and local rebellions were often the result of the brutal and lawless depradations of these mounted warriors. William took the threat in the north more seriously. In Scotland Malcolm III was threatening invasion while providing a safe haven for the English prince and legitimate claimant to the throne, Edgar the Aetheling. Malcolm also married Edgar's sister, Margaret, so there was a real possibility that the disgruntled northern shires might simply secede to Scotland: the Anglo-Scottish border had been fluid for centuries, the people a mixture of British, Anglo-Saxon and Danes. England and Scotland were not clear-cut national entities and the northeast had been buffered from the expanding power of the English kingdom in the south by the presence of the Norse in York and the territory beyond.

When William made a serious response, moving north with a powerful force, establishing Nottingham Castle and occupying York, Malcolm decided on discretion and sued for peace. However, the northern English were less cautious. When Robert de Commines, William's recent appointment as Earl of Northumberland, arrived in Durham, his force of several hundred knights was massacred in a local uprising on 28 January 1069. This was the signal for a widespread revolt across the north.

William responded with enormous force and brutality, not just sacking York but ravaging and laying waste Yorkshire, Northumberland and then Cheshire, where Chester was the focus for rebellion. The Anglo-Norman monk and historian Orderic Vitalis, who was not without sympathy for the natives as his mother was English, put these words into William's mouth as he lay on his deathbed: 'I fell on the English of the northern counties like a raving lion, subjecting them to the calamity of cruel famine and by so doing ... became the barbarous murderer of many thousands, young and old, of that fine race of people.' A northern chronicler provided an even more graphic description of the results of William's handiwork. It could be a scene in Kosovo, or Rwanda, in the twentieth century:

> So great a famine prevailed that men compelled by hunger devoured human flesh ... and that of horses, dogs and cats ...
> [Some] sold themselves to perpetual slavery ... It was horrific

> to behold human corpses decaying in their houses, the streets and on the roads, swarming with worms while they were consuming in corruption with an abominable stench ... There was no village inhabited between York and Durham; they became lurking places to wild beasts and robbers, and were a great dread to travellers.

William suppressed opposition in the north with a scorched-earth policy, destroying crops, villages and towns, and slaughtering the local population. They were not going to provide succour, support and fodder for his enemies. The population of northern England was set back for a generation by William's deliberate act of genocide.

The notoriously unruly and unrulable Welsh were not such a direct threat to William's authority. In spite of Offa's Dyke, the Marches were a permeable frontier zone through which the Welsh and English had raided and traded for centuries. English kings had usually preferred to keep the problem of this thinly populated, unstable backwoods area at arm's length. Edward the Confessor had even invited some of his tough and not necessarily compliant Norman henchmen to carve out lordships there in the 1050s, when Gruffudd was proving troublesome. The *Anglo-Saxon Chronicle* for 1051 reported: 'The foreigners had built a castle at Herefordshire in Earl Svein's territory and inflicted every possible injury and insult they could upon the men in those parts.'

This was the first use in England of the new word 'castle' (from the Latin *castrum* – 'camp'). The English themselves had constructed fortified towns and *burhs* as community defences against the Danes. Archaeological excavations at Goltho, Lincolnshire, have also revealed the defended homestead of an Anglo-Saxon thegn. This is not dissimilar to the so-called 'ringwork' castles often built by Normans; but the motte and bailey, with its elevated tower, was something new in the English, Welsh and, eventually, Irish landscape. They were bases for aggressive newcomers, a platform from which to suppress the native peoples. The pre-Conquest castles were probably built at Ewyas Harold, in Herefordshire, Hereford itself and Richard's Castle, south of Ludlow. For the English and Welsh it was a foretaste of things to come. Castles had probably developed and multiplied in Normandy in the anarchic days of the early eleventh century, when freebooting lords looked to their own interests and there was little centralised authority. In contrast, southern and eastern England, after Alfred, was a more orderly society, and the ringworks around the homesteads of thegns, such as Goltho, were more a sign of lordly status than of hostile intent or need for security. As the young William gradually took a grip on his duchy, he seems to have spent much of his early career capturing and taking control of the independent castles that had spread like a rash across his realm.

After the Harrying of the North, William was determined to maintain his grip on his new subjects, but seems to have lost any empathy for them that he might have had. He gave up learning English and spent more time in Normandy, leaving his most trusted lords to tighten the vice; and nowhere is this tough policy more apparent than in the Welsh Marches. One of William's closest allies, Roger de Montgomery was made Earl of Shrewsbury and granted vast estates in Shropshire and Herefordshire. With them came the right and responsibility to keep this wild west frontier in some kind of order. In return Roger soared up the Norman rankings of importance: he is listed third, behind only William and his brother Odo.

We have a very detailed picture of the tough life on the frontier because for almost thirty years the archaeologist Philip Barker systematically excavated Roger's castle of Montgomery, known today by its Welsh name: Hen Domen, the 'Old Mound'. This strong motte and bailey, with multiple lines of defence, was carefully sited to control an important nodal point, where roads met and forded the River Severn. Inside, the motte was topped with a massive timber tower at least two storeys high, approached by a twelve-foot-wide flying timber bridge of the kind illustrated on the Bayeux tapestry. The bailey was packed with timber buildings. Frontier life in Castle Montgomery was tough and there were few comforts for the garrison.

Roger and his followers planted castles throughout the central Marches. There are eighty-five known in Shropshire alone. The other marcher lords Hugh d'Avranches, in Chester, and the fitzOsberns, Earls of Hereford, were equally dynamic castle-builders and these became a platform for incursions into Wales. The Earls of Hereford built Monmouth and Chepstow as bases for the conquest of Gwent.*

From their castles in Chester, Shrewsbury and Hereford and across the Severn estuary, the Norman marcher lords launched a four-pronged attack on Wales, building more castles to hold their conquered territories: Glamorgan, for example, has thirty stone castles. At first the advances were dramatic, but the Normans had taken on too much: the geographic

---

* It is often claimed that the superb stone tower or hall-keep of Chepstow is the earliest stone building of its kind in England. It is more likely that the fitzOsberns built a conventional motte and bailey and William himself constructed the Chepstow stone keep after the fitzOsberns had fallen from grace. Chepstow, like the Tower of London, sent a clear message to those in its shadow, as did the stone fortresses of Monmouth, Montgomery and Rhuddlan.

and social structure of Wales – mountainous, tribal and fragmented – told against them. The Welsh fought back in the 1090s, pinning the Normans into a narrow coastal strip by the Dee estuary; and in mid Wales even the Montgomery castle of Hen Domen fell, in 1095. In the south-west the Normans desperately clung to their stronghold in Pembroke while the Welsh took control of the inland areas. Only in the castle-studded south-east of Wales did the Normans successfully hold on to their territories.

Like Harold, the Normans came to the conclusion that the conquest and subjugation of Wales were not worth the effort required. By the twelfth century a kind of stalemate was achieved with zones later known as Marchia Wallie (the 'March of Wales') under Anglo-Norman control, and Pura Wallia, under the rule of Welsh dynasties (Gwynedd, Powys, Ceredigion and Ystrad Tywi (roughly Carmarthenshire). Though the Welsh built some castles themselves, the vast majority of the four hundred or more in Wales reflect the advance of the incomers.

The Marchia Wallie was a relatively small zone, mainly along the Marches and south coast. Most of inland Wales remained native British and tribal, based on territories known as the *cantref* or the *cwmwd* (the 'commote' – the smaller units), each with a court of *llys*, where the tribal chieftains held court. Welsh rulers also had a hereditary servile class of peasants, the *taeogia*, the equivalent of villeins in England. Traditional pastoral farming remained the predominant way of life for this bastion of Britishness. The nobility still gathered in the halls of the tribal chieftain to enjoy his hospitality and the entertainment of bards. But even if tribal Wales could fight off the Norman invaders it could not keep out the influences of the modern world. Welsh rulers such as Owain Gwynedd (d. 1170) introduced new agricultural practices and traded with the enemy, using new coinage. Traditional life was inevitably transformed.

As the period of chronic instability in the eleventh century came to an end, Wales as a whole benefited from improved farming, trade and the use of coinage. From 1070 to 1300 the population probably increased threefold. Marchia Wallie also saw the first major development of towns with some fifty, albeit small, urban centres by 1170, such as Rhuddlan,* which had eighteen burgesses in 1086, and Brecon, where its burgesses lived in the castle bailey. Others, such as Pembroke, grew up outside the castle, partly to provide services to the garrison and specialised crafts and markets for the rural hinterland. By 1170 Wales had about fifty

---

* Rhuddlan was the site of the Saxon *burh* of Gledemutha, established by the Anglo-Saxons about AD 921, but this was an exceptional outpost of urbanisation.

places which could claim urban status and perhaps 5 per cent of the population were town-dwellers. Most of these towns must have felt insecure, Anglo-Norman islands in a Celtic sea: 86 per cent had defences compared with 38 per cent in England. The Normans did not simply rely on their mounted knights. While those fighting men provided their services to their lords, in return they were granted estates of their own, which were opportunities for incoming colonists. The colony of Pembrokeshire, still called 'Little England Beyond Wales', attracted Flemish settlers. The Welsh Chronicle the *Brut* recorded the reaction of the local inhabitants to these newcomers in south Pembrokeshire:

> A certain folk of strange origin and custom ... were sent by King Henry [Henry I, in about 1108]. And that folk seized the whole cantref [territory] of Rhos ... after having driven out the inhabitants ... who have lost their rightful land and their rightful place from that day to this.

The *Welsh Chronicle* goes on to say that these people from Flanders had inhabited a crowded land threatened by the sea. The Flemings had a reputation for being able to drain and reclaim land and their experience was put to good use in Britain. But they were not just peasant farmers. Gerald of Wales in 1188 described their versatility and energy:

> a brave and sturdy people, mortal enemies of the Welsh, with whom they engage in endless conflict; a people skilled at working wool, experienced in trade, ready to face any effort or danger at land or sea in the pursuit of gain; ... quick to turn to the plough or to arms.

The Flemings had distinctive names like Lamkin, Freskin and Wizo; and the Flemish language was spoken in Pembrokeshire until at least 1200.*

Welsh place names were abandoned in favour of Anglo-Norman ones. Pembrokeshire has 155 places with the suffix '-ton' (such as Templeton, probably a planted village) and Monmouthshire has 35. The fertile Gower became a Norman estate, ringed with castles, dotted with nucleated villages and covered with manorial open fields.

Many of these peasant newcomers were arable farmers. The increasing population stimulated the demand for crops and for corn mills, all of

---

* The Flemings were great colonists in eastern Europe, and also had considerable impact on Scotland. A group settled in Upper Clydesdale as tenants of King Malcolm IV (reigned 1153–65). Freskin and Berowald the Fleming moved further north into Moray and Elgin. A Michael Fleming was Sheriff of Edinburgh in about 1200 and two of Scotland's leading aristocratic families, Douglas and Moray, had Flemish ancestry.

which increased the power and wealth of the aristocracy. The Church was also a part of that aristocracy. Priests and monks may have taken vows of poverty, but the higher-ranking — those who ruled minsters and monasteries — lived in substantial buildings and ate well, surrounded by the trappings — vestments, books, altar cloths, metalwork — of high status. Most abbots and bishops were also recruited from aristocratic families, in stark contrast to the ill-educated, poor, local clergy. The extension of Norman power coincided with the great period of reform inspired by the Rule of Benedict in the Church in the eleventh century. With Lanfranc, formerly abbot at Caen and product of the reforming abbey at Bec, as Archbishop of Canterbury from 1070, the Church was as much under new management as the landed estates. The dynamism of the Norman-French Church is still apparent from the great buildings of the age, such as Durham Cathedral.

In Wales, William fitzOsbern's Benedictine priory at Chepstow, founded in 1071, was as important an element of Norman culture and control as his castle. It was the first of dozens like it in Wales. Ewenny, established by Maurice de Londres, is the most impressive, a cell of the Abbey of Gloucester. The Abbot of Gloucester wrote to the prior of Ewenny to remind him to strengthen the lock on his doors and make sure he had a good ditch and an impregnable wall. The house of God was clearly not thought to be safe from the Welsh neighbours. For security's sake, though, most Benedictine and Augustinian monasteries were sited by the new Norman boroughs. In Wales, native saints fell down the pecking order of holy influence. St Stephen took over from St Tathan in Caerwent, St Peter from St Teilo at Llandaff. Even St David was less influential, though a Romanesque nave was added to his cathedral. The bishops of Welsh dioceses were forced to acknowledge the supremacy of Canterbury. In reaction, Welsh princes endowed their own Cistercian monasteries, such as Strata Florida and Aberconwy, where devotions, artistic work and contribution to Welsh life gave them a unique place in the affections of the native community.

In 1066 fortune was in William's favour. The next two decades proved to be more onerous for the Norman king. England was not an easy place to control. It demanded a massive programme of castle-building and a transfusion of fresh blood from France. The destruction of the native aristocracy, unresolved threats from usurpers and invaders, and the ambitions of William's own land-grabbing lords exacerbated the difficulties. Yet William was not a short-term opportunist. As King of England he meant business; and he knew how to run one. He was no mere mounted thug, though he could behave like one: William appreciated that information was also power.

His most remarkable initiative was launched at Gloucester in 1085: the Domesday Inquest. William wanted to know the details of his kingdom — in the words of an English author writing in the *Anglo-Saxon Chronicle*:

> ... how it was occupied or with what sort of people. Then he sent his men over all England into every shire and had them find out how many hundred hides there were in the shire, or what land and cattle the king himself had in the country, or what dues he ought to have in twelve months from the shire. Also he had a record made of how much land his archbishops had, and his bishops and abbots and his earls — and though I relate it at too great length — what or how much money it was worth. So very narrowly did he have it investigated, that there was no single hide nor virgate of land, nor indeed ... one ox nor one cow nor one pig which were left out, and not put down in his record; and all these records were brought to him afterwards.[7]

Now this is a slight exaggeration because it is clear from the statistics that some of William's subjects, two-legged and four, escaped the audit. Nevertheless, the Domesday Inquest was a remarkable project, probably unparalleled in medieval Europe, in terms of scale,* though, in David Roffe's words, 'there was a long tradition of smaller-scale inquests in Anglo-Saxon England going back to Edward the Elder and even his father, Alfred'.[8]

The statistics are impressive: in thirty-three counties, 25,000 named landholders for 1066; 19,500 lords and tenants in 1086, 13,000 named settlements, 270,000 unnamed inhabitants, 2,061 churches, over 6,000 mills, etc. It is not surprising that, as Richard fitzNeal reported about 1179, the great survey 'the King's Book' was known by the native English as the book of 'Domesday' — the Day of Judgement.

Historians have debated for many years why William should have made such an effort at that particular time. Some have argued that the Domesday Book was a means of collecting *geld* — the royal taxes used to pay for the English army and the defence of the country. Certainly it was the sophistication of English government, unparalleled in Europe

---

* The two-volume Domesday Book can be found in the National Archives at Kew. The first volume, the Great Domesday Book, is a 382-folio (764-page) account of England south of the Tees, minus Norfolk, Suffolk and Essex and those parts of Wales not controlled by the Normans in 1086. The second volume, the Little Domesday Book, describes the three eastern counties more expansively in 450 folios.

(except, perhaps, in Sicily), that made it attractive to successive invaders. The local government and administration could effectively raise taxes and siphon off the wealth of the country, whether to pay for armies or to buy off blackmailing Vikings. The King needed such a system, but so did his subjects to ensure fairness and to protect small men from the magnates and their retinues. Hence the objective Inquest was needed so that returns were not based on dubious and biased local reports.

The *Anglo-Saxon Chronicle* makes it clear why William needed to raise cash and resources in 1085:

> In this year people said and declared for a fact that Cnut, King of Denmark, son of King Svein, was set out in this direction and meant to conquer this country with the help of Robert, Count of Flanders, because Cnut was married to Robert's daughter. When William, King of England, who was then in Normandy … found out about this, he went to England with a larger force of mounted men and infantry from France and Brittany than had ever come to this country, so that people wondered how this country could maintain all that army. And the King had all the army dispersed all over the country among his vassals, and they provisioned the army each in proportion to his land.

The Cnut threat was serious. Three times in William's reign – in 1069, 1070 and 1075 – large Danish fleets had invaded England and they had stimulated English uprisings and unrest among the Norman lords. The alliance with Robert of Flanders, who could provide an invasion base only a short ferry ride across the Channel, made the Danish spectre even worse. In these circumstances it looks as if William stayed remarkably cool and clear-headed. There was an urgent need for money, but William did not want unnecessarily to alienate his subjects, whether English or Norman. The Domesday Inquest would provide an up-to-date record of landholdings and resources. In particular, this army which William had brought from Normandy needed to be billeted on people 'in proportion to [their] land'.

The Inquest had the added advantage of sorting out landholding after two decades of land-grabbing. For William's potentially troublesome and restive lords the survey would confirm their rights to their English estates. This may be why William also organised a grand oath-swearing for 1086.

In the event the crisis evaporated. Cnut's assassination meant that no Scandinavian fleet ever threatened England again. The Viking Age was, in effect, over. Thanks to this threat, though, we have a remarkably detailed picture of England in 1086 and changes in landholding and value since Edward the Confessor's day. The devastation and suffering caused by the Harrying of the North are detectable in the bland and neutral report of the Inquest: over a thousand villages, mostly in the west and North Ridings of Yorkshire were described as 'waste'. Whole quarters of towns, such as Oxford, had also been flattened to make way for castles. In Warwick 166 English houses had disappeared, in Lincoln another 166 and in Cambridge 27.*

The urban population of England had increased fourfold since the ninth century. The Normans appreciated that they needed to control these places by constructing castles and also by acquiring urban property themselves. While most town-dwellers were English, the immigrants established French quarters – for example in Southampton and Norwich – to promote trade. The spread of castles and monasteries in the longer term stimulated urban growth as communities developed outside the castle or monastery gates. The result was a revolution in urban topography.[9] The Domesday Book does not mention Abingdon, for example, but it does record ten traders outside Abingdon Abbey's gate. Domesday provides a basic urban hierarchy (though it fails to mention some major towns at all). Lincoln has 936 inhabited messuages (4–5,000 people), Stamford 500 (2–3,000 people), and Torksey has 102 burgesses (500 people). So Lincoln was about ten times the size of Torksey and similar in scale to Norwich and York. These urban populations had to be fed from the surrounding countryside and to pay their way the townspeople developed crafts, which have left their marks in street names such as Shoemaker Street, Tanner Street and Shieldmaker Street in Winchester.

Most Domesday entries are brief, encoded statements. Christopher Dyer has examined one: the manor of Pinbury, on the Cotswold slopes above Cirencester.[10] William had granted it to the nuns of Caen in his homeland. Helpfully, the nunnery produced its own survey thirty years later, which expands and clarifies the brief Domesday statement: 'There are 3 hides. In demesne 3 ploughs 8 villeins and a smith with 3 ploughs. There are 9 slaves. A mill at 40d. It was and is worth £4.'

The '3 hides' is simply a term of tax liability, putting the estate in the lower bracket. The 'demesne' is the estate land, cultivated for its own purposes with three ploughs, which would be powered by twenty-four oxen. The later survey of 1120 tells us that 205 acres were under crops – wheat,

---

* Ironically, the castle mounds may have preserved some of the best evidence for Anglo-Saxon towns. When part of the mound of Wallingford Castle was excavated, a remarkable cob (dried-mud) building survived beneath it, still standing to the height of a man.

rye, and oats — which, assuming half the land was fallow, means the demesne consisted of about 400 acres. The ploughing was completed with the assistance of three further ploughs belonging to the villeins, or free peasants, who must have had about three oxen apiece, which they combined to make up plough teams for their own holdings — totalling about 300 acres — and to help on the larger demesne. Domesday does not mention it, but the later survey says that the villeins owed the lord five days' work per week.

The nine slaves were the lord's full-time labour force and the smith serviced the community by producing ploughshares, sickles, tools, nails and parts for vehicles. Their descendants turned into village garages in the twentieth century. Domesday does not record any animals at Pinbury — a common omission; but in 1120 there were a horse, 17 cattle, 122 sheep and 10 pigs. As the lords (or ladies) lived on the other side of the Channel, it is likely that much of the produce was sold in the local market and the £4 a year owing to the lord (the nuns of Caen) paid in cash.

On the basis of these figures, which were accumulated for tax purposes not as a census of the whole population (William was not concerned with public services), we can attempt to estimate the numbers and density of people in 1086. At Pinbury the eight villeins, nine slaves and a smith probably represent eighteen households. In 1120 there is also a priest, though neither he nor a church are recorded in the Domesday Inquest (was the church built after 1086? or simply ignored?). The household multiplier, to estimate the total number of people, is a contentious issue amongst historians, but a reasonable average number for a household may be 4.5 to 5. So Pinbury village might have had a population of eighty to ninety people. Christopher Dyer summarises: 'We can begin to visualise the village surrounded by about 700 acres of cornfields, but with some pasture and meadow for feeding the animals, and perhaps a small wood, which would not be mentioned in Domesday if it did not provide revenue for the lord, but was a source of fuel and pasture for the peasants.'

William had taken over a going concern. Between the ninth and the eleventh centuries farming in much of the Midlands and south had become more systematically organised, based on open fields with intermixed strips, adapted to an improved plough. The recorded boundaries of Anglo-Saxon estates, such as the strip parishes which can still be seen running into the Vale of the White Horse onto the chalk downland, incorporate land suitable for cattle and sheep grazing, arable, water supplies and woodland.[11] The increase in arable production was an understandable reaction to population expansion. Experiments with modern cereals have produced 5,183 dietary kilocalories per hectatre, compared with 884 for milk and 312 for beef.[12] As in the late prehistoric and Roman period, so in the ninth to late-thirteenth century arable farming increased to feed a growing population. And in the river valleys such as the Thames and the Nene alluvium or flood silts were laid down in the valley floor providing a high water mark of arable intensification as woodland was cleared, pasture ploughed up and soils eroded into the river systems.

Domesday historians have attempted to work from the particular entries to a generalised picture of England, its regional variations and its population. The survey records 13,000 places, 269,000 individuals on manors and just over 20,000 people and properties in towns. Nevertheless, we know that many people and places are missing, notably the households of lords, the garrisons of castles, priests, monks and nuns, everyone in the four northern shires and many people in towns – even large ones such as London, Bristol and Winchester. In Gloucester it is likely that Domesday records less than a quarter of the population. Six thousand mills are recorded but only eight millers, an estimated million-plus sheep (almost certainly an underestimate by Domesday), but only ten shepherds in the entire country. Taking these difficulties into account, a reasonable (but not indisputable) population for Domesday England would be about 2.5 million. Population densities calculated from Domesday returns indicate that East Anglia, with over fifteen and even twenty persons per square mile, was the most populous rural area – and Norwich the largest town after London. About a quarter of the population of England lived in Lincolnshire, Norfolk and Suffolk. The south coastal strip, east of Southampton, Kent and the chalk scarpland and vales, from Hampshire through Wiltshire, Berkshire and Oxfordshire, were also relatively well populated. In contrast, in the Welsh borders, Cornwall and the entire north above the Humber and the Mersey inhabitants were very thinly spread, with fewer, sometimes much fewer, than five persons per square mile. There were virtually no settlements high in the Pennines, but the lowlands of Yorkshire were fully occupied: five out of six known villages were already in existence by 1086. About 8 million acres were cultivated (30 per cent of the land) and half as much was woodland. Traditionally woodland was an asset to the poor; but not royal forests, which the Normans imposed as hunting preserves under strict Forest Law.[13] These out-of-bounds places entered English mythology – and not without reason: Domesday blandly reports that people at Downton (Wiltshire), 'dwelling there, were driven out on account of the King's forest'.

In the next two hundred years, thanks to improved agricultural techniques, relative stability, climatic improvements and a developing economy, the English population doubled to 4–5 million; but there is little doubt that William had won himself a valuable prize: a kingdom with the capacity to feed its population and with potential for growth.

About 90 per cent of the population worked on the land and most were ethnically English – that is Anglo-Scandinavian and British stock – rather than Norman-French, who represented a small ruling minority, or 'kleptocracy', as Fleming called them.[14] In two decades, between 4,000 and 5,000 Anglo-Saxon lords were replaced by 144 Norman barons. This new elite signalled its status by, among other things, speaking a different language. When Cnut was king, English was the court language and Old Norse virtually died out as a common language in England. But not before it infiltrated everyday speech. Very ordinary, down-to-earth words originating in the mouths of Scandinavians entered English – words such as 'sister'; words for body parts: 'leg', 'neck' and 'skin'; the weather: 'fog'; basic adjectives: 'ugly' and 'fat'.

The modern English word 'bread' comes from Old Norse. The Old English word for bread – *hlaf* – now survives as 'loaf'. These verbal acquisitions show the close relationships that must have existed between English- and Norse-speakers: people who lived in the same village, or even in the same families, such as the bilingual children of Anglo-Norse marriages, especially in the north of England and southern Scotland (*kirk* is the Norse word for 'church').*

When I was a child in Yorkshire, I used to *laik* football, and my mother would tell people, 'He's out laiking somewhere' – often down by the beck or the laithe. In the heartlands of Scandinavian settlement these Norse words for 'play', 'stream' and 'barn' are still in common usage – as is 'gate' to mean 'street' – like Kirkgate in York – 'Church Street'. Some Norse words proved to be more convenient than English ones and were adopted: the pronouns 'they', 'them' and 'their' are of Norse origin. The Old English equivalent: *hie, him* and *hiiera,* easy to confuse with 'him' and 'her', were abandoned.

Surprisingly, perhaps, the English word 'law' is of Scandinavian origin and its adoption marks the point that there was more to the Norse than the stereotyped rapacious Viking of popular history. The legal code was a matter of great importance to Scandinavian communities. William's Domesday Inquest was part of this Anglo-Norse tradition of kings and lords making decisions and charging dues on the basis of fair and objective assessment; but his participation in Anglo-Norse culture did not go

*The hard 'k' sound is Norse, as opposed to the softer English 'ch' of church. 'Shirt' is English, 'skirt' is Norse; both originally meant a short garment.

so far as speaking English. Norman-French and Latin were the prestige languages of the new elite, the military and the Church. The vast majority of people, though, continued to speak their native tongue, adopting loan words which trickled down from London, the capital, the court, the castle and the church. As a result, English now contains a huge number of French words. Unlike the Norse ones, which came from the grass roots, they tend to be rather elevated: lordly titles – 'sovereign', 'baron', 'prince'; words for rules and administrators – 'government', 'parliament', 'nation', 'chancellor'; for the religious establishment and their activities – 'abbey', 'saint', 'parish', 'friar' and 'prayer'; and of course for the military (my own name, Miles, was the Norman-French word for soldier) – 'castle', 'armour', 'war'; and the arts – 'fashion', 'music', 'beauty' and 'colour'.

The Normans may have been tough, hard-nosed land-grabbers, but they shifted the cultural influences in Britain from the Norse world southwards to the more modern, technically advanced cultures of France, Europe and Christendom. English retained the homely words of the ordinary folk (itself an English word; 'nation' is the Frenchified equivalent). The French borrowings often have a flavour of the formal and refined: 'manor' and 'palace' as opposed to 'home' and 'house'; 'butler' and 'servant' versus 'maid' and 'man'. English persisted and eventually won the linguistic battle because it was, in the key areas, the language of the majority; but until the later fourteenth century French and Latin remained stepladders for the ambitious.

About 1330 a monk in Chester called Ranulph Higden wrote a universal history in Latin with the grand title of *Polychronicon*. The work starts by describing the languages of Britain and complains that:

> [the] corruption of the mother-tongue is because of two
> things. One is because children in school, contrary to the
> usage and customs of all other nations, are compelled to
> abandon their own language and to construe their lessons
> and their tasks in French, and have since the Normans came
> to England. Moreover, gentleman's children are taught to
> speak French from the time they are rocked in their cradle ...
> and rustic men want to make themselves like gentlemen, and
> strive with great industry to speak French, in order to be
> more highly thought of.

However, linguistic fashions were changing. The language of the Normans itself was gradually modified in England, and Anglo-Norman French came to seem provincial on the Continent to speakers of the elite

Parisian French of the court. The two languages, or dialects, were further divided when King John lost Normandy to France in the early thirteenth century. Anglo-Norman estates were severed from each other and those lords who decided to commit themselves to England also irrevocably committed themselves to English.

By the fourteenth century French was a language that had to be taught in England. As a sense of national identity and pride exerted itself, English began to gain in prestige. Nowhere is this more apparent than in the great flowering of literature, best known today from the work of Geoffrey Chaucer, particularly *Troilus and Criseyde*, written about 1380, and that great portrait of the English *The Canterbury Tales*, penned over the following two decades.

The English in Ireland, like ex-pats today, were concerned about their identity and imported works of literature. In England itself regional identities and accents remained strong.

Ranolph Higden complained in 1330, or thereabouts, that English children had to be educated in French. His work was translated into English by a Chester monk, John of Trevisa, a contemporary of Chaucer, who in 1385 added a comment of his own about teaching in French: 'This custom was much in use before the first plague ("furste moreyn" – the Black Death of 1349) and since then has somewhat changed ... in the year of Our Lord 1385, in the ninth year of King Richard II, in all the grammar schools of England children are abandoning French, and are construing and learning in English.'

Trevisa goes on to make a complaint of his own which would echo down the centuries: though the children learn more quickly in their mother tongue, they know no more French than their left heel and find it difficult to converse when travelling abroad.

The year before Chaucer's death in 1400, the last obstacle to English linguistic supremacy fell. Henry IV seized the throne and, for the first time since 1066, England had a king who was a native speaker. In Wales and Ireland the offshoots of the original British languages still flourished. The position in multicultural Scotland was more complicated, where the Norse had a strong cultural influence in the Northern Isles and Gaelic was spoken in the Highlands. The Lowland Scots had their own form of English – or 'Inglis' – a branch of Northumbrian Old English, with the distinctive pronounciation that is still characteristic today in words such as 'haim', 'bairn' and 'nicht'. Gaelic seems to have had remarkably little influence, with few loan words. The growing prestige of southern English, and the influence of literary figures such as Chaucer made an impact on Scots English. Most influential, in the sixteenth century, was the spread of southern English translations of the Bible.* 'Inglis' became less common as a literary language and southern English became the medium of the educated Scots.

At the end of the eleventh century the Norman rulers of England and the Welsh Marches were the dominant power in the British Isles. Improvements in farming, trade, technology and military organisation, combined with growing population, provided the resources for the elite of Europe to conquer and colonise old rivals and new lands. Frankish knights pushed into Sicily, Italy and on to the Holy Land in the name of the Crusades; German knights conquered and settled Slavic territory beyond the Elbe, and in Spain the Arabs were in retreat. This expansionism was inevitably a threat to the native kings and chieftains of Wales, Scotland and Ireland.

The Norman marcher lords divided Wales into Pura Wallia and Marchia Wallie. In the north the Anglo-Scottish borders had been permeable for centuries. However, the firm wedge of Scandinavian influence in northern England had buffered the Scots from the expanding power of the Wessex kings. The Viking threat had also brought the Scots, Picts and Britons of Dal Riáta together to create a Scottish kingdom, while at the same time sheltering it from the larger and ambitious rival in the south.

Under Malcolm (Canmore) III (1058–93) – whose last name translates as 'Bighead', and well it might, as he disposed of Macbeth on his way to the throne – the Scots invaded England five times between 1061 and 1093 and prompted the inevitable backlash. The Norman strongholds of New Castle, on the Tyne (1080), and Carlisle (1091) were the result, bulwarks from which the Normans could exert growing pressure on Scotland. Following Malcolm's death in an English ambush there was a series of short-lived monarchs in Scotland, often dependent on Anglo-Norman support. The accession of David I (reigned 1124–53), the youngest son of Malcolm Canmore, introduced Anglo-Norman rule by proxy. He was raised in England at the royal court as David fitzMalcolm,† Earl of Huntingdon and Northampton. He was supported by the forces based in Newcastle and Carlisle and was virtually a marcher-style lord before his accession, owing allegiance to Henry I. Once on the throne he dispensed huge estates in southern Scotland to his Norman followers: Renfrewshire went to Walter FitzAlan, who in Scotland then

---

* The Bible was not widely available in Scots until 1983![15]
† 'Fitz' (or '*fils de*') was the Norman term for 'son of', like 'Mac' in Scots, 'Map' in Welsh, 'O'' in Irish. As surnames became common, the Welsh added an 's' to the end of a name; hence the frequency of Davies, Williams, etc.

took the name 'Steward' from the office he and his family held at the royal court. By the fourteenth century Walter's descendants were calling themselves the 'Stuarts'.

Another incomer with a famous name was Robert Bruce (or 'de Brus'), Lord of Brix in the Cotentin peninsula of Normandy and of Cleveland in Yorkshire. One of David's first charters grants him Annandale. Professor G.W. S. Barrow has examined this feudal takeover: 'We have the impression of a country far from depopulated but settled loosely and extensively enough for newcomers to enter by royal favour and practise a more extensive exploitation of resources.'[16] As in England, the new bosses knew how to squeeze more out of the business, out of the land and out of the peasants. They brought in new workers as willing labour, settlers eager to carve out a living on the latest frontier. Although the Stuarts and Bruces came to represent Scottish patriotism and independence, their origins lay with the Norman colonisers and they had little in common with the British of the Highlands. Newcomers also came to the string of new towns founded or encouraged by David; Stirling, Roxburgh, Berwick and Edinburgh flourished, and trading privileges, granted for tolls and oiled by Scotland's first coinage, attracted English and Continental merchants. Fifteen royal burghs are known by the end of David's reign, in 1153, the greatest single upsurge of urbanism in Scotland until the metropolitan expansion of the eighteenth and nineteenth centuries.

David introduced, first at Roxburgh in 1120, an office that came to be identified with Scotland though it took its name from England: that of the sheriff, or 'shire reeve'. The Scottish sheriff took on a new character – as well he might, as there were no shires in Scotland (counties did not emerge until 1889). In the less centralised circumstances of Scotland the sheriff's role was more that of a judge based in a place of royal power such as a castle.

Ireland was another Celtic area vulnerable to the Norman modernisers. Brian Boruma had risen to the top of the jostling throng of competing chieftains to attain the position of High King usually held by the O'Neills. With his death in 1014 the competition was open once again. In the eleventh and twelfth centuries there was constant small-scale warfare as these rutting monarchs butted for supremacy.

In the mid-twelfth century a powerful figure emerged: Muirchertach MacLochlainn, King of Cenél nEogain (the north central area of Ireland). He achieved the title 'King of Ireland without opposition' until the people to the south of his home territory rose in opposition and killed him. Fatefully, on 1 August 1166, Muirchertach's most powerful ally, Diarmait MacMurchada, fled overseas.

MacMurchada sailed to Bristol and then on to Aquitaine. There he met King Henry of England and swore an oath of fealty promising to hold his kingdom, if with England's help it was returned to him, as a fief of the Crown of England. MacMurchada then went to Pembrokeshire, which traditionally had close links with Ireland, and, promising land and riches, recruited supporters from among the still land-hungry Anglo-Norman Fleming community. Under the leadership of Richard fitzGodebert (ancestor of the Roche family) his force crossed to Ireland in August 1167. Diarmait MacMurchada regained the core of his kingdom in the south-east corner of Ireland around Wexford and Waterford, two of Ireland's main trading ports; but he had ambitions beyond this to regain the whole of Leinster. This became a reality with the arrival of thirty knights, sixty men-at-arms and 300 archers in three ships at Bannow Bay, in County Wexford, in early May 1169. The new Norman force was led by Robert fitzStephen of the Barry family. His nephew, Gerald de Barry, better known to Latin-, English- and Welsh-speakers as Giraldus Cambrensis (Gerald of Wales, Gerald the Marcher or Gerault Cymro), became the historian of the Irish invasion. Gerald's ancestry shows the complexity of Britishness.[17] He was born about 1146 at Manorbier Castle, Pembrokeshire. He was three-quarters Norman and a quarter Welsh. His father, William, came from Normandy and took his family name from Barry Island, near Cardiff. His mother Angharad was the daughter of the Welsh noblewoman Nest (herself a daughter of Rhys ap Tewdr) and Gerald of Windsor, famous for his defence of Pembroke Castle. Gerald declared: 'I am descended from the princes of Wales and the barons of the March ... and I hate to see injustice in either nation.'

The Anglo-Norman expeditions were uncoordinated small-scale affairs until 1170. Then the big guns arrived: the Lord of Pembroke and Strigoil, Richard de Clare, known as 'Strongbow'. MacMurchada had met Strongbow in Wales and made him an offer which apparently he could not refuse: the succession to his kingship and his daughter Aoife's hand in marriage. Strongbow was backed by a hundred knights and a thousand troops. This episode of Norman private enterprise stimulated by an Irish quisling was beginning to look like a serious invasion.

Strongbow captured Ireland's second port Waterford and, after marrying Aoife, moved on to Dublin, which fell with great slaughter. Some of the Ostmen took to their ships and headed for the Isle of Man or the Northern Isles. A few months later, in 1171, Diarmait MacMurchada died. He had served his purpose and provided the Normans – or rather the mixture of English, Welsh, Flemings, Anglo-Normans and French –

with the bridgehead and the excuse to colonise Ireland. Gerald de Barry, in his account of the invasion, *Expugnatio Hibernica* ('The Irish Conquest'), was clear about the nationality of those who took part in the invasion. He called it the '*adventus Anglorum*' (the 'arrival of the English'), reflecting the famous phrase used for the fifth-century arrival of the English in Britain, the '*adventus Saxonum*'. The *Irish Annals* called the foreign invaders 'Saxanach', or 'Engleis'.

Henry II was the most powerful ruler in western Europe, with an empire that stretched from the Scottish border to the Pyrenees. Yet Henry could not ignore Strongbow's impressive conquests in Ireland. He had to exert his rights as the supreme feudal lord and take control. So in 1171 Henry II became the first reigning English monarch to visit Ireland; and, like William the Conqueror, he had papal authorisation, from Pope Adrian IV, to eradicate certain evils prevalent among the Irish – notably their supposed non-standard marriage practices of polygamy and serial monogamy. The Norman Archbishop of Canterbury spouted the standard anti-Irish propaganda: 'It is said that men exchange their wives as freely and publicly as a man might exchange his horse.' Another cleric complained that the Irish had 'a law of marriage which [was] rather a law of fornication'.

The English did not take over the whole of Ireland. Strongbow succeeded to the kingdom of Leinster in the south-east and allocated estates there to his family, companions and allies, who thus owed him rents and military service. To counterbalance Strongbow, the King granted the central lands of Meath to Hugh de Lacy, the great marcher lord. These new lords needed to defend themselves and their acquisitions from hostile neighbours while keeping a grip on their new territories. As in England, the solution was to build castles. New boroughs were established alongside many of them, which encouraged immigration from across the Irish Sea for the next hundred years.

As a result of this colonisation the economy, culture and population of Ireland, particularly in the eastern and central areas, were transformed. In the course of the next century these Anglo-Irish lords and colonists continued to think of themselves as the 'English of the land of Ireland', though they increasingly resented interference and arrivals from the old country. In the fourteenth century and during the long reign of Henry II the colonisation of Ireland continued – and much of the countryside adapted to the Anglo-Norman manorial system. While the lord held good land for himself in demesne, tenants worked the strips of large open fields, distributed so as to provide a range of land of varying quality. Ireland's famous forests were rapidly depleted as more land was brought into cultivation to feed both the expanding number of mouths and a hungry tax system. The open fields, as in Britain, were usually run on a three-course rotation of winter corn, spring corn and fallow. The countryside was dotted with new buildings from monasteries and churches to castles, manor houses and mills. By 1300 'the British Isles were altogether a much more English-dominated and English-influenced collection of societies ... than they had been two centuries earlier.'[18]

The history of colonisation is often written in terms of the great Norman lords, but behind them came massed ranks of peasantry as well as soldiers – in the words of the *Anglo-Saxon Chronicle*, 'brought in to fill the land'. When, in 1092, William Rufus founded Carlisle Castle to dominate the British-speaking region of Cumbria, he posted a company of knights and 'sent thither a great multitude of lowly folk with women and cattle to dwell and till the land'. In north-west Wales the great survey of 1334 of lands granted by Edward I to the Earl of Lincoln reveals the deliberate colonisation with English settlers from Pontefract, Skipton and Castleford in Yorkshire, Blackburn and Clitheroe in Lancashire and Sunderland in the north-east of England. Some 10,000 acres of good arable in the Clwyd valleys was handed over to the newcomers, while Welsh peasants were removed to the mountains. English lords, soldiers and peasants then operated within a framework of English law. As the Welsh chronicles recorded, an 'Englishry' had been established. The lords planted people as well as castles, burghs and crops, which together provided a quicker and more secure return.

As a result of the Domesday Inquest it is possible at least to estimate the population of England in the late eleventh century. No such figures exist for Ireland, Scotland or Wales, although contemporary comments indicate that the population density was low compared with England, for example in Pembrokeshire and Gower.[19]

Ireland also seems to have had a sparse if not precisely calculable population. English colonies of 2,000 to 4,000 newcomers were apparently substantial enough to withstand local pressure and to make an impact on Irish place names. About 8,800 out of 62,000 townland names are English, the vast majority of which arrived in the medieval period.[20]

By 1300 one distinctive group of people had disappeared from Britain, ejected by Edward I in 1290. These were the Jews. Their ancestors had first come over from France and the Rhineland in the wake of the Conqueror, who needed their financial acumen and connections to fund his military activities and his castle- and church-building activities. Canon law forbade Christians to lend money on interest so the Jews occupied this necessary and useful niche in medieval society, promoting trade, lending capital and charging high rates of interest. At the same time they were forbidden to enter a trade or a craft themselves since membership required the applicant to swear an oath to the Holy Trinity. The Jews came specifically under the protection of William and the succeeding English monarchs, who taxed them highly and treated them like a valuable flock of sheep: always available for shearing; always vulnerable to wolves. The Jews provided English kings, nobles and churchmen with the capital for major projects: their palaces, houses, cathedrals, such as Lincoln and Peterborough*, and the great monastic building programmes such as the Cistercian houses of Yorkshire. As a result, attitudes to the Jews were contradictory: they were useful and even, at times, popular with their clients; they were also despised and resented for their wealth and financial power.

For over a century after the Conquest they played a valuable role in building Anglo-Norman England and resentment was kept in check. Jewish communities were established in the principal trading centres. In London the Old Jewry developed near the Cheapside markets and the Guildhall. This was no ghetto, however, as Jewish and Christian merchants lived alongside each other. Outside of London the largest Jewish communities appear from Treasury records in the early years of Henry II's reign to have been in Norwich, Lincoln, Winchester, Cambridge, Thetford, Northampton, Bungay, Oxford and Gloucester.[21] Other sources also indicate that Jewish families lived in Bristol and York.

In the relative insecurity of medieval towns Jewish financiers, who handled bullion and cash in quantity, needed secure buildings. Like other wealthy merchants they built strong stone houses to protect their property from the two principal threats: fire and thieves. These were the first stone domestic buildings to appear in England since the Roman period. But like Roman villas these houses reflected the wealth and status of their owners, rather than simply the need for security.[22] None survives in London where the earliest were built about 1100 on the north side of Cheapside, near the river on Thames Street and Milk Street. Canterbury had about 30 stone houses in the twelfth century, which included the large building belonging to Jacob the Jew on the corner of High Street and Stour Street (which was known in the Middle Ages as Hethenmanne

---

* These cathedrals contracted loans with the wealthiest Jewish financier of the twelfth century Aaron of Lincoln. When he died Henry II appropriated his wealth including debts to the tune of three quarters of the annual royal income in a normal year. Aaron's bullion was shipped to France to finance the English wars against Philip Augustus but sank in February 1187 on the voyage from Shoreham to Dieppe.

Lane). About 1180 Jacob acquired three plots on this site to build his house which was later occupied by his sons Aaron and Samuel. They sold it to Christ Church and the monks leased the property to another Jew, Cressel, for 11 shillings a year.

As in London the early stone houses of Canterbury were destroyed in subsequent re-developments of the towns. However, two survive in Lincoln: the Norman House (previously and erroneously called Aaron's House) on Steep Hill and the Jew's House on The Strait, where the Jewish Lady Belaset lived in the late thirteenth century. Both these houses were built about 1170 at the height of Lincoln's medieval prosperity, when the city ranked below only London, York and Norwich. Economic recession in the fourteenth century ensured the survival of these small but solid houses, with their grand, arched doorways and exterior chimney breasts.*

The Jews prospered and experienced relative toleration during the reign of Henry II with new arrivals coming from France, Spain and even Russia. Henry's death in 1189, papal antagonism, and the growing enthusiasm of the English for Crusades marked the start of a century of increasing oppression. The pogroms began immediately on 3 September 1189 at the coronation of the new King, Richard Lionheart. The Jewish delegation, which came bearing gifts, was attacked and the violence spread to the Jewry, where Jewish homes were burnt and thirty people killed, including Rabbi Jacob of Orleans who had only recently come to London from the Continent. The new King sent dispatches around the country ordering that 'his' Jews be left alone. However, in December he left the country for six months to raise forces in France.† In his absence crusading zeal spread through England along with a vehement hatred of Jews. Violence erupted in February in Lynn (Norfolk) – now Kings Lynn – and spread to Norwich, Stamford, Lincoln, Colchester and Thetford. In Dunstable the small Jewish community accepted baptism to save their lives.

The most violent episode of all took place in York on the site of what is now the rather austerely respectable monument of Clifford's Tower. The Jews in York probably numbered about thirty households, or 150 people, prominent among whom were the financiers Josce and Benedict of York, and the scholar Rabbi Yomtob from Joigny in France. The trouble began

---

* Enclosed fireplaces and chimneys were the privilege of the wealthy in the twelfth century.
† When Richard was held for ransom by the Duke of Austria on his way back from the Third Crusade, it was the Jews who put up a disproportionately large share of the money. London Jews paid £486 9s 7d and Jacob the Jew in Canterbury, alone, raised £115 6s 8d. The contributions were decided in Northampton in March 1194 and the so-called Northampton Donum lists twenty major Jewish communities and several smaller ones.[23]

one night in March 1190 when an armed gang burst into the house of Benedict of York. He had been amongst the delegation attacked at Richard's coronation and he had died of his wounds on the return journey northwards. The attackers, led by Richard Malebisse and other creditors of York's Jews, murdered Benedict's widow and the rest of the occupants, plundered the house and burnt it down. Next morning the terrified Jews, led by Josce, fled to the protection of the King's castle, into the wooden keep of Clifford's Tower. Those left outside were butchered. The Jews in the castle were besieged for about ten days. When the siege engines were finally dragged into place, on the night of Friday 16 March, the eve of the great sabbath before Passover, the defenders realised that they could not hold out much longer. Rabbi Yomtob* proposed that they should all commit suicide rather than submit to the tender mercies of their Christian besiegers. The wooden tower was set on fire and the mass immolation was carried out. The next morning a few survivors emerged from the castle, having been promised clemency. They were immediately hacked down by the mob. Richard Malebisse and his fellow conspirators immediately went to the Cathedral where the Jewish financiers had deposited their bonds for safekeeping. Malebisse's gang piled the bonds onto the floor of the church, set fire to them and destroyed the evidence of their debts.

In spite of this horrific incident Jews returned to York. Vivid evidence of their presence was found in the early 1980s when archaeologists from the York Archaeological Trust excavated nearly 500 burials in the Jewbury cemetery just north-east of the city walls. It seems that in the first century after the Conquest the only formal Jewish cemetery was in London.† The bodies of the dead had to be carried there. The Jewbury cemetery was first recorded about 1230, but was probably established several decades before that. Like other Jewish cemeteries or Hortus Judeorum (Jewish gardens) such as Oxford's, it was placed away from the inhabited area and surrounded by a wall and a ditch, probably to protect it from vandals. Desecrating Jewish graves is a long and dishonourable tradition. The Jews interred their dead, laying them in no fixed orientation but were meticulous about not disturbing the bodies once they had been placed in the ground.

After the archaeological exacavation at Jewbury the remains were rapidly re-buried, so forensic analysis was limited. However, the measurements of the bones of 116 females and 135 males indicated that the

---

* The Rabbi was a poet and one of his hymns is still regularly chanted on the Eve of Atonement.
† Eventually there were ten Jewish cemeteries in England. Only three have been examined by archaeologists: seven graves in London, ten in Winchester and 482 in York.[24]

Jewish men were slightly smaller than their Christian neighbours, averaging 1.7 metres. (York gentile males ranged from 1.55 metres to 1.90 metres, with a mean of 1.72 metres, the female mean height was 1.58 metres.)* Life expectancy at birth was about 24 years and an additional 22 to 23 years at the age of 14. Few people lived more than the biblical span of 70 years.† A rough estimate can be made for the Jewish population using the cemetery over about a century. This varied between about 196 and 362 people, though some of these may have been brought to York for religious burial from other places, such as Lincoln.

Through the thirteenth century conditions for the Jews in England deteriorated. The loss, by King John, of the Normandy territories in 1204–6 severed the routine business and cultural links between the English and French Jewish communities. In 1210, returning from his ill-fated campaign in Ireland, King John confiscated Jewish property on a massive scale and executed those who resisted. The crown was no longer the protector of the Jews. Even Magna Carta (1215) wracked up the miseries of the Jews in England by removing the obligation to pay interest on certain debts. Then three years later the instruction of the Fourth Lateran Council (held in 1215) was implemented: that Jews and other infidels should wear a prominent badge to differentiate them from Christians. This consisted of two strips of yellow cloth six inches long and three inches wide to be worn at all times on the outer garment.

Christians were especially infuriated by one of their own who dared to convert to Judaism. In 1222 a Christian deacon married a Jewess and adopted her religion. In righteous fury the sheriff of Oxfordshire, Fawkes de Bréauté, had him burnt,‡ 'consigning him to hell', he said, 'without his paramour'.

There were wild accusations of ritual murder, notably the infamous case of Little Hugh of Lincoln. This unfortunate child probably fell accidentally into a cesspit and drowned in August 1255. Childhood accidents, from fire, cooking pots and deep holes, were common in the medieval world. This time the Jews made a convenient scapegoat. And Little Hugh

---

* People in the past were not, given reasonable environmental conditions, significantly smaller than today. Modern height averages in Britain are 1.61 metres for females and 1.74 metres for males.[25]

† The oldest medieval king at death was Edward I who was sixty-eight years old when he died in 1307. Demographic statistics show that in British ducal families life expectancy for males (from 1480 to 1679) was 30.1 years, rising to 62.5 (from 1880 to 1954). Women rose from 33.9 years to 70.2 in the same period.

‡ This execution set the common law precedent for the punishment of heretics by burning.

was given a martyr's burial in the cathedral choir.*

The crusading King Edward I introduced the Statute of Jewry in 1275 which made the practice of usury illegal and put the Jews out of business (though this did not prevent the Italians with papal protection from taking over the banking role). In the same year Edward ordered the Jews of Marlborough to move to Devizes, those in Gloucester to Bristol, in Worcester to Hereford and Cambridge to Norwich. In Lincoln the Jewess Belaset, who occupied the stone Jew's House, was accused of coin clipping and hanged. In the same year, 1290, Edward expelled the remaining, now virtually destitute, Jews from his kingdom.

By 1300 the British Isles were a distinctly more integrated and anglicised world – through law, language, finance and trade. That is not to say they were unified. Wales, Ireland and the Highlands and Islands of Scotland retained a distinctive Gaelic tradition, especially in the mountainous and broken country where guerrilla warfare could take its toll against the mounted troops which were most effective in flat, open country. In one of his earlier 'pro-English' phases Gerald of Wales reported that some people 'judge that it would be safer and wiser to abandon such a rough and trackless country (whose inhabitants are quite untameable) to wild animals and turn it into a game preserve'.

As he grew older and more sympathetic to the Welsh, Gerald emphasised their simplicity, generosity, wit and humour, their tartan clothes, obsession with cleaning their teeth and above all their choral abilities: 'The Welsh do not sing their traditional songs in unison, but in many parts, and in many modes and modulations. So that in a choir of singers – a customary thing among these people – you will hear as many different parts and voices as you see heads: but in the end they all join together in a smooth and sweet B-flat resonance and melodic harmony.'[26]

However, anglicisation did not just depend upon conquest. In the relatively strong kingdom of Scotland, Englishness was adopted without force: through urbanisation, trade, finance, mixed marriages (Anglo-Norman names were increasingly given to children) and adoption of English law. Lothian had been English-speaking for several centuries, but by the thirteenth century the language had spread north of the Firth of Forth and Gaelic was in the long process of retreat that continued until the twentieth century. Ranolf Higden, the Chester monk who bemoaned the use of French in his *Polychronicon*, reported that in his day the Welsh

---

* The story became the stuff of popular legend and features in Chaucer's *Canterbury Tales* ('The Prioress's Tale'). Hugh's body was found near the house of the Jew Copin who was tortured until he confessed, dragged around Lincoln's steep streets tied to a horse's tail and then hung on the instructions of the King who had arrived in Lincoln to join in the anti-semitic jamboree.

aped civilised English behaviour, tilling gardens, living in town, sleeping under sheets and wearing shoes and stockings:

> *So they seemeth now in mynde*
> *More Englische men than Walsche kynd.* [27]

Across Europe a similar process of modernisation and integration was taking place.[28] The English colonisation of Ireland was backed by Italian bankers and Jewish merchants, who followed in the wake of William the Conqueror. Frankish military power made itself felt from Cumbria to Sicily and into southern Greece, where sun-baked castles such as Monemvasia (Malmsey) looked out over the Mediterranean. The lands of Church and lords were more intensively cultivated and new lands, from the forest and fen, were brought into cultivation. People moved about to seize new opportunities. In the manor of Stoneleigh (Worcestershire) in 1305 at least 14 out of 134 men who paid taxes were incomers from surrounding shires. Increasingly, unfree bondsmen, living in highly populated areas such as Norfolk and Somerset, made *chevage* payments which allowed them to live outside their native manors. They were probably off in pursuit of new recently drained land or seasonal work to better themselves and their families. Populous East Anglia also supplied immigrants – and a new dialect – to London by the 1300s. London grew to a city of 100,000 people as international markets developed for wine, wool, hides and grain. The earlier medieval period was blessed with a relatively good climate. For a range of complex reasons the population in the eleventh and twelfth centuries in Britain and much of Europe grew at a substantial rate. Absolute and precise numbers are difficult, but it is possible to draw conclusions from documentary evidence such as the 1377 poll-tax returns.[29]

In 1300 the average estimated population density in Essex was in the region of 95 to 108 persons per square mile. This was high; it compares favourably with 136 persons per square mile in the same area in 1801 – a level reached after half a century of rapid growth, as population expanded in the hinterland of London. Leicestershire in the fourteenth century was even more densely settled than Essex, averaging between 108 and 122 persons per square mile in 1300. In counties where the population statistics for 1801 and the estimates for 1300 can be compared the figures are not significantly different. It seems likely that the number of people in England in 1300 could not have been less than 5.5 million and may have been as many as 6.5 million.[30]

Most were country-dwellers but England and Wales had about 1,500 market towns into which they could bring their products. Rural manors, like Roman villas, had become farms designed to feed the market. Ten million sheep produced 40,000 sacks of wool a year for the international cloth market. London was, massively, the largest town. In the next rank York, Norwich and Coventry had 10,000 to 13,000 inhabitants apiece. In spite of internal colonisation, much of the land of Britain was still marshy or wooded. Many of the poorer peasants and unfree did not have sufficient land to feed themselves and their families. They worked for wages, emigrated to towns, assarted (cleared) land from the forest or assisted in the large-scale drainage projects in Lincolnshire, Somerset and Kent.

The Scots, Irish and Welsh had visions of finally pushing back the English. Robert Bruce's brother, Edward, led a campaign into Ireland. The Welsh showed little enthusiasm for Bruce's ambitions. In addition to the devastation of the famine Ireland and northern England were ravaged by the Scots in 1318 and 1319. Emboldened by their successes thirty-nine Scots earls and barons came together under Robert Bruce to proclaim their national rights. The Declaration of Arbroath declared: 'Thus our people lived free and in peace till the noble Prince Edward King of England, father of the present king, attacked our kingdom under the guise of friendship and support when it was without a head.' It went on to request Pope John XXII's support. A reader of this eloquent document might not appreciate that Robert Bruce had been excommunicated for fourteen years and the Scots had done far more damage to the English in recent years, as the villages of Cumberland, Yorkshire and Lancashire could testify. The situation was reversed five years later. Edward III (reigned 1327–77) reopened the war in 1325 and came within an ace of taking over Scotland until he was distracted in 1337 by a small matter with the French – the Hundred Years War.

If this ongoing series of skirmishes and raids punctuated by serious battles in the north was not debilitating enough for the British, then there were natural disasters to make things much worse. The worst of these was the Great Famine of 1315–22. This started with a bad harvest in 1314, then two years of wet, miserable weather and crops rotting in the fields. Better harvests followed, but before full recovery could take place a further disastrous harvest coincided with widespread sheep and cattle disease in 1319–21. Manorial records show catastrophic crop yields: in Winchester wheat was down by nearly a half in 1315 and 1316; in Bolton Priory, Yorkshire, the rye crop was far worse. This meant that, after keeping back seed for the following year, there was virtually nothing for man nor beast to eat. But there were not many beasts left. On Bolton Priory's estate the number of cattle fell from 225 to 31. Wheat and barley prices rose by about 300 per cent and the average labourer earned enough in a year – about 30 shillings, to feed his family for six months. People with small amounts of land began to sell it to buy food; others took to crime. Many simply died of starvation. Manorial court records indicate death tolls of 10 to 15 per cent and even more, for example at Longbridge Deverall, Wiltshire. Typhus compounded the problem. This was the worst famine in English history.

After 1322 the weather improved and the surviving population expanded rapidly in the following decade. The dead left vacancies and land to be filled. At such times couples married earlier and produced more children, and young men looking for opportunities married landed widows. In 1316 John Attepond of Redgrave (Suffolk) paid 5 marks for the hand of Agnes, widow of John. Agnes's sister was less of a prospect, her husband only paid 2 shillings.

Then, in 1348, the *Pestilentia* arrived in Britain. Dorset provided the point of entry for the Black Death from Gascony:

> In this year 1348, in Melcombe [near Weymouth], in the
> county of Dorset, a little before the Feast of St John the
> Baptist [24 June], two ships, one of them from Bristol, came
> alongside. One of the sailors had brought with him from
> Gascony the seeds of the terrible pestilence and through him,
> the men of that town of Melcombe were the first in England
> to be infected.

The pestilence soon took hold in the busy ports of the south – in Bristol and Southampton; in Jersey and Guernsey fishermen were already dying. Once the painful swellings of lymph nodes (or 'buboes') became visible in the groin, neck or armpit the victim usually died within a few days.

The bubonic plague arrived in the early summer and flourished in the warm weather. In the winter pneumonic plague took over, infecting the lungs and spreading rapidly through coughs and sneezes.

> *Ring-a-ring o' roses,*
> *A pocket full of posies,*
> *A-tishoo! A-tishoo!*
> *We all fall down.*

The nursery rhyme makes a harmless game of what was virtually a death sentence. No family, high or low, remained untouched. Edward III had triumphed over the French at Crécy and over their allies the Scots at Neville's Cross, Durham, capturing King David II, son of Robert Bruce.

The King's triumph was reflected in the inauguration, on 10 August 1348, of the Order of the Knights of the Garter, Edward's Arthurian fantasy of twenty-six knights of the Holy Grail who processed to the specially built and glorious Chapel of St George at Windsor.* At the height of his triumph Edward received a harsh reminder that even royalty was mortal: his daughter Joan was struck by the plague while travelling to Spain for her wedding. She died on 2 September 1348. Princes of the Church were not immune either. The Archbishop of Canterbury had died a week earlier. Within three years they were joined by about half the British population.

> Sceptre and crown
> Must tumble down,
> And in the dust be equal made
> With the poor crooked scythe and spade.[31]

The suffering of the British Isles was not exceptional. Across Europe and Asia, in towns, cities and the countryside people were dying in their millions. As often happened with plagues, the disease had hitched a ride with a mobile army and then boarded trading ships bound for Europe, Africa and the Near East.

The Mongol army of Kipchak Khan Janibeg was probably the vehicle that brought the bacillus of wild rodents, living in the steppes of central Asia, to the west. According to an Italian lawyer, Gabriele de Mussis, the Mongols besieged the Crimean port of Caffa in 1346, held by the Genoese, and resorted to the well-known siege tactic of hurling dead and decomposing bodies into the city. These Mongol corpses had died of the plague. Within a year the disease was rife in Genoa, Venice, Padua and Florence. Following Europe's trading routes, it spread to the ports of the Mediterranean, and then inland to the great cities of Paris and Vienna.

In 1348 London had an estimated population of about 60,000 people, living cheek by jowl with each other, as well as their livestock and vermin. Such overcrowding and insanitary conditions were ideal for the spread of plague. The rich often shared bedrooms and beds; the poor slept on reed-strewn floors, sharing their cramped quarters with chickens and pigs as well as with the uninvited black rats which acted as hosts for the plague bacillus. Castles and monasteries had lavatories, or garderobes, which poured down outside walls, like an open bowel, into moats or rivers. The Thames was an open sewer. The Fleet Prison ditch was in

---

* St George, the mounted knight and slayer of dragons, was a third-century Roman soldier and martyr who lived in the eastern Mediterranean. He was adopted by the crusaders as their icon and became patron saint of England, as well as of Germany and Ethiopia.

1355 reported as choked with the sewage from eleven latrines and twelve sewers, so no water flowed through it. In 1347 one Londoner complained that his next-door neighbours were piping their sewage directly into his cellar. Many simply used stone-lined latrine pits in their back yards — a common discovery for any urban archaeologist — often within seepage distance of the household well. Mortality rates in towns were horrendous even before the arrival of the pestilence.

Butchers were a particular source of complaint. The prior of St John of Jerusalem complained about the butchers of St Nicholas Shambles (a shambles was a butchers' area) near Fleet Prison because, as a result of killing and disembowelling, 'great beasts abominable and filthy stinks proceed, sicknesses and many other evils have happened to such as have abode in the said city!'[32] First the butchers' site was moved to Stratford and Knightsbridge, suitably remote sites east and west of the city, and finally their stinking debris was dumped in the Thames.

We know of such cases because the city authorities were aware of the squalor and made attempts to do something about it; but the arrival of the plague threw these rudimentary public-health provisions into chaos. Street cleaners, night-soil (sewage) collectors, nurses, apothecaries, friars and priests died like everyone else. Excavations at East Smithfield have revealed hundreds of bodies, often in family groups, neatly stacked in rows. A Florentine commentator describes a similar scene with an Italian culinary image which shows how people can become accustomed to the shocking: 'In the morning when a large number of bodies were found in the pit, they took some earth and shovelled it down on top of them; and later others were placed on top of them and then another layer of earth, just as one makes lasagne with layers of pasta and cheese.'[33] In other London cemeteries and in Hereford even this sense of order in death disappeared and bodies were unceremoniously tipped from carts into open pits.

From its entry point in the English ports of the south coast in the summer of 1348, the plague coursed through the country: into London and the east-coast ports of Ireland by late summer 1348, penetrating South Wales by March 1349, the English Midlands in 1349, and raging in northern Scotland in 1350. The network of towns, villages and hamlets was such that there were few obstacles to the spread of the disease. The plague was carried by fleas (*Xenopsylla cheopis*) living on black rats (*Rattus rattus*). There is archaeological evidence that the black rat was enjoying a population boom in the fourteenth century. In Southampton dockside excavations rat bones increased significantly from the later thirteenth century, as did those of cats and terriers, probably brought in as predators. Similar patterns of rats, cats and small dogs also appeared at the same time in rural sites, such as Hatch Warren, near Basingstoke. The black rat likes its creature comforts and is attracted to human habitations, burrowing into earthen walls and thatch, stores of grain and bales of wool. If the plague bacillus also crossed to the human flea (*Pulex irritans*), this might explain the rapid transmission across country. The finger has even been pointed at the rabbit; after all, the marmot was the favoured host rodent in Mongolia. Some historians have argued that because of the speed and virulence of the plague it might have included diseases such as anthrax and haemorrhagic fever. Professor Didier Raoult has now firmly indentified the bubonic plague bacterium (*Yersinia pestis*) in samples taken from the pulp tissue of the tooth of a plague victim who died in Monpellier in the south of France. This technique could potentially clarify the epidemiology of the disease through the rest of Europe.

Mild, wet weather and dense populations could have encouraged the spread of the plague. There is some evidence that the Gaelic-Irish, spread thinly through the mountains, were less badly affected than the Anglo-Irish in their relatively dense settlements in the fertile lowlands.[34]

However, in Scotland, the Highlands and Lowlands were both badly hit.

One of the most terrifying descriptions comes from the Welsh poet Jeuan Gethin writing in 1349:

> We see death coming into our midst like black smoke,
> a plague which cuts off the young, a rootless phantom which
> has no mercy for fair countenance. Woe is me of the shilling
> in the arm-pit; it is seething, terrible, wherever it may come,
> a head that gives pain and causes a loud cry, a burden carried
> under the arms, a painful angry knob, a white lump. It is of
> the form of an apple, like the head of an onion, a small boil
> that spares no-one. Great is its seething, like a burning cinder,
> a grievous thing of an ashy colour. It is an ugly eruption that
> comes with unseemly haste … It is a grievous ornament that
> breaks out in a rash. They are like a shower of peas, the early
> ornaments of black death … It is a grievous thing that they
> should be on a fair skin.*[35]

Across the British Isles people and communities succumbed to the dreaded disease. In Llanllwch near Carmarthen eleven out of twelve tenants died (and presumably their families); over half the population on

---

* Within days this desperately eloquent man was dead.

the manors of Glastonbury Abbey, over 40 per cent of the parish clergy across England and 27 per cent of the nobility. The death toll among the aristocracy may have been relatively low because they lived in more spacious stone houses, less permeable by rats.

After the dramatic growth of the eleventh and twelfth centuries suddenly, within a few years, the towns and countryside of Britain seemed like stricken places. The survivors wondered why — and phlegmatically got on with their lives. One young Irishman wrote on Christmas Eve 1350 of his fear of dying: 'In the second year after the coming of the plague into Ireland … And I myself am full twenty-one years old, that is Aedh, son of Concubhar MacAodhagani, and let everyone who shall read this utter a prayer of mercy for my soul … may He put this great Plague past me and past my friends and may we be once more in joy and happiness.'

A year later, still alive, he wrote: 'A year ago this night since I wrote these lines … and may I by God's will reach the anniversary of this night. Many changes. Amen. Pater Noster.'

The young man was right. In Ireland and across Britain there had been many changes: in population, economy and language, in rural and in urban life, in the Church and in the State. The Norman Conquest had looked disastrous for the people of England and the rest of Britain. But from it had emerged a vibrant, if often violent people. Now, it seemed, God was punishing them for their hubris. But with change comes opportunity; and, as in the interlude after the Great Famine, the British would seize it and adapt to new ways.

Seven Changing Worlds

A SHORT WALK from Oxford's great Norman motte, along Worcester Street, is the boundary wall of Worcester College. For several years I had an office that overlooked the wall and the college gardens inside. One day out of my window I witnessed an alarming sight – at least, it was alarming for an archaeologist. A yellow JCB was digging a trench along the edge of the garden. Now this was no mere patch of lawn. In the fifteenth century a tenement of houses had stood there whose inhabitants had been victims of the Black Death. Such abandoned and decaying buildings had caused property prices in Oxford to collapse, and colleges were able to take advantage. Worcester – originally Gloucester College, because it was a house of learning for the monks of Gloucester Abbey – had expanded its holding to the street. Worcester College was not, and is not, amongst the wealthier of Oxford colleges, and, as far as I knew, had never built on its expanded property. So the remains of the ill-fated tenement probably still lay beneath the lawn and in the path of the growling machine that was gobbling up the ground as I watched.

The Provost of Worcester College was then Sir Asa Briggs, one of Britain's most distinguished historians. I immediately rang his office and within an hour the machine was browsing carefully, to the instructions of a team of archaeologists. Over the next few days the foundations of the medieval houses, remnants of the Black Death, emerged.

To people in the fourteenth century it must have seemed that their world, as well as many of the buildings and settlements around them, was collapsing. After three centuries of economic expansion and population growth, up to the early 1300s, there was now an overwhelming sense of decline, decay and loss: in a contemporary schoolbook of phrases to be translated into Latin, pupils read: 'The roof of an old house had almost fallen on me yesterday.'[1] In 1376 Parliament recorded a depressing conclusion: 'There is not a third part of the people or of other things that there used to be.'*

In the 1390s the poet John Gower wrote:

The world is changed and overthrown
That it is well-nigh upside down
Compared with days of long ago! [2]

Conventionally historians have portrayed the fourteenth century as a grim, dark age. Barbara Tuchman, for example, in her book *Distant Mirror*, echoes Gower: 'This was an upside-down world, a troubled, feverish world.' But it was also a time of change and opportunity, a time to challenge convention and exploit the cracks and the gaps that appeared in the feudal structure of medieval society. The British, like their Continental neighbours, had suffered dreadfully, and they were to recover even more slowly. Mediterranean areas such as Tuscany and Provence were hit as badly as England in the mid-fourteenth century but recovered more quickly.†

After the demographic catastrophe of the mid-fourteenth century the population of Britain remained doggedly low for 150 years. That of England, Wales and Scotland numbered no more than three million and Ireland about half a million in the later fourteenth century, half the level in 1300. By the early 1520s it was scarcely higher. [4]

This was, in part, because the epidemic did not cease. The new disease, 'the first pestilence', which struck Britain in 1348–50, delivered the most catastrophic blow, but more were to follow. The arrival of the plague was the start of a process; the most populous towns, such as London and Norwich, became endemic centres of infection. The survivors of 1348, if they were fit and well fed, retained a degree of immunity; but this did not necessarily apply to the new generations, unborn in 1348. Another outbreak, in 1361, particularly affected the young and so was known as the 'mortality of children'. Other national outbreaks followed, in 1369 and 1375, which killed a further 10 per cent of the population. More regional flare-ups occurred every decade into the sixteenth century; Scotland suffered eight plague years between 1349 and 1420 and Wales even more.

The result was that the British population remained persistently low. Famine was less of a threat, as from 1375 the price of bread and other

---

* In England, Wales, Scotland and Ireland death rates from the plague are estimated at 30 to 50 per cent – as many as two million people. Surprisingly few burial pits, like that excavated at East Smithfield, Tower Hill, London, have been found.

† Thanks to detailed taxation returns the population growth rates in Tuscany can be calculated at about 0.7 per cent per annum from 1420 to the mid-sixteenth century, while Provence's population expanded at about 1 per cent per annum. In much of southern Europe the population had recovered to pre-plague levels by about 1550. [3]

foodstuffs fell. Only from 1437 to 1440 did disastrous weather cause the last great medieval famine. For the most part the diet of the majority of people improved and some diseases declined – leprosy, for example, arguably because of a better diet or because the climate had become cooler. The analysis of late-medieval human skeletons (7,929 females and 8,494 males have been studied from excavated remains) does not indicate that food shortage was a persistent or widespread problem.[5] In spite of the popular misconception that people in the past were small, the analysis of skeletal remains across Britain reveals a mean height for men of 1.71 metres (5 feet 7 inches) and for women of 1.59 metres (5 feet 2 inches). Height is mainly influenced by genetic factors, though poor diet in infancy limits the ability to reach our full potential growth.

The staple diet of the peasantry was carbohydrate-based: dark bread, made mostly of rye, porridge and ale; milk in the form of buttermilk, whey, curds and cheese,* and more beef, pork and fish for the better-off. Cabbage and leeks are the vegetables most frequently referred to in medieval documents, along with fruit such as apples and pears. The poet William Langland describes a frugal peasant diet, in the lean winter months, consisting of bread, cheese, curds and vegetable pottage. Root vegetables and onions were also winter staples. Honey was the major sweetener and used to make mead. Sugar was still an expensive rarity, imported from the thirteenth century at 2 shillings a pound in 1264, and still 7 pence a pound in 1334.

London was an enormous consumer of rural produce and producer of fast food. In *Piers Plowman* the street sellers cry: 'Hot pies, hot! Good piglet and geese, go dine, go'; but we are also told the urban brewers, bakers and cooks 'poison the people secretly and often'. The town authorities constantly passed by-laws to control prices and quality – baking a rabbit or a capon in pastry should only cost a penny, for example, and there were checks on pastry cooks to prevent them disguising rotten meat in their pies. Many subsisted on ale – a heavy nutritious drink made of barley and oats, while the better-off drank wine from Gascony and Anjou. London was bursting with taverns but home – brewing was common. As always drunkenness led to violence and accidents.

If the upper echelons of late-medieval society had any dietary problems they seem to have been those associated with eating too much – the Fat Friar Tuck Syndrome. At St Swithin's Priory, Winchester, late-fifteenth-century monks gobbled down on average 1.5 pound of meat a day, five

---

* The word 'dairy' comes from '*deye*', a medieval word for a female servant, who presumably made butter and cheese.

eggs, vegetable soup and plenty of bread and ale (the average for the population was 3 pints a day in the 1340s). This might account for the presence of Prestier's disease, or Diffuse Idiopathic Skeletal Hyperostosis (DISH), observable mostly in males and particularly those buried in monastic cemeteries. DISH is clinically associated with obesity and while it was scarcely observable in York's Jewish cemetery, over 11 per cent of those buried at Eynsham Abbey in Oxfordshire suffered from the condition. Nearby, at Abingdon Abbey, and at the Blackfriars Friary, Ipswich, and Mottisfont Abbey, Hampshire, DISH was also prevalent.

Monastic evidence suggests that life expectancy continued to decline in the later fourteenth and fifteenth centuries. At Westminster Abbey the monks lived, after the age of twenty, on average for another thirty years in the early part of the fifteenth century, but for ten years less by the end of it. In other words, average age of death dropped from fifty to forty. Given that these men were relatively well fed and housed, their mortality rates were most likely affected by the infectious townspeople who crowded around the skirts of the monastery. Essex peasants in the late fourteenth century had the benefits of a healthier rural way of life and, if they avoided childhood diseases, could expect to live to an average of fifty-four years. Their descendants a century later lived, on average, to forty-eight. Infant mortality remained high and the hazards of childbirth still ensured that women, on average, died younger than men.

Medieval understanding of childbirth is set out in the encyclopedia *De Proprietatibus Rerum* ('On the Properties of Things') written by the Franciscan friar Bartholomew the Englishman in the mid-thirteenth century. It was still sufficiently authoritative to be printed by Wynkyn de Worde in 1495 and, again, in 1535 and 1582. Bartholomew said that a child was formed by the father's seed mixing with the matter from the mother. If the embryo that formed grew on the woman's left side, it became a female; if on the right, then a male. The relative size of the mother's left and right breasts indicated the sex of the child. As childbirth was a risky business, churches such as Canterbury Cathedral lent holy girdles (St Anselm's belts) to safeguard pregnant women. Royalty had even more poweful protection: they could borrow the Virgin Mary's girdle from Westminster Abbey. Fortunately the Virgin had others, which could be found at Bruton Abbey (Somerset) and Dale Abbey (Derbyshire). The finger of St Stephen, held in Kelham Church (Nottinghamshire) also provided protection. Pregnant women sought security in amulets of aetites or eaglestone (a form of iron ore), rock crystal, jasper and malachite. Bartholomew assumes that at the birth the mother will be accompanied by a woman ('midwife' means 'with the wife') who 'hath craft to help a woman that travaileth of child, that she bear and bring forth her child with less woe and sorrow'. But all these devices had limited success: in the late Anglo-Saxon rural church cemetery at Raunds (Northamptonshire) 44 per cent out of all adult females died between the ages of seventeen and twenty-five, the optimal time for childbearing, and there was little improvement throughout the Middle Ages.[6]

Population estimates for a generation after the Great Plague are given a degree of precision by the statistics from the first poll tax of 1380/1. This was levied at the reasonable rate of 4 pence per person and so avoidance was probably not widespread. In 1377 the total number of tax-payers was 1,355,201 in England, which excluded beggars, the inhabitants of Durham and Chester palatinates, clergy and children under fourteen. From this it can be calculated that the population of England was in the order of 2.5 million. By 1520 it was scarcely any different.[7]

High mortality caused by endemic plague is usually assumed to have been the major factor in keeping the British population low; but population change is influenced by the balance between death and birth rates. Late medieval families seem to have been relatively small – often two adults and two children. Statistics are lacking to explain the cause: late marriage, high infant mortality, missing generations caused by the removal of young, fertile people – young adults killed by the plague, or the knock-on effect of the 'children's plague' of 1361–2 impacting on births twenty to thirty years later?

Logically, the reduced population should have led to a labour shortage, more available land and jobs, earlier marriage and a surge in population. The Continent experienced these trends but not Britain. If the causes of low population in the later fourteenth and fifteenth centuries are uncertain, the effects are more apparent. Labour shortage cut a swathe through the restraints of the medieval feudal system. Serfs demanded more freedom and if it was not forthcoming they voted with their feet. In Scotland the institution disappeared. Lords fulminated and threatened but with work available elsewhere the serfs' previous status was easily forgotten, or ignored.

There was no love lost between the peasantry and their landlords. For a time the boot was on the other foot: with tenants in short supply landlords had to reduce their rents. Nevertheless the lords retreated only when they had to; where possible, they exploited their powers and the persistence of villeinage to their own advantage and to the abhorrence of their tenants and serfs – an ongoing conflict which would erupt in the future.

The catastrophic population collapse of the mid-fourteenth century, combined with economic and political factors and worsening climate, caused the abandonment of some marginal areas; the populations of the fenlands of East Angia, the Kent and Sussex marshes and the Thames estuary declined as flooding encroached.[8]

The environmental impact was exacerbated by the lack of manpower: there were few labourers to maintain the dykes, drains and sea defences — much as happened in some areas at the end of the Roman occupation in the later fourth and fifth centuries. People abandoned their moor-edge communities in Cornwall and Devon, and in Northumberland, where Scottish raiding made life even more uncertain. But people were not simply victims of environmental pressures; they adapted. In Cornwall in 1351 tin miners struggled to produce a quarter of their 1342 output, but by 1386 they were back to earlier levels. In the infertile, sandy brecklands of Norfolk the locals took up large-scale rabbit farming, exploiting an animal that had been brought to Britain by the Normans. But the biggest impact of depopulation was on the extensive ploughlands, particularly of midland England. There, abandoned village earthworks and the distinctive corrugated pattern of ridge and furrow cover the modern landscape — at least they did until recently: the powerful machinery of modern arable farming has unfortunately scoured many of these traces away.*

One area of prominent earthworks survives on the borders of Oxfordshire and Northamptonshire, preserved in the parklands of Tusmore. Trevor Rowley, a landscape archaeologist from Oxford University, and I spent several days surveying this place — planning the crofts and tofts, the enclosures of medieval gardens, the platforms where houses once stood and the streets hollowed by generations of feet and hooves. Tusmore village is now just a series of slight swellings beneath the turf of the great park of Tusmore House. However, it is famous among medieval historians because it is one of the few villages known to have been deserted because of the Black Death. The plague delivered literally the killer blow to a community already in decline. Tusmore is on the edge of a breckland area, once used as a medieval military training ground, a place for jousting. The strains of the early-fourteenth-century climatic deterioration, relatively poor soils and their isolated position were already driving the people of Tusmore away. The plague was the last straw. As there was no one left in the deserted village, the lord obtained permission to empark his land.

* Maurice Beresford and John Hurst's classic study in 1971 of deserted medieval villages and hamlets lists 2,263 places abandoned or severely reduced at various times (often undated) in the later medieval period.

Midland villages were deserted in large numbers, but for complex and varied reasons and at different times. Counties such as Leicestershire and Warwickshire contained some of the heaviest and, potentially, most fertile arable land in Britain – provided that there were enough peasants to cultivate the claylands thoroughly and that the weather co-operated by not being too wet at the wrong time.* Otherwise the system could collapse.

The shortage of manpower, increasing wages, falling grain prices and bad weather continued to cause problems. When W. G. Hoskins surveyed the villages of Leicestershire in 1950, he reported that at least one-sixth – about sixty places – had disappeared between 1450 and the early seventeenth century.

The first arable farmers, in prehistoric Britain, selected the light, well-drained, easily cultivable soils of the river valley gravel terraces and the chalk and limestone slopes. The heavier clay soils of Warwickshire and Leicestershire were partly cleared of forest later, as populations expanded, by the Romano-Britons and by the Anglo-Saxon peasants prior to the Norman Conquest. These new arable fields were hard work, but could be prolific, rewarding their cultivators with burgeoning harvests if their luck held. The early cultivators were able to buffer their risk by maintaining pasture and woodland as insurance against crop failure. By the early fourteenth century much of this non-arable land had been whittled away by the demands of a growing population. There were more mouths to feed, increasing pressures and risks, and crop failure could mean disaster.

Ironically, after the Black Death, the reduced population of the later fourteenth century increased the risk factor of cultivating both the marginal lands and the heavy clay soils of the English Midlands. The latter required intensive and reliable labour. And recovery was not just slow: 'one of the most sustained and severe agricultural depressions in documented English history'[9] hit the country between about 1430 and 1470. In a world already turned upside down more disasters were to come: further severe outbreaks of plague, a disastrous famine (1438–9) following three wet summers, epidemics which laid waste the herds of cattle and flocks of sheep. With a depressed population and low demand, grain prices continued to fall in the 1440s. At the same time the wool and cloth trades were also hit: customs records show an enormous slump in exports in 1448–50. In 1449 royal finances collapsed and salaries went unpaid; royal debt had doubled to £372,000 since 1433; 1450 was an 'annus

---

* Ideally a dry autumn for ploughing, a cold winter to break up the ground and a dry spring for sowing. Two years of wet autumns and springs could bring famine.

horribilis' for the English King Henry VI. His most powerful and corrupt adviser, William de la Pole, Duke of Suffolk, was murdered while fleeing across the Channel. Jack Cade led the men of Kent and Sussex in a protest march on London, perhaps naively expecting that the law would provide justice and redress for modest people. More radical mobs executed royal advisers and chanted 'The King is a fool'. They demanded that land rents should be lowered below 2 pence per acre. Later in the year groups of young men, mainly tanners, thatchers, masons, smiths and dyers gathered to threaten the authorities and listen to the rhetoric of reformers.

In France artillery, introduced by the French with Italian expertise since 1420, was crashing through walls of English garrisons such as Bayeux (Normandy). Artillery was decisive in the last battle of the Hundred Years War, at Castillan (1453).*

At home trade, prices, rents, grain yields, wool and milk production all fell.† This was, in part, due to the continuation of the increasingly disastrous war in France. Normandy and Gascony were lost and by 1453 only Calais remained of England's once extensive French territories. In all this chaos the State and the Crown also lost control at home; private armies backing noble factions wreaked havoc on local economies and frightened away foreign traders. In 1439 Londoners built a public granary in Leadenhall so that they would never again have to resort to an emergency diet of peas, beans and barley. The hardest burdens, however, fell on the peasants, who lacked the resources to help them through hard times.

Yet many people flourished in this fragmented and changing world. The years after the first great plague provided the peasantry with opportunities to break free from their feudal shackles – the chance to move from their traditional homes, to exploit the labour shortage by demanding wage increases or negotiate better terms for land tenancies. Nevertheless, the forces of reaction were powerful: the poor were expected to know and keep their place. Any problems and they should appeal to 'their very dear, honourable and rightful lord'.[10] In 1362 Parliament ordered all pleas to be heard in English, so peasants now understood in their own language when their 'dear and honourable' lords trampled on them.

Not surprisingly, those who had taken the opportunity to rise above

* Shakespeare's portrayal of the loyal and conscientious John Talbot, Earl of Shrewsbury, who died with his son at Castillan, is completely inaccurate.
† Between 1438 and 1448 export of broadcloths averaged 55,000 a year and fell to 34,000 between 1448 and 1471.

their servile status wanted to reflect their new position in life while their feudal superiors preferred the old order. In 1363 sumptuary legislation attempted to tell people what they could and could not wear in order to convey their proper station in life. Only royals and earls, bishops and barons, knights and their ladies with an income over £100 per year should bedeck themselves in fur, which is why Jack Cade wore a blue velvet gown lined with fur on his people's progress into London. Ploughmen and shepherds should not presume to wear cloth valued at more than 12 pence a yard. Fourteenth-century lawmakers probably justified this attack on 'excessive apparel' on two grounds: workers with money to spend were pushing up the demand and, therefore, the prices of clothing; and if the symbols of authority — such as fur and silver buckles — were devalued by the *nouveaux riches*, then the privileged positions of the aristocrats themselves might be undermined.

We do not know what an up-and-coming cloth dealer like Emma Erle in Wakefield thought of these — probably futile — attempts to keep her in her place. Her business was worth at least £50 per year in 1395. Or Joan Edwaker, who drove a cart in Eynsham, traditionally a man's job. We only know about Joan because she was killed on the job in 1389 and an inquest recorded her death. This was still a man's world, but some women, through determination and intelligence, exploited the informal opportunities to get ahead which opened up in the later fourteenth century. Others preferred the security and clarity of the old medieval three orders: ideally chivalrous knights protected the peasants who did the work, while the priests prayed. And women looked after the household and raised children — except if they became nuns, in which case they could also spend their lives in prayer. William Langland reflected the conservative view in his great poem *Piers Plowman* (*c*.1372): 'And I have dreamt a marvellous dream. I saw a fair field of folks rich and poor ... The commons pursued different occupations, and in particular they produced ploughmen, who were to labour and till the ground for the good of the whole community.'

Piers is the ideal peasant personified: trustworthy, hard-working, straight-talking, a no-nonsense son of the soil. He accepts his lot in life. Unfortunately he saw his world undermined by greedy wage earners, work-shy, 'sturdy' beggars and grasping friars. Langland's poem appealed to the sentiments of the wealthy elite, who did not welcome the loosening of social and economic bonds, the undermining of the old order by wage negotiations, or uppity labourers with money in their pockets and pretensions to consumerism. They responded by passing the Ordinance of Labourers (1349) and the Statute of Labourers (1351), which made it an offence to demand or offer to pay rates higher than those in use before the pestilence.

The Ordinance also prohibited alms-giving to beggars and made it illegal to refuse work – for example to turn down a year's contract (it was to the labourers' advantage to take short-term contracts, then renegotiate or move on). These laws were enforced by Justices of the Peace, who certainly had an interest in them, as they were themselves recruited from the major employers. Not surprisingly, those brought before the courts were workers who had accepted higher wages, never the employers who had offered them.

The old order was clearly buckling under the pressures of change in spite of futile legal attempts to buttress it. The role of the warrior aristocracy, the knights in particular, was being questioned. Their job in the medieval world's ideal three orders was to protect the labourers, not subject them to a protection racket. They were failing to deliver their side of the bargain. Wars, raids and skirmishes had dragged on in France for decades. In the 1340s and 50s the English won famous victories at Crécy and Poitiers, where the Black Prince captured King Jean II.*

The English troops made a profit by ransoming the French King and his nobles, and by pillaging their countryside.†

By 1370 a fragile truce had collapsed and the war had turned sour. The French raided the English coast, as they had before, at the start of the war, when they sacked Southampton in October 1338. Edward III, however, had ensured that the war would be fought on French soil by destroying the French fleet at Sluys in 1340. In the 1370s the French controlled La Manche once again. They occupied the Isle of Wight and only left after they had received a large payment. As English arms became enfeebled, the burden on the taxpayer increased. This was not how the feudal plan, the ideal world of *Piers Plowman*, was supposed to work. In order to stimulate revenues, and to spread the burden onto wage earners, poll taxes were raised in 1377, 1379 and 1381. The third was crippling, demanding three groats – or one shilling – from everyone over fifteen years of age. Tax avoidance was widespread: families took to the woods;

---

* The Black Prince of Wales, Edouard, born in Woodstock was a native French-speaker who spent most of his life in France and never set foot in Wales. He was, however, made the first ever Duke in England (of Cornwall) in 1337 – a new title which reflects the growing concern of the aristocracy to reinforce its hierarchical structure.

† Ransoms were often so great that the men who collected them could retire to grand houses. Sir Roger Fiennes, veteran of Agincourt, used his winnings to build Herstmonceux (Sussex) in 1441, importing Flemish builders and bricks. However, the tables could be turned: the bankers Filippo Borromici and Co. transferred £1,631 4s 11d from their London branch to ransom Sir Thomas Rempston in 1429.

masters whisked their young servants out of sight or insisted that they were under the taxable age. Between 1377 and 1381 over 450,000 people disappeared from the tax list — a major display of passive resistance. Resentment of the poll tax was enormous; another nail in the coffin of social cohesion. Peasants who had survived the horrors of the plague and taken advantage of the new opportunities created by demographic collapse found landlords dragging out the arcane technicalities of feudalism to exploit and oppress them. Now the poll tax sought to strip them of the little wealth they had acquired.

The popular uprising of 1381 in south-east England, the so-called 'Peasants' Revolt', though it was neither led by peasants nor strictly a revolt, was sparked by officials checking poll-tax evasion in Kent and Essex. The causes were more complex and drew in not simply poor peasants but worldly-wise Londoners and the relatively successful upper echelons of village communities, who had lost faith in the competence of government and the legal system. Respectable, hard-working and patriotic yeomen saw their modest achievements threatened by greedy and backward-looking magnates. It is not surprising that they felt stressed to breaking point. Peasants had also become more mobile, in pursuit of wage-earning jobs in mining, fishing, craftwork and agricultural labouring. They had cash in their pockets, increased expectations, and resented the traditional restrictions. Women especially were on the move, most taking up jobs as servants. The poll-tax returns of 1377 show that in towns such as Worcester and Northampton 19 per cent and 30 per cent of the tax-paying population were servants. Women often outnumbered men in towns and vice versa in the countryside.

The decade before 1381 had been one of the most terrible in British history: the renewed war with France fuelled heavier taxation; the lethal famine of 1370 was outdone in severity only by that of 1315–17; plague flared up in 1369 and 1374–5 and was then followed by a massive slump in grain prices and fall in land values. In the years after 1375 there was widespread unrest amongst the peasantry and an increasing intolerant and self-fulfilling fear of uprising amongst the magnates and landlords. Their attempts to frustrate the economic opportunities of workers caused seething resentment.

The rebels of 1381, mainly from relatively prosperous areas such as Essex, Hertfordshire, East Anglia and Kent, retained a touching loyalty and a fatal deference to their young King Richard II, son of the Black Prince and hope of the future*; but his advisers had earned neither

---

* Richard was born in Bordeaux in 1377.

respect nor loyalty — especially not his uncle, the warmonger John of Gaunt, or the officials most closely associated with the hated poll tax. In Essex, on 10 June, the rebels set about systematically destroying the poll-tax records.[11]

Across East Anglia, Essex and Kent they attacked and occasionally killed officials and ransacked their files to remove the evidence of the abhorrent tax.

This was a well-organised rebellion and the demands were well thought out: a radical attack on almost five centuries of peasant exploitation in England. Magna Carta in 1215 may have defined royal powers for the benefit of the aristocracy, but it did precious little for one of the most effectively harnessed and hard-driven peasantries in Europe. When the population of medieval England was at its peak, in the 1290s, some 60 per cent of the rural tenantry were unfree.*[12]

The feudal landlords of Britain looked down on their calloused peasantry with contempt; the *villani* were 'lowly people and lacking in substance', which sounds even more derogatory in the original Latin: '*viles et inopes personae*'.[13] These peasants may not have been able to understand the languages of their rulers, but they got the message.

Now there was the whiff of revolt in Rainham, Billericay and Mucking — and not just among the most poor and downtrodden. Most of the rebels were landholders, with between five and twenty acres, owners of sheep, cattle and pigs. They included craftworkers and townspeople from St Albans, Canterbury and even as far afield as Scarborough, York and Bridgwater. The leaders of the rebellion were responsible types who had held office in their local communities, as jurors, constables and reeves. They rose not in despair but to demand a better future, brighter prospects and a fair stake in a changing world. God had stricken everyone with the plague; so why should the lowly not challenge their masters? In Kent the rebels elevated an ex-serf from Colchester, Wat Tyler, to be their military leader. Another Colchester man took charge of spiritual affairs: John Ball was an excommunicated priest who wished to scour the country of all greedy bishops and lords — except for the new post of Bishop of the People, to be occupied by one J. Ball.

The chronicler Froissart reports John Ball's rousing sermon, reminding his listeners of the Christian doctrine of equality:

> Are we not descended from the same parents, Adam and
> Eve? And what can they show or what reason can they give

---

* J. Hatcher (1981), 'English serfdom and villeinage: towards a reassessment', in *Past and Present* 90, 34.

why they should be more masters than ourselves? They are clothed in velvet and rich stuff, decorated in ermine and other furs while we are forced to wear poor clothing. They have wines and spices and fine bread while we have only rye and refuse of the straw and when we drink it must be water. They have handsome manors ... while we must brave the wind and rain in our labours in the field and it is by our labours that they ... support their pomp. We are called slaves and if we do not perform our services we are beaten and we have no sovereign to whom we can complain.

In a vicious display of English jingoism, the rebels turned on foreign scapegoats; specifically they singled out the Flemings, who perhaps were seen as competing in the wool and textile trades. Thirty-five of these poor souls were hauled out from their supposed sanctuary in St Martin-in-Vintry and decapitated on a block, one after the other. Flemish ladies of ill repute fared slightly better: their brothel on London Bridge was put to the torch – but probably because it belonged to the hated Lord Mayor of London, William Walworth.

The clichéd image of the Peasants' Revolt is that of the remarkable cool fourteen-year-old Richard, every inch a Plantagenet monarch on this occasion, confronting the rebels led by Wat Tyler, at Smithfield. In this tense face-off, a fracas breaks out and Walworth, the Lord Mayor, cuts down the presumptuous Tyler. Richard exerts royal leadership: 'You shall have no captain but me,' he calls to the rebels, who remain docile and quietly disperse. Three days later the royal reckoning begins. Ringleaders are rounded up and executed. At Waltham the King now changes his tune. He tells the previously trusting rebels: 'Give this message to your colleagues. Rustics you were and rustics you are still: you will remain in bondage not as before but incomparably harsher.'[14] In spite of the royal rhetoric many landlords, including the ever pragmatic John of Gaunt, took a more softly-softly approach to their tenants. Life, work and taxation had to go on.*

Yet Richard II himself, in his two meetings with the rebels in London, had initially agreed to their remarkably radical proposals: to abolish

---

* Not that the future Archbishop of Canterbury William Courtenay, son of the Earl of Devon, moderated his contempt for his inferiors. In 1390 six of his tenants at Wingham delivered their customary dues of hay discreetly, on foot so as not to be noticed. They had a good reason: these serfs were now prosperous people, and ashamed of their servile status. The Archbishop, though, was determined to exert his own status in the medieval hierarchy – and theirs. His court sentenced the six to parade as penitents, half-naked, around Wingham Church, carrying sacks of hay.

serfdom, to put a limit of 4 pence an acre on the rental value of servile land and allow anyone to sell their goods in all cities, boroughs and markets. The *Anonimalle Chronicle* also records Wat Tyler's demand that outlawry should be abolished. This was not simply an exercise in anarchy. The age of the romantic literary outlaw, like Robin Hood, was in part encouraged by the increasing application of outlawry to labourers and servants who violated the labour legislation of 1349–51 and fled rather than stand trial.*

Tyler had another demand: that 'all warrens, as well as fisheries as in parks and woods should be common to all, so that throughout the realm … poor as well as rich might take venison and hunt the hare in the fields'. Freedom to hunt and fish was one of the great dreams of the English peasantry. And so it largely remained – though it was to fulfil that dream that English settlers transported trout to Australian rivers five hundred years later; and perhaps it was this folk memory that in part led a Labour government to clamp down on foxhunting in 2005: the peasants' revenge on the mounted classes, at last.

Edward II and his magnates may have rejected these demands, but the peasantry had dared to voice them. Over the long term the inevitable tide of change brought on by demographic collapse worked in favour of the majority – wages and labour costs rose, food became cheaper and the prices of manufactured goods increased, putting more money into the purses of craftspeople. After 1381, when peasants negotiated with their lords to convert labour service to money rents or to remove feudal dues, the memory of the rebellion weighed in the balance. The peasants had flexed their muscles and could do so again. Most lords were willing to compromise rather than risk the threat of a future uprising, or drive their tenants away at a time of labour shortage. As a result, serfdom disappeared during the fifteenth century.

Not all landlords saw it this way, however. The English marcher lords were used to having their own way and, faced with reducing incomes, piled the pressure on their Welsh tenants. When the relatively moderate John of Gaunt died, in 1399, his son and heir Henry, Duke of Lancaster, demanded a payment of £1,575 from the people of Cydweli. Other

---

* The earliest definite reference to Robin is in Langland's *Piers Plowman*, written in the 1370s, where the character Sloth says:

> '*I kan noght parfitly my Paternoster as the priest it syngeth,*
> *But I kan rymes of Robyn Hood and Randalf of Chestre.'*
> ['I do not know my Paternoster perfectly as the priest sings it,
> But I know rhymes of Robin Hood and Randolph, Earl of Chester.']

This suggests that rhymes of Robin Hood were already well known in the fourteenth century.[15]

marcher lords increased rents, demanded feudal dues, exploited their monopoly of local mills and maintained restrictions on Welsh commercial activity around the colonial towns. The result was a revolt against English rule in 1400 led by Owain Glyn Dwr, an ex-law student at Westminster, a hardened soldier and member of the Welsh gentry. He declared himself Prince of Wales. For a decade Owain ruled in Wales, negotiated with the Pope and formed treaties with the French. His status was such that the great English nobleman Edmund, Earl of March, gave his daughter in marriage to him. To the Welsh, Glyn Dwr was their Arthur and his residence at Sycharth their Camelot.

> *There'll be no lack of gifts*
> *No fault, no famine, no shame*
> *Nor thirst ever in Sycharth,*

wrote the poet Iolo Goch (d. 1398). In 1402 the London Parliament outlawed Welsh minstrels. In reality Wales was no Shangri-La during Glyn Dwr's reign. For seven years the rival forces despoiled Welsh towns and countryside. At least forty towns went into serious decline, including Cardiff; but those that recovered, like Carmarthen and Caernarfon, attracted more Welsh settlers and were no longer identified so clearly as English colonies. Refusal to pay rents — passive as well as violent resistance — in the long run forced the marcher lords to moderate their authority and accept that even their world was changing. For the Welsh there was a downside to the revolt. Racial discrimination was institutionalised in the Penal Laws of 1401–2. These were often ignored, but they were there when the English needed them. In the ravaged countryside, further depopulation also resulted in the concentration of estates into fewer, privileged hands.

Within Europe the shifting epicentres of economic power also had an influence in Britain. The most advanced economies and progressive agriculture in medieval Europe were centred around the large commercial cities of Italy and Flanders. After the expulsion of the Jews from England, Lombards played a major role in financing the English Crown — the name of Lombard Street, for example, in the City of London, is a reminder of their presence.*

In the years before the Peasants' Revolt Florentine banking companies — the Bardi, Riccardi, Peruzzi and Frescobaldi — moved into London. The first English gold coin, the florin, took its name from them. In the

---

* Evidence of the international contacts of these Lombards came when I excavated a site in another Lombard Street, in Abingdon. The most spectacular discovery was a fragment of a medieval mosque lamp.

fifteenth century wool and cloth made up about 90 per cent of English exports. German merchants, from Cologne, Lubeck and Hamburg, united in 1281 to form the 'Hanse' trading league and established a centre, principally to export wool and cloth, near London Bridge at the Steelyard. Hans Holbein painted the portraits of such earnest Steelyard characters as Georg Gisze (1532) standing at his work table, which is covered with an imported Turkey carpet, surrounded by the attributes of his trade. The Germans were the dominant merchants in London through the fourteenth century, though their influence declined thereafter and Elizabeth I, suspecting that they were too close to the Spaniards, closed them down. It could be precarious being a foreigner in London, as the unfortunate Flemings had discovered during the Peasants' Revolt. The chronicler Matthew Paris complained as early as 1255 that the city was 'overflowing with Poitevins, Provençals, Italians and Spaniards'.

As so often happened, foreigners were welcome when they brought much needed skills, a factor still repeated in today's asylum debates and in the government's proposals for immigration restrictions. Medieval England was a great producer and exporter of wool, but an importer of expensive, finished cloth. In 1337 Edward III announced: 'All the cloth workers of strange lands, of whatsoever country they be which will come to England ... shall come safely and securely, and shall be in the King's protection and safe conduct, to dwell in the same lands choosing what they will.' There is little evidence for the numbers of foreigners who came to England until, in 1440, Richard II introduced a tax on all foreigners living in the country – except the Hanse merchants, who had special privileges. Most were in the City of London, which housed 1,500 immigrants, and there were a further 350 in Southwark. These aliens included Welsh, Irish and Scots – but the largest group were Dutch – or, in Latin, '*Theutonici*' – which included Flemings, Germans and Brabanters from the Low Countries. These were followed by Italians and French, a few Greeks and Icelanders, six Portuguese sailors and six Jews, in spite of the official expulsion. At this time Jews in London were usually sanctioned as Christian converts from Spain or Turkey.

The Dutch made important contributions to goldsmithing, leatherworking and tailoring. They also pioneered new technologies: in printing, clock-making, optics, brewing and brick-making.[16] One Englishman, at least, appreciated them. He wrote from Havering-atte-Bower to a friend near London, in 1469, asking him to find 'a mason that is a dutchman or a flemyng that canne make a dowbell [double] chemeney of brykks for they can best fare'.[17]

Between 1440 and 1501 the number of 'aliens' in London doubled to at least 3,000 out of a population of 50,000. This reflected the growing economic development of Britain and in particular of London at the same time as power and wealth in Europe were shifting westwards to Portugal, Spain and the Atlantic coast. The textile trade shows the shift of balance of the English economy. Medieval exports of wool peaked in 1308 at 46,382 sacks and remained relatively high until about 1360. At this time manufactured cloth exports began to climb steadily, overtaking wool exports after 1420 and substantially outpacing them for the next century. The English clothiers now supplied their own market and their lightweight, fairly cheap products sold well in southern Europe. Lincoln 'scarlets' and 'Northamptons' were well known abroad. Eastern English towns such as Stamford and Norwich became important manufacturing centres and worsteds — tightly spun, close-woven and hard-wearing cloths — took their name from the village of Worstead north of Norwich. Some textile towns, such as Coventry and Colchester, even increased in size in the post-Black Death decades* in spite of the general urban decline. Individuals such as the Scottish merchants Adam Forester of Edinburgh (d. 1405) and John Mercer of Perth (d. 1380) did well out of wool, but the general decline in raw-wool exports hit east-coast ports from Aberdeen to Hull and Yarmouth and inland collecting points such as Melton Mowbray. Scotland suffered particularly badly as its customs revenues fell from £9,000 per annum in the 1370s to £2,500 in the mid-fifteenth century and only picked up to a meagre £3,000 by the end of the century.

As the cloth business expanded, London increased its dominance to the disadvantage of towns such as Bristol. In the early fourteenth century, before the Black Death, London had had an estimated population of 80,000. In the 1520s 60,000 lived in the City, about 9,000 in Southwark (which had grown considerably) and 3,000 in Westminster. London's port provided a link between the east and south coasts of Britain and the Continent; the Thames was an artery into midland England. Foreigners were welcomed by the authorities when they brought money or skills that were economically useful, but occasionally local resentment boiled over. 'Evil May Day' in London, in 1517, was such an occasion. Several foreign bankers went bust and fled, leaving debtors in their wake. At the

---

* Coventry's population went from about 5,000 to 9,000, but fell after 1523; Colchester's from 4,000 to 6,000. Many others suffered severe decline, especially after 1400. Winchester fell from about 12,000 in 1300 to less than 8,000 in 1417 and 4,000 in 1524. York, Lincoln, Lynn and Grimsby were badly affected. At least nine Welsh boroughs disappeared entirely and twenty Scottish burghs failed to develop.

same time the story spread that an honest Englishman had been cuck-olded by an oversexed, overpaid and over-here Lombard merchant, Francesco di Bardo. These two events provided the excuse for an aggres-sive mob, many of them underemployed youths in a self-righteous frenzy, to go on the rampage, attacking foreigners and smashing up their homes and workshops, mainly in Leadenhall and Fenchurch Street. The authorities, who appreciated the economic value of the foreign commu-nity, did not approve. The Tower of London once again showed its true purpose – by turning its guns on the City. Three hundred rioters were arrested and several horribly executed. When the authorities inflicted hanging, drawing and quartering on its victims, they intended to make a statement. Londoners were forcefully reminded that the business of the City was business.*

As the legal and royal centre, London attracted the great magnates who by 1520 had built seventy-five town houses. It provided opportuni-ties for the ambitious, the hopeful and the desperate, even if the streets were not literally paved with gold. Richard Whittington came from Gloucestershire, the younger son of a knight with no prospect of inherit-ing the family estate. Instead he took his chances in London where, in the 1380s and 90s, he sold silks to royal and aristocratic households, moved into wool trading, lending money to the King, and became Lord Mayor three times. London craftsmen were the best in the country: goldsmiths, bell-founders, brass-makers – whose products decorate tombs across the country. London merchants were equally dominant, not only in cloth, but in the by-products of the trade such as dye-stuffs and alum, handled by grocers, who dealt in products by weight, including the growing mar-ket for spices. Northern consumers who could afford ginger, pepper, dried fruit and sugar made their purchases from London wholesalers. In 1400 every county in England owed debts to London.

England in 1300 was a relatively urbanised country; about 20 per cent of the population were town-dwellers, though many of these towns were extremely small, with 3,000 inhabitants or less. In spite of the Black Death and the high death toll in crowded, unhygienic towns, the propor-tion remained at about this level over the next two centuries. In Wales the successful towns of the south and west, such as Cardiff and Haverfordwest, relatively declined, but there was expansion in the north-east, at Denbigh and Wrexham – though these were small even by

---

* In the late-sixteenth-century play *Sir Thomas More* (in a section probably written by Shakespeare), More confronts the mob and persuades them, temporarily, that order is the best policy. In particular, he argues, banishment would cause them to become 'strangers' themselves in a foreign city.

English standards, scarcely reaching a population of one thousand apiece. In Scotland Edinburgh developed from a minor town before the Black Death, partly as an exporter of wool, stimulated by the English capture of Berwick (which gave Edinburgh a new hinterland) and the decision by James III (reigned 1460–88) to make it the centre of Scottish administration.

The Scottish authorities planted a rash of new towns between 1350 and 1520, especially in the decades on either side of 1500, including ten royal burghs and fifty-nine burghs of barony and regality. These were granted rights to fairs, markets and trading privileges as a stimulus to urbanisation. Many failed to take off – Scottish urbanism was still more fragile than England's; but others such as Hawick and Paisley were successful. High wages in towns attracted people from the countryside, as in Wales. In the south skilled craftsmen such as carpenters and builders were earning £6 per year, and they were looked down on by tailors and shoemakers, who were presumably earning more. Higher up the social scale a third-generation town-dweller such as Sir John Rutherford (d. 1528) of Aberdeen, a port past its peak, nevertheless successfully traded in cloth, grain, salmon, salt and wine. He acquired peat cuttings, fisheries and sheep pasture – and married twice with the daughters of local aristocrats.

By 1500 money was beginning to speak louder than feudal status; and with money came a desire for comfort and possessions to reflect one's place in the world. John Symond of Wickham Market, Suffolk, was a barber and dealer in wax. In 1481 he left a will, which listed his household goods: a feather bed and bedclothes, six pewter plates, twelve silver spoons, several pewter salts, a wooden chest, four metal candlesticks, a brass pot, five irons, rosary beads and a saddle and bridle for his horse. He was not wealthy, but these possessions show that he enjoyed a degree of material comfort unknown to his ancestors. And with increased wages came a concern for productivity and timekeeping. Church towers began to acquire clocks in this period; used at first like bells, to regulate services, they increasingly served to fix the time of the working day. Masters could now specify working hours more precisely to their small workforces – and small they still were. In 1457 Thomas Downton's pewter workshop in London employed eighteen people – the largest workforce recorded at the time. Downton was a specialist. As specialists congregated together, standards and knowledge improved: cutlers in Sheffield, metalworkers in Birmingham, potters in Surrey and brewers in Burton-on-Trent. Beer, containing hops, was a Dutch brew, which supposedly arrived in Britain at the end of the fourteenth century. There is, however, evidence for the presence of hops in England by the tenth century. Labelled 'a wicked and pernicious weed' by traditionalists, hops, a preservative, gave beer a longer life than ale. Increasingly, brewing became a bigger operation in fewer hands. The earlier small-scale operation was often undertaken by women. In Oxford between 1311 and 1500 those brewing and selling ale declined from 250 to 24. Presumably Oxonians drank as much as ever. Although beer became the national brew, conservatives initially objected, coining the memorable if inaccurate doggerel: 'Hops, Reformation, Beys and Beer / Came to England in one bad year.'

When the upper classes of Dunfermline threw a Christmas party in 1503, they blew over 60 per cent of the budget on beer, 29 per cent on wine and 6 per cent on ale; the rest on bread and coal. There is no mention of whisky, which only appears for the first time in royal accounts about this time. Whisky may have been a drink of the poor in Scotland by 1500.

Rising labour costs and demand also encouraged efficiency and productivity. Yorkshire iron-makers introduced water-powered hammers and bellows, and blast furnaces with water-powered bellows, which increased both production and temperatures. It became possible to make cast iron. In cloth-working areas such as the Stroud valley, in Gloucestershire, fulling mills, known since before 1200, spread rapidly. Wales had 202 of them by 1547. As a result, manufacturers and traders made money, which they invested in fine houses, like those in Lavenham, or Thomas Paycocke's in Coggeshall, Essex. Sir Robert Vaughan built one of Wales's finest timber houses by 1470 at Tretower in the Rhiangoll valley. He was a Yorkist and his superb house appeared just before the start of that ugly series of dynastic squabbles known as the Wars of the Roses. Over twenty years there were some extremely brutal skirmishes and battles, like those at Towton, Tewkesbury and Bosworth field. The remarkable letters of the Paston family — the first of their kind in British history — describe how mafia-like gangs besieged their homes in East Anglia. But most English people were relatively unaffected by these magnates' quarrels, which consisted of long periods of boredom interspersed with occasional outbreaks of nasty, but fairly small-scale violence. Following the death of the Yorkist King Richard III at Bosworth Field on 22 August 1485, the Tudor Henry VII seized and stabilised the throne — and as a result many great British myths were born, not least thanks to William Shakespeare, writing at the height of Tudor power.

Not everyone benefited from the growing prosperity of the later fifteenth and sixteenth centuries. Just as manpower costs affected manufacturing, so in the countryside landowners reacted to labour shortage, higher wages and the low price of corn by increasing their efficiency and productivity. Few places were depopulated specifically because of the Black Death in 1348, but over the next two centuries the shock waves continued to ripple through British society. One effect was the growing attempts by landlords to splice small landholdings together to make large, more efficient ones – the 'engrossing' of farms and the enclosing of open fields. This happened all over the country and led to substantial rural depopulation. In 1489 the government became concerned about the Isle of Wight (site of the French invasion), where engrossing had so reduced the population that its defences were compromised. In the Midlands, heavily populated by arable farmers before the famine and plagues of the fourteenth century, landowners ejected their workers and converted the labour-intensive heavy claylands to pasture. The Catesbys held the manor at Rabbourne, in south-east Warwickshire. Originally an arable village populated by peasants, it had been converted by 1443 'to a single pasture without any arable or tenants'. In the process the Catesbys introduced 1,643 sheep, ejected the peasants and increased the estate value from £19 to £64.

Another example, among hundreds, is the village of Knaptoft, south of Wigston, in Leicestershire, famously studied by W. G. Hoskins, the father of historical geography. Knaptoft appears in the Domesday Book, when the community is mainly made up of servile tenants. By 1279 there were thirty-two households in this small place, dependent upon arable farming. In the late 1400s the Turpins, new lords with new ideas, took over. By 1507 the manor was fully enclosed and converted to pasture. A few miles to the south, at Buttesby, in October 1494 the Earl of Shrewsbury evicted the entire population of sixty people and replaced their arable fields with sheep and cattle pastures.

John Rous (d. 1491), an idealistic priest, regarded this clearance of the countryside, the depopulation of Warwickshire, as a disaster caused by 'the plague of avarice'. He listed sixty villages that he knew to be abandoned or severely reduced in size. Rous's pragmatic villains included wealthy families such as the Verneys, who acquired the village of Compton Murdack, cleared out its tenants about 1447, and subsequently changed its name to Compton Verney. Only a manor house and church remained where once twenty-seven families had lived. At the end of his list of lost villages Rous invokes God's vengeance on the men who, out of greed, had caused these disasters. He also persistently petitioned the authorities. There is no evidence that they or God took any notice of him – though another idealist returned to the theme. In his *Utopia* (1516) Thomas More wrote of 'sheep [which] had become so great devourers and so wild that they eat up and swallow the very men themselves. Then consume and destroy and devour whole fields, houses and cities.'

More highlights a process that had been going on for decades, stimulated in part by the high value of cloth exports, but also by the urban demand for cattle produce: meat, milk and hides. The myth — which appealed to William Langland — of feudal stability, where everyone knew their place, was over. As in all times of change, some people benefited, and many, like the evicted peasants of Warwickshire, did not. Henry Waver knew his place. His peasant family left their hamlet of Cestersover, near Coventry, to look for a better life. Henry prospered as a London draper and alderman from 1465 to 1470. In 1466 he bought his old hamlet — and turned it into a park. Henry was a moderniser.

I cannot think of a place that more vividly demonstrates the differences and the similarities between the medieval and the modern worlds than the Spitalfields excavations in the City of London in 2002.

Surrounded by the gleaming glass-and-steel monuments of modern capitalism, archaeologists from the Museum of London uncovered the graves of 10,500 of the inhabitants of the medieval city buried in the graveyard of the Hospital of St Mary Spital. In total nearly 18,000 people had supposedly been laid to rest here between the thirteenth and sixteenth centuries to await the call of the Last Trump. In the twenty-first century they had to give way to the demands of the mercantile city. The huge number of burials was far too many for the Hospital itself — even given the dubious achievements of medieval medicine. In fact the monks of St Mary's were also into big business: the burial business. This was a profitable enterprise — there was an endless demand for plots in a burgeoning city with a horrendous death rate. By charging for burials in an overcrowded city St Mary Spital became one of the richest monasteries in the country, and a tempting target for Henry VIII when he decided to put them out of business during the Dissolution.

The archaeologists found other evidence of the Church's money-making activities, in the form of four lead seals. These were papal indulgences, probably issued in the fourteenth century from Avignon, where the great Papal Palace still dominates the town and the famous bridge. In the dance of death, however, the chances of a rapid transfer to Heaven were considerably enhanced by papal support — at least that is what the fourteenth-century Londoners believed who had paid up for their celestial passports. These people were not uneducated, superstitious peasants, but some of London's wealthier citizens, trying to maintain control over death, to reduce the odds in the afterlife — people like Johanna, wife of the wealthy mercer William Eynsham, who funded the stone chantry chapel in the cemetery.*

The English word 'chantry' comes from the Latin *cantana* – a place for singing, specifically singing the Mass on behalf of departed souls. 'Mass' is the western name for Christianity's central act, the service of the Eucharist. The word is taken from the odd dismissal at the end of the service: '*Ite missa est*' – 'Go, it is sent.'†

The drama of the Mass joined Christ and his people, reminding them of his place in the physical world of bread and wine and of his triumph over death. It was such a potent ceremony that in the Middle Ages the laity rarely approached the altar table – perhaps at Easter only, and then to receive only the bread, not the wine. In the western Church the potency of the Mass was given a further powerful purpose when it came to be seen as a kind of current, or conduit, through which people could be steered past the shoals and perils of death into the ultimate bliss of the afterlife. The more Masses said on your behalf the stronger the current and the quicker the progress to Heaven. So medieval churches in the west accumulated altars and side chapels to contain them, where Masses could pour forth for the benefit of deceased benefactors.

By the twelfth century the sophisticated intellectuals and administrators of the Church had developed a more complex geography of the afterlife than the simple alternatives of Heaven and Hell of the New Testament.[18] They gave the name Purgatory – the place of purging and cleansing fire (and limbo for unbaptised children and Old Testatment patriarchs) to this ante-room of Heaven; and the precise, bureaucratic minds of churchmen developed a finely calibrated system for easing the burden of those weighed down in Purgatory by the ballast of their sins. The chantry was the mechanism by which masses could be fed into the system for the living to assist the dead. At the same time in this cycle of mutual aid the dead mitigated the sins of the living by passing their time in Purgatory in prayer. The living and the dead were joined in a comforting cycle of intercession on each others' behalf.

As Diarmaid MacCulloch states: 'No wonder Purgatory was one of the most successful and long-lasting theological ideas in the western Church. It gave people a sense that they had some control over death, before which humanity has always stood baffled and powerless.' After the

---

* The Spitalfields chantry was a good-quality building, but not on the scale of the most elaborate chantries, such as that of the endowed association, or *collegium*, of priests organised to pray for the souls of the dear departed of the Hundred Years War, now known as All Souls College, Oxford.
† As an altar boy, attending Mass almost every day at the age of ten and eleven, I assumed that the service was like a telegram to God.

terrors and chaos of the Black Death it is not surprising that people attempted to take a grip on the whole business of death through their elaborate rituals and careful arrangements for the afterlife. Yet it was in northern Europe, rather than southern, that communities invested most in chantries and indulgences, like those found at St Mary Spital, to bank their spiritual investment as payments for the future demands of Purgatory.

Fifteenth-century London was a vibrant, youthful, cosmopolitan city inhabited mostly by people who had come from somewhere else looking for a better life. With its bankers, merchants, lawyers, ale-, wine- and food-vendors, craftsmen and servants it was, for its time, a modern city. Henry Waver, the draper and alderman of London who purchased his home village, was a man of his times, moving from the medieval to the modern world. But such terms are the artificial constructs of historians. The Battle of Bosworth Field, the end of the Wars of the Roses, with the ascent to the throne of Henry Tudor, in 1485, is a convenient terminus to the Middle Ages for textbooks – and for Tudor propagandists glorifying the new regime. In reality the deeper, slower tides of history allow for no such sudden turning points. Nor do the minds of people like Henry and those buried in the Spitalfields cemetery – city movers and shakers making the best of their circumstances, yet with a deep attachment to their Catholic religion – Britons who were both ancient and modern.

Eight Expanding Horizons

WHEN I STUDIED the Tudors for A level at an English grammar school in the 1960s, it was obvious that this period was a watershed in English, British and European history: a time of larger-than-life monarchs such as Henry VIII and Elizabeth I, of Shakespeare* and Marlowe, masters of the English language. Sitting at our wooden desks in black blazers (or red, if you were a prefect: the English still favoured such distinctions), we heard and read about constitutional affairs, the problems of royal succession, the political machinations of Thomas Cromwell and Cardinal Wolsey, the Reformation, the creation of the Church of England and the rivalries with Spain, France and Scotland. But neither teachers nor textbooks mentioned the most powerful engine of change: population growth.

From 1525 the demographic brakes were at last released, and the stagnant British population accelerated into rapid growth. Within fifteen years there were an additional half a million English people – an increase of about a quarter. Under Queen Mary – the unluckiest of the Tudor monarchs – outbreaks of famine and epidemics (probably of influenza) in 1557–9 caused short-term setbacks in the general trend. By the end of the sixteenth century, however, the English population reached 4 million and the Welsh had grown from approximately 210,000 in 1500 to 380,000 in 1603. Irish figures are harder to come by, but recovery there seems to have been even slower.§

In a relatively short space of time parts of Britain seemed, to its inhabitants, populous once more: 'pestered with people', in the words of Sir Humphrey Gilbert; 'more populous than heretofore', according to Richard Hakluyt, the great chronicler of the Age of Exploration. Hakluyt was not quite correct. The population level that he observed in 1584 may

---

* The economist John Maynard Keynes made a perceptive comment, long ignored by mainstream historians: 'We were just in a financial position to afford Shakespeare when he presented himself.'[1]

still have been lower than that of Roman Britain at its fourth-century peak. Nevertheless, in an agrarian society where 90 per cent of the population lived on and off the land, more people meant an expanding economy – unless, with bad harvests, communities hit the Malthusian buffers. In sixteenth-century Britain this was not generally the case; the population expanded rapidly from a low base and for the most part remained able to feed itself.

Henry VIII significantly assisted the study of historical demography when, as part of his attempt to create a modern, bureaucratic state, he required parishes to maintain records of births, marriages and deaths. For the first time in English history we have a closer insight into population structure, family size and the make-up of individual households. The population of Tudor England was young; half were under twenty-five and only 10 per cent or less reached the age of sixty. Families were relatively small and nuclear – parents and children lived together, but not with lots of relatives. By 1550 fertility rates had improved and children were not a major financial burden for the poor, as they were usually put to work from around the age of six. People could also expect to live longer in the second half of the sixteenth century, though the figures varied regionally and were not impressive by modern standards. Life expectancy varied between thirty-five and forty-two years, averaging about thirty-eight. At the same time, a minority reached a reasonable age, and those who achieved sixty years were not regarded as particularly old. The 1570 census of the poor for Norwich records two men and five women in their nineties out of a total of 1,400 people (women generally lived longer than men, if they survived the dangers of pregnancy); and about 30 per cent of the Norwich poor were over fifty and 15 per cent had reached sixty. Of course, at the time of most rapid population expansion in the sixteenth century the young predominated: 39 per cent were under fifteen.[2]

The savage spectres of famine and disease did not entirely disappear, however, and Malthusian crises continued to threaten some areas. There were bad harvests in most decades throughout the sixteenth century, especially in 1555–7 and 1596–8, when rain lashed the crops and flooded the valleys. The worst impacts remained regionalised: while some areas were hit, others escaped. As a result of poor transport and communications and weak integration of regional markets, relief was not forthcoming for those that suffered most – a problem which afflicts part of Africa today. In the largely pastoral upland areas growing conditions for grain were marginal at best. As the population expanded, there was an increasingly risky dependence on this marginal land. When northern pastoralists lost their local bread supply and their incomes plummeted during bad harvests, grain prices in the arable south and east soared. The northerners starved while the southerners prospered.[3]

Disease also continued to strike, though now more locally. Smallpox, bubonic plague and influenza remained killers, but at least outbreaks in rural areas such as Devon, in 1546–7, did not spread far.* In the densest centres of population, London and the towns of eastern England, plague remained endemic and flared up frequently. London, in particular, consumed its children, its rapid population growth depending entirely on the high rate of immigration to compensate for the city's deadly environment. Nevertheless famine and disease struck a significantly smaller proportion of the expanding population, and the rural surplus was sufficient to supply the stream of urban immigration.

In tough times, for example the 1550s, marriage rates declined as people lacked security and confidence in their prospects. The less well-off delayed marriage until they could support themselves. Peasant couples needed a smallholding of about fifteen acres, along with a cottage, in order to survive without other income from crafts or industry. Labourers could only risk starting a family if work was plentiful, and artisans once they had mastered a trade. By modern standards illegitimacy rates were remarkably low – about 2 per cent – and most such births were the result of failed betrothals. Both Church and society abhorred 'fleshly meddling' outside marriage; and many young people, living within the domestic and economic constraints of apprenticeships and servitude, meddled at their peril.

In England the Church frowned on adultery as a sin and a crime to be punished. Those who threatened the stability of family and society by failing in the Catholic duties of good behaviour could find themselves reported by disapproving neighbours to the Church courts. The flow of defamation suits, mostly for accusations of sexual misconduct, increased through the sixteenth century. A woman slandered by foul-mouthed neighbours as a 'privy whore' or a 'hedge whore' might take her own case to court, to strike first in self-defence and protect her reputation. Loss of it could have serious consequences. The legal penalties for adulterous women remained severe: they were commonly whipped and had their hair shaved off. Not so the men.

---

* Through the study of wills from 1485 to 1538, and thereafter parish registers, Paul Slack has tackled the issue of local mortality rates.[4] In Devon the severe plague of 1546–7 hit twenty-six out of thirty-three parishes, and in most of these the burial rate doubled. The national death rate, however, was much less severe because these outbreaks of plague were localised and relatively brief. In league tables of national death rates 1546–7 comes only thirty-third out of the forty-five worst years.[5]

The House of Commons confidently displayed its double standards when, in 1601, the all-male membership was faced with a proposal to reduce the penalties for female adultery offences to those imposed on males. All the House cried 'Away with it' and gave a monstrous great 'No'.[6]

For a man to be branded a 'horned cuckold' was no mean slur to his reputation, as Shakespeare was well aware when he had Iago pour sordid taunts into Othello's vulnerable ears – in a play written the year after Parliament's misogynistic bawlings. In spite of the sexual tittle-tattle and gossip that enlivened and bedevilled Tudor communities, single unions for life were the ideal. But in the sixteenth and seventeenth centuries life-long marriages averaged less than twenty years. Because of the universal dangers of childbirth, many men outlived their wives and remarried. This is reflected on church monuments, where the husband is often portrayed with all of his wives, like that of John Borworth, dated 1674, at Long Itchington (Warwickshire). Borworth's is, however, one of the last. After this date such representations seem to have been regarded as insensitive, or flouting the ideal. Marriages almost always ended in the death of a partner, partly because of the fragility of life but also because divorce was not recognised by the Church of England. Couples could and did separate and live apart, without any licence to remarry. Divorce, with permission to remarry, onerously required a private Act of Parliament. In the 318 years from 1539 to 1857 only 317 divorces were allowed in this way.[7] Henry VIII would make divorce an international affair.

Gaelic Ireland, as in the early Middle Ages, still took a different approach to marital and sexual matters. Marriage was a secular (not an ecclesiastical) business. Consequently trial marriage was common, divorce easier and legitimacy a matter of no great concern. The English viewed these relaxed Irish affairs with po-faced disapproval. They live 'diabolically without marriage', muttered Sir Thomas Cusack, the Master of the Rolls in Dublin in 1541, from within the defensive Pale.* This was not quite accurate; but beyond the Pale the Irish did practise serial marriage, and children born out of wedlock were accepted into their fathers' families.

Most medieval people, as we saw in the Spitalfields cemetery, sought solace in the Church and accepted its authority. But not all. The first popular heretical movement in England was that of the Lollards – a sarcastic term for those who 'mumbled' the gospels to themselves. Lollardy

---

* The defensive earthwork known as 'the Pale' was constructed to protect the last territory to which the English clung around Dublin in about 1450. Beyond, Gaelic Ireland depended on subsistence agriculture and pastoralism and was controlled by its rival clans.

emerged from the teaching of John Wyclif, an austere academic in Oxford who wrote in Latin. His ideas might never have travelled much beyond the River Cherwell if his colleagues had not translated, summarised and propagated them to a less erudite audience. Wyclif placed great emphasis on the authority of Scripture – 'the mirror of eternal truth' – which God had provided for all, not just priests. As he pointed out, there was no word for 'pope' in the Bible. Wyclif believed in predestination – God has always known what is to happen – so he saw no value in the official Church and its hierarchies, in pilgrimage, indulgences or the veneration of images. Many of his arguments foresaw the central tenets of sixteenth-century Protestantism, initiating 'the premature reformation'.

The greatest achievement of Wyclif and his followers was the translation into English of the whole of the Scriptures. For the first time Holy Writ was available to ordinary people in their mother tongue (if they could read or had access to someone who could read to them). There were political implications to all this. For those who resented the power of the Pope and the Church, Wyclif's message was a welcome one. To others it represented a threat to authority and even to the property-owning class. Reading the Bible had dangerous implications – hence, in 1409, Archbishop Arundel banned both the possession and reading of the Scriptures in English. The Lollards played into the hands of their opponents when, led by Sir John Oldcastle, Lord Cobham, they attempted a coup against Henry V in 1414. Any official support or high-ranking patronage withered away and the heresy retreated underground. The ideas survived, nourished particularly by what their opponents derided as those 'most foolish' Lollard women 'who publicly read and taught in a congregation of men' and 'those women which makes themselves so wise by the Bible'. Lollardism as a religious movement sought refuge in the home, where it was promoted by women such as the Suffolk housewife Agnes Young who 'could read very well'.[8]

Nevertheless its impact lingered; Lollards had received support from a number of influential landowners – families such as the Cheyneys, in Buckinghamshire. A detailed study of hundreds of late – medieval English wills shows that many people left money to pay for Masses and prayers for the dead: Norfolk was a notably devout area. By contrast, in Buckinghamshire and Berkshire there was far less interest in the Purgatory business. Lollard ideas may have introduced and cultivated a strain of scepticism there. Such scepticism eventually erupted on a volcanic scale on the Continent with the declarations of Martin Luther. Traditionally Germans mark 31 October 1517 as Reformation Day, when Luther nailed what might seem a rather pedantic and technical list of lecture notes to the church door at Wittenberg. But Luther hammered home his ideas at a time of enormous excitement and heightened anxiety in Europe. On 29 May 1453 Constantinople, the capital of the eastern Roman Empire and Byzantine Christianity, fell to the twenty-year-old Sultan of the Ottoman Empire, Mehmed II.

In western Europe Christians feared that God had sent Mehmed and the Ottomans for a purpose. The Last Days just might be at hand. Partly in reaction to the triumph of the Ottomans ('Turk' was still an insulting name for an Anatolian peasant), the popes in Rome determined to glorify their crumbling city and hasten the rebuilding of St Peter's. For this, Leo X needed money, and with the papal bull *Sacrasancti*, in 1515, he determined to extract it from the faithful through the sale of indulgences on an unprecedented scale. The Fugger Bank in Augsburg was roped in and a crass Dominican friar, John Tetzel, appointed as chief salesman, promised buyers that they would have 'a divine and immortal soul, whole and secure in the Kingdom of Heaven'.

You did not need to be Martin Luther to find the papal campaign vulgar, mercenary and a stain on the spirit of Christianity. Luther's complaints sparked a chain of reaction, particularly in Germany, where there had previously been the most avid demand for indulgences. In contrast, in Italy there had never been much interest; indulgences were not seen as an issue. Luther could not have picked a better time in which to voice his criticisms of the Pope. His words cascaded from the new printing presses. In 1523 alone 390 editions of his writings poured forth. Millions of pamphlets circulated across Europe.

Nevertheless in Britain Luther initially had limited impact, though his books rapidly found their way to the universities and the Inns of Court (the place of education for the laity). Humanists such as Erasmus and Thomas More thought Luther had gone too far in undermining the Church and its sacraments. Henry VIII himself, in early 1521, set about writing a condemnation of Luther entitled *Assertio septem sacramentorum adversus Martin Lutherum* (he probably had some help from professionals such as John Fisher and More).* On 12 May 1521 a huge crowd gathered in front of St Paul's to watch the burning of Luther's books.

---

* The language of theological debate in the sixteenth century could be subtle – or not. Luther wrote that Henry was a liar, a pig, a dog who deserved to be covered in shit. Thomas More, erudite lawyer, humanist and author of *Utopia*, replied in Latin and in kind. Luther, he writes, celebrates Mass '*super foricam*' – on the lavatory; he is a shit-devil ('*cacodemon*'), who should have his mouth shat into ('*incacrere*'), or pissed into ('*meiere*'). He is an ass, a drunkard, an ape – '*Asinus! Potista! Simium! Pediculosus fraterculus!*' – a lousy little friar. In reality, More was closer to the sensual, sexual and scatalogical imagery of the medieval world than he was to the rationalism of Paul Scofield's portrayal of him in the film *A Man For All Seasons*.[9]

Henry's book, on the other hand, was solemnly presented to Pope Leo X, who was informed that there was 'no nation which more impugns this monster, and the heresies broached by him'. In return the Pope awarded Henry the title of '*fidei Defensor*' — 'Defender of the Faith', which in spite of subsequent events remains on coins of the realm.

More strongly disapproved of ordinary people reading the Bible in the vernacular, and of possessing the wrong books. These he righteously burned along with their owners. When the London leather merchant John Tewkesbury, who had previously recanted his heretical views, was found with banned books, More sentenced him to death. He declared that Tewkesbury was clearly a man who 'reverted to heresy as a dog returns to his own vomit', and so he was 'burned as there was never wretche it were better worthy'. Richard Bayfield, an ex-Benedictine monk and dealer in banned books, was also, in More's words, 'well and worthely burned in Smythfelde'.

More was not averse to reform but feared that to undermine the Church fundamentally and to tempt the secular authorities, notably the monarch, to defy the Pope would generate chaos. Ultimately that is precisely what Henry VIII, Defender of the Faith, did in the cause of seeking an heir. The Act of Supremacy of 1534 confirmed More's worst fears — 'Be it enacted by authority of this present Parliament that the king our sovereign lord, his heirs and successors kings of this realm, shall be taken, accepted and reputed the only supreme head on earth of the Church of England called Anglicana Ecclesia ...'[10] — and he was executed in 1535 for failing to support Henry's demand for a divorce from Catherine of Aragon.

Significantly, from the point of view of liturgy and belief, Henry remained a Catholic until his death, in 1547.

There was a long way to go in the development of the English Reformation, but in rejecting the Pope Henry had opened the door to more radical reformers. William Tyndale, a supporter of Luther, with puritanical views close to those of John Calvin and the Swiss theologians, was determined to lay the words of the Scriptures before the eyes of his fellow countrymen 'in their mother tongue'. His English translation of the Bible was printed in Worms, in Germany, and successive editions, starting with 3,000 copies of the New Testament in 1526, poured into Britain. As the size and the price of books fell (from octavo to quarto, costing 4 shillings) Tyndale's samizdat translation was smuggled into the country through eastern ports, where reforming networks flourished. In Bremen, Hull sailors were said to pack the Bibles into casks of grain or wax to sneak them past the eyes of the customs authorities.

Heretics were not the only victims to be burned in England's religious reformation. Henry's dissolution of some 750 monasteries and convents, starting in 1534, sanctioned a century or more of drastic iconoclasm – the destruction of Catholic medieval art.[11] Sculptures and paintings blazed on bonfires throughout Britain; stained-glass windows were smashed to flood newly whitewashed churches with the light of Protestantism. Parish churches were scoured of their history and culture. Occasional images surface, like the Wenhaston Doom (in Suffolk), a powerful depiction of the Last Judgement (c.1490), which was only found when rain washed away its whitewash coating; or the Abergavenny Jesse, a magnificent figure of the prostrate Jesse carved from the trunk of an oak. This ancient symbol of life has its roots in the pagan beliefs that created Seahenge four thousand years ago.

Those who objected to the dissolution, like the ancient Abbot of Glastonbury, could find themselves on Henry's gibbet (in his case hung from the tower on Glastonbury Tor). Far more gained advantage. Vast quantities of monastic land were redistributed, giving the gentry a vested interest in the survival of the Anglican Church. The social, medical and educational services provided by the monasteries became the responsibility of local communities. Most monks and nuns were pensioned off. Others left for the Continent. Margaret Clement, foster-daughter of Thomas More, spent thirty-eight years as prioress of St Ursula's Convent at Louvain, where she was joined by other English nuns. Through the following century English convents were established in Rouen, Dunkirk, Paris, Bruges and many other centres in France and Belgium. The daughters of Catholic families congregated there. In Bruges there were Pastons, Arundels, Fitzherberts, Englefields; at Liège there were Cliffords, Ropers and Dormers.

The Protestant Reformation did not spread uniformly and consistently across the British Isles. Wales remained rural and fragmented, its scattered population divided by a rugged topography and isolated by dreadful roads: travellers referred to Breconshire as 'Breakneckshire'.* The Tudor English caricatured their western neighbours as garrulous leek- and cheese-eating thieves, speaking a language that sounded like

---

* The population of Wales was not formally counted until the census of 1801. Demographic growth was slow after the Black Death but in the sixteenth century and after it became the main engine of socio-economic change. Population can only be estimated:

Year	Population
1530	c.230,000
1670	c.370,000
1750	c.489,000

'the gobbling of geese and turkeys'. Against the odds the spread of Protestantism promoted the Welsh language and probably led to its survival.

The Welsh in the sixteenth century had a strong sense of communal rather than national identity. They were divided, north from south, by mountains and language; dialects were varied and pronounced. The humanist William Salesbury, in one of the first printed books in Welsh, in 1547, wrote: 'A Welshman today does not know what patriotism consists of.' From London, Wales was seen as unruly and backward – and the possessor of a long coastline vulnerable to invaders. The Tudors had reason to know: Henry Tudor had landed on the Pembrokeshire coast in 1485 before travelling through central Wales to Bosworth for his fateful encounter with Richard III.

Modernisers such as Thomas Cromwell, Henry VIII's chief policy-maker, wanted control over provincial government as well as supremacy over the Church – a 'unitary realm' that extended into peripheral areas like Wales and Ireland. The process of assimilation culminated in the Acts of Union of 1536–43. Wales was divided into thirteen shires, although six of them (Anglesey, Caernarfonshire, Cardiganshire, Carmarthenshire, Flintshire and Merionethshire) had existed since 1284. The seven new counties (Breconshire, Denbighshire, Glamorgan, Montgomeryshire, Monmouthshire, Pembrokeshire and Radnorshire) were partly an administrative device to put an end, finally, to the fractious and violent marcher lordships. The Welsh shires and towns now sent twenty-seven representatives to Parliament in Westminster. Few Welsh lived in towns, and few urban centres had more than 1,500 inhabitants. It is clear that the English, in assimilating Wales, intended to promote their own language. The 1536 Act of Union puts its linguistic cards on the table: '... the people ... have and do daily use a speech nothing like nor consonant to the natural mother tongue used to within this realm ... all justices in and other officers ... shall proclaim and keep the ... courts in the English tongue ... no person or persons that use Welsh speech or language shall have or enjoy any manner of office or fees ... unless he or they use and exercise the speech or language of the English.'[12]

The Welsh gentry put up little or no resistance to the union with England: they saw where power and their own future prosperity lay. Nor did they object to Cromwell's hit squads which, in 1536, set about dismantling Wales's forty-seven monastic houses. The orgy of licensed vandalism and redistribution of wealth known as the Dissolution of the Monasteries stimulated outbreaks of protest in some traditional areas of England – notably the Pilgrimage of Grace in the north, where the bonds of medieval lordship still persisted,* but in Wales the gentry looked to their own interests. The King needed money; they helped him to grab it and retained a slice for themselves.

The Welsh gentry provided no leadership or encouragement to those rural Catholics who preferred the comfort of their traditional religion. From the point of view of belief and liturgy Henry VIII remained a Catholic until his death in 1547. The Protestant revolution accelerated during the brief six-year reign of his son and successor Edward VI (1547–53). The remaining monasteries in Britain and Ireland were dissolved, chantries robbed, church walls whitewashed. The Protestant English Book of Common Prayer replaced Catholic liturgy. This was too much for the Cornish, who sent 'Articles of Supplication' to the King's Protector, Lord Somerset, asking to be allowed to keep their holy statues and the use of Latin in their services. To the Cornish, Latin in the church was equated with the use of their native language in the home. English was a threat to Cornish identity. Somerset rejected their request and the Cornish marched on Exeter, declaring: 'And so we Cornishmen (whereof certain of us understand no English) utterly refuse this new English.' The Cornish stood little chance against the professional English army. The rebels were put to flight and the English set about 'the good works of hanging'. The Cornish called it the 'Commotion Time'.

Ironically the Cornish 'Prayer Book Revolt' probably helped the cause of Welsh identity. The Welsh may have been 'much given to superstition and papistry' and slow to convert to Protestantism. Yet they did not revolt or appear disloyal to the Tudor monarchy, whose Welsh connections they appreciated. In the reign of Elizabeth I a group of progressive Welsh clerics led by Richard Davies, Bishop of St David's, persuaded the English that religious unity should come before the aggressive promotion of linguistic unity.

To the Cornish and Irish, Protestantism was an alien English imposition; to the English, the native British tongues were the languages of popery and sedition. However, an Act of Parliament of 1563 established

---

* A crusade of 40,000 gathered in the north, under the banner of the Five Wounds of Christ and the impression that theirs was not a rebellion but an attempt to petition the King. Henry did not see the challenge to his authority in the same way. Faced with this massive force he sent the Duke of Norfolk, the late Anne Boleyn's pragmatic uncle, to Doncaster, supposedly to do a deal. As with the Peasants' Revolt, the participants thought their arguments had won the day and dispersed. Henry sent orders to Norfolk: 'Our pleasure [is] that you shall cause such dreadful execution to be done upon a good number of every town, village and hamlet that have offended as they may be a fearful spectacle to all other hereafter that would practise any like matter.' Even Henry's scorched-earth policy could not eradicate the cultural, religious and social divisions between the north and south of his kingdom, which persisted for generations.

Welsh as the official language of worship and authorised the translation of the Bible and the Book of Common Prayer into Welsh. William Morgan's Welsh Bible of 1588 became a medium by which the Welsh could retain their identity and assimilate the new Protestant thinking.

This was also the year of the Spanish Armada. Increasingly Catholicism was becoming identified with the threat of foreign invasion and oppression. John Foxe, compiler of the enormously influential English *Book of Martyrs*, which encouraged English Protestants to see themselves as both victims and the elected people of God, preached outside St Paul's Cathedral in London on Good Friday 1570:

> For the Turk with his sword is not so cruel, but the bishop of Rome on the other side is more fierce and bitter against us; stirring up his bishops to burn us, his confederates to conspire our destruction, setting kings against their subjects, and subjects disloyally to rebel against their princes, and all for thy name. Such dissention and hostility Satan hath sent among us, that Turks be not more enemies to Christians, than Christians to Christians, papists to protestants, yea protestants with protestants do not agree, but fall out for trifles'.[13]

Such popular printed books as the *Book of Martyrs* also influenced language in the British Isles and promoted the dominance of Standard English. The popularity of major poets such as Chaucer had an impact on Scottish written language, but English translations of the Bible had even more, especially the Calvinistic Geneva Bible of 1560. Books in southern English were printed in Scotland in the late sixteenth century and by the seventeenth century southern English was the norm for literary output. Scots English dialect continued to be spoken, and promoted by the nationalist dialect movement, initially by Allan Ramsay (1686–1758) and most famously by Robert Burns (1759–96). Such dialect literature is not the same, however, as a standard literary language. Southern English, helped by the Bible and the Prayer Book, was permeating Britain.

To many Protestants, Latin was the medium of the papist plot, an arcane priestly code meant to exclude lay people from the Good News of the Scriptures. More importantly, with the increasing dominance of the nation-state, people came to identify with their own country and its vernacular language. The schoolmaster Richard Mulcaster put the feeling into words: 'I love Rome, but London better, I favour Italie, but England more, I honour the Latin, but I worship the English.'[14] National administrators and monarchs encouraged such sentiments. So did bookprinters, who needed to promote the national language and iron out the vagaries of dialect and spelling in order to appeal to as wide a market as possible. Some groups, notably doctors, preferred to keep their professional arts arcane, and clung to the use of Latin, which retained enormous prestige as the language of international intellectuals and administrators.

From the early sixteenth century, grammar schools taught Latin grammar. Even the great scientific works of the seventeenth century – Gilbert on magnetism (1600), Harvey on the circulation of the blood (1628) and Newton's *Principia* (1689) – were written in Latin. By Newton's time the use of Latin was in serious decline and his *Opticks* (1704) was in English. Latin promoted the feeling that writers were part of educated Christendom, but the tide was running against this scholarly internationalism.*

Many who were less educated – traders, soldiers, sailors, craftsmen – were crying out for manuals and handbooks in their own language. There were also ambitious, and successful, attempts to build a national literature to compete with the classical models of Homer and Virgil: works such as Spenser's *Faerie Queen* (1590) and, in the next century, Milton's *Paradise Lost* (1667). Even today the most widely read works in English – by Shakespeare, and the King James Bible – emerged in this period of enormous creativity, when no more than 5 million people spoke English.

It was not a universal acceptance, however; early Modern English was regarded by the educated as an unsophisticated language lacking the subtlety, range and eloquence of Latin. Ralph Lever, in 1563, complained of his native language that there were 'more things, than here are words to express things by'. Early Modern English was a magpie of a language: it stole words that glittered. The English had picked up the habit centuries earlier because of the importance of French as the language of the royal court and their rulers. As English matured as a tool of literature, science and administration, it borrowed loan words from Latin at an enormous rate. In the late sixteenth and seventeenth centuries, as the English discarded Latin as a living language, they nevertheless ransacked it for useful words, or ones that merely sounded impressive: Shakespeare satirised Holofernes in *Love's Labours Lost*, the user of so-called 'inkhorn terms'. Not that Shakespeare was averse to word-collecting himself; and many of these pompous Latinisms now nestle comfortably within the language like natives – words such as 'spurious', 'defunct' and 'strenuous'.[15]

---

* *Utopia*, written by Thomas More for fellow intellectuals, was in Latin. However, More's religious polemics and debates were intended for a wider audience and so were composed in English.

The English were also happy to loot words from their Continental neighbours, mostly the French, who contributed military and scientific terms such as 'bayonet' and 'muscle', and even such mundane words as 'entrance'. From Spanish came commercial terms — 'cargo' and 'sherry' — and from the Age of Exploration 'cannibal' (from 'Caribes', the native people of the West Indies), 'chocolate' and 'canoe'. The Dutch were a rich source: such good English words as 'deck', 'yacht', 'cruise', 'skipper' and 'booze' were originally shipped into the language from their prosperous neighbours across the North Sea.

The demand for books also encouraged the spread of paper-making.* Paper arrived in Europe from China via the Arabs in the late fourteenth century. Manufacturing was initially dominated by the Italians and then the French — *The Canterbury Tales* was printed in Oxford on French paper. There were very few paper mills in sixteenth-century England, but about a hundred existed in 1696, many established by French religious refugees.

The French Huguenots (see below) — white, Protestant, possessing valuable skills and hard-working — were able to make their mark in Britain relatively free from prejudice. These foreigners† had the right qualities, and their legacy is still significant.[16] I work today with some of their descendants in England: Oliviers and Batchelors; visit the art gallery established by the Courtaulds and buy spectacles from the Dollands; and in France many are my neighbours. This morning, as I walked into the village of Lasalle in the Cevennes to buy bread, I heard some of their descendants singing lustily in their 'temple'. The hymn was 'Let's go gather at the river' — almost the anthem of American pioneers in John Ford's westerns. At Lasalle the classical 'temple' of the Protestants faces the medieval church of the Catholics across the market place. Once a river divided the two congregations; now it runs underground, its erosive scar in the granite hillside covered by the village boule court.

In sixteenth-century France religious differences were a matter of life and death. About 1560 Calvinist French Protestants became known as Huguenots. The origin of the word is uncertain: some link it to King

---

* Vellum, made of sheepskin and used for manuscripts, was essentially a luxury product. Each volume of the Gutenberg Bible in its vellum edition took 170 sheepskins. Volume – and cheapness – through printing would not have been possible without paper.

† In Tudor England the word 'foreigner' did not necessarily mean someone from another country; it could refer even to someone from outside the county. At the age of eight, before television brought regional dialects into everyone's home, I came to London for the first time from Yorkshire to watch the Rugby League Cup final at Wembley. After the match we all travelled into the West End. I can still remember the strange accents of Londoners, and I asked my father why the place was full of 'foreigners'.

Huguet's Tower in Tours, a supposed Protestant meeting place; others to the term '*Eidgenoss*', used in Geneva to mean 'confederate'. Whatever its origins, by the mid-sixteenth century 'Huguenot' was the common term for Protestants in the geographical area of modern France and the French-speaking Low Countries (the people known as Walloons). In the second half of the seventeenth century the Huguenots began to have considerable success: well educated and organised, backed by Calvinist missionaries trained in Geneva, the Reformed Church won over many of the French aristocracy. Although probably no more than 12 per cent of the population of France were Huguenots, their disciplined national and international movement, crossing class and state boundaries, was seen as a serious threat to the Catholic Church and the monarchy. The danger of instability was made worse by the accession to the French throne in 1560/61 of a nine-year-old boy, Charles IX, whose royal hand was held firmly by his foreign mother and regent, Catherine de Medici. Their joint rule was notable mainly as a period of feuding, rivalry and assassinations, with ambitious families such as the Catholic Guises vying for power with the Protestant Condes, who had a great deal of influence in areas such as Normandy, Languedoc and Lorraine.

A series of vicious civil wars ensued, with both sides attempting to terrorise local populations. The tensions were also exacerbated by the campaigns of the Spanish King Philip II, or rather his brutal regent the Duke of Alva, against their reluctant Protestant subjects in the Netherlands. There was the danger that French Protestants would become involved on the side of their co-religionists in the north. In England Elizabeth feared a Franco-Spanish Catholic alliance. Hunger and rising grain prices did nothing to calm a dangerously volatile situation. On 22 August 1572 Paris was full of Huguenots gathered for the wedding of the Protestant Henry of Navarre and Margaret de Valois. Catholics were repulsed by the idea of the marriage; even more so by the event itself, which took place outside the Cathedral of Notre Dame, as Henry refused to enter or attend Mass. That evening the Catholic militia and the mob took to the streets. In the next three days, in an orgy of killing known as the St Bartholomew's Day Massacre, they slaughtered 3,000 Huguenots. The bloodbath spread to other cities, such as Lyon and Bordeaux, where a further 10,000 were butchered.

In the southern Low Countries the Duke of Alva systematically sacked Huguenot towns, and the Protestant leader Willem van Oranje (William of Orange) retreated to Holland. Protestant resistance in France was concentrated in the south and west, around Nîmes and La Rochelle, areas with a strong sense of regional identity, antipathy to Paris and a well-developed commercial sector of clothiers, artisans, merchants, teachers and lawyers. As in Britain, Protestantism was not the religion of the traditional peasantry, who disliked its work ethic and antagonism to their few sources of pleasure: the tavern, the carnival and festivals. Nevertheless, the Protestants had neither the power nor the numbers effectively to challenge the French Catholic Church and monarchy. Increasingly they sought a compromise, which came with the Edict of Nantes in 1598, which offered toleration, at least in theory.

During the worst of the troubles many Huguenots left France and the Netherlands. As Protestant traders and merchants they belonged to wide international networks and had some choice of refuge. It is uncertain how many chose to come to Britain in the later sixteenth century. However, in London the authorities compiled relatively precise statistics of aliens for several reasons: concern that the locals would riot if they perceived an economic threat from immigrants; fear of foreign plotters; and, more importantly, to keep account of foreigners who could be taxed. Immigration clearly increased in Elizabeth's reign – partly because, compared with her predecessors, she settled on a moderate approach to religion. (Henry VIII would burn Protestants and Catholics with equal enthusiasm if they questioned his role as Head of the Church; Edward VI swung strongly to the Protestant cause and Mary veered back again to the Catholics.) In 1568 6,704 aliens were recorded in London (plus over 2,300 in Westminster), rising to 7,143 in 1573 and over 7,000 in 1593. In 1573, the year after the St Bartholomew's Day Massacre and the campaigns of the Duke of Alva, the returns record that of 7,143 aliens in the city, 2,561 had come 'onlie to seeke woorck'. Clearly a considerable number of the others were religious refugees, but how many is not recorded.

In Rye, Sussex, the mayor reported that over six hundred refugees had arrived between 27 August (just after the slaughter) and 4 November 1572. There were four thousand aliens in Norwich at this time – a third of the city's population – because of traditional trading links with the Netherlands, but no evidence that they were joined by refugees. There does, however, seem to have been an influx into Sandwich and then into Canterbury. Probably by 1573 there were at least ten thousand Protestant refugees in England. The numbers were reduced by plague – over seventy died in Southampton in 1583–4 – but overall they increased, thanks to a flourishing birth rate. In Colchester, of 1,293 Dutch inhabitants 504 were children born in England.

The Huguenots were the best-known immigrants into England in the sixteenth century but they were not the only ones. Some came from further afield and not usually by their own choice.[17] A small group of Africans were recorded at the court of King James IV of Scotland in the early 1500s. They had probably been taken from a Portuguese slave ship by the Barton brothers, Scottish privateers acting with the King's permission. On 11 December 1504 one of these 'Moor lasses' was baptised – the 'More lass wes crestinit', according to the Scots account. One of the black men was a drummer who, in 1505, choreographed the Shrove Tuesday festivities. The King bought him a horse and a yellow coat, and paid his doctor's bills. He also tipped a nurse 28 shillings to bring this 'Moris barne' – the black baby – for him to see. Perhaps this was the drummer's child. These Africans were obviously a great curiosity and relatively well treated. Two years running the King championed one of the black ladies in the tournament, spending £29 on a damask-and-taffeta dress and black leather gloves for her. Ninety years later there is a record of 'a Black More', possibly a descendant of this group, taking part in a pageant to celebrate the birth of Henry, James VI's son. The earliest black man recorded in Tudor London was a trumpeter referred to as 'John Blanke'. In 1507 Henry VII paid him 8 pence per day and he is probably the man who twice features on the painted roll of the 1511 Westminster Tournament, to celebrate the birth of a son to Catherine of Aragon.

In the summer of 1555 a group of five black Africans arrived in England from the coast of what is now Ghana. It seems they were being taught English to help open the way into the closed Portuguese West Africa trade in slaves, gold, ivory and pepper. They were said to be tall and strong men who found English food palatable, though 'the coulde and moyst ayer doth sumwhat offende them': the Africans did not like English weather. Such a common-sense account of Africans, observed at first hand, is extremely unusual. The English were normally fed travellers' tales and fantasies about dog-headed Africans and '*anthropophagi*' – 'man-eaters'; lustful beasts who fell upon the nearest woman. To Europeans Africans were less than savages; they were subhuman. This kind of racism justified their exploitation as animals and beasts of burden. It was only a matter of time before the English broke into the trans-Atlantic slave trade.

The dubious privilege of being first fell to John Hawkyns, who undertook a voyage from Africa in 1562. There he bought slaves from African merchants, stole more from Portuguese slavers and kidnapped others. In total he carried 300 people from the Guinea coast to Hispaniola (now Haiti and the Dominican Republic) and exchanged them for pearls, hides, sugar and ginger worth £10,000. Queen Elizabeth was sufficiently impressed by his spirit of enterprise, and the profitability of his venture, to provide him with a six-hundred-ton vessel, the *Jesus of Lubeck*, for his next voyage. And to Hawkyns's coat of arms was added a crest showing 'a demi-Moor proper' — a half-length figure 'in natural colour' of a bound captive. On the coat of arms itself were three black men shackled with slave collars.

From the 1570s African slaves began to arrive in England in small numbers. Most worked as household servants, some as court entertainers; others were exploited in the Tudor sex industry. Most found themselves in London, but some are recorded in the provinces. Nicholas Wichehalse of Barnstaple includes 'Anthonye my negarre' in his will of 1570. A child was baptised in Plymouth in 1594 whose mother was 'a negro of John White's', the father a Dutchman. By the end of the sixteenth century it was starting to be fashionable for wealthy families to have a black slave among their retainers: Sir Walter Raleigh's wife was one of the first to acquire such an exotic status symbol. Fifty years later it was all the rage — but not without opposition from the Queen, who, at a time of population growth and intermittent food shortage, declared that there were enough mouths to feed in her kingdom without importing 'blackmoores'. She informed the Lord Mayor of London and the mayors of other towns on 11 July 1596 that they should get rid of these blacks living in their midst: 'Her Majestie understanding that there are of late divers blackmoores brought into this realme, of which kinde of people there are already here to manie … Her Majesty's pleasure therefore ys that those kind of people should be sent forth of the land.' A week later Elizabeth sent out another letter. She informed local mayors that a certain Lubeck merchant, Caspar van Senden, had arranged for the release of eighty-nine prisoners held by the Spanish. In return the Queen required public officers to help him round up 'blackamoores' — with the consent of their masters who, according to the Queen, 'like christians rather to be served by their owne countrymen than with those kinde of people, will yielde those in their possession to him'. In other words, English slave-owners should hand over their possessions to a Lubeck slave-trader so that the Queen could recover English prisoners without it costing her anything.

Elizabeth clearly overestimated her subjects' Christian patriotism and her own authority. Five years later, in 1601, she is stamping her foot and declaring herself 'highly discontented to understand the great number of negars and Blackamoores which (as she is informed) are crept into this realm'. She goes on to declare that, as they eat too much and, in any case, are mostly infidels, 'the said kind of people should be with all speed avoided and discharged out of this Her Majesty's dominions'; and again she gave the job to Caspar van Senden – though it seems with no more success than the first time. Black people continued to live in Tudor and Stuart England as servants, pages, laundrymaids and musicians.

As horizons widened, another continent and its people began to feature in British consciousness. Evidence for this, rather surprisingly, can be found in the small Cotswold town of Burford. Burford's fine limestone houses still stand on the end of their narrow medieval burgage plots, fronting the High Street, as they have for centuries. Now they house antique dealers and tea shops catering to visitors drawn to Burford's mellow charms. Burford is one of Britain's best-preserved medieval wool towns, because its prosperity declined in the sixteenth century. The neglect of poverty was eventually transformed into the respectability of age, helped by the fundamental qualities of good local building material. At the foot of the High Street, almost hidden from view, is Burford's grandest building and one of England's most surprising churches. St John's contains the earliest representation in Britain of American Indians. They cavort around the tomb of Edmund Harman (d. 1569), barber to Henry VIII. Below them, in a regimented rank, are Harman's wife and children. Why he and his family wished to portray native Americans no one knows, though the images may have been copied from a Flemish book. Perhaps as the medieval world came to a close in Burford, Harman's family wished to emphasise the new opportunities that were opening in the west.

The decline in the Antwerp cloth trade may have provided a stimulus to those seeking new opportunities. The English had been relatively slow to see the potential of the Americas, though only four years after Columbus's first voyage Henry VII had commissioned John Cabot and his son to seek out lands across the Atlantic. Their Newfoundland expedition came to have great symbolic importance but, at the time, made relatively little impact and the English displayed no great enthusiasm for exploration or long-distance trade.

During Elizabeth's reign English sailors began to comb the world's oceans, mainly as pirates and plunderers, parasites on the Spanish, who had established the models for imperial expansion in the Caribbean and South America.* Expeditions such as Francis Drake's 1579 voyage in the

---

* The Spanish and the Portuguese were the big players in early European colonisation. The Spanish conquered the empires of the Aztecs and the Incas, helped by superior weaponry, horses and the dreadful impact of European diseases on native communities. The brutal Spanish regimes were rewarded with the vast outputs of South American gold and silver mines. The Portuguese played a different game – from Brazil, along the African coast to India and China they established trading bases through which they exported valuable exotic products.

Golden Hind, raiding along the Pacific Coast of America and then return-ing around the Cape of Good Hope, provided an enormous return for private investors (including Queen Elizabeth, who gained 4,700 per cent). They were encouraged to create squadrons of ships, which ulti-mately strengthened English sea power.

In the 1570s the English, God's chosen people, began to have imperial fantasies of their own: a Protestant empire to rival the Catholic mon-opoly. John Dee, Elizabeth's mathematician, astrologer and magus,* encouraged the Queen with stories of her Tudor ancestors: King Arthur with his imperial expedition to the Continent and 'twenty kingdoms', or Prince Madog of Wales, who had supposedly discovered America. The Arthurian myth of 'Britaine' was linked to the recent conquest of Ireland, which was increasingly under Tudor military control. In the *Faerie Queen*, written in honour of Elizabeth, Spenser elevates 'Mightie Albion, father of the bold / And warlike people, which the Britaine Islands hold.'†

As Peter Ackroyd writes in his book *Albion*, 'The English genius busily conflated past and present.' Elizabeth made grandiose noises, objecting to the papal division of the world between Spain and Portugal. Is not 'the use of the sea and the air … common to all?' she asked rhetorically, but she lacked the resources to become much of a player in the international stakes. Anxious to avoid unnecessary trouble with Spain, she vowed to plant English colonies in lands where Europeans had not settled. Nearly a century after Columbus's first voyage it was apparent that he had found a new continent – now named after Amerigo Vespucci. Adven-turers such as Martin Frobisher (between 1576 and 1578) persisted in the search for a North-West Passage to the Indies. He did not reach Asia but he did find an Eskimo with Asiatic features, and sparkling rocks which stimulated a Fool's Gold Rush. Many adventurers lusted for gold; more righteous Protestants proclaimed that England would not success-fully plant colonies unless it approached the problem in a spirit of evan-gelical righteousness. However, early attempts at colonisation were mostly approached with a mixture of greed and incompetence. Some attempts, such as that of Sir Humphrey Gilbert in 1583, sank at sea. Sir Walter Raleigh may have excelled at chivalry (supposedly by placing his cloak over a puddle for the Queen) and at butchering Irish men, women and children, but his colonising ambitions were misplaced. His first expedi-tion left England in April 1585 to deposit 107 men at Roanoke Island, off

---

* Dee fixed the propitious date for Elizabeth's extravagant coronation, when she entered Fleet Street as Deborah, 'the Judge and restorer of Israel'.
† Spenser wrote the *Faerie Queen* from his house in Ireland.

North Carolina. Things went badly from the first: the colonists lost their supply ship and had to scrounge off the local Indians. When, during a long winter, the natives' charity wore thin, the settlers resorted to threats, so the locals tried to starve them out. In June Sir Francis Drake came sailing to the rescue and carried the desperate colonists back to England.

Raleigh (who never actually set foot in the New World) was not about to give up. Another band of colonists, this time a more mixed group consisting of 110 men, women and children, were shipped off to Roanoke. Their leader was John White, a painter, who produced some of the most vivid early images of New World natives. White's paintings reflect very clearly the attitude of the English to the 'savages' they encountered. Their view was not racist in the modern conventional sense. Savagery was a cultural state, the precursor of civilisation. Savages could be educated and developed, not enslaved. Colonist William Strachey, author of *The Historie of Travaile into Virginia Britannia* (1612), wrote of the Indians: 'We are taught to acknowledge every man that beareth the impression of God's stamp to be not only our neighbour but our brother.' The colonists noticed the copper colour of the natives but believed that, were it not for painting their skin and daubing themselves with anti-mosquito grease, they would, in fact, be white. The English also believed that their own ancestors had progressed from savagery thanks to their beneficial conquest by the Romans. White specifically painted images of ancient Britons, woad-daubed, semi-naked and long-haired prior to the civilising effects of the Romans. So what the Romans had done for them, the English would now, generously, do for the natives of North America. William Strachey posed the question: 'Why, what injury can it be to people of any nation for Christians to come unto their ports, havens and territories?' He clearly knew little of the activities of Sir Walter Raleigh.

The second expedition to Roanoke Island resulted in the first births of English children in the New World. One of them was White's granddaughter. After only a few weeks with the settlers, White sailed back to England to pick up supplies. War with Spain delayed his return until 1590. By the time he got back there was no sign of his family or any other colonists. They had disappeared without trace – to become part of America's founding myth of the Lost Colony. So a century after Columbus's first expedition England's attempts to settle the New World were fairly pathetic. They hardly looked like potential rivals to the Spaniards, or even the French, who were expanding their activities in the St Lawrence and making inroads into Canada.

The English, however, were learning the dark arts of colonisation closer to home. In Ireland Henry VIII had developed a policy of filling the top jobs in the administration – the Law and the Church – with new English courtiers and officials – imported from England – rather than the Old English, the descendants of the Anglo-Norman colonisers. This simply exacerbated Anglo-Irish hostilities. Henry's newcomers combined arrogance with incompetence, cultural misunderstanding and absenteeism. Henry decided to bring in the troops, which served only to make matters worse. The commander-in-chief of the expeditionary force, the Earl of Surrey, believed that the Irish problem could be settled by full-scale military conquest: put down the native Irish; make the Anglo-Irish lords conform to English law; and ensnare the country in a net of military bases, new towns and castles, all cemented with new English settlers. Henry could not afford this ambitious plan and instead formulated a policy based upon the rule of English law. Perhaps, he reasoned, the Irish rebelled because they were denied access to law and legal title to lands. Give them English law and they would behave like Englishmen! Unfortunately Irish warlords could not so easily be turned into English landlords.*

There was a fundamental culture clash. In English law the principle of primogeniture meant that the eldest legitimate child inherited property and titles. In Ireland all offspring had rights, including bastard sons. The eldest did not naturally succeed – hence Irish inheritance could be a bloody and prolonged struggle, which promoted a feudal mafia system.†

Lordship was not simply a question of ownership of land; rather it was a right to tribute and services – so the Church at Armagh, for example, owned its estates but paid the O'Neill of Tyrone, in what was a complex protection racket known as '*slainte*' in Gaelic. The test of lordship was the ability to levy tribute, to punish those who failed to pay and to retaliate against those who injured the lord's subjects. 'Spend me and defend me' was the Irish expression in the sixteenth century. Failure to defend meant that a subject switched to a new lord. Ultimately the system was based on violence and the effectiveness of the mercenaries hired by Irish chieftains: the gallowglasses (axemen loyal to the highest paymaster) and kerns (or footsoldiers, of notorious toughness). In the primitive Irish economy, where cash was a rarity, lords maintained their retinues by billeting them on their subjects. Modernisers and reformers in Dublin and Westminster abhorred this practice of 'coyne and livery', which, they said, was 'invented in hell'.

---

* The phrase is taken from Sean Duffy,[18] who points out that the 'same conflict between coercion and conciliation underlay British policy towards Ireland until the twentieth century'.
† Henry Og O'Neill, in 1493, murdered his elder brother to obtain the chieftaincy of Tyrone. Henry's bardic poet celebrated the victor's might and right.

The Irish revolts against the Tudors were the equivalent of the Pilgrimage of Grace: attempts by a violent, traditional feudal society to stave off the changes imposed by a 'modernising' state. Some in Ireland, notably within the Pale and town-dwellers in Galway, Kilkenny and Cork, welcomed the changes; but for the rural Gaelic-Irish the struggles were intensified by the fervour of religious differences.

Irish feudalism was gradually ground down by the English. The House of Kildare was overthrown in 1530; in 1576 Connaught was divided into the English-style counties of Sligo, Galway, Roscommon and Mayo, and a decade later the lords of Connaught agreed to pay rent and military service to the Crown. Ulster remained a bastion of Gaelic feudalism and Hugh O'Neill would not compromise. In September 1595, like his ancestors, he took himself to the Stone of Tullaghoge, to be inaugurated as the O'Neill, clan chieftain and Prince of Ulster. During the ensuing war O'Neill came close to taking control of Ireland. After his victory on 14 August 1598 at the Battle of the Yellow Ford, Munster rose in revolt and English settlers were massacred. Revenge was in the air, emphasised by a piece of English propaganda, a leaflet grimly entitled *A Supplication of the Book of the English most lamentably murdered in Ireland, crying out of the earth for revenge*. But it was not simply a case of English Protestants versus Irish Catholics. The Munster revolt was led by Anglo-Irish lords; the Gaelic McCarthys held back. In April 1599 the Earl of Essex landed with an army of over 12,000 troops. The campaign came to nothing. By the end of the year O'Neill issued a proclamation demanding the restoration of the Catholic Church and Irish clergy, and the confirmation of the lands and privileges of the great lords the O'Neills, O'Donnells and Desmonds. Irish bards began to celebrate the whole of Ireland as the fatherland – *athardha* – and 'a fortress of Paradise', reflecting Gaunt's description of England in Shakespeare's *Richard II*: 'This other Eden, demi-paradise, / This fortress ...'

Ireland's two Catholic communities, the Gaelic and Anglo-Irish, could unite against the heretic interlopers. Pope Clement VIII gave a crusading indulgence to the troops of O'Neill, 'captain general of the Catholic army in Ireland'; but Irish optimism was doomed. In September 1600 the Spanish landed on the south coast at Kinsale and were rapidly besieged by the English. O'Neill headed south to join them. On Christmas Eve he engaged the English at Kinsale and was routed. The cost was terrible for both sides. Elizabeth appreciated that the war had brought 'the alienation of our people from us' and that, in Lord Cecil's words: 'That Land of Ire has exhausted this land of promise.'

For Ireland the impact of the struggle was even worse. Unlike virtually every other country in Europe, Ireland's population failed to grow in the sixteenth century. To violence and lawlessness were now added famine and despair. The economy was wrecked, Ulster a backward wasteland and the Irish lords reduced to embittered feuding gangs. When O'Neill himself finally surrendered to the Queen of England on 30 March 1603, he did not know that she had been dead for several days. On 23 March she had indicated that James, King of the Scots, should be her successor. Nearly five years later, in 1607, O'Neill and his ally Rory O'Donnell, now pardoned, were confirmed as the Earls of Tyrone and Tirconnell by King James. Nevertheless rumours of Spanish plots continued to flourish, exacerbated by the activities of Guy Fawkes and his fellow conspirators in England. In September 1607 the earls, fearing arrest, fled to the Spanish Netherlands and then to the papal court in Rome to seek help. None was offered and the earls never returned to their homeland. The flight of the earls represented the end of independent Gaelic power in Ireland – and paved the way for the English and Scottish Plantation of Ulster over the next three decades.

The British population boom of the sixteenth century brought advantages economically, socially and culturally. It also created new strains and stresses in Tudor society — inflation, land-grabbing, underemployment, poverty and vagrancy. In the fifteenth century rents and prices remained low and wages relatively high, reflecting the persistent manpower shortage. But after 1520 more people generated a growing demand for work, food, clothing and other goods, which burst the bubble of artificial prosperity born of stagnant population.[19] As extra labour flooded the market, wages fell and the demand for foodstuff rose. People had to eat, and the prices of necessities rocketed, further stimulated by short-term agricultural crises.

After a century of stable prices inflation increased dramatically. Henry VIII came to the throne aged eighteen in 1509. By his death, in 1547, prices had risen by 270 per cent. Two years later they hit an unprecedented 409 per cent, thanks to Henry and his son Edward's habit of debasing the currency. After an initial fall, prices climbed once again throughout Elizabeth I's reign to an increase of 685 per cent in 1598.* With more mouths to feed there was a surge in the demand for bread. The prices of wheat, barley, oats and rye shot up even faster than those of other foodstuffs such as milk, eggs and cheese. With increasing prices and profitability land rents soared, by as much as ten times through the sixteenth century. In such a market landowners saw the opportunities

---

* The price index is based on the equivalent of a supposed building craftsman's wages, from a base rate in the late fifteenth century.[20]

and pursued the 'engrossment' of farms at the expense of small tenants and peasants. Commercialised and increasingly efficient farming, however, contributed to Tudor England's principal success: its ability to feed an expanding population, at a time when the country experienced both high birth rates and increased life expectancy.

High prices encouraged farmers to produce for the urban market, rather than for local subsistence. The rural poor drifted towards the towns while increasingly prosperous landowners indulged in Britain's greatest period of country house building since the burgeoning of Roman villas over a thousand years earlier. Rich landowners displayed their wealth and status increasingly in bricks and mortar. Henry VIII had shown the way before 1547 with his extravagant building programme. He remodelled Hampton Court and the rambling complex of Whitehall; above all he displayed himself as a true Renaissance prince by erecting the extravagant château of Nonsuch Palace in Surrey. He left his children so well endowed with royal real estate that none of them needed (or could afford!) to build another palace. Other lesser magnates did feel the need to imitate Henry and had the cash to do it.

Cold and draughty barrack-like castles and fortified houses were no longer necessary in England and Wales. Strong central government delivered a more secure and peaceful country. Domestic life became less military and masculine for the upper echelons. Somerset House (the predecessor of the building that now stands on the Strand) and Longleat were built by Sir John Thynne as exemplars of the French and Italian Renaissance styles. Thynne, like Lord Burghley or Elizabeth Talbot ('Bess of Hardwick') were dedicated amateurs. The profession of architect had not yet crossed the Channel. Their so-called 'prodigy-houses' proudly exposed their handsome façades outwards, reflecting their masters' − or, in Bess's case, the mistress's − wealth and taste to the outside world. Inside, the great chambers and long galleries provided space for formal gatherings, the reception of guests, preferably royal ones, and the display of works of art − particularly portraits. Henry VIII had patronised artists such as Holbein, who for the first time created a national portrait gallery of admittedly upper-crust images. He was the artist, it is said, who showed the English what they looked like. Tudor faces such as those of Thomas, Lord Vaux or Thomas More and his family gaze out, like real people posing awkwardly and self-consciously for the artist.

Today the gallery of Tudor portraits in the National Portrait Gallery presents the earliest ensemble of lifelike, if often highly symbolic, images of English characters. Henry Howard, Earl of Surrey, is every inch the educated Renaissance man in his spectacular Italian costume, the height of fashion in about 1546. Even more spectacular is the incredibly over-the-top costume of Richard Sackville, third Earl of Dorset, who poses theatrically between ruched curtains, on a 1613 portrait in Ranger's House. This may be his outfit for the wedding of Princess Elizabeth to the Elector Palatine on 14 February, which the Master of Ceremonies declared 'dazzled the eyes of all who saw'. Clearly Sackville outshone the bride. Not surprisingly, he was reported by Clarendon to be 'a licentious spendthrift'.[21]

Queen Elizabeth, however, controls her austere image at all times. Her portraits resemble medieval icons, the ageless Virgin Queen, in her symbolic and luxurious clothing, surrealistically decorated with ears and eyes. In the Rainbow portrait she grasps the rainbow which symbolises the peace she has restored to a divided realm. In the Armada portrait her hand rests on a globe, touching the Americas, while in the background the Spanish Armada is attacked by English fireships and smashed to pieces on the storm-wracked coast of Ireland.

The fashion for greater comfort and privacy in housing trickled down the social scale. William Harrison, in his *Description of England* of 1577, recorded that the old men of Essex reported three notable changes in houses in their lifetimes: a multitude of chimneys, more pillows and mattresses and the exchange of treen (wooden platters and spoons) for pewter, tin and silver.

The 'Great Rebuilding' had a long pedigree, beginning with the transformation of rural houses in the fourteenth century. For the first time since the Roman period the houses of yeomen were deliberately built with a degree of permanence. The late-medieval timber-framed Wealden House had a central hall open to the roof with an open fire in the middle. Life was thus both communal and smoky. Tudor yeomen, first in Kent and East Anglia, began to alter these houses, inserting a ceiling into the hall, with a chamber above, and adding storerooms and sleeping quarters for servants. With the ceiling in place smoke could no longer seep through the roof, so a fireplace and chimney were needed — hence the observation of the Essex elders.

Brick-built structures sprouted in East Anglia and around London, replacing timber framing, which still provided the main material for vernacular architecture in Kent, Berkshire, the Welsh borders and the northwest. In the central limestone belt of England, notably in the Cotswolds, handsome gentry houses became a distinctive feature of the landscape. With the Dissolution of the Monasteries around 1536–40, local landowners not only stripped great buildings like Glastonbury Abbey and Abingdon Abbey of materials such as timber, lead and stone; in some cases they actually moved in, converting the monastic remnants for their own domestic purposes. Sir Edward Carne made a manor house out of the core of Evenni Priory (Glamorgan) with all Tudor mod cons: hall, dining room, study, gallery, parlour and a multitude of bedrooms and service rooms.[22]

But whereas in Wales the gentry developed into sophisticated residents in the English style, in Ireland, Scotland and the northern border country, residences retained their grim medieval character. And as the population grew across Britain the simple houses of the peasantry multiplied: mostly one-bay cottages of stone or timber, wattle and daub, usually, by the later Elizabethan period, with a fireplace and chimney. In the early sixteenth century it was the upper classes, eager to secure their dynasties and their landholdings, who organised the marriages of their children at a relatively youthful age. The poorer sort married late and had fewer offspring.

William Harrison, in his *Description of England*, divided his fellow countrymen into four 'sorts': gentlemen, citizens or burgesses, yeomen and artificers or labourers. The major distinction was between 'gentlemen' and the rest. The upper tier included peers of the realm, knights and esquires. In sixteenth-century England it was a matter of fierce debate who or who was not a gentleman: whether the position could be earned by virtue, education and wealth, or whether pedigree alone provided entry into the show ring of English society. Harrison supported a relative meritocracy where lawyers and graduates, and those who 'can live idly and without manual labour and ... will bear the port, charge and countenance of a gentleman will be taken for one'.[23]

In the later sixteenth century the writer Thomas Nashe emphasised the emergence of new hierarchies to replace the medieval ones of *Piers Plowman*. 'In London the rich disdain the poor. The courtier the citizens. The citizen the countrymen. One occupation disdains another. The merchant the retailer. The retailer the craftsman. The better sort of craftsman the baser. The shoemaker the cobbler.' [24] Tudor society retained a degree of openness through the sixteenth century but in such a time of flux the interest in genealogy, 'ancient blood' and family lineage became an obsession.*

Heralds exploited this mania, both in their own interests and in those

---

* One of the most evocative series of monuments erected to a single family is in the Church of St Mary, Lydiard Tregoze, on the outskirts of Swindon. Here the StJohns began to commemorate themselves from 1592. The most dedicated genealogist, Sir John StJohn (1586–1648), was a royalist whose five sons had divided loyalties during the Civil War. The three who sided with their father all died.

of the old aristos and the *nouveaux riches*. Between 1560 and 1640 the College of Heralds granted arms to about 6,000 men. In most parts of England the eldest son inherited family land and property. This principle of primogeniture did not apply, however, in the remoter areas of the west and north, and surprisingly, perhaps, in the Weald of Kent. For the rest, though, this snakes-and-ladders system favoured the head of the family, who became wealthier, while the other siblings could find themselves on the slippery slope of economic decline, or in need of another livelihood. In 1601 Thomas Wilson put it bluntly: the eldest son 'must have all, and all the rest of them that which the cat left on the maltheap, perhaps some small annuity'.[25]

Through the second half of the sixteenth century and into the seventeenth century population rose hand in hand with the other major engine of change, an unprecedented rise in prices. At the same time most people found themselves working for wages which bought much less than in previous decades. For the burgeoning numbers of youngsters in the countryside 'of the meaner sorte', desperate to earn a living, the answer was to travel – taking the lane to the nearest town, or increasingly the high road to London. In the mid-sixteenth century about 1,250 youths arrived in London to take up apprenticeships. Of the 32,000 apprentices recorded in sixteenth-century London all but 73 were male and only 2 per cent of them worked for women – usually the widows of craftsmen.

In the sixteenth and seventeenth centuries London mushroomed. Unfortunately, precise population figures are impossible to come by in what has been described as 'the obscurely illuminated, if not totally "Dark Ages" of English demographic history'.[26] Nevertheless, from a variety of sources such as tax lists and ecclesiastical censuses, the trends are clear. London's population, including Westminster and Southwark, rocketed from some 50,000 to 60,000 in the 1520s to about 200,000 at the end of the century. It reached 400,000 by 1650 and an estimated 575,000 by 1700. London was the largest city in western Europe. Only Constantinople, in eastern Europe, was larger, with about 800,000 inhabitants. Paris probably had half a million inhabitants, Naples 300,000 and Amsterdam 200,000.

In the period in which England's population doubled (between 1520 and 1700) London's increased tenfold, and the proportion of Londoners in relation to the population as a whole soared from 2 per cent to about 11 per cent. London was an irresistible people-magnet; and for a variety of reasons: it was the royal and administrative capital of an increasingly unified nation; geographically it acted as a gateway between Britain and the Continent, particularly into the prosperous Netherlands. Trade, like the Thames, flowed through London, a cornucopia of riches piled into its markets; foodstuffs from Wales, Scotland, northern and midland England fed London's gigantic stomach. The enormous population attracted manufacturers — of hats, shoes, cloth, bells, weapons, boats, carriages, food and drink. As John Stow noted: 'There was no want of anything to him that wanted not money.'

Stow's great *Survey of London* of 1598 captured the city at the height of its throbbing expansion. For some it was a place of luxury, a haven of intrigue, a cultural cornucopia. Londoners could catch Shakespeare's latest offering on the south bank, across what was still London's only bridge over the Thames. The Rose and the Globe theatres rose out of the stew of Southwark, but green fields were still only five minutes' walk away, and cattle and pigs were a commoner sight in the street than carriages. A delicate foreign ambassador, well able to resist London's charms, noted the stench of the city, which, he claimed, was the filthiest in the world. Not everyone prospered amongst London's fertile mulch. In 1597 *A Midsummer Night's Dream* was performed for the first time, and wages hit their lowest level in seven centuries. Two years earlier there had been food riots both in London and in the provinces, exacerbated by grain speculators hoarding to take advantage of price rises and led by apprentices, masterless men and ex-soldiers. Immigrants arrived in London in their thousands, full of hope or desperation; but cities — and particularly London — continued to be unhealthy environments where life expectancy was low. Overcrowding, poverty and plague were the common lot of the least fortunate urban immigrants. Children and young people were the principal victims of disease-ridden towns, whose rising population levels were constantly topped up by the influx from the rural population boom. Sir John Reresby had a point when he wrote, in 1680: 'London drained all England of its people.'

London was overwhelmingly the dominant city in Britain, but the burgeoning population of the countryside also flowed into regional urban centres. Between 1500 and 1650, as the national population doubled, the proportion of people resident in towns of 10,000 or more actually tripled. As farming became more efficient, many landowners prospered and the landless and jobless rural poor headed for town. But at least, for the most part, food supplies into urban markets improved.

Beyond London the largest towns were Norwich, Bristol, Exeter, York, Salisbury and King's Lynn, although none had over 12,000 inhabitants in Henry VIII's reign. Norwich climbed to about 18,000 in 1579 but was then cropped by a severe outbreak of plague. When Elizabeth I died, in 1603, Norwich's population had risen back to 15,000, Bristol and York to about 12,000; Exeter and Newcastle-upon-Tyne both had about 9,000 inhabitants. There was also a string of regional centres like Oxford, Cambridge, Chester and Ipswich, which housed between 5,000 and 8,500 people.

In Scotland by 1550 only about 1.5 per cent of the population (13,000 people) lived in towns of more than 10,000 compared with 3.5 per cent in England and Wales. This doubled in the next fifty years. Plague slowed the urban expansion, but by 1700 Scotland's urban population rose to about 53,000, about 5 per cent of the population compared to 13 per cent in England and Wales. In this period Edinburgh, by far the largest Scottish town, expanded from 12,000 in 1560 to 30,000 in 1640 and about 45,000 by the end of the century. Glasgow was still some way behind as the second city.

Provincial towns experienced varying rates of growth, all dependent on immigration rather than their own natural fertility and upon economic success. In late-sixteenth early-seventeenth-century Norwich the textile industry drew the workers; in Plymouth the dockyards were the magnet for those seeking employment.* Newcastle's population probably trebled, or even quadrupled, in the sixteenth and seventeenth centuries, from about 4,000 inhabitants to 16,000 in the 1690s, mainly as a result of its thriving coal trade to London. In the second half of the sixteenth century coal imports to London rose from 33,000 tons to 163,000 tons a year, launching the capital's reputation for being smog-bound and soot-laden. New urban communities were also beginning to emerge out of developing industries. Between 1550 and 1700 Birmingham's population rose from 1,500 to about 8,000, as metalworking industries expanded, unhindered by the protectionist medieval guilds and trade restrictions which had developed in older towns.† Manchester, driven by its textile industry, was growing at about the same rate as Birmingham. In 1538 Leland described it as 'the fairest, best buildid, quickest and most populous towne of all Lancastreshire'.

In 1700 Liverpool was just beginning to expand, and had a mere 5,000 inhabitants. In contrast, the ancient port of Chester had 9,000 people, though the silting of the River Dee was placing a severe handicap on its role as the major overseas port and commercial centre of the north-west. Within fifty years Liverpool would be twice as large as Chester and the dominant port for Ireland and the American colonies.

Like all rapidly expanding cities, London was a tough place to be

---

* Plymouth's population rose from about 4,000 in 1550 to almost 8,000 by 1603.

† Though as early as 1540 it was said of Birmingham: '[A] grate parte of the towne is mayntayned by smiths.'

down and out. People arrested for vagrancy were sent to Bridewell for punishment. The Bridewell's Court Books clearly demonstrate the enormous increase in vagrancy in London between 1560 and 1625, rising from 69 cases to 815 – a much faster rate than that of the population increase.[27]

Amongst the statistics a bald account in the Bridewell Court Book for 18 May 1603 nevertheless conveys the sheer misery of vagrancy:

> Frances Pulmer, a vagrant sent in by Mr Dale's warrant out of Southwark, having two children begotten in whoredom, says that one Thomas Wood, servant with Sir Edward Wotton, is the father of them, and the place where she was delivered was openly in the street, two or three doors off from the Cross Keys, and they died and were buried in Allhallows parish in Gracious [i.e. Gracechurch] Street, and she was after her delivery taken into Cross Keys. Ordered to be punished and delivered.

Many of London's vagrants must have arrived as hopeful immigrants – large numbers came from East Anglia, Yorkshire and the counties to the west of the city. They found themselves eking out a living in the suburbs, in Clerkenwell, Southwark, Fleet Street and Westminster. The rich still occupied the ancient centre, while the poor congregated in the suburban stews that clung to its skirts. John Stow, in his *Survey*, described slums emerging in Whitechapel and Southwark: 'nurseries and seminary places of the begging poor that swarm in the City'. Most of the Bridewell vagrants were remarkably young. In 1602, of thirty-seven whose ages were recorded thirty were between eleven and twenty, only one was over twenty-one, and most were boys. Unable to find secure and respectable employment, they did odds and ends of market work, begged, sold ballads and pamphlets, shined shoes, picked pockets, shoplifted and nicked lead off roofs.*

For the first time in almost three centuries the population of Great Britain was expanding and society was in flux. People left the countryside to seek their fortunes in the volatile environment of towns and cities. But they had alternatives: there were lands to colonise across the Irish Sea and beyond the Atlantic Ocean.

---

* *Plus ça change* ... Shortly after writing this I read in the *Observer*, 18 July 2004: 'In an interview last week to mark the end of his time as Metropolitan Police Commissioner, Sir John Stevens said that each London borough had between 20 and 60 feral children causing vast levels of crime ... Feral children are blamed for a quarter of street assaults and robberies. He said the issue would be second only to terrorism in the list of priorities for his successor.'

Nine Departures and Arrivals

ON 16 MARCH 1994 I flew into the Caribbean island of Montserrat. I had been asked by the Overseas Development Agency to carry out an archaeological survey of the island, as part of the plans to build a new airport: I could see why they might need one. I had crossed from Antigua in a packed flight of a dozen people and banked alarmingly over the gaping mouth of a volcano before dropping precipitously on to a tiny airstrip clinging to the shoreline.

The next day was 17 March: St Patrick's Day. Montserrat is the only country besides Ireland where St Patrick's Day is a national holiday, to celebrate an unsuccessful slave rebellion on 17 March 1768. Unknown to the rebels, this was a particularly inappropriate day for a slave rising: St Patrick was the only slave from the millions in the Roman world whose written words have survived. His feast day was already commemorated by the white population on Montserrat in 1768 because quite a few of them were Irish. Now he became a patron of black slaves. Montserrat was given its name by Columbus, who sailed by on 11 November 1493 – the serrated volcanic mountain peaks reminded him of Montserrat, behind Barcelona. No Europeans settled there for nearly 140 years until, in 1632, a group of Irish Catholics arrived, forced off the nearby island of St Kitts by aggressive English Protestants. They were soon joined by Irish refugees from the Virginia colonies. On 26 January 1634 a Jesuit priest travelling from the American colonies to England wrote in his diary: 'We came before Montserrat, where is a noble plantation of Irish Catholique, whom the Virginians would not suffer to live with them because of their religion.'

Fifteen years later Oliver Cromwell shipped even more Irish Catholics to the island, after his brutal Irish campaigns of 1649–51. In the 1650s as many as a hundred thousand Irish Catholics were transported across the Atlantic, manacled below decks in conditions little better than the black slaves who were to follow them in even larger numbers in the later seventeenth century. Other poverty-stricken Irish and English people came voluntarily as indentured labourers – tied to the land for a fixed period of service. In the West Indies conditions were notoriously difficult for workers from temperate climates – as I myself found on Montserrat when wielding a machete to remove the undergrowth around ruined plantation sites and trying to avoid the manchineel plants, which spray acidic sap on the unwary.

In 1677 the Leeward Island governor, William Stapleton, commissioned the first official census of Montserrat. It revealed that there were 1,869 Irish, 761 English, 52 Scots and 992 black slaves. Already the backbreaking, energy-sapping work of tobacco and sugar cultivation was being imposed on African slaves.

Increasingly the Irish on Montserrat realised that the island was less of a Catholic haven and instead just another place run by the British. They secretly negotiated with the French, who landed at the Irish settlement of Kinsale. For the transplanted Europeans Montserrat had become a mirror of home, with its religious, nationalist and ethnic prejudices.

But black Africans were in demand. In the 1620s the white farmers complained that slaves were in short supply. Only two slave ships had come to the island with 300 slaves, and half of them had been dead. Attempts were made to speed up delivery from Africa. By 1707 there were 3,580 slaves on the island, 5,858 by 1729 and some 10,000 by 1774 – just a small part of the massive British mercantile system that operated in the West Indies.

The combination of population pressure, religious rivalries and economic stress at home meant that the inhabitants of the British Isles continued to pursue their overseas fantasies of treasure, prospecting or freedom. The breakthrough in the New World came in 1606 with the establishment of the Jamestown colony, which eventually provided the foothold for English settlement along the east coast of North America. In spite of its royal name the colony was not launched with royal support. Three small ships, the *Susan Constant*, the *Godspeed* and the *Discovery*, left Blackwall docks in London in late December 1606 carrying about 105 colonists and thirty-nine crew. They were all launched thanks to private enterprise, financed by the Virginia Company of London, in the hope of locating precious metals and other New World riches.

The ultimate survival of the Jamestown colony was a matter more of luck than judgement. The emigrants transported their attitudes with them and half of them were 'gentlemen'. Muscular pioneering and hard work were not part of their game plan. In 1665 George Chapman satirised such colonists going to Virgina: 'Do nothing; be like a gentleman, be idle, the curse of man is labour.'

Such an attitude frustrated one of the Jamestown colonists – Captain John Smith, son of a Lincolnshire farmer, professional soldier fighting the Ottomans and himself an ex-slave. He appreciated that, whatever poets and gentlemen might think, toil was necessary, and so was a *modus vivendi* with the native residents (in the case of Jamestown the thirty thousand or so members of the Powhatan confederation). For a variety of reasons – uncertainty about the newcomer's real strength, the possibility of retaliation, their potential use against native rivals – the Powhatans (led by a chieftain also called Powhatan) chose not to wipe out the weak and mostly incompetent settlers. This was in part because John Smith played a tough and risky hand, exploiting Chief Powhatan's uncertainties; he also had the luck to attract the interest of Powhatan's eleven-year-old daughter, Pocahontas.

Later, in April 1614, Pocahontas converted to Christianity, taking the name Rebecca, and married colonist John Rolfe, whose wife and daughter, Bermuda, had died in America. The Virginia Company were keen to bring Pocahontas to England. Investors had lost interest in the company, which had promised much and delivered nothing. Even the most optimistic and naive had given up their fantasies of gold, silver and pearls; even the promised return on more mundane products such as lumber, flax, pitch and hemp was not forthcoming. The Virginia Company resorted to running lotteries, its printed flyers decorated with exotic Indians. Pocahontas provided it with the opportunity to attract attention by displaying a real Indian; she was a New World princess, moreover, an exotic savage converted to Christianity.

Pocahontas landed in Plymouth with her husband and young son Thomas about 3 June 1616. With her was a retinue of about ten of her fellow Powhatans. One was a native shaman, Tomocomo, who had been ordered by Powhatan himself to report back on the state of the English. His first task was to count the number of people by making notches on a stick, but almost as soon as he arrived, in the busy port of Plymouth, Tomocomo threw his stick away. This was hardly surprising. The Powhatans came to England in the middle of a rapid demographic upturn, which contributed in no small part to the persistent enthusiasm for overseas colonisation. In the mid-sixteenth century the population is estimated to have been about 3 million people, rising to 4.1 million in 1603 and continuing to rise to 5–5.2 million in 1650 (thereafter flattening off for the next fifty years or more). If Tomocomo with his stick could not count them, nor could the contemporary authorities.

If the Indians were startled by the bustle of Plymouth, London must have been a total shock. Its population of 200,000 seethed within narrow streets and crowded buildings, piled several storeys high. The city lay under a dismal pall of coal smoke, and the pungent smell of human waste and horse dung permeated everywhere. Nevertheless Pocahontas, an intelligent, curious and broad-minded woman, clearly enjoyed her experience of what was to her a fascinating New World. She was fêted around London society and even met King James, though she did not realise who this unappealing specimen was; overweight, with rotten teeth and an aversion to washing himself or changing his clothes, he was not a Powhatan model of leadership. Rebecca/Pocahontas was not with her husband when she met the King. Perhaps John Rolfe, a pioneer of tobacco cultivation in Virginia, was aware of James's aversion to the noxious weed and stayed away.*

Unfortunately, it was the London air, rather than tobacco, that disagreed with Pocahontas's lungs. She wanted to remain in England, but John Rolfe's business in Virginia required his presence. They boarded the ship *George*, and almost immediately Pocahontas fell seriously ill. The ship anchored at Gravesend, where Pocahontas died on 21 March 1617, probably of pneumonia or tuberculosis, aged about twenty-one. She lies in a grave still marked in the churchyard of St George's – the first known American to be buried in English soil.

Rolfe left his young half-Indian son behind in England, fearful, he said, of the 'hazard of his health'. He returned to Virginia, to his ever-increasing tobacco fields. In 1617, the year of his return, exports of tobacco from the fragile colony amounted to 20,000 pounds in weight; by 1621 the commercial crop had increased massively to 350,000 pounds. Rising numbers of colonists put increasing pressure on the natives, demanding more and more land. In 1622 the Indians attacked Jamestown, killing some 350 settlers and bringing the colony to 'a very low and calamitous condition'.[1] However, it survived, though the company's days were numbered, and in 1624 it was abolished by royal decree. Virginia became the first royal colony in the New World, established by the King and not by Parliament.

In spite of his aversion to tobacco, King James was even more averse to empty coffers. He thus decreed that all Virginian tobacco, regardless of its ultimate destination, should pass through specified English ports. This

* In his *Counterblaste to Tobacco* (1604) James pronounced that smoking pollutes men's 'inward parts ... with an unctuous and oily kinde of soote, as hath been found in some great tobacco takers, that after their deaths were opened'. Tobacco smoking, according to James, was 'a custom loathsome to the eye, hatefull to the nose, harmefall to the brain, dangerous to the lungs ...'

kept the trade under the fiscal control of the British monarchy – an issue that would fester and contribute to the revolution of 1760. The wealth generated from tobacco also helped to create the class of American landowners which eventually led the forces of insurrection against the British.

In the mid-seventeenth century, however, tobacco made the colony in Virginia viable – it was a taxable commodity much in demand at home. If the Spanish relied on gold and silver mines, the English in the New World depended upon a cash crop. Tobacco was soon to be supplemented by indigo and sugar.

For the first time in the history of the British Isles (with the possible exception of the fifth century), more people departed the islands than immigrated. In the seventeenth century over a third of a million people left in search of a new life – mostly young men seeking employment. Surprisingly, perhaps, to a modern audience, the biggest proportion headed for the West Indies, then the Virginia colonies, followed by Catholic Maryland and the Puritan haven of New England, where seekers of religious toleration outnumbered economic migrants. Not everyone bound for America went by choice. In the seventeenth century there was an increasing obsession about public order and crime: arguably more a perception of disorder and a popular paranoia rather than a real crime wave. Prosecutions significantly increased: in Cheshire there were twice as many felony indictments in the 1620s as in the 1580s, and three times as many in the 1660s. The county of Devon averaged twenty-five executions a year in the first decade of the sixteenth century, and London held 150 executions a year from 1600 to 1625. At the same time transportation to the Americas became more common even for relatively minor offences, particularly vagrancy (peaking in the 1650s). Most emigrants did not find the good life in the New World: instead disease, malnourishment, harsh winters, bad water and Indian attacks killed the early generations of settlers in droves.

Not all migrants headed west, however. As many as 30,000 to 40,000 Scots lived in Poland during the seventeenth century, where the word Scot ('Szkot') meant a pedlar or commercial traveller. As early as 1569 Sir John Skene noted 'a great multitude of Scots pedlars in Cracow'. The outward flow of men may partly explain the relatively slow population growth from 1300 to well into the sixteenth century, as most of these migrants were young men; many married abroad and became integrated into their new European homelands. Their names assumed a local flavour: in Poland Gordon became Gordonowski; Ramsay, Ramze; Chalmer, Czamer.* Gdansk still has an area known as Stary Szkoty –

'Old Scotland' — and the Poles retain the expression '*skapy jak Szkot*' ('as mean as a Scot'). Most of these Scottish pedlars came from the east coast, routinely crossing the North Sea. When the population of Scotland was less than a million they represented a high proportion — more, in fact, went to Poland than left for America or Ulster in this period of significant emigration.

The accession of James I (James VI of Scotland) and the Regal Union of 1603 caused consternation in the Westminster Parliament. Would England be swamped with Scottish migrants? 'The multiplicities of the Scots in Polonia' were a dreadful warning of the fate awaiting England if the Scots became naturalised subjects.[2]

The Scots not only had a reputation for driving a hard bargain; they were known as fearsome soldiers, fighting not only for their livelihoods but also as crusaders for the Reformation in the seventeenth century. During the cataclysmic Thirty Years War (1618–48), when Europe was convulsed by the conflict between Protestantism and the Catholic Hapsburg Empire, as many as 66,000 Scots aided the Protestant cause. From 1625 to 1642 the Scots Privy Council authorised over 47,000 men to join foreign armies. The Munros of Easter Ross alone provided the Swedish King, Gustavus Adolphus, with three generals, eight colonels and three dozen lesser officers. Some Scottish soldiers found fame and fortune; most ended up as cannon fodder, or victims of the deadly 'army fever', a concoction of contagious diseases, which hung like a shroud over armies of this period.

The Scots were economic migrants on a scale equalled only by the Swiss (also tough soldiers, who were recruited to guard the Pope) — a reflection of their poverty and the austerity of their land, its soil described as 'skin over bone' by Neal Ascherson.[3] In the first half of the seventeenth century an average of 2,000 Scots left their homeland each year from a population of no more than 1.2 million.

In the early seventeenth century the Scottish population was, at last, increasing and, as in England, there was a perception that the country was populous. However, increasing numbers of people were also dreadfully vulnerable to Malthusian catastrophe, relying as they did on subsistence farming, which clung to such fragile soils and was battered by inclement weather. In 1623 a severe famine struck the country, killing up to a third of the population of Dunfermline, and 15 per cent of the people of Dumfries. Such a catastrophe set in train a further wave of emigrants: unemployed farm workers and farm tenants unable to pay their rents were scoured

---

* Alexander Chalmer from Dyce became Mayor of Warsaw.

from the land. Many joined the English in the 'Plantation' of Ireland.

James VI/I also had ambitions to bring the fractious and feudal kingdom of Ireland into his modernised, unified state. The Tudor monarchs had reason to fear Ireland. Two serious conspiracies had attempted to use Ireland as a launch pad to overthrow Henry VII. (Lambert Simnel was crowned King of England, France and Ireland with the support of the Butlers in Dublin Cathedral in 1487. A second Yorkist pretender, Perkin Warbeck, appeared in Ireland in 1491.) With the growth of European national animosities, fuelled by religious differences, Ireland became even more of a threat − a potential base from which England's enemies could launch an invasion.

Following the devastations of the Tudor campaign, Ireland's population was probably a mere half to three-quarters of a million people. Ulaid, or Ulster, the most traditionally Gaelic area, home of the O'Neills, was particularly thinly populated, and English was rarely heard. Like America, here was land awaiting colonisation, sparsely inhabited by native unbelievers, who might soon be outnumbered and displaced by the righteous. Six new counties − Armagh, Cowan, Fermanagh, Derry, Donegal and Tyrone − were pronounced Crown Property and ripe for plantation. Only a few 'deserving' natives would retain their land, providing that they built English-style dwellings and adopted English farming methods and tenancies.

This venture was a British, not a purely English, undertaking. The three kingdoms of Scotland, Ireland and England were unified in the person of King James in 1603. In Scotland James already had experience of handling his own Gaels in the Highlands and Islands, whom he was determined to bring under central control. He warned his son that the Western Isles were barbarous and 'without an shew of civilitie'. His solution was to plant colonies of his supporters to 'reforme and civilise the best inclined among them; rooting out or transporting the barbarous and stubborn sort and planting civilitie in their rooms'. Various failed attempts were made to settle the Isle of Lewis with lowlanders, and a series of military expeditions from 1596 to 1607 reduced the power of clan chiefs. Their sons were sent off to the lowlands to learn 'civilitie'; they were discouraged from carrying arms and indulging in communal drinking bouts. After fifteen hundred years or more Tacitus remained the handbook on how to handle wild Gaels.

James already had experience of internal colonisation and a mind-set that classified the Gaels as barbarians who needed the benefits of civilised authority. After 1603, with the King's enhanced power base, it became possible to drive a Protestant wedge between the Gaels of

Ireland and Scotland. This created an Anglo-Scottish partnership, 'the first joint "British" enterprise of the new Kingdom of Great Britain'.*[4]

As the Ulster Plantation was a joint Anglo-Scottish venture, roughly equal areas of land were reserved for the Scots and the English (and Welsh) — about 81,000 acres apiece. There were varied reasons why the Ulster Plantation should appeal to the Scots. In the early seventeenth century the Scottish economy was sluggish, and wealthy landowners and merchants needed new outlets for investment. In the south-west the aggressive Clan Campbell and its leader the Earl of Argyll were displacing and evicting their McDonald tenants. In the Borders, recently the lawless frontier between the two kingdoms, reiver families with surnames[†] such as Maxwell, Graham, Armstrong, Nixon, Davison, Charlton, Robinson and Milburn had lived by raiding and rustling across Liddesdale, the upper Tyne and the Cheviots. With the Union of 1603 the Borders came under increasing control as James cleared out the unruly and replaced them with loyal and well-behaved tenants from the lowlands. Many of the displaced migrants in time replaced the Irish in East Ulster. One unusual aspect of the Ulster Plantation was the involvement of the City of London. In 1610 it agreed to organise the settlement of the county of Coleraine and the reconstruction of its main towns Coleraine and Derry — hence 'Londonderry'. City companies organised plantations and new towns, which were named after them, such as Draperstown and Salterstown.

By 1641 about 70,000 English and Welsh settlers had poured into Ireland, and a further 100,000 immigrated during the Cromwellian period. By 1672 some 100,000 Scots had joined them, and a further 50,000 came in the fifteen years after 1690. This influx converted the immigrants into a majority in Ulster. Yet despite the original plantation strategy, which virtually advocated ethnic cleansing, many Catholic Irish survived in Ulster as disaffected and resentful tenants. They were even joined by other Catholics, Hebridean Gaels tidied away by James to the Antrim estates of Sir Randall MacDonnel — an Irish Gaelic lord who had avoided the taint of rebellion and retained the favour of the King.

In 1600 about 2 per cent of the Irish population had English or Scottish blood, but just over a hundred years later the figure had risen to 27 per cent. Irish culture changed dramatically along with its social

---

* The new settlers were 'British' families and of 'British birth and descent'. To James the Ulster venture was much more important for the future security and prosperity of his kingdom than the risky, tobacco-growing outposts on the shores of the distant Americas.
† The term 'surname' was first recorded in 1498.

structure, economy and landscape. Its famous forests, for example, disappeared, chopped down and shipped to England. The Irish language faded as rapidly as the woodlands, and more quickly than any other Celtic language in recent times. The Irish Catholics may have adopted the tongue of their Anglo-Scottish neighbours, but their resentment has persisted until today. The Scots, with their tradition of mobility, had uprooted themselves for Ireland. They retained the habit and many continued on to America in the eighteenth century.

No country in Europe exported so many of its people as Britain and Ireland in the seventeenth century, but the majority of those on the move stayed closer to home, transferring from the country into the town. London became the great magnet for internal migration in the century between 1550 and 1650.

London's population grew by about 3,300 a year in spite of its appalling death rate, which exceeded the birth rate by about ten per thousand. This meant a shortfall of about 2,500 people a year. In other words, net immigration of 6,000 people each year was needed to maintain London's growth rate. So about half the population increase in England was drawn to London. There were also a significant number of Welsh in Tudor London. A survey of 1638 identified 1,079 Welsh surnames: probably about 6,000 Welsh in total – and nearly four times as many in 1695.

Charles I ascended the throne in 1625 and, fatally, set about offending a significant proportion of his subjects. In Scotland he tried to give the bishops a major role in government and meddled in sensitive issues of landownership. The Scots Presbyterian majority hated bishops and valued its own property. In England the King fell out with Parliament over taxation and decided to rule without them; and as if that were not enough, the English Puritans were deeply suspicious of Charles's Catholic sympathies. The Anglo-Catholics in Ireland, at least, ought to have been sympathetic; but the King offended them by first promising some religious freedoms, accepting £120,000 as a sweetener, then failing to keep his part of the bargain.

When Charles attempted to foist an English prayer book on Scotland, the Presbyterians formed the National Covenant to demand the removal of Anglican bishops. The King twice raised an army to invade Scotland, but lacked resolution. The Scots responded by marching into England in 1640 and occupying Newcastle – the so-called Bishops' Wars. The following year the Irish Catholics rose in rebellion, slaughtering about 3,000 of the Protestant settlers (who by then numbered up to 40,000). Many of the rest fled to England to spread stories of Catholic barbarism. Charles and Parliament were at loggerheads. When his attempted coup failed, he fled to York. Both sides rallied their forces.

The resulting conflict is often known, Anglo-centrically, as the English Civil War. The Irish, more accurately, know it as the Wars of the Three Kingdoms. Certainly all three kingdoms were closely involved and the populations of Ireland and Scotland suffered far more than the English. Unlike the Wars of the Roses, the Civil Wars impacted on all levels of society. Neighbours, families and communities were divided in their loyalties and set upon each other. The populous and prosperous south-east, London and East Anglia were strongest in their support for Parliament. The west, including Wales, was mainly for the King. The Irish Catholics eventually came over to the King, as did the highland Catholics, but the Scots Presbyterians remained adamantly against him. Defeat by Oliver Cromwell and Sir Thomas Fairfax on 2 July 1644 at Marston Moor, west of York, put the King's campaign into reverse. The following year his Scottish supporters were smashed by the Covenanters at Philiphaugh. Charles's urban strongholds, such as Chester, Exeter and Oxford, then came under attack.

I had a vivid insight into this vital period of English history when excavating in Abingdon (Oxfordshire) a few years ago.* We uncovered a large number of skeletons laid in regular graves orientated north–south. These were in the grounds of Abingdon Abbey – in fact in its vineyard – but were also close to an earlier Roman building. Because of the orientation – Christian burials are customarily placed east–west – we assumed the graves belonged to Roman Britons. Then we noticed lots of tiny metal shroud pins on the bodies. These could not be Roman in date but had to be later. Eventually we cracked the problem: Abingdon was a front-line Parliamentary garrison facing the King's forces in Oxford. The town was also a bastion of Puritanism and opposed to the Anglican Church and its bishops. Thanks to the presence of the army, Abingdon was ravaged by disease, carried by the troops – the dreaded 'army fever'. A new burial ground was urgently needed, so the Puritans simply took over the vineyard. As they felt no need to apply for a licence from the Anglican bishop, there was no documentary record of the cemetery's existence. They then proceeded to bury their dead lying north–south in defiance of tradition.

One of the graves was particularly interesting. It contained the bodies of seven young men. Some had musket balls lodged in their chests. We subsequently found out why. Seven Irish soldiers of the King had been captured and brought to Abingdon. The Parliamentary commander, a

---

* The same dig as attracted the DNA hunters; see p. 470.

Colonel Brown, had them summarily executed. The grave-digger was paid sixpence for each body and placed them together, side by side, in one grave.

This ground is a slice of British history. Initially it was part of an Iron Age *oppidum*, then a Roman town, and later an Anglo-Saxon and medieval monastery. After the Dissolution the land eventually passed into the hands of the Verney family. Sir Ralph Verney was the King's standard-bearer and was killed at the Battle of Edgehill, in 1642. His hand, it was said, was found on the battlefield still clutching the standard. Parliament confiscated the family's Abingdon property, which was then available for the burial ground. After the war it was returned to the family and the 2,000 souls buried in the vineyard were forgotten.

The King's death made a bigger impact. When his head was struck off, in Whitehall on 30 January 1649, the crowd groaned and the shock waves reverberated around Europe.

The King did not suffer alone. In August 1649 Oliver Cromwell and 3,000 of his Ironsides landed in Ireland to accomplish his 'great work against the barbarous and bloodthirsty Irish'. On 11 September he sacked Drogheda, massacring the garrison, which included a large proportion of English royalists, the Catholic clergy and some of the townspeople. He then marched on Wexford, where his troops, their bloodlust up, ran amok and killed 2,000 people. After a campaign which shocked even the brutalised Irish, Cromwell left for England in May 1650 having achieved his purpose: 'by the assistance of God, to hold forth and maintain the lustre and glory of English liberty in a nation where we have an undoubted right to do it'.[5] Many defeated Irish officers and their troops left to join Continental armies. The poor were transported in their thousands to labour in the West Indies.

While the English set about developing new prejudices for a New World, some of the traditional medieval ones were undergoing a change. In 1656, 366 years after they had been expelled, the Jews were allowed to return. In fact they had never entirely gone away. As Jews were the best doctors, various English monarchs had required their services. Even Dick Whittington arranged for a Jewish doctor, Samson de Mirabeau, to care for his wife. Spanish and Portuguese Jews (the Marranos) also operated, discreetly, amongst London's financial community. There may have been about forty Jewish families in Elizabethan London, some of whom were known to Shakespeare; but they had to keep a very low profile, holding services in a private house owned by Alvaro Mendes.[6] It would be some time before a Jew was presented favourably on the English stage.

It was during the Commonwealth that a distinct change of attitude took place, for reasons that were part theological and part economic. In 1654 Cromwell wrote: 'I desire from my heart, I have prayed for it, I have waited for the day to see union and right understanding between Godly people — Scots, English, Jews, Gentiles, Presbyterians, Independents, Anabaptists and all.' ('All' did not, of course, include Catholics.)

By this time the Marranos, prosperous merchants and financiers, were living in the Fenchurch Street and St Mary Axe area of the City of London and had a house, used as a synagogue, in Creechurch Lane. The authorities turned a blind eye. The Jews were a valuable link to continental mercantile and military intelligence. Cromwell appreciated the potential economic value to the country of a more open society, where Continental Jews could operate freely. He also had a religious motive. According to the Scriptures (Daniel 7: 7 and Deuteronomy 28: 64), Jews had to be scattered to all corners of the world before the Messiah would return. Augustine of Hippo in the fourth century, emphasised that God then intended to convert the Jews en masse in time for the Last Trump. The Last Days loomed large in Puritan thinking; they were imminent and the Jews had a part to play. Jews had recently set foot in America; it only remained to bring them back to England for biblical prophesy to be fulfilled.

Rabbi Menasseh ben Israel was a highly respected member of the Jewish community in Amsterdam. Aware of the changing views in England, he appealed to the 'tender-heartedness' of Oliver Cromwell. Rabbi Menasseh was also encouraged by the practical arguments of John Thurloe: a British trading empire in the Atlantic would be greatly assisted by the Jews' inside information on the main rivals, the Spanish, Portuguese and Dutch.

Cromwell called a five-day conference in the Council Chamber in Whitehall, attended by theologians, lawyers, Members of Parliament, merchants and other interested parties. The subjects for discussion: was it lawful for Jews to return? If so, on what terms? The answer to the first question was relatively simple: the Jewish expulsion was by royal decree, so there was no legal reason why they could not return. The second question allowed all the old prejudices to surface: the Jews would try to convert Christians; English trade and traders would wilt under Jewish competition; Jews really wanted to convert St Paul's into a synagogue. Cromwell realised he was not going to achieve a straightforward declaration of support. So he adopted an English compromise. He disbanded the conference, said Parliament would consider the conference's advice, then let it be known that the Jewish presence was legitimate.

Jews gradually came to England, mainly from Spain, Portugal,

Amsterdam, Hamburg and the south of France. In London they formally established a synagogue at Creechurch Lane in 1657 (see above), where five years later there was a congregation of 100 men and boys. Samuel Pepys attended on 14 October 1663 and was shocked to observe 'the disorder laughing, sporting and not attention but confusion'. He did not realise that he had walked in on Simchat Torah, the one festival where Jews were allowed to let their hair down, to sing, dance, drink and generally misbehave.

For the first time since the thirteenth century the Jews acquired an official cemetery in England. Unfortunately it was soon needed, for twenty-one victims of the Great Plague of 1665. Samuel Pepys reported the ensuing panic, when the wealthy, including physicians, fled the city, the population of which now numbered over 400,000. One disaster followed another. The following year the Great Fire swept through London. Many Londoners blamed God, Catholics or foreigners; in fact it started as an accident in a baker's shop in Pudding Lane, fanned by a gusting wind. Because of complex landownership and determined occupants the medieval warren of streets and building plots survived. The fire, however, cleansed as it destroyed. Out of the ashes rose Wren's St Paul's, and the spires of his churches which soared over the city until the Blitz.

The Jewish community expanded and by 1673 the extended Creechurch Lane synagogue housed 174 men and 84 women. These prosperous merchants, bankers and dealers in precious stones were Sephardim — Jews of Mediterranean and Middle Eastern origin, mainly from Spain and Portugal — who had established communities in Amsterdam and Hamburg. New Jewish immigrants — Ashkenazim — began to arrive from central and eastern Europe. These people were mostly less well educated and earned their living as pedlars, street traders and rag merchants. By 1690 they were numerous enough in London to have their own synagogue, not far from the Sephardim, in Duke's Place, Aldgate. By the end of the seventeenth century the Jews in London numbered about one thousand. In 1701 the Sephardi community opened a new synagogue in Bevis Marks, just round the corner from the modest building in Creechurch Lane. They took with them some of the simple, hard wooden seats as souvenirs of the old synagogue. These were the only simple things in a new magnificent building, which proclaimed the presence of a proud and confident community.* The Bevis Marks Synagogue

---

* There was, in fact, one other simple thing. Queen Anne sent the Jews an oak beam from a Royal Navy ship, which was incorporated into the roof. The lavish interior was modelled on fashionable Amsterdam synagogues, though the builder was a Quaker named Avis, who refused to take a profit for building a House of God.

has survived unchanged, apart from some IRA bomb damage – both the building and the bomb were legacies of Oliver Cromwell.

The Jews were not the only incomers during this century of emigration. Huguenot immigrants continued to flow into Britain and parts of Ireland through the seventeenth century. By the 1590s Church records recorded over 15,000 attending services at foreign churches in England, most of whom would be French and Walloon Protestants. The situation in the Netherlands eased after 1609 with the creation of the independent United Provinces and fewer Walloons sought sanctuary. In spite of the Edict of Nantes, the French Protestants were not completely secure – in the 1620s Southampton received forty-two refugees driven out by Cardinal Richelieu and Louis XIII.

Numbers increased substantially with the renewed persecution by Louis XIV from 1679 and dramatically after 1681 when the Sun King began to billet hostile, aggressive troops, the *dragonnades*, on known Protestant families.* If they did not reject their religion, these people would eventually become destitute from bearing the costs of demanding Catholic soldiery. To make matters worse, their children could be removed for re-education and the women sent to convents. Emigration was, however, forbidden. Nevertheless they fled in greater numbers to England after 1687, when the Catholic King James II issued his Declaration of Indulgence, confirming his subjects' rights to liberty of conscience and the free practice of their religion. Most Huguenots headed for towns in the south-east, the east and London, traditionally home to Flemish weavers and a refuge for earlier Huguenots. Many also settled in Ireland (Dublin), though few went to Scotland. In Bristol 80 per cent of immigrants came from Poitou and Saintonge, areas which, through the Middle Ages, had traded wine to Bristol. In London and Canterbury most arrived from Normandy.

By 1700 there was a clear pattern of Huguenot settlement in London from Spitalfields in the east to Leicester Fields and Soho in the west. Their formal place of worship was the French Church of London, in Threadneedle Street. French Protestants were long established in the City, families such as the Delmes, Lefroys and Papillons, who were able to offer assistance to new refugees. Pierre Delme was already a pillar of the London establishment and his eldest son became Lord Mayor and Governor of the Bank of England. By 1700 there were 23,000 Huguenots in London (including Westminster) – about 5 per cent of the population of half a million (and a population of England and Wales of about 5 million).

---

* The English term 'to dragoon' comes from this activity.

For many refugees the journey to England was not easy. Henry Portal, a young boy, stowed away at Bordeaux in a wine cask. Jean Desaguliers travelled inside a barrel from La Rochelle.* Many never made it to their destination. French ships intercepted them and packed them off to royal slave galleys. Those refugees who reached England, on the whole, received a hospitable reception – Protestant propaganda preceded them, castigating the enormous cruelty of the French Catholic regime and the sufferings of 'poor French Protestants'. The Great Plague of the 1660s had also knocked back the English population, so there was a perceived shortage of manpower, at least on the part of the authorities.

The most fortunate refugees found that English hospitality could include soup kitchens and the offer of lodgings.† When Jacques Fontaine arrived with a shipload of fellow refugees in Barnstaple, the townspeople immediately offered them shelter in their own homes. They were 'kindness itself', he wrote. He perhaps had a more balanced view of his new neighbours, some years later, when his successful shop in Taunton attracted their envious attention. Someone brought Fontaine before the mayor, calling him a 'French dog'. Though the case was dismissed, Fontaine decided to leave town.

The arrival of Huguenot workers did not meet with universal approval. People complained that they worked too cheaply, drove up the rents and the prices of timber and coal, polluted rivers, ate strange food – such as garlic, snails, oxtail soup and root vegetables. The number of refugees was exaggerated. Popular prejudice blamed them for the Great Fire of London in 1666, and illogically assumed that they were papist agents of the powerful French state. Spain was the traditional enemy during Elizabeth I's reign but by the later seventeenth century France had taken up the role of principal villain. As Samuel Pepys recorded in his diary: 'We do naturally all love the Spanish and hate the French.' Nevertheless, on 1 December 1655, he married Elizabeth, fourteen-year-old daughter of Alexandre le Marchant de St Michel, lately of Paris. The stresses were greatest among the poorly paid textile workers of the East End, who saw the immigrants as a threat to their livelihood. Riots in

---

* Jean went on to develop the first air-conditioning system, which was installed in the House of Commons.

† Dr Samuel Byles, a medical officer at London's French Hospital in the nineteenth century, wrote a song, 'The Huguenot Refugee', to be sung lustily at the hospital court dinner. The chorus encapsulated the tolerant (perhaps self-satisfied) view of its time:

> *Hey, for our land, our English land*
> *The land of the brave and free;*
> *Who with open arms in the olden time*
> *Received the Refugee.*

London in the summer of 1675 were partly caused by the fear of new foreign technology – a premonition of the Luddites of the Industrial Revolution. 'That devilish invention of looms brought in by strangers … with looms of 12 to 24 shuttles' caused 'the destruction of many poor' was a complaint of the Company of Silkweavers to James I. In 1675 the rioters smashed looms and attacked the French weavers and their homes. The authorities had to take steps 'to awe the rabble'.

Certainly the Huguenots were a challenge to traditional practices; many immigrants arrived possessing the skills and trade secrets of the French industry. They also understood French taste and fashion. And the art of creating a demand. The generation that arrived after the Massacre of St Bartholomew's Day in 1572 boosted the provincial English textile industry with their skills in lace-making, stocking-knitting and ribbon production. Norwich was in decline until the foreigners arrived with their baffling variety of products: 'bays, fustians, pachmentiers, camientries, tufted mockadoes, currelles, tooys, bussins, mockadoes, valures all of linen cruell, carletti, damaske, says of dry cruel (after the fashion of Lille, of Amiens, and of Muy), dry grograynes, double mockadoes, bombasines of taffety, all silk … etc, and other outlandish inventions'. The local Norwich craftsmen were bamboozled by the sheer range, but suspected a degree of French salesmanship. The newcomers invented names, they complained, to make their products 'more vendible'. Nevertheless the new draperies boosted Norwich's economy: between 1660 and 1749 almost half the freemen of the city were employed in the textile industry.

Anyone visiting the new British Galleries at the Victoria and Albert Museum* cannot help but be impressed by the obvious impact of Huguenot skills on British industry in the seventeenth and eighteenth centuries.[7] They helped to put an unsophisticated economy onto the path of manufacturing that led to the Industrial Revolution. The Weavers' Company of London, in 1684, records the impact made on them by two new arrivals, seeking admittance:

> John Larquier and John Quet, who lately came from Nimes
> in Languedoc, now appeared and declared that they were …
> fully enabled to weave and perfect lutestrings, alamodes and
> other fine silks … [They were then asked to demonstrate their
> abilities.] John Larquier now produced a piece of alamode
> silk … This Court considered thereof, and conceiving the like

---

* These innovative and informative galleries, which opened in 2001, are devoted to the history of design and manufacture in Britain from 1500 to 1900.

hath never been made in England and that it will be a great
benefit to this nation, do agree that the said John Larquier be
admitted a foreign master gratis.

With one condition: that he employ English workers.

In Spitalfields such abilities transformed the industry, producing
satins, damasks, taffetas and brocades in an incredible variety of floral
patterns, which came to have a distinctly English style. An English-
woman, Anna Maria Garthwaite, was the most prolific textile designer of
the mid-eighteenth century and over 800 of her designs still survive.

Huguenot craftsmen were highly influential in other forms of manufacturing: clocks, guns, swords, gold and silversmithing, scientific instruments, perfume, wigs and hats. In the West End their shops introduced
French taste and sophistication into Britain. When Napoleon dismissed
the British as a nation of shopkeepers, he conveniently ignored the fact
that many of the shops had originally been opened by French immigrants. Paper-making was another speciality. Gerard de Vaux set up in
Southampton where one of his trainees was Henry Portal, from Poitiers.
Portal, in turn, established a paper mill at Bere Mill, near Whitchurch in
Hampshire. By 1724 the Bank of England had commissioned him to
manufacture paper for their 20, 30, 40, 50 and 100 pound notes. His
hard, textured material took detail well and reduced the risk of forgery. In
1743 the now familiar '£' sign ('L', for *librum*) was added to the notes.

Huguenots also brought skills to Britain that are now traditionally
associated with the natives. In particular they developed horticulture,
and the obsessive pursuit of perfection in growing particular varieties of
flowers, especially carnations, auriculas and — above all — tulips.*

In Chelsea, where they established market gardens, Huguenots popularised cut flowers and in Dublin retired Huguenot army officers set up a
Florists' Club. In Norwich they 'advanced the use and reputation of
flowers' and it was there that the first English 'florists' feast' was held in
1631. The English flower show was born.[9]

The current debate about 'genuine' refugees fleeing danger as opposed
to economic migrants is an old one. Daniel Defoe's fictional Huguenot
Roxana reports that the French:

---

* The tulip may have come to England with the Huguenot botanist Matthias de l'Obel (the lo-
belia, commonest of English bedding plants, is named after him). He lived in Lime Street, near
another Huguenot gardener, James Garrett. Both worked closely with John Gerard, author of
Gerard's Herball. Garrett was well known for his yellow, white, purple and red tulips, which he
grew in his garden at London Wall.[8]

flock over in Droves, for what they call in *English* a Livlihood: hearing with what Open Arms the REFUGEES were receiv'd in *England*, and how they fell readily into Business, being, by the charitable Assistance of the People in London, encourag'd to work in the Manufactures, in *Spittle-fields*, *Canterbury* and other Places … My Father, *Iray, told me*, That he was more pester'd with the Clamours of these People, than by those who were truly REFUGEES, and fled in Distress, merely for Conscience.

While these words appear in a novel, Defoe, like any good journalist, would reflect the views that he had heard reported.

Attitudes in the seventeenth century were changing. Elizabeth I might have wished to reduce the number of her black subjects, but a century later Daniel Defoe voiced the opinion of many commentators who saw immigrants as a benefit: 'People are indeed the essential of commerce, and the more people the more trade the more trade, the more money, the more money the more strength, and the more strength the greater the nation.' And it is worth remembering the sheer size of France at the end of the seventeenth century compared with its puny British neighbour across the Channel. France had the largest population of any west-European country, with about 20 million people; in contrast, Britain scarcely topped 6 million. France had an enormous peasantry cultivating a productive countryside. They, however, remained poor in order that a large aristocracy might indulge in a lifestyle of prodigious wealth and luxury. This elite provided a market for luxury goods and set the fashions for the rest of Europe, basking under the influence of King Louis XIV. The monarchs of early modern Europe excelled at competitive display, in dress, gardens, palaces, even ships.* Louis XIV outshone all his rivals, and Versailles, the greatest of his palaces, acted as a showcase for French craftsmanship, much of it — tapestries, silk hangings and carpets — produced in state-run and subsidised factories.

If the Huguenots helped their adopted country to appreciate the good things of life, they also contributed in a much more robust and bloody manner to British history. After the death of Cromwell, on 3 September 1658, and the Restoration of Charles II, the country was still racked by fears of papist plots and the threat of the great Catholic power across the

---

* Charles I had a three-decked warship, *Sovereign of the Seas*, built at vast expense: £65,587 was ten times the price of an average fifty-gun warship. Over 10 per cent of the cost was for elaborate carving. The ship was like an expensive towering wedding cake – not much use in battle, but a floating display of Charles's magnificence.

Channel. The succession of James II, aged fifty-two, without a son and a Catholic sympathiser, exacerbated these fears among ordinary people. They were also aware that James had two daughters, Mary and Anne, neither of whom was in their father's religious camp. Mary, the elder, was married to the Continental hero of the Protestant cause and arch-enemy of Louis XIV, Willem van Oranje (William of Orange), Stadtholder of the United Provinces.

Protestant propaganda portrayed William as the righteous leader resisting the bestial papist troops of the French monarch. Brilliantly gruesome Dutch illustrations vividly depicted the Catholics supposed speciality: impaling Protestant babies. The English rightly feared another religious war, like the Thirty Years War, which had ravaged Europe until 1648. If it had to be fought again, they knew which side they wanted to be on. But James's loyalties were less clearly defined. He sought greater toleration for Catholics in his kingdoms and even attempted to improve the Catholics' lot in Ireland and reverse the brutal effects of the generations of colonial wars. With bigotry ripe on all sides, however, James's more powerful subjects were not about to contemplate any move in the direction of Catholic France. King James had something else in common with Louis XIV besides religion: both were absolutist monarchs who firmly believed in the Divine Right of Kings. They were chosen by God, and so, by God, they knew best. James, pig-headed to a fault, believed that if he insisted on having his way, then the aristocrats and gentry, and particularly the Tories,* would have no alternative but to support him. As royalists they had had nowhere else to go.

He ignored the presence of Princess Mary and her husband, William of Orange. Mary's proposed succession had a veneer of legitimacy until, in June 1688, James's second queen delivered a healthy son and heir. The plot to usurp the Catholic Stuarts and to put power into the hands of a Protestant successor went ahead nevertheless. To William it was an opportunity to increase his anti-French power base and, at the same time, ensure that Britain did not become a French ally.

Whig historians, such as Lord Macaulay, subsequently portrayed these events as the Glorious Revolution of 1688, the finale of a long-drawn-out struggle between the monarchy and Parliament over their

---

* In the latter years of Charles II's reign the English political ruling classes were divided. One group was derisively labelled 'Tories', after the Irish name for Catholic rebels. They saw themselves as latter-day Cavaliers, essentially supporters of the monarchical ideal, who wanted to stop Parliament from dictating royal succession. The opposing bunch were sarcastically labelled 'Whigs', or 'Whigamores', a Scottish name for Covenanters – those who expected the monarch to enter an agreement or covenant with his subjects. The Whigs expected Parliament's views to be paramount.

supposed contractual constitution. Yet in many ways it was also part of a nasty, lengthy and bloody religious struggle, which convulsed the people of the British Isles and Ireland for generations.[10] According to the Whig version of history, the so-called 'Immortal Seven' invited William to assist them in their pursuit of a constitutional monarchy and a bloodless revolution. In reality, William did not need much assistance from these seven politicians: he had already been planning an invasion. In June he requested an 'invitation', which promptly arrived from Henry Sidney, Charles II's envoy to the Dutch, the Earls of Danby and Shrewsbury, the Bishop of London and others. William had to plan how to avoid the superior English navy. James was unaware of the plot and did not consider that his daughter would sanction such an attack. Nevertheless William landed at Torbay with 600 Dutch ships and 20,000 crack Dutch, Huguenot, German and Danish troops. This was not so much a Glorious Revolution as an unopposed invasion by Continental Protestants. James II, deserted by his generals, promptly fled to France and William marched into London. He summoned Parliament, which conveniently declared that they 'found the crown vacant'. 'We found it so, we did not make it so,' in the words of the lawyer Sir George Treby. The King had not been deposed; there had been no rebellion. William refused to be a regent, tied to 'his wife's apron strings', as he put it. So Parliament declared William and Mary King and Queen of England.

The Scots, where the Stuarts had reigned since 1371, had also lost a king, though no one had asked their opinion. As usual, opinion was divided, but John Graham, Viscount Dundee, rallied the Highland clans. At the Pass of Killiecrankie 2,000 claymore-wielding Highlanders charged through a hail of musket balls, to butcher the foreign troops before they could reload. Dundee's death during this gory mayhem rendered the Scots' victory Pyrrhic. His supporters disintegrated into a feuding rabble and the new King William III attempted to impose a public oath of allegiance on the clans. Where the Gaelic communities could not be persuaded to co-operate, they would be coerced. William's troops burned villages and killed the rebels. A notorious instance occurred on the Hebridean island of Eigg. When William's enforcers arrived, the local men were away fighting, so the soliders attacked the women instead, raping and murdering them.

New Year's Day 1692 was set as the deadline for the oath of allegiance, and plans were put in place to make an example of those who failed to co-operate. John Dalrymple, King William's adviser, wrote of his pleasure that the people of Glencoe had not taken the oath. Their failure to co-operate provided a perfect opportunity 'to extirpate that den of thieves

... It were a great advantage to the nation that thieving tribes were rooted out and cut off.' At the beginning of February 1692 120 soldiers under the command of Captain Robert Glenlyon, a member of the loyalist Campbells, tramped into Glencoe. For over a week, in bitter weather, they lodged among the local villagers. Then the order arrived from their commander, the Earl of Breadalbone, 'to fall upon the rebels, the Macdonalds of Glencoe, and put all to the sword under seventy'. In the early hours of the morning the troopers went from house to house, shooting and stabbing the local men, stripping the women and children and leaving them to freeze.

In the darkness some of the intended victims escaped and carried the news of the massacre to the outside world. In Edinburgh and London the authorities feigned shock and disapproval. A Commission of Enquiry decreed that the troops and their officers had been overzealous and had gone too far.*

However, the punishments were token and soon rescinded. Such was the standard reaction of imperial powers to non-cooperating, traditional communities standing in the way of the imperial project, from the Roman legions at Hod Hill and Anglesey to the British troops at Amritsar and the US Seventh Cavalry at Wounded Knee. General Philip Sheridan summed up for modernisers throughout history with his famous remark: 'The only good Indians I ever saw were dead.' Within Scotland, England and Ireland there was an ongoing clash of cultures: between those (usually Catholic) based on traditional bonds of kinship, lordship and honour – the enemies of law, industry and trade, in Macaulays account of Glencoe – and the modernisers, in pursuit of commerce, conformity and the nation-state. What might come as a surprise to anyone observing the downtrodden Highland Scots in 1692 was how they, like the Tungrian garrison on Hadrian's Wall, would within a generation find themselves at the cutting edge of the British imperial project.[12]

Huguenots and other Continental Protestants played an important part in the rise of British military power. William's foreign troops had been forged in the toughest European arena, fighting the French. In response to Louis XIV's policy of religious persecution, many of his own highly trained officers and men switched sides, now highly motivated to

---

* Lord Macaulay's version of the Glencoe events makes fascinating reading. Hugh Trevor-Roper called it one of Macaulay's most 'brilliant pieces of sophistry and special pleading'. In plain English: a whitewash. Macaulay refers to the Macdonalds as a 'tribe', a 'den of robbers', brutes who burned the whole congregation of Culloden church alive while playing the bagpipes. A third part of Scotland was 'in a state scarcely less savage than New Guinea'.[11]

fight their fellow countrymen. One of these was Samuel de Pechel, upon whose family the *dragonnades* descended at Montauban in August 1685. They terrorised his pregnant wife and young children and threw them out of their home; his mother and sister were incarcerated in the local convent and his children taken away to be indoctrinated. Samuel himself was imprisoned and then transported to San Domingo in 1687. He escaped to Jamaica in an English ship and made his way to London, from where he discovered that, although his wife and son had escaped to Geneva, most of his family were either dead or held in Montauban. He joined the cavalry regiment of the Duke of Schonberg, William's second-in-command. Schonberg had himself served in the French army, but switched sides following the revocation of the Edict of Nantes. Thousands of Protestants did the same.

On 12 March James II landed in Ireland, hoping to establish a power base to resist his daughter and son-in-law. He advanced on London-derry, where the Protestant Apprentice Boys barricaded the gates and maintained a fifteen-week siege, paralleled only by Mafeking in British mythology. James's army moved south while 10,000 foreign troops, under the Duke of Schonberg and including the now Lieutenant Samuel de Pechel, landed near Belfast. Ironically, James was reinforced by 7,000 French troops in March 1690, half of whom were Walloon and German Protestants.

On Tuesday, 1 July 1690* the two European armies faced each other at the River Boyne. William's army included some Ulster Protestants, but the vast majority were Continentals: 7,000 Danes plus French Huguenots, Swiss, Dutch and German troops. Despite subsequent mythologising, the Boyne was not a particularly bloody defeat for James and the Irish Catholics, who lost no more than a thousand men.†

Nevertheless it was crucial, and followed by James's much more severe defeat by the Dutch General Ginkel and his army at Aughrim (County Galway) when 7,000 Catholic Irish troops perished on 12 July 1691. By the end of the year 12,000 Jacobite survivors set sail for France – the so-called 'Flight of the Wild Geese'. Any Irish Catholic hopes that they might secure their lands and position were finally dashed.

Instead they were barred from Parliament and forbidden to bear arms.

---

* 12 July in the old calendar – still the date on which the battle is commemorated.

† William lost his commanding officer. The Duke of Schonberg, aged seventy-five, was caught in the thick of the retreating Catholics and accidentally shot by his own men, a victim of 'friendly fire'. Samuel de Pechel founded an English military dynasty: his son Jacob became a lieutenant colonel, his grandson, Sir Paul Pechell, also a lieutenant colonel, his great-grandson, Sir Samuel Pechell, a rear admiral. His great-great-grandsons were Rear Admiral Sir Samuel Pechell and Admiral Sir George Richard Brooke Pechell.

They were also prohibited from owning a horse worth over £5, sending their children to school overseas or maintaining Catholic schools in Ireland. Nor could they acquire land from a Protestant or inherit land in total (it had to be divided, unless the eldest son converted). Catholic clergy were expelled from the country and, in 1728, Irish Catholics were denied the vote. Protestants were in the ascendant.

As King William became older, without direct heirs, the question of a constitutional union between Scotland and England became more pressing. After Cromwell's experiment there was little enthusiasm for a republic. A joint monarch was needed, but not a Catholic Stuart, as this would threaten the Protestant ascendancy. What was needed, according to the English oligarchs, was another William III: a Protestant foreigner who would spend a lot of time abroad and leave Parliament to rule the country – preferably one who would produce some heirs. There was also the problem of Scotland, which had a right to choose its own king and retained a fondness for the Stuarts. As the Scots were virtually bankrupt, the English feared that Louis XIV might beg, bribe or bully them into accepting one of the Stuarts whom he kept for such occasions stored away in France.

Desperate to avoid such a situation, Parliament passed the Act of Settlement in 1701 – while William was still on the throne. It finalised the question of royal succession, and has functioned ever since. The Act overruled the hereditary rights of the House of Stuart and the legitimacy of fifty-seven potential Stuart Catholic claimants, giving the House of Hanover a position of priority, to take over as constitutional monarch subservient to Parliament. The Hanoverians were minor German princes, conveniently lacking any real Continental power base; Protestants of no strict convention, they had a thin streak of Stuart blood, lots of fertile offspring, and spoke absolutely no English. These immigrants would be welcomed with open arms when the time came.

William III died in March 1702 and the last Stuart monarch, the childless and Protestant Anne, became Queen in England and Scotland. Two years later the Scottish Parliament passed the Act of Security, making absolutely clear its right to choose the Scottish monarch. The English reacted by threatening to deport all Scottish residents in England. Having wielded the stick, they offered the carrot: a Bill of Union accompanied by a large financial settlement. The Scottish Parliament accepted and abolished itself. The Scots retained their system of law, their currency, municipal corporations and Church. They would send forty-five members to Parliament in Westminster, which would act as the legislature for the new joint state. The independent Scottish monarchy, which dated back to

Cinaed mac Alpin (Kenneth MacAlpine) in the ninth century, would cease to exist when Queen Anne died.

The new Anglo-Scottish state was to be known as the 'Kingdom of Great Britain' and the Union flag devised by James I would fly over it. The British people would be subjects of a British monarchy, ruled by a British Parliament with a British government and protected by a British army. The British Empire was just emerging.

Queen Anne ruled until 1 August 1714. She had given birth to nineteen children, mostly stillborn and no surviving ones to complicate the arrangement with Hanover. In preparation for the succession, George Ludwig van Braunschweig-Luneburg, Elector of Hanover, was naturalised as an English subject in 1705. He was not the ideal family man – he had divorced his wife, imprisoned her in one of his castles and refused to speak to his son – but, then as now, model families were not part of the royal job description.

The Royal Assent to the Act of Union on 6 March 1707 was only one of several agenda items. As Norman Davies observes: 'There is something exquisitely inappropriate in the fact that the act embodying the fundamental constitutional treaty between England and Scotland was given the same weight on the agenda as an act for trying to stop the escape of convicts and another for mending the roads between the villages of Hockliffe and Woodborne.'[13] The Queen did, however, go on to deliver a short speech emphasising the importance of the Union. In it she said: 'I desire and expect from all my subjects of both nations, that from henceforth they act with all possible respect and kindness to one another, that so it may appear to all the world they have hearts disposed to become one people. This will be a great pleasure to me.'

Three weeks later, on 1 May 1707, a British Parliament met for the first time. It still had a Stuart monarch descended from a Scottish-Norman family. It was not until 1 August 1714 that the final piece of the British jigsaw could be put in place: Anne died and George, Elector of Hanover, was proclaimed King of Great Britain, France and Ireland.

Ten An Industrious People

I SPENT MY early childhood in the Calder valley, in West Yorkshire. We lived in a terraced house dominated by a 'dark satanic' mill, though to me it seemed quite a friendly place. The workers sat on the wall outside our house chatting at break-times and our next-door neighbour, Dick Barber, would take me to see the mill's gleaming steam engine on Sunday mornings, which he polished lovingly and called 'Mary Ellen'. There was a panoramic view of the valley from the millstone grit outcrops that edged the nearby moor. William Wordsworth's sister, Dorothy, had enjoyed this countryside as a child in the 1780s, 'walking wild', gathering bilberries and following the mossy paths by the River Calder, where a passer-by could 'catch the silvered glances of the trout / seen in the bottom of the lucid wave'.[1]

The first worsted woollen mill opened a few years later and the Calder valley began to change. In the 1950s I counted over a hundred mill chimneys along the valley, next to the canal, the railway and the slick River Calder, which now flowed a gaudy shade of pink or mauve from dye effluent. The trout were long gone. This was the heartland of the Industrial Revolution. Or so I was told. Nowadays historians are more circumspect about using terms such as 'revolution'. It is possible to observe a series of longer-term changes coming together and gathering pace in the late eighteenth and first half of the nineteenth century; but this phenomenon has many strands, which go back further in time.

In England the Georgian era did not begin on a wave of optimism. The hunger problem was less severe than in the past as England achieved a balance between food production and population. The fear of plague persisted and in the early 1720s it was raging in the south of France. The English could not know that they had seen the last of it.

Not that plague was the only health problem. Samuel Pepys records in his diary that he suffered from colds over a hundred times in the ten years he was writing it. He took to wearing a hare's foot for protection. It was as good as anything else available. The new experimental natural philosophy, which would transform Britain, was only just beginning to make inroads into the understanding of the human body. William Harvey (1578–1657), who first discovered the principles of the circulation of blood around the body, was one of the pioneers. Born in Folkestone and trained in Padua, he became a physician and public dissector at St Bartholomew's Hospital. He believed in observation and experimentation rather than the acceptance of classical dogma passed down from Galen: 'I profess to learn and teach anatomy not from books but from dissections ... not from the tenets of Philosophers but from the fabric of Nature.' Like Pepys, however, Harvey was a complex man of his time. If he realised that the Ancient Greek Galen was not the infallible font of all medical wisdom, he was still an enthusiastic supporter of Aristotle and the belief in the importance of the soul.

To the modern mind seventeenth-century science and religion may seem uneasy bedfellows. The Royal Society was established in 1662 to 'promote the welfare of the arts and sciences', though founder member Robert Boyle still advocated crushed mistletoe as a treatment for epilepsy. Boyle believed in religious cures but sought a scientific explanation. Isaac Newton pursued alchemy while producing his great work the *Principia* in 1687, which firmly established the scientific model as the most effective in the pursuit of knowledge.

Another physician, Thomas Sydenham (1624–89), was lauded as the 'English Hippocrates', and also favoured observation over speculation. As Sydenham served in the Parliamentary army he must have observed a multitude of deaths from the prevalent 'army fever', which struck the Parliamentary garrison at Abingdon, and the epidemic diseases that ravaged the population of London in the 1660s and 70s. He decided that the ague, the annual fever epidemic that occurred from March to July, resulted from the warmth of the sun acting on humours that had built up in the blood during the winter. For smallpox, the speckled monster and one of Europe's most virulent killers, Sydenham prescribed 'cool therapy' – plenty of fluids and moderate bleeding to cool the patient. This treatment was, at least, preferable to that previously inflicted by doctors: bury the patient under a pile of blankets and provide him or her with hot cordials to sweat out the disease.*

* If there was one thing more dangerous than a complete lack of medical attention, it was too much. Charles II underwent the customary torture of the royal deathbed, inflicted by a surfeit of competitive quacks. After the King suffered a stroke, the physicians flocked around him, experimenting with bleeding techniques, cupping glasses, emetics, purgatives and red-hot cautery. As Dr Charles Scarburgh, one of the dozen physicians in attendance, explained, 'nothing was left untried'.

It was not until after 1750 that Robert Sutton and his sons developed a simple and safe form of inoculation that they were able to administer cheaply on a large scale. Edward Jenner (1749–1823) was a country doctor who inoculated his Gloucestershire patients. He learnt from them that cowpox, a cattle disease contracted by dairymaids, also seemed to confer immunity from smallpox. As cowpox was benign in humans, Jenner reasoned that inoculation from the cowpox pustule should be safer than the current method. Experimentation proved him to be right. From 1798 Jenner's method of inoculation spread round the world. Napoleon had his army vaccinated. In 1802 Parliament rewarded Jenner with a payment of £10,000 and took steps to promote vaccination. At last the state was beginning to appreciate that it had a responsibility for the health care of its citizens.

Science was of limited use in the earlier eighteenth century, when the country was stricken by successive bouts of smallpox, fever and agues* (possibly typhus, typhoid and influenza transmitted from pigs and ducks) between 1727 and 1731 and again in 1740–42.[2]

These lethal epidemics were another serious demographic setback. They erased the small increase in population which had been gained since the 1670s. Dr Hillary, in Ripon, reported that 'many of the little country towns and villages were almost stripped of their poor people'.[3] Fever remained a more dangerous killer than war and, combined with emigration and low fertility levels, served to keep the population low. In 1721 the population of England and Wales was about 5,200,000, no more than that of Cromwell's time.

By the mid-1740s, however, there was a demographic upturn. The reasons are uncertain. Food prices had been low for twenty years as a result of low demand (fewer people) and a run of good harvests. Corn output increased by over 10 per cent in the first half of the eighteenth century. The surplus was exported or distilled into gin, whose production in 1743 was six times higher than at the turn of the century. The cost of bread went down, reducing the cost of living, especially for the poor, whose health improved in the 1730s and 40s – if they kept off 'Mother Gin', whose influence is so graphically portrayed by William Hogarth in *Gin Lane*.† Low prices drove some farmers out of business but inspired

---

* The folk remedy for ague was extracted from the bark of the white willow (*Salix alba*) on the grounds that the tree grew where ague abounds. The Reverend Edmund Stone of Chipping Norton, Oxfordshire, reported that he was experimenting with willow bark because of 'the general maxim, that many natural maladies carry their cures along with them'. In 1899 a new name was invented for the drug acetylsalicylic acid, extracted from willow bark (salicin) and meadowsweet (salicylic acid): it was called aspirin and became the most popular drug in the world.

others to greater efficiency, innovation and productivity. As usual when labour was in short supply and expensive, farmers attempted to maximise income by reducing labour costs. They also attempted to extend the acreage of useful land. They drained fens and marshes, brought so-called 'waste' under the plough and experimented with fertilisers, such as seaweed and marl.

At Holkham, in Norfolk, Thomas Coke was the great publicist of such improvements. From 1778 he turned his sandy soils into productive cornlands and increased the value of his estate from £5,000 to £20,000. He was not the only practitioner: neighbours such as the Townsends and Walpoles were enthusiastic agricultural improvers, participants in a rural change that had developed through the fifteenth and sixteenth centuries. With enclosure, engrossing and improvement rural society had been in a constant state of flux for decades. The agrarian world was dominated by capitalist farmers, not necessarily owners, but tenants of the large gentry landlords. Changes in agriculture speeded up in the eighteenth century, though the term 'Agricultural Revolution', which is often used, fails to recognise the duration and variation of the process. The historian E. L. Jones has observed that:

> in terms of efficiency of resource use and the absolute
> increase of output the achievement of British agriculture
> during the eighteenth century was a considerable one. It was
> not, however, dramatic or dramatically brought about ... no
> convincing starting date can be found during the century for
> any process that might be labelled an 'agricultural revolution'.
> [It was] a part of the history of an expanding universe, not
> something that began with a big bang.[4]

However, in the eighteenth century stockholders, for example Robert Bakewell in Leicestershire, applied more systematic, scientific techniques to animal breeding: he called his sheep '[machines] for turning grass into mutton'. Many well-known breeds appeared at this time, such as Hereford cattle and Southdown sheep; and the finest, inflated specimens posed for their portraits, the pride of their owners and creators. Animals could be controlled more successfully in an enclosed landscape than upon the open, common fields of medieval England. Enclosure of

† In a period of increasing prosperity Hogarth's prints (which made him rich) appealed to the rather self-satisfied and judgemental class of shopkeepers, tradespeople, artisans and merchants. Hogarth signed himself 'Britophil' and spoke for the respectable people, satirising and condemning the undeserving poor, debtors and drunks. Life is not to be celebrated by moralising Protestants like Hogarth.

common fields had been put in place by local agreement since Tudor times, but in 1750 the first of over 4,000 parliamentary Acts of Enclosure was enacted, bringing compulsion into the process, imposing a green grid on the countryside. In Scotland, Wales and Ireland enclosure was not so predominant as in England; however, there was massive clearance of woodland and the open land was then used for sheep. Permanent upland farms replaced the traditional upland shielings, or shelters, used for transhumance (the seasonal movement of flocks and herds), and the *hafod* and *uvest* smallholdings of upland Wales.

On the lowlands fodder crops were used to improve grazing; soil fertility was improved by growing nitrogen-fixing legumes and clover. Viscount Townsend in Norfolk achieved fame as 'Turnip Townsend' and turnips were grown as winter fodder for the increasingly large numbers of livestock from the 1730s. Soil improvement, under drainage and rotation systems, removed the necessity for wasteful fallow periods. More fodder allowed for more and bigger animals, more manure and better yields of cereals. Wool flowed into the textile trades and roast beef into the stomachs of the well-to-do. The poor subsisted mainly on bread and cheese, though Arthur Young, journalist and advocate of improvement, noted in 1767 that 'rye and barley bread are looked on with horror even by poor cottagers'. The tables of the 'better sort' groaned with the roast beef of Old England, supplemented by an occasional helping of vegetables towards which there was a traditional antipathy. A Swedish visitor in 1748 commented that English cooking did not extend much beyond roast beef and plum pudding – accompanied by plenty of alcohol. Early in the eighteenth century the annual consumption of spirits in London was about 7 gallons per adult. Northampton had 160 inns and alehouses: about one per thirty inhabitants. Beer was still the standard drink and safer than water.

Productivity was also increased by technical improvements to agricultural machinery. Jethro Tull produced his seed drill in 1701, though it took eighty years before it was widely used. Agricultural societies and the proliferation of handbooks spread the knowledge and virtues of new techniques, but eighteenth-century agriculture still depended upon animal and human power. The most important stimulus for efficiency came in the nineteenth century with the invention of new ploughs and the harnessing of steam power for agricultural purposes.

The great landowners and enterprising farmers mostly thrived in this drive for improvement and productivity. Poorer people, as ever, were the victims of all this change. Many small cultivators, peasants and cottagers, depended upon the so-called 'waste': spare land which provided food for a few geese, a family pig or cow. The peasants could gather fuel there, produce charcoal and trap rabbits. For smallholders the extras from the 'waste' were vital: without these they were reduced to penury; and they could not afford the fences, hedges and ditches required to enclose and demarcate their small parcels of land. Davis Davies, Rector of Cookham, Berkshire, observed: 'An amazing number of people have been reduced from a comfortable state of partial independence to the precarious condition of mere hirelings, who when out of work immediately come on the parish.' Arthur Young, in spite of his enthusiasm for improvement, admitted: 'By nineteen out of twenty Enclosure Bills the poor are injured and most grossly ... The poor in these parishes may say with truth, "Parliament may be tender of property; all I know is, I had a cow, and an Act of Parliament has taken it from me."'

The changes were even more drastic in the Highlands of Scotland. The 'Young Pretender', Charles Edward Stuart (Bonnie Prince Charlie), grandson of James II, landed in the Hebrides in July 1745. He was the great hope of the Jacobites — the mixture of Catholics, traditionalists and displaced Irish who hated Hanoverians and the Protestant state of Britain and prayed for the return of the Stuarts and the old ways. Charles raised an army of 2,500 Highlanders, took control of most of Scotland, including Edinburgh, and defeated a small British force at Prestonpans. With an army now of 5,000 men he marched through northern England, reaching as far south as Derby. The English were shocked to discover that a raggle-taggle mob of Highlanders, generally considered as Gaelic barbarians by the Sassenachs — Scottish lowlanders and the English alike — could trample its way through a supposedly modern country. 'That it had achieved so much with such minimal resources was a testament to the Jacobite army's mettle and leadership, and to the ineptitude of much of the formal machinery of the British state.'[5] The British had a professional army of 62,000 men, most of whom were campaigning in Germany and Flanders. In spite of the Jacobite threat, the defence of the realm had been severely negelected. Fortunately for George II, the 'Young Pretender' was pursuing a lost cause. Except for the poorer Highland clans only a handful of English and Welsh rallied to his cause. Even in Scotland the prospering inhabitants of the major towns, the commercial and manufacturing centres, wanted nothing to do with this romantic throwback.

As the powerful Hanoverian state eventually geared itself for action, Charles was forced to retreat northwards. He foolishly, and suicidally, decided to launch his Highlanders against the steel wall of Lord Cumberland's army at Culloden (near Inverness). Charging uphill, screaming their Gaelic war cries, the Jacobites were torn apart by the regimented muskets and cannon and impaled on the bayonets of the British army – a force which contained more Scotsmen than their own.

Bonnie Prince Charlie survived to become a figure of sentimental legend; in reality he wandered the courts of Europe, an embarrassment descending into alcoholism. The British army rolled on through the Highlands, threshing the chaff of the clan system in a campaign of what would today be called 'ethnic cleansing'.

After the '45 Jacobite rebellion government authority was finally imposed across the Highlands. Military control, however, was only part of the story. Creating the British state also meant establishing the British Museum and publishing the *Encyclopedia Britannica*. In the developing urban and industrialised economy of Scotland there were overwhelming pressures to produce more food and raw materials: cattle, timber, fish and slate. The traditional tribal values of kinship and obligation were swept away as clan chiefs adopted the new ways of the Scottish and English lowland landowners and reorganised their estates. In the new order commercial influences superseded traditional loyalties: clan chiefs became landed gentlemen; landlordism replaced tribalism. And landed gentlemen kept an eye – and both hands – on rents. In Skye these trebled, and Norman MacLeod of Macleod and Sir Alexander MacDonald of Sleat concocted a scheme to deport their poorer tenant families and sell them as indentured labour to the American plantations. Their scheme was a scandal at the time, and a forerunner of the later Highland Clearances.

The clan chiefs of Gaeldom increasingly adopted the attitudes of the lowland landed class (amongst whom they were now educated), participating enthusiastically in the fashion for competitive display. Traditional agriculture with its meagre returns was inadequate for Highland landowners seeking to ape the grand houses and lifestyles of the south. Clearances and dispossession could be morally justifiable to those who viewed the Gaelic peasantry as backward, feckless and inefficient. Agricultural improvement was often presented by landowners as a necessary evil. As cattle and black-faced sheep became profitable, supplying the hungry towns and the expanding woollen industries, Highland tenants were shifted to coastal townships, where they had to scrape a living from crofting. Crofting was not designed to provide a complete livelihood; typically crofters needed at least an extra 200 working days a year off their holdings if they were to avoid destitution. Kelp manufacturing (the production of fertiliser from seaweed) filled the gap for up to 40,000 people in the Hebrides. Fishing, withy-making and service in Highland regiments — led by the landowners — were other means by which crofters were turned from farmers to labourers and soldiers. In the long run the policy was to prove disastrous.

Ireland was subjected to much the same pressures as Scotland. Live-stock farming expanded to meet the demands of a growing internal population, the city of Dublin and, above all, the English market for beef and butter; but as the rural population expanded, rented farms were divided until tenants were struggling to subsist on smallholdings, dependent upon potato cultivation to avoid starvation. The proliferation of Georgian houses across Ireland shows the profitability of commercial farming and the taste of their owners.[6]

The elite in England also signed up for Palladian country houses and landscape parks,[7] such as Sir Richard Temple, later Viscount Cobham, who created the monument to Whig history at Stowe (Buckinghamshire). Between 1714 and 1779 almost anyone who was anyone in garden design worked at Stowe: Bridgeman, Vanbrugh, Kent, Gibbs, Capability Brown. Kent brought his knowledge of Italian Renaissance gardens to the project, but the Temple of British Worthies and Gibbs's Gothic Revival Temple celebrated English freedom brought by German (Anglo-Saxon) ancestors. Cobham was elevated to the peerage by the House of Hanover in 1714, aged forty. He then married a wealthy brewing heiress and launched into his grand garden project.

Britain had wealthy aristocrats, but there were not too many of them. In 1688 England and Wales had 160 peers; by 1832 they had increased to 350. In the mid-eighteenth century the country gentry numbered about 1,500. An estate of a thousand acres was the minimum necessary to bring in the rents to sustain a gentleman in the style to which he was accustomed. However, these numbers were tiny compared to the Continent. On the eve of the Revolution, in the 1780s, France had 120,000 nobles — enough to fill the tumbrils for months. Spain had half a million.

If the British elite was the smallest in Europe, it was also the richest. In the parliamentary papers called the 'New Domesday', which recorded the ownership and values of estates in the 1870s, two-thirds of the United Kingdom's total land area was held by fewer than 11,000 owners. Henry VIII's Dissolution of the Monasteries in the sixteenth century had the effect of transferring land from the Church to the secular elite. Activities such as engrossing and enclosure thrust more land into fewer hands. This trend towards larger holdings was then maintained by strict settlement — passing entire estates intact to the next generation; by marriage settlements which united landed dynasties; and by the increasing ability of the wealthy to borrow more money as mortgages to fund new land purchases. Out of this process emerged the great landed estates and grand country houses, such as Holkham Hall, built for Thomas Coke, Earl of Leicester, from 1734 and designed by William Kent (creator of the Monument to Whig Heroes at Stowe). Unlike the Tudor gentry, whose houses nested cosily within the village, grand Georgian mansions sat four-square, isolated from the hoi-polloi by their landscaped parks and ha-has.* These landowners, in their domestic temples of taste, no longer wished to mix with their less privileged neighbours.

If an existing village threatened to spoil the view of the grandees, the solution was simple: move it. The Irish poet Oliver Goldsmith idealised village life, evoking a lost world and damning selfish landlords in his poem *The Deserted Village*:

> *Sweet smiling village, loveliest of the lawn,*
> *Thy sports are fled, and all thy charms withdrawn;*
> *Amidst thy bowers the tyrant's hand is seen,*
> *And desolation saddens all thy green:*
> *One only master grasps the whole domain ...*
> *Ill fares the land, to hastening ills a prey,*
> *Where wealth accumulates, and men decay;*
> *Princes and lords may flourish or may fade —*
> *A breath can make them, as a breath has made;*
> *But a bold peasantry, their country's pride,*
> *When once destroy'd, can never by supplied.*

Goldsmith penned these words after visiting Nuneham Courtenay, south of Oxford, in 1761. In 1755 Simon, Earl Harcourt, had decided to build himself a new, stylish Palladian villa. His family seat at Stanton Harcourt, on the flat lands of the Thames above Oxford, did not have the potential for fashionable undulating landscaping. At Nuneham, however, with its view towards Oxford and along the river, Lord Harcourt could perceive a passing and desirable resemblance to the Seven Hills of Rome. There was a minor problem: the Earl's manor house at Nuneham was surrounded by a church and a village. The Earl demolished the lot, then erected a new house and an acceptable church in the style of a Greek temple. One old woman, Babs Wyatt, did not wish to leave her 'clay built cott', so she was graciously allowed to remain in the grounds in the guise of an 'Arcadian shepherdess'. In spite of Goldsmith's disgust, the other villagers were probably satisfied to move into their new brick cottages,

---

* Sunken fences or ditches, invisible at a distance, so that garden and landscape beyond looked as one. When one came upon the ditch it was a surprise: hence 'ha-ha!' The earliest example is Vanbrugh's at Blenheim, constructed in 1709.

which the Earl built nearby, alongside the main road to Oxford. They are still standing, probably more desirable residences than the 'clay built cotts' that they replaced.*

In the 1760s the writer Tobias Smollett, in one of his better moods, benignly surveyed the land: 'I see the country of England smiling with cultivation: the grounds exhibiting all the perfection of agriculture, parcelled out into beautiful enclosures, corn fields, hay pasture, woodland and common.' However, growing prosperity did not depend simply upon agricultural production. With the accession of William III, Parliament provided the monarchy with a stable financial base in return for legal supremacy.

Unlike the Tudors and Stuarts, William was granted regular public funding and a new political bargain was reached. In the words of Erskine May's *Parliamentary Practice* of 1844: 'The Crown demands, the Commons grant, and the Lords assent to the grant.' Fiscal agreement replaced constant bickering and rivalry. The royal budget increased fourfold and within several decades the Crown was able to float loans for levels of interest that were comparable with those that had made the Dutch so commercially successful. Not only did capital flow into the state, but ordinary people began to trust the capital markets and invest their surplus cash. No longer did they keep it under the mattress or, like Samuel Pepys, bury it in the garden when the Dutch fleet threatened London.

While improving agriculture fed the growing population, investment and wage surpluses stimulated manufacture. The falling percentage of agricultural workers acts as a barometer of modernisation and rising prosperity. In 1700 about 60 per cent of the British population worked in agriculture, decreasing to 40 per cent by 1800 (in 1700 one farm worker fed 1.7 persons; in 1800 one farm worker fed 2.5 persons). After the Napoleonic wars the figure dropped dramatically, reaching 10 per cent before World War I and 2 per cent in the late twentieth century. In the same period in North America the agricultural labour force fell from 70 per cent of the total population to less than 2 per cent and real per capita GDP increased thirtyfold. In spite of the hardships of the poor and the displaced, clearer ownership rights led to experimentation, investment and vastly improved yields.†

---

* Goldsmith's warning about 'fading princes' was prophetic. The Earl of Harcourt, as Chancellor of the Exchequer in London, did not visit his elegant pile very often. On one such occasion he wandered through his park, unaware of the location of the village well. He fell down it and met an untimely end.

† The maxim attributed to Laurence Summers, former US Treasury Secretary, in the *Wall Street Journal*, the in-house newsletter of capitalism, captures the principle: 'No one in the history of the world ever washed a rented car.[8]

Throughout the eighteenth century Britain was usually at war, and usually with the French. Whereas in the previous century religious differences had fuelled conflict, now resources and the control of trade became major issues. And the costs of warfare rose: William Pitt the Elder, the British Prime Minister, called it 'breaking windows with guineas'. Overseas conflict in the Americas and Asia stimulated the growth of the navy, at vast expense. Nelson's flagship HMS *Victory*, now a romantic and colourful relic in Portsmouth harbour, actually cost five times as much to build as Abraham Crowley's steelworks, one of the major investments in the Industrial Revolution.[9]

As military techniques and equipment advanced, they invariably became more expensive. The flintlock gun, developed between 1680 and 1730, had been charged down by wild Highlanders at Killiecrankie in 1689; but the armies of Frederick the Great of Prussia developed disciplined mass fire which soon became a European standard – and ratcheted up the spiralling costs of warfare. The size of armies also increased. The French Revolution introduced the concept of the mass levy of young men conscripted into the national army. As a result Napoleon had enormous armies to throw against the Russians, Prussians and British. In 1759 the British deployed 5,000 infantry at the Battle of Minden; at Waterloo, in 1815, they had 21,000, many from the Celtic fringes. Yet these were tiny forces compared to the French Grande Armée. The British response was to subsidise foreign allies to participate as their proxies.

Warfare helped to keep grain prices high, but the principal factor in the last three decades of the eighteenth century was accelerating population growth. In 1789 wheat sold for 45 shillings a quarter. By the end of the century, in eleven years, it had shot up to 84 shillings and then to 102 shillings by 1814 – an unheard-of price. Large landowners grew fat on the profits. On English estates rentals went up as much as 90 per cent, in Wales by slightly less; in Ireland increases averaged 90 per cent and in Scotland they increased eightfold between 1750 and 1815.[10]

Even the once 'backward' Highlands now attracted southern investors. After Napoleon's final defeat and the Congress of Vienna, in 1815, grain prices fell and there was an agricultural slump. Nevertheless ten years later rentals of land stabilised at double the pre-1790 figures, while unemployed farm workers flooded into the urban and industrial labour market. Their wages declined for about five years, but then began a steady increase.

Industry had been changing and developing through the eighteenth century, stimulated by the growing population and the needs of the military. However, its roots are much older. The Dutch historian Jan de Vries has developed the concept of the 'industrious revolution'. He argues that in parts of northern Europe this meant using family labour more efficiently by buying in goods and services from outside, not just being self-sufficient. For example, the consumption of coffee and tea, along with sugar and white bread served on mass-produced plates and cups, became a new ritual: breakfast, which 'gave people a higher calorific intake, a new time discipline and a new pattern for sociability and emulation in the household'. So the English breakfast boosted consumerism, trade in international foodstuffs, in disposable crockery, itself subject to fashion, rather than wooden or pewter platters which had been in the family for years. The industrious revolution, with Huguenots leading by example, instilled a new sense of time discipline into British society. Before any of the factories appeared in the Calder valley Daniel Defoe came to visit. He crossed the Pennines in August – and, ever the dramatist, makes them sound like the Alps in winter: 'It is not easy to express the consternation we were in when we came up near the top of the mountain … The ground also was covered with snow that we could see no track, or when we were in the way, or when out; except when we were showed it by a frightful precipice.'

Eventually Defoe descends into the Shangri-La of Halifax.[11] The hill slopes are dotted with houses but there are no people about. They are all indoors, industriously attending to their business, '[which] is the clothing trade, for the convenience of which the houses are thus scattered and spread upon the sides of the hills … The reason is this; such has been the bounty of nature to this otherwise frightful country, that two things essential to the business as well as the ease of the people are found here; I mean coals and running water over the tops of the highest hills.' In local cottages 'dwell the workmen which are employed, the women and children of which are always busy carding, spinning, etc., so that no hands are unemployed and all can gain their bread'.

As with the Huguenot families of Smithfield, or the metalworkers of the Severn valley, in the early eighteenth century the people of the infertile Yorkshire hillsides were already bent to the discipline of manufacture and dependent on a cash economy rather than agricultural self-sufficiency. The easy flow of goods into and out of such a remote area depended upon improving transport. The road repairs on the same agenda as the 1707 Act of Union may seem trivial compared with Anglo-Scots unity, but they were fundamental to the industrialisation and modernisation of Britain. Before 1700 the responsibility for roads was local; it lay with the parish to patch and mend what was still a primitive and localised network of tracks. As demand and the need to travel longer distances increased, a new system developed in response: turnpike roads, which passed the cost to the users by charging a toll.

In 1750 there were less than 5,000 kilometres of such roads, yet by 1770 there were 25,000 kilometres, densest in south-east and central England. They were the responsibility of turnpike trusts, and standards were consequently still variable. They were also authorised by individual Acts of Parliament (452 Acts in fourteen years from 1760) until the General Turnpike Act of 1773. This was the golden age of coaching and coaching inns; Britain had a European reputation for good roads and service stations. In 1754 a Manchester newspaper advertisement boldly declared: 'However incredible it may appear this coach will actually arrive in London four days after leaving Manchester.' By the 1780s this journey time had been halved. The Edinburgh to London journey time had also been sliced, from thirteen days to two and a half days by 1796, by which time John McAdam's hard and dry macadamed roads allowed coaches like the *Independent Tally Ho* to fly between Birmingham and London at 15 miles per hour. For the first time roads in Britain were better than those built by the Romans 1,700 years earlier.

By the 1830s fifty-four coaches a day carried passengers each way between London and Manchester and 700 mail coaches criss-crossed the country. The adventurous and imaginative speculated about new forms of transport: Erasmus Darwin considered steam-driven balloons. But in the late eighteenth and early nineteenth centuries the horse was still the fastest form of transport, as demonstrated at the Derby, the Formula 1 Grand Prix of its day, which was first run in 1780.

Faster road transport was not a solution to the increasing need to move bulky industrial commodities. The overland transport of heavy materials remained a problem until a network of 'dead water' canals, using pound locks, was in place. Britain was late into canal-building. As usual, the centralised and strategically organised French government provided funding for a canal system, linking the large estuaries, long before Britain's haphazard system of private enterprise stirred into action. The first British canal construction, the Newry Canal, was built in Ireland between 1735 and 1740, though it was the Duke of Bridgewater's project linking his Worsley coalfields to Manchester and Liverpool in 1760–61 that initiated the boom in canal-building to service the developing heavy industries. The canal halved the price of coal in Manchester and profits from Bridgewater's mines rocketed from £406 in 1760 to £48,000 in 1803. In the 1760s and early 70s, a rare period of peace, money was cheap and private enterprise, in the form of bankers, merchants and the landed gentry, rushed to invest in what became a nationwide transport network without parallel in Europe.*

Armies of navvies ('navigators'), mostly Irish and ex-farm workers, were needed to hack and haul the titanic amounts of rock and earth displaced by the increasingly heroic schemes of inspired engineers such as Thomas Telford ('The Colossus of Roads').†

He was responsible for a Welsh Wonder of the World at Pontcysyllte, where his spectacular aqueduct carried the Ellesmere Canal in a cast-iron trough 127 feet above the River Dee. An admiring French engineer wrote, in 1816:

> A sky-born canal, whose iron trough is held up by piers
> which are both sturdy and elegant. Heavily laden boats and
> the horses which haul them may safely cross this passage
> over an abyss and carry away towards Ellesmere the coal,
> limestone and iron from the mine, quarries and foundries of
> the Vale of Llangollen … Never had I seen such an imposing
> sight … There were blast furnaces, forges, limekilns, piles
> of coal being coked, workshops, fine mansions, villages built
> into an amphitheatre around the flanks of the valley. At the
> bottom was a foaming torrent, while above it the canal,
> enclosed in its iron envelope, hung like something enchanted,
> on its high slender pillars, a supreme work of architecture,
> elegant and unadorned.[12]

The Grand Trunk, over 90 miles long, linked the Mersey and the Trent, providing an outlet for barges laden safely, and at a quarter of the cost of road transport, with the mass-produced plates and teacups of the Potteries. The major rivers were eventually connected by canals: the Severn and Mersey (in 1727), the Trent and Mersey (1777), the Severn and Thames (1789), and the Mersey, Trent and Thames (1790). As a result the cities of the north, Midlands and south of England were tied into a 2,500-mile-long artery of duty-free trade, which encouraged the production and movement of goods – and of people – across the country.

The government took a more proactive role in the improvement of

---

* The canals were not a true national system, as there were different widths and varying ownership.

† Telford was another self-taught, if not quite self-made, Scot. Born in 1757 at Glendenning, son of a shepherd, he worked on Somerset House as a stonemason. He caught the eye of Sir William Johnstone, 'the richest commoner in Britain', who put him in charge of building work in Portsmouth Dockyard. From there his career blossomed: he built the biggest bridge in the world across the Menai Straits to Anglesey, and his superb roads through the Highlands opened them up to the new tourist industry inspired by Sir Walter Scott.

transport in the Celtic west, investing partly for military reasons and also to inhibit overseas emigration by providing work (the Irish and Scots made good soldiers and their loss was a concern to recruiting officers). Parliament voted over half a million pounds for roads and bridges and promoted the Caledonian Canal to inhibit 'the present rage for Emigration and prevent its future Progress'. But local tycoons invested in the Monklands Canal to transport Lanarkshire coal to Glasgow, where there was a shortage, and the Forth–Clyde Canal to shift Glasgow tobacco eastwards and into the European markets. Between 1760 and 1800 the upper Clyde was transformed from an unnavigable river into one of the world's best ship canals.

Whether we call it the Industrial Revolution or not, British commercial and industrial activity shifted up a gear in the late eighteenth century. There are many indicators: from 1780 pig-iron production doubled every eight years; 976 new patents for inventions were taken out between 1760 and 1789 (there were only 210 patents in the country prior to 1760); coal production doubled between 1750 and 1800; cotton imports increased by five times in the twenty years up to 1800. Scotland's linen industry doubled its output and trebled its value between 1746 and 1790. And all these figures soared exponentially in the nineteenth century. The inventors of the period were not blue-skies scientists; they were a varied bunch, but mostly practical men with business acumen. A Greenock instrument-maker, James Watt,* designed pumping machinery to ensure that tobacco ships could be careened more quickly, which was necessary, as they were regularly exposed to the toredo worm-infested waters of Chesapeake Bay on the east coast of America.

Watt turned his attention to the steam engine, applied the idea of separate condensation, which enabled it to generate a constant motion, and, in 1791, devised a rotary motion. Watt, with his ceaselessly moving pistons, had revolutionised power and the supply of cheap energy to drive the technological improvements which came thick and fast in the later eighteenth century: Cartwright's power looms, Crompton's mule, John Kay's flying shuttle, the spinning jenny.

With his partner, the Birmingham ironmaster Matthew Boulton, Watt had a monopoly of steam-engine production for a quarter of a century and turned the engines from being basically water pumps into the essential drivers of innumerable industries. Matthew Boulton declared in 178: 'The people in London, Manchester and Birmingham are all steam mill mad.'

---

* Watt was largely self-taught, but he personified the principles of the Scottish Enlightenment: 'common-sense, experience as our best source of knowledge, and arriving at scientific laws by testing general hypotheses through individual experiment and trial and error'.[13]

When James Boswell visited the Soho works, near Birmingham, Boulton infomed him: 'I sell here, Sir, what all the world desires to have: power.' Yet at the same time, like Josiah Wedgwood, Boulton the manufacturer searched through illustrations of Renaissance and Ancient-Greek pottery for inspiration to satisfy the mania for vases. Also like Wedgwood, he had a flair for publicity and marketing, linking his products to the tasteful aristocracy to encourage the trickle-down effect into the large middle-class market, which could be supplied via the canals alongside his factory.

The swelling middle class fuelled the consumer society. 'The English', according to Josiah Tucker, 'have better conveniences in their house and affect to have more in quantity of clean, neat furniture, and a greater variety of such as carpets, screens, window curtains, chamber bells, polished brass locks, fenders, etc. – things hardly known abroad among persons of such rank – than are to be found in any other country in Europe, Holland excepted.' They are, he said, 'the customers to and the manufacturers for each other'.*[14]

Less glamorous products were every bit as important for the national economy. New technology made manufacture quicker, easier and cheaper and put traditional workers out of business. The Luddites retaliated by smashing the hated machinery. Nevertheless the British prided themselves on not just making inventions, but developing and applying them. Between 1780 and 1800 the value of cotton exports leapt from £236,000 to £5,371,000.†

Industrial development in Britain was a highly regionalised phenomenon, as Adam Smith realised in the 1760s: 'All over Great Britain manufacturers have confined themselves principally to the coal countries.' Water and wind powered early mills, but coal powered industrial expansion. George Stephenson, the railway entrepreneur, declared: 'The strength of Britain lies in her iron and coal beds ... The Lord Chancellor now sits on a bag of wool [the woolsack] ... He ought rather to sit on a bag of coals, though it might not prove so comfortable a seat.'

Abraham Darby, a Quaker ironfounder, pioneered the use of coal – or rather coke – when, in the early eighteenth century, he moved from

---

* Wedgwood knew what he was doing when he produced 'Queen's Ware' pottery, with its regal connotations, for sale in his London showrooms, visited by 'shoals of ladies'. But the internal market was not the only one: thanks to his trade catalogues, often published in foreign languages, 80 per cent of Wedgwood's products were sold abroad.

† In India a local hand-spinner took 50,000 man hours to process 100 pounds of cotton; in 1780 a Crompton mule did the same job in 2,000 hours; a hundred-spindle mule, in 1790, took 1,000 hours, and a power-assisted mule, in 1795, 300 hours. By 1825 the Roberts automatic mule processed the cotton in a mere 135 man hours.

Bristol up the Severn to Coalbrookdale, Shropshire, and used it to fuel his blast furnace there in the early eighteenth century. The iron rods he manufactured went to the Birmingham area, where hundreds of small-scale metalworkers squatted on the common land, digging out the shallow coal for fuel, and making locks, scythes, nails, hinges, tools, buttons, buckles, guns, pans and myriad other metal objects. William Hutton, a visitor to Birmingham in 1741, marvelled at the activity of the Brummies: 'I was surprised at the place, but more so at the people. They were a species I had never seen. They possessed a vivacity I have never beheld: I had been among dreamers but now I saw men awake.'

Coalfields were being mined in South Wales, Cumberland, West Yorkshire, Derbyshire and Nottinghamshire, around Bristol, Staffordshire, Shropshire, Warwickshire and the Forest of Dean. Largest of all were the north-east coalfields, which supplied London and the east coast. By the early eighteenth century the coalfields of Durham and Newcastle had an extensive system of wooden waggonways, or 'railways', as they would become known. Thomas Newcomen's steam engine was first used successfully in 1712 at Conygree, near Dudley, to pump water from coal mines. In 1750 the output of coal was 4.3 million tons a year; by 1800, with Watts' improved steam engines, it was 14 million tons.

All this changed the way the British worked and lived and where they lived.

In the nineteenth century the number of coal miners in Britain rose to nearly half a million, concentrated in mining communities such as Merthyr Tydfil, Abergavenny, Tynemouth, Durham and Wigan: the 1851 census records that in these places between a quarter and a third of the population were coal miners. In agricultural societies the harvest was paramount; people were dependent on the local ecosystem for vegetable outputs — for food, shelter and clothing — because transport was expensive, low-capacity and unreliable. Coal and cheap power removed what the economic historian E. A. Wrigley has called the 'photosynthetic constraint'.[15] When coal is consumed, it produces 400 times more energy than is taken to extract it and only the equivalent of a sixth of that energy is used to transport it.[16]

Manufacturers needed power, transport, communications and an amenable labour force. Regional specialisation clustered in what had previously been peripheral areas of the country where power was plentiful and, as it happened, regulations and controls were lax. Factory production with armies of 'operatives' encouraged even denser clusters of population, most of whom were recruited from the immediate countryside.

Cotton manufacturing was well established in Lancashire by the early 1700s, but the second half of the century saw fundamental changes in the methods of production. Steam-powered machinery replaced hand working and production was reorganised to put all the various processes in one building. Instead of working at home on part of the process Lancastrians were regimented into factories to tend machines. The processes were broken down into tasks that were relatively simple and required little skill and could even be undertaken by children. Richard Arkwright, ex-barber and wig-maker, was the organisational genius responsible. He developed cotton mills along the River Derwent and the Cromford Canal in Derbyshire in the later eighteenth century, housing his workers around the towering six- and seven-storey factories.

In 1789 Lord Tirrington commented that the levels of population in Cromford made it look 'like a Chinese town. The simple peasant is changed into the impudent mechanic.' Arkwright's example was emulated by others: Jedediah Strutt at Belper, with its famous waterwheel; Thomas Evans at Darley Abbey, also on the River Derwent, where the workers lived in three-storey terraced dwellings. In 1785 Arkwright and his partner David Dale built the first of the great mills at New Lanark, on the Clyde. Low Scottish wages, Arkwright boasted, would allow him 'to take a razor to the throats of the mills of Lancashire' – if he could attract the workers. David Dale provided houses for 200 families from Skye as encouragement to choose his mill rather than emigration to America.[17] Dale's advert sought families 'having three children fit for work, above nine years of age'. There were about 900 cotton mills in Britain by 1797 but only a third operated on the Arkwright model. Most were smaller and more specialised. Spinning was more suited to the factory system than weaving, so 50,000 hand-loom weavers were still at work in the cottages in Lancashire in the mid-nineteenth century.

As Britain became the workshop of Europe, it also began to export people. Aberdeen was a centre for agricultural improvement and from there specialists went as far afield as Russia and the Ukraine to sell their skills. Engineers and miners went round the world. Between 1760 and 1780 there was an increase in emigration. In a revolutionary period the most adventurous became economic migrants. The government was so concerned at the loss of tenants and workers that it carried out an investigation between December 1773 and March 1776 into the causes and composition of migration. Lacking statistics, the government ordered customs officers to keep a tally of departures. A study of 9,500 emigrants has shown that the largest proportion came from London, Yorkshire, Northern Ireland, central Scotland and the Highlands. The southerners were mainly young, single, underemployed tradesmen 'bound for temporary servitude in Pennsylvania, Maryland and Virginia'.[18] The northerners went mainly as families, even with servants. They were older, more financially sound, and did not arrive in America as bonded servants. Instead they were looking for land in the New World. The outbreak of the American War of Independence put a temporary halt to the flow of British emigrants. However, in 1803 the government passed the Passenger Act, which attempted to support the interests of landlords, especially in the Highlands, who complained about the loss of tenants. The Act demanded high standards from passenger ships but increased the costs beyond the reach of poorer emigrants. This, though, was the last decade when a British government would have a perception that the country was short of people.

When Defoe descended from the bleak moors towards Halifax, he noted the scattered cottages of the home textile workers. By the mid-nineteenth century the factory system dominated the Calder valley, as it still did (though rapidly disappearing) when I counted the chimneys in the late 1950s. Small villages and scattered hamlets had swollen and coalesced into an almost continuous urban ribbon: mills, pubs, chapels and ranks of stone terraced houses were hemmed within the steep valley slopes from Dewsbury, Brighouse, Elland, Halifax, Sowerby Bridge to Mytholmroyd. The mill at Copley, where my father was working when it closed in the early 1970s, is well known to industrial historians. The mill complex was launched on a wave of Victorian optimism at the same time as the Great Exhibition in Crystal Palace (which opened on 1 May 1851), where Yorkshire woollen manufacturers proudly displayed their wares. Edward Akroyd was a prosperous Halifax worsted manufacturer who had inherited £1.75 million from his father. (In the 1950s, although the industry was on the skids, the mill-owners still drove along the Calder valley in their Rolls-Royces and parked their Mediterranean-going yachts on the canal.) He decided to build a model village at Copley, a street of sturdy back-to-back houses leading to the mill with its barbican of an entrance. In 1859 he constructed a more ambitious village, modestly named Akroydon, next to his Haley Hill mills. The great Victorian architect George Gilbert Scott was the master-planner and architect of the soaring All Souls Church. The Gothic style was used, with plenty of expensive carved detail, as 'Mr Akroyd is very desirous of keeping up the old English notion of a village'. Already the English were unsure about their Industrial Revolution, with its noise, dirt and grime; even mill-owners like Akroyd harked back to a mythical medieval rural idyll. But not Titus Salt. He revelled in the achievements of industry and the promise of the future.

In the Aire valley, alongside the Leeds and Liverpool Canal and the Leeds to Skipton railway he conceived a new mill and its satellite town: Saltaire. When the complex opened, in 1853, Titus Salt declared:

> I looked around for a site suitable for a large manufacturing establishment ... It is also, from the beauty of its situation, and the salubrity of the air a most desirable place for the erection of dwellings. Far be it from me to do anything to pollute the air or the water of the district ... I hope to draw around me a population that will enjoy the beauties of this neighbourhood – a population of well-paid, contented, happy operatives.[19]

Unfortunately in most of the country industrialisation did not take place in such a planned or philanthropic manner. Industrial settlements – not always obviously urban – spread like a fungus. Power reduced distance, and shrank geographical space (it was said that the railways had the effect of making Britain one-sixth of its former size) and it also made the country and its regions much more varied in terms of industrial specialisation, energy consumption and the agglomeration of people.*

The coalfields, London and other ports boomed while some agricultural areas changed little. In the first half of the nineteenth century the share of the national total of business income taxes paid by Lancashire and Yorkshire residents rose from 11 per cent to 23 per cent, while London's fell by about a third to 27 per cent. Population rose much faster in the industrial areas – trebling in Lancashire, Yorkshire, Cheshire and Monmouthshire – while in most rural counties in the south and east, the population did not even double. Nineteen of the twenty fastest-growing towns in Britain in the eighteenth century were to be found on or near coalfields. By 1841 thirty-five of the fifty biggest towns were close to coalfields. So national statistics, which appear with increasing frequency at this time, can be misleading. Between 1750 and 1800 real wages rose by 20 per cent in the industrial north-west, while the national average fell by 60 per cent. In 1830 farm labourers' wages were pitiful: they bought only half the bread and a quarter of the beer that they could acquire a century earlier.[21]

Poor-relief payments shot up – in the agricultural areas of the south and east. In contrast, the standard of living of industrial workers rose. It is not surprising that John Naismith commented in 1790, about Scotland's

---

* In peasant economies geographical variation produces differences in energy consumption of 20:1 – varying with the natural productivity of the Earth. With the capture of mineral energy differences increased to 1,162:1.[20]

linen industry, which employed about quarter of a million men, women and children: 'The linen manufacture has been the most universal source of wealth and happiness introduced into Scotland. To how many thousands has it afforded bread for these forty years past?'[22]

Unfortunately, in spite of John Naismith's optimistic words, happiness was not universal. Unplanned industrialisation and mushrooming urban growth inflicted drastic problems of pollution and public health in the crowded rookeries and tenements. In the most backward agricultural zones peasants clung to minute landholdings, only surviving from one potato harvest to the next.

Those who suffered most, however, were the involuntary migrants – black African slaves transported like cattle to plantations in the Americas. These unfree workers fuelled Britain's industries overseas. They generated much of the wealth that paid for the great Georgian country houses, provided the surplus for investing in Britain's industrial revolution and laid the foundation for the British Empire. Many also came to Britain to live as slaves in the homes of wealthy families, or found themselves eking out a living in the ports.

When I worked on the West Indian island of Montserrat in the mid-1990s, one of our first tasks was to try to locate the sites of plantations, which had covered much of the island from the seventeenth century. One day, following a track through the middle of the rainforest, Julian Munby (my colleague in the project) and I found ourselves standing on a tall, elegant, ashlar-stone bridge. This spanned a deep ravine, or *ghaut* (the word was imported from India), and looked completely anomalous. We soon discovered why the bridge was there in the middle of the forest. It led to 'Paradise', a grand Georgian house that would not have looked out of place in a Jane Austen novel. The ground outside was littered with sherds of Staffordshire teacups, Bristol wares, plant pots and clay pipes. 'Paradise' was derelict; enormous palms with massive buttressed roots grew through the building. The rainforest had regenerated, and reclaimed the plantation.

In the seventeenth and eighteenth centuries 'improving' British plantation-owners were horrified by this dark, miasmic, primitive forest. It cried out for the axe and the torch. To the British, forests were a health risk; they exuded harmful vapours that caused fevers and agues. Open vistas conformed to the British aesthetic ideal. Today the nearby island of Antigua appears barren, yet in 1671 it was heavily forested – that is until the governor brought in 4,000 slaves to clear the woods 'for more health for the English'.[23] When the soil then eroded from the hills, the slaves carried it back up again.

Our plantation may have been named 'Paradise', but this must have been deeply ironic to the slaves who worked it. The British did not develop West Indian islands as self-contained sustainable societies: rather they were a network of slave-driven factories manufacturing tobacco, indigo and, above all and most profitably, sugar and rum. Montserrat is dotted with the ruins of windmills, which mark the plantations, and were one source of their power. Most energy came from slaves. While Britain itself underwent an energy revolution, plantations relied on human muscle in the West Indies. The British imperial vision looked west. Canada had vast resources of fish, fur and timber; the American colonies, as well as being a source of raw materials, were an increasingly properous market for British goods; the West Indies generated wealth from the slave trade and its plantations.

Sugar plantations began on Barbados in the mid-seventeenth century. Within a decade the island supported 40,000 people (still mainly white indentured labour), and was one of the most densely populated agricultural regions in the world. Within a generation all of the forest had been cleared and the soil exhausted. So another European species – cattle – was imported in an attempt to improve fertility.

Jamaica was the most profitable of the islands for the British. The first state-sponsored colony – by Cromwell – it was nevertheless a frontier society, Britain's Wild West.[24] Jamaica was ten times as big as all Britain's other sugar-producing islands. By 1673 there were 10,000 black slaves on the island; thirty years later 45,000 laboured on about 245 plantations. By then the number of whites on Jamaica had gone down to 7,000. Sugar plantations were brutal but well-organised factories. Cane had to be cut, and crushed and boiled within forty-eight hours or else the juice would spoil. It was tough, hot, back-breaking work. On average a slave produced between one and two tons of sugar, then died.

As many as 12 million Africans may have suffered the transatlantic Middle Passage to the New World from West Africa. An estimated 2 million did not survive the dreadful treatment on board. At the same time Native American populations were not just decimated: they probably lost about 90 per cent of their numbers owing to their lack of resistance to European diseases such as smallpox, measles and influenza. The Native Americans were largely replaced by white Europeans and black Africans in the world's largest transfer of populations. Slavery had been taken for granted for centuries, but now, at its peak, attitudes began to change.

As early as 1787 a tract was published in London entitled 'Thoughts and sentiments on the evil and wicked traffic of the slavery and commerce of the human species'. The author knew what he was writing about. His name was Ottobah Cuguano. This African demanded freedom for his people and forecast calamity for those 'criminal nations' who profited from slavery.

Two years later, in 1789, a friend of Cuguano's and fellow abolitionist published his autobiography: *The Interesting Narrative of the Life of Olaudah Equiano, or Gustavus Vassa the African*. Equiano's book was remarkable not just in that an African slave – seized when he was about eleven years old, from his village in eastern Nigeria – was able to tell his story directly to a white audience, but in that he also turned it into a successful business opportunity. Rather than seeking sponsorship from Quakers or other abolitionists, Equiano published the book himself, by recruiting subscribers, and sold it for 7 shillings from key London bookshops. By 1794 the book had gone through nine editions; it was also published in America and translated into German, Russian and Dutch. Equiano had a best-seller on his hands – a picaresque tale, but one which presented an African as a cultivated, Christian human being – and slavery as a thoroughly rotten system. His publishing success came just in time: the Pitt government and the war with France had by 1793 turned the tide against the reformist wave which promoted abolitionism and the ideas of Tom Paine. The abolitionist cause was suspended for the duration of the war.

When only about twelve years old Equiano had been bought in Virginia by an English naval lieutenant, Michael Pascal, who had given him the name 'Gustavus Vassa' – and regular blows to remind him to answer to it. At least the disorientated and lonely young slave had been fortunate, on his voyage to England in a cargo vessel carrying tobacco, to be befriended by a kindly young American of sixteen named Richard Baker. Baker had died at sea two years later and Equiano remembered him fondly: 'A man superior to prejudice, and who was not ashamed to notice, to associate with, and to be the friend and instructor of one who was ignorant, a stranger, of a different complexion, and a slave.'

Like many black slaves Equiano had served in the Royal Navy, experiencing the shocking violence of life on a warship fighting the French in the Seven Years War; but he had also benefited from the companionship of many other children on board (Royal Navy recruits could be as young as six or eight)[25] and educated sailors such as the ship's clerk on the *Aetna*, in 1762, who had taught him writing and arithmetic. On the *Namur* there had been a school for the young sailors, where he had learned to read. After an eventful six years, which took him from Orkney and Turkey to Canada with General Wolfe, Equiano had found himself based on the Isle of Wight – 'this delightful island' – where he had met another black slave, who rushed to greet 'one of his own countrymen ... as if I had been his brother, though we had never seen each other before'. Then he was back into action against the French.

When, in December 1762 at the end of the war, his ship had been ordered to London to be paid off, Equiano had been happy, believing that, as a baptised Christian, he would be given his liberty.* But Captain Pascal's charity had its limits. In Deptford Equiano had suddenly been bundled into the ship's barge and, in spite of the protests of his ship-mates, ferried to Gravesend, into the hands of James Doran, captain of the *Charming Sally,* bound for the West Indies, who had told the sixteen-year-old, 'You are now my slave.' In return for over five years of faithful service Pascal had repaid Equiano by keeping his pay, his prize money and even his coat and his books.

The distraught young man had found himself bound for the tiny vol-canic island of Montserrat. There he had had the relative good luck to be purchased by a reasonable owner, the Quaker Robert King.†

Though he records the everyday cruelties which he witnessed on Montserrat and many other islands, Equiano was able to make and save enough money to buy his freedom after three years and return to London in 1766. The parish register in Soham, Cambridgeshire, records that on 7 April 1792 under the name 'Vassa', he married Miss Susanna Cullen, daughter of Mr Cullen of Ely. Unfortunately his wife and first daughter were both dead within five years. On the wall of St Andrew's Church, Chesterton, a plaque records:

ANNA MARIA VASSA
Daughter of Gustavus Vassa the African
She died July 21 1797
Aged 4 years

... know that there lies beside this humble stone
a child of colour happily not thine own,
Her father born of Africa's sun-burnt race,
Torn from his native fields, ah, foul disgrace ...

Equiano died himself shortly afterwards, on 31 March 1797, leaving his remaining daughter well provided for. Like St Patrick 1,200 years earlier,

* Slavery was partly justified by characterising black people as heathens. In the eighteenth and nineteenth centuries there is increasing evidence in English parish registers of slave baptisms, for example Benjamin Moor in York Minster in 1777, and 159 black baptisms in London between 1780 and 181.
† By 1763 the Society of Friends had set itself firmly against slavery, but Robert King clearly ignored the strictures of his religion.

Equiano emerged from the anonymous barbarism of slavery to record for posterity the voice of a courageous, determined and incredibly adaptable human being, 'the most important single literary contribution to the campaign for abolition'.[26]

From the 1760s opposition had increased to slavery. For decades there had been confusion about the status of blacks in England. In 1706 Lord Chief Justice Holt had ruled 'that as soon as a Negro comes into England he becomes free'. However, this was not universally accepted. A ruling in 1729, as a result of lobbying by West Indian slave-owners, declared: 'We are of the opinion, that a slave, by coming from the West Indies, either with or without his Master, to Great Britain or Ireland, doth not become free ... and baptism does not bestow freedom on him ... We are also of the opinion, that the master may legally compel him to return to the plantation.'[27]

However, in 1762 the Lord Chancellor interpreted the law differently again, stating that a black slave who entered England was free and could not be held against his will. The matter was finally settled, thanks to a long campaign by an obscure but remarkably obstinate, determined and principled clerk from Durham named Granville Sharp. Sharp's brother William was a surgeon in Mincing Lane, London, who gave free medical advice to the poor. One morning in 1765 Sharp found a black teenager on his brother's doorstep, half beaten to death. The young man, Jonathan Strong, told them his story. A Barbadian planter and slave-owner called David Lisle had brought him to London, beaten him over the head with a pistol and thrown him out into the street. The Sharp brothers took Jonathan to hospital, where he lodged for four months until he had recovered. They then provided him with clothes and lodgings and found him a job as an errand boy in Fenchurch Street.

Two years later Lisle spotted his former slave in the street and tracked him to his lodgings. He hired two slave-hunters to seize Jonathan and handed him over to a Jamaican slave-owner, one James Kerr. This man would pay £30 when his new property was stowed on a ship bound for Jamaica. When Granville Sharp discovered that his godson (Jonathan had been baptised) was incarcerated, he applied to the magistrates for Jonathan's release. At the Mansion House the Lord Mayor said 'the lad ... was not guilty of any offence, and was therefore at liberty to go away'.

That was not the end of the matter. Kerr, the Jamaican slaver, issued a writ claiming £200 damages. Sharp's solicitors, influenced by the 1729 ruling, advised him to settle. Sharp was damned if he was going to compromise with these brutal bullies − or listen to vacillating lawyers. He took up the case with a vengeance, and educated himself in the laws of the land. He won his case and went on to challenge the 1729 ruling with his publication *A Representation of the Injustice and Dangerous Tendency of Tolerating Slavery; or of Admitting the Least Claim of Private Property in the Persons of Men, in England* (1769). In it he stated that 'a toleration of Slavery is, in effect, a toleration of inhumanity'. As a result of his campaign Granville Sharp became a champion of kidnapped slaves.

Still the law could not make up its mind. Matters came to a head with the case of James Somerset, who had escaped from his American owner in England and been recaptured. The case came before Lord Chief Justice Mansfield in 1771. Mansfield listened to the arguments and then declared that he could not decide immediately, as 'Almost insurmountable embarrassments assail us on either side. On one hand we are assured, that there are no less than 15,000 slaves now in England, who will procure their liberty should the law decide in their favour, and whose loss ... will amount to not less a sum than £700,000.' On the other hand, he went on, colony slave laws were 'altogether foreign to the object of our present enquiry'.

He dropped a broad hint that the American, Mr Stewart, should free his slave and not bring this awkward issue to a legal conclusion. Nevertheless, a judgment was sought and came down in favour of James Somerset. Blacks could not be held against their will. There was cheering and joy in the courtroom, especially on the part of the black people who had anxiously awaited the decision. However, the Mansfield judgement did not ban slavery in Britain, as is sometimes claimed. It simply said that a master could not force a slave to leave England. Over the next twenty years many slave-owners ignored the ruling and attempted to challenge it in Parliament, arguing that slavery was essential to British prosperity. The opposition sought outright abolition. Public opinion swung in their favour with the *Zong* scandal in 1781, when 133 slaves were thrown overboard from the Liverpool slave ship so that the master could claim the insurance. Olaudah Equiano and Granville Sharp took up the case. Nevertheless, the murderers went unpunished, as slaves were mere chattels; and MPs from London, Bristol and Liverpool fiercely resisted the moderate reforms that were proposed. A 1792 pamphlet published in Liverpool pronounced: 'Africans being the most lascivious of all human beings ... may it not be imagined, that the cries they let forth at being torn from their wives, proceed from the dread that they will never have the opportunity of indulging their passions in the country to which they are embarking.'

In the same year 500 petitions against the slave trade were collected from all over Great Britain.

To the British government the West Indies were the biggest colonial prize, worth more than North America. Up to 1773 the little island of Nevis, next door to Montserrat, exported three times as much to Britain as New York. Coffee, chocolate and tea were bitter drinks that appealed much more to British taste when laced with sugar. After about 1680 these drinks were fashionable, a respectable alternative to alcohol and a social stimulant. The sweet-drinks revolution had arrived.[28]

The West Indian colonies enabled the British to control this valuable — though from a purely calorific point of view useless — product. By 1801 8.3 million English people consumed about 17 pounds of sugar apiece, much of it going into the increasingly popular cup of tea and the famous English puddings. Samuel Pepys recorded in his diary in 1660 that he had come across tea, 'a China drink of which I never had drank before'. Within a century it was a national institution. In the later eighteenth century all tea came to England from China, imported by the East India Company — or smuggled illegally as the government imposed a tax of over 50 per cent. Lord North plunged relations with the 3 million colonists in North America into an irretrievable low when he had the bright idea of selling surplus tea to them at a much-reduced tax rate. He hoped that with an eye for a bargain the Americans would not notice that they were paying a tax, albeit a small one, to Britain. They did. 'No taxation without representation,' became an American battle cry. By this time the Americans were prosperous and well able, so the British thought, to contribute in taxation. Defeating the French in North America during the Seven Years War had been done at vast cost to the home country. Americans were coining money from their slave plantations and from smuggling sugar out of the West Indies to trade tax-free rum, particularly to the Indians. The British government thought that it was reasonable for its prosperous colony to contribute to its own defence.

Roderick Gordon of Carnoustie, a doctor turned trader and slave-owner, summarised the benefits of life in Virginia in 1734 with Scots phlegm:

> My situation in this Colony is tolerable and we live in the
> most plentifull country in the world, for all necessities of life;
> for our estates consist chiefly in land and negros; which negros
> make grain in plenty to raise all necessary provision within
> ourselves, as also a great deal for export; which returns us
> rum, sugar and molasses from the Caribee Islands and wines
> from other islands; and the tobacco made at the same time by
> these slaves, return us from England all necessary apparrel

for ourselves and slaves … I beg pardon for this tedious
description of our society but did thousands in Scotland know
it they would desire banishment never to return.[29]

The Americans seemed to be riding a gravy train without paying the
fare. They, of course, did not see it that way. So when the tea duty came
in, on 16 December 1773, a group of men from Massachusetts, dressed
as Indians, clambered aboard three ships loaded with tea in Boston harbour and tossed the lot into the Charles River. Tea became a talisman of
the American Revolution. (The Canadians still consume four times as
much per head as the Americans.)

The careless loss of the American colonies in 1783 might have seemed
like a serious blow to British imperial ambitions. In fact, it proved to be
no major handicap. The ex-colonies still contrived to trade with Britain,
which turned its imperial attention to the east. In Asia the East India
Company had first gained a toe-hold in India with its coastal trading
posts at Bombay, Madras and Calcutta, then in China, in 1713, at
Canton. By 1815, after a century or more of warfare with France, Britain
was the dominant world power. Instead of acquiring an empire 'by accident', through its trading companies, the British government set about
more systematically colonising territory in India, Malaya and the Pacific
– following James Cook's exploratory voyages between 1768 and 1778.
Within a decade the first colony was established in New South Wales
(1787) and then Van Diemen's Land (Tasmania, in 1803). The Reverend
John Entick proudly proclaimed in *The Present State of the British Empire*
(1794): 'The British empire is arrived at the height of Power and Glory,
to which none of the States and Monarchies upon Earth could ever lay
the like claim.'

In India alone Britain had gained a massive market for its manufactures and a reservoir of manpower to supplement its own limited population. Increasingly its human resources would be grown by seeding 'white'
colonies with loyal imperial subjects. A surprisingly large number of
those loyal subjects were Scots. One of them, a minister's son named
James Thomson, composed the words for 'Rule, Britannia' in 1740:

> *When Britain first, at heaven's command,*
> *Arose from out the azure main,*
> *This was the charter of the land,*
> *And guardian angels sung this strain:*
> *'Rule, Britannia, rule the waves;*
> *Britons never will be slaves.'*

Britannia, originally personified by the Romans, now had her own divinely inspired empire; and if the Scots and their Pictish ancestors had not been part of the first, they certainly saw the benefits of partnership in the new Britannia.*

Often the partnerships were personal: marriage between the English, Scots, Welsh and Irish elites became common. In the last third of the eighteenth century the British aristocracy went through a demographic crisis. For reasons which are unclear they failed to breed – many simply did not marry; others did not produce sons. Distinguished families such as the Queensberrys became extinct in the male line. In Monmouthshire and Glamorgan, Cambridgeshire and Yorkshire gentry families effectively disappeared. As a result about a third of landed estates passed into the hands of newcomers. Those successful in this game of territorial musical chairs accumulated land throughout the country. The Butes, for example, managed to attract four heiresses in three generations and so acquire vast estates, of 40,000 acres, in England, Wales and Scotland. Such families became British through their possessions. In the second half of the eighteenth century Scottish peers married off more than twice as many of their daughters to Englishmen as in the first half; and in the nineteenth century well-bred Scottish girls married more Englishmen than fellow countrymen. This partly reflected the fact that prosperous Scottish, Anglo-Irish and Welsh peers could afford to spend the social season in London. The Englishman George Granville Leveson-Gower landed a double Scottish catch in 1785: he married Elizabeth, Countess of Sutherland and gained 800,000 acres of her home country. Marriage was one way that the Scots infiltrated the national conduits of power; the army and colonial opportunities were others.

For centuries the Irish and Scots had travelled through Europe as mercenaries and as intellectuals. By 1800 the English had developed a taste for bellicosity, stimulated by fear of French invasion and the arch bogeyman Bonaparte. The British population was overwhelmingly young – 55 per cent were under twenty-five and a considerable propor-tion of these were red-blooded, macho males who wanted to bash foreigners. Linda Colley describes it as 'the cult of heroic endeavour and aggressive maleness that was so pronounced in patrician art and litera-ture at this time' and 'in popular ballads and songs'.[30] Newcastle colliers sang:

---

* Both in their architecture and their tombs the British emulated the Romans. In St Patrick's Cathedral, Dublin, General Sir Samuel Auchmuty appears on his tomb in the guise of a stoical, imperial Roman.

Then to parade the pitmen went
We hearts both stout and strong, man,
God smash the French we are so strong;
We'll smash them every one, man ...

If the British felt themselves ready and able to take on the world, they were joined in the enterprise by Irish Catholics, who were recruited into imperial armies in greater numbers than the Scots, Welsh and English combined. After the Act of Union of 1800 'the Irish of all descriptions entered enthusiastically into the business of empire'.[31] For them Ireland was not a land of opportunity; the expanding British empire was.

Sir Walter Scott, whose novels, along with macadamed roads, opened Scotland to a new tourist industry, recalled: 'I was born a Scotsman and a bare one. Therefore I was born to fight my way in the world.' Many, such as James Murray, did this literally. He fought alongside General James Wolfe in Quebec and in 1760 became Britain's first Governor of Canada. India, however, was where the Scots made their biggest impact, as the backbone of the East India Company.

From its initial trading posts the company found itself ruling several million Indians, thanks to the effective if brutal behaviour of Robert Clive. During the Seven Years War the Nawab of Bengal attacked the Bombay settlement of Bengal, incarcerating about a hundred British in the infamous Black Hole of Calcutta. Clive, with an army made up mainly of Indian allies, counter-attacked and defeated the Nawab at Plessey. In the words of a contemporary Indian historian Cholam Hossein Khan: 'those merchants ... found the means of becoming masters of the country'. Under the Treaty of Allahabad the East India Company gained the right to administer and tax over 20 million people.

Most mornings I walk to work in London across Horseguards Parade. The imposing statue of Clive of India guards the steps between the Treasury and the Foreign Office. He looks calm and dignified – not at all like a manic-depressive opium addict who eventually committed suicide (though Britain was notorious for suicides in the eighteenth century). The authorities replaced him with Warren Hastings, who went to school in Westminster a stone's throw away from where Clive's statue now stands. Under Hastings even more Scotsmen came to Bengal (about half the East India Company employees in his time were Scots), and with them the enquiring minds of the Scottish Enlightenment. Like Hastings, the Governor-General, many of these men studied local languages and literature. Although the British were primarily there to make money,[32] many developed a great regard for Indian culture. Hastings founded a

Madrassa – a Muslim law school – in Calcutta, claiming: 'Muslim law is as comprehensive, and as well defined, as that of most states of Europe.' Some of the East India men adopted Indian ways at home and took Indian wives. John Maxwell from near Aberdeen had at least three children by Indian women. William Fraser from Inverness subjugated the Ghurkas and married several local women, by whom he had many children, who were 'Hindus and Muslims according to the religion and caste of their mamas'.* Such liberal multiculturalism was frowned on later by the nineteenth-century imperialists of the Raj and tended to be written out of their histories of the British in India.[33]

The eighteenth-century dandy and gallant gave way to a different concept of the gentleman. The Evangelical movement encouraged the imperialist ruler to be dutiful, manly, responsible and brave. The public schools turned out such paragons (Stalky and Co.) and ensured that they experienced the whiff of cruelty that was good for their character. The Sahib – the Master – was responsible for his subjects. Increasingly the master race saw their subjects as a lesser breed. By the mid-nineteenth century the word 'nigger' appears more frequently in private correspondence. Shortly before the Indian Mutiny of 1859 one traveller commented: 'Now one hears ordinarily and from the mouths of decent folks nothing but contemptuous phrases (nigger, etc.).'[34]

Not all the Britons who went to India flourished and prospered. Half the recorded administrators in Bengal died there, succumbing to drink, drugs or disease. In spite of the fortunes that had been made the company was in debt to the tune of £8.4 million in 1784. When Hastings returned to Britain the following year, he was impeached and faced disgrace. There were military battles still to be won, too. Tipu Sultan, ruler of Mysore, mounted a ferocious campaign against the British – just one of the many problems that beset the East India Company in the late eighteenth century.† For the Indian peasantry ravaged by famine, the situation was far worse.

As a result of the company's disastrous rule in India, the India Act was passed and responsibility taken over by the government. Governor and

---

* The British nabobs, like Hastings, could return from India with fabulous wealth and set themselves up in grand country houses, targets for *femmes fatales*, like Becky Sharpe in Thackeray's *Vanity Fair*, who fantasises herself as married to an 'enormously rich' nabob, 'arrayed in an infinity of shawls, turbans, and diamond necklaces, and … mounted on an elephant'.
† One of the star exhibits in the Victoria and Albert Museum is the figure of a very jolly tiger. He is eating an Englishman, whose hat remains firmly in place. This is 'Tipoo's Tiger', actually an organ built for Tipu Sultan, a great enemy of the British. As the Victorians had to see a moral in everything, they displayed 'Tipoo's Tiger' to emphasise Britain's 'civilising mission' among the benighted people ruled by such a sadistic despot as Tipu.

generals would be appointed by the Crown and administered by the Indian Civil Service. As in Britain, the rights of peasants were swept aside for the benefit of an upcoming Bengali gentry. Tipu Sultan died fighting the British in 1799; following the example of the Romans, whom they had come to emulate, the British took his sons as hostages. Four years later the Mughal emperor bowed before British military power. By the early nineteenth century Britain ruled 40 million Indians.

India, though, was not a destination for many British emigrants. It was the more temperate colonies – North America (Canada), then Australia and New Zealand, with vast areas of available land (once the natives were wiped out by disease or aggression). In the eighteenth century the patterns of emigration in Britain were very varied. At a time when the population of England and Wales (at 8.7 million) was over six times that of Scotland (1.265 million) both nations were providing similar numbers of colonists to America; and the biggest group of all were Ulster Presbyterians – the much mythologised Scots-Irish. In the early 1720s Daniel Defoe remarked: 'If it goes on for many years more Virginia may be rather call'd Scots than an English Plantation.' It was relatively easy for the Scots to head for America, as there was regular shipping from the Clyde and even small east-coast ports. They could act as ballast on ships that had unloaded bulky American cargoes of sugar, rice and tobacco.

Similarly, ships transporting linen seed docked in Northern Ireland and returned with human cargoes. Not that a sea voyage of six to eight weeks was a pleasure cruise in the pre-steamship era: cramped, claustrophobic, disease-ridden and stinking, it was a dangerous ordeal to be endured. Janet Shaw was a cabin passenger in 1774, so relatively comfortable. She describes a twelve-day storm, waves 'mountains high', and the ship turning on its side, before the masts snapped and it righted itself. Below decks the poorer migrants stood in the dark for days, in pouring water, with no food.

After France's defeat in the Seven Years War (1763) British land speculation swept through north-east America, launching mass emigration of all classes of people from many parts of Britain. In the forefront were the 'notoriously migratory' Scots, so described by Samuel Johnson during his tour of the Highlands with James Boswell – the locals, he said, had an 'epidemick disease of wandering'; and the greatest travellers were Orcadians, recruited by the Hudson Bay Company. Their employers were confident that men brought up in such a harsh climate could endure the rigours of the Canadian fur trade, and they were not wrong. In 1800 80 per cent of the company men were from Orkney. Some returned with their savings; others married Native American women and remained in Canada.

Because of concerns about emigration and the loss of manpower it entailed, Britain kept detailed statistics in the form of a Register of Emigrants between December 1773 and March 1776. Of 9,808 men, women and children 40 per cent were Scots and the vast majority of these headed for the thirteen colonies of North America (92 per cent) — the remainder to Canada or the West Indies. Surprisingly, perhaps, most of these people came from the relatively prosperous lowlands, where they were farmers or artisans. They were not dirt-poor and desperate. As the cost of emigration was about £10, the poorest — as at all times — did not have the choice: they could not afford to leave. The exception to this was 150 indentured labourers: they had their passage paid in return for a fixed period of servitude.

Why would these people choose to leave an improving economy when Glasgow was the fastest-growing city in Europe? Behind the general economic trends there were short-term and general problems. In the countryside of Angus, Ayrshire and Lanarkshire the equivalent of English 'engrossment' was pushing large numbers of people off the land, less dramatically than the Highland Clearances, but just as effectively. To make matters worse, in 1771–2 the so-called 'rotting rains' fell incessantly. At the same time the textile industry was in crisis and thousands of weavers were thrown out of employment. In a country such as Scotland, with well-developed links to America and a transport system in place, resilient and determined people with rising expectations could make the decision to seek a better life.

However, the biggest group of British migrants at this time was from Ireland, and principally from Ulster. Between 1700 and 1820 between a quarter and half a million Irish left for America: almost a third of all immigrants into America. No group has been more mythologised than the 'Scots-Irish'[35] — a term coined in America to distinguish respectable Presbyterians from the huddled, impoverished Catholic masses who flowed into the country after the Great Famine of 1840: 'the most undesirable, the most mischievous, the most damnable element of population that could have been scraped out of the corners of the earth'.

The Scots-Irish, in contrast, were portrayed as sturdy, independent frontiersmen — and women (the northern Irish were unusual in the eighteenth century in emigrating with their families). They crossed the Allegheny Mountains, the Potomac and the Shenandoah, into the Carolinas and Georgia, through the Cumberland Gap into what became Tennessee and Kentucky; and they gave birth to heroes: Davy Crockett, Sam Huston, Stonewall Jackson; to statesmen and presidents such as Andrew Jackson, son of a Carrickfergus weaver; and to captains of industry: the Gettys from Londonderry, the Mellons from County Tyrone.

Forty per cent of the immigrants (about 250,000 people) who moved into eighteenth-century colonial America were from Ulster and half as many from the Catholic south. It is not surprising that the American statesman Benjamin Franklin visited Dublin, in 1771, to try to recruit Irish support in his struggle with the British. Nearly half his fellow countrymen were of Irish stock.

The Ulster migrants had a particularly strong sense of identity. 'Ostentatiously separate', they crossed the Atlantic in community and family groups. Most were not well-off and they were under increasing economic pressure from their populous Catholic neighbours, with whom they competed for tenancies. In Ulster there was a tradition of moving in search of opportunity. Their co-religionists who had already made the crossing reported that in America land was cheap, their religion was tolerated and there were plenty of opportunities. The ships that arrived in Londonderry laden with American flax seed for the Ulster linen industry were a ready means of transport; and for those who could not afford the price of the ticket, signing on as an indentured servant for up to seven years meant a 'free' passage. In their thousands they chose to start a new life in America. In the next century many more Irish migrants were to make the crossing, but with a greater sense of desperation.

Eleven

Living in the City

IN THE EARLY 1970s, while undertaking research on Irish archaeology, I spent a couple of winters on the island of Omey, off the Galway coast. Reachable at low tide across a wide strand of sand, Omey is a low out-crop of pink-and-grey granite. On a bad day Atlantic waves lash its west-ern coast and to the east the mainland is scarcely visible through the banks of low cloud. Then, when the skies clear, there are magnificent views across to the peaks of the Twelve Bens in Connemara.

Only a handful of people then lived on Omey. The landscape was dot-ted with the hummocky, turf-covered ruins of black-houses, the long thatched dwellings where a decreasing number of people had eked out a living as fishermen and smallholders until the early part of the twentieth century. The few survivors had moved to a string of single-storey houses built by the Irish government along a new track — though they still had no electricity or running water. The island was almost entirely pastoral when I was there; stone walls built as part of a government relief programme divided it into fields. A few people looked after the cows that grazed there, which were taken to the mainland for fattening and sale. Everywhere there were signs that Omey had once been a busy, well-populated, if not necessarily thriving, place. A surface like corduroy ran beneath the pastoral enclosures — the narrow ridges and furrows of so-called 'lazy beds'. Most of the island was covered with these tell-tale signs of cultivation. Once large numbers of peasant smallholders had system-atically dug, with spades and hoes, every square foot of land that they could get their hands on.

The most westerly house, at the end of the track near to the ocean, be-longed to a man named Bill. Sitting almost in the dark by his peat fire, we would drink brews of strong 'tay' (tea-drinking only became common in western Ireland in the nineteenth century and the then Gaelic-speakers adopted the French name: *thé*) and Bill would talk about the old days, be-fore the stone walls had been built. How the grandmothers would watch the few hobbled cattle to prevent them from straying into the crops; how the house had been full of people before almost everyone in his large family had left for the USA or for the building sites and mills of England. He himself had worked most of his life in England until he had had to return to look after his elderly parent. Bill had never married and had been left alone when his parent died. Bill was typical of his generation, born in the 1920s in western Ireland.

The 1841 Irish census recorded a population of 8,175,124 (in 1700 it was probably no more than 2 million). Disraeli said that Ireland was the most densely populated country in Europe. In fact, the census-takers probably erred on the low side, missing people who did not want to be counted. Contemporary estimates, supported by modern historical research, put the figure for the Irish population in 1841 as high as 9 million.[1]

This was an enormous number for a small country lacking in such essential resources for nineteenth-century success as coal and iron. Even Ireland's existing industries, notably textiles, were in decline and, for an island surrounded by rich seas, its fishing industry was in a poor state. Consequently, Ireland's burgeoning population was largely poor and rural. It was so numerous thanks to a relatively recent immigrant from South America: the potato.

The potato (*Solanum tuberosum*) was cultivated by the Incas on the irrigated terraces of the Andes and introduced into Europe before 1600 by the Spanish. By the later eighteenth century it had become the staple for poor Irish people. The advantages of the spud were obvious: it was nutritious, rich in vitamins B1, B2 and C, and could almost alone sustain life; it grew prolifically in the temperate, damp climate of Ireland; it was cheap and it was easy to store through the winter. The poor became dangerously dependent upon the potato, which was notoriously vulnerable to disease. Between 1816 and 1842 the crop failed, at least in part, in fourteen seasons out of twenty-seven. Many voices were raised in warning, but the Irish peasantry were trapped in a cycle of poverty, driven by high fertility and a notoriously unjust system of landholding. The high population and competition for work drove down wages: agricultural labourers earned between 8 pence and a shilling a day. The same factors kept rent high and landholdings small. Nothing generated carbohydrates more rapidly than the potato; but Ireland was a demographic disaster waiting to happen.

The population had rocketed partly because the potato was so easy to grow. Poor people married early because they could erect a simple cabin on a small patch of land, rear a family and survive on the potato crop (one acre could support a family of six) supplemented with milk, cheese and the products of the family pig. Improved medicine and peaceful conditions meant that more of their children survived. More children meant security in old age.*[2]

Irish peasants were virtually excluded from the capitalist market of distribution and exchange. Lacking cash, they owned remarkably few goods from the prolific manufactories of Britain. They were almost entirely self-sufficient and dependent on one plant. It was a dangerous strategy and there was no lack of warnings.

The crisis began in 1845 with the arrival in Ireland of a new fungal disease, *Phytophthora infestans*, which thrived in the climate and blighted the potato crop. On 7 October 1845 300 members of the Royal Agricultural Improvement Society sat down to a banquet 'comprising all the choicest viands and the rarest delicacies of the sea ... The wines, including champagne and claret, were of the richest vintage and choicest aroma.' The Earl of Devon addressed the assembly: 'The condition of the people of Ireland is steadily improving,' he asserted with lordly confidence. Another speaker announced that Ireland should imitate England, 'the proudest nation on the face of the earth'. On the same day the *Cork Examiner* reported: 'As regards potatoes, we cannot shut our eyes to the fact that the disease is extending its ravages amongst them to an extent that will not be generally known or acknowledged till the period for the digging out of the crop.' Later October saw the main harvest. Reports came in from Kilkenny, Drogheda, Limerick, and from at least seventeen other counties, of rotten, evil-smelling potato crops. On 21 October the *Wexford Independent* asked: 'What is to become of the poor people? There is a serious danger that even seed for next year may not be preserved.'

The newspaper was right: the blight returned in 1846. In 1847 it did not reappear, but the poor had no seed potatoes to plant anyway. Then the blight reappeared in 1848, to a lesser extent in 1849, and by 1850 it had run its course. The result was a catastrophe of biblical proportions. It struck hardest in the west of Ireland – in Kerry, through Galway to Mayo – where small-scale subsistence farming predominated. People began to die of starvation and far more from the disorders that preyed on the weak: dysentery, scurvy and typhus – which became known as 'Irish fever'. About a million Irish people died in the late 1840s from the effects

---

* Early marriage in Ireland may pre-date potato consumption. Dramatic population increase came at the end of the eighteenth century as children were cheap to raise and their labour was useful. The population of Ulster rose spectacularly without depending upon the potato – they preferred porridge and root vegetables. By 1820 population pressure was pushing down the age of marriage, encouraging emigration and lowering the rate of growth.

of the Great Famine, and one and a half million deserted the country, mainly for England and America. By 1911 the Irish population had halved to 4.4 million. Possibly no government of the period could have completely mitigated such a disaster[3] – certainly not one like the British government, shackled by its racial and economic prejudices.

One of the biggest political issues of the time was the question of the Corn Laws. Traditionally European countries had controlled the price of corn and the tax on imports. *Laissez-faire* economists in England, led by industrialists who wanted cheaper food for their workers, argued for a free market, where corn could be bought cheaply at its 'natural' price. The economic view of the time was that governments should not interfere and food supply should be left to private enterprise and the market. The anglophobe view of the famine, however, tends to underestimate the attempts made by the British to tackle a catastrophic situation. The government launched public works to assist with relief, such as road-building and the harbour construction at Kingston (now Dun Laoghaire); it introduced price controls, soup kitchens and food depots to distribute Indian meal – unpopular stuff, but edible nevertheless. However, contemporary economic theories hampered the aid and too little was done too late and often too bureaucratically. The economists criticised Ireland's 'want of capital' and 'want of industry' and the dreadful tendency to allow excess population to 'loiter upon the land'.

Scotland also suffered serious crop failure at the same time as Ireland. There, landlords were able to feed their tenants, which rarely happened in Ireland. The large Irish landlords and the English were not forgiven for their failure, though neither were entirely to blame. In the post-famine period middle-size farmers prospered as their holdings increased and livestock-rearing expanded. The division of land between sons was abandoned and instead one son inherited it. This resulted in an increase in the age of marriage and, in some cases, a reluctance to marry at all. As the peasantry died or fled the country, the proportion of Catholic priests in the population doubled from 1: 3,000 to 1: 1,500.

The Irish migrants were often weak, sick and poverty-stricken. They did not usually find a charitable welcome on their arrival – if they arrived alive. When Dr John Griscon descended into the hold of the *Ceylon*, newly arrived at Staten Island from Liverpool, he witnessed a scene from Hell: 'emaciated half-nude figures – crouching in their berths', covered in sores and their own filth and unable to move since leaving Liverpool. On board there were 115 cases of typhus. Dr Griscon reported: 'The Black Hole of Calcutta was a mercy compared with the holds of such vessels.' Just a short, breezy boat ride away from Staten Island lies the cemetery of New York's black slaves, on Wall Street. The Irish refugees entered the throbbing, violent, exciting New World one layer above the blacks in the competitive compost heap of New York.

In attempting to escape the stark realities of subsistence farming, the Irish peasants who crossed the seas to Liverpool, Glasgow or New York found themselves in the maw of a new phenomenon: the disease-ridden industrial mega-city. In Boston, Massachusetts, a city census reported that the children of the Irish districts were 'literally born to die' – the average age of the dead was under thirteen and a half years. The twin evils of the city: crime and disease, were seen as part of the Irish problem. As British industrial cities grew apace, local authorities and the medical profession could not cope with the enormous public-health problems. The Irish were made convenient scapegoats.

Thomas Carlyle, one of the most influential of nineteenth-century commentators but no friend of the supposed lesser species of humans such as 'poor blackhead niggers' or the Irish, wrote, in 1839, how these members of the Celtic or Milesian race 'darken all our towns'. In their depravity, he claimed, the Irishman would tackle any work, whatever the wage, provided it kept him in potatoes. These immigrants worked too hard and too cheaply. Lodged in his pigsty the Celtic savage drove out the honest Anglo-Saxon and: 'There he abides in his squalor and unreason, in his falsity and drunken violence, on the ready-made nucleus of degradation and disorder.'[4] Anthony Trollope satirised Carlyle in *The Warden* (1855) as Dr Pessimist Anticont, the Scotsman who could not write English, yet 'popularity spoilt him for all further use, as it has done many another'.

With pundits of the day like Carlyle pumping out such stuff from his Chelsea study it is hardly surprising that the Irish were blamed for the social and environmental evils in which they found themselves – not just in England and the United States. Presbyterian Scotland erected a bulwark of anti-Papist and anti-Irish societies, tracts and papers, such as *The Protestant*, which appeared in Glasgow as early as 1818. By the mid-century the drums of tribal hostilities were beating louder. The Scottish Protestant Associations and the *Scottish Protestant* newspaper emerged as the 1851 census showed that the Scottish population of 2,888,742 included 207,367 Irish immigrants. John Steill published a racist tract entitled *Scotland for the Scotch*, bewailing the dreadful consequences of Irish immigration, which brought 'clouds of the vilest specimens of the human animal on the face of the earth', infecting the pure, hard-working Protestant Scotch with 'Irish crime, Irish dirt, Irish disease and Irish degradation'.[5]

Much early industry had developed in rural areas, along rivers, such as the Severn, Derwent and Calder. The phenomenon of the age, however, was the industrial city and it was this, with its opportunities for work, that attracted the Irish most of all people. In the late eighteenth and nineteenth centuries Liverpool expanded faster than any other place in Britain. In 1700 there were a mere 1,210 Liverpudlians, and it ranked 257th in the urban league tables. In 1801 the population had risen to just over 92,000, by which time it was the third-ranking city in Britain, and then soared to over 286,000 in 1841.[6]

Liverpool's mushrooming success had little to do with the expanding economy of London or southern England. The place was relatively isolated from the south: not a single stagecoach ran to London (or anywhere else) and there were only four carriers a week to the capital. Instead Liverpool looked west. One hundred and twenty-five vessels a week plied the Irish Sea, while 106 vessels departed for North America and the West Indies and forty-eight for Africa. In comparison a mere twenty-eight vessels a week were destined for Continental Europe.[7]

Liverpool also dominated the Atlantic slave trade, surpassing London and Bristol, partly because of its proximity to the new northern manufacturing areas and their saleable goods. Over a hundred slaving ships, mostly specially designed for the purpose to minimise space and maximise efficient delivery of the goods, were plying their trade when the British abolished slavery in 1807. Needless to say, Liverpool merchants prophesied total doom if the trade — what British sugar merchant John Carey described, in 1695, as 'the most profitable of any we drive' — should cease.[8] As the abolitionists ratcheted up the anti-slavery movement from the 1780s, Liverpool merchants and politicians were among their most vociferous opponents, arguing that the slave trade was essential to their city's prosperity, and to the nation's. They were supported by their commercial rivals in other slave ports from Glasgow, Whitehaven, Lancaster and Bristol to Southampton, Portsmouth, Cowes and Poole. In the end these descendants of Sir John Hawkins, the first English slave-trader in 1562, were overtaken by the mood of the times. A small group of Quakers along with ex-slaves such as Equiano, launched the anti-slavery movement; their ideas chimed with the thinking of the industrial age and were echoed by the increasingly influential Baptists, Methodists and even economists.

In Birmingham the Baptists grew in the first half of the nineteenth century from a minor sect to a congregation of 4,000 members in ten churches. With an all-encompassing missionary zeal Baptists believed every soul could potentially be converted and saved. For the purpose of evangelising the world God had given Britain an empire 'on which the sun never set', declared Birmingham preacher John Angell James. With the imagery of the improving agriculturalist he urged his young listeners to rise to the challenge of saving souls:

> But yours is the task, the glorious and immortal work of
> enclosing, and draining and cultivating this mental waste,
> of sowing it with the seeds of thought, of causing it to bring
> forth and blossom, and of adding it to the territory of mind,
> from which it now seems almost entirely cut off. Your object
> is compassionate … to terminate the reign of evil for the
> universal empire of mercy!

Samuel Pearce, minister of Cannon Street in Birmingham, declared: 'A Christian's heart ought to be as comprehensive as the universe. The Asiatic, the Americans and the Africans – all are our brethren.'[9]

Practical manufacturers and utilitarian theorists had less pious motives for their opposition to slavery: they were advocates of the concept of free trade and free labour; of their rights to hire and fire as the market demanded. To them slavery, the ultimate system of tied workers, was an inefficient anachronism, a relic of the world of feudalism. To many workers, imbibing the intoxicating ideas of Tom Paine and the American and French revolutionaries, slavery was anathema, the ultimate stain on the rights of man.*

Ironically, it was also in part because of free-trade '*laissez-faire*' economics that the conditions in early industrial cities were so awful. It was not government's job to interfere in the manufacturers' right to make money. In theory – and the theory contained a degree of truth – British industry had thrived precisely because it was not subject to a centralised, interventionist bureaucracy like that of France. Burgeoning cities – Liverpool, Glasgow, Manchester, Leeds and Birmingham – spread without planning, infrastructure and public services. These monster cities, with their crowded, insanitary conditions, were breeding grounds for disease. Tuberculosis – the 'consumption' seen in romantic novels and operas – killed one in four of its victims (and 40 per cent in Paris – Britain was not unique). Fevers were rife: diphtheria and scarlet fever decimated the young. 'Enteric fevers', notably typhoid, scythed through the urban poor and sometimes the more privileged. Typhoid, probably bred in the cesspools of Windsor Castle, claimed the life of Prince Albert in 1861.

International communications brought new killers. Cholera seeped

---

* Thomas Paine, the Thetford (Norfolk) radical, published *The Rights of Man* in 1791/2 in response to Burke's *Reflections on the Revolution in France*. In it he advocated democracy, civil rights and social security. He asked: 'Why is it that scarcely any are executed but the poor?'

out of India in the 1820s, first reaching China, Japan and Russia. A second pandemic began in 1829, descending on London in 1832, where 7,000 died, and then the slums of Manchester. Victims suffered a particularly foul death — racked by diarrhoea, vomiting, cramps and a raging thirst.[10] The big cities, with their open sewers, fetid streets and tenements packed with people and livestock, were killing grounds for their own population and particularly the young. Of 350,000 deaths in England and Wales in 1842 nearly a quarter were children less than a year old, and 140,000 were children under five years. At the same time life expectancy at birth in Liverpool and Manchester was 28.1 years and 26.6 years respectively. In Glasgow the average dropped from thirty-five years in 1820 to twenty-seven years in 1841. People's chances in the statistics of death depended upon where they lived. Even in the cities the leafy gardens of the middle classes and the factory owners — 'the breezy heights of Cheetham Hill, Broughton and Pendleton', in Manchester — were safer than the crowded tenements. Yet cities were not as severely segregated and zoned as some commentators implied. Cholera and TB were no respecters of class. Between 1820 and 1870 there was no significant improvement in the expectation of life in England. The rapid rise in the proportion of people moving into deadly industrial cities almost certainly accounts for this.[11]

Voices were raised in opposition to this casual and careless waste of life. Edwin Chadwick, the son of a Nonconformist and one-time assistant to the great utilitarian philosopher Jeremy Bentham, had written: 'In England, abundance of useful things are done by individuals which in all other countries are done by government or not at all.' Fire services, madhouses and gaols might be privately owned, but Chadwick realised that if the public health problem was to be tackled, then government needed to put a national policy into action. In 1842 Chadwick produced his *Report on the Sanitary Conditions of the Labouring Population of Great Britain*. It made an enormous impact. No one yet understood the science of killer diseases, but Chadwick rightly assumed filthy conditions had something to do with it. In Glasgow, 'There were no privies or drains there, and the dung heaps received all filth which the swarm of wretched inhabitants could give; and we learned that a considerable part of the rent of the houses was paid by the produce of the dungheaps!'*

---

* Earlier commentators made similar observations. At the time of the Great Plague of 1665 William Boghurst in *Loimographia* noted that the causes of the plague were ... 'thickness of the inhabitants; those living as many families in a house; living in cellars; want of fitting accommodations, of good fires, good dyett, washing, want of good conveyances of filth; standing and sticking waters; dunghills, excrements, dead bodies lying unburied and putrefying; churchyards too full crammed; unseasonable weather ...'[12]

In the industrial cities open cesspools and drains, rubbish heaps and even burial grounds seeped into and mingled with the water supplies. Families and their animals crowded promiscuously into damp cellars. And conditions were not just bad in the large cities. The Brontë sisters lived in Haworth, a Yorkshire mill town on the River Worth, south of Keighley. This was not an isolated rural 'Brigadoon' world, as portrayed by their first biographer, Mrs Gaskell, and by Hollywood; it was the heartland of the burgeoning Industrial Revolution. When Patrick Brontë arrived as minister to Haworth in April 1820, the population had risen by a fifth in the previous decade to 4,668; and it grew by another third in the next twenty years. As Haworth became more crowded, its inadequate water supply, polluted by the 'effluvium' from middens and privies, became increasingly lethal. Haworth was as deadly a place as the worst rookeries of London: over 40 per cent of its children died before reaching the age of six, and the average age of death was twenty-five. When tuberculosis (consumption) struck down Emily Brontë, aged thirty, she was, like many of her less illustrious neighbours, the victim of her toxic environment. Charlotte wrote: 'The galloping consumption has merited its name.'[13]

In 1845 a young German immigrant produced a bitter polemic against such conditions. His name was Friedrich Engels. *The Condition of the Working Class in England* made much less impact at the time than Chadwick's report of three years earlier, not least because it was published in Germany, and only appeared in Britain, in English, in 1892. Engels was not a practical reformer. For him Manchester was a laboratory experiment: a place where manufacture and the working class would act as a catalyst for revolution. Engels described the foul living conditions, the polluted landscape, child labour, the sexually rapacious mill-owners (Engels came to Manchester to work in his father's textile business, Ermen and Engels) and — inevitably — the most abject of humans, the Irish. Engels peered at them through the magnifying glass of his political theory as if they were an alien species: 'The facile character of the Irishman, his crudity, which places him but little above the savage, his contempt for all humane enjoyments, in which his very crudeness makes him incapable of sharing, his filth and poverty, all favour drunkenness.'[14]

Engels conveyed the impression that all Manchester's workers, a lumpenproletariat, lived in abject poverty — there was no 'respectable', wage-earning working class in his analysis. Manchester's porters, clerks, weavers and shop assistants did not suit the bourgeois revolutionary's promotion of the proletarian uprising. Engels's wished-for revolution never came and he took to fox-hunting in Cheshire, holding soirées at his

London home in Regent's Park and subsidising Karl Marx's great endeavours in the British Library.

In contrast, the Welsh and northern working classes took to Methodism,* the 'real religion of Yorkshire', as it was known. John Wesley's evangelical 'Society of Methodists' separated from the Church of England in 1795. In spite (or because) of the fact that Methodists and other Nonconformists were riven by dissent and argument they gained huge numbers of converts in the new raw industrial camps, where people were seeking to build some sort of communal life at a time of cholera and, often, unemployment. Methodism advocated personal self-control, temperance and teetotalism as a solution to the chaos and arbitrariness of the contemporary world; and in the valleys of South Wales and West Yorkshire choral singing (from the later nineteenth century) provided entertainment and inspiration in a hard world.† The first religious census in Wales, in 1851, recorded 2,813 chapels and meeting houses attended by 87 per cent of worshippers.‡

Nonconformists increasingly became a radical political force. Pressure from them induced Parliament to pass the first piece of UK legislation (and the first Act to treat Wales separately from England since 1543) to treat Wales as a separate ethnic unit: the 1881 Sunday Closing Act for Wales, which forced Welsh pubs to close on Sundays.[15] Later, Conservative, Liberal and Labour clubs appeared to provide a respectable front for those who wanted a drink on Sundays.

The issue divided the Welsh; one frustrated and thirsty worker wrote to the *Merthyr Express*:

> How would these very good people like to live days, weeks
> and months underground without a sight of the pub? ...
> Oh, these very generous people have their nice cosy clubs or
> homes which they enjoy every day. But the collier has to live
> in discomfort in a small home, and for nearly six months
> in every year never sees the sun, except on the first day of
> the week.

---

* The Welsh Methodists were distinctly Calvinistic and labelled liberal Wesleyans ... as 'Arminianist'.

† When I worked in a Huddersfield foundry, in 1969, some of the men, members of the famous local choral society, would discuss the technicalities of singing Handel and Wagner over their tea break.

‡ It also recorded a large number of non-church-attenders. Victorian England and Wales became increasingly secular. 'It is not that the Church of God has lost the great towns,' the Reverend A. F. Winnington-Ingram wrote in 1896; 'it never had them.'

One solution was to walk three miles: a *bona fide* traveller was entitled to a drink.

At the end of the first decade of the twentieth century two-thirds of the Welsh population lived in Glamorgan and Monmouth. Between 1851 and the turn of the century the population of Cardiff rose from 18,000 to 164,000; and 400,000 left the rural areas. The rural–industrial division in Wales was also becoming pronounced politically, with the Liberals most focused on agrarian problems. In 1900 the Scot Keir Hardie (1856–1915) became Wales's first Labour Member of Parliament, for Merthyr. Five years later it was rightly predicted that Wales, 'a hot-bed of Liberalism and Non-conformity in the past ... would become a hot-bed of socialism and real religion in the future'.[16] By the end of the Great War class, rather than religion and ethnicity, was the fundamental issue in Welsh politics. When Lloyd George's Liberal government decided not to nationalise the mines in Wales in 1921 there was a decisive shift to Labour. Rural Welsh-speaking areas were politically marginalised and in the English-speaking industrialised south, ancient battles continued to be waged on the rugby pitch at Cardiff Arms Park.

In spite of alarming medical reports and lurid political polemics the nineteenth-century industrial cities were not simply places of filth, degradation and oppression. Workers came to them usually by choice, to improve their wages, to escape the grind and poverty of agriculture, the uncertainty of cottage industries, the power of landowners, and to enjoy the excitement and vitality of urban life.

Awareness of the problems began to stimulate action. A rash of reports into the social conditions of British towns highlighted the squalor, the lack of clean water, adequate sanitation and decent housing. The cholera epidemics of 1832 and 1837–8 shocked even British politicians out of their customary apathy where such issues were concerned. One Leeds Nonconformist minister argued that the city was 'the nidus of a new commonwealth' and that the 'operatives' should not be thought of as the insensate 'masses' – a term which denied the individuality and energy of real people.[17] The new industrial towns were themselves distinctive places in their own right, not simply a uniform species of urban 'Coketowns' as depicted so effectively by Charles Dickens in *Hard Times*:*
'It was a town of unnatural red and black like the painted face of a savage, inhabited by "the Hands" – a race who would have found more favour with some people, if Providence had seen fit to make them only hands,

---

* Dickens was much influenced by Thomas Carlyle and his belief that the industrial city promoted social degeneration, spiritual collapse and materialism. Dickens wrote to the great panjandrum: 'No man knows your book better than I.'

or, like the lower creatures of the seashore, only hands and stomachs'.

To Dickens the industrial city was hostile, repetitive, mechanistic and, most demeaning of all, utilitarian and Gradgrindish: 'Every inch of the existence of mankind from birth to death was to be a bargain across a counter.' In so effectively visualising this industrial dystopia, in bemoaning its lack of humanity, Dickens uncharacteristically failed to appreciate the humanity of the people who actually made their lives in Manchester, Birmingham and Leeds and had the energy and creativity to remake their cities. Dickens could not foresee a better future; but it was to come, as city-dwellers set about improving their own environment.

In the year of the Great Exhibition – 1851 – there was a national census: the population of England and Wales was about 18 million; Scotland had 2.9 million inhabitants and Ireland 6.5 million. For the first time in history more Britons (in the mainland countries) lived in towns than in the countryside. Agriculture was still the largest industry but agricultural labourers continued to desert England's green and not-so-pleasant land to take up urban life. British agriculture was hit by a deepening crisis when the North American prairies were opened up to agriculture in the 1870s, as the brief but colourful reign of the horse-riding Cheyenne, Lakota and Comanche came to an inglorious end.

By 1870 the United States had over 53,000 miles of railways. Grain could be shifted cheaply from the prairies to Chicago and the coast, where transatlantic steamers transported it to Europe. Between 1873 and 1884 the cost of sending one ton of grain from Chicago to Liverpool fell from £3 7s to £1 4s. Other European countries such as Germany, France and Russia defended themselves with import taxes. In Britain Cobden's free-trade dogma, which had abolished the Corn Laws in 1846, ruled the roost. The impact was profound. The global revolution in food production of the late 1870s and 1880s transformed the structure of wealth and the identity of the 'ruling class' in Britain far more profoundly than the agricultural and industrial revolutions of a hundred years before.[18] As wheat prices tumbled, British grain production fell; 65 per cent of wheat was imported and nearly a million labourers left the land to energise the new industries in Britain and also in the USA, Canada and Australia. In Britain the tide of world trade inexorably tugged the country into unexplored territory, into the world of the capitalist city, a new phenomenon never before experienced. As the British made the journey, commentators looked back over their shoulders wistfully towards the never-never land of a romanticised rural and feudal past.

In 1851 there was a belief that further urbanisation was scarcely possible, yet fifty years later, at the turn of the twentieth century, 80 per cent of the inhabitants of England and Wales were town-dwellers — the largest proportion of any European country. In 1901 there were seventy-four towns with more than 50,000 inhabitants and the largest of all, London, the capital not just of a nation but of an empire of 400 million souls, grew from 2.3 million in 1851 to 4.5 million in 1911 (with another 2.8 million in its suburbs). The biggest growth of all was in what the Victorians called 'conurbations' — the sprawl around the cities that still exists today, for example the M62 belt between Liverpool, Manchester, Huddersfield and Leeds. In 1911 Britain had seven conurbations when they were scarcely known in the rest of Europe — in Greater London, south-west Lancashire, Merseyside, the West Midlands, West Yorkshire, Tyneside and Clydeside, all with population concentrations of over 1.5 million people.

The new economy of the Industrial Revolution in the first two generations poured vast wealth into the pockets of its investors, factory and mine-owners and manufacturers. The operatives — the 'hands' — existed at subsistence level. The 12,000 workers in Glasgow's cotton mills in 1833 mostly earned less than 11 shillings a week; and in Manchester about a shilling more, on average. At the same time the mill magnates accumulated more money than they knew what to do with. Some of it went into railway investment, the mania of the 1830s and 40s. No phenomenon of the industrial age caught the imagination or aroused virulent opposition* like the railway. Almost overnight speeds of up to 60 m.p.h. became possible. The fact that, unlike with canals, few railway investors made much of a profit did not stop the rich from dipping into their swollen pockets. And they gained in other ways. A new railway track gobbled up about 300 tons of iron every mile. Between 1830 and 1850 the output of iron in Britain trebled; so did the production of coal. The railways stimulated the modernisation of the heavy industries, which had lagged behind cotton production in terms of efficiency.

Steam locomotives first operated in the pre-Victorian era,† transporting heavy loads in the north-eastern coalfields and the mines of Cornwall. The opening of the Stockton–Darlington line, in 1825, to carry freight from the Durham coalfields, conventionally marks the start of the Railway Age. The Liverpool and Manchester Railway was the project that launched the railway as we know it; it opened on 15 September 1830, running on its own reserved track, carrying passengers in purpose-built carriages to a regular timetable.*

---

* The Duke of Wellington and William Wordsworth were among its opponents.
† Iron rails laid on wood were first used in 1767, in Coalbrookdale. In 1787 John Curr of Sheffield produced a flanged or plate rail.

Acts of Parliament provided privately funded British railways with powers of compulsory purchase, so that by 1850 over 6,000 miles of railway stitched the principal conurbations together.† Railways were an instant hit — those who could afford it loved to travel at speed. The nation, in effect, shrank and previously remote areas became accessible. In 1840 1,250 passengers went on an outing from Leeds to Hull, reversing the old saying recorded by Daniel Defoe: 'From Hell, Hull and Halifax, Good Lord deliver us.'‡ Railways were vital to the success of the Great Exhibition in 1851.

London's first railway opened between Greenwich and Bermondsey in 1836 and the capital was linked to Birmingham the following year. Rival companies developing the northern routes established termini at St Pancras, King's Cross and Euston and, in 1838, the Great Western built another; close to the present Paddington Station, which was completed by Brunel in 1854. So by the time the Great Exhibition opened London was the focal point of a national network of railways owned by rival entrepreneurs. These businessmen realised that their trains needed to appeal to a mass market and not just the well-to-do. Cut-price excursions and weekend specials were concocted, promoted by Mr Thomas Cook, ex-estate worker and wood-turner from Derbyshire. A committed member of the Temperance Association, Cook initiated a new travel industry when he arranged an excursion for 570 teetotallers from Leicester to a large temperance rally in Loughborough on 5 July 1841. This was the first public rail excursion in Britain. As a result of the demand Thomas Cook and the Midlands Railway chief, John Ellis, saw the Exhibition as a great business opportunity. Cook toured the towns of the Midlands and north promoting savings clubs to collect the fifteen-shilling fee for the proposed outing to London. Canny northern workers held on to their brass — they predicted that rival railways would set about slashing prices. The *Leeds Intelligencer* reported rather archly: 'The working classes seemed to have a kind of prescience that the competition for their patronage would be so strong between the rival railway companies as to cause the fares to be reduced much below the scale which was then stated to have been agreed upon by the respective boards of directors ...'[19]

Sure enough, by late July train prices began to tumble — though they

---

* The Rainhill locomotive trials were held on the Liverpool and Manchester line in 1829. Robert Stephenson's *Rocket* was the clear winner, moving its train along easily at 30 m.p.h. With its multi-tube boiler, blast-pipe exhaust and pistons attached to the driving wheels the *Rocket* was the model for the first generations of locomotives.

† By the end of the century there were 18,680 miles of railway.

‡ Halifax still has a Gibbet Street, a reminder of the reason for the expression.

were not so cheap as the steamships out of Hull. The railways reflected the sharpening distinctions of the class system:* on Saturday 19 July 1851 Great Northern Railways offered first-class fares at £1 12s, second-class at £1 4s and third-class at 11s. Two days later the third-class fare was cut to 9s.

In Bradford Thomas Cook sent his son round the town with a brass band announcing the latest reduction. A price war between the Great Northern and the Midland eventually settled at 5 shillings for the trip to London. Many of Cook's customers were his loyal teetotallers. They went in their thousands to the Crystal Palace and began an impromptu choral performance in Welsh. As a result of the fracas that developed the Great Exhibition executive committee decided to ban singing. Nevertheless, thanks to the trains, the Exhibition was 'a stupendous beehive' (6 million people visited over its six-month run).† However, the stiff competition meant that most of the railway companies made little profit: the Midland Railway's share price fell from 55d. to 37d. during the exhibition.

The Great Exhibition conveyed the impression of a hyper-industrious Britain. A few years later the *Mechanics Magazine* (27 April 1860) wrote: 'There is no doubt that the people of England work harder, mentally and physically, than the people of any other country on the face of the earth.'

The English, though, had learned to love an excursion and a bargain; particularly after the introduction of the Bank Holidays Act of 1871, seaside resorts and great sporting events would prosper. By the 1890s the workers of the northern mill towns decamped for 'wakes week' (or at least went for a day trip) to Blackpool, the world's first working-class holiday resort. The holiday Mecca of the Lancashire coast had a population of 47,000 by 1900, which tripled at peak periods. Originally planned as a watering hole for the better-off in the 1860s, Blackpool began to attract the mill workers as wages increased in the 1880s and 1890s. Entrepreneurs like Bill Holland realised that the new audiences wanted less genteel entertainment: they preferred the leggy Tiller girls to opera singers. 'Give them what they want' was Holland's motto. The opening of Blackpool Tower in 1894 (five years after the Parisian prototype) started an escalating competition to provide more and more spectacular venues for sensation-craving workers: from aquaria to zoos; from ballrooms,

---

* Disraeli, in his novel *Sybil* (1844), dramatised British classes into the Rich and Poor. Marx and Engels, four years later in the *Communist Manifesto* (1848), emphasised the gaping breach between the bourgeoisie and the proletariat. Mrs Gaskell emphasised geographical distinctions in her novel *North and South* (1855).

† Six million people visited the Millennium Dome in 2000, but that was perceived as a failure partly because 12 million were predicted and most of the content was rubbish.

circuses, Ferris wheels and piers to tramways and winter gardens. Not everyone approved. The Reverend J. S. Balmer, minister of Blackpool's United Methodist Free Church and opponent of drinking and dancing, was horrified when he put a penny into the 'Parisian scenes' slot machine to discover not panoramas of the city, nor cultural highlights of the Louvre, but that he was 'looking through the gateway to perdition'. The Reverend Balmer and Bill Holland, who lived amicably on the same street, nevertheless represented the opposing poles of Victorian society: the proper and puritanical versus the popular; godliness next to rowdiness.

Bracegirdle Hemyns estimated that there were at least 80,000 prostitutes, mid-century, in London. In addition there were the amateurs — 'dollymops' — servant girls and nursemaids who succumbed to 'scarlet fever' — the charms of lusty soldiers. Victorian values were not always ones to which Mrs Thatcher would have wanted to return. Henry Mayhew* reported: 'The costermongers, taken as a body, entertain the most imperfect idea of the sanctity of marriage ... the expense of a church ceremony is considered as a useless waste of money.' One eighteen-year-old girl told Mayhew: 'I dare say there ain't ten out of a hundred gals what's living with men what's been married Church of England fashion.' She then went on to describe the casual brutality of the men, their habit of plying girls with drink so as to have sex with them and their tendency to abandon their pregnant girlfriends to the workhouse.

Queen Victoria's reign also saw the banning of popular Georgian blood sports (at least officially) such as cock-fighting and bull-baiting. Respectability put an end to traditional country entertainments. The Scouring of the White Horse on the Berkshire Downs, for example, had attracted tens of thousands, including every pickpocket around, to watch the back-staff champions of Berkshire and Wiltshire split each other's skull with staves for substantial prize money; and women competed to see who could keep a pipe of tobacco alight the longest: their prize — a barrel of gin. Such entertainments fell out of fashion later in the nineteenth century as more regulated sporting events gained in popularity. Some Victorian inventions, such as the Oxford and Cambridge boat race, retained opportunities for anarchy, hard drinking and police-bashing (usually by university undergraduates). The Derby attracted all

---

* Henry Mayhew was one of the founders and an editor of *Punch*, which first appeared on 17 July 1841. His great work of journalism, *London Labour and the London Poor*, began as a series of articles for the *Morning Chronicle* in 1849 and 1850 and was published in book form a decade later. Mayhew had great compassion and respect for the poor; he did not patronise or judge them, nor did he smother his readers in typically Victorian sentimentality.

classes and provided the greatest opportunity for popular but illegal gambling. Football clubs, such as Liverpool and Everton, Glasgow Rangers and Celtic, provided Saturday entertainment for urban workers, and an outlet for their traditional Protestant or Catholic prejudices.

Improved transport strengthened the political clout of the industrial workers. *The Times* commented: 'When it was rumoured during the struggle over the Reform Bill (in 1832) that over 50,000 men from Birmingham were coming to London to present a petition, a great authority wondered "Where will they find shoes?" Now, nineteen years on, 'the artisans of Birmingham have achieved their threatened march on the metropolis on shoes of iron.' The British middle classes and their rulers found it harder to ignore the dreadful conditions in towns as the poorer occupants became more vociferous and communications improved. Rail transport allowed people to see the state of the country for themselves; newspapers and the 'penny post' mail* were delivered rapidly and reliably. The country's half-dozen time zones were also unified, thanks to the railways, and Greenwich Mean Time became standard. The repeal of the stamp duty on newspapers (1855) and the excise duty on paper (1861) encouraged the spectacular expansion of the Victorian press. There were 129 regular magazines and newspapers at the beginning of the nineteenth century and over 4,800 at the end of it. In this period their popularity rose eight-fold and paper production sixtyfold.[20]

The Great Exhibition of the Industry of All Nations showed off the products of the workers. Increasingly, those who had benefited from industry realised that these workers were more than 'hands' and had a voice. From the beginning of the nineteenth century there were insistent and irresistible pressures for greater civil and religious equality and for an extension of the parliamentary franchise. In the first part of the century the Tory forces of reaction controlled the country. The peaceful demonstrators at St Peter's Field in Manchester, in 1819, during the depression following Waterloo and the end of the French wars, were confronted by the mounted, sabre-wielding Manchester Yeomanry, who left eleven dead and about five hundred wounded – what became known, infamously, as the 'Peterloo Massacre'.

The early nineteenth-century franchise in England and Wales was still based on restrictive and exclusive principles established by Parliament in 1430 'to exclude people ... of no value'. There was little consistency in how this was applied: in Preston every adult male was entitled to vote; in

---

* Rowland Hill conceived the standardised postal scheme in 1839 and the adhesive stamp followed two years later. In the 1840s the number of letters sent through the Post Office quadrupled.

other places a small elite elected their representatives. Rotten boroughs such as Old Sarum (Wiltshire), little more than a prehistoric hill fort above Salisbury, returned a member to Parliament as did the Universities of Oxford and Cambridge (until abolished by the 1945 Labour Government), but the relatively new industrial towns were grossly underrepresented. In Scotland only those owning estates with a medieval pedigree — 'land of old extent' — could vote and several towns were lumped together for the privilege of sending a single MP to Parliament. Edinburgh's member was chosen by a select group of thirty-three men. In Ireland Catholics were almost completely disenfranchised until the Catholic Emancipation Act of 1827.

The political system — designed for the benefit of landowning aristocrats — had not kept pace with the transformation of Britain into an industrial, urban society, nor with the radical views of its people — particularly the large working class and the increasingly confident and often Nonconformist middle class. With the death of the reactionary King George IV and the fall of the Duke of Wellington's Tory government (both in 1830), the main obstacles to reform were removed. Not that the 1832 Reform Act had an easy passage; the result was a typically British fudge and compromise. Parliamentary seats were redistributed more fairly to the new centres of population — Manchester, Birmingham, Leeds and Sheffield had their own MPs for the first time — and in Wales, Scotland and Ireland. The franchise was still restricted, however, to the better-off and the electorate only expanded by 45 per cent — to about 18 per cent of adult males in England and Wales.* In Scotland the minute electorate expanded considerably but was, nevertheless, a smaller proportion of the total than in England and Wales. Most adult men and all women were still excluded from the franchise, and many elections remained 'open' and subject to bribery and vote-rigging. Whatever its limitations, the 1832 Reform Act was the start of a more transparent and coherent electoral system — and it raised great expectations. Many of the working class, who had struggled hard for reform, felt betrayed and demanded more radical action. The Chartist movement called for universal male suffrage and secret ballots.

Parliament simply turned its back on Chartist petitions and, in the face of protests and agitation and threats of insurrection, deported Chartist leaders and mustered the troops. The ruling elite were divided in how to respond to widespread protest and unrest. Old-fashioned Tories such as Wellington believed in keeping the lower orders in their place by

---

* The pool of prospective voters increased from 435,000 to 650,000.

taking a tough line and reasserting the time-honoured habits of 'obedience, order and submission. [21]

Even the Whig government of Lord Grey, aristocratic to a fault, supported the Reform Bill, to enhance rather than undermine the hierarchy, which they feared was discredited by corruption and rotten boroughs – 'to bind firmly and kindly the different classes of society together', in Lord John Russell's words. To restore 'tranquillity and subordination' it was necessary to 'associate the middle with the higher orders of society in the love and support of the institutions and government of the country'.[22]

The Whigs saw British society as divided into three classes. In their opinion the property owners large and small (the Whig concept of 'the people') had better stick together unless they wanted to be overrun by 'the mob' and 'the rabble'. For the Chartists and the recently formed 'Political Unions of the Middle and Working Classes'* Parliament was insulated by wealth and privilege from the needs and concerns of the majority of people. To them the great Reform Bill was smoke and mirrors. The *Poor Man's Guardian* summarised the confidence trick: 'The promoters of the Reform Bill projected it, not with a view to subvert or even re-model our aristocratic institutions, but to consolidate them by a reinforcement of sub-aristocracy from the middle classes.' The result was to unite 'all property against all poverty'.[23]

The propertied middle classes had climbed on to the ladder of political power from the backs of the working-class radicals, who felt betrayed as well as disenfranchised. The great Reform Bill had, however, succeeded in taking the impetus out of the Chartist cause, which is often portrayed as a working-class movement. Commentators such as Engels failed to notice that the workers were not a monolithic mass. They were regionally varied and included factory operatives, domestic workers, craftsmen and farm workers with little sense of collective identity: as the economist T. Thornton commented, in 1846: 'The labouring population has been spoken of as if it formed only one class but in reality it is divided into several.' The Chartist view that Britain was divided by a 'great gulf'† between rich and poor, the haves and the have-nots, was too simple a representation of the realities of nineteenth-century Britain's social structure, with its subtle gradations.

---

* First established in Birmingham, in 1829, and then spread throughout the country.
† The fictional Chartist John Barton uses the expression, in Mrs Gaskell's novel *Mary Barton: a tale of Manchester life* (1855).

I spent my childhood in a nineteenth-century built environment (as the jargon goes nowadays). Our first house, hard by the mill wall, was a back-to-back, two-up-two-down, mid-Victorian terraced house with an outside lavatory in a small adjacent yard – typical of the West Riding. We had the proverbial tin bath in front of the coal fire beloved of coal miners and featured in D. H. Lawrence novels. Most of the women who lived in Dewhurst Buildings worked in the mill of the same name and were obsessively house-proud – they washed the front steps every week and holystoned them so that they looked spick and span.*

These were the smallest houses, rented by the 'hands' from the mill-owner. As my father was promoted, we moved a hundred yards to another terrace. Here the houses had three bedrooms, an inside bathroom, and a small garden both front and back. Later he was offered a manager's house – a grand, four-square building that stood just across the road in its own walled grounds, surrounded by enormous chestnut trees. On a damp, moonlit evening it looked like a scene painted by Atkinson Grimshaw. But I did not know that in 1958. We did not move there, because my mother thought it would need too much housework; she did not come from the class that employed cleaners.

The point is that this industrial community had a whole range of houses within two minutes' walk of each other, which reflected the social and economic structure of operatives, skilled men who had done apprenticeships, clerks, foremen (or 'overlookers' – there were no forewomen) and mill-managers. Mixed in with these were retired people, the corner shopkeeper, some unemployed and the resident jail-bird – an ex-soldier with six pallid children who lived on a diet of chips and Wagon Wheels (Engels would have beamed in on this family). As my father became a local councillor, I saw for myself how varied were their political views, attitudes and aspirations. Some, but not many, might have agreed with the Reverend Marmaduke Pritchett of Trinity College, Cambridge, who pronounced, in 1838, 'that the order of human society is established by God'. Or with Lord John Manners, friend of Disraeli, who, like many in the mid-nineteenth century, hankered after a *Piers Plowman* world of fixed and certain hierarchies, where: 'Each knew his place – King, peasant, peer or priest, / The greatest owed connection with the least.' This paternalist view appealed to many of the industrial oligarchs, who adopted Gothic styles of building to hark back to the medieval Christian world of order, hierarchy and chivalry. Gothic symbolised 'an integrated system of society.' [24]

* Richard Hoggart, in *The Uses of Literacy*, Penguin edn (1990), refers to them as 'well-scrubbed wives with well-scrubbed doorsteps'.

Pugin,* the Victorian Gothic architect par excellence, showed a limited knowledge of history when he pronounced in 1843: 'We are not Italians, we are Englishmen ... Our climate remains precisely the same as formerly ... we are governed by nearly the same laws and the same system of political economy [as in the Middle Ages].' So, he said, the Gothic revival '[is] warranted by religion, government, climate, and the want of society. It is the perfect expression of all we should hold sacred, honourable and national, and connected with the holiest and dearest associations'.

As Catholics in Britain grew in confidence, Pugin was the man to demonstrate their presence. He designed St Chad's, Birmingham (1839–56), with its Germanic spires, and St Giles, Cheadle (1841–7), which fellow Catholic convert Cardinal Newman called 'the most splendid building I ever saw'. The novelist William Makepeace Thackeray described Britain in 1850 as a 'Gothic society, with its rank and hierarchies, its cumbrous ceremonies, its glittering and antique paraphernalia'.[25]

The style certainly appealed to the wealthy oligarchs of the industrial towns, impressed by the architect's talk of muscularity, virility, sternness and strength. Marx and Engels in the *Communist Manifesto* (1848) took them to task: what 'the reactionary forces so greatly admire about the medieval period' is its 'brutal expression of strength'. It is not surprising that the historian Eric Hobsbawm, doyen of the left, castigates the wealthy burgers of the industrial cities, who 'even began to celebrate their collective glory by constructing those shocking town halls and other civic monstrosities in Gothic and Renaissance imitations, whose exact and Napoleonic costs their municipal historians recorded with pride.'[26]

Mark Girouard offers a different perspective. To him 'the corporations of Victorian towns, especially northern industrial towns', were heroes. 'With unfailing energy and resourcefulness they took over services from inefficient private enterprise and made them prosperous and fruitful, leaving behind them a rich harvest of town halls, court houses, market halls, schools, viaducts, bridges, reservoirs and pumping stations, all proudly flaunting the corporation coat of arms from ripely ebullient architecture.'[27] There is no doubt that the Victorians learned how to build and live in cities.

Following the Reform Act of 1832, the Municipal Corporations Act of 1838 led to the reorganisation of 178 existing corporations to be elected by ratepayers (still only 3–10 per cent of adult males) – in practice a middle-class electorate could vote in their fellows, often

---

* 'To Puginise: to mix up political and theological speculations with architectural ones' – W. H. Leeds (1843); quoted in Cannadine (1998), p. 96.

Nonconformist Liberals rather than the old Anglican Tories, who no longer presided over the courts or appointed the clergy. The opportunities of exercising local power, supported by the rates, attracted dynamic new blood into local government. Councils bought up private gas and water companies, improved paving and drainage, water supplies, public baths, lighting, tramways, museums and art galleries, municipal parks and cemeteries.

Following the 1835 Act, in the rest of the century 135 municipal boroughs successfully sought incorporation: Birmingham and Manchester in 1838, Bradford in 1847, Halifax and Huddersfield in 1848, Rochdale in 1856. These confident and aggressively boosterish councils were not afraid to use money to improve the lives of their citizens. The civic fathers had seen the catastrophic impact of the cholera epidemics of the 1830s and 40s and determined that water supply was too vital a matter to be left to private companies. In the latter part of the nineteenth century Bradford spent £3 million on its water supplies and £300,000 on sewerage and drainage systems. Liverpool Corporation invested over £1.3 million in its water supply in the 1880s. With Haussmann's Paris as the example, many corporations took to widening their streets, easing traffic flow and clearing away the rookeries and dung-ridden courts. Corporation Street in Birmingham, Victoria Street in Liverpool and New Oxford Street, Shaftesbury Avenue and Charing Cross Road in London swept away some of the worst urban slums, albeit provoking further housing shortages.

On 14 October 1859 Queen Victoria, probably coaxed by Prince Albert, boarded the steamboat *Rob Roy* to cross Loch Katrine in weather of 'a truly Highland character'. Her purpose was to open the new aqueduct tunnel built to supply Glasgow with 50 million gallons a day of clean Highland water. Glasgow's civic fathers had spent £1.5 million so that the city's inhabitants would no longer poison themselves with the deadly stew of the River Clyde. The *Glasgow Daily Herald* praised the project for satisfying 'a community thirsty for good water on the one hand and abhorrant of high taxes on the other'. This was a Scottish project delivered on time and to budget.

The previous summer (1858) Londoners had not had to drink the Thames to experience its noxious flavour. It was the year of the Great Stink, when the river, in Disraeli's words, became 'a stygian pool reeking with ineffable and intolerable horrors'. The stench drove members from the grand new Houses of Parliament; the government, after years of indifference, was forced to address the problem of the open sewer swilling beneath its windows. Fortunately, an engineering Hercules was at hand to tackle this great labour and clean London's Augean Stable. He was Joseph Bazalgette, chief engineer of the Metropolitan Board of Works, who masterminded the construction of an eighty-two-mile network of multi-levelled sewers beneath London, from Hampstead and Pimlico to the Isle of Dogs.

At a cost of £4 million Bazalgette's sewers conveyed London's effluvia fourteen miles downriver and out to sea. By constructing the Victoria Embankments (opened in 1870) to carry his east–west low-level sewers, Bazalgette changed the face of London, and the Thames, which he constrained between banks of suitably imperial solidity.

Attempts were also made to improve the dreadful housing conditions of the urban poor. In the second half of the nineteenth century fifty statutes were passed, such as the 1885 Housing of the Working Classes Act and the 1888 Local Government Act. In Scotland, in this period, the average number of people per house dropped from almost 8 to 4.7. At the same time crude death rates fell, from 21.6 per thousand in 1841 to 14.6 in 1901. Improved hygiene and better diet were the main reasons: with higher wages poorer people were able to spend more on food. As the population rose, the number of doctors increased from 14,415 in England and Wales in 1861 to 22,698 in 1901 – of whom 212, or just under 1 per cent, were women.*

This was also the great age of hospital-building, though medical science still had a long way to go: as great a proportion of British children died in their first year at the end of Victoria's reign as they had at the beginning of it. There were major scientific advances in the understanding of disease; most of these, however, came from the Continent. In Britain opposition to animal vivisection limited experimentation for medical research. Instead the British became obsessed with hygiene and the avoidance of contagion – from the 'great unwashed', from foreigners, from toilet seats and even from telephones, as shown by patent applications about 1900.

From the mid-century anaesthesia – the use of ether and then chloroform – made surgery a less terrifying performance, though unsterilised equipment caused a high level of fatalities. Joseph Lister made a major breakthrough (learning from Louis Pasteur's laboratory work) when he developed antiseptic procedures using carbolic acid, in Edinburgh in 1869. As the male-dominated medical profession resisted the entry of women, it increasingly took over responsibility for the delivery of babies. Childbirth did not became any safer, mainly owing to practices such as

---

* The British Medical Association was founded in 1856.

the use of forceps, which could cause puerperal fever and high maternal mortality.*

At the opposite end of the medical spectrum some traditional methods were no more successful: on St Kilda, in the Outer Hebrides, midwives anointed the severed umbilical cords of the newborn with the oil of a local seabird, the fulmar. The result was that puerperal fever virtually wiped out the St Kilda's infant population and was a major factor, ultimately, in the abandonment of the island. Women, though, did find an increasing role as nurses. Most mornings I walk to work past one of London's finest monuments. In Waterloo Place, the magnificent statues of Florence Nightingale and her grizzled cohort of Crimean veterans, in busbies and greatcoats, look down towards St James's Park. Florence Nightingale became a legendary heroine of the imperial age, and the first woman to receive the Order of Merit, for the work of her nurses at Scutari — an antidote to the well-publicised incompetence of the military authorities in the Crimea. She may not have understood germ theory (she held to miasma theory — that disease was caused by corruption of the atmosphere), but she did appreciate that cleanliness and order make hospitals less deadly places to be incarcerated.† She emphasised in her *Notes on Hospitals* (1859) that the first obligation of the hospital was that 'it should do the sick no harm'. Thanks to Florence, the image of nursing improved and it became a respectable profession for women, with improved training and a career structure.

Posterity has, until recently, succumbed to amnesia as far as another imperial heroine is concerned. Mary Seacole was a Jamaican nurse whose exploits in the front line of the Crimean War made her as famous in her day as Florence Nightingale — and more loved by the troops. Aged forty-eight, after years of experience and ministering to troops around the West Indies and Central America, she came to Britain to volunteer to help in the Crimea. She was shocked at the racial prejudice of the authorities. Undaunted she took herself out to the Crimea, as a butler — to supply the troops with provisions. In practice she ran a store-cum-dispensary and hospital treating the soldiers whether they could pay or not. *The Times* war correspondent W. H. Russell made her famous in Britain with

---

* 'In the worst Victorian maternity hospitals, between 9 and 10 per cent of women entering might leave in a coffin ... Maternal mortality – the outcome of sepsis (puerperal fever), haemorrhage or toxaemia (eclampsia) – maintained its tragic plateau from mid-Victorian times until the 1930s. But the majority of deaths could have been prevented by better obstetrics.' Low-status midwives had little training, GPs not much more. Hospital doctors were 'trigger-happy' with forceps and careless about cross-infection. In short, the safest form of childbirth was traditionally 'away from hospital and the doctor's clutches'.[28]

† An issue, still, today with the problems of MRSA virus infection in NHS hospitals.

his dispatches from the front. On 14 September 1855 he reported: 'This kind and successful physician doctors and cures all manner of men with extraordinary success. She is always in attendance near the battle-field to aid the wounded, and has earned many a poor fellow's blessings.'

At the end of the war Mary Seacole was left bankrupt. A letter to *The Times* asked: 'Where are the Crimeans? Have a few months erased from their memories those acts of comforting kindness which made the name of the old mother venerated throughout the camp? While the benevolent deeds of Florence Nightingale are being handed down to posterity ... are the humbler actions of Mrs Seacole to be entirely forgotten?'

The troops rallied to her aid and a four-day festival of music, with nine military bands, was held in her honour in Kennington. At an official dinner Mary Seacole was 'cheered and chaired ... by the adoring soldiers'. W. H. Russell wrote a preface to her vivid memoirs *Wonderful Adventures of Mrs Seacole in Many Lands*. 'I trust that England will not forget one who nursed her sick, who sought out her wounded to aid and succour them, and who performed the last offices for some of her illustrious dead.' Mary Seacole died on 14 May 1881 and was buried in Kensal Green Cemetery.*

Most black Victorian Britons received less generous treatment than Mary Seacole. Lascars, or seamen from south Asia, made up the majority. Their numbers increased as steam power generated a need for stokers on ships to work in literally hellish conditions. Few European sailors fancied the job, or the low pay. Unfortunates were often dumped by their ships in ports such as London, Liverpool, Glasgow, Hull and Cardiff – where in 1881 a Sailors' Rest was set up for them. Cardiff was second only to London in the proportion of its people that were foreign-born, and prior to World War I some 700 were African or West Indian in origin. There was talk of repatriation, until the outbreak of war in 1914 generated a huge demand for munitions workers and merchant seamen. In 1918 there were an estimated 10,000 black people in Britain.

Not all Victorian black Britons led quietly anonymous lives, however. William Cuffay had the distinction of being put on trial for 'levying war' against Queen Victoria in 1848. William was a disabled tailor, only 1.5 metres (4 feet 10 inches) tall – not an obvious warrior; nevertheless, he

---

* Mary Seacole is now increasingly recognised. Thames Valley University has a Mary Seacole Centre for Nursing Practice. Her memory has been revived thanks to Ziggi Alexander and Audrey Dewjee (1982), *Mary Seacole: Jamaican national heroine and 'doctress' in the Crimean War*, Brent Library Service; and Peter Fryer (1984), *Staying Power: the history of black people in Britain*, Pluto Press, London, pp. 246–52. Her story has also been told recently by A. N. Wilson (2002), *The Victorians*, Hutchinson, London, pp. 178–80, and by Jane Robinson, *Mary Seacole*, Constable, London.

made a marvellous nuisance of himself. He was the grandson of an enslaved African and the son of a St Kitts slave, who, gaining freedom, crossed the Atlantic as a cook on a British warship. William was born in Chatham in 1788 and, having a deformed spine, took up the trade of a tailor. He seems to have worked quietly and industriously for many years, until he went out on strike with his trade union and was sacked. In 1839 he joined the Chartists, who demanded universal suffrage, secret ballots, reformed electoral districts, the abandonment of property qualifications for MPs and the redistribution of land. Cuffay quickly rose to a position of authority. The Westminster Chartists elected him their representative in 1841 on the Metropolitan Delegate Council, and the following year found him chairing a 'Great Public Meeting of the Tailors'. *The Times*, not usually to be found in the forefront of reform movements, referred to the London Chartists as 'The Black man and his Party'.

By the crisis year of 1848 Cuffay was one of the most determined Chartist leaders, chairman of the committee responsible for organising the march to take a petition of almost 2 million signatures from Kennington Common to the House of Commons. The authorities were so alarmed at the prospect of a working-class invasion of central London that the Queen was packed off to the Isle of Wight for her protection and even the British Museum was provided with 50 muskets and 100 cutlasses. Seven thousand soldiers and heavy guns were placed along the embankment and 4,000 police blocked the bridges to protect Parliament from the people. Faced with such a dangerous force, the Chartists' procession was called off – much to William Cuffay's disgust.

On 16 August 1848 a number of leading Chartists were arrested, supposedly for planning arson. *The Times* thundered: 'Cuffay … is half a nigger', 'the very chief of the conspiracy'. 'Some of the others are Irishmen. We doubt if there are half-a-dozen Englishmen in the whole lot.'

At his trial Cuffay pleaded not guilty and demanded a jury of his peers, 'according to the principles of the Magna Carta'. He was found guilty on the evidence of two paid police spies and *agents provocateurs*. In a defiant, dignified final speech he accused the court of rigging the witnesses and the press of condemning him by ridicule. Every proposal that was likely to benefit the working class, he said, had been set aside in Parliament, but a measure to restrain their liberties had been passed in a few hours.

Cuffay was sentenced to transportation, for life, to Tasmania. 'A severe sentence, but a most just one', according to *The Times*. In contrast, the *Northern Star* – a Chartist newspaper – reported: 'The conduct of Cuffay throughout his trial was that of a man. A somewhat singular appearance, certain eccentricities of manner, and a habit of unregulated speech, afforded an opportunity to the "suckmug" reporters, unprincipled editors and buffoons of the press to make him the subject of ridicule … In a great measure Cuffay owes his destruction to the Press-gang. But his manly and admirable conduct on his trial affords his enemies no opportunities either to sneer at or abuse him … Cuffay's last words should be treasured up by the people.'

Another pro-Chartist newspaper, the *Reynolds' Political Instructor*, pronounced its own verdict: 'Whilst integrity in the midst of poverty, whilst honour in the midst of temptation are admired and venerated, so long will the name of William Cuffay, a scion of Africa's oppressed race, be preserved from oblivion.'*

While most Indians living in Britain in the nineteenth century were poor seamen, there was also a small number of businessmen, students and teachers. Some of these people were in the forefront of the movement to promote democracy in India and arouse the liberal conscience of imperial Britain. One of these was Dadabhai Naoroji, the first Asian to be elected to the House of Commons. Naoroji was born in Bombay, in 1825, and by the age of twenty-nine was the first Indian professor of mathematics and natural philosophy. In 1855 he came to Britain and took up the post of Professor of Gujerati at University College, London. From then on he became the voice of India in London, constantly prodding the conscience of the British, constantly appealing to their much-vaunted sense of fair play.

In 1886 Naoroji stood for the parliamentary seat of Holborn and lost. Lord Salisbury catapulted the failed candidate to national fame when he declared: 'However great the progress of mankind has been, and however far we have advanced in overcoming prejudices, I doubt if we have yet got to the point of view where a British constituency would elect a black man.' In response the National Liberal Club gave a banquet with Naoroji as guest of honour, 'to mark their disapproval of Lord Salisbury's intolerant language' – and, no doubt, to embarrass a political opponent.

In 1892, in spite of Tory claims that he was a fire-worshipper,† Naoroji was elected Liberal MP for Central Finsbury – by a majority of three votes; hence his nickname: 'Narrow Majority'. Naoroji devoted himself,

---

* George Reynolds was both a sensation-seeking journalist and the Derby representative of the Chartists, best remembered for the *Reynolds' News*, which I used to read in my grandmother's house in the 1950s. Cuffay, always one of the awkward squad, even challenged Reynolds' credentials to be a Chartist – he thought the journalist was too middle-class.

† In 1861 Naoroji helped found the London Zoroastrian Association, dedicated to the welfare of Parsees in Britain. The name of Uhuru Mazda, the Zoroastrian fire god, was used in Britain for a brand of light bulb.

though, to the cause of Indian welfare and independence from the British.

Over the next thirty years a succession of Indian intellectuals attempted to persuade the British, on home soil, that illiteracy, famine and economic decline in India were the bitter fruits of empire. Liberal democratic ideals, they proclaimed, should be applied in India as well as at home.

The British were quick to forget the part played by black sailors in the Royal Navy in the most dramatic decades of its history. In World War I their contribution was also great. Over a thousand black sailors from Cardiff alone were killed at sea; and Sir Harry Johnston, friend of Henry Morton Stanley, wrote a book entitled *The Black Man's Part in the War*, praising their 'pluck, gallantry and devotion' and 'courage in the face of machine-gun fire'.

At the end of World War I many soldiers from West Indian and West African regiments were demobilised and stayed in Britain. In the 'land fit for heroes' the blacks were the first to feel the rigours of unemployment and were often deliberately cheated out of unemployment benefit. In Liverpool, after the war, the black population rose to as many as 5,000. Early in 1919 about 120 black workers were suddenly sacked from the sugar refineries, where they had been employed for years, because whites refused to work with them. There were constant reports of attacks on blacks, many of whom were crippled ex-servicemen. The secretary of the Liverpool Ethiopian Association told the Lord Mayor of Liverpool that over five hundred black men, mostly discharged soldiers and sailors, were unemployed and 'practically starving'. As tensions heightened, inter-racial violence increased and policemen were injured. In one incident a mob of two hundred stone-throwers chased Charles Wotten, a demobilised West Indian ship's fireman. They hurled Wotten into the Queen's Dock and pelted him with stones until he drowned.

No one was arrested from the lynch mob. Instead, for several days gangs of white youths rampaged around the streets of Liverpool beating and stabbing any black they came across, burning and looting their houses and hostels. The *Liverpool Courier*, on 11 June 1919,[29] stoked the violence: 'You glimpse black figures beneath the gas lamps, and somehow you think of pimps and bullies, and women, and birds of ill-omen generally.' Its editorial further fanned the flames of self-righteousness: 'One of the chief reasons of popular anger behind the present disturbances lies in the fact that the average negro is nearer the animal than is the average white man, and that there are women in Liverpool who have no self-respect. The white man ... regards [the black man] as part child, part animal and part savage ...'

In contrast the *LiverpoolWeekly Post* (14 June 1919) reported the words of a local magistrate: the white mobs were 'making the name of Liverpool an abomination and disgrace to the rest of the country'. Liverpool was not alone. In Newport and Cardiff equally vicious mobs attacked the black community of about 3,000 people, killing several and injuring many more. The damage could have been much worse if Dr Rufus Leicester Fennell, a West Indian dentist and army medic, had not helped to organise disciplined self-defence forces of ex-black soldiers and negotiated with the authorities to calm the situation.

Rioting also spread to London, notably Cable Street, Stepney, in April and Limehouse the following month. When the blacks defended themselves, they were often blamed and arrested. The *Manchester Guardian* (less liberal in those days) whinged: 'The quiet, apparently inoffensive, nigger becomes a demon when armed with revolver or razor'; and they would insist on stirring up red-blooded white men by associating with white women. Such things 'revolt our very nature', according to a letter in *The Times* (14 June 1919) from Sir Ralph Williams, ex-governor of the Windward Islands.

A few days later *The Times* published a blistering response from Felix Hercules, an important figure in the black liberation movement. He pointed out that for generations young black girls had been debauched to satisfy 'the base lust of white seducers' and the world was full of half-caste offspring to prove it:

> I do not believe that any excuse can be made for white men who take the law into their own hands because they say they believe the association between the men of my race and white women is degrading. Sir Ralph Williams and those who think like him should remember that writing in this way gives a stimulus to those racial riots and can only have one ultimate result, the downfall of the British Empire.*

Such talk set the alarm bells ringing. In the United States and across the British Empire black people had experienced the hardships of the

---

* This was not just rhetoric. Marion, Lady Nugent, lived in Jamaica from 1801–5 as the wife of the Governor. She thought that the white rulers set a dreadful example to black slaves: 'White men of all descriptions, married or single, live in a state of licentiousness with their female slaves; and until a great reformation takes place on their part, neither religion, decency, nor morality, can be established among the negroes ... The overseers, too, are in general ready adventurers without either principles, religion, or morality. Of course their example must be the worst possible to these poor creatures.'[30]

war, seen the good and bad sides of their white officers and fellow soldiers — and the survivors had benefited from military training. In the crisis year of 1919 black and white rivalry for jobs was intense, and the clashes bitter. This generation of black ex-soldiers and their radical spokesmen, such as Felix Hercules in England and Marcus Garvey in America, challenged the racialism of white society and its imperial assumptions; and they noted its collective amnesia: the 1919 race riots were conveniently forgotten.

Black Africans and West Indians made up a minority of immigrants in Britain. The later nineteenth and early twentieth centuries saw an influx on a much larger scale: the Jews from the Russian Empire. Today millions of Britons carry a reminder of one of these immigrants on the label of their underwear. He was a young man who left Polish Russia and arrived in Hartlepool in 1878. His name was Michael Marks, and when he died, aged only forty-eight, his son Simon memorialised his father's name in the St Michael label for the family firm of Marks and Spencer. Like many poor immigrants Michael Marks took to the road as a pedlar. After a few years he became a salesman for the Leeds-based clothing business of Isaac Dewhirst. From there he set up a market stall in Leeds and came up with a great idea: 'Don't ask the price,' he told his customers. 'It's a penny!' The penny bazaar was born — rapidly producing offspring across the West Riding and Lancashire. As the business grew, Marks took on a partner: Dewhirst's cashier, Thomas Spencer. In 1894 they formed Marks and Spencer and in a decade they had forty shops.

Marks was not the only hard-working Jewish immigrant to make a success of the schmutter trade. In London the Moses brothers took their modest second-hand clobber upmarket and became Moss Bros.* Montague Ossinsky, a fifteen-year-old Lithuanian, arrived in Chesterfield, where he worked in a shop. He changed his name to Burton and in 1909 moved to Sheffield, where he sold men's off-the-peg suits for the expanding middle class. By the mid-twenties Montague Burton had built up the largest retail business in Europe and his impressive marble-fronted shops stood in every high street. On the eve of World War II his 600 shops were supplied by his Lancashire factories employing 20,000 workers. Soon they were turning out millions of uniforms.

---

* Another Yiddish word, 'nosh', has entered the language and recently been translated into Cockney rhyming slang as 'Becks and Posh'. In *Piers Plowman* (1362) the word 'cockney' refers to a misshapen egg – as if laid by a cock. Chaucer used the word to mean a mother's favourite. By the sixteenth century a cockney was a town-dweller in general and by the early seventeenth century specifically someone born in London – within hearing distance of the Great Bell in Bow.

Marks, the Moses brothers and Montague Ossinsky were some of the great success stories. Most of their fellow immigrants had tougher and less financially rewarding lives. They were all part of a stream of 3 million refugees fleeing tsarist Russia, particularly after the assassination of the relatively moderate Alexander II, in 1881. Two thirds of them crossed the Atlantic to create the vibrant Jewish culture in America; about 150,000 came to Britain. Conditions for Russians were never easy, but they deteriorated even further during the reign of Tsar Alexander III. In 1882 he passed laws to restrict Jewish ownership of land, forbade them to work on Sundays and forced half a million Jews to move into towns, or *shtetls*, in the so-called Pale of Settlement – the strip of Russian and Polish provinces from Yalta on the Black Sea to Kovino in the north. In this area the expanding Jewish population was confined with few and restricted job opportunities, short of food and subject to arbitrary pogroms culminating in a particularly vicious one in Odessa in 1905.

To escape the grinding poverty and persecution Russian Jews boarded ships in Hamburg, Bremen, Gdansk and Odessa, often having to bribe officials or pay middlemen, agents and ships' officers to arrange passages. At ports such as Tilbury and Hull the sharks were circling, ready to strip the unwary or seize vulnerable victims for the flourishing Victorian sex industry. Those who left the Pale had to be enterprising and determined – to set out into the relatively unknown, with few possessions, little money and usually no English. They were strangers in a not entirely strange land. In the early nineteenth century about 18,000 Jews lived in London. Service in the Napoleonic wars, at a time of heightened British patriotic fervour, had improved their standing somewhat. Nathan Mayer Rothschild, founder of the London branch of the famous banking family was even a major source of intelligence for the British government during the war, through his network of Continental contacts. He informed the Prime Minister, Lord Liverpool, of the result of the Battle of Waterloo thirty hours before the news arrived from Lord Wellington.

The Rothschilds were one of the pre-eminent Jewish families in London, part of 'the Cousinhood' – so called from their habit of marrying each other – which also included the Cohens, Goldsmidts, Montefiores, Samuels and Sassoons. The records of the Bevis Marks Synagogue, in East London, list the birth, in 1804, of one Benjamin Disraeli. When Disraeli junior was twelve his father fell out with the Bevis Marks elders and had his children baptised as Christians. When Benjamin entered public life and eventually became Prime Minister he made no secret of his Jewish origins – and his name advertised them. In fact, he seems to have been 'gifted with a superiority complex'[31] – not surprisingly, as he was accustomed to mixing with the Rothschilds in their palatial mansions at Waddesdon and Mentmore.

Jews were distinguished in other and varied walks of British life: Daniel Mendoza (1764–1836), the British boxing champion, came from a Bethnal Green family of Spanish Jews. In his first professional fight, in 1784, he beat Harry the Coalheaver over forty rounds. His scientific style, swift footwork and clever defence made him a British sporting hero, patronised by the Prince of Wales. He made boxing so fashionable that Lord Byron became a pupil at Mendoza the Jew's Boxing Academy, in Bond Street. If the British loved a sportsman, they were equally fond of animals – at least, they developed this reputation, thanks to Lewis Gomperz – the Jewish founder of the Royal Society for the Prevention of Cruelty to Animals (RSCPA).

Although many Jews were socially and economically successful in nineteenth-century Britain, they still suffered civil disabilities in a country whose laws gave primacy to Protestantism. Jews were barred from Oxford and Cambridge Universities, from the Bar and from Parliament, thanks to the Test and Corporation Act of 1673, which required all government officials to take an oath reflecting loyalty to the established Church (so Catholics and Presbyterians were also excluded). Partly to compensate for these restrictions wealthy Jews helped to set up London University in 1826 (later University College), which allowed in students of any or no religion.

The Test Acts were repealed in 1828 and the Catholic Emancipation Act the following year removed restrictions on Roman Catholics. The House of Lords, however, insisted on retaining a Christian form of words in the Oath of Allegiance, which resulted, still, in excluding Jews from Parliament and other offices. It took several more decades for all the barriers to come down. The Christian form of words was set aside so that Moses Montefiore could become Sheriff of London as late as 1937. In 1902, at the peak of Jewish immigration, Marcus Samuel became the fifth Jewish Lord Mayor of London and, accompanied by the Household Cavalry, the Brigade of Guards and the Jews' Orphan Society band, the Lord Mayor's Parade processed through the main Jewish areas of the East End.

Immigrants were not always made to feel so welcome. The arrival of so many poor, culturally distinct and Yiddish-speaking foreigners caused alarm in the 1880s – and not just among the Anglo-Christian population: the established, Anglicised Jewish community also had its concerns, in spite of their success and acceptance by at least part of the Establishment.* The Jewish community still feared an anti-Semitic backlash.† A pogrom in Brick Lane was not out of the question and exotic, Yiddish-speaking Polish Jews with black hats, sidelocks and long coats made an obvious target.

Many English Jews were poor and relied on the charitable system supported by the more prosperous. Fear that this would break down under pressure from needy immigrants caused the Jewish Board of Guardians to inform its correspondents on the Continent: 'In order to avoid trouble in the coming days we beseech every right thinking person among our brethren in Germany, Russia and Austria to place a barrier to the flow of foreigners, to persuade these voyagers not to venture to come to a land they do not know.' But the flow of eastern immigrants was unstoppable, and the resident English community decided acceptance and integration were the only option. The Chief Rabbi, Hermann Adler, preaching in the Princelet Road Synagogue in the East End of London in 1893, reminded his congregation of their duty to help those 'who have newly arrived here from the country where they have been so cruelly oppressed ... Shall we join the hue and cry which is raised in certain quarters and signify our assent to any measures that may prevent immigration of "detestable aliens" as they are called? No, my brethren, emphatically no.' He then reminded his congregation of the words of the Torah (Exodus 23: 9): 'Also thou shalt not oppress a stranger: for ye know the heart of a stranger, seeing ye were strangers in the land of Egypt.'

The Jewish elite threw their charitable resources behind programmes to teach English and job skills and to promote British patriotism – while retaining Jewish identity and religious practice. The *Jewish Chronicle* claimed that a Polish child placed in the Jews' Free School in Bell Lane (Petticoat Lane) would be turned out a young Englishman – complete, in the school photographs, with Eton collar, neatly parted hair and plus fours. State schools proliferated as a result of the 1870 Education Act (469 appeared in London by the early 1900s). East-European Jewish immigrants were suspicious of them, however, as they suspected from their homeland experience (and Christian charity in Britain often came with strings attached) that state schools might have missionary ambitions to convert them to Christianity. Suspicions were overcome by appointing a Jewish headmaster, Abraham Levy, to the Old Castle Street Board School in the East End. Within a few years 95 per cent of its 1,500 pupils

---

* Sir Ernest Cassel was such a close friend of King Edward VII that he was nicknamed 'Windsor Cassel'.
† In 1883 the *Jewish Chronicle* warned: 'An outcry will arise against the newly-come Hebrews which will react terribly upon the comfort and reputation of the older settlers.'

were Jewish, and by 1900 there were sixteen 'Jewish' Board Schools in London. The headmaster of Deal Street School claimed that he produced 'Jewish lads who ... will grow up to be intelligent, industrious, temperate and law-abiding citizens and ... will add to the wealth and stability of the British Empire'.

In 1908 the *Daily Chronicle* reported enthusiastically how adult immigrants rushed from work to join evening classes in English, eager 'to be English, to work for England, fight for England. England is the only western European nation that has been wholly just to the Jews and in return England is the only country where the Jew is as proud of his nation as of his race.' In spite of such an outburst of patriotic optimism, conditions in Britain for first-generation immigrants were not easy. Housing conditions were crowded. In Whitechapel, an almost entirely Jewish area on Russell and Lewis's map 'The Jews in London', the average number of inhabitants per house rose from nine in 1871 to fourteen at the turn of the century. Grandparents, parents, children and lodgers often crowded into small partitioned rooms. Not surprisingly, life spilled out into the streets packed with Jewish shops and stalls, bath houses, fried-fish shops and synagogues. The Jews took over and subdivided the houses of the earlier Huguenot settlers. A Huguenot church on the corner of Brick Lane and Fournier Street, which had become a Wesleyan Chapel in 1819, was converted to a synagogue in 1898. Today it is a mosque. Eventually the East-End Jewish population spread beyond the Whitechapel Road–Hanbury Street triangle, beyond Brick Lane, north towards Bethnal Green and south to Cable Street, where they bordered on the massed ranks of Irish immigrants. Hackney, Shoreditch, Stepney and Bethnal Green remained largely English and here the British Brothers' League thrived far into the early 1900s, encouraging anti-alienism. The jingoistic Conservative MP for Hoxton, Claude George Drummond Hay, campaigned, in 1906, to a song whose words reflected and encouraged the fears of his native constituents:

> *Hay has stood up for Hoxton,*
> *Treated us fair and square,*
> *Guarded our work and wages.*
> *Houses and food and air.*
> *He'll see no Alien Sweater*
> *Rob us of our work today.*
> *Hay is the man we'll vote for,*
> *No-one but Claudie Hay.*

Hay was not averse to dirty tricks. He distributed a spurious statement, supposedly on behalf of his Liberal opponent, Henry Ward: 'In London, where thousands of *foreign paupers* come every year, who fill our *gaols and workhouses, overcrowd* our houses and cut down *wages,* I think perfect freedom should prevail ... *Free trade* means *Cheap* Labour, and as the Polish or German Jew will work for *half the price of an Englishman,* he should not only be welcomed but encouraged to come in greater numbers.'

Fifty years later an early issue of the *East London Black Shirt* (1953) set its sights on a new target, asking: 'Are Coloured Men Becoming a Menace?' and demanding a stop to the 'invasion of Britain by aliens and coloured men'.[32]

It was amongst these poor communities* in the crowded warren of Whitechapel that the most notorious and publicised of English murders took place over a matter of ten weeks in 1888. The sensational Jack the Ripper case thrust the Jewish East End into English mythology[33] – but also increased awareness of the poor housing conditions and dreadful sanitation. The East End was without clean water until 1903. The *East London Observer* reported that, after the first murders – of Polly Nicholls, on 31 August in Durward Street (then Bucks Road), and Anne Chapman, on 8 September in Hanbury Street – hostile crowds began to threaten 'the Hebrew population of the district. It was repeatedly asserted that no Englishman could have perpetrated such a horrible crime as that of Hanbury Street, and that it must have been done by a Jew ... Happily the presence of a large number of police prevented a riot actually taking place.'

The Jack the Ripper case may have been a godsend to the editors of lurid Victorian tabloid newsheets; but the immigrants, like the Irish before them and many since, were busy working all hours that God sent – fifteen hours a day, according to the TUC Congress of 1894 – on a diet of bread and cheese, turning out clothing, shoes and furniture in rudimentary workshops. It was a Jewish tailor in New York, Isaac Singer, who invented the Singer sewing machine, turned thousands of living rooms into sweatshops and revolutionised the ready-made clothing industry.† For several decades after the 1880s over half of Jewish men and women worked in the tailoring trade, mostly stitching ready-cut material for between £1 and £2 10s a week – Jewish tailors went on strike in 1889,

---

* On Charles Booth's 1889 maps of social characteristics and poverty many of the streets in these areas were categorised (and how Victorian boffins loved to categorise!) as 'lowest class, vicious, semi-criminal', or 'very poor, casual, chronic want'.

† Beatrice Webb surveyed the new ghetto for Charles Booth's *Life and Labour of the People in London* (1889) and recorded over a thousand workshops. Manchester (Strangeways), Hull and Leeds (Leylands) also acquired new Jewish enclaves.

demanding the luxury of a twelve-hour day and a six-day working week.

These sweated immigrants were at the bottom of the Victorian social hierarchy. In some respects they resembled the rag-scavenging, street-sweeping, ash-grubbing paupers whom Mayhew had interviewed and recorded for the *Morning Chronicle* in the 1850s. There was a fundamental difference, however: Mayhew's poor were mainly self-employed, grimly hanging on to the grubby skirts of the city, 'survivors from the pre-industrial system',[34] like the poorest inhabitants today in cities such as Cairo or Istanbul. The sweatshop and home workers of the late nineteenth and early twentieth centuries worked for small-scale capitalists, churning out cheap mass-consumer goods or elements in a more complex industrial process. This kind of work was distinctly modern – looking forward to the south-Asian producers of trainers and sportsware of the twenty-first century, rather than backwards to Mayhew's archaic urban survivors.

Immigrants formed the backbone of another modern industry. Cigar-making was traditionally associated with the East End, introduced by Dutch Jews before the onset of east-European immigration. In 1883 the American tobacco industry introduced revolutionary cigarette-making machines, which were taken up by Wills of Bristol – whose monument is the stub-like Wills Memorial Building, which now dominates the university quarter of the city. In London Bernhard Baron exploited a different machine and expanded the Carrera business to mass-produce Craven A cigarettes. Louis Rothman – Rothman's of Pall Mall – dominated the upmarket end of the booming cigarette trade. Thousands of more modest entrepreneurs made caps, rabbit-fur capes and slippers; they fried fish – the archetypal British fast food – baked bagels and ran scores of corner shops. Joseph Lyons opened a tea shop; by 1914 he owned 200 of them, with his famous Corner Houses providing a comfortable retreat for lady shoppers and the growing armies of city office workers.

Though the British labour force engaged in manufacturing reached its peak in 1901, the service sector was already expanding rapidly. In the four decades from 1871 the number employed in clerical, commercial, retail and transport occupations rose by 400 per cent. In the same period the gross national product increased by 150 per cent and the financial services sector by 1,100 per cent. In 1911 three-quarters of a million men and women worked as clerks. Free trade, a generation after the repeal of the Corn Laws, was generating the first global economy. In London Joseph Lyons provided cups of tea to thousands of clerical workers; Montague Burton dressed them respectably and in provincial towns Marks and Spencer supplemented the products of the local market with goods from around the world.

Twelve **New Britons**

BRITAIN WAS NOT in the forefront of modernisation in every respect. In probably no other west-European country was such a large proportion of land held by the descendants of the feudal and court aristocracy. A new Domesday survey, commissioned by the government in 1874–5 and published as *The Great Landowners of Britain and Ireland* (1877), showed that British landownership was scarcely touched by a century of industrial development nor by decades of political reform and market economics.

Fewer than a million people out of a population of 31 million owned any freehold land.* Eighty-five per cent of these owned less than an acre, while according to the report: 'Four thousand five hundred persons held half the area of England and Wales, one thousand seven hundred held nine-tenths of Scotland,' and of the 2,500 'great landowners', of whom 400 were peers, most belonged to families who had held their estates since the sixteenth century. Primogeniture, strict settlements and careful marriages meant that Britain was owned by Europe's smallest but most successful tribe. Quantity of land did not necessarily equate with economic success, but as Trollope's Archbishop Grantly so rightly commented: 'Land gives so much more than rent. It gives position and influence and political power, to say nothing of the game.'

As the new Domesday survey appeared, however, times were changing for the Dedlocks of Britain and Ireland.† They were hit by competition from the great prairie producers of North America, a string of dreadful

---

* There were over five times as many both in France and Germany.
† Dickens captured the spirit of the traditional landowner (in *Bleak House,* 1852):

> 'Sir Leicester Dedlock is only a baronet, but there is no mightier baronet than he. His family is as old as the hills, and infinitely more respectable. He has a general opinion that the world might get on without hills, but would be done up without Dedlocks. He would on the whole admit Nature to be a good idea (a little low, perhaps, when not enclosed within a park fence), but an idea dependent for its execution on your great country families.'

harvests, mass migration to the towns and tumbling grain prices (at their lowest for a century, by the 1890s). The decades on either side of 1900 saw the start of a transformation 'in the economics, politics and social structure of landed property in the United Kingdom – a revolution that was in context dramatic and highly visible, in other contexts largely imperceptible to the majority of contemporaries'.[1] In Ireland the Land Acts of 1885 and 1903 led to the transfer of about two-thirds of agrarian freehold land from landlords to former tenants. Land also lost status in an increasingly urban and capitalist society and, for the first time, new peers were not necessarily sizeable landholders. Landed estates began to be fragmented and sold to tenants. It was said, in 1900, that half of Scotland was for sale in the hands of one Edinburgh lawyer. By 1910, eighty of the hundred wealthiest families in Britain had made their fortunes from manufacturing.

The greatest change was in Ireland, where, following the famine and years of large-scale emigration, there was also the greatest pressure. The publication of the 1861 census highlighted the issues: out of a population of 5.75 million, 4.5 million were Catholics. Fewer than three-quarters of a million people were members of the established Church. The Irish revolutionary movement, the Fenians,* aimed 'to make Ireland an independent democratic republic' – though they chose the wrong time to rise up: the night of 5 March 1867, when heavy snow fell and the Fenians became literally bogged down. Later in the year there were incidents in Manchester and Clerkenwell, when a policeman and innocent bystanders were killed. Gladstone did not react by initiating draconian suppression: rather he pursued reform to address what he saw as legitimate Irish grievances. Gladstone's Church Act of 1869 severed the official connection between Church and State: Protestantism's ascendancy had peaked. Gladstone also initiated a series of Land Acts, which radically altered the tenure of land in Ireland.

In spite of the reforms the 'Irish Problem' did not go away. Lord Belmore's agent reported in August 1880: 'I have been for the last two days in the County Leitrim which is in a very disturbed state. The authorities would not let me move about without a guard of police. They appear to dread the people coming down like Zulus from the hills and carrying the country by storm.' This was written at about the same time

---

* Founded on St Patrick's Day 1856 by James Stephens, the Fenians took their name from the legendary warrior cohort of Fionn Mac Cumhaill the Na Fianna. Stephens's time in America brought him into contact with many hard-bitten Irish soldiers, trained and toughened by their experiences in the Civil War – and keen to get at the English. Clan na Gael, the Irish-American Fenian Society, was the start of the longer-term American support for Irish republicans.

as Captain Boycott (agent for Lord Erne) was deliberately abandoned by virtually all the estate staff and 150 Orangemen from the north gathered the harvest, protected by armed guards of the Royal Irish Constabulary. Boycott's letter to *The Times*, bemoaning his situation, made him a household name and gave a new word to the English language.

In October 1881 Sir William Gregory, demonstrating a stiff upper lip, wrote:

> I am in the land of the living, albeit the landlord shooting
> season has set in with great briskness in my county ...
> all around me there prevails an absolute reign of terror ...
> Besides assassinations successful and assassinations incom-
> plete, there is cutting off ears, and desperate assaults, and
> mutilation of cattle, and orders, which dare not be resisted to
> servants to leave their masters' houses, and to shepherds and
> herds to leave their flocks ... A single emissary of the Land
> League exercises more terror and authority over a whole dis-
> trict than all the magistrates, police and priests put together ...
> Threatening notices of murders are flying like snowballs ...'2

The land question had, however, generated a well-organised political party structure in Ireland, substantially due to Charles Stewart Parnell (1846–91), an Irish Protestant. Parnell's divorce scandal in 1890 com-promised the ultra-respectable Victorian values of Gladstone – the Irish best hope in England – not to mention good Catholics. Parnell was seri-ously undermined and the strain told on his health. He died in Brighton in 1891, but he left a legacy: the question of Irish Home Rule was now high on the British political agenda and would not go away.

At the same time as political activism boiled up in Ireland so did a renewed enthusiasm for Irish culture. The status of the Irish language had withered dramatically since the overthrow of the native aristocracy, the chief patrons of bards, music and poetry, in the seventeenth century. While Welsh had become the symbol of national identity and the medium of religious expression, the Irish language was dangerously close to being ignored as the archaic mumblings of a depressed peasantry. With the dramatic rise of the population, by the early nineteenth century there were probably more Irish-speakers than at any time in history, but they were the poorest and weakest members of society. The native language was already in decline before the Great Famine, migration and English prejudice ripped the heart out of it. Fortunately, new enthusiasts were at hand to resuscitate the cause just before the condition became terminal. They formed the Gaelic League – Conradh na Gaeilge – to foster the language and embed its teaching within the educational system, and established a weekly paper, *Fainne an Lae* ('Dawn of the Day'). One of the founders of the league was Douglas Hyde, son of an Anglican clergyman. In November 1892 he told his Dublin audience straight, in a lecture entitled 'The Necessity of de-Anglicising Ireland': '[The Irish public] continues to apparently hate the English and at the same time continues to imitate them; how it continues to clamour for recognition as a distinct nationality, and at the same time throws away with both hands what would make it so.' The study and translation of ancient texts such as the *Tain Bo Cuailnge*, Ireland's great epic, reminded the Irish of a fact largely forgotten since the Tudor catastrophe: they were the possessors of the oldest vernacular literary tradition in western Europe.

There were also robust Irishmen who wanted to de-Anglicise games and sports. Michael Cusack, from Clare, established the Gaelic Athletic Association to organise and promote hurling and Gaelic football. Several of his co-organisers in the GAA were Fenians: the promotion of Irish identity was closely allied with political activism, and also with the concept of severing economic, linguistic and political dependency on Britain. So a new organisation dedicated to independence took the name Sinn Fein, meaning 'We Ourselves' (sometimes translated as 'Ourselves Alone').*

In 1912, with the powers of the House of Lords curtailed and the Liberal government of Asquith dependent on Irish nationalist support, a Home Rule bill looked likely. Protestants hated the idea and found a powerful spokesman in Dublin: Sir Edward Carson, an Irish lawyer totally opposed to Irish independence.† Carson had a knack for theatrical oratory, rousing the mass rallies that gathered to hear him speak. The sparks of intransigence and threats of violence in Ulster were fanned, across the water, by the new leader of the British Conservative Party, a Canadian-born Ulsterman, Andrew Bonar Law. He practically cocked the Orange rifles when he declared: 'If an attempt were made to deprive these men of their birthright they would be justified in resisting by all means in their power, including force … I can imagine no length of resistance to which Ulster can go in which I would not be prepared to support them.' With the establishment of the Ulster Volunteer Force, a well-armed military organisation committed to maintaining the *status quo*, it was evident that Home Rule for Ireland was not going to be straightforward.

* The phrase was put forward by Maire Butler, ironically a cousin of Edward Carson, the ultimate promoter of Unionism.
† Carson had been a student with Oscar Wilde at Trinity College but represented Lord Queensbury in Wilde's prosecution which led to his imprisonment in Reading Gaol.

The revolution eventually erupted when, on Easter Monday, 24 April 1916, about a thousand Irish volunteers seized the General Post Office in Dublin, raised the tricolour and proclaimed a provisional government. In the heavy fighting that followed 450 people died and the elegant Sackville Street (now O'Connell Street) was almost reduced to rubble by British artillery. The Irish republicans were overwhelmed by a combination of their own incompetence, British military superiority, and bad luck. Nevertheless, the British managed to sour their own victory: the internment and executions* which followed the Easter Rising presented the Irish with a whole host of martyrs to inhabit the national mythology. A previously apathetic public became determinedly anti-British.†

In the first years of the Great War 100,000 Irish had volunteered to join the British forces. Yet the British government, as always during European conflicts, feared the possibility that Ireland would offer a back door to the enemy – an anxiety exacerbated when Sir Roger Casement attempted to ship arms into Ireland in a German submarine and a steamer, the *Aud*, on the eve of the Easter Rising.‡ Sinn Fein benefited from the changing mood. One of the victors in the 1917 by-election was Eamonn de Valera, who was to become the dominant figure in Irish politics in the first half of the twentieth century. He had survived the Easter Rising and just been released from prison, fortunate not to have been translated into the ranks of the martyrs himself. De Valera had a Spanish father and an Irish mother, and had been born in New York. From among the possible permutations of ethnicity he chose Irishness. His American citizenship, however, probably saved him from execution. The British government, under David Lloyd George (showing no sympathy for his fellow Celts), continued to detain its opponents, who responded with hunger strikes.

The British claimed to have fought the Great War partly to improve the lot of small, beleaguered nations. The Armistice in November 1918 provided an opportunity to see what this meant for Ireland. Nationalists fought the election, which rapidly followed the end of the war, demanding

---

* Fifteen people were executed between 3 May and 12 May, extending the agony and infuriating the Irish – a public-relations disaster for the British, who displayed crass stupidity rather than the fair play on which they prided themselves.

† Thomas Ashe, a hero of the Easter Rising, died as a result of force-feeding. Huge crowds attended his funeral, and were addressed by a twenty-seven-year-old, then unknown, firebrand named Michael Collins, who was to become one of the most charismatic leaders of the independence movement.

‡ In the last desperate months of the war, Lloyd George proposed to make conscription compulsory in Ireland (the number of volunteers had dropped dramatically). This inflamed anti-British sentiment. The arrest of supposedly pro-German Sinn Fein leaders drove opposition underground.

an end to Irish MPs in Westminster and the establishment of a national assembly. They even appealed to the Versailles Peace Conference to recognise the Irish right to independence. The 1918 election was the last pan-Irish parliamentary election in the twentieth century. Sinn Fein won seventy-three seats (it had had only seven before). Irish politics was transformed and the majority wish for complete independence from Britain could not be ignored.

Predictably, the Sinn Fein MPs refused to take their seats in Westminster and instead set up the Dáil Éireann ('Assembly of Ireland'), which was boycotted by the Unionists. Inspired by their American cousins, the Dáil announced a Declaration of Independence. On 1 April 1919 de Valera was elected President of the Dáil and he chose a team of ministers, an alternative to the Dublin Castle regime. A group of about two thousand volunteers was elected to defend this new government and became known as the Irish Republican Army (IRA). The killing, on 21 January 1919, of two Royal Irish Constables started a nasty and vicious campaign of guerrilla warfare and assassination. Both sides were ruthless. On Sunday morning, 21 November, Michael Collins's hit squad murdered eleven suspected British intelligence officers; that afternoon the Black and Tans retaliated.* They opened fire on a crowd of innocent football spectators, killing twelve. Ireland had its first Bloody Sunday. The vicious cycle of reprisals came to an incendiary climax when the Black and Tans torched the town centre of Cork in revenge for an IRA attack.

This kind of neo-colonialist thuggery did enormous damage to Britain's international reputation. Consequently, in 1921, Lloyd George pursued a truce to the Anglo-Irish War, demanding that the IRA should first disarm.† The IRA, of course, refused. Nevertheless, a truce was agreed on 11 July 1921 and the rival parties met: de Valera was offered Dominion status (like Canada) for Ireland — excluding the six counties in the north-east. This was unacceptable to the Dáil, as it would partition Ireland. However, the nationalists were in dire economic straits and could scarcely afford to reopen active warfare with the British. The new delegation (from which de Valera wisely excluded himself) had an impossible task.‡

---

* The Black and Tans were former British soldiers recruited in 1920 to support the Royal Irish Constabulary. They got their name from their odd mixture of uniforms, and their reputation from their ruthless and often downright lawless behaviour. They contributed to the British government's loss of any moral high ground.

† As so often in Irish history events seem to repeat themselves.

‡ The delegation was a mutually suspicious bunch that included a reluctant Michael Collins, the Sinn Fein leader, Arthur Griffiths, who rejected the use of force, and Erskine Childers, author of *The Riddle of the Sands* and a gun-runner.

There was no way that the shrewd and manipulative Lloyd George was going to agree to an Irish republic. Compromise was inevitable, but was likely to be reviled by die-hard republicans. After stressful and protracted negotiations agreement was finally reached at 2.10 a.m, on 6 December 1921, to establish the 'Irish Free State' – Saorstát Éireann – as a Dominion of the British Empire. Predictably, communal violence broke out in Belfast, where several hundred died and the Royal Ulster Constabulary, backed by 16,000 part-time 'B-specials', was established as what amounted to a Protestant militia.

In Dublin the Dáil was dramatically riven. A small majority supported the proposed treaty and de Valera resigned as President. Civil war broke out between former comrades, who now slaughtered each other over the fine print of the treaty, in a season of collective insanity. The pro-Governmment Kevin O'Higgins signed the death warrant of the IRA stalwart Rory O'Connor, who had been best man at his wedding less than a year before. Michael Collins predicted his own fate: he was gunned down, aged thirty-one, in County Cork. Ireland was traumatised as its children consumed and eventually exhausted themselves, but not before 4,000 of its most patriotic activists lay dead.

Lloyd George had persuaded the Irish treaty delegation to set aside the important issue of the six north-eastern counties and await a Boundary Commission report. The republicans were aware of northern demographics. In the 1911 census only three counties – Antrim, Derry and Down – had had Protestant majorities* and even within these, particularly Derry, there were significant areas where Catholics formed the majority. There were clear Catholic majorities in the other three counties – Tyrone, Armagh and Fermanagh.

The Irish delegation who signed the 1921 treaty had persuaded themselves that Lloyd George's Boundary Commission enquiry would show that a separate Northern Union was not viable. The expectations of the Nationalists were dashed – the border was not altered and proportional representation was replaced by the British first-past-the-post system of voting, which solidified the monopoly of power of the Unionist majority. Ulster Prime Minister Craig pronounced the new, ostentatious Stormont Parliament building, 'a Protestant parliament for a Protestant people'.[3] Religion and ethnicity still ruled in Irish politics. In England, though, Irish politics were relegated to a side show. Since 1801 the presence of Irish MPs in Westminster had made Irish issues

---

* Protestantism in the north was not unified: it included Anglicans, Nonconformists and Presbyterians.

central to British political life. Now the removal of over eighty Irish Nationalist members pushed Ireland off the agenda and fatally wounded the Liberal Party.

Even as late as 1953 the leader of the Irish Labour Party, Brendan Corish, could announce to the Dáil: 'I am an Irishman second; I am a Catholic first'.[4] In the severely economically depressed new state, controlled by an unimaginative gerontocracy of aged revolutionaries* and where marriage, education and even publication were dominated by the Catholic Church, many Irish people, especially the young, chose the ancient solution: emigration. In the 1950s and 1960s they left in large numbers to take up work in the thriving English job market.

Irish immigrants to Britain in the nineteenth century had often been met with hostility and prejudice. Yet in comparison with many countries Victorian Britain was relatively liberal. Certainly Indian and black Britains often met with crude racial taunts, but there were opportunities to succeed and to make a decent life: from George Rice, a black doctor in South London, to Joe Clough, the first West Indian bus-driver in London, to Samuel Coleridge-Taylor, a leading composer – when he died prematurely the funeral route through Croydon was lined with mourners. Black football players also strode the pitches of Preston North End, Tottenham Hotspur and Glasgow Rangers.

Arthur Wharton was the first black professional, a goalkeeper for Sheffield United, Preston North End and Rotherham. Walter Tull was an outstanding player from Glasgow Rangers. Grandson of a Barbadian slave he was brought up in an orphanage in Bethnal Green. He left Rangers to join the army, where he became the first black officer in the history of the British forces (or at least since the Romans occupied the country). He was killed in the last few weeks of the Great War.

Unfortunately, their efforts were rewarded with a century of racist chanting, which has besmirched the so-called 'beautiful game'. From the 1970s and 80s the Football Association and British clubs tried hard, and largely successfully, to stamp out racist abuse from the terraces, as teams such as Arsenal and Liverpool became dependent on black players. Even in 2004, black players Shaun Wright-Phillips and Ashley Cole had to put up with the moronic racist abuse of the Spanish crowd in Madrid's Bernabeu Stadium. At the same time, Britain's Olympic medal tally would be seriously depleted without its black athletes and heroines such as Kelly Holmes, and new stars like the young boxer Amin Khan.

If there were glimmers of growing tolerance in Victorian society, they

---

* Éamonn de Valera was returned as Taoiseach in 1957, aged seventy-five, and subsequently served two seven-year terms as President.

soon faded. Imperial setbacks in India and South Africa combined with the anti-Jewish backlash towards the end of the nineteenth century to make Britain a less hospitable society for foreigners. With little real evidence, hysterical commentators warned of the waves of immigrants supposedly swamping the country – an image revived by Margaret Thatcher. In fact, far more people left the country than entered it in the four decades from 1870. Almost 2 million Britons departed for America, Australia, Canada, South Africa and New Zealand – part of what was regarded as 'the British world movement'. If arrivals in Britain were often portrayed as cast-offs and dregs, British migrants were the torch-bearers of civilisation, permeating the darkness of barbarism. In New Zealand there were 'waste lands calling for civilisation'.[5]

The final wave of the 'agricultural revolution', which had arrived on British shores about 6,000 years before, was now transported to the Antipodes: forests were cleared, sheep, cattle and rabbits (Australia had 600 million by 1950) pushed aside indigenous species – including humans, who, as in America, succumbed to western diseases in large numbers. Around the southern hemisphere the English language, along with cricket, rugby and Gothic architecture, etched the high-water mark of the imperial project. It was not really a project, however, nor a national mission: there was no coherent programme of mass emigrations. Freedom of movement across the pink parts of the globe was made possible by the Pax Britannica – though the indigenous peoples of Australia, New Zealand and South Africa learned the hard way that the Pax came out of the barrel of the Colt Navy pistol and the Maxim machine-gun.

As the British responded to the tug of urbanisation and industrialisation most migrated internally – to Belfast, Glasgow, Birmingham or London. Thousands of individuals and families, but still a minority, made more adventurous decisions – drawn to new cities like Sydney, the latest gold rush, or the wide-open spaces. Unlike the plantation-owners of the West Indies, or the imperial administrators of India and parts of Africa, these people went to settle.*

Early migrants from Britain to Australia were as powerless as black slaves. The first deportees were shipped out in 1782 to relieve the pressure on prisons: six ships caried 737 convicted men, women and children. Mary Haydock, born in 1777 in Bury (Lancashire), was arrested at the age of thirteen for stealing while dressed as a boy, and transported to Sydney in 1792. John Caesar, nicknamed 'Black Caesar', was born in

---

* In 1890 Britain had a population of about 34 million and 290,000 emigrated. At that time there were about 3 million British- and Irish-born people living in the USA, half a million in Canada, 800,000 in Australia and 150,000 in South Africa.[6]

Madagascar and arrested at twenty-three years of age for stealing £12 in Deptford, where he was employed as a servant, and transported on the first penal fleet. If British emigration (with the exception of prisoners and the Catholic Irish) was seen as heroic, immigrants were more often regarded as pathetic or parasitical. Tracts such as *The Alien Invasions* by William Wilkins of the Society for Preventing the Immigration of Destitute Aliens (founded 1891) accused Jews of stealing British jobs and forcing up rents. Local politicians complained about 'Yids' creating 'a foreign town', of Englishmen driven from their homes by 'the off-scum of Europe' and 'alien invasions'.*[7]

A youthful Winston Churchill came forward bearing the shield of tolerance, though he was about to stand as a Liberal, in 1904, for the seat of North-West Manchester, which had a large Jewish population. He wrote to *The Times* in support of 'the old tolerant and generous practice of free entry and asylum to which this country has so long adhered and from which it has so greatly gained'. Nevertheless, the Tory government succumbed to the prevalent anti-immigrant pressure and, on 10 August 1905, passed the Aliens Act. For the first time there was an official bar on entry to Britain. For another century the immigration issue would become a political football. Xenophobia was made respectable.

East-European Jews were not the only targets of hostility. Gypsies deported from Holland were sent back.† The Chinese were marked out as the 'Yellow Peril' and characterised as Dr Fu-Manchu-like villains running opium dens and the white-slave trade.‡ The popular imagination preferred to ignore official reports that the Chinese community (largely made up of ex-sailors) was remarkably law-abiding and mainly engaged in laundry work.

In practice, the Aliens Act was more symbolic than effective and relatively few immigrants were denied entry. With the outbreak of World War I, however, a much more draconian regime was put in place with the Aliens Restrictions Act. Britain had many German inhabitants – butchers,

---

* H. G. Wells tapped into this fear with his book *The War of the Worlds*, which appeared in 1898.
† Gypsies or 'Egyptians' were first recorded in Britain in Scotland in 1505, and in England a decade later, when a gypsy fortune teller is mentioned. Their travelling way of life has attracted the hostility of the settled population ever since. The Criminal Justice Act of 1994 removed thee local council obligation to provide traveller encampments. Following a tabloid newspaper hate campaign in 2004 Nick Williams of the Metropolitan Police said, 'I think some newspaper headlines have been outrageous'. The *Observer* (14 November 2004) reported, 'Racism against gypsies has been so severe that it is akin to the way black people were treated in the sixties'. For a sympathetic account of gypsies see Judith Oakley (1983).[8]
‡ In 1913 Arthur Ward, using the exotic pen name 'Sax Rohmer', created his arch-villain Dr Fu-Manchu, who became a stereotype of the sinister oriental. Evil aliens also loom large in the work of Arthur Conan Doyle.

bakers and bankers – whose businesses were hit by a Trading with the Enemy Act – and more literally by hostile English mobs, who smashed their windows and looted shops from London to Keighley and Crewe. The *Daily Mail*, following its traditional policy of righteous racism, in August 1914 called for German waiters to be sacked – and many wère. In an era of populist newspapers and populist politics public opinion was manipulated and scapegoats demonised. Horatio Bottomley, editor of *John Bull*, the biggest-selling weekly, called for 'a vendetta against every German in Britain ... you cannot naturalise an unnatural beast – a human abortion – a hellish freak. But you can exterminate it. And now the time has come ... the moral leprosy of the tribe to which he belongs must be emphasised by a boycott in every station of life' (15 May 1914). Anti-German riots spread through London, Liverpool, Manchester and other Lancashire towns in Britain's *Kristallnacht*.*

Ironically, many Germans had emigrated to Britain and established businesses here specifically because they opposed Prussian militarism. One woman, Mrs Elizabeth Palowker, was abused by an angry mob who assumed her name was German. In fact, her husband was half-Indian, and her sons were serving with the army in France. Mrs Palowker decided to Anglicise her name to Wilson – an example followed by another family: the Saxe-Coburg-Gothas became the Windsors, and their relatives, the Battenbergs, changed their name to Mountbatten.†

As a baby-boomer, born just over two years after the end of World War II, I spent my childhood immersed in films, comics, songs and images of the war. An enormous, dank air-raid shelter dominated our junior school's playground; an ageing Churchill was the national hero, and my father and uncles regularly talked about their war-time experience: D-Day and the invasion of Europe, life in India or on convoys crossing the Atlantic and visits to Jack Dempsey's club in New York; the reaction of young Communists in Archangel to seeing a crucifix. My mother was a land girl and my grandmother, a widow, left at home with her youngest son, was better off than she had ever been, as her older children sent money home (and civilian mortality rates fell, partly due to the diet imposed by rationing). World War II seemed almost an enjoyable caper – an opportunity to see the world.‡

* Two thousand properties were attacked in London, and 500 in Liverpool.
† King George V, crowned on 23 June 1911, was born George Frederick Ernest Albert of Saxe-Coburg und Gotha. His queen, Mary, had previously been Princess Victoria Marie von Teck-Württemberg (though born in Kensington Palace). Kaiser Wilhelm II was King George's cousin. However, from the Hanoverian George I to George V these imported Protestant monarchs had provided essential stability in Britain, and every British monarch from 1714 to Victoria's death in 1901 had a German spouse.

In comparison, in our community, the impact of World War I – the Great War – still seemed overwhelming. My own family was fortunate to have no serious casualties in World War II, yet my maternal grandfather had died in 1932 from severe wounds, which included being gassed and losing a leg, fighting with the Canadians at Vimy Ridge. I was close to my father's father, and I was dreadfully shocked when, standing next to me at a rugby match, he vomited blood and collapsed – gas, which had corroded his lungs since 1918, had insidiously killed him forty years later. On Armistice Day in the 1950s the pall of sadness at the war memorials in virtually every town and village still seeped in from the Great War. The troops' cynical songs – 'We've seen, we've seen 'em, hanging on the old barbed wire' – had none of the patriotic romanticism of Vera Lynn or the cheerfulness of Glen Miller in World War II.

The poetry of Wilfred Owen, Siegfried Sassoon, Isaac Rosenberg or Edward Thomas conveyed an overwhelming regret and bitterness. Aside from the character of World War I and the sheer bloody awfulness of the Western Front, the cold statistics explain the impact on Britain and its families. Between 1914 and 1918 723,000 British servicemen died in action (compared with earlier wars relatively fewer died from disease or infected wounds); and of 5.2 million who served in the army nearly one-third were wounded – so everyone knows veterans like my grandfathers: men with limbs missing, blinded or gassed. In World War II 264,000 servicemen and women died, and 77,000 civilians, 30,000 of whom were women. In 1939 the British population was larger than in 1918, yet the number serving in the forces was 1.4 million fewer. In World War II 5.6 per cent were killed compared with 11.8 per cent in the Great War. Simply in demographic terms these were losses that could soon be made up by a healthy population. Other national combatants fared worse: Germany suffered 2 million military casualties in World War I, France 1.3 million, Russia 1.8 million, and Serbia lost some 6 per cent of its entire population – in comparison Britain lost 1.6 per cent. Emotionally, though, the shock to the British people was intensified by the fact that most of the casualties came from such a youthful group – 37 per cent of the dead were aged twenty to twenty-four. Because of the carnage to locally recruited 'pals' regiments, small communities found they had, overnight, lost a generation of young men. Twenty per cent of Oxford and Cambridge graduates who joined up were killed: officers were trained to lead from the front.

---

‡ I got a very different impression of the war when I first went to Germany, aged twelve, and visited the Dachau concentration camp; also when I went to Russia a few years later.

The Great War seems like a watershed, but in many ways it was not. In the big picture of British history the most significant changes began to accelerate in the later nineteenth century. These dramatic social and economic transformations generated conflicts around the world (particularly in Europe), which became unmanageable by 1914. The spread of railways and steamships created global networks earlier in the nineteenth century; rival industrial economies sprang up across North America, Europe and as far afield as Japan. With this came new competitive economic pressures, imperial ambitions, all fuelled by the powerful press and public opinion. By 1914 there were a hundred times as many newspapers across the world as there had been in the late eighteenth century. These pressures generated an arms race between the superpowers. Britain produced steel monsters like the almost 18,000-ton ship *Dreadnought* and Germany launched a submarine fleet. On 25 July 1909 Louis Blériot became the first person ever to fly into Britain, taking off in his monoplane from France, near Calais, and landing near Dover Castle. A new form of transport was born that would also deliver warfare directly to civilian populations.

The Census of 1871 showed that almost half the population of England and Wales lived in the countryside and small towns. Farming still employed as many people as mining, textiles and transport put together. There was also 'a remarkable sense of unbroken ethnic continuity with past times: the inhabitants of the different localities of the United Kingdom were still perceived as the direct descendants of Saxons, Angles, Danes, Celts, of those who had risen with Jack Cade and Wat Tyler'.[9] In spite of industrialisation and urbanisation most families remained rooted in the locale that they had occupied for centuries. Even town- and city-dwellers mainly migrated from the immediate hinterland.[10]

In the decade after the 1871 Census the countryside drastically lost its population while the towns expanded by over 25 per cent (and by three times as much in the major metropolises). Even today on a train rolling out of Manchester, Leeds or London the suburban skirts of red-brick houses seem to spread endlessly over what were principally green fields until the 1870s. By 1911 the population had risen to 45 million, 7 million of whom lived in Greater London. The railways and the Underground enabled Londoners increasingly to surf the transport system to dormitories on its outer edges, encouraged by new, romantic and misleading names, such as Chalk Farm and Golders Green.*

---

* Even the masterly Underground map gives the impression that the suburbs are closer than they actually are.

On the eve of World War I the proportion of people employed in agriculture was down to 8 per cent (France and Germany had, relatively, four and three times as many) and in the largest-expanding towns half the population had come from somewhere else – usually, in fact, from the nearby countryside; and these people were young, and disproportionately female. As a result eight out of ten children were born in towns and cities in the first decade of the twentieth century. In the four decades prior to World War I about 6 million Britons – many of whom were male agricultural workers – emigrated. The number of immigrants, in spite of all the fuss, was relatively small: about 400,000 actually settled as British citizens, a third of whom were east-European Jews. The Census of 1911 recorded a mere 4,000 Britons of Asian origin, 12,000 from Africa and 9,000 from the West Indies. Almost all of them lived in large cities. Across the shires and in rural Scotland and Ireland virtually the whole population was made up of ancient Britons.

Between 1871 and 1911 these Britons bred with remarkable facility – increasing the population by half – from 31 million to 45 million. Yet the concerns of the day shifted: from the Malthusian fear, in mid-century, that food supply could not keep pace with the multitudes of mouths, to anxiety about declining birth rates. The new urban-dwellers preferred small families. Victoria herself, with nine children, was a typical mother of the early Victorian period (except that, unusually, her children all survived). By the end of her reign women were being exhorted to have more children. But it was the most prosperous who set the example, by having few, if any at all.

Marriage also went out of fashion in the early 1900s, with half the male population unmarried by the age of thirty.* In the mid-nineteenth century the average number of surviving children per marriage was over five. Fifty years later the number had fallen to three† – a pattern of decline which has continued in Britain and the rest of the modern, urban world (except for a brief post World War II increase, and amongst first-generation immigrants).

There is no shortage of theories to explain the reduction in family size: attempts to maintain living standards at times of depression and wage reduction; the increasing cost of education for the middle classes; and the introduction of compulsory state education in the 1870s, which took young children out of the labour market and made them an expensive

---

* When I married for the first and only time, in 1969, three-quarters of British males had followed suit by the age of thirty.

† In 1871 the annual reproduction rate for live births was 34.1 per 1,000, falling to 24.5 per 1,000 in 1910–12.

item for working-class families.* Other explanations have focused less on economic factors and more on education, literacy and the dissemination of knowledge about contraception. Declining fertility was not restricted simply to Britain or to urban populations, however; it was a widespread phenomenon, probably caused by varied and complex factors. And it was not simply that infant-mortality rates declined, as they remained high in the later nineteenth century, rising suddenly to 163 per 1,000 in 1899 and only improving dramatically after 1902.†

The general decline in mortality rates in Britain was partly influenced by developments in medical science and their availability, improvements in diet as incomes rose, better housing, hygiene and public services. Cigarette-smoking was rare before the 1890s so did not kick in as a major killer until the twentieth century.

By the onset of World War I many aspects of the modern world were well developed: the demographic revolution, the dramatic improvements in the infrastructure of cities, in transport, communications, food pro-duction, leisure and entertainment, education and consumerism and stable, family-centred life. Nearly a million men were employed in mines producing 300 million tons of coal a year. Yet Britain's world dominance in industry was already over. In 1870 it possessed almost a third of the world's manufacturing capacity; by 1910 this figure had slipped to 15 per cent as the USA and Germany forged ahead.

My own early childhood, in the late 40s and early 50s, was in many ways closer to the experiences of my grandfather at the same age in the early 1890s than to those of my own children. Life was still centred on the local mill, the pub and the clubs, the chapel (in our case the Catholic church) and Sunday school, the allotments and the family. None of our neighbours owned their own house, had a car, a television or a telephone. On Mondays the women did the washing by hand with a posser (a plunging device, and a word that seems to have disappeared from every-day use in the past fifty years) and washing lines filled the streets with the effect of billowing sails. Many women worked in the mills, but not usually when their children were young, and I do not think anyone in the neigh-bourhood was divorced.‡

Older women had brown, toasted shins from sitting close to coal fires;

* Though in 1901 300,000 children were found to be in regular employment.
† Rates were closely linked to class and poverty. In the East End of London, mortality rates were over 200 per 1,000 and less than 80 in the healthier and wealthier suburbs like Hampstead. In Dublin infant mortality hit the dreadful rate of 269 per 1,000 in 1874 - probably exacerbated by the lack of mains drainage, which only arrived in 1906.
‡ Though in the late 40s divorce rates soared for the first time, as post-war romances fractured in the face of reality.

the men hawked and spat a lot. Everyone went to Blackpool, Filey, Scarborough or Bridlington for their holidays – usually at the same time, in late July, when the factories closed for Wakes Week. Our local small town had two cinemas,* men worked on Saturday mornings and went to rugby league or football matches in the afternoons – often with their fathers, sons or brothers, rarely with their wives or girlfriends.

The big shift, from my personal experience, came in 1952 – *The Archers* started on radio, the first soap opera and the first time the usually welcoming next-door neighbours insisted I shut up or clear off when I wandered into their house. Shortly afterwards, following the Coronation in June 1953, everyone began to hire a television; and from 1955 schoolmates who had ITV boasted about how much better it was than the (then Reithian) BBC. I saw a coloured man for the first time – a Sikh pedlar started knocking on doors, carrying a suitcase from which he sold nylons and other luxuries to local housewives. Darshan Singh was probably the first Sikh pedlar in Yorkshire.† He arrived in 1938, based himself in Bradford, then set up shop in Leeds, from where he promoted a network of Sikh salesmen.

When I started at a Catholic primary school, in 1952, I first made friends with foreign children – mainly Poles and Ukrainians whose families had arrived after the war. At the age of five I used to call '*Djindobri, babska*' – 'Good-day, granny' – to the black-swathed Polish old ladies who waited by the school gate every afternoon to collect their grandchildren. The Polish families served borscht when I went to visit – we only ate Heinz tomato soup at home; the fathers drank vodka and hated the Russians.

Foreigners livened up the early 50s world where I lived as a child – a period often referred to as 'drab', though it didn't seem so at the time. At the end of my grandmother's road there was a large shed. Inside there were rows of bright-red bins – full of ice cream made by a local Italian family. I ate the ice cream in the form of a cornet – an Anglo-Italian solution to the complaint of a *Lancet* report in 1879. In London Italian organists, particularly around their enclave in Clerkenwell, had taken to selling roasted chestnuts in winter and ice cream in the summer. The organists' music became a sales pitch for the ice cream, which survives today in the chimes of the ice-cream van. Much of the ice cream was made in desperately unhygienic conditions and served in small glasses, which then received a rudimentary swill and a wipe with a dirty rag. Cholera was still

---

* In 1946 a third of the population went to the cinema once a week and 13 per cent went twice. As a result *Gone with the Wind* is the most watched film in British cinema history.
† The first Sikh gurdwara, or temple, opened in Shepherd's Bush in 1911.

a major urban killer and the *Lancet* pointed an accusing finger at the Italian cottage industry, particularly its dirty glass containers.

The conical wafer – which always reminded me of communion wafers – was the more hygienic response. Italian ice-cream parlours were especially popular in Scotland. Before World War I Glasgow had about three hundred of them. Italian men were also popular with British women – and most married locally. The offspring of one Italian and his Irish wife was Guglielmo Marconi who, in 1901, transmitted the first radio message across the Atlantic and won the Nobel Prize for Physics eight years later.

To get to my grandmother's house and the ice cream, we always travelled on a double-decker bus. Within a few years most of the conductors on these buses, from Halifax to Huddersfield, were West Indians, and at the local mill, which was managed by my father, Pakistani men arrived to work on the night shifts – newly introduced to make the most of modern German spinning machines. Local women would not work nights and most men regarded the mill as a place where women worked for low wages.

In 1951 the number of men working in manufacturing jobs in Britain peaked at 6 million (40 per cent of the labour force). As the post-war economy boomed, over half a century of low birth rates and emigration kicked in and generated a labour shortage. For the first time the Empire, which at its peak had contained a quarter of the world's population, began to export its people back to the home country. First, though, the British government looked to sources closer to hand. Interviewers from the Ministry of Labour visited displaced persons' camps across Europe at the end of the war to select people in good health to come to Britain to work in areas of labour shortage – in textiles, coal mining and farming. Ninety-one thousand of these European volunteer workers, mainly Russian, arrived to help fill the labour gap. About 145,000 Poles also took up residence in post-war Britain – mainly ex-soldiers and their families whose contribution to the war, including the Battle of Britain, was often overlooked.

These workers were needed. The period from the end of World War II to the oil crisis of the early 70s saw the most rapid economic expansion in recorded history. From 1950 to 1970 the European gross domestic product grew at the rate of about 5.5 per cent per annum. Britain, now with no rural masses to draw on, suffered a labour shortage through the 50s and 60s.

Some of the potential labour force had arrived before the war. About 70,000 middle-Europeans, fleeing from Hitler and the Nazis with increasing desperation, fetched up in Britain between the early 1930s and the start of World War II.[11] About 55,000 became permanent residents. This was an exceptionally well-educated, self-disciplined group whose determined promotion of civilised values made a remarkable contribution to British cultural life in the second half of the twentieth century. In my own professional field the German archaeologist Gerhard Bersu fell foul of the Nazi regime and escaped to Britain. There he found himself classed as an enemy alien and transported, like many frustrated victims of the Third Reich, to the huge internment camps on the Isle of Man.* There Bersu made a major contribution to the archaeological investigation of the island before bringing German excavation methods to the mainland with his pioneering work, stripping large open areas with bulldozers, at the Iron Age settlement of Little Woodbury.

Like many of his fellow émigrés Bersu was a successful member of the German establishment. A large proportion were Jews, but these secular, internationally minded intellectuals, lawyers, architects, publishers, musicians and scientists often regarded themselves, principally, as Germans — members of a unified, economically successful, cultured modern state. 'To my parents,' recalled Claus Moser, 'especially my father, being German came first.' (Moser senior was a banker who had fought in World War I.) 'That's why so many of them thought — tragically wrongly — that things would be all right, that this Hitler thing would pass over and they would be OK. It wouldn't touch people like them (they thought) because, above all, they were such good Germans!'[12]

In the period in which I lived in Oxford — from the early 70s — the city and the university still clearly felt the influence of its émigré population. Once, at a Christmas Day party, I found myself talking, or rather listening, to an incredibly dynamic little man with a German accent; it was several minutes before I realised that he was the philospher Sir Isaiah Berlin — one of my academic heroes. A great friend in Oxford was Barbara Gomperts. She and her Dutch husband had lived in Berlin in the 1930s — next door to Himmler. So with neighbours like that they fled to the Netherlands and on to Britain. Barbara's house in Oxford was full of art — her own paintings and photographs and a fantastic collection of pots — many made by her friend and fellow émigré Lucie Rie — probably the most influential potter of the post-war period in Britain. During the war Lucie Rie made buttons for a living. When she visited Barbara she brought sweets as a present — packed in pots which would become icons of modernist art.

* Michael Foot, later leader of the Labour Party, reacted to indiscriminate internment by asking ironically in the *Evening Standard*: 'Why not lock up General de Gaulle? France has recently been occupied by the Germans.'

Other émigrés from Hitler rejuvenated post-war British publishing — George Weidenfeld from Austria, André Deutsch from Hungary, Paul Hamburger (Hamlyn) from Berlin (also, like Claus Moser, a great promoter of music) and Bela Horovitz from Vienna. Others wrote books — and none more prolifically than Nikolaus Pevsner, trained in Leipzig and Dresden, whose vast output of Penguin volumes on the 'Buildings of England', made the natives aware of their heritage, even as they enthusiastically demolished it.*

Many of the 1930s immigrants became super-anglophiles, or at least absorbed in the culture of their newly adopted country. While Pevsner promoted buildings, Ernst Gombrich† wrote *The Story of Art*, published by Phaidon (set up by Bela Horovitz, who, like Paul Hamlyn, exposed the British to books on art) in 1950 and still in print, having sold over 6 million copies.

The British film industry was given an enormous boost by the arrival of the Hungarian Alexander Korda, who established London films, with its Big Ben trademark, in Denham. His 1933 film *The Private Life of Henry VIII* attracted a cinema audience of almost 8 million — still one of the most successful English films of all time. Some of his finest output was the result of the collaboration between Imre (renaming himself Emeric) Pressburger, from the part of the Habsburg Empire that is now Romania (via Prague and Berlin), and the Englishman Michael Powell. Their post-war masterpieces include *A Matter of Life and Death*, *The Red Shoes* and *The Tales of Hoffmann*. This Anglo-Hungarian partnership combined European Expressionism and English quirkiness with a powerful emotion and an unparalleled intensity of saturated colour. The simple and affecting use of English was characteristic of the multi-lingual Pressburger; like another central European immigrant, the novelist Joseph Conrad, he literally mastered his adopted tongue.

These immigrants transformed visual culture in other significant ways — particularly introducing the sometimes reluctant backward-looking

---

* Nikolaus Pevsner, in 1955, delivered the prestigious Reith Lectures from the BBC: his subject was 'The Englishness of English Art'. Although a modernist, advocating the industrial efficiency and social equality of the Bauhaus philosophy, Pevsner still appreciated the backward-looking, pastoral Arts and Crafts movement of William Morris – the English had, after all, experienced the worst of the Industrial Revolution, with its unplanned and uncontrolled urban squalor.

† London's centre for art history, the Warburg Institute, where Gombrich worked, was originally established in Hamburg by Aby Warburg, a Jewish banker and art historian. It transferred to London, with its great collection of books and pictures, as the Nazis came to power in 1933. Gombrich provided a home for Karl Popper, the philosopher, when he and his wife arrived in England.

Brits to the modernist architecture of central Europe. Out of the wreck-age of bomb-damaged Britain there emerged new schools, theatres, hospitals and houses designed by émigré modernist architects. Peter Maro was a member of the LCC team that created the Royal Festival Hall for the 1951 Festival of Britain — 'an extraordinary rich, sophisticated achievement for its date and the haste with which it was built'.[13]

Eugene Rosenberg formed a partnership with F. R. S. Yorke and the Finn Cyril Mardall to design new schools such as the Susan Lawrence School in East London, which showcased prefabricated building, and Barclay School, Stevenage (Hertfordshire) — the first significant second-ary school to be built after the war and probably the only one to have its own Henry Moore sculpture, *The Family of Man*, in its forecourt.

The reputation of high-rise apartments might have fared better in Britain had they all been of the quality of Berthold Lubetkin's innovative Spa Green Estate in East London, built after 1945 to house people who had lost their homes in the Blitz. The Russian architect Lubetkin came to Britain, via Berlin and Paris, in 1931; his best-known modernist icon is a home for penguins rather than people, at London Zoo. Another high-rise, and now a highly desirable address, is Trellick Tower in Kensington, designed by the Hungarian Erno Goldfinger,* who also worked on the Festival of Britain, not to mention the more controversial Alexander Fleming House at the unloved Elephant and Castle.

British people saw more black faces during the war than at any time previously. A million and a half American troops fetched up in the UK — 'overpaid, oversexed and over here' — and about 130,000 of them were black. These forces, from the land of the free and the home of the brave, brought with them their blatant racist and segregationist attitudes. The British often objected. One West Country farmer told the *New States-man*: 'I love the Americans — but I don't like those white ones they've brought with them.' The Commander-in-Chief, General Eisenhower, was puzzled: 'The small-town British girl would go to a movie with a Negro soldier quite as readily as she would go with anyone else'; and when the white Americans objected with their fists, the British press sup-ported the Negroes.[14]

Britain had been drained, battered and bankrupted by the war and after 1945 suffered five more years of rationing. Many of the British rul-ing class still imagined that this victorious 'island race' ruled the world. The 1948 Nationality Act gave a boost to the myth of empire: it gener-ously provided the right of free entry into Britain for all imperial

* Ian Fleming so disliked Goldfinger's work that he named one of the most memorable Bond villains after him.

subjects. The Tory MP David Maxwell Fyfe proclaimed: 'We are proud that we impose no colour-bar restrictions ... We must maintain our great metropolitan tradition of hospitality to everyone from every part of the empire.' Many Britons, anxious about housing, jobs and wages or simply having coloured foreigners for neighbours, would not agree with him.

At the end of the war 10,000 West Indian troops returned home; but in the forces they had glimpsed a different world, where whites behaved like ordinary people rather than colonial rulers. Jamaicans came home to find an island recently devastated by the worst hurricane for a generation, an agricultural depression, few jobs and no planning for their arrival. To them Britain was the mother country; they had read English school books full of imperial derring-do and taken the names of British heroes such as Nelson and Winston, played cricket and sung the National Anthem.*

Cy Grant – who became famous for his performances on the BBC's *Tonight* programme, and whom I saw playing Othello in the mid-6os – said: 'Jamaica was a colony ... I didn't want to live in a colony. When I went back to Jamaica it was shocking.'†

On 21 June 1948 the *Daily Express* reported:

EMPIRE MEN FLEE NO JOBS LAND:
500 MORE HOPE TO START A NEW LIFE TODAY[15]

The *Empire Windrush* has since become the mythical ark of West Indian emigration – their *Mayflower*. The people who boarded the ex-troopcarrier came under their own steam and initiative: the British government only discovered they were on their way shortly before their arrival.

George Isaacs, Minister of Labour, said in the House of Commons a week before the ship docked at Tilbury: 'All I know is that they are in a ship and are coming here. They are British citizens and we shall do our best for them when they arrive ... I hope no encouragement will be given to others to follow them.'

Of course others did – often, however, with official encouragement including that of Enoch Powell as Health Minister, to meet labour shortages in the National Health Service, London Transport and the textile industries of the north. Pulled by jobs in Britain, West Indians were also

* The last time I saw an ostrich-plumed, white-uniformed English diplomat accompanied by a column of red-coated troops armed with Brown Bess rifles was on a Montserrat cricket field in 1995; it was a scene that could have taken place a century earlier – except, perhaps, for the girls with spectacular hairstyles who watched with great amusement – it was their uniformed boyfriends playing soldiers that they found funny.

† Cy Grant joined the RAF in 1941 and was shot down over Germany. After the war he qualified as a barrister and became an actor and singer.

pushed by unemployment at home and restrictions on entry to the United States as a result of the McCarron Act of 1952. Pakistani and Indian workers also began to arrive in Britain in the early 1950s, followed by a mass exodus of Indians from East Africa from 1967 — expelled by aggressively independent governments pursuing policies of 'African-isation'.

The 1971 Census calculated that there were 1.5 million immigrants from what was by then known as the 'New Commonwealth'.* About 30 per cent were from the West Indies, and over 50 per cent were Pakistani, Indian or East African Asians — not many out of a total UK population of almost 56 million. However, these immigrants had congregated where they could find work, housing and support from their families and friends. In Bradford there were 30,000 Pakistanis, 10 per cent of the local workforce; London boroughs such as Hackney, Brent, Lambeth and Harringay had large concentrations of immigrants, as did towns such as Wolverhampton, Leicester and Derby. A coloured face was still a rarity in Scotland, Northern Ireland and the rural shires of England. The Irish — from north and south — continued to desert their depressed homeland for better economic prospects in England. In the 1960s they avoided the traditional stamping grounds — the declining cities of Liverpool and Glasgow — and made instead for more prosperous cities, such as London and Birmingham.

Inevitably there were pressures. In Huddersfield, on South Street, where my grandmother lived, large numbers of West Indians arrived. Increasingly, houses in the street began to be bought up by immigrants and filled with single men desperate for somewhere to stay. This was exactly what had happened a generation earlier, when many of these houses had been used to accommodate Irish labourers — sleeping on benches with their heads resting on tables, according to my mother, who used to run errands for them. My grandfather had a small shop — recom-pense for his war injuries — from which he used to sell them a pinch of tea and sugar to make a brew. Black neighbours came in and out of my grandmother's house in the late 50s, but even as a child I was aware that

---

* Since 1999 countries outside the Commonwealth 'family of nations' and the European Union have been the principal providers of immigrants to Britain. In 2003 new British citizens from Somalia far outnumbered the combined total from the West Indies, Canada, Australia and America In 1991 Afro-Caribbeans outnumbered black Africans by more than two to one. In 2001 the gap closed; there were 560,000 Afro-Caribbeans compared to 485,000 Africans in Britain. Labour force surveys now indicate that the latter have moved ahead, with about 618,000 at the present estimate. The arrival of Africans has gone relatively unnoticed by politi-cians and commentators because the newcomers do not present much of a problem. They are mostly young, healthy, Anglophone and well educated.

the white population was resentful, felt threatened and still referred to 'Pakis' and 'Niggers'. They didn't like the loud music, flashy clothes and different cooking smells — though nothing was worse than English over-cooked cabbage, in my opinion; and the whites did have an in-built racial superiority complex: the presence of blacks lowered the tone of the neighbourhood, in their opinion.

The arrival from about 1960 of Pakistanis, many from the remote Mirpuri area near the Kashmir border, did not make the local English any happier — except for those who ran the textile mills and needed cheap labour. Mirpuris were peasant farmers who had traditionally sup-plemented their meagre incomes by joining the British army. The con-struction of the Mangla Dam inundated over 240 Mirpuri communities. They spent their compensation money on tickets to Britain — especially aiming for the mill towns of Lancashire and Yorkshire. These were very conservative people who lived, several generations together, in one house, and for whom marriage was a means of forming alliances in which women were bargaining counters. They were religious Muslims and teetotal. Not surprisingly, the English and the Mirpuris did not always understand each other.

In contrast, the Uganda Asians, like many Indians expelled from the subcontinent, aspired to self-employment. So did the Cypriots, about 40,000 of whom came to Britain during the civil war that racked the divided island during the 50s. When Cyprus became an independent republic, in 1959, the British forces withdrew and many of the jobs asso-ciated with their bases disappeared. Suddenly Turkish Cypriot restau-rants, coffee shops and greengrocers appeared in places such as Stoke Newington. The Green Lanes area of Harringay in North London* became the largest Cypriot community outside of Nicosia — and the English could buy an aubergine, though it took a few more years of Mediterranean holidays, cookery writers like Elizabeth David and visits to Turkish restaurants before they came to appreciate the delights of an Imam Bayildi, of hummus and taramasalata.

As the British learnt to love foreign food and music, others spread a gospel of hatred. Oswald Mosley had learned nothing from the war ex-cept to switch his nasty attentions predominantly from Jews to coloured people. Right-wing groups began to stir up race hatred, issuing pamph-lets and encouraging gangs to attack immigrants, their homes and busi-nesses. In 1958 there were brutal incidents and riots in Nottingham and Notting Hill, where 6,000 West Indians lived near desperately poor

* Greek Cypriots congregated in Camden.

whites, and where Mosley had, provocatively, opened his Union Movement office.*

As had happened before in such circumstances, following the Notting Hill Riots politicians demanded greater controls on immigration, blaming the victims not the aggressors. The Commonwealth Immigrants Act became law on 1 July 1962, and required immigrants (excluding the Irish) to have a work permit. In the previous year 130,000 immigrants rushed in to forestall the closing barrier – more than the total number for the previous five years. Following the Act, West Indian immigration declined sharply. The Act, however, allowed family unification – so many men, particularly Pakistanis and Indians, who were mainly working in Britain temporarily, to finance relatives at home, now sent for their families and became permanent settlers. In 1961 only one-sixth of immigrants were women; by 1971 women and children made up three-quarters of the total immigrant population. In the face of racial and political pressure the diverse Caribbean communities in London got together to create the Notting Hill Carnival as an expression of solidarity and British identity. Notting Hill in the early 50s was seen by the respectable British as a kind of Wild West London – a very different image from that presented in the film *Notting Hill* (2000) (in which there was scarcely a black face to be seen), a place where estate agents thought they had died and gone to heaven.

If Notting Hill in the west was changing, so was the East End of London. Streets that once had housed industrious Huguenots, then Jews and Irish labourers, now saw a new generation of newcomers arrive. These were Bengalis, many of whom had left their homeland, the future Bangladesh, to escape the wars between India and Pakistan. They found themselves in another war – one launched by the National Front and their skinhead allies, descendants of the 50s Teddy boys. Paki-bashing, and worse, became a local sport. Through the 70s there were beatings and murders culminating in a protest march of 7,000 people conveying the coffin of a murdered Bengali, Altab Ali, from Brick Lane to Downing Street.

Despite the violence life went on: 50,000 Bangladeshis created 'Banglatown' around Brick Lane, which had over forty curry houses. Chicken tikka marsala replaced fish and chips as the British national dish.§16

* The following year a thirty-two-year-old carpenter from Antigua, Kelso Cochrane, was stabbed to death by a gang of white youths. The police denied a racial motive and failed to find the killers. It was the start of a generation of mistrust of the Metropolitan Police, depressingly mirrored by events around the murder of Stephen Lawrence, in Eltham, in 1988.

On the corner of Fournier Street and Brick Lane one building in particular encapsulated the history of the East End. In 1743 the Huguenots had opened a chapel there, which was then taken over by the Wesleyans until, in 1898, the local Jews converted it into the Spitalfields Great Synagogue. By 1976 the old chapel/synagogue had become the Jamme Jarshid Mosque.*

Population statistics about immigration have often been a matter of myth, assumption and exaggeration. The 1991 Census for the first time provided reasonably accurate data, by asking questions about ethnic origin.

Population by ethnic group (in thousands and percentages) 1991:

	Black	*In/Pk/Bl*	*Other*	*White*	*% Ethnic*
Britain	891	1,480	645	51,874	5.5
England	875	1,431	605	44,144	6.2
Wales	9	16	16	2,794	1.5
Scotland	6	32	24	4,936	1.3

The most obvious fact about ethnic minorities in Britain is that they cluster in certain areas, notably London boroughs such as Brent (including, at 45 per cent, the highest proportion in the country), Tower Hamlets, Hackney, Brixton; in Slough and Luton on the periphery of London, in Bradford in the north and in the West Midlands. Britain's multiracialism was clear from the statistics of church membership. The majority white population became increasingly secular; only 15 per cent (6.44 million) claimed membership of traditional Christian churches – the lowest in western Europe. Recent immigrants and their families continued to practise their faiths with greater regularity – over half a million Muslims, 280,000 Greek Orthodox, 270,000 Sikhs and 140,000 Hindus. New elements were added to the cultural landscape of Britain. By the mid-90s Muslims had established 600 registered mosques in England and Wales, the Sikhs had 300 gurdwaras and the Hindus 200 temples or *mandirs*. In contrast Christian church membership showed significant decline.† Anglican numbers fell from 2.55 million in 1970 to 1.81 million; Methodists from 69,000 to 46,000 and Catholics from 2.71 million to 2.04 million. Ireland, both north and south, remained the one part of the British Isles to buck the secular trend.

* The first mosque in Britain, the Shah Jehan Mosque, was opened in Woking in 1889.
† On Christmas Day 1990 fewer than one in five children (between eight and fourteen years old) attended any religious service.

Religion still provides a powerful element in the sense of identity to the Irish — both Catholic and Protestant. Of Ireland's population of 3,917,203 (in 2002), over 3,462,000 classified themselves as Roman Catholic, and 154,000 as Protestant of one denomination or another. In Northern Ireland 86 per cent identify with some religion compared with 77 per cent in England and Wales. It remains to be seen whether Ireland's remarkable growth of prosperity and recent scandals of priestly paedophiles will undermine the Irish commitment to religion.

At the time of writing this chapter (November 2004) Ireland had just been placed top in a survey of the pleasantest countries in the world in which to live — a remarkable turn-around for a place which until recently was abandoned by its children in droves.

Population of Ireland (Eire) 1901–2002

Year	Total Population
2002	3,917,203
1996	3,626,087
1991	3,525,719
1981	3,443,405
1971	2,978,248
1961	2,818,341
1951	2,960,593
1946	2,955,107
1936	2,968,420
1926	2,971,992
1911	3,139,688
1901	3,221,823

The transformation probably began when Ireland and the UK entered the European Economic Community, in 1973 — the former with more enthusiasm than the latter. Since then Ireland has been firmly at the heart of Europe, in spite of its peripheral geographic location. As a small, and in the 70s a relatively poor country, Ireland benefited financially from its EEC membership, particularly in the agricultural sector, which declined in numbers but increased dramatically in prosperity. Nevertheless, in the 1980s Ireland see-sawed from one political and economic crisis to another, unemployment soared and emigration returned to the levels of the 50s (note the minimal growth in population from 1981). Stability returned in the late 80s, when the Haughey government and the Fine Gael opposition finally agreed to tackle the juggernaut of government expenditure. The 'Celtic Tiger' was conceived. The explanation for Ireland's economic success in the 90s is still much debated: the enthusiastic embrace of the single European market at a time when the Thatcher government in the UK appeared, at best, lukewarm; the 'social partnership' which provided a stable period of industrial harmony; government investment in infrastructure such as telecommunications and a well-educated, youthful and English-speaking labour force. These were certainly factors that attracted inward investment. The Irish gross domestic product, per head, overtook that of the UK and the OECD ranked Irish purchasing power as fourth in the world. Ireland's image changed, thanks to its cheerful football fans, its much-admired female head of state Mary Robinson, who showed that a president could be personable, its world-class writers and its far-from-world-class singers, who nevertheless won the Eurovision Song Contest with monotonous regularity.*

The raucous tribalism of Northern Ireland is still all too obvious, though, in the close-packed streets of Belfast. The Dutchman King Billy rides out of the end of terraced houses above pavements painted red, white and blue. Ragged Union Jacks, Scottish saltires and Israeli flags hang like ancient trophies, displayed virtually next door to more sophisticated Catholic paintings of hunger-strikers and houses adorned with Palestinian flags and the Irish tricolour. Both sides, however, lay claim to the ancient Irish hero Cú Chulainn, as if, when people feel that their cultures are under threat, they revert to the security of familiar mythology. Appropriately, Cú Chulainn is an Irish Arthur, complete with his magical sword – a saviour and defender of his people. Belfast Catholics and Protestants alike have adopted the image of the bronze statue of Cú Chulainn in the Dublin Post Office on O'Connell Street which commemorates the Easter Rising – a surprising symbol of their mutual suffering and overlapping identities.

One Protestant inhabitant of north Belfast took me down Lower Newtonards Road, past an abandoned pub – 'closed', he said, 'because the landlord wouldn't pay protection money' – and past Catholic houses barricaded behind high wire fences. The public identities of Protestants and Catholics were now being more visibly displayed, with murals and flags. He told me: 'Since we stopped shooting each other, people are less scared to show who they are.' Some sort of progress,

---

* An event only illuminated by the cynical commentary of Terry Wogan, himself living proof that the BBC believed the Irish spoke the most mellifluous English. That is, unless spoken by an Ulsterman. To the English the northern Ulster accent is personified by the strident voice of the Reverend Ian Paisley, the rhetorical descendant of Sir Edward Carson.

though, in a place with few immigrants, minorities such as the Chinese were increasingly being targeted by white racist gangs looking for someone new to blame. At the bottom of the road we saw the great yellow cranes that dominate the Harland and Wolff shipyard. Twenty thousand workers once worked here, and built the *Titanic*. Now only the cranes remain. They were built by Krupps. As we looked at the *Titanic*'s slipway, the Stenna Line ferry came in – the world's biggest, so they claim – bringing back the Irish from their rendezvous with the nearest Ikea store, in Scotland. The Vikings still control trade around the Irish Sea.

On census day, 29 April 2001, the population of the United Kingdom was 58,789,194.

2001 population by UK countries

	Population	% of total
England	49,138,831	83.6
Scotland	5,062,011	8.6
Wales	2,903,085	4.0
Northern Ireland	1,685,267	2.9

As an archaeologist I am more accustomed to looking into the deep past, but there are trends within the national statistics that point to the future.

In a relatively small collection of islands nearly 60 million people might seem a lot – especially as the British insist on congregating in the booming bottom right-hand corner. The population of the south-east has grown by over 19 per cent in the past twenty years, while in Scotland and the north-east and north-west of England there has been a decline in population. Wales's population has expanded by 3 per cent (89,600 people) and Northern Ireland has experienced the largest relative growth in the UK of 9 per cent in twenty years.[17]

Northern Ireland also has the youngest population the UK – 24 per cent are under sixteen years of age (compared with 20 per cent in the UK as a whole). Recent UK population growth is modest compared with many countries. Since 1951 it has increased by 17 per cent, lower than the European Union average of 23 per cent and minuscule compared with the massive increase of 133 per cent in Australia and 80 per cent in the United States, largely the results of immigration (and high birth rates among young immigrants).

In 2003 there were 621,469 live births in England and Wales, an increase of 4.3 per cent on 2002 and the largest number since 1999. This rate still only represents an average of 1.73 children per woman. In other words, the British population is not replacing itself, as the replacement rate is 2.1 children per woman.* And as more women have easily available contraception, earn salaries and help pay mortgages† to maintain a desired standard of living, the average age of women that give birth has risen to 29.4 years (and 30.6 years in Ireland).

One of the clearest social trends in Britain has been the remarkable increase of live births outside marriage – from 32 per cent in 1993 to 41 per cent in 2003. The British may like attending *Four Weddings and a Funeral* in the cinema, but they have fewer opportunities in real life.

At the World Economic Forum in Davos in January 2004 some economists (such as David Bloom of Harvard University) argued that booming birth rates explain burgeoning economies.[18] America is outperforming Europe economically and in the maternity ward. (US women each have 2.0 live births on average) – and, according to such demographic determinists, economic dynamism is the result. This might seem simplistic stuff, but Britain's demographic trends do have implications for the future; and women are not likely to develop, suddenly, a mass fondness for large, early Victorian-style families: the trend for smaller families has been with us for a century. Like almost every other developed country, Britain hugely subsidises the old in comparison with the support provided for families with young children. Yet even in France, where childbearing was encouraged with financial rewards (and surveys suggest the French have sex more than anyone else), state interference made little difference.

The British population is on course to shrink and become older. The 2001 Census showed, for the first time, that there are more Britons aged sixty and over than there are under sixteen.‡ So one way to keep the population stable and the economy prosperous, and solve the pensions problem, which is of increasing concern, is to live and work longer. It helps to stay healthy. The British already work longer hours than the EU average, to make up for the lower productivity. They are also longer-lived but not necessarily healthier. In the 2001 Census 9.2 per cent of the population of England and Wales reported that their health was 'not good'.*

---

* Germany and Japan have even lower figures of 1.4 and 1.3 respectively.

† The average house price has risen from £68,085 in 1997, when the Labour government came into power, to £160,857 in 2004.

‡ Over-sixties make up 21 per cent of the population and children 20.2 per cent in England and Wales. There has also been a large increase in the number of people aged eighty-five and over, now over 1.1 million, or 1.9 per cent of the population.

* Durham, Merseyside and Tyne and Wear had the highest proportion of 'not good' responses in England, and South Wales the highest of all: 17.3 per cent in Merthyr Tydfil. Buckinghamshire had the lowest figure (5.8 per cent) of any county.

Until the later nineteenth century the medical profession was almost dismally irrelevant to health – except negatively, with its aptitude for killing patients, particularly pregnant women. That changed as medicine became more scientific and made real breakthroughs, which in the last fifty years have saved more lives than in any epoch since medicine began.[19] The great medical essayist Lewis Thomas (1913–93) highlighted the changes during his own career, which began in the 1930s: 'The major threats to human life were tuberculosis, tetanus, syphilis, rheumatic fever, pneumonia, meningitis, polio and septicaemia of all sorts. These things worried us then the way cancer, heart disease, and stroke worry us today. The big problems of the 1930s and 1940s have literally vanished.'

Medical and technical advances – such as antibiotics, the contraceptive pill, transplant surgery, psychotrophic drugs to treat mental illness, genetic screening, ultrasound and CAT scans – have made an enormous contribution to health; but at a great financial cost. In the most health-conscious countries, such as France and the USA, with its system of medical licensed robbery, between 10 and 15 per cent of gross national product is spent on health. 'The irony is that the healthier western society becomes, the more medicine it craves … What an ignominious destiny if the future of medicine turns into bestowing meagre increments of unenjoyed life.'[20]

In the West the greatest increments for health potentially come from lifestyle improvement rather than from inflated expectations of the medical profession: from better diet, avoidance of tobacco and other harmful drugs, exercise and environmental improvements. Scientific medicine cannot always stay on top of the Darwinian forces of ceaseless adaption. Over 25 million people died in six months in the influenza pandemic that raged across the world in 1918;* and in recent years new forms have emerged from China, spreading from domestic birds to people. AIDS (Acquired Immune Deficiency Syndrome) has proved to be the greatest unexpected problem of the late twentieth century, as the human immunodeficiency virus (HIV) mutates rapidly and provides a difficult, rapidly moving target for vaccines and anti-viral drugs.†

The original 'gay plague', accompanied by an outbreak of moralising

---

* Two hundred thousand died in England and Wales, half a million in the USA; Samoa lost a quarter of its population.

† AIDS probably originated in sub-Saharan Africa as a disease of apes, possibly confined for many years to a relatively small niche in the Africa rainforest. Suddenly it broke out and was first recognised in 1981 in the USA (the HIV virus was identified in 1983). It has been suggested that AIDS was stimulated into activity by the World Health Organisation anti-smallpox programme, when needles were re-used many times and live smallpox vaccines could have provoked human immune systems. It spread rapidly, like Chinese flu, thanks to modern global communications.

and inflamation of blame culture, has now been transformed into a disease that is most prevalent among the African poor, particularly women and young children, and in the West among drug users.

In spite of this, life expectancy is increasing in Britain, but averages often mask reality and, in particular, the differences between rich and poor. Maps produced by the Office for National Statistics in 2001, which chart the patterns of disease and death across Britain, provide very clear illustrations of regional differences.[21] The prevalence of heart disease presents the most vivid contrast between north and south, and is largely determined by poor diet and smoking.* Parts of Scotland, South Wales and the Black Country have the highest rates – areas of industrial decline, high unemployment, poor housing and low educational attainments.† Heart disease is complemented by lung cancer, which has similar distribution among lower social classes and areas of declining industry, including the poorer boroughs of London. At present, women live significantly longer than men, though this could change if the current fashion among young women for binge drinking and smoking continues.

To retain their current level of economic prosperity the British could improve their lifestyle and work longer. They could also accept more immigrants – at least as long as birth rates remain high and incomes low in Africa and South-East Asia, and there is a pool of willing migrants. On present estimates the British are short of about 166,000 babies a year, if the population is to stay at its current level. One possible solution is to double the number of immigrants to Britain.‡ As one commentator wrote: 'We're not being over run by immigrants; we need them.'

New arrivals in a small cluster of off-shore islands, a place with remarkable continuity, where regional diversity of cultures and accents is almost as great as its variation of landscape. A country refreshed and stimulated by new arrivals who, despite the difficulties, merge with its people to create a constantly changing new Britain.

---

* The wealthy used to be more prone to heart disease because they had a richer diet. When Michael Brown and Joseph Goldstein discovered the dangers of cholesterol, the wealthy modified their diet. The poor stuck with junk food.

† The government, in its report *A New Commitment to Neighbourhood Renewal*, pledged that 'within 10 to 20 years no one should be seriously disadvantaged by where they live'; but the problem is not *where* people live – but how. The well-off and well-educated are now more likely to fall victim to the diseases of affluence – breast cancer (a greater risk for women who delay child-bearing) or prostate cancer for men (why is uncertain, but higher rates may simply reflect better detection.

‡ In 2002 359,000 people left the UK to live elsewhere and 513,000 arrived to stay at least one year. Therefore there were 153,000 more immigrants.

Picture Credits

Map 1. Spread of Celtic settlement and influence, first millennium BC

Areas of settlement of Celtic-speaking people
Centres of Celtic influence
Allobroges Celtic groups
ILLYRIANS Other ethnic groups

Iverni
Caledonii
Brigantes
Iceni
Silures
Atrebates
Veneti
Parisii
Belgae
Treveri
Aedui
Bituriges
Arverni
Allobroges
Aquitani
Gallaeci
BASQUES
Lusitani
Celtiberians
IBERIANS
TARTESSIANS
PHOENICIANS
PHOENICIANS
GERMANS
Volcae
Helvetii
Insubrese
Senones
ETRUSCANS
Rome
ITALICS
GREEKS
Scordisci
Dardani
ILLYRIANS
SCYTHIANS
THRACIANS
Delphi
GREEKS
Athens
Pergamon
Tectosages
Tolistobogii
Trocmi

Map 2. The tribes of late Iron Age Britain and main tribal centres

⊙ Dun Ailinne   Main tribal centres

Novantae   Tribes

Clickhimin
Mousa ⊙

ATLANTIC
OCEAN

Dun Carloway ⊙

Cateni Cornavii
Carnonacae Smertae
Lugi
Decantae
Boresti Taexall
Vacomagii
Creones
Caledonii
Venicones
Traprain Law
Dumnonii
Selgovae Votadini
Novantae
Carvetii
Robogdii
Navan Fort
Black Pig's Dyke Darini
Nagnatae Voluntii
Dorsey
Cruachain ⊙
Ebdani
Tara ⊙
Cauci
Dun Aengus ⊙
⊙ Dun Ailinne
Auteini   Manapii
Gangani   Usdiae
Velabori   Coriondi
Brigantes
Iverni

Setantii
Brigantes
Stanwick ⊙
Parisi

North
Sea

Irish
Sea

Deceangli
Ordovices
Cornovii
Corieltauvi
(Coritani)
Iceni
Catuvellauni
Trinovantes
Demetae   Salmonsbury   Grim's Ditch
Bagendon ⊙   Colchester ⊙
Wheathampstead ⊙
Silures   St Albans ⊙
Dobunni   Dyke Hills ⊙
Durotriges   Silchester ⊙
Hod Hill ⊙   Atrebates   Canterbury
Hengistbury   Winchester ⊙   Cantiaci
Maiden Castle ⊙
Dumnonii

Celtic
Sea

0 20 40 60 Miles
0 20 60 100 Km

Julius Caesar
55–54 BC

migration c.100BC

trading link
100BC

English
Channel

Belgae

Map 3. Evolution of Britannia as Roman province through 1st to 4th century AD

ANTONINE WALL

HADRIAN'S WALL

Britannia

◖ Legionary bases

◯ Tribal capitals

◯ Urban centre

Belgae Tribal name

Principal roman roads

■ Colonia

Irish Sea

Celtic Sea

North Sea

English Channel

Carvetii

Carlisle
Luguvalium

Brigantes

Parisi

Aldborough
Isurium Brigantum

York
Eburacum

Brough-on-Humber
Petuaria

Deceangli

Chester
Deva

Lincoln
Lindum

Cornovii

Ordovices

Corieltauvi

Leicester
Ratae Corieltavorum

Iceni

Wroxeter
Viroconium Cornoviorum

Caistor
Venta Icenorum

Demetae

Carmarthen
Moridunum

Cirencester
Corinium

Catuvellauni

Colchester
Camulodunum

Gloucester

Dobunnorum

Trinovantes

Caerwent
Venta Silurum

Silures

Dobunni

St Albans

Atrebates

Chelmsford
Caesaromagus

Caerleon
Isca

Bath
Aquae Sulis

London
Londinium

Canterbury
Durovernum Cantiacorum

Silchester
Calleva Atrebatum

Ilchester
Lindinis

Winchester
Venta Belgarum

Cantiaci

Exeter
Isca Dumnoniorum

Durotriges

Belgae

Regni

Dumnonii

Dorchester
Durnovaria

Chichester
Noviomagus Regnorum

0   20   40   60   Miles

0   20   60   100   Km

Map 4. The people of Britain, 5th to late 7th century

Area of British influence

Area of Anglo Saxon influence

Early royal centres

+ Early ecclesiastical centres

LINDSEY Early kingdoms

Map 5. Settlement of Danes and Norwegians, 9th to 10th centuries

Main areas of Danish influence
Areas of Wessex/English influence
Norse settlement
Ⓜ Five Boroughs of the Danelaw
Ⓞ Alfred's *burhs*
Ⓜ Other Anglo-Saxon *burhs*
◈ Other Danish centres
Ⓤ Viking *longphorts* in Ireland
✝ Monastic site

EARLDOM
OF ORKNEY

CAITHNESS

MORAY

SCOTIA

STRATHCLYDE

ATLANTIC

OCEAN

GALLOWAY

NORTHUMBRIA

✝ Lindisfarne

North
Sea

✝ Jarrow

NORTHERN
UÍ NÉILL

Lough
Neagh

CONNACHT

SOUTHERN
UÍ NÉILL

Ⓤ Annagassan

Lough Ree Ⓤ

Irish
Sea

Ⓤ Dublin

Ⓜ York

Lincoln ◈

LEINSTER

Ⓤ Arklow

Ⓤ Limerick

Ⓜ Chester

GWYNEDD

Nottingham Ⓜ

Derby Ⓜ

Leicester Ⓜ

Shrewsbury Ⓜ

MERCIA

Stamford Ⓜ

Thetford ◈

MUNSTER

Waterford Ⓤ

Ⓤ Wexford

Northampton Ⓜ

Huntingdon Ⓜ

Cork Ⓤ

Ⓤ Youghal

Hereford Ⓜ

Worcester Ⓜ

Cambridge ◈

DEHEUBARTH

Cricklade Ⓞ

Bedford Ⓜ

Colchester ◈

Celtic
Sea

MORGANNWG

Oxford Ⓜ

Wallingford Ⓞ

Malmesbury Ⓞ

London Ⓜ

Bath Ⓞ

Sashes Ⓞ

Southwark ◈

Axbridge Ⓞ

Shaftesbury Ⓞ

Chisbury Ⓞ

Wilton Ⓞ

Eashing Ⓞ

Pilton Ⓞ

Lyng Ⓞ

Winchester Ⓞ

Burpham Ⓞ

Eorpeburnan Ⓞ

Langport Ⓞ

WESSEX

Lewes Ⓞ

Hastings Ⓞ

Lydford Ⓞ

Southampton Ⓞ

Clichester Ⓞ

Porchester Ⓞ

Exeter Ⓞ

Bridport Ⓞ

Wareham Ⓞ

Christchurch Ⓞ

Halwell Ⓞ

English Channel

0 20 40 60 Miles
0 20 60 100 Km

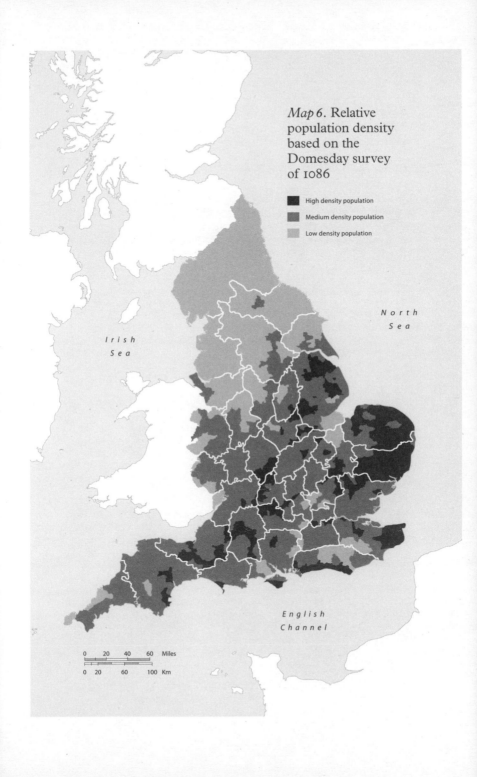

Map 6. Relative population density based on the Domesday survey of 1086

High density population
Medium density population
Low density population

North Sea

Irish Sea

English Channel

0   20   40   60   Miles
0   20   40   60   100 Km

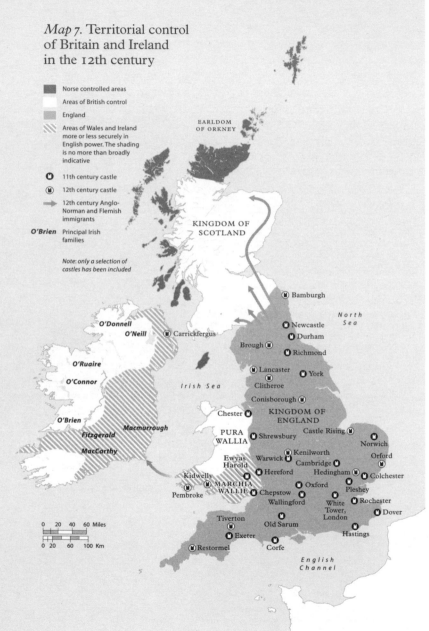

Map 7. Territorial control of Britain and Ireland in the 12th century

Norse controlled areas

Areas of British control

England

Areas of Wales and Ireland more or less securely in English power. The shading is no more than broadly indicative

11th century castle

12th century castle

12th century Anglo-Norman and Flemish immigrants

O'Brien   Principal Irish families

Note: only a selection of castles has been included

EARLDOM OF ORKNEY

KINGDOM OF SCOTLAND

North Sea

Bamburgh

Newcastle
Durham
Brough
Richmond

O'Donnell
O'Neill   Carrickfergus

O'Ruaire

O'Connor

Irish Sea

Lancaster   York
Clitheroe

Conisborough

Chester

KINGDOM OF ENGLAND

O'Brien

PURA WALLIA   Shrewsbury   Castle Rising

Macmurrough

Fitzgerald

MacCarthy

Norwich

Kenilworth
Warwick   Cambridge   Orford

Ewyas Harold
Kidwelly   Hereford   Hedingham   Colchester

Pembroke   MARCHIA WALLIE   Oxford   Pleshey

Chepstow   Rochester
Wallingford   White Tower, London   Dover

Tiverton   Old Sarum
Hastings

Exeter

Restormel   Corfe

English Channel

0   20   40   60 Miles

0   20   60   100 Km

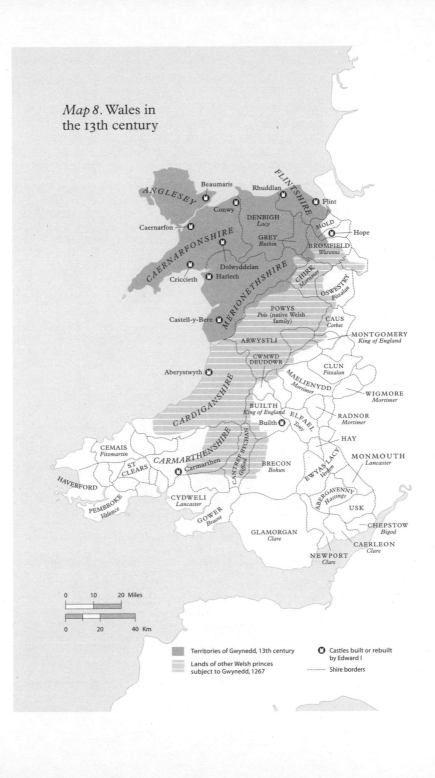

Map 8. Wales in the 13th century

ANGLESEY

Beaumaris

Rhuddlan

FLINTSHIRE

Flint

Conwy

Caernarfon

DENBIGH
Lacy

MOLD

Hope

GREY
Ruthin

BROMFIELD
Warenne

CAERNARFONSHIRE

Criccieth

Dolwyddelan
Harlech

MERIONETHSHIRE

CHIRK
Mortimer

OSWESTRY
Fitzalan

POWYS
Pole (native Welsh
family)

CAUS
Corbet

Castell-y-Bere

MONTGOMERY
King of England

ARWYSTLI

CWMWD
DEUDDWR

CLUN
Fitzalan

Aberystwyth

MAELIENYDD
Mortimer

WIGMORE
Mortimer

CARDIGANSHIRE

BUILTH
King of England

ELFAEL
Tony

RADNOR
Mortimer

Builth

HAY

CEMAIS
Fitzmartin

CARMARTHENSHIRE

CANTREF
BYCHAN
Giffard

MONMOUTH
Lancaster

ST
CLEARS

Carmarthen

BRECON
Bohun

EWYAS LACY
Verdon

HAVERFORD

CYDWELI
Lancaster

ABERGAVENNY
Hastings

USK

PEMBROKE
Valence

GOWER
Braose

GLAMORGAN
Clare

CHEPSTOW
Bigod

CAERLEON
Clare

NEWPORT
Clare

0   10   20 Miles

0   20   40 Km

■ Territories of Gwynedd, 13th century

▨ Lands of other Welsh princes
subject to Gwynedd, 1267

Ⓦ Castles built or rebuilt
by Edward I

········· Shire borders

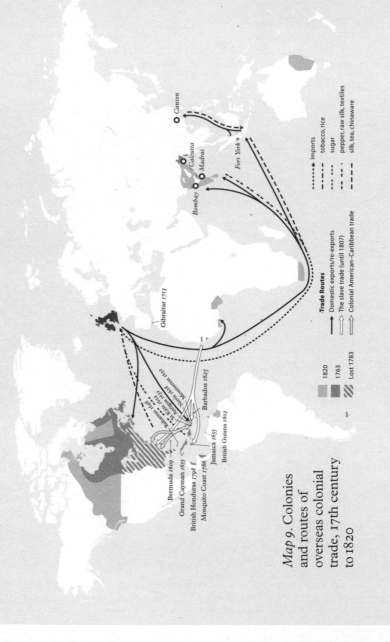

Map 9. Colonies and routes of overseas colonial trade, 17th century to 1820

Bermuda *1609*
Grand Cayman *1655*
British Honduras *1798*
Mosquito Coast *1786*
Jamaica *1655*
British Guiana *1803*

Bahamas *1648*
St. Kitts *1624*
Nevis *1628*
Antigua *1632*
Montserrat *1632*
Barbados *1625*

Gibraltar *1713*

Canton
Calcutta
Madras
Bombay
Fort York

Trade Routes
→ Domestic exports/re-exports
⇒ The slave trade (until 1807)
⇒ Colonial American–Caribbean trade

‑‑‑‑► Imports
‑ ‑ ‑ tobacco, rice
‑‑‑‑ sugar
····· pepper, raw silk, textiles
– – – silk, tea, chinaware

1820
1763
Lost 1783

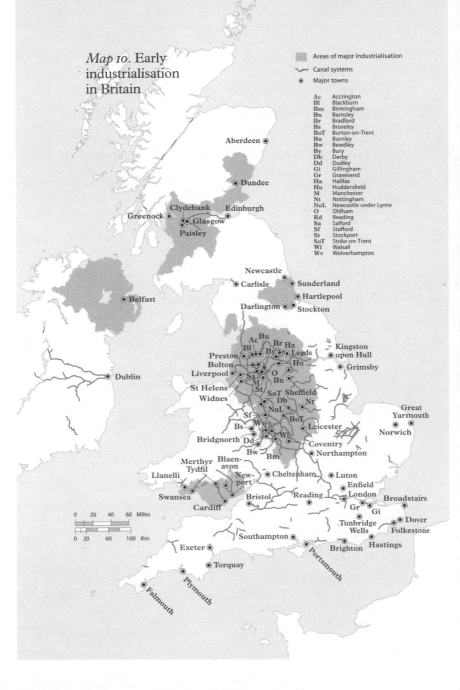

Map 10. Early industrialisation in Britain

Areas of major industrialisation
Canal systems
Major towns

Ac	Accrington
Bl	Blackburn
Bm	Birmingham
Bn	Barnsley
Br	Bradford
Bs	Broseley
BoT	Burton-on-Trent
Bu	Burnley
Bw	Bewdley
By	Bury
Db	Derby
Dd	Dudley
Gi	Gillingham
Gr	Gravesend
Ha	Halifax
Hu	Huddersfield
M	Manchester
Nt	Nottingham
NuL	Newcastle under Lyme
O	Oldham
Rd	Reading
Sa	Salford
Sf	Stafford
St	Stockport
SoT	Stoke-on-Trent
Wl	Walsall
Wv	Wolverhampton

Aberdeen

Dundee

Clydebank   Edinburgh
Greenock   Glasgow
Paisley

Newcastle
Carlisle   Sunderland
Hartlepool
Darlington   Stockton
Belfast

Ac Bu
Bl   Br Ha
By   Leeds   Kingston
Preston   O   Hu   upon Hull
Bolton   Sa   Bn   Grimsby
Liverpool   M   Sheffield
St   SoT   Db   Nt
Dublin   St Helens   NuL   BoT
Widnes   Sf   Wv   Leicester   Great
Bs   Wl   Northampton   Yarmouth
Bridgnorth   Dd   Coventry   Norwich
Bw   Bm
Merthyr   Blaen-   Cheltenham   Luton
Tydfil   avon   Enfield
Llanelli   New-   Reading   London
port   Broadstairs
Swansea   Bristol   Gr   Gi
Cardiff   Dover
Tunbridge   Folkestone
Wells   Brighton   Hastings
0 20 40 60 Miles   Southampton
0 20   60   100 Km   Portsmouth
Exeter
Torquay
Plymouth
Falmouth

REFERENCES

Introduction

1 See BARRY CUNLIFFE (2001), *The Extraordinary Voyage of Pytheas the Greek: the Man who Discovered Britain*, Allen Lane, London.

2 NATHANIEL PHILBRICK (2000), *In the Heart of the Sea*, HarperCollins, pp. 95–8.

3 T. M. DEVINE (1999), *The Scottish Nation 1700–2000*, Penguin edn (2000), pp. 3–4, 16.

4 Quoted in STEVE JONES (1996), *In the Blood: God, genes and destiny*, Flamingo paperback edn (1997), p. viii.

5 STEPHEN JAY GOULD (2003), 'The Geometer of Race', in *I Have Landed: splashes and reflections in natural history*, Vintage, London, pp. 356–6.

6 'On Reading the Poems of Phillis Wheatley, the African Poetess', *New York Magazine*, October 1796.

7 PHILLIS WHEATLEY (2001), *Complete Writings*, Penguin Classics, p. xxxvii.

8 RICHARD DAWKINS (2004), *The Ancestor's Tale*, Weidenfeld & Nicolson, London, pp. 336–7.

9 NORMAN DAVIES (1999), *The Isles: a history*, Macmillan, London.

10 E. G. BOWEN (1972), *Britain and the Western Seaways*, Thames and Hudson, London; B. W. CUNLIFFE (2001), *Facing the Ocean: the Atlantic and its Peoples*, Oxford University Press, Oxford.

11 JOHN MCWHIRTER (2002), *The Power of Babel*, Heinemann, London.

12 MARTIN JONES (2001), *The Molecule Hunt: archaeology and the search for ancient DNA*, Allen Lane, London, p 11.

13 JOHN COLLIS (2003), *The Celts: origins, myths, inventions*, Tempus, Stroud, pp. 218–22.

14 See STEVE JONES (1996), *In the Blood: God, genes and destiny*, Flamingo paperback edn (1997), London, pp. 152–4.

15 BRIAN SYKES (2001), *The Seven Daughters of Eve*, Bantam Press, London, p. 179.

16 CHRISTOPHER SMITH (1992), 'The Population of Late Upper Palaeolithic and Mesolithic Britain', *Proceedings of the Prehistoric Society*, 58, 37–40; but see also CLIVE GAMBLE (2002), 'Early Beginnings 500,000–35,000 Years Ago', in Paul Slack and Ryk Ward (eds.) (2002), *The Peopling of Britain: the shaping of a human landscape*, Oxford University Press, Oxford, p. 30.

17 STIG WELINDER (1979), 'Prehistoric Demography', *Acta Archaeologica Lundensia*, Lund.

18 Figures taken from the US Board of the Census, International Programs Center, 'Historical Estimates of the World Population': http://www.census.gov/ipc/www/worldhis.html

19 T. MCKEOWN (1976), *The Modern Rise of Population*, Edward Arnold, London.

Chapter One

1 C. LYELL (1863), *The Geological Evidence of the Antiquity of Man with Remarks on Theories of the Origin of the Species by Variation*.

2 NICHOLAS BARTON (1997), *Stone Age Britain*, English Heritage / Batsford, p. 100.

3 STEPHEN ALDHOUSE-GREEN (ed.) (2000), *Paviland Cave and the 'Red Lady': a definitive account*, Western Academic Press, Bristol.

4 BRYAN SYKES, (2001), *The Seven Daughters of Eve*, Bantam Press.

5 GRIP (1993), 'Climate Instability During the Last Interglacial Period Recorded in the GRIP Ice Core', *Nature* 364, 203–7.

6 *See* www.nhm.ac.uk/hosted_sites /ahob

7 W. A. BOISIMIER (2002)'Lynford Quarry: Neanderthal Butchery Site', *Current Archaeology* 182, November 2002, 53–8.

8 ABIGAIL HACKETT AND ROBIN DENNELL (2003), 'Neanderthals as Fiction in Archaeological Narrative', *Antiquity*, 816–827.

9 See C. B. STRINGER AND R. MCKIE (1996), *Africa Exodus: The Origins of Modern Humanity*, London, Jonathan Cape.

10 M. KRINGS et al. (1997), 'Neanderthal DNA Sequences and the Origin of Modern Humans', *Cell* 90, 19–30.

11 B. COLES (1998), 'Doggerland: a speculative survey', *Proceedings of the Prehistoric Society*, 64, 45–81.

12 'Shells could have been strung as a necklace. Shells point to origin of human mind', *New Scientist*, 24 April 2004, 17. www.newscientist.com

13 PAUL BAHN (2003), 'Art of the Hunters', *British Archaeology*, September 2003, 9–13.

14 S. MITHEN (1996), *The Prehistory of the Mind: a search for the origins of art, religion and science*, Thames and Hudson, London.

15 A. J. LEGGE AND P. A. ROWLEY-CONROY (1988), *Star Carr Revisited*, London.

16 JOHN LEWIS (2000), 'Hunters in the Cold', *British Archaeology*, October 2000, 14–17.

17 *See* www.ncl.ac.uk/howick

18 CHRISTOPHER SMITH (1992), 'The Population of Late Upper Palaeolithic and Mesolithic Britain', *Proceedings of the Prehistoric Society*, 58, 37–40.

19 CLIVE GAMBLE (2002), 'Early Beginnings 500,000–35,000 Years Ago', in Paul Slack and Ryk Ward (eds.) (2002), *The Peopling of Britain: the shaping of a human landscape*, Oxford University Press, Oxford, p. 30.

20 MARINA GKIASTA et al., (2003), 'Neolithic Transition in Europe: the radiocarbon record revisited', *Antiquity*, 45–62.

21 COLIN RENFREW (1987), *Archaeology and Language: the puzzle of Indo-European origins*, Jonathan Cape, London.

22 J. P. MALLORY (1989), *In Search of the Indo-Europeans: language, archaeology and myth*, Thames and Hudson, London

23 ALEXANDER BENTLEY, R. L. CHIKHI AND T. DOUGLAS PRICE, (2003), 'The Neolithic Transition in Europe, Comparing Broad Scale Genetic and Local Scale Isotopic Evidence', *Antiquity*, 63–5.

24 PETER ROWLEY-CONWY (2002), 'Great Sites: Balbridie', *British Archaeology*, April 2002, 22–4.

25 MARTIN JONES (2001), *The Molecule Hunt: archaeology and the search for ancient DNA*, Allen Lane, London, p. 126.

26 GORDON NOBLE (2003), 'Islands and the Neolithic Farming Revolution', *British Archaeology*, July 2003, 20–22.

27 ALEXANDER FENTON (1978), *The Northern Isles: Orkney and Shetland*, Tuckwell Press, East Lothian (1997 reprint), pp. 459–60.

28 JOHN HEDGES (1982), 'An Archaeological Perspective on Isbister', *Scottish Archaeological Review*, 1, 5–20; JOHN HEDGES (1984), *Tomb of the Eagles: a window on Stone Age tribal Britain*, John Murray, London.

29 K. M. WEISS (1973), 'Demographic Models for Anthopology', *American Antiquity*, 38.

30 FRANCIS PRYOR (2003), *Britain* BC: *Life in Britain and Ireland before the Romans*, HarperCollins, London.

31 D. W. A. STARTIN and R. BRADLEY (1981), 'Some notes on work organisation and Society', in *Prehistoric Wessex in Astronomy and Society in Britain during the Period 4000–1500* BC, Eds. C. L. N. Ruggles and A. W. R. Whittle, BAR 88, Oxford, 289–96.

FROM TECHNICAL NOTES

32 *See* KATE WONG (2003), 'An Ancestor to Call Our Own', *Scientific American,* January 2003, 42–5.

33 ROBIN DUNBAR (1996), *Grooming, Gossip and the Evolution of Language,* Faber and Faber, London.

34 *See* ANDREW WHITE and RICHARD W. BYRNE (eds.) (1997), *Machiavellian Intelligence II*, Cambridge University Press.

35 N. HOWELL and V. A. LEHOTAY (1978), 'Ambush: a computer programme for stochastic microsimulation of small human populations', *American Anthropologist*, 80, 905–22.

36 CLIVE GAMBLE (2002), 'Early Beginnings 500,000–35,000 Years Ago', in Paul Slack and Ryk Ward (eds.), *The Peopling of Britain: the Shaping of a Human Landscape,* The Linacre Lectures, Oxford, 11–37.

37 And for further progress see PÄÄBO and C. STRINGER (2002), 'Modern human origins: progress and prospects', Phil Trans Royal Soc, Lond B 357, 563–579.

38 L. CHICKL, R. NICHOLS, G. BARBUJANI and M. A. BEAUMONT (2002), 'Y Genetic Data Support the Neolithic Diffusion Model', *Proceedings of the National Academy of Sciences, USA* 99, 11008–11003.

39 M. V. RICHARDS, E. MACAULEY, HICKEY, et al. (2000), 'Tracing European Founder Lineages in the Near Eastern mt DNA Pool', *American Journal of Human Genetics,* 67, 1251–76.

40 T. DOUGLAS-PRICE, J. H. BURTON and R. A. BENTLEY (2002), 'Characterisation of Biologically Available Strontium Isotope ratios for the Study of Prehistoric Migration', *Archaeometry,* 44, 117–35, and T. DOUGLAS-RICE, R. ALEXANDER BENTLEY, J. LUNING, D. GRONESBARN and J. WELSH (2001), 'Prehistoric Human Migration in the Linearbandkeramik of Central Europe', *Antiquity,* 75, 593–603.

Chapter Two

1 For details see website: www.wessexarch.co.uk

2 FRANCIS PRYOR (2003), *Britain* BC: *life in Britain and Ireland before the Romans,* HarperCollins, London.

3 EDRIC ROBERTS (2002), 'Great Orme: Bronze Age Mining and Smelting Site', *Current Archaeology* 181, 29–32; www.greatorme.freeserve.co.uk

4 Suggested by P. HERRING (1997) in 'The Prehistoric Landscape of Cornwall and West Devon: economic and social contexts for metallurgy', in P. Budd and D. Gale (eds.) *Prehistoric Extractive Metallurgy in Cornwall,* p. 12–22. For an up-to-date survey of Bronze Age mining *see* S. TIMBERLAKE (2001), 'Mining and Prospection for Metals in Bronze Age Britain', in *Bronze Age Landscapes: tradition and transformation,* Joanna Bruck ed. 179–192, Oxbow Books, Oxford.

5 'Earliest Evidence of Lead Mining at Cwmystwyth', *British Archaeology,* April 2001, 4.

6 P. Clark (ed.) (2004), *The Dover Bronze Age Boat,* English Heritage, Swindon.

7 *See* M. PARKER PEARSON and RAMILISONINA, ' Stonehenge for the Ancestors: the stones pass on the message', *Antiquity* 72, (1998), 308–26.

8 ALISTAIR BARCLAY (2003), *Lines in the Landscape*, Oxford Archaeology Monograph No. 15, Oxford.

9 I have taken these figures from COLIN BURGESS (1980), *The Age of Stonehenge*, J. M. Dent, London.

10 FRANCIS PRYOR (2003), *Britain BC*, HarperCollins, London.

11 STUART PIGGOTT (1931), 'The Uffington White Horse', *Antiquity* V, 17, 44–5.

12 MORRIS MARPLES (1949), *White Horses and other Hill Figures*, Country Life, p. 46.

13 D. YATES (2001), 'Bronze Age Agricultural Intensification in the Thames Valley and Estuary', in Joanna Bruck (ed.), *Bronze Age Landscapes: tradition and transformation*, Oxbow Books, pp. 65–82.

14 FRANCIS PRYOR (2001), *The Flag Fen Basin: archaeology and environment of a fenland landscape*, English Heritage, London.

15 FRANCIS PRYOR (1996), 'Sheep, Stockyards and Field Systems: Bronze Age livestock populations in the fenlands of eastern England', *Antiquity* 70, 313–24.

16 DAVID FIELD (2001), 'Place and Memory in Bronze Age Wessex', in Joanna Bruck (ed.) *Bronze Age Landscapes: tradition and transformation*, 56–64.

17 DAVID MC'OMISH, DAVID FIELD and GRAHAM BROWN (2002), *The Field Archaeology of the Salisbury Training Area*, English Heritage, Swindon.

18 ANDREW FLEMING (1988), *The Dartmoor Reaves: investigating prehistory land divisions*, Batsford, London.

19 S. P. HALLIDAY (1993), 'Patterns of Fieldwork and the Burnt Mounds of Scotland', in V. Buckley (ed.), *Burnt Offerings International Contributions to Burnt Mound Archaeology*, Wordwell, Dublin, pp. 60–61.

20 G. WHITTINGTON and K. J. EDWARDS (2003), 'Climate Change', in K. J. Edwards and I. B. M. Ralston (eds.), *Scotland after the Ice Age*, Edinburgh University Press, pp. 18–19.

21 JOHN EVANS (1884), 'On a Hoard of Bronze Objects Found near Wilburton Fen nearby Ely', *Archaeologia* 48, 106–14.

22 C. B. BURGESS (1974) (ed.), 'The Bronze Age in Renfrew', *British Prehistory: a new outline*, 165–232, 291–329, Duckworth, London.

23 RICHARD BRADLEY (1990), *The Passage of Arms: an archaeological analysis of prehistoric hoards and votive deposits*, Cambridge University Press, Cambridge.

24 NAOMI FIELD, MIKE PARKER PEARSON and JIM RYLATT (2003), 'The Fiskerton Causeway: research, past, present and future', in S. Catney and D. Start (eds.), *Time and Tide: the archaeology of the Witham valley*, Witham Valley Arch. Res. Comm., Sleaford, pp. 16–23.

25 I. M. STEAD, J. B. BROOKE and DON BROTHWELL (1986), 'Lindow Man: the body in the bog', British Museum Publication, London.

26 MARSHA A. LEVINE (1993) 'Social Evolution and Horse Domestication', in C. Scarre and F. Healey (eds.), *Trade and Exchange in Prehistoric Europe*, Oxbow Monograph No. 33, Oxford, pp. 135–141.

27 JOHN COLES (2003), *The Celts: origin, myths and inventions*, Tempus, Stroud.

28 J. V. S. MEGAW and M. R. MEGAW (1993), '221 Cheshire Cats, Mickey Mice, the New Europe and Ancient Celtic Art', in C. Scarre and F. Healy (eds.), *Trade and Exchange in Prehistoric Europe*, Oxbow Books, Oxford.

29 J. R. TOLKIEN (1963), 'English and Welsh in Angles and Britons', O'Donnell Lectures, Cardiff, University of Wales Press.

30 M. DILLON and N. CHADWICK (1972), *The Celtic Realms*, Weidenfeld & Nicolson.

31 B. CUNLIFFE (2001), *The Extraordinary Voyage of Pytheas the Greek: the man who discovered Britain*, Allen Lane, London, p. 169.

32 Translation from Cunliffe (2001), p. 106.

33 BARRY CUNLIFFE (1983), *Danebury: the anatomy of an Iron Age hill fort*, Batsford, London.

34 See SIMON GILMOUR and MURRAY COOK (1998), 'Excavations in Dun Vulan: a reinterpretation of the reappraised Iron Age', *Antiquity* 72, 327–37.

35 M. MARKEY, E. WILKES and I. DARVILL (2002), 'Poole Harbour an Iron Age Port', *Current Archaeology* 181, 7–11.

36 B. W. CUNLIFFE (1987), *Hengistbury Head, Dorset, Volume 1: The prehistoric and Roman Settlement, 3500 BC– AD 500*, Oxford University Committee for Archaeology Monograph No. 13, Oxford.

37 CAESAR, *De Bello Gallico*, V, 12.

38 CAESAR, *De Bello Gallico*, V, 12.

39 *See* R. S. O. TOMLIN (1983), 'Non Coritani sed Corieltauvi', *Antiquaries Journal* 63, 353–5.

Chapter Three

1 Tab. Vindolanda 11.164 Pl v.

2 W. J. M. WILLEMS (1986), *Romans and Batavians: a regional study in the Dutch East River Area*, (2nd edn), Amsterdam University Press.

3 ANTHONY BIRLEY (2002), *Garrison Life at Vindolanda: a band of brothers*, pp. 41–4.

4 Quoted by ALAN K. BOWMAN (1994), pp. 56–7.

5 TACITUS, *Annals of Imperial Rome*, 1.

6 DIO CASSIUS, LV, 19, 1.

7 See KEVIN TROTT and DAVID TOMALIN (2003), 'The Maritime Role of the Island of Vectis in the British pre-Roman Iron Age', *International Journal of Nautical Archaeology* 32.2, 158–81.

8 S. S. FRERE and M. G. FULFORD (2001), 'The Roman Invasion of AD 43', *Britannia* 32, 45–56.

9 J. MANLEY (2002), *AD 43. The Roman Invasion of Britain: a reassessment*, Tempus, Stroud.

10 DIO CASSIUS, LX, 21.

11 'Ad Quintum Fratrem', 21 (III, 1) 10, in D. R. Shakleton Bailey (ed.) (1988), *Cicero: Epistulae ad Quintum Fratrem et M. Brutum*, Cambridge.

12 For a more recent three-fold division of the landscape see B. K. ROBERTS and S. WRATHMELL (2000), *An Atlas of Rural Settlement in England*, English Heritage, London.

13 A. S. HOBLEY (1989), 'The Numismatic Evidence for the post-Agricolan Abandonment of the Roman Frontier in Northern Scotland', *Britannia* 20, 69–74.

14 W. S. HANSON (2003), 'The Roman Presence: British interludes in Scotland', in *After the Ice Age: Environment, Archaeology and History 8000 BC–AD 1000*, K. J. Edwards and Ian B. M. Ralston, (eds.) 195–216.

15 S. DUFFY (2000), *The Concise History of Ireland*, Gill and Macmillan, Dublin, p. 38.

16 H. E. M. COOL (2004), *The Roman Cemetery at Brougham, Cumbria*, Britannia Monograph Series 21, London.

17 M. J. JONES, DAVID STOCKER and ALAN VINCE (2003), *The City by the Pool. Assessing the archaeology of the city of Lincoln*, Oxbow Books, pp. 22–7.

18 TONY GREGORY (1991), 'Excavations in Thetford 1986–92', *East Anglia Archaeology* 53, Norwich.

19 *See* P. SALWAY (1981), *Roman Britain*, Oxford University Press, Oxford, p. 152.

20 H. HURST (2000), 'The fortress-colonia of Roman Britain', in *Romanisation and the City: creations, transformations and failures*, ed. E. Fentress, Journal of Roman Archaeology Supplementary Series 38, 105–114.

21 TACITUS, *Annals*, 3, 43.

22 *Current Archaeology*, November 2002, 182, 48.

23 *See* DUNCAN JONES (1982), *The Economy of the Roman Empire: quantitative studies*, Cambridge University Press, Appendix 10, pp. 348–50.

24 DIODORUS SICULUS, 5, 26, 3.

25 *See* K. BRANIGAN and D. MILES (1989), *The Economies of Roman Villas*, Sheffield University, Sheffield.

26 HENRIETT QUINNELL (2004), *Trethurgy: excavations at Trethurgy Round, St Austell: community and status in Roman and post-Roman Cornwall*, Cornwall County Council.

27 T. W. POTTER and C. JOHNS (1992), *Roman Britain*, British Museum Press, p. 68.

28 M. MILLETT (1990) *The Romanization of Britain: an essay in archaeological interpretation*, CUP, Cambridge, p. 185.

29 CHARLOTTE ROBERTS and MARGARET COX (2003), *Health and Disease in Britain: from prehistory to the present day*, Sutton, Stroud, p. 108.

30 D. J. MATTHEWS (1999), 'Death into Life: populations statistics from cemetery data', in *Theoretical Roman Archaeology and Architecture*, Alan Leslie (ed.), Guthrie Press, pp. 141–161.

31 PETER SALWAY (1981), *Roman Britain*, Oxford University Press, Oxford, p. 552.

Chapter Four

1 A. BOYLE, A. DODD, D. MILES and A. MUDD (1995), *Two Oxfordshire Anglo-Saxon Cemeteries: Berinsfield and Didcot*, Thames Valley Landscapes Monograph 8, Oxford.

2 J. BLAIR (1994), *Anglo-Saxon Oxfordshire*, Alan Sutton, Stroud.

3 PHILIP RANCE (2001), 'Attacotti, Deisi, and Magnus Maximus: the Case for Irish federates in late Roman Britain', *Britannia* 32, 243–270.

4 M. WINTERBOTTOM (ed. & trans.) (1978), *Gildas: The Ruin of Britain and other documents* Phillimore, London; M. Lapidge and D. Dumvile (eds.) (1984), *Gildas: new approaches*, Boydell; N. HIGHAM (1994), *The English Conquest*, Manchester University Press, Manchester.

5 NICHOLAS HOWE (1989), *Migration and Mythmaking in Anglo-Saxon England*, Yale University Press, New Haven.

6 B. COLGRAVE and R. MYNORS (1969), *Bede's Ecclesiastical History of the English People*, Oxford University Press, Oxford.

7 ERIC JOHN, *Reassessing Anglo-Saxon England*, Manchester University Press, p. 5.

8 HAROLD MYTUM (1992), *The Origins of Early Christian Ireland*, Routledge, London.

9 CHARLES THOMAS (1990), '"Gallici nautae de Galliarum provinciis" – a sixth/seventh century trade with Gaul, reconsidered', *Medieval Archaeology* 34, 1–26.

10 *The Táin*, trans. Thomas Kinsella (1970), from the Irish epic *Táin Bo Cuailgne*, Oxford University Press, Oxford.

11 SAM LUCY (2000), *The Anglo-Saxon Way of Death*, Sutton, Stroud.

12 H. HARKE (1990), 'Warrior Graves? The back ground of the Anglo-Saxon

weapon burial rite', *Past and Present* 126, 22–43.

13 H. HARKE (1998), 'Archaeologists and Migration: a problem of attitude', *Current Archaeology* 39, 19–45.

14 J. LLOYD JONES (1997), 'Calculating Bio-distance Using Dental Morphology', in S. Anderson and K. Boyle (eds.), *Computing and Statistics in Osteoarchaeology*, pp. 23–30.

15 R. GOWLAND (2002), *Age as an Aspect of Social Identity in Fourth- to Sixth-Century England*, University of Durham, PhD dissertation.

16 COLIN RENFREW and KATIE BOYLE (eds.) (2000), *Archaeogenetics: DNA and the population prehistory of Europe*, McDonald Institute Monograph, Cambridge, p. 4.

17 B. SYKES (2001), *The Seven Daughters of Eve*, Bantam Press, London.

18 CATHERINE HILLS (2003), *The Origins of the English*, Duckworth, London, pp. 57–71.

19 J. F. WILSON et al. (2001), 'Genetic Evidence for Different Male and Female Roles During Cultural Transitions in the British Isles', *Proceedings of the National Academy of Sciences* USA 978, 5078–83.

20 WEALE et al. (2002) 'Y Chromosome Evidence for Anglo-Saxon Mass Migration', *Molecular Biology and Evolution* 19, 1000–21.

21 J. HINES (1997), 'Archaeology and Language in a Historical Context: the creation of English', in R. Blench and M. Spriggs (eds.), *Archaeology and Language II*, Routledge, London, pp. 283–94; CATHERINE HILL (2003), *The Origins of the English*, Duckworth, London, pp. 41–55.

22 SALLY M. FOSTER (2004), *Picts, Gaels and Scots*, Batsford/Historic Scotland.

23 KATHERINE FORSYTH (1997), *Language in Pictland: the case against non-Indo European Pictish*, Utrecht.

24 STEPHEN DRISCOLL (2002), *Alba: the Gaelic kingdom of Scotland* AD *800–1124*, Edinburgh.

25 D. N. DUMVILLE (2002), 'Ireland and North Britain in the Earlier Middle Ages: context for Miniugud Senchasa Fher nAlban', in C. A. Baoill and N. R. McGuire (eds.), *Rannsachadh na Gaidhlig* (2000), Aberdeen, pp. 185–211.

26 ANDREW REYNOLDS (1999), *Later Anglo-Saxon England: life and landscape*, Tempus, Stroud, p. 67.

27 M. CARVER (1998), *Sutton Hoo Burial Ground of Kings*, British Museum Press, London.

28 JOHN BARRETT and KEN SMITH (2004), *The Peak District: landscapes through time*, Windgather Press, Macclesfield.

29 *The Prittlewell Prince: the discovery of a rich Anglo-Saxon burial in Essex*, Museum of London Archaeology Service (2004).

30 A. BOYLE, D. JENNINGS, D. MILES and S. PALMER (1998), *The Anglo-Saxon Cemetery at Butler's Field, Lechlade*, Thames Valley Landscapes Monograph 10, Oxford.

31 J. BLAIR (1994), *Anglo-Saxon Oxfordshire*, Sutton, Stroud, p. 41.

32 MICHELLE P. BROWN (2003), *The Lindisfarne Gospels: society, spirituality and the scribe*, British Library, London.

Chapter Five

1 R. I. PAGE (1987), *Runes*, University of California Press and British Museum, London; JULIAN D. RICHARDS (2000), *Viking Age England*, Tempus, Stroud.

2 P. Sawyer (ed.) (1977), *The Oxford Illustrated History of the Vikings*, Oxford University Press, Oxford.

3 JULIAN RICHARDS (2001), *Blood of the Vikings*, Hodder and Stoughton,

London; Mark Rednap (2000), *Vikings in Wales: an archaeological quest*, National Museum and Galleries of Wales, Cardiff.

4   *See* DAIBHI O'CROININ (1995), *Early Medieval Ireland, 400–1200*, Longman History of Ireland, Longman, p. 235.

5   JAMES GRAHAM-CAMPBELL (1989), *The Viking World*, Frances Lincoln, London.

6   *See* O'CROININ (1995), p. 245, for refs.

7   MICHELLE P. BROWN (2003), p. 36.

8   BARBARA E. CRAWFORD (1987), *Scandinavian Scotland*, Scotland in the Early Middle Ages 2, Leicester University Press.

9   See H. H. LAMB (1981), 'Climate from 1000 BC to AD 1000', in M. Jones and G. Dimbleby (eds.), *The Environment of Man*, British Archaeological Report 87, Oxford, pp. 53–65.

10 J. J. Tierny (ed.) (1967), 'Dicuili "Liber de mensura orbis terrae"', Scriptores Latini Hiberniae, VI, Dublin.

11 For the 'Blood of the Vikings Genetics Survey', by University College, London, *see* http://www.bbc.co.uk/history/programmes/bloodofthevikings/genetics.

12 *Orkneyinga Saga*, chapter 106.

13 Joan Radner (ed.) (1978), *Fragmentary Annals of Ireland*, Dublin, p. 120.

14 *See* REDNAP (2000), pp. 19–21.

15 J. H. F. Peile (trans.) (1934), *Life of St Wulfstan, Bishop of Worcester*, Oxford, pp. 64–5.

16 *See* REDNAP (2000), pp. 32–5.

17 M. BIDDLE and B. KYOLBY-BIDDLE (1992), 'Repton and the Vikings', *Antiquity* 66, 36–51.

18 RICHARDS et al. (1995), 'The Viking Barrow Cemetery at Heath Wood, Ingleby, Derbyshire', *Medieval Archaeology* 39, 51–70.

19 SEAMUS HEANEY (1975), p. 8.

20 JULIAN D. RICHARDS (2000), *Viking Age England*, Tempus, Stroud.

21 GREG SPEED and PENELOPE WALTON ROGERS (2004), 'The Burial of a Viking Woman at Adwickle-Street, South Yorkshire', *Medieval Archaeology* 48, 51–90.

22 DAWN HADLEY (2002), 'Invisible Vikings', *British Archaeology* 64, 16–21.

23 Quoted in REDNAP (2000), p. 40.

24 D. M. HADLEY (1997), '"And they proceeded to plough and support themselves": the Scandinavian settlement of England', *Anglo-Norman Studies* 19, 69–96.

25 D. M. HADLEY (1996), 'Multiple Estates and the Origins of the Manorial Structure of the Northern Danelaw', *Journal of Historical Geography* 22, 3–15.

26 TOM HASSALL (1987), *Oxford: the Buried City*, Oxford Archaeological Unit.

27 J. D. RICHARDS (2000), *Viking Age England*, Tempus, Stroud, p. 59.

28 ALAN VINCE (1990), *Saxon London: An Archaeological Investigation*, Seaby, London.

29 ALAN VINCE (1990), *Saxon London*, Seaby, London pp. 72–4.

30 ANN WILLIAMS (2003), *Aethelred the Unready: the ill-counselled King*, Hambledon and London, p. 53.

Chapter Six

1   JOHN BLAIR (1994), *Anglo-Saxon Oxfordshire*, Tempus, Stroud, pp. 159–61, 167–8.

2   R. ALLEN BROWN (1984), *The Normans*, Boydell Press, Woodbridge; R. D. H. GEM (1980), 'The Romanesque Rebuilding of Westminster Abbey', *Proceedings of the Battle Conference on Anglo-*

Norman Studies iii, 33–60

3 B. GOLDING (1994), *Conquest and Colonization: the Normans in Britain 1066–1100*, New York, St Martin's Press.

4 DAVID HEY (2000), *Family Names and Family History*, Hambledon and London, p. 33.

5 D. HEY (2000), pp. 33–4.

6 *See* NICHOLAS ORME (2001), *Medieval Children*, Yale University Press, New Haven and London; PHILIP NILES (1982), 'Baptism and the Naming of Children in Late Medieval England', *Medieval Prosography* 3, 95–107.

7 *Anglo-Saxon Chronicle*, 16, 1–2, quoted in DAVID ROFFE (2000), *Domesday: the Inquest and the Book*, Oxford University Press, p. 1.

8 DAVID ROFFE (2000), p. 2.

9 R. FLEMING (1991), *Kings and Lands in Conquest England*, Cambridge University Press, Cambridge.

10 CHRISTOPHER DYER (2002), *The Origins of the Medieval Economy c.850–c.1100*, Yale University Press, pp. 92–4.

11 DELLA HOOKE (1987), 'Anglo-Saxon Estates in the Vale of the White Horse', *Oxoniensia* 52, 129-143.

12 D. GIGG (1982), *The Dynamics of Agricultural Change*, London

13 JAMES BOND (1994), 'Forests, Chases, Varrens and Parks in Medieval Wessex', in M. Aston and C. Lewis (eds.), *The Medieval Landscape of Wessex*, Oxbow, Oxford, pp. 115–58.

14 R. FLEMING (1991), *Kings and Lords in Conquest England*, Cambridge University Press, Cambridge.

15 BRUCE WEBSTER (1997), *Medieval Scotland: the making of an identity*, Macmillan Press, London, 2nd edn, p. 138, note 1.

16 G. W. S. BARROW (1980), *The Anglo-Norman Era in Scottish History*, Oxford University Press, Oxford,

pp. 61–4, and quoted in BRUCE WEBSTER (1997), *Medieval Scotland and the Making of an Identity*, Macmillan Press, London, p. 30.

17 CHARLES KIGHTLY (1988), *A Mirror on Medieval Wales: Gerald of Wales and his journey of 1188*, CADW, Cardiff.

18 R. R. DAVIES (2000), *The First English Empire: power and identities in the British Isles 1093–1343*, Oxford University Press, pp. 143–4.

19 THOMAS JONES (1955), *Brut y Tywysogyon, or The Chronicle of the Princes*, Peniarth MS20 version, Cardiff, 1941–52, p. 42.

20 A. COSGRAVE (ed.) (1981), *A New History of Ireland, vol. II: Medieval Ireland 1169–1534*, pp. 212–13, 404–10.

21 CECIL ROTH (1941), *A History of the Jews in England*, Oxford University Press, Oxford.

22 ANTHONY QUINEY (2003), *Town Houses in Medieval Britain*, Yale University Press, New Haven

23 ROTH (1941), p.27

24 JANE M. LILLEY, G STROUD, D R BROTHWELL and M H WILLIAMSON (1994), *The Jewish Burial Ground at Jewbury, The Medieval Cemeteries: the Archaeology of York 12/3*, The Council for British Archaeology, York.

25 CHRISTOPHER DANIELL (1997) *Death and Burial in Medieval England 1066–1550*, Routledge, London

26 Quoted in CHARLES KIGHTLY (1988), *A Mirror of Medieval Wales: Gerald of Wales and his journey of 1188*, CADW, Cardiff, p. 91.

27 R. R. DAVIES (2000), *The First English Empire: power and identities in the British Isles 1093–1343*, Oxford University Press, Oxford, p. 170.

28 ROBERT BARTLETT (1993), *The Making of Europe: conquest and colonization and cultural change, 950–*

1350, BCA, LondonCA, London

29 RICHARD SMITH, 'Plagues and Peoples: the long demographic cycle, 1250–1670', in Paul Slack and Ryk Ward (eds.), *The Peopling of Britain: the shaping of a human landscape*, Oxford University Press, pp.177–210.

30 For a discussion of wide-ranging population estimates *see* E. MILLER and J. HATCHER (1978), *Medieval England: rural society and economic change 1086–1348*, Longman (1985 edn), London, pp. 28–9.

31 JAMES SHIRLEY (1596–1666), from *The Contention of Ajax and Ulysses* (1659).

32 Quoted in PHILIP ZIEGLER (1969), *The Black Death* (1991 edn), Alan Sutton, p. 120.

33 Quoted in COLIN PLATT (1996), *King Death: the Black Death and its aftermath in late medieval Europe*, London, p. 4.

34 MANA KELLY (2001), *A History of the Black Death in Ireland*, Tempus, Stroud, p. 27.

35 Recorded in W. REES, 'The Black Death in England and Wales as exhibited in Manorial Documents', *Proceedings of the Royal Society of Medicine*, XVI, part 2, 34.

Chapter Seven

1 Recorded in CHRISTOPHER DYER (2002), *Making a Living in the Middle Ages: the people of Britain 850–1520*, Yale University Press, p. 265.

2 Quoted in E. B. FRYDE (1996), 'Peasants and Landlords', in *Later Medieval England*, Alan Sutton, p. 2.

3 *See*, for example, S. R. EPSTEIN (1991), 'Cities, regions and late medieval crisis: Sicily and Tuscany compared', in *Past and Present* 130, 3, 50.

4 RICHARD SMITH (2002), 'Plagues and Peoples: the long demographic cycle 1250–670', in PAUL SLACK and RYK WARD, *The Peopling of Britain: the shaping of a human landscape*, Oxford University Press, p. 180.

5 CHARLOTTE ROBERTS and MARGARET COX (2003), *Health and Disease in Britain: from prehistory to the present pay*, Alan Sutton, pp. 244–6.

6 SALLY CRAWFORD (1999), *Childhood in Anglo-Saxon England*, Sutton, Stroud, p. 63.

7 Based on JOHN HATCHER (1977), *Plague, Population and the English Economy 1348–1530*, and Edward Miller (ed.) (1991), *Agrarian History of Wales, volume III, 1348–1500*, Cambridge University Press. J. CORNWALL (1970), 'English Population in the Early Sixteenth Century', in *Economic History Review*, 2nd series, 23, 44 puts the numbers slightly lower.

8 M. BAILEY (1991), 'Per impetum maris: natural disaster and economic decline in Eastern England 1275–1350', in B. M. S. Campbell (ed.), *Before the Black Death: studies in the 'Crisis' of the early fourteenth century*, Manchester University Press, pp. 184–208.

9 MIRI RUBIN (2005), *The Hollow Crown: a history of Britain in the late Middle Ages*, Allen Lane, London, p. 265.

10 ASA BRIGGS (1994), *A Social History of England: a new edition from the Ice Age to the Channel Tunnel*, London, p. 93.

11 NICHOLAS BROOKS (1985), 'The Organisation and Achievements of the Peasants in Kent and Essex in 1381', in H. Mayr-Harting and R. I. Moore (eds.), *Studies in Medieval History Presented to R. H. C. Davis*, London.

12 Christopher Dyer estimates that about half the English rural popula-

tion was unfree – see *Standards of Living in the Later Middle Ages: social change in England c.1200–1520,* Cambridge (1989), p. 137 – although E. B. Fryde suggests that both these estimates are too low.

13 E. B. FRYDE (1996), *Peasants and Landlords in Later Medieval England,* Sutton Publishing, p. 10.

14 Quoted in E. B. FRYDE (1996), *Peasants and Landlords in Later Medieval England,* Sutton Publishing, p. 243.

15 J. C. HOLT (1982), *Robin Hood,* Thames and Hudson, London, p. 16.

16 Nick Merriman (ed.) (1993), *The Peopling of London: fifteen thousand years of settlement from overseas,* Museum of London, p. 40.

17 SYLVIA THRUPP (1969), 'Aliens in and around London in the fifteenth Century', in A. E. J. Hollander and W. Kellaway (eds.), *Studies in London History,* London.

18 DIARMAID MACCULLOCH (2003), *Reformation: Europe's house divided, 1490–1700,* Allen Lane, London.

Chapter Eight

1 J. M. KEYNES (1930), *A Treatise on Money, volume 11;* quoted in ASA BRIGGS (1999), *A Social History of Britain,* 3rd edn, p. 110.

2 ANNE LAURENCE (1996), *Women in England 1500–1760: a social history,* Phoenix, London, pp. 28–9.

3 J. WALTER and R. S. SCHOFIELD (1989), 'Famine, Disease and Crisis: mortality in early modern England', in J. Walter and R. S. Schofield (eds.), *Famine, Disease and the Social Order in Early Modern Society,* Cambridge University Press, pp. 1–74.

4 P. SLACK (1985), *The Impact of Plague in Tudor and Stuart England,* Routledge and Kegan Paul, London,

pp. 79–110.

5 E. A. WRIGLEY and R. J. SCHOFIELD (1981), *The Population History of England 1541–1871: a reconstruction,* Harvard University Press, Cambridge, MA, p. 653.

6 Quoted in SUSAN BRIGDEN (2001), *New Worlds, Lost Worlds: the rule of the Tudors 1485–1603,* Penguin, London, pp. 64–5.

7 LAWRENCE STONE (1990), *The Road to Divorce: England 1530–1987,* Oxford University Press.

8 MAURICE KEEN (1990), *English Society in the Later Middle Ages 1348–1500,* Penguin, London, pp. 290–95.

9 PETER ACKROYD (1998), *The Life of Thomas More,* Chatto and Windus, London, pp. 226, 296–8.

10 G. R. ELTON (1982), *The Tudor Constitution,* 2nd edn, Cambridge University Press, pp. 364–5.

11 ANDREW GRAHAM-DIXON (1996), *A History of British Art,* BBC, London.

12 NORMAN DAVIES (1999), *The Isles, a History,* Macmillan, London, p. 493.

13 DIARMAID MACCULLOCH (2003), *Reformation: Europe's House Divided 1490–1700,* Allen Lane, London, p. 346.

14 PENRY WILLIAMS (1995), *The Later Tudors: England 1547–1603,* the New Oxford History of England, Oxford University Press, p. 395.

15 CHARLES BARBER (1993), *The English Language: a historical introduction,* Canto edition (2000), Cambridge, pp. 179–182.

16 ROBIN GWYNN (2001), *Huguenot Heritage: the history and contribution of the Huguenots in Britain,* Sussex Academic Press, Brighton.

17 PETER FRYER (1984), *Staying Power: the history of black people in Britain,* Pluto Press, London.

18 SEAN DUFFY (2000), *The Concise History of Ireland,* Gill and Macmillan, Dublin, p. 97.

19 JOHN GUY (1988), *Tudor England,*

Oxford University Press, Oxford.
20 E. H. PHELPS BROWN and S. V. HOPKINS (1956), 'Seven Centuries of the Prices of Consumables, Compared with Builders' Wage Rates', *Economica* NS 23 (1956), 296–314.
21 Karen Hearn (ed.) (1995), *Dynasties: Painting in Tudor and Jacobean England 1530–1630*, Tate Publishing.
22 PENRY WILLIAMS (1995), *The Later Tudors, England 1547–1603*, the New Oxford History of England, Oxford University Press, p. 208.
23 Quoted in PENRY WILLIAMS (1995), *The Later Tudors, England 1547–1603*, the New Oxford History of England, Oxford University Press, p. 211.
24 ASA BRIGGS (1999), *A Social History of England*, 3rd edn, p. 120.
25 F. J. Fislo (ed.) (1936), *The State of England, 1600, by Sir Thomas Wilson*, Camden Society, 3rd series, 52, Camden Miscellany 16, London, p. 24.
26 PENELOPE CORFIELD (1990), 'Urban Developments in England and Wales in the Sixteenth and Seventeenth Centuries', in Jonathan Barry (ed.), *The Tudor and Stuart Town: a reader in English urban history 1530–1688*, Longman, London, p. 39.
27 A. L. BIER (1990), 'Social Problems in Elizabethan London', in John Barry (ed.), *The Tudor and Stuart Town: a reader in English urban history 1530–1688*, Longman, London, pp. 121–38.

FROM TECHNICAL NOTES

28 E. A. WRIGLEY and R. S. SCHOFIELD (1981), 'Social Problems in Elizabethan London', in John Barry (ed.), *The Population History of England, 1541–1871*, Cambridge University Press, Cambridge

Chapter Nine

1 JOHN C. APPLEBY (1998), 'War, Politics and Colonization, 1558–1625', in NICHOLAS CANNY, *The Origins of Empire, volume 1*, the Oxford History of the British Empire, Oxford University Press, pp. 55–78.
2 For the Scots in Poland and references, see T. M. DEVINE (2003), *Scotland's Empire 1600–1815*, Penguin edn (2004), pp. 10–11.
3 NEAL ASCHERSON (2002), *Stone Voices: the search for Scotland*, Granta Books, London, p. 27.
4 T. M. DEVINE (2003), *Scotland's Empire: 1600–1815*, Penguin edn (2004), p. 20.
5 SEAN DUFFY (2000), *The Concise History of Ireland*, Gill and Macmillan, Dublin, p. 116.
6 GERRY BLACK (2003), *Jewish London: an illustrated history*, Breedon Books, Derby.
7 MICHAEL SNODIN and JOHN STYLES (2001), *Design and the Decorative Arts in Britain 1500–1900*, V&A Publications, London, pp. 89–92.
8 See ANNA PAVORD (1999), *The Tulip*, Bloomsbury, London, pp. 15, 104–5.
9 R. E. DUTHIE (1982), 'English Florists' Societies and Feasts in the Seventeenth and first Half of the Eighteenth Centuries', *Garden History* 10, 18, 33.
10 MARK KISHLANDSKY (1996), *A Monarchy Transformed: Britain 1603–1714*, Allen Lane, London.
11 LORD MACAULEY (1848–61), *The History of England*, Hugh Trevor-Roper (ed.), (1979), Penguin Books.
12 LINDA COLLEY (1992), *Britons: forging the nation 1707–1837*, Yale University Press, New Haven and London.
13 N. DAVIES (1999), *The Isles: a history*, Macmillan, London

Chapter Ten

1 ROBERT GITTINGS and JO MANTON (1985), *Dorothy Wordsworth*, Oxford University Press, paperback edn (1988), Oxford, pp. 4–5.

2 ROY PORTER (1997), *The Great Benefit to Mankind: a medical history of humanity from antiquity to the present day*, Fontana paperback edn, (1999), London, pp. 133–4.

3 Recorded in ROY PORTER (1991), *English Society in the Eighteenth Century*, revised Penguin edn, London, pp. 202–3.

4 E. L. JONES (1981), 'Agriculture 1700–1800', in *The Economic History of Britain since 1700: Volume 1, 1700–1800*, eds. Roderick Floud and Donald McCloskey, Cambridge University Press, p. 66.

5 LINDA COLLEY (1992), *Britons: forging the nation 1707–1837*, Yale University Press, New Haven and London, p. 158.6
VALERIE PAKENHAM (2000), *The Big House in Ireland*, Cassell, London.

7 DAVID WATKIN (1982), *The English Vision: the picturesque in architecture, landscape and garden design*, John Murray, London.

8 Quoted in WILLIAM J. BERNSTEIN (2004), *The Birth of Plenty: how the prosperity of the modern world was created*, McGraw Hill, New York, p. 213.

9 JOHN RULE (1992), *The Vital Century: England's developing economy 1714–1815*, Harlow, p. 276; C. A. BAYLEY (2004), *The Birth of the Modern World 1780–1914*, Blackwell Publishing, p. 92.

10 Quoted in LINDA COLLEY (1992), p. 80.

11 DANIEL DEFOE (1724-6), *A Tour through the Whole Island of Great Britain*, Penguin (1971), London.

12 BARRIE TRINDER (1982), *The Making of the Industrial Landscape*, Phoenix edn (1997), London, p. 92.

13 See ARTHUR HENMAN (2002), *The Scottish Enlightenment: the Scots invention of the modern world*, Fourth Estate, London, p. 272.

14 ROY PORTER (1991), *English Society in the Eighteenth Century*, Penguin, 2nd revised edn, London, p. 318.

15 E. A. WRIGLEY (1994), 'The Classical Economists, the Stationary State and the Industrial Revolution', in G. D. Snooks (ed.), *Was the Industrial Revolution Necessary?*, Routledge, London, pp. 27–42; *see* p. 33.

16 H. T. ODUM and E. L. ODUM (1976), *Energy Basis for Man and Nature*, McGraw Hill, New York, p. 52.

17 MARJORIE HARPER (2003), *Adventurers and Exiles: the Great Scottish Exodus*, Profile Books, London, p. 6.

18 ERIC RICHARD (2004), *Britannia's Children: emigration from England, Scotland, Wales and Ireland since 1600*, Hambledon and London, p. 92.

19 BARRIE TRINDER (1982), *The Making of the Industrial Landscape*, Phoenix edn (1997), London, p. 207.

20 Figures quoted in JOHN LANGTON (2002), 'Prometheus Prostrated?', in Paul Slack and Ryk Ward (eds.), *The Peopling of Britain: the shaping of a human landscape*, Oxford University Press, Oxford, pp. 243–54.

21 I. DYCK (1992), *William Cobbett and Popular Rural Culture*, Cambridge University Press, Cambridge, p. 135.

22 JOHN NAISMITH (1790), *Thoughts on Various Objects of Industry Pursued in Scotland*, Edinburgh, p. 93. Quoted in T. M. DEVINE (2004) *Scotland's Empire 1600–1815*, Penguin, London, p. 337.

23 LYDIA M. PULSIPHER (1986), *Seventeenth-Century Montserrat: an environmental impact statement*, Historical Geography Research Series, p. 17.

24 CATHERINE HALL (2002), *Civilising Subjects: metropole and colony in the English imagination 1830–1867*, Polity Press, Cambridge, p. 69.

25 N. A. M. RODGER (1986), *The Wooden World: an anatomy of the Georgian navy*, Fontana Press, London, p. 27, and N. A. M. RODGER (2004), *The Command of the Ocean: a naval history of Britain, 1649–1815*, Allen Lane, London, pp. 508–12.

26 PETER FRYER (1984), *Staying Power: the history of black people in Britain*, Pluto Press, London, p. 107.

27 PETER FRYER (1984), p. 114.

28 FELIPE FERNANDEZ-ARMESTO (2001), *Food: a history*, Macmillan, London, p. 178.

29 Quoted in MARJORIE HARPER (2003), p. 19.

30 LINDA COLLEY (1992), *Britons: forging the nation 1707–1837*, Yale University Press, New Haven and London, p. 303, and for demographic and marriage information, pp. 156–161.

31 THOMAS BARTLETT (1998), '"This famous island set in a Virginian sea": Ireland in the British Empire, 1690–1801', in P. J. Marshall (ed.), *The Oxford History of the British Empire, volume 2: the eighteenth century*, Oxford, pp. 273–4.

32 NIALL FERGUSON (2003), *Empire: how Britain made the modern world*, Allen Lane, London, pp. 42–7.

33 WILLIAM DALRYMPLE (2002), *The White Mughals: Love and Betrayal in Eighteenth-century India*, HarperCollins, London.

34 Lawrence James (1997), *Raj: the making of British India*, Abacus edn (1998), London, p. 158.

35 *See* for example RORY FITZPATRICK (1989), *God's Frontiersmen: the Scots-Irish epic*, Weidenfeld and Nicolson, London.

Chapter Eleven

1 R. F. FOSTER (1988), *Modern Ireland 1600–1972*, Penguin edn (1989), p. 331. Foster estimates a population of 8.2 million and suggests that the growth rate had slackened by 1841, from 17 per cent twenty years earlier to 5.25 per cent.

2 For a more complex view of Irish demography based on the work of Kenneth Cullen, see R. F. FOSTER (1988), *Modern Ireland 1600–1972*, Penguin edn (1989), pp. 217–20.

3 *See* R. F. FOSTER (1988), p. 325, for a balanced account.

4 T. CARLYLE 'Chartism', *Selected Writings*, London (1986), quoted in TRISTRAM HUNT (2004), *Building Jerusalem: the rise and fall of the Victorian city*, Weidenfeld and Nicolson, London, p. 25.

5 COLIN KIDD (1997), 'Sentiment, Race and Revival: Scottish identities in the aftermath of the Enlightenment', in L. Brockliss and D. Eastwood (eds.), *A Union of Multiple Indentities. The British Isles c.1750–c.1850*, Manchester University Press, p. 116.

6 J. LANGTON (2000), 'Urban Growth and Economic Change from the Seventeenth Century to 1841', in P. Clark (ed.), *Cambridge Urban History of Britain II*, Cambridge University Press, pp. 253–90.

7 J. LANGTON (2002), in P. Clark (ed.), pp. 249–50.

8 J. WALVIN (1992), *Black Ivory: slavery in the British Empire*, Blackwell, Oxford, 2nd edn (2001), p. 260.

9 CATHERINE HALL (2002), *Civilising Subjects: metropole and colony in the English imagination 1830–1867*, Polity Press, Cambridge.

10 ROY PORTER (1997), *The Greatest Benefit to Mankind: a medical history of humankind from antiquity to the*

present, Fontana edn (1999), London, pp. 401–3.

11 E. A. WRIGLEY and R. SCHOFIELD (1989), p. 475.

12 *See* J. A. I. CHAMPION (1993), 'Epidemics and the Built Environment in 1665', in J. A. I. Chapman (ed.), *Epidemic Disease in London*, University of London Institute of Historical Research, Working Papers Series 1, pp. 35–54; see p. 39.

13 JULIET BARKER (1994), *The Brontës*, Phoenix paperback edn (1995), pp. 92–9, 575–6.

14 F. Engels (1987 edn), *The Condition of the Working Class in England*, p. 290.

15 Prys Morgan (ed.) (2001), *The Tempus History of Wales: 2500 BC–AD 2000*, Tempus, Stroud, pp. 200–205.

16 K. O. Morgan (ed.) (1963), *Wales in British Politics 1868–1922*, Cardiff, p. 210.

17 ASA BRIGGS (1994), *A Social History of England*, BCA, p. 214.

18 JOSE HARRIS (1993), *Private Lives, Public Spirit: Britain 1870–1914*, the Penguin Social History of Britain, paperback edn (1994),London, p. 252.

19 MICHAEL LEAPMAN (2001), *The World for a Shilling: how the Great Exhbition of 1851 shaped a nation*, Review paperback edn (2002), London, pp. 225–7.

20 MICHAEL TWYNMAN (1970), *Printing 1770–1970: an illustrated history of its development and uses in England*; JAMES RYAN (2001), 'Images and Impressions: printing, reproduction and photography', in John M. MacKenzie (ed.), *The Victorian Vision: inventing new Britain*, V&A Publications, London, p. 216.

21 DAVID CANNADINE (1998), *Class in Britain*,Yale University Press, New Haven and London, p. 73.

22 Quoted in DAVID CANNADINE (1998), p. 74.

23 DAVID CANNADINE (1998), p. 77 and p. 79 for references.

24 J. MORDAUNT CROOK (1987), *The Dilemma of Style: architectural ideas from the picturesque to the post-modern*. John Murray, London, p. 47.

25 A.W. PUGIN, *True Principles of Pointed and Christian Architecture*, p. 56.

26 ERIC HOBSBAWM (1962), *The Age of Revolution 1789–1848*, Abacus edn (2001), p. 62.

27 MARK GIROUARD (1990), *The English Town*,Yale University Press, New Haven, p.8.

28 ROY PORTER (1999), *The Greatest Benefit to Mankind: a medical history of humanity from antiquity to the present*, Fontana Press, pp. 711–12.

29 *See* PETER FRYER (1984), *Staying Power: the history of black people in Britain*, Pluto Press, London, p. 302.

30 Quoted from Frank Cundall (ed.) (1907), *Lady Nugent's Journal: Jamaica one hundred years ago*, A. & C. Black, London; see SUSIE STEINBACH (2004), *Women in England 1760–1914: a social history*, Weidenfeld & Nicolson, London, p. 197.

31 A. N. WILSON (2002), *The Victorians*, Hutchinson, London.

32 Quotations from CHRISTOPHER T. HUSBANDS, 'East End Racism 1900–1980', the *London Journal* 8, 3-26.

33 GERRY BLACK (2003), *Jewish London: an illustrated history*, Breedon Books, Derby, pp. 100-104

34 JOSE HARRIS (1993), p. 132.

Chapter Twelve

1 JOSE HARRIS (1993), *Private Lives, Public Spirit: Britain 1870–1914*, Penguin edn (1994), London, p. 102.

2 VALERIE PAKENHAM (2000), *The Big House in Ireland*, Cassell, London, pp. 159–63.

3 SEAN DUFFY (2000), *The Concise History of Ireland*, Gill and Macmillan Ltd, Dublin, p. 206.

4 SEAN DUFFY (2000), p. 216,

5 W. K. HANCOCK (1937–68), *Survey of British Commonwealth Affairs* II, part I, Oxford University Press, p. 56

6 ERIC RICHARD (2004), *Britannia's Children: emigration from England, Scotland, Wales and Ireland since 1600*, Hambledon and London, p. 280.

7 Quotations from ROBERT WINDER (2004), *Bloody Foreigners: the story of immigration to Britain*, Little Brown, London, p. 196.

8 Judith Oakley (1983), *The Traveller-Gypsies*, Cambridge University Press, Cambridge.

9 JOSE HARRIS (1993), *Private Lives, Public Spirit: Britain 1870–1914*, Penguin, London, p. 42.

10 I. D. WHYTE (2000), *Migration and Society in Britain 1550–1830*, Macmillan, London; C. G. Pooley and J. Turnbull (1990), *Migration and Mobility in Britain since the 18th Century*, UCL Press, reprinted Routledge (2003).

11 DANIEL SNOWMAN (2002), *The Cultural Impact on Britain of Refugees from Nazism*, Chatto and Windus, London.

12 *See* SNOWMAN (2002), pp. 8–9.

13 ELAINE HARWOOD (2003), *England: a guide to post-war listed buildings*, Batsford, London, p. 688.

14 ROBERT WINDER (2004), *Bloody Foreigners: the story of immigration to Britain*, Little Brown, London.

15 Quoted in MIKE PHILLIPS and TREVOR PHILLIPS (1998), *Windrush: the irresistible rise of multi-racial Britain*, HarperCollins, paperback (1999), p. 53.

16 See ROZINA VISRAM (2002), *Asians in Britain: 400 years of history*, Pluto Press, London, pp. 37–43. By 1914 there were a few 'Indian' restaurants in Soho and the Piccadilly area of London. Since then, thanks mainly to the efforts of Bangladeshi seamen, they have spread through the entire country, concocting vindaloo and other dishes for the British market. In recent years a new generation of upmarket restaurants providing more authentic and sophisticated Indian food has arrived.

17 Figures from *Regional Trends 2001*, HMSO, London.

18 'Do We Need a Baby Boom? A declining population doesn't necessarily mean a failing economy though it makes succeeding harder', by WILL HUTTON, the *Observer*, 25 January 2004, 30.

19 ROY PORTER (1997), *The Greatest Benefit to Mankind: a medical history of humanity from antiquity to the present*, Fontana Press, London, p. 715.

20 ROY PORTER (1997), pp. 717–18.

21 *Geographic Variations in Health*, Office for National Statistics (2001), London.

TECHNICAL
APPENDIX
(marked with § in text)

Chapter One

p. 39 **DNA evidence**
Any simple human chromosome is a mosaic of haplotype blocks. Our genome sequences are largely identical – there is only 0.1 per cent variation – and this variation can be observed in the haplotypes. A recent study of 928 of these haplotype blocks in Africans, Asians and Europeans found that half were found in all three continents, nearly three-quarters in two and over a quarter in one continent only. Of the haplotypes found in one continent, only 90 per cent were from Africa. African DNA sequences also differ more among themselves than they differ from Asian or European DNA sequences. See Solvante Pääbo (2003), 'The Mosaic that is our Genome', *Nature* 421, 23 January 2003, 409–12.

For the development of archaeogenetics see MARTIN JONES (2001), *The Molecule Hunt: Archaeology and the Search for Ancient DNA*, Allen Lane, London; STEVE OLSEN (2002), *Mapping Human History: Discovering the Past through our Genes*, Bloomsbury, London; LUIGI LUCA CAVALLI-SFORZA (2000), *Genes, Peoples and Languages*, Allen Lane, London.

p. 40 **Ice cores and analysis of oxygen isotopes**
Deep-sea cores provide stratified columns through the mud deposits on the ocean bed.

We can establish temperatures in the past from ice cores and 'forams' (see below), because there are two isotopes of oxygen. Oxygen-18 is the heavier and molecules formed from it do not evaporate from the sea as easily as those made from the lighter Oxygen-16. However, Oxygen-18 condenses more rapidly to form snow. In colder periods there will be more of the lighter Oxygen-16. By measuring the ratio of the two forms of oxygen centimetre by centimetre in ice cores taken from Greenland or the Antarctic, it is possible to monitor changing climate. In the sea, microscopic animals known as foraminifera absorb oxygen and use it to make their shelly exoskeletons. By analysing these it is possible also to monitor temperature change: when it is cold there will be more of the heavier Oxygen-18 in sea water because the lighter isotope will have evaporated more quickly. Within these columns are the remains of foraminifera, which can act as a guide to global climate, to the changing volume of ice and temperature changes in the oceans.

Forams can tell us this because each of these single-celled creatures absorbs the oxygen isotopes 16O and 18O from sea water. As they are short-lived and occur in vast numbers, there is a constant drizzle of forams descending to the seabed, which becomes a necropolis of calcium carbonate skeletons containing a long-term climatic record. The proportion of the two oxygen isotopes varies according to temperature and the quantity of ice in the world. A graph of the last 800,000 years shows some nineteen stages – hence they are known as Oxygen Isotope Stages (OIS). Each warm period has an odd number (we are living in OIS 1) and each cold period an even number. *See* N.J. SHACKLETON, and N.D. OPDYKE (1973), 'Oxygen Isotope and Palaeomagnetic Stratigraphy of Equatorial Pacific Core V28–238, *Cont Quaternary Research*, 3, 39–55.

p. 42 **Hominid evolution in Africa**
There is no doubt that our earliest human ancestors evolved in one

continent: Africa. The first tool-using hominids, who walked upright, lived in sub-Saharan Africa about two million years ago. Their fossils were first found in 1959/60 by Mary and Louis Leakey, who named the species *Homo habilis*: 'handy man'. With this ancestor of ours emerged the key human ability to manipulate the environment, butcher the carcasses of dead animals and split the bones to obtain nutritious marrow. Meat eating became an important element of hominid diet.

In the past forty years the number of human fossils from Ethiopia to South Africa has increased substantially. One of the most important is that of a young adolescent known as the Nariokotome Boy, who died about 1.5 million years ago of septicaemia caused by an infected root canal in his lower jaw. This tall, slim young man would probably have grown to about 6 feet tall and had the light build of the Masai who live in Kenya today. Nariokotome Boy belonged to the species now classed as *Homo ergaster* – 'work man': bare-skinned, with signs of a pronounced nose developing, he was adapted to a hot, dry climate. The nose ensured that moisture was retained when he breathed out. His slim hips were those of an active, fast-moving runner. But they required the *H. ergaster* offspring to be born early if the infant skull was to fit through the birth canal. So Ergaster society had to be capable of looking after vulnerable children. *Homo ergaster* was the mobile, questing hominid who first walked out of Africa, through the Middle East and into the Far East. They were the ancestors of the first hominids to be found in Britain.

The east-African Rift Valley is a geological supermarket with 4,000 miles of sparsely-stocked, rocky shelves exposed to the hunters of hominidae fossils.* In contrast, west Africa with its different geology, wetter climate and denser vegetation is more difficult territory.†

If the family hominidae includes all the species from us back to our remote ancestors, after the split with the chimpanzees 4 to 6 million years ago (on the basis of molecular evidence), defining hominids anatomically is a problem: bipedalism and transformation of the canine are the most distinguishable traits. The story of human evolution is constantly adapting to new discoveries and to developing theories. It now looks as if about 10 million years ago the earth was more tropical than today. Fifty or more species of apes lived and competed in this Garden of Eden. The apes were not ejected from the garden; rather the garden was taken away in an environmental holocaust. Between 8 and 6 million years ago there was a mass extinction as a drying climate reduced the forest in eastern Africa to a patchwork. Earth was no longer the planet of the apes.‡

Some, however, had already adapted to bi-pedalism – walking on the back two legs – possibly for reasons to do with sexual display and competition. A male with his hands free could collect extra food to attract a partner; females who chose these helpful types could spend more time rearing children. In a drier world of open savannah these upright

---

* The discoverer of *Sahelanthropus tchalensis*, Michel Brunet of Poitiers University, argues that this is the oldest hominid so far. Others would classify it as an ape.[32]

† Some palaeontologists have argued that the Rift Valley formed a climatic and a genetic barrier between apes to the west and hominids to the drier east. Discoveries in the Chad's Djorab Desert arguably push the hominid range 2,500 kilometres to the west of the Rift Valley and back to 7 million years ago. The Rift Valley developed from about 15 million years ago.

‡ The apes were eventually reduced to gorillas, orang-utans, chimps and humans. Initially monkeys out-competed apes because they could subsist on poorer food. Apes cannot neutralise tannin in unripe fruits, so the monkeys, who can, eat them first.

characters had an advantage: they could walk out of the forest (bi-pedalism is not a great way of sprinting but it is good for long-distance foraging);* they could see further and less of their bodies was exposed to the sun in this open environment.

The big advantage of walking on two legs, regardless of environment, is that it frees the front ones to develop hands and to improve food-collecting and make tool-making possible. With technology, hominids became more adaptable; they could exploit a wider range of resources and a richer diet. Predators were the main threat to small hominids. Fortunately this way of life promoted an increase in size. It also encouraged brain growth: a phenomenal 250 per cent over 2 million years, the most rapid physical change known in any species. Although the brain consists of only 2 per cent of human body weight on average, it consumes 20 per cent of our energy – that is, pound for pound, ten times the rest of the body. Humans have the largest brain relative to body size of any animal that has ever existed. Why put so much effort into brain growth?

Social life and communication are fundamental to apes and hominids. For a successful kill a lion has to get within 30 yards of its prey – a leopard within 10 yards. Social groups with lots of eyes have an advantage, as a defence mechanism. They can also gang up on the predator. But living in groups is not without its stresses and strains. We need to get on with each other – develop a balancing act between outside threats, overcrowding and the desire for social proximity.[33]

Monkeys interact through grooming – to communicate, dominate, subordinate and make friends. They spend up to 20 per cent of their time in this form of social behaviour. Grooming, like jogging around Central Park, stimulates endorphins – a mildly relaxing narcotic. By the standards of most animals apes are complicated characters. They can calculate the effects of future actions and use them for selfish purposes, forming alliances and tactical deceptions such as deliberately conning other group members out of food or pinning the blame on someone else. This is intelligence, albeit of a Machiavellian variety:[34]

> For a prince … It is not necessary to have all the [virtuous] qualities, but it is very necessary to appear to have them … [It] is useful, for example, to appear merciful, trustworthy, humane, blameless, religious – and to be so – yet to be in such measure prepared in mind that if you need to be not so, you can and do change to the contrary.
> (MACHIAVELLI, 1514)

The bigger the group and the greater the social interaction and complexity, the more a member needs brainpower to cope and to thrive. Brain tissue has a high metabolic cost but it is a good investment – especially the neocortex, the part where conscious thought resides. While for most mammals the neocortex represents less than 40 per cent of brain volume, for humans it is 80 per cent. And neocortex seems to increase with social-group size. Robin Dunbar has attempted to predict ideal group size from the development of neocortex. He calculates that humans evolved to deal with a close-knit community of about 150 members. Small-scale mobile hunting bands tend to consist of about thirty people (five to six families). Tribes are often about 1,500–2,000, made up of bands or clans of the predicted 150 people. This is the

---

* A recent theory is that bi-pedalism promoted long-distance running so that scavenging hominids could reach carcasses quickly, ahead of the competition.

size of group which can interact well: an effective breeding unit,[35] about the size of an army company, the size at which businesses need to put more formal management structures into place and of many church congregations.

In groups of this size grooming takes too long. Robin Dunbar suggests that language evolved as vocal grooming, to allow us to gossip and interact more effectively with more companions. Big brains have knock-on effects especially for a narrow-hipped, upright species: human babies would take twenty-one months to reach full term if they waited for their brains to develop fully. Instead they are born 'premature'. So they need an exceptional amount of parental care and stable families to protect them. Brains also need high energy input; rapid brain expansion may go hand in hand with organised hunting and meat eating. So large groups needing large resources require bigger territories. The hominids needed to move out of Africa.

p. 45 Age of the Lynford site and Optical Stimulated Luminescence
The Lynford site's date of about year 60,000 BP was established by Optical Stimulated Luminescence (OSL) in the Oxford Laboratory for Art and Archaeology. This method utilises the fact that minerals like quartz are bleached of their stored electrons by exposure to sunlight. Once the minerals are buried and no longer exposed to sunlight the minerals begin to accumulate electrons again at a predictable rate. In the laboratory this accumulation can be driven off and measured to calculate the approximate date of burial. The silt from the base of the Lynford hollow gave a date of between 60,000 and 65,000 years ago. In this period of the Middle Palaeolithic Neanderthals had moved into Britain during a relatively warm spell. The Ice Age (known as the Devensian) had begun about 115,000 BP and reached an exceptionally cold trough about 70,000 BP. Thereafter the climate improved a little and the Neanderthals moved northwards, recolonising Britain. About 20,000 BP the cold took a harsher grip again, Neanderthals had become extinct and modern humans (*Homo sapiens*) like the Red Lady of Paviland could only move in and out of Britain in the short intervals of ameliorated climate.

p. 46 Population density
This is based on a high population estimate of 0.09 persons per km² and a low one of 0.02. The land mass of the British Isles is 303,000 km².[36]

p. 47 Neanderthal DNA
Pääbo and his colleagues analysed the mitochrondrial DNA of the original Neanderthal remains, now preserved in Bonn. They found that no living humans whose mitchondrial DNA has been analysed (and there are many whose has not!) had a Neanderthal relative through the maternal line.[37]

p. 67 DNA analysis
Sykes and his team used bones from Abingdon, where excavations had provided a couple of thousand Roman, medieval and Civil War burials. In the lab they decided to target mitochondrial DNA (mt DNA) for the amplification process, principally because cells have at least a hundred times more mt DNA than any other genetic material. Mitochondrial DNA was the easiest target to hit. It also happens to be found in the cell body, rather than the nucleus. Cavalli-Sforza's work was based on nuclear DNA, which we inherit from both our parents in the unpredictable process known as 'recombination'. Consequently, after many generations of recombination, the tracks of our evolutionary trail left by nuclear DNA are confused and indistinct.

Mitochondrial DNA leaves a clearer

and simpler track because you inherit it entirely from your mother. This is because the male sperm – single-minded and stripped for action – is purely a nucleus driven by a tail. The female nucleus is surrounded by cytoplasm containing the mitochondria which act as the powerhouse of the cell. During fertilisation the male nucleus combines with the female but brings with it no mt DNA of its own. As a result mt DNA consists of central stepping stones each laid by the mother. This provides a clear path – but it should be appreciated only one of the many that existed. Mitochondrial DNA would not, for example, register a bunch of rapacious Viking males contributing their genes to a Northumbrian village, or oversexed, overpaid and over-here American soldiers exerting their charms on the female population of wartime Norwich.

Mitochondrial DNA does, though, have other advantages: its high mutation rate leaves a distinct path for the historical geneticist to follow. However, this is a rapidly changing field, dependent, so far, on relatively small samples. A recent study of Y chromosome haplotypes from modern Europeans favours the demic diffusion model, proposing that 50 per cent of the gene's contribution came from immigrant farmers.[38]

This appears to contradict seriously the 20 per cent contribution proposed by Sykes and others.[39] However, these discrepancies may be more a matter of sampling and data analysis than reality. It is worth bearing in mind the different perspective given by the different genetic approaches. While mt DNA is transferred through the female line, Y chromosomes come through the male. If colonising farmers were in small groups then there could be significant differences at the local scale – for example, if male immigrant farmers took local wives.

A recent method has been claimed for distinguishing between 'locals' and 'immigrants' through the comparing of strontium isotope signatures in human bones with regional geochemical characteristics.[40]

Chapter Two

p. 81 **Oxygen Isotope Analysis**
OIA can provide a general idea of where we were brought up. Everyone absorbs oxygen as they breathe, eat and drink. Oxygen has three forms, or isotopes, which have different physical properties owing to slight variations in their weights. The oxygen absorbed into the teeth comes mostly from the water we drink while our teeth are forming. The drinking water, from rain and snow, has oxygen isotopes which vary with latitude, altitude, distance from the sea and temperature. By analysing the oxygen in a person's teeth we can establish the kind of climate in which they lived while young and compare the oxygen values with oxygen isotope maps. In this way we can establish, roughly, where the person was brought up. The oxygen isotope maps, it must be emphasised, give only a coarse picture, so precision is rarely possible. There can also be complications if, for various reasons, the water supply a person drank is not local (for example brought by aqueducts, pipelines or from deep wells).

p. 86 **Prestige pots**
There are interesting documented examples of how prestige objects can spread through society. For example, in the mid-nineteenth century American Indians, demoralised by disease and the fragmentation of their way of life, seized on the Peyote Cult as a way of asserting their identity and seeking comfort. The cult involved sacred rattles, feather fans, drums and crescent-shaped altars of clay. In a relatively short time, after 1850, these objects spread with the cult from

Mexico to Canada. In post-Roman Europe Christian cult objects spread from the Mediterranean to northern Europe.

Chinese porcelain provides a well-documented case study for the spread of high-status ceramics, but without any mass movement of people. One of the earliest pieces to reach the west was the Gagnières-Fonthill vase, made in China in the early 1300s. A Nestorian Christian embassy from China, visiting the Pope in Avignon, brought the vessel with them and gave it to the King of Hungary in 1338. By 1689 it was in the collection of porcelain belonging to the Grand Dauphin of France and was bought by William Beckford on one of his shopping expeditions to revolutionary France. It now lives in the Victoria and Albert Museum in London.

The prestige of Chinese porcelain is illustrated by its prominent appearance in Giovanni Bellini's famous painting *The Feast of the Gods* (National Gallery of Art, Washington), created for the Duke of Ferrara about 1514. By then Lorenzo de Medici had built up an impressive collection. Britain came late to collecting Chinese procelain but began to acquire pieces from the 1560s mainly by seizing Spanish and Portuguese cargoes. The eastern trade passed to the Dutch in the early seventeenth century. Chinese potters began to modify porcelain vessels for the European market and by the early eighteenth century had developed a mass export trade.

In 1684 John Dwight of Fulham obtained a patent for the Dutch process of copying Yixing ware, and by 1690 Staffordshire potters were also making Chinese-influenced vessels. The first high-quality porcelain in Europe was made at Meissen from 1709, in factories sponsored by Augustus the Strong, Elector of Saxony and Europe's greatest collector of Chinese porcelain. He lusted after it so much he once traded 600 soldiers for 151 pieces. Now imagine how

archaeologists, if they had no historical records, would describe the four-hundred-year story of these prestige pots.

Chapter Eight

(p. 296) **English population totals, 1525–1601**[28]

Year	Totals (*in millions*)
1521	2.26
1541	2.77
1551	3.01
1561	2.98
1581	3.59
1591	3.89
1601	4.10

Chapter Twelve

(p. 443) **Sake Deen Mahomed**
A simple tombstone in St Nicholas's churchyard, Brighton, marks the grave of Sake Deen Mahomed (1759–1851) who deserves to be remembered for his contributions to Anglo-Indian culture. Born in Patna, Bihar Mahomed joined the British army in India aged eleven and later moved to Cork. In 1794 he wrote his *Travels*, the first book to be written and published in English by an Indian. In 1807 Mahomed moved from Cork with his Irish wife Jane to London, and established in 1810, at 34 George Street, the Hindoostan Coffee House, where he produced Indian dishes 'unequalled to any curries ever made in England', according to his adverts.

In 1814 Mahomed moved to the rapidly expanding health resort of Brighton, where he set up the Indian Vapour Baths and Shampooing Establishment – the word 'shampooing' was thus popularised in the English language – 'a sort of stewing alive by steam' one cynic called the process.

INDEX

Acknowledgements

An author unwise enough to tackle a book of such a scope as this one is, inevitably, indebted to a vast number of specialists (archaeologists, historians, demographers and scientists) whose work lies behind my synthesis, generalisations and simplifications. Some are mentioned here by name and in the bibliography, but I am grateful to the many others whose publications I have not systematically referenced for the sake of brevity.

My first thanks must go to the publishers, particularly Michael Dover, who commissioned this book and showed great patience and calmness during its gestation, and to Catherine Bradley who has encouraged and cajoled the author, and positively shaped the book. Without her I would not have completed the task.

I wrote this book while working as Chief Archaeologist at English Heritage. I have benefitted from the expertise and assistance of many of my colleagues, particularly Alex Bayliss, Bob Bewley, Martin Cherry, Edward Impey, Simon Mays, Adrian Oliver, Gill Hummerstone, Sebastian Payne, Chris Scull, Tony Wilmott and Pete Wilson. I am grateful to the staff of the National Monuments Record in Swindon and, above all to the ever-helpful stalwarts of the English Heritage Library in Savile Row, who diligently pursued my need for obscure research material and reference works from libraries around the country.

Others whose brains I have picked over the three years this book has been in the writing (and long before) include John Blair, Richard Bradley, Clive Gamble, Gill Hey, Richard Hingley, Julian Richards, Francis Pryor and Maisie Taylor, Nicholas Johnson, Martin Jones, Mike Parker-Pearson, John Barrett, Alan Saville, Chris Stringer and many members of staff from the Museum of London, Cadw in Wales, Historic Scotland, the Department of Environment Northern Ireland, the Irish Heritage Service, Duchas, as it then was, and the Isle of Man Heritage Service.

Various members of my family have supplied my personal history, notably my mother, Norah Bullett *nee* Graham and my mother-in-law Sylvia Morgan *nee* Axford.

My greatest debt is to my wife, Gwyn Miles, who has put as much effort into this book as I have, reading and commenting on drafts, word processing and lugging the boxes of research material between London and France, where most of the writing was done.

DAVID MILES
Millbank and Lasalle, March 2005